Joseph Alois Schumpeter

Joseph Alois Schumpeter

THE PUBLIC LIFE OF

A PRIVATE MAN

· *WOLFGANG F. STOLPER* ·

PRINCETON UNIVERSITY PRESS

PRINCETON, NEW JERSEY

Library of Congress Cataloging-in-Publication Data

Stolper, Wolfgang F.
Joseph Alois Schumpeter : the public life of a private man / Wolfgang F. Stolper.
p. cm.
Includes bibliographical references and index.
ISBN 0-691-04305-1
1. Schumpeter, Joseph Alois, 1883–1950. 2. Economists—United States—
Biography. 3. Economists—Austria—Biography. 4. Economics—History—20th
century. I. Title.
HB119.S35S76 1994 330'.092—dc20 93-50667 CIP
[B]

This book has been composed in Sabon Typeface

Printed in the United States of America

1 3 5 7 9 10 8 6 4 2

G . S .

J . A . S .

M . V . S .

IN MEMORIAM

AND

M . D . G .

IN GRATITUDE

"I have never met a person with your ability to and eagerness to understand the other fellow's point of view and to do him justice."

—Letter of Ragnar Frisch to Schumpeter, dated October 13, 1939, Oslo

"It is our responsibility as scientists, knowing the great progress which comes from a satisfactory philosophy of ignorance, the great progress which is the fruit of freedom of thought, to proclaim the value of this freedom; to teach how doubt is not to be feared but welcomed and discussed; and to demand this freedom as our duty to all coming generations."

—Richard P. Feynman, "The Value of Science," in *What Do You Care What Other People Think? Further Adventures of a Curious Character*

· CONTENTS ·

JOSEPH A. SCHUMPETER

JOSEPH A. SCHUMPETER was born in 1883, the year in which John Maynard Keynes was born and Karl Marx died. In recent years there has been a veritable flood of writings on him, innumerable articles, and a large number of monographs. They include *The Life and Work of Joseph Schumpeter* by Robert Loring Allen (1991), vol. 1, Europe, and vol. 2, America; *Schumpeter: A Biography* by Richard Swedberg (1991); a collection of articles by Schumpeter, *Joseph A. Schumpeter: The Economics and Sociology of Capitalism*, edited and introduced by Swedberg (1991); *Joseph Schumpeter: Scholar, Teacher and Politician*, by Eduard März, with a foreword by James Tobin (1991); and *Joseph Alois Schumpeter: A Reference Guide* by Massimo M. Augello (1990), with a full bibliography of Schumpeter's writings and a list of about 1,900 articles, papers, and other writings on Schumpeter.

Shortly after Schumpeter's death three volumes of his writings were published in Germany, edited by his student Erich Schneider and his colleague Arthur Spiethoff. They are *Aufsätze zur Ökonomischen Theorie* (Essays on economic theory), 1952; *Aufsätze zur Soziologie* (Essays on sociology), 1953; and *Dogmenhistorische und Biographische Aufsätze* (History of economic doctrine and biographic essays), 1954.

Finally, I will mention three fascinating volumes by Wolfgang Stolper and Christian Seidl, an Austrian economist who was professor in Graz and is now professor in Kiel. The first book is titled *Joseph A. Schumpeter: Essays on Economic Policy (Aufsätze zur Wirtschaftspolitik)*, 1991; and the second, *Joseph A. Schumpeter: Political Speeches (Politische Reden)*, 1992. A third volume, *Aufsätze zur Tagespolitik* (Essays on Current Policy), appeared in 1993.

The titles of these books are wholly insufficient to indicate their rich content—for two reasons. First, they contain not only Schumpeter's articles and speeches but also letters, memoranda, and other items. Second, there are invaluable introductions and comments by the editors that reflect an enormous research effort.

This volume by Wolfgang Stolper has a great advantage over all the others in that the author had close personal connections with Schumpeter. He was a student of Schumpeter in Bonn and in Harvard, and his father, Gustav Stolper, and his stepmother, Toni Stolper, were close friends of Schumpeter.

Gustav Stolper had a most remarkable career. In Vienna he became editor of the influential weekly magazine *Der Österreichische Volkswirt* (The Austrian economist). In 1925 he left little Austria and went to Germany, where he started a second career. After becoming a German citizen, he was elected to the German parliament as a member for the Democratic party. He founded the weekly magazine *Der Deutsche Volkswirt* (The German economist), which was a great success from its beginning in 1926. Schumpeter regularly contributed articles, all of which are reprinted in the volumes by Wolfgang Stolper and Seidl. When Hitler came to power in 1933, Gustav Stolper had to leave Germany and went to the United States, where he started his third career. All this time Stolper and his wife, Toni, kept close contact with Schumpeter.

Schumpeter was undoubtedly one of the greatest economists, sociologists, and social scientists of our century. Two names are mentioned as possible rivals—John Maynard Keynes and Max Weber. It can be argued that Schumpeter was superior because Keynes was not a sociologist, and Max Weber was a sociologist and an economic historian but not an economic theorist. But we should remember that Goethe said when told that people were discussing whether he or Schiller was the greatest poet: "That's foolish. People should be glad that there are two such fellows around."

Schumpeter had an unhappy life. Until World War I, however, things went well except for the early death of his father. At the age of thirty-two, when he already had two major books to his credit and was well known in Europe and the United States, he became the youngest full professor in Austrian history—at the University of Czernowitz, in the easternmost part of the Habsburg empire, where several Austrian economists started their career.

During and after World War I, one tragedy followed another. As an admirer of Britain, he was unhappy about the war, which destroyed his fatherland. In the new republic of Austria, he became minister of finance, a post in which he ultimately failed. After that he became president of a bank, which failed and left him with a large debt. Another disappointment was that he was never offered a chair at his own alma mater, the University of Vienna. Thus, Schumpeter found it necessary to accept an offer to go to uncongenial Bonn. The worst of all tragedies followed—the death of his mother, of his deeply beloved second wife, in childbirth, and of his son. No wonder the young optimist became cynical and pessimistic. Because of his close personal connections with Schumpeter, Stolper's discussions of these tragedies and their impact on his work are especially insightful. They make his book unique, compared with all the other biographies.

Schumpeter gained a lift from his third marriage to Elizabeth Boody, a fellow economist. Without her help he could hardly have established his residence in Cambridge. She had a country house they used for vacations, in which Schumpeter spent the last days of his life. Elizabeth assisted him in his research, and her own research on Japan was congenial. Finally, with the help of some of her friends, notably the late William Fellner, she edited Schumpeter's last book, the massive *History of Economic Analysis*.

This is what one competent critic had to say:

The appearance of Schumpeter's *History of Economic Analysis* constitutes a major event in the history of the *Dogmengeschichte* of our discipline. It is a book large in its physical proportions; its text proper amounts to over 1,000 pages. It covers its subject matter from Ancient Greece to Keynes. It aims to account for every writer who made a significant contribution to the development of economic theory. Greek, classical Latin, mediaeval Latin, Italian, Spanish, Swedish, and Dutch contributions, as well as, of course, German, French, and English literature, are reported on from their original texts. Most important of all, this is a history of theory written on the grand scale by an economist who was an original, a powerful, and a versatile theorist on his own account. Schumpeter, moreover, was interested, deeply interested, in apparently the entire range of matters intellectual, was learned beyond the normal capacities of economists, could exercise with facility and with power the whole range of skills which the economic theorist employs; static analysis, dynamic analysis, historical analysis, mathematical and statistical analysis, partial- and general-equilibrium analysis, and so forth without visible end. He was able to deal familiarly with all ages and with the materials of a wide range of disciplines: physics, psychology, history, sociology, mathematics, philosophy, jurisprudence, and perhaps still others. This is a work written in the polymath manner by perhaps the last of the great polymaths.[1]

The life of Schumpeter has often been compared with that of Keynes, and it has been said, rightly I believe, that Keynes was much luckier; first, unlike Schumpeter, Keynes, for well-known reasons, had no marital problems, and, second, he spent his entire life in Kings College, Cambridge, where articles and letters written or received by him, and other materials, were preserved. This enabled the Royal Economic Society to publish the magnificent thirty-volume *The Collected Writings of John Maynard Keynes*.

The publication of *The Collected Writings of Joseph Alois Schumpeter* will be a much more difficult problem, especially tracing his enormous correspondence with economists all over the world. My guess is that it would run to perhaps thirty volumes.

May I suggest that Stolper himself should take on this task. He has, after all, already done a lot of work in the present volume and in the three volumes he and Christian Seidl published. He would of course mobilize the Schumpeter Society. Perhaps a committee should be set up to help him.

Gottfried Haberler
Washington, D.C.

---

[1] See Viner (1991), 327.

THE IDEA FOR this book goes back a long way, and the premise was simple: to put Schumpeter's thoughts and actions into a historical context that I perhaps understood most clearly because it was partly my own. It has been suggested that I omit the account of Schumpeter's Austrian troubles or at least severely cut them. Upon reflection, I did cut back on this section, but did not eliminate it entirely, and not only because much time and effort was spent on archival research on just these problems. There was also the matter of setting the record straight: to this day, Schumpeter's behavior as minister and bank president is considered not quite aboveboard, though time has changed violent disapproval to amused acceptance. This is also why I felt it necessary to let Schumpeter speak for himself. Many of the quotations reproduced herein refer to German documents that are not generally available. I felt it was important to quote both English and German sources to ensure that my interpretation of Schumpeter's theories are not mistaken for my personal idiosyncrasies.

It is my pleasant duty to acknowledge the help of many people. The readers of the manuscript, Mark Perlman and Richard Swedberg, whose names were, with their permission, revealed to me, wrote flattering, detailed, and encouraging comments. I have followed many, although not all, of their suggestions.

In Vienna, my work was at the very beginning greatly facilitated by the secretary of state in the Ministry of Finance, now retired, Professor Hans Seidl, who made possible quick access to the files of his ministry and documents in parliament. At the time, the files were not yet as easily available as they are now, because the Staatsarchiv had not yet been built. My special thanks go to Professor Dieter Bökemann of the Technical University Vienna, who helped with introductions and the collection and reproduction of documents.

In the Oesterreichische Staatsarchiv and the Verwaltungsarchiv, my work was initially helped by Dr. Hubert Steiner. Drs. Jeřabek and Gertrud Enderle-Burcel of the Staatsarchiv helped in many ways. Dr. Enderle-Burcel, in an act of extraordinary professional courtesy, made her own Schumpeter file available, which shortened my search considerably. I hope that in a small way I could add to her collection items that I discovered. They also directed me to and made contact with other archives, which led to some discoveries that had eluded me and other researchers simply because we had looked in the wrong places.

Dr. Günther Schefbeck, the Archivist of Parliament, dug up the file of the report to the parliamentary investigation into the affairs of the Biedermann Bank, which Schumpeter had been unable to obtain.

Finally, there were the libraries of the Handels- and the Arbeiterkammer. The former had a complete newspaper file of the *Neue Freie Presse*, the latter a valuable "morgue" of newspaper clippings which were most helpful.

I also consulted the archive of the Archdiocese of Vienna, which has the papers of Monsignor Ignaz Seipel, who was during Schumpeter's ministerial days the parliamentary leader of the Christian Social Party and, later, chancellor. His diary is, however, an appointment book, and although it listed when he had lunch with Schumpeter, and when he first saw Schumpeter's successor Reisch, it revealed nothing about what was discussed. A visit to the University of Vienna Archive was unsuccessful.

I visited the University of Oslo Archive to look into the Ragnar Frisch papers, where I found the most cordial help. The visit also allowed me to discuss matters with Mr. Andvig and Mr. Fagerberg. I also went through the Spiethoff papers, deposited in the University of Basel Archive, whose help I gratefully acknowledge. Docent Rolf Henriksson of the University of Stockholm kindly made his research on Schumpeter's visit available.

I am particularly grateful to the Harvard University Archives. My interest concentrated on letters written and received by Schumpeter. I have, however, deliberately refrained from reading Schumpeter's diary or anything very personal, except where already published elsewhere.

In Berlin, my old friend from high school days and retired member of the library staff of the Free University, Christa Schulze-Krantz, was enormously helpful in doing much archival research for me. However, neither she nor I were successful in locating relevant files in the Prussian Archives in Merseburg. Inquiries by letter and lengthy telephonic discussions yielded no results.

Richard Nelson read the pages dealing with his and Winter's book, made comments, all of which I used, and also generally approved in Winter's name of my summary of their book. He did not, however, see the final and shortened version.

Rudolf v. Albertini, Emeritus Professor of History at the University of Zürich, led me to and through historic literature to understand events of over one hundred years ago. So did my sister, Dr. Joan Campbell, a historian specializing in modern German history. F. M. Scherer read and commented on several chapters.

There are several persons who must be singled out for special thanks. Dr. Herbert Fürth has an unparalleled first-hand knowledge of the historical, political, and juridical situation in the Double Monarchy and the later Republic. While my stepmother, Dr. Toni Stolper, was still alive, I frequently telephoned to ask her what it was really like at that time. Dr. Fürth checked my historical and juridical statements, corrected or approved them, and frequently led me to look in additional places for information. His and my generation are about to die out. There is a function of grandfathers in the transmission of knowledge to grandchildren, a knowledge which comes from having been part of that history and not merely having read about it. The imponderables surrounding facts are frequently as important as the facts themselves.

Paul Sweezy read the chapters on socialism. I accepted most of his comments. The remaining disagreements, as he himself pointed out, are really not so much with my descriptions of Schumpeter's thought, as with Schumpeter's thoughts themselves. Sweezy was a friend of Schumpeter in a way I was not. Though only a few years older than myself, there was between Sweezy and Schumpeter a sense of friendship among equals, while with me there always remained a sense of a generational difference. I wish this had not been so, but, though a friend of Schumpeter, I never was on equal terms with him as Paul was.

Professor Yuichi Shionoya, president of Hitotsubashi University, very carefully read the first ten chapters. I have followed all his suggestions.

The late William Mirsky, who had been professor of engineering at the University of Michigan, sparked my interest in chaos theory. When I first read Gleitz's book, which Mirsky had given me, my reaction was: "This is precisely what Schumpeter was talking about."

Whether this is so is perhaps too early to say. But it is clear that I could not have done without the substantial and substantive help of Carl Simon, professor of mathematics and economics at the University of Michigan. He helped me to understand at least in principle what the mathematics of nonlinear systems was all about, what I could and could not say. He also drew my attention to more technical articles, which he helped me to read.

Irita Grierson did the painstaking work of preparing the manuscript to the precise requirements of Princeton University Press. But in addition she occasionally questioned formulations, leading, I am certain, to improvements.

There are still others who had an influence on this project. Foremost is Jack Repcheck, who as editor suggested some tightening of the manuscript. But there were many whose names I do not know. As the manuscript developed I talked about the various parts I was working on to various groups in the United States, Germany, Switzerland, and Israel. The questions asked helped improve later formulations. I am conscious of the help received, although I can not express specific thanks to particular individuals.

A grant from the Earhart Foundation helped finance trips to Vienna, the substantial amount of xeroxing necessary, and many of the expenses incidental to the preparation of a manuscript. It allowed me also to pay a small honorarium for secretarial help. I am most grateful for this help.

Grateful acknowledgment is also made to the following:

Chicago University Press, for F. A. v. Hayek, *The Constitution of Liberty*, Chicago, 1960.

Harper Torchbooks, for Joseph A. Schumpeter, *Capitalism, Socialism and Democracy*, 3d ed., New York, 1970.

Harvard University Press, for Richard R. Nelson and Sidney P. Winter, *An Evolutionary Theory of Economic Change*, Cambridge, Mass., 1982.

Macmillan, for J. M. Keynes, *A Treatise on Money*, London, 1930.

McGraw-Hill, for Joseph A. Schumpeter, *Business Cycles*, New York, 1939.

Michigan University Press, for Arnold Heertje and Mark Perlman, eds., *Evolving*

Technology and Market Structure in Schumpeterian Economics, Ann Arbor, 1990.

Richard D. Irwin, for Frederic C. Lane and Jelle C. Riemersma, eds., *Enterprise and Secular Change, Readings in Economic History*, Homewood, Il., 1953.

W. W. Norton & Co., for Herbert Butterfield, *The Whig Interpretation of History*, New York, 1955 and later.

Joseph Alois Schumpeter

The Aim of This Biography

THIS BOOK IS conceived as a somewhat different kind of biography. Recently three major biographies of Schumpeter have appeared which recount many of his private affairs and inner torments.[1] I do not want to retell what has been well told elsewhere.

Some knowledge of what happened in his life is nevertheless of interest. But this biography will limit itself to those matters where Schumpeter's behavior can perhaps be viewed in a somewhat different light by being put into the specific historical and political context of the times.

I have also refrained on the whole from reading memoirs when actual contemporary documents were available. This is, for instance, true for the memoirs of Richard Kola, since I have found the stenographic transcripts of the hearings of the commission of enquiry into the so-called Kola affair set up by the German-Austrian government. This is also true for the memoirs of Otto Bauer.

Schumpeter is known today primarily for his theoretical writings. But he was also an immensely ambitious man with a meteoric career, which made him many enemies. He described himself as a snob in his youth in order to illustrate why firms survived beyond their original innovative actions.[2] His "three" ambitions to be the best horseman, lover, and economist have been told and retold and have gained with each retelling. But he also confessed on the occasion of a party given on his sixtieth birthday that he had wanted to be a success in politics and an expert in art.[3] He did not mention that he also wanted to be a success in business.

He did become an expert in art, particularly of the French gothic cathedrals, where he was an amateur in the original sense of the word: a lover, but not a dilettante. But successes in business (except for the early Cairo interlude) and in politics eluded him.

---

[1] I refer to the biographies of März (1983), Allen (1990), and Swedberg (1991b), who deal with those personal aspects of Schumpeter's life which I have avoided. For a novelist, the private life of his characters is essential to understand what makes them tick. But the mere facts of a situation even when they can be established beyond doubt need to be put into a context of the man's psychological makeup, and the same facts may mean something very different in different situations. Not being a novelist, I simply did not trust myself to explain so complicated a man as Schumpeter.

[2] "When I first lived in England as a young man and a great snob, I would no more have thought of calling the spurs one used in fox hunting spurs than of calling a hound a dog. They were called latchers and it was only from the firm of that name from which it was correct to buy any spurs." Letter to George Stocking, September 19, 1949. In the Harvard University Archive.

[3] Letter by Theodore Morgan to *The Economist*, July 24, 1983.

There is, as I hope to show, a remarkable unity about Schumpeter's theoretical thought and his political and policy actions. He saw reality as being constantly in flux brought about not only by external events, but by its own logic. This implied a theoretical formulation that could deal with historically unique facts. His theory tried to formulate a way of dealing with irreversible real, as well as with reversible theoretical, time. At the same time, any policy application had to allow for the unique historic situation in which it was to be applied. It is necessary to present in detail how he envisaged this relation between uniqueness and repetitiveness of reality.

At the same time, Schumpeter's political activities and his policy prescriptions seen both in the context of their theoretical basis and their historical context have so far not been adequately researched.[4] They are of interest in themselves. And events in Eastern Europe reflect a frightening relevance of the events of 1919. For this reason, I believe an account of Schumpeter's minister of finance days has more than historical interest. But there is also the methodological aspect that the need to make decisions at a specific time in a specific historical context, neither of which can be chosen by the decision maker, quickly shows how good the theoretical view of the world is, and indeed whether there is any such view at all, or whether one's actions are simply reactions to events.

THE STRUCTURE OF THIS BOOK

I want this book to be treated as more than a series of unrelated essays, unified only by the fact that they all refer to Schumpeter the theorist, adviser, or man of action. To start with, it is necessary to lay out what Schumpeter's theory actually says. Many critical discussions of the theory suggest that this is not an unnecessary task. Moreover, Schumpeter's view of the nature of the world and the problems this poses are slowly gaining ground, and the theory itself has undoubtedly significant possibilities of development.

A theory is not so much right or wrong, provided it has no inherent logical flaws, but rather useful or useless. A theory may be useful if it clears up confusion, one hopes for good, to allow further development. Haberler's *Prosperity and Depression* is a brilliant example of this kind of usefulness. But usefulness may also consist of presenting a different view, capable of development, and Schumpeter's theory is this kind of usefulness. Hence the structure of this book.

After a brief outline of Schumpeter's public life in the next chapter, and such personal characteristics as seem relevant or seem to have been frequently misunderstood, Part I, The Theoretical Bases of Economic Policy, tries to

---

[4] März makes little use of cabinet protocols or documents of the socialization commission in his discussion of Schumpeter's politics. There may be a reason for this: they were possibly not yet available at the time März wrote.

document Schumpeter's methodological and theoretical views. It gives the analysis of an economy in steady flux, change coming from inside the economy being its essence. Its methodological nature is that of a "real type" in Spiethoff's, not of an "ideal type" in Max Weber's terminology. That is, its assumptions as well as its choice of problems to be analyzed are derived from an anteceding analysis of reality, from what Schumpeter calls his vision.

Part II, Socialism, seems a logical topical sequel; its theoretical purpose is to show that Schumpeter's definition of socialism follows naturally from his analysis of the developmental processes of capitalism. One of its central concerns is to work out how differently Schumpeter defines capitalism and socialism from Mises and Lenin/Stalin, who between them have been allowed to define the problems and to dominate the discussion, unfortunately so in my view.

Parts III and IV are accounts of historical interludes, but they are meant to be more. Part III deals with Schumpeter's political activities, his attempts to become a sort of éminence grise. They bring out his strong progressive-conservative views in the manner of Winston Churchill. But this section also serves the *theoretical* purpose of identifying the role of the State which, while considered a disturbing factor, is yet an essential part precisely of an individualistic market economy. Part IV discusses Schumpeter, the minister of finance, the active politician. There is no way to understand this period without the historical background in which these activities took place. But here, too, it is hoped that Schumpeter's picture of the world is not lost in the details of the historical situation. Part V deals with Schumpeter the investment banker. Here the connection between theory and action is really quite obvious. Schumpeter saw himself as an idea man, an entrepreneur who nonetheless left the day-to-day running of his enterprises to others whose abilities and character he badly misjudged.

Part VI analyzes Schumpeter's views of fiscal and monetary policies, again as an outsider but with very definite theoretical and political ideas. The epilogue attempts to summarize Schumpeter's failures and successes.

A Brief Curriculum Vitae

SCHUMPETER WAS BORN on February 8, 1883 in Triesch—now Trest—in Moravia. His father was a manufacturer who died while Schumpeter was a child. His mother remarried a high-ranking officer from whom she was later separated. After a short move to Graz, she relocated to Vienna where Schumpeter attended the Theresianum, a school founded by Maria Theresia, whose students were drawn from the civil service and the aristocracy.

Schumpeter studied law and economics in Vienna, where he earned his doctorate in 1906. A visit to England led to his first marriage to Gladys Ricarde Seaver, said to have been a stunning beauty and the daughter of an Anglican churchman. In 1907–1908 the Schumpeters went to Cairo, Egypt, where Schumpeter practiced law before the Tribuneaux Mixtes, acquired a considerable private fortune in the process, and produced his Habilitationsschrift, *Das Wesen und der Hauptinhalt der theoretischen Nationalökonomie*, which appeared in 1908. This book was never translated into English, though a Japanese translation exists.

Schumpeter was appointed Privatdozent in Vienna in 1909, and in the same year Extraordinarius at the University of Czernovitz.[1] While an outpost of the Austro-Hungarian Monarchy, Czernovitz had a lively Jewish and German cultural life, as attested by Eric Roll.[2]

In 1911 Schumpeter became full professor (Ordinarius) at the University of Graz, thanks to the protests of the law members of the faculty who objected to the list of proposed appointments submitted by the economists, and the intercession of Böhm-Bawerk.[3] In the same year *Die Theorie der wirtschaftlichen Entwicklung* appeared, which established his international reputation, but which was not translated into English until 1934. In 1913 he was the first Austrian exchange professor at Columbia University, which conferred upon him an honorary degree.

The visit to Columbia University marks the high point of Schumpeter's

[1] Czernovitz had been in a part of the Turkish Empire under Austrian administration for decades. In 1908, it was formally annexed by Austria. After the First World War it became Romanian as Cernauti. After the Second World War it became Soviet Russian, and in 1991, Ukrainian, with yet another change in name.

[2] Lord Eric Roll (1988). A 1992 *New York Times* report mentioned the lively cultural life of earlier days which had completely disappeared with the departure of Jews and Germans.

[3] Böhm-Bawerk somewhat later had a controversy with Schumpeter about the latter's interest theory. This did not, however, prevent him from appreciating Schumpeter's genius. This comment is made because it is assumed that Schumpeter was jealous of Keynes. Neither Schumpeter nor Böhm-Bawerk allowed their scholarly opinions to be influenced by their personal feelings and vice versa.

worldly success. The First World War, which he had opposed from the beginning, was to Schumpeter a major tragedy. In 1918 he became a member of the German Socialization Commission and in 1919 the German-Austrian minister of finance, a position in which he lasted almost seven months. After a brief return to Graz, he became president of the Biedermann Bank. He was gently but decisively forced to leave in 1924.

Schumpeter remarried in 1925. It is occasionally stated that this was a bigamous marriage, an assumption based on the fact that no document of divorce has so far been found and that Gladys, from whom he had apparently separated earlier, had threatened a scandal. This episode of Schumpeter's life remains puzzling. In the questionnaire which Schumpeter had to fill out in connection with his becoming finance minister, he listed himself as married; in the questionnaire filled out in connection with a criminal investigation in the Braun-Stammfels affair, Schumpeter listed himself as unmarried rather than as divorced. This suggests that Schumpeter considered his marriage to Gladys to have been annulled or otherwise invalid.

Until 1938, family law in Austria was a matter for the churches, not the State. A Catholic could not legally get a divorce from another Catholic, though a partner could enter into a so-called dispensation marriage, provided the other partner did not object. To get an annulment, as a Catholic married to a non-Catholic, would have been a lengthy and difficult matter. Perhaps the English marriage had only been a civil ceremony. A complication might have arisen in this case because Gladys was not Austrian. I do not know how international private law would have decided this case, but Gladys may have fought the annulment as not recognized by the English.[4]

In any case, Schumpeter left the Catholic church and became a Lutheran. Annie Reisinger was his great love, and their marriage marked the high point of his private life. The marriage ended in tragedy: in 1926 mother and child died in childbirth, and their death followed by only a few months the death of his mother, to whom he had been greatly attached. This triple blow of fate, coming after the collapse of his beloved Double Monarchy, the loss of his private fortune, and constant attacks on his personal honor, was the final blow which turned Schumpeter from a man of immense vitality into a depressed and emotionally broken man.

This change in his personality was noticed by persons who knew him well in earlier days. A personal letter from a friend expressed this change in a touching manner: My God what a famous man! Do they have anywhere a

---

[4] If a German wanted to marry a Swiss or a Dutch woman he had to get a statement from the German police that there was no objection to that marriage in Germany. However, this need not have been recognized in Switzerland or Holland. Thus, if a devout Moslem wanted to marry a Swiss or Dutch woman as his fourth wife as permitted by the Koran, the statement that the Saudi-Arabian police saw no obstacle to such a marriage because the groom had only three wives would hardly have been recognized. After 1933, a German Jew could not get such a certificate if he wanted to marry a non-Jewish woman. The Swiss recognized this as a valid legal obstacle to the marriage, but the Dutch rejected it as immoral.

bust of you? But I don't quite know, I always believe your heart is lost in the process. This is clumsily said and does not say what I want to say. There is always such a strange breath in your letters. It really looks as if you no longer cared for anything in this world.[5]

In 1925, Schumpeter was appointed to the chair of public finance at the University of Bonn, largely due to the efforts of his friend Arthur Spiethoff. It has been said that Spiethoff prevented Schumpeter from teaching theory. This statement can be dismissed. He certainly did teach theory in his lectures and seminars, as I can attest from personal experience. The misunderstanding probably arises from a neglect of the manner in which the teaching of economics was organized in Bonn: There was the chair of theory held by Spiethoff, of economic policy held by Herbert v. Beckerath, of public finance, and of business, held by Rössle. However, the teaching of statistics was a part-time appointment in Bonn.

In 1927 Schumpeter visited Harvard. In 1931 he again visited Harvard and also spent a month in Japan, which left him with a lifelong admiration for Japanese culture. In 1932 he moved to Harvard for good. He died in his sleep on January 8, 1950 in the Connecticut summer home of Elizabeth Boody Schumpeter, his third wife.

ASPECTS OF SCHUMPETER'S PERSONALITY

It seems appropriate to describe how Schumpeter affected his surroundings. Although numerous scandalous stories circulated about him, it is remarkable that all of them refer to his Austrian period, and that not one story has surfaced concerning his visit to Columbia University or his Bonn or Harvard years. This perhaps tells more about the Viennese atmosphere than about Schumpeter.

Schumpeter always took his teaching duties seriously. His Czernovitz students—unlike his Graz students—adored him, and well they might since he fought a duel with the librarian to gain them better access to books. Of particular interest is Friedrich von Wieser's assessment of Schumpeter. After Schumpeter had been appointed minister of finance on March 17, 1919, Wieser wrote in his diary that he had seen Schumpeter, who was in superb spirits and who did not "hide that under Emperor Karl he had wanted to become Minister of Finance and that he had several times reason to believe that he would have success."[6]

Wieser also wondered how Schumpeter had thought this feasible, and if this would have meant that Wieser himself would be dropped from the cabi-

    [5] Letter sent from Baden, a spa south of Vienna, January 7, 1936. My translation. In the Harvard University Archives.
    [6] Nachlass Wieser in the Haus- Hof- und Staatsarchiv, typewritten entry of March 19, 1919. The relevant extracts from Wieser's Diary are reproduced in Schumpeter (1992). Gertrud Enderle-Burcel of the Staatsarchiv Vienna drew my attention to the Wieser Diary.

net. Schumpeter also informed Wieser that he did not think much of his fellow ministers, except for Otto Bauer, who in turn reciprocated the feeling of respect "despite all differences of opinion." Wieser's opinion of Schumpeter is of great interest because Wieser was an economist of first rank, the teacher to whom Schumpeter felt closest. Wieser had different methodological opinions from Schumpeter about the need of psychological assumptions in equilibrium theory, but here the interest is Wieser's reaction to Schumpeter the public figure, an opinion that changed back and forth.

Wieser's opinion became favorable upon hearing Schumpeter's speech about the future of Austria.

> I must give him the testimonial that he has spoken as intelligently as conscientiously. The unfavorable impression I recently had when he performed his somersaults for my benefit (als er mir seine Capriolen vormachte) has been entirely overcome. He sees clearly and recognizes the essential points, does not allow himself to be sidetracked by prepared slogans. The connection with the public is not sought out of vanity (although he probably pleases himself in this) but he recognizes precisely that he needs this connection to be effective.[7]

Yet a month later there is again Wieser's questioning and rather harsh assessment:

> I'll mention Schumpeter on the side whom I have heard speak once more. Superb (glänzend) without a doubt. I esteem his courage of spirit. His vanity is spurred on by the difficulties of the situation in order to find clarity, and he has found clarity. He suns himself in the feeling that he has found it. To that extent his vanity is good, but it has no limits in effectiveness. [The German is not quite clear: . . . aber sie hat an Wirksamkeit nicht ihre Grenzen.] He does not really care about the general misery, and he will thus not do his utmost to escape the misery. As soon as his vanity is no longer satisfied, as soon as he believes that the difficulties cannot be conquered, he will retire. He was so naive to say this publicly: "Do you think that I want to remain Minister of a State which goes bankrupt?" From there it is only one step to kid himself (täuschen) in his vanity and to think away (wegtäuschen) the difficulties in order to remain in the glory of the position.[8]

Undoubtedly Wieser's judgment is too harsh, as future developments (discussed in Part IV) show. But they are symptomatic of the ambiguous impression Schumpeter made on his surroundings, and they come from a man who is certainly above reproach. In any case, it was not Schumpeter who chose to retire.

Wieser also records the precipitous decline of Schumpeter after his dis-

[7] Wieser Diary, entry of May 13, 1919 (Schumpeter 1992, 11). My translation.

[8] Wieser Diary, entry of June 24, 1919. When reading the German version it is not self-evident why Schumpeter's statement should have been so offensive to Wieser. Since Wieser is an outstanding witness, one would suppose that there was something in the inflection of Schumpeter's speech that caught the ear of the listener.

missal from cabinet, though Wieser himself did not join the chorus of detractors:

> During the day there was much talk about Schumpeter. Kelsen who during his time of power clung to him, drops him entirely. It seems that in the opinion of all parties and of all educated people Schumpeter is finished. As Kelsen told me, even the younger economists who considered him their leader, have turned their back on him and given up on him also scientifically; nothing could any more be expected of him.[9]

Well, not everyone: In a letter to Kurt Singer, Gustav Stolper wrote that he "actually liked the man."[10]

As minister, Schumpeter was accused in public of being overoptimistic to the point of being irresponsible. But no one ever accused him of being illogical. If anything his fault was that his intellectual horizon went too far into the future, much beyond the horizon of most, even of most intellectually aware people. Regarding his contributions to the *Deutsche Volkswirt* in the 1920s, he wrote to Gustav Stolper, the founder, publisher, and editor, that his aim would be to educate people to economic thinking and to rescue economics from the accusation that it was not a science but just a defense of special interests.

WAS SCHUMPETER ANTI-SEMITIC?

In Graz, Schumpeter was considered a *Judenfreund*. And when it became known that he would leave for Bonn, a rightist newspaper ran a piece to the effect that Schumpeter was a member of the Austrian marginal utility school, which originated in Galicia (where Menger was born) and that Böhm-Bawerk, a half-Jew, had been his teacher!

There certainly are some utterances of Schumpeter which by today's sensibilities sound somewhat anti-Semitic. But all the evidence is against Schumpeter having any such prejudices. One such utterance refers to Viennese newspapers of world renown which were edited and owned by Jews. Schumpeter wanted to establish a paper of equally high standards which would serve the conservative cause.[11] Another relates to a correspondence with Ragnar Frisch in which Schumpeter worried that a clannishness of Jews and Socialists would prevent the appointment of Erich Schneider as fellow of the Econometric Society. Ragnar Frisch wrote Schumpeter that this had not been the case and he chided Schumpeter for his racial and political prejudice. Schumpeter reacted to the accusation explicitly: "My dear Frisch, no. You do me an injustice. I am not so narrow as to object to someone because he is a socialist or anything

---

[9] Wieser Diary, entry of November 19, 1919. My translation.

[10] This letter is reproduced in Schumpeter (1985).

[11] See below the account of the Harrach letters, which are reproduced in Schumpeter (1992).

else in fact. If I did take political opinion into consideration I should be much in favor of including socialists in our list of fellows. Nor am I or have ever been anti-Semitic."[12]

Some of the impression of anti-Semitism may be due to his at least initially ambivalent attitude toward the rise of National Socialism. He had not much liked political and social developments in Weimar, Germany, which had led to a near-paralysis of decision making, and he was initially skeptical toward all stories coming out of Germany, considering them "Greuelpropaganda." This was, of course, quite common at the time and continued to the point at which no one could believe stories about what really happened in concentration and extermination camps. Certainly, the confusion, to use a neutral term, of the political landscape in the 1920s and early 1930s contributed to many otherwise intelligent and decent people seeing Hitler as a savior from chaos and bolshevism.

It is only natural that Jews, for whom there was no possible accommodation with Hitler, should oppose him at any cost. Churchill and Roosevelt had Jewish friends and advisers, but their opposition to Hitler had nothing to do with this. In Schumpeter's case one has to remember also that he considered war a major tragedy and quite anticapitalistic.

It may be useful to make these matters explicit because of the unconscious habit of applying present moral values and sensitivities to an earlier time when they had no place, were associated with quite different imponderables, and hindsight did not exist.[13] There is no sense in condemning Schumpeter because of a disregard of the historical context.[14] I will, therefore, stress the historical context in the political and policy chapters.[15]

In any case, Schumpeter soon learned better, and while he evidently underestimated the menace of Hitler, he also evidently thought that to deal with the human tragedies arising from Hitler's menace was not a war, but a personal effort to help Hitler's victims. Thus he wrote a letter to a number of people: "I am writing today to solicit your interest and cooperation in the work of a small committee which Wesley Mitchell and I are trying to get together to consult what can be done for those German economists who have been re-

[12] Letter to Ragnar Frisch, on Harvard letterhead. November 3, 1932. In the Frisch papers in the manuscript collection of the University of Oslo.

[13] I never heard Schumpeter use words like *wop, Jap, frog, Kraut,* or *kanuk,* which were in the 1930s used quite carelessly even by people without derogatory intent and provable absence of racial prejudice.

[14] A particularly nasty example of the total disregard of the historical context appeared in 1992. Despite coming from a historian, who really should have known better, I do not want to give a reference but rather spread the mantle of Christian charity over it.

[15] The late President Theodor Heuss told me once in a personal conversation that Hitler's coming to power was all the fault of his parents. When I asked just what this was supposed to mean his answer was literally: "So wie wir erzogen wurden, konnten wir uns eine solche Schlechtigkeit einfach nicht vorstellen" ("The way we were brought up we simply could not imagine such evil").

moved by the Hitler Government and now find themselves in what undoubtedly is a very serious situation."[16]

On April 22, 1933, Schumpeter had written to Mitchell:

> Allow me to add that a few days ago I had proof of how desperate things look in Germany. I always refuse to believe excited reports and am still convinced that things are not half as bad as they look from outside. Yet a very funny thing happened. My friend . . . wrote me from Spain where this amiable *viveur* passed his Easter holiday and asked half jokingly and bitterly in earnest to the other half, whether I could not get him some instructorship or job as a young man in Cook's travelling office because, he said, he doubted how much longer it would be possible to serve at the same time science and Germany honorably. Now this proves very much because the man is not a Jew. . . . Now if he begins to feel uncomfortable, things must indeed be a bit thick.

In any case, as Alvin Johnson wrote to Schumpeter, the issue was not so much political as what happened to the Republic of Letters, which was very much the concern of scholars. So Schumpeter tried also to help non-Jewish scholars who could not stomach the fascist regimes, among them Cyriacy-Wantrup, Georgescu-Rögen, Karl Bode, and Herbert Zassenhaus. Naturally, the problem of Jewish scholars was more urgent and personal.[17] Schumpeter also had a long correspondence with Cläre Tisch, sending her affidavits, but Cläre Tisch sacrificed herself to take care of Jewish orphans in Germany. Her last letter asked Schumpeter not to send another affidavit and not to write anymore, as her address would be unknown. It was Auschwitz.[18]

---

[16] Such a letter was sent at the end of April and/or May, 1, 1933 among others to Frank Fetter, Irving Fisher, James Angell, Edmund Day, the Rev. Fosdick. Alvin Johnson, who at the time was trying to organize the University in Exile, was also informed in order to get his blessing and to be assured that the Mitchell-Schumpeter enterprise would not interfere with Johnson's efforts.

[17] Schumpeter's list, found in the Harvard University Archive, is (in his order): Dr. Gustav Stolper, Dr. Jakob Marschak, Dr. Hans Neisser, Professor Karl Mannheim, Professor Emil Lederer, Professor Adolf Löwe, Professor Gerhard Colm, Professor Karl Pribram, Dr. Altschul.

[18] This should suffice to show that Schumpeter certainly was not anti-Semitic. He threatened to resign after Harvard's initial failure to give Samuelson an appointment. His bitter comments have been distorted in continuous retelling. I remember him telling me "Es ist nicht Anti-semitismus, denn sie haben nichts gegen. . . . Es ist nur, dass er besser ist, als sie" ("It is not anti-Semitism, for they have nothing against. . . . It is just that he is better than they are.") This has been distorted into meaning that Schumpeter could understand if it were anti-Semitism. The actual context is perhaps another comment Schumpeter made: the first reaction to a young man's new ideas is to ignore them; the second is that it is all wrong; and the third reaction is: we have known this all along. Actually, there are numerous letters in the files of Schumpeter worrying about Samuelson's future, precisely because his brilliance and originality would not be understood by the profession. Similarly, a story to the effect that Schumpeter was against Samuelson because Jews mature early is provably just a mix-up. Not only was this argument used against the non-Jew Schumpeter. The identical story was told by Machlup to Mrs. Carver. When Machlup visited Professor Degenfeld to solicit his support for an appointment as Privatdozent, Degenfeld raised another objection: "There is another reason why I cannot vote for you. The Jews are precocious. With this precociousness they appear much brighter at an earlier age. If we then pick the Jew who shows promise at an earlier age, we would really be discriminating against the

Schumpeter as Feminist

Schumpeter might even be considered an early feminist. When still in high school he had, so he told us, a female friend who was already at University. The emperor had issued a decree to admit female students to all courses. One professor, however, refused to lecture as long as female students were present, and the male students took his side. Schumpeter, on the grounds that he was going to study law, was asked to write a petition to the emperor, protesting the action of the professor. The females also mobilized their male friends to protect them against the hostile male students when attending the lecture.

This occurred around the turn of the century. But in 1936, Schumpeter suggested to President Conant, who had asked Schumpeter's advice, that he invite Ragnar Frisch and John R. Hicks to join Harvard:

> The latter has a wife who is also a very good economist who would be useful in her own right, so the invitation could be extended to both of them. In making my suggestions I have submitted to the apparently invincible Harvard prejudice against women. But Mrs. Joan Robinson of Cambridge, England, an economist of international fame, would be an extremely good acquisition. . . . I may add that if there were any wish to break with that antifeminist tradition, which seems to me, frankly, to be somewhat reactionary, her appointment would afford an excellent opportunity.[19]

Lack of Character, Jealousy of Keynes, Lack of Seriousness?

Schumpeter's meteoric rise won him many enemies. He was accused of shady dealings during his ministerial and banking days, which played a major role in his possible appointment in Berlin. The details of the Berlin affair will be taken up below. It is, however, remarkable that there were numerous enquiries about his availability before Berlin, and none of the other universities raised questions about his character or supposed lack thereof. Thanks to the efforts of Professor Klaus O. W. Müller of the University of Leipzig, a possible appointment to the University of Leipzig in 1916 has come to light, as a successor to Karl Bücher. This appointment was supported by Wundt, who particularly mentioned that Schumpeter might continue to work along the lines of the "Swiss Wallras."[20] The main opponent of the appointment was a Professor Stieda, who thought "Wallras . . . unproductive and his general direction a dead end (Holzpfad)" (Müller 1990, 18), and who objected to Schumpeter as too young, a non-German and antinational, and who also

---

Aryans, the non-Jews. And hence, I cannot vote for a young Jew" (Earlene Carver, "The Emigration of Austrian Economists," *History of Political Economy*, vol. 18, no. 1, 1986, p. 24).

[19] Letter to President James B. Conant, December 7, 1936.

[20] The misspelling of Walras's name is in the original faculty minutes (Müller 1990), 17.

thought that one had to look at Schumpeter's personality more closely. The last obviously could not have been a reference to Schumpeter's ministerial or banking days.

This was done by requesting a letter from a former colleague of Schumpeter at the University of Czernovitz, Professor Kronmeyer, who stressed that Schumpeter was a pleasant social companion and an excellent teacher whom the students adored.[21] "He does not exhibit an undue self-importance. He is so sure of himself as befits his importance, which may, of course, annoy smaller minds" (Müller 1990, 20). He loved paradoxes in conversation but was serious in his scientific work, and Kronmeyer did not perceive an antinational attitude.

Of course, Czernovitz occurred before the First World War, and the Secret Memoranda (see chapter 12) were still to come. Yet Schumpeter's decidedly unfavorable opinions about the war and German policies evidently had leaked out.

After his return to Graz but before becoming bank president, Schumpeter received and accepted an appointment to the Handelshochschule Berlin as successor to Werner Sombart, who had moved to the University. Schumpeter's acceptance was, however, qualified by his right to withdraw. The discussion in the faculty was polite and favorable to Schumpeter, though doubts were expressed whether he would accept. The first contacts with Schumpeter had been made while he was a member of the German Socialization Commission. It is fairly clear that Schumpeter kept several options open. At one time he apologized for his delay in answering a letter, explaining that he felt that he could not accept the appointment until he had liquidated all his political connections. He finally withdrew his acceptance, expressing his regrets that unforeseen personal matters made his acceptance impossible. The personal matters were not further elaborated, but Schumpeter shortly thereafter became president of the Biedermann Bank.[22]

Soon after his resignation from the presidency of the bank, Schumpeter had a luncheon with Professor J. H. Rogers of Yale University in which Schumpeter described his departure from the bank as more voluntary than it was according to most accounts.[23] Rogers wrote to L. C. Marshall of the University of Chicago that during the luncheon he, Rogers, had brought up the bank failure (which was certainly not that of the Biedermann Bank, which went into liquidation only in 1926). Schumpeter explained that the Biedermann Bank had "suffered considerable losses [in 1924] as had most of the others and on that account that he had continued as President until he could get the affairs of

---

[21] This was quite different from his experience in Graz in 1912 where the students boycotted his classes and protests mounted because he was considered too difficult an examiner.

[22] The voluminous file of 76 pages is found in the Archive of Humboldt University, Berlin. I owe its discovery to Ms. Christa Schulze-Krantz whose enormous help in this and related matters is here gratefully acknowledged.

[23] Letter by J. H. Rogers to Professor L. S. Marshall, University of Chicago, dated September 29, 1925. I am grateful to Professor Swedberg for telling me about this letter.

the Bank again into a healthy condition. This he says he has accomplished, and had recently resigned to take up academic work again." The purpose of Rogers' letter was to inform the University of Chicago of Schumpeter's availability, which suggests how highly Schumpeter was considered in American academic circles.

Before accepting Bonn, Schumpeter was also offered a position at Tokyo University as successor to Emil Lederer, and inquiries about his availability continued after his move to Bonn. The University of Freiburg suggested a visit, which he accepted at the insistence of Spiethoff. This offer had followed a "completely uninteresting" invitation from Prague. The Prussian Ministry of Education in turn was anxious to keep Schumpeter and offered him a post at any other Prussian university should he wish to leave Bonn because the loss of his wife and child had made the place intolerable. The University of Kiel also made a special effort to recruit him. All of this elicited Schumpeter's comment: "These Prussians are really delightful."[24] None of these universities expressed any of the moral qualms about Schumpeter's character that were later expressed in Berlin.

Schumpeter never had any doubt that he was an original and superior thinker. Nevertheless, he gladly recognized his equals, and in some cases his superiors. His sharp review of Keynes's *General Theory* is frequently attributed to jealousy of Keynes's success, which began to overshadow Schumpeter's influence. This is not so, as Schumpeter had been an unabashed admirer of Keynes. But this did not prevent Schumpeter from disagreeing with Keynes about certain aspects of his *Tract on Monetary Reform* (see chapter 22). Similarly, in letters to Irving Fisher he frequently expressed criticisms about Fisher's work.

Some of Schumpeter's letters contain positive reactions to Keynes, such as his refusal to be party to criticisms of Keynes's plan on how to pay for the war, which Schumpeter welcomed as a return to a positive attitude toward savings. Schumpeter was certainly upset about the *General Theory* and its influence, which he considered less than beneficial. Schumpeter's criticism of the *General Theory* was that it did not address itself to the central features of the real economy, that it was a throwback to earlier days, that every one of its propositions could be duplicated from earlier analyses, all of which was by no means only Schumpeter's opinion.[25]

[24] Letter dated February 5, 1927, reprinted in März (1983), 174–75. Kiel, now in Schleswig-Holstein, was at that time Prussian.

[25] See, for example, Henriksson (1989). Henriksson reports on a lecture in Stockholm by Keynes on October 1, 1936 on "My grounds for departure from orthodox economic traditions" which was not very well received by, among others, Lundberg, Myrdal, and Svennilson. Professor Swedberg drew my attention to Mr. Henriksson's research. I am most grateful to Mr. Henriksson for making it so readily available to me.

Professor H. W. Singer, who has the distinction of being one of the few people who were intimate students of both Schumpeter and Keynes, suggested in a letter that the comparative coolness'between Schumpeter and Keynes had not so much scholarly roots as the differences in the cultural milieu in which they were brought up.

Equally remarkable was Schumpeter's willingness to learn from others and to change his mind radically. In a letter to Alvin Johnson he wrote that he considered Tinbergen "one of the foremost and most significant figures among economists alive or dead."[26] In a letter to Taljin Koopmans he even expressed a willingness to throw over everything he had believed if it disagreed with Tinbergen:

> I am so great an admirer of Professor Tinbergen and I hope so much from the line of advance which he has opened up that I am truly grieved to find that as yet I cannot get over certain objections on general logical grounds. I have a feeling that these objections are really antiquated and that the success of Tinbergen's work should inspire us to reconstruct our statistical theory rather than to condemn him on the basis of it. You will therefore understand how grateful I am for any attempt which competently espouses his cause as yours does.[27]

On the other hand, Schumpeter avoided public controversy except with so outstanding and otherwise respected a scholar as Keynes. There is a friendly but nevertheless doubting review of Hayek's *Road to Serfdom*,[28] whose conclusions he questioned essentially on the grounds of an inadequate analysis of reality. Schumpeter did, however, reject Mises's and Hayek's economic theories. In a letter to Gottfried Haberler, with whom Schumpeter had an extensive exchange of letters and whom he estimated very highly,[29] Schumpeter wrote:

> I am not astonished that you begin to find fault with the Mises-Hayek theory. What I was astonished about is that you ever had a taste for it even to the point of expounding it in your Chicago address which I was very sorry to read, for really you ought to tell people of results of your own and if you allow me to say so, that address would have been a mistake even if that theory was more valuable than it is.[30]

No one has ever claimed that Schumpeter was jealous of Haberler, whose achievements he greatly admired.

There is no question that Schumpeter was a conscientious teacher, as evidenced in a letter by Max Weber to the Viennese faculty that strongly favored Schumpeter for an appointment and stressed that he was indeed a brilliant

---

[26] Letter dated August 22, 1940.

[27] Ibid.

[28] Schumpeter (1946), 269–70.

[29] In a letter to Gustav Stolper in the Bundesarchiv, Koblentz, Schumpeter asked Stolper to use his influence to secure a professorial chair for Haberler at the University of Königsberg—now Kaliningrad—the University of Immanuel Kant and the city of Käthe Kollwitz. He referred to Haberler as "the best horse in the Viennese stable."

[30] Letter to Gottfried Haberler, March 20, 1933. The letter is reproduced in Swedberg (1991b), 215. Original in the Harvard University Archives. Haberler, stressing the many merits of Hayek as a scholar, nevertheless was critical of Hayek's business cycle theory, mainly because he could not accept the "nature of the maladjustments—the key concept of his theory." Haberler (1986).

teacher.[31] Perhaps I can characterize his teaching as that he did not so much want to prepare his students for exams as to set trains of thought into motion so that years later they might suddenly say: so that is what he really meant. A university was for him not a high school with teachers and students, but an association of equals where it was not so much the business of the older to teach as of the younger to learn.

There is the report of a mixed reaction to a speech of Schumpeter's which shows him to have been a brilliant speaker—something to which many people can bear testimony—but also a speaker who could enjoy being more playful than serious. Henriksson reports on an affair at the Stockholm Student Economic Club in May 1932 at which the German economist Gerhard Mackenroth was the invited speaker and Schumpeter the special guest of honor. Svennilson related in a letter to Lundberg what occurred that evening:

> "Schumpee" however was the memorable experience. He opened and finished the discussion with incomparable speeches, eloquently verbose with an extraordinary vitality. He virtually leaped back and forth in the room. Then at Metropol (a restaurant frequently visited by the members of the Stockholm group) he gave a real table performance for the remainder of the evening. He was greeted with a flattering speech by Myrdal but was then the one who did the entertaining, merrily summing marginal utilities and so forth, but also wriggling away from and dodging all questions with the most rapturous dialectical ingenuity. He was at the same time a great acquaintance and a great disappointment. After this probably none of those present will read his works with confidence any more.[32]

This was a rather harsh judgment which, one hopes, Svennilson later reconsidered. Schumpeter may simply have felt that a dinner speech with good food and good wine, both of which he appreciated greatly, was hardly the occasion for a serious economic discussion, particularly as it was Mackenroth rather than he who should have been discussed.

Schumpeter was also reluctant to speak on economic policy in public. His letters provide enough evidence to be certain of his reasons. One example may suffice. In 1933, he wrote to Irving Fisher why he found it difficult to express himself briefly on such an important matter as the depression:

> [M]y reluctance to express myself in public is increased in this case by the impossibility to add the necessary qualifications when speaking to an audience of a popular kind. As things stand, I am of course in favor of a measure of inadvertent inflation, but I could not stand for it unless precautions are taken at the same time and within the same measure to stop the inflationary impulse at once when it has done its duty.[33]

---

[31] The letter seems to be in the files of the Zentralarchiv, Merseburg (former German Democratic Republic). Mr. Swedberg kindly drew my attention to this letter. When I asked for a copy in Merseburg it could not be found.

[32] The letter is dated May 25, 1933. As reported by Henriksson (1989).

[33] Letter to Irving Fisher, dated February 10, 1933.

SCHUMPETER'S "IRAN-GATE"?

Schumpeter was accused in the Viennese Press of having been a real cloak-and-dagger conspirator against the Bolshevist regime in Hungary.[34] The story it told was that of a counterrevolutionary conspiracy against the Hungarian Embassy in Vienna which ended in a successful take-over of the embassy by a bunch of excitable and evidently highly incompetent Hungarian aristocrats, whose attempt to invade Hungary and topple the regime ended in a total and ludicrous failure.[35]

The plans of the counterrevolutionaries were known to the British representative Cunninghame. Ashmead-Bartlett mentions that both the Hungarians and the Russian Bolsheviks were rumored to have large sums of money in Vienna to finance an attempt to install a Soviet regime in Austria,[36] which both the Entente and the Bolsheviks considered pivotal. Bauer and Deutsch, the minister of defense, are referred to as Bolsheviks, and the Austrian government as semi-Bolshevik (ibid., 157), which was somewhat of an exaggeration. The plans of the counterrevolutionaries lacked money and evidently competent leadership. The whole affair was in Ashmead-Bartlett's view a mixture of tragedy and musical comedy. The Viennese, despite their desperate food situation, were not in a very revolutionary mood. When arriving in Vienna, "instead of finding Vienna in flames, I found the town absolutely quiet." Reports of past outbreaks were vastly exaggerated and "the work of comparatively few Hungarian and Russian agitators" (ibid., 148). "The weather is beautifully fine and this is a most important factor in keeping a Viennese mob in a good humor" (ibid., 149). The expected unrest at a May First demonstration failed to materialize because there were more onlookers than participants in the parade. The counterrevolutionaries themselves lived in the comparative luxury of the Hotel Sacher, financed, until better times, by that staunch royalist Frau Sacher of Sacher torte fame. It was in connection with financing the counterrevolution that Ashmead-Bartlett went to

> [S]ee Schumpeter, the Austrian Minister of Finance, and endeavor to arrange a loan for the Counter-Revolution from him. Schumpeter is a young man, still in the thirties, of great intelligence, who has spent many years in America and speaks English perfectly. We discussed the future of Austria. He is bitterly opposed to the "Anschluss," the proposed union with Germany. Schumpeter is not

[34] "Schumpeter als Geheimbündler," *Der Montag mit dem Sportmontag*, August 6, 1923. I owe this reference to Dr. Gertrud Enderle-Burcel.

[35] The *Montag*'s account, though substantially correct, nevertheless shows a certain sloppiness. It refers to a work of memoirs—no further title is given—of E. A. Bartlett, a correspondent of the *Daily Mail*. There was in fact a correspondent working in that part of the world, though not in Austria, by the name of Vernon Bartlett, whose novel *Tomorrow Always Comes* I happened to have read. The author turned out to be Ellis Ashmead-Bartlett, CBE, who was a correspondent of the *Daily Telegraph* and whose book was called *The Tragedy of Central Europe*, (1923). I mention this because it took me a long time to straighten out the *Montag*'s misinformation as to the source.

[36] Ashmead-Bartlett (1923), 158.

even a Socialist or Republican. I speedily discovered that he is quite out of sympathy with Deutsch and Bauer, and wishes to see a moderate constitutional regime installed in both Austria and Hungary. Having found the ground so favorably prepared, I was able to approach the real object of my visit—the raising of funds for the Counter-Revolution. There was no need to be cautious or to indulge in half-measures. Schumpeter declared without reserve that all his sympathies were with us and that the only way to eliminate the Red Danger from Vienna was to drive the Soviet Government out of Hungary. I then explained the great difficulties we were experiencing, and the obstacles that Louis Rothschild was putting in our way.[37] Schumpeter was most sympathetic and replied: "Had I not got to account for the money afterwards to Parliament, I would willingly advance it myself from the Austrian Treasury." He then suggested a more practical scheme. He undertook to see Louis Rothschild and to tell him that he could withdraw ten million from the banks without any questions being raised by the Treasury.[38]

So Schumpeter was involved in a kind of "Iran-Contra" affair except that German-Austria had as yet no constitution and the Austrian parliament had passed no law. There was nothing illegal about Schumpeter's actions; but as Gustav Stolper pointed out, he did intrigue against Bauer, the foreign minister, he did make his own foreign policy which clashed with the official policy of the cabinet (though the Christian-Socialists were probably not too unhappy about it), and he thus laid the basis for the later revenge of the social democrats in the Kola affair, in which Schumpeter was innocent.

It might also be noted that Ashmead-Bartlett considered it quite natural to be involved in a conspiracy while a journalist. At the time this evidently posed no ethical questions.

Schumpeter's behavior was careless, to say the least. On May 2, 1919, "Schumpeter, the Austrian Finance Minister . . . came to lunch with me at Sacher's. Schumpeter, in spite of his official position, entered fully into our plans, gave us some excellent advice, and also promised to help to raise money by any means in his power. . . . We then induced Schumpeter to send Rothschild a note telling him he could safely lend us money as he would guarantee the repayment from the Treasury."[39]

Cunninghame, the British representative, also appeared later at the lunch "and was surprised to find Schumpeter taking part in our deliberations" (ibid.). That same evening, "Schumpeter's secretary came in [at Rothschild's] and said: 'I have a message from Mr. Schumpeter for Baron Rothschild. There is no need for him to advance any money as it has been raised elsewhere'" (ibid., 164).

Ashmead-Bartlett assumed that Schumpeter was willing and able to use

---

[37] There had been an attempt to raise money with Rothschild.

[38] Ibid., 159, dated May 1, 1919.

[39] Ibid., 162. The newspaper account got the substance of the passage right, except that it omitted without indication of having done so the bracketed sentence—forgivable in a newspaper account; less forgivable that it had the note sent to Count Schönborn.

treasury funds, but there is no "smoking gun" to prove that this was so, and in view of Schumpeter's earlier hesitations about his need to account to parliament for the money spent, it would require the further belief that Schumpeter had somehow succeeded in finagling the books.

In any case, since the counterrevolutionaries succeeded in capturing the Hungarian embassy and in the process captured 135 million kronen and about 300,000 Swiss francs, there was no need to raise money elsewhere.

Of course, Bela Kun protested the violation of his Embassy's extraterritoriality. But he then "formally surrendered his extraterritorial rights, and formally asked the [Austrian] Government to take possession of the Embassy and to arrest the raiders" (ibid., 172). This led to the possibility that the counterrevolutionaries would be returned to Hungary, where they were sure to be shot. So on May 4, Ashmead-Bartlett again had lunch with Schumpeter at Sacher, where Ashmead-Bartlett raised the feared extradition. But "Schumpeter promised as a member of Government that under no circumstances would this happen" (ibid., 173).

In the aftermath of the attempted invasion of Hungary, which was a botched and incompetent affair—an invasion originally planned with 3,000 men and finally executed with 30—Schumpeter was asked by a Hungarian countess to intervene with the Austrian government in favor of the somewhat disgraced Hungarian aristocracy (ibid., 182).

Bauer was furious with the police for failing to trace the 135 million kronen. Eventually, about 50 million kronen (but no Swiss francs) were recovered, "but the police for their part guaranteed not to hand the money over to the Bolsheviks, but to hold it in trust for the new Government when it is established. Schober[40] in parting said: 'If you enter any other movement, please do it in a more intelligent manner.' Thus ends the miserable badly organized fiasco at Bruck. Those who took part in it are, for the time being, somewhat discredited, which perhaps is a good thing" (ibid., 184).

Ashmead-Bartlett probably did not mean to include Schumpeter among the discredited. But the episode does put Schumpeter in a somewhat strange light. There is his almost fatal liking for an aristocracy which, on the one hand, he believed indispensable (see Chapter 12) yet whose political acumen he estimated rather low (see his letters to Lammasch). There is also a certain vanity not only that he did see things right (which was probably true) but that he could single-handedly put them right. And there is his taste for intrigue, executed in a blatantly open manner, that helped to undo him.

Of course, the same actions can also be interpreted quite differently: there was a man who deeply cared for his country and fought for what he believed to be essential even if the odds for succeeding were not good. And he certainly broke no laws and did not act in secret.

[40] Ashmead-Bartlett got the name wrong, spelling it Schrober. He also misspelled Prater (as Isherwood's *Prater Violet*) Prada.

PART I

The Theoretical Bases of Economic Policy:

Statics, Dynamics, and Evolution

or

History Matters

The volume and complexity of historical research are at the same time the result and the demonstration of the fact that the more we examine the way in which things happen, the more we are driven from the simple to the complex. . . . Perhaps the greatest of all lessons of history is this demonstration of the complexity of human change and the unpredictable character of ultimate consequences of any given act or decision of man; . . . this is a lesson that can only be learned in detail.

. . . What we have a right to demand of [the historian] is that he shall not change the meaning and purport of the historical story in the mere act of abridging it.

—Herbert Butterfield, *The Whig Interpretation of History*

Economics as a Science

METHODOLOGICAL VIEWS

Schumpeter always warned against mixing theory and practical policy advice ostentatiously based on theory. At the same time he himself was, of course, greatly interested in economic policy, not in abstracto but as a publicist and a formulator and executor on the highest political level; and he tried his hand at investment banking as well. It is all too easily assumed that his advice was the result of his failures in "real" life.[1] This is probably not so and is in itself a perfect example of the dangers of deriving conclusions from circumstantial evidence alone.[2]

Das Wesen und der Hauptinhalt der theoretischen Nationalokonomie (*The Nature and Main Content of Theoretical Economics*, cited hereafter as *Wesen*), dated March 2, 1908, Cairo, which was written in 1907 when Schumpeter was twenty-four years old, is proof to the contrary.[3] It was written when he was a highly successful lawyer, full of energy and hope, characteristics which he preserved throughout his minister of finance and investment banker days.[4] The *Wesen* makes quite clear that Schumpeter's warning was based on different considerations.

First, he insisted that economic theory had to be *wertfrei* and that it was possible to make it so. In a letter to Gustav Stolper in connection with the

---

[1] Schumpeter's failures are occasionally contrasted with Keynes' successes. There is some justice in this assessment, but a comparison seems instructive. Both men "succeeded" as publicists and public speakers. Keynes succeeded in business where Schumpeter, after an initial success in Cairo before the First World War, failed. But both must be considered political failures until and including the Great Depression. Keynes's warning about the Treaty of Versailles fell on deaf ears as did Schumpeter's desperation about the Treaty of St. Germain. Both opposed postwar deflationary policies. Keynes's opposition to a return to prewar parity of the pound-sterling was no more understood than Schumpeter's insistence that the war-devaluation of the Austrian krone should not be reversed but only halted.

Keynes's policy successes started with the *General Theory* and his wartime and postwar influence. But there is no evidence that he had any effect on New Deal policies. Keynes's thought did eclipse Schumpeter's after the appearance of the *General Theory*. Schumpeter, in a slightly different context, explained Keynes's success by giving respectability to an already prevailing antisaving attitude in America which Keynes did not create but which Schumpeter considered a grave danger to America's future.

[2] An example of such an unjustified inference from internal logic without corroborating fact in an entirely different field is found in C. S. Lewis (1926). Lewis gave a specific example to warn "critics who attempt to date ancient texts too exactly" from internal evidence (ibid., xv). Throughout this study I shall do my best to stick to facts and eschew amateur psychology.

[3] Page references without specific source refer to *Das Wesen* (1908). My translations.

[4] This is attested to by the entry into Wieser's diary already quoted.

founding of the *Deutsche Volkswirt* and Schumpeter's role as a regular contributor, Schumpeter expressed his desire to use the articles to teach the public economic thinking by discussing current problems, and to rescue economics from ideological misuse.[5] Economics was to Schumpeter a serious science. The issue was precise thinking. From the very beginning, Schumpeter championed the use of mathematics (although he never became proficient in it himself)[6] not instead of but in addition to history and sociology. Schumpeter expressed his ideas of what mathematics could do in a fascinating letter to E. B. Wilson in 1937.

May 19, 1937

Professor E. B. Wilson
42 Brinkton Road
Brookline, Mass.

Dear Wilson:

In thanking you the other day for your permission to attend your course I was not able to express my gratitude, independent of the gratitude I feel for what the course has given me personally, for the impulse and support you have again extended to a line of advance which at Harvard has still to fight for its existence and which nevertheless is, I feel convinced, indispensable if economics and economic policy is ever to emerge from the stage of phraseology on the one hand and of pedestrian fact-collecting on the other.

The reason for this letter, however, is to make another, though cognate point. I was strongly impressed with the immense value to the economist of such lectures as you gave in the first part of the course. I perfectly agree with those who object to the practice of some economists, simply to copy out what they believe is an economic argument from textbooks of pure mathematics or of theoretical mechanics or physics, and I hope you will not interpret what I am about to say in the sense of that practice, which sometimes comes near being ridiculous.

But it is one thing to copy and another thing to learn how to apply existing, and to derive the stimulus for constructing, new mathematical tools in the face of difficult factual patterns. We must not copy actual arguments but we can learn from physics how to build up an exact argument.[7] Moreover we can learn to understand the relation of mathematics to the reality to which it is applied. Most important of all is the consideration that there are obviously a set of concepts and procedures which, although not belonging to the field of pure mathematics, but to the field of more or less applied mathematics, are of so general character as to be applicable to an indefinite number of different fields. The concepts of Potential

[5] Letter from Schumpeter to Gustav Stolper, dated Bonn, May 28, 1926. Reprinted in Schumpeter (1985).

[6] "Ueber die mathematische Mehode der theoretischen Oekonomie," reprinted in Schumpeter (1952), appeared already in 1906.

[7] Richard Feynman, a Nobelist in physics, in his *You Can't Be Serious, Mr. Feynman*, uses a nonmathematical sociological investigation as an example of good scientific procedure!

or Friction or Inertia are of this kind, and the problems and difficulties to which they give rise are formally much the same, whatever the subject matter.

There is, as it were, a kind of science which is not simply pure mathematics, but is yet neither mechanics, nor acoustics, nor economics, nor anything in particular, and this science ought to be known to every scientific worker, whatever his field. Every one would, besides learning useful techniques, also acquire in studying it, a broadening of his horizon and a better understanding of his instruments.

Such a science is extremely difficult to learn or to teach. There is no book on it, nor any literature about it. It must be pieced together. And this can only be done by a man who has wide experience with a large number of fields. Well, and all I want to say is that you are just such a man for that important and difficult task and that economists who cannot without an unreasonable amount of work, do the job for themselves, would have to be particularly grateful to you if you undertook it.

What I am suggesting is, therefore, that you consider the expansion of what you told us in the first part of this spring into the main content of such a half-course.

Cordially yours,

Joseph A. Schumpeter

This letter clarifies important issues about how Schumpeter envisaged his scientific task. It is certainly far removed from the usual "mathematics for economists." It talks about the development of new mathematical tools—which has since happened—and about difficult factual patterns, which is the major problem of *Business Cycles*.

Traditional equilibrium analysis cried for the application of calculus; indeed, the rise of marginalism is a rediscovery of calculus. Yet Schumpeter was for very good reasons dissatisfied with the state of affairs. His formulation of the problem did indeed call for a different kind of mathematical approach, and a case can be made (and has been made by a mathematical colleague) that Schumpeter's ideas anticipated later mathematical developments of nonlinear dynamic systems of higher order.

Moreover, while in 1908 he specifically rejected an analogy to the biology of the time for equilibrium economics, he later did state that for evolutionary economics there were intellectual relations to mutations and *évolution créatrice*.[8] Mechanical analogies made perfectly good sense for the explanation of parts of reality, but not for dealing with evolution as a whole. What mattered to Schumpeter was finding ways to bring order into chaos, to allow for organization of the host of unique facts.

Interestingly, E. B. Wilson in turn urged Schumpeter to teach the kind of course which was being pushed out of the liberal arts curriculum and which was unjustly stigmatized as a "snap course." Wilson vigorously defended snap courses as being every bit as difficult as "hard" courses: "I take it that a

---

[8] In a letter to Jakob Marschak, parts of which are reproduced in the Epilogue.

liberal as contrasted with a technical education means primarily that a person is aware of problems, has some notion of what people have thought about them, and in particular has a keen appreciation of the difference between the problems that can be definitely solved, and those that certainly give no evidence of definite solutions."[9]

This certainly was as far removed from a survey course as was Schumpeter's search from the usual course on mathematics for economists.

These two letters make the important methodological plea of, on the one hand, ever improving the level of technical analysis, but on the other hand, not disregarding facts and developments simply because more precise methods of analysis were not yet at hand. Between them, Wilson and Schumpeter almost seem to call for an approach which in earlier days was claimed to be fulfilled— up to a point—by theology, but with a consciousness of the limits of human capabilities.

Wertfreiheit, Science, and Ideology

There was a more substantive basis for Schumpeter's warning. "Theoretical economics" or "economic theory" meant at the time static economics, equilibrium theory. It was the best worked out part of theory, in fact, the only one that was reasonably well worked out on the basis of the marginal principle, though, of course, much remained to be done. But in the *Wesen*, Schumpeter showed that the applicability of stationary static theory was severely limited. Because of these limitations, policy prescriptions based on equilibrium theory were not always relevant to the real world. The real world was dynamic, evolutionary, developmental. In the static world important economic phenomena—such as productive interest—had no logical place. And policies which in a static world were clearly indefensible might make some sense when evolutionary problems were considered. In any case, it seemed nonsensical to derive important conclusions on the basis of data for only a few years.

Schumpeter never deviated from this view that economics had to be free of value judgments, wertfrei. If anything it became more pronounced. In 1943, he wrote: "Is it not possible that an author presents facts and arguments in little self-contained miniatures which are intended to stand by themselves and to be judged on their own merits and demerits without trying to put all of them into the concentration camp of his personal value judgments—in which they would, just as human beings do, lose all their individuality and flavor?"[10]

---

[9] Letter dated November 4, 1943. In the Schumpeter papers, Harvard University Archives.

[10] Letter to Dr. Waldemar Gurion, editor of *The Review of Politics*, Notre Dame, Indiana, dated February 5, 1943, in the Harvard University Archives. Schumpeter is really just pleading for some common sense. In strict logic, we cannot, of course, escape the limits of our humanity. But, as Schumpeter was fond of saying, "The fastest way to complete nonsense is to be ruthlessly logical." An analogy might make clear that this is not a cynical bon mot. Is it really impermissible to measure the surface of a kitchen table by plane geometry when the earth is really round and hence, in strict logic spherical geometry should be applied? On the political level, we find all the

Schumpeter continued to the last to think about "Science and Ideology," the title of his presidential address to the American Economic Association.[11]

Of course, we all have our value judgments and ideological prejudices, but "Science is technique" (ibid., 268). Developing techniques is independent of value judgments. It is indeed "misconduct to bend either facts or inferences from facts to make them serve either an ideal or an interest. But such misconduct is not necessarily inherent in a worker's arguing from axiological premises or in advocacy per se" (ibid.).[12]

"*Ideologies are not simply lies*; they are truthful statements about what a man thinks he sees" (ibid., 271, italics in original). There is the initial vision, which is prescientific but not irrational. Everybody is subject to ideological preconceptions in this sense; Schumpeter credits Marx for this analysis.

Schumpeter gives three examples from the history of economic thought. The first is Adam Smith, whose ideological preconceptions have no effect on his analysis. But in both Marx and Keynes the original vision does get in the way of analysis. In Marx's case, "the increasing misery of the masses . . . [was] untenable and at the same time indispensable for him" (ibid., 277). In Keynes's case, it was "modern stagnationism" (ibid.) "which Schumpeter traced already to the *Economic Consequences of the Peace,* judged to have remained a side issue in the *Treatise on Money,*" but no longer in the *General Theory*" (ibid.).

Characteristically, however, it is *not* some individuals who could completely free themselves from all preconceptions which might make them harmless. It is first that any "initial vision . . . induces fact finding and analysis . . . [which] tend to destroy whatever will not stand their test. [Hence] no economic ideology could survive indefinitely ever in a stationary social world." Even so, "some ideology will always be with us" (ibid., 281).

> But this is no misfortune. It is pertinent to remember another aspect of the relation between ideology and vision. That prescientific cognitive act which is the source of our ideologies is also the prerequisite of scientific work. No new departure of any science is possible without it. Through it we acquire new material for our scientific endeavors and something to formulate, to defend, to attack. Our stock of facts and tools grows and rejuvenates itself in the process. And so, although we proceed slowly because of our ideologies, we might not proceed at all without them. (ibid.)

---

time that in a dispute between parties the one which has committed heinous crimes will always argue that the other side also is not perfect, which is undoubtedly true but irrelevant.

[11] J. A. Schumpeter, "Science and Ideology," Presidential Address at the 61st. Meeting of the American Economic Association, 1948. Reprinted in Clemence (1950). All page references are to this reprint.

[12] Of course, all science starts, I believe, with an act of faith that there is indeed something in the real world that can be logically explained, which is not identical with a belief in a deterministic universe. And any science is, I believe, only possible on the basis of the strong belief that truth matters. Schumpeter's position might perhaps be paraphrased: errors are unavoidable and forgivable; lies are not.

Even here it is ultimately Schumpeter's vision of reality as an evolutionary process which leads him to an optimistic conclusion about the progress of science.

Wertfreiheit, Vision, and Ideal and Real Types

Schumpeter's notion of "vision" seems worthy of further discussion. It is this point that the concept of a stationary equilibrium economy is inadequate to deal with reality, which explains his sympathy for some aspects of the German Historical School, whose program he considered closely related to that of Wesley Mitchell.[13] It explains his frequently expressed opinion that the *Methodenstreit* made no sense, that the actual scholarly work of economists would simply ignore it. And it also shows his affinity to the work of his friend and colleague Arthur Spiethoff. It is also important to understand Schumpeter's difference from the methodological and hence analytic approach of Max Weber. It is central to understand how Schumpeter envisaged the basic task of theory and the interrelation between historic uniqueness and theoretical generality.

The word vision seems to have put many readers off Schumpeter's work. The issue is: just how do you arrive at the initial assumptions of your theoretical analysis? Just how do you decide what it is you want to analyze? Max Weber gave one answer, Spiethoff and Schumpeter another.

Max Weber developed the concept of an ideal type in 1904.[14] It is simplest to quote the original essay because there seems to me to be some inner contradiction. On the one hand, Weber speaks

> [O]f an idealized picture (Idealbild) of events on the market for goods with a social organization based on exchange, free competition and strictly rational actions. This abstraction (Gedankenbild, thought construct) combines particular relationships and events of historical life into an internally consistent cosmos of *imagined* (*gedachter*) connections. In its content this construct has the character of a *utopia* which is found by a *thought* process of exaggeration (*gedankliche* Steigerung) of certain elements of reality. Its relation to the empirical facts of life consists only in that wherever connections of the kind which the construct pictures abstractly . . . are supposed to exist we can visualize the individuality (Eigenart) of these connections by means of an *ideal type* . . . it is not a "hypothesis" but it wants to show the way to the formulation of hypotheses. It is not a *picture* (*Darstellung*) of reality, but it wants to provide unambiguous (eindeutig) means of expression for the picture. (ibid., 190; italics in original; my translation)

---

[13] "Gustav v. Schmoller und die Probleme von heute," originally 1926. Reprinted in Schumpeter (1954), 148–99.

[14] "Die "Objektivität sozialwissenschaftlicher and sozialpolitischer Erkenntnis," reprinted in Weber (1922), 146–214. Part 1 of this essay (pp. 148–61) reflects the opinion of all editors of the *Archiv für Sozialwissenschaft und Sozialpolitik*. Part 2, the remainder of the essay, expresses only Max Weber's opinion. The idea of the "ideal type" apparently antedates Max Weber's use of it, but Max Weber's use is entirely original.

So far, there is a connection made with reality, though in a somewhat ambiguous way. There is a call for internal consistency which for me is essentially an equilibrium characteristic. There is a call for strict rationality which is here not further defined but which evidently is meant to exclude all considerations that have no place in the construct. All of this already distinguishes this approach from those of Spiethoff and Schumpeter.

But a few sentences later Max Weber explains:

> The *ideal type* . . . is arrived at by a unilateral *exaggeration* of one or a few points of view and by combining into a consistent (einheitlich) thought construct (Gedankengebilde) many scattered and discrete *individual* phenomena which exist here more or less and *elsewhere not at all.* This thought construct does nowhere exist in reality. It is a utopia and the historian's work is to determine in the individual case how near or how far reality comes to the individual picture. (ibid., 191; italics in original; last italics added; my translation)

When it comes to the idea of a "capitalistic culture," Weber states specifically:

> [I]t must be considered as certain . . . that . . . numerous utopias of this kind may be sketched of which none resembles any other, and even more, of which none may be observed in reality . . . but of which each nevertheless may claim to picture the "idea" of capitalistic culture and of which *each can* claim this, as each is indeed derived from certain in its *individually (Eigenart) significant* features of reality and brought into a consistent ideal picture. (ibid., 192; italics in original; my translation)

Thus, for Weber there are in principle any number of capitalistic ideal types which may even contain features not found in reality and whose only purpose is to be confronted with reality!

It is not my intention to analyze Max Weber. But it must be pointed out that unlike Spiethoff's real types or Schumpeter's vision, the ideal type is *not* an abstraction of reality. Real types on the other hand are derived from observed reality, or at the very least insist that reality conforms to them in *all* important features. Spiethoff distinguishes for subtypes. "Type 1. The model which mirrors a real institutional situation and is arrived at by economic Gestalt theory. Type 2. The model in pure theory arrived at by abstraction from reality."[15] These two types are of interest here, the latter characterizing Schumpeter's approach. Real types need not be, and indeed as a rule are not, internally consistent: "exceptions are taken for granted" (ibid.). And there can be only *one* real type of capitalistic reality.

---

[15] Arthur Spiethoff, "Pure Theory and Economic Gestalt Theory: Ideal Types and Real Types," in Lane and Riemersma (1953), 457. The editors also have provided a very useful introduction to Spiethoff's methodological views. Spiethoff's term "anschauliche Theorie" has, with his consent, been translated as Gestalt Theory. The term "anschauliche Theorie" did not originate with Spiethoff but was suggested by his friend, Edgar Salin.

At this point a decisive difference between the ideal-type and the real-type economic style becomes evident. While there may be numerous ideal types possible to picture the capitalistic way of economic life, there can be only one real type of the capitalistic economic style. There is only one purpose that guides the selection of characteristics to be combined in that real type: completeness of the causal elements. Which these elements are is not a matter to be settled once and for all. They may vary according to the progress of research. But one thing is settled, namely, the point of view from which the elements are selected. To sum up, economic style models of type 1 are not ideal types, they are real types, which aim at reflecting historic reality.[16]

The point expressed here is also relevant to the definition of socialism, whose coming Schumpeter "predicted," for it is precisely the change in the course of economic development which is crucial, and not a set of attributes selected once and for all.

Spiethoff quotes with approval the following passage from Schumpeter's second (1926) edition of the *Theorie*, which was omitted from the English translation of 1934: "To quote Schumpeter: 'No doubt, our picture is only a schema. But it is a schema which is linked to reality by an unbroken analytical chain. This analysis has selected what seems to be essential to the economic process while it has left out what is neither a causal factor nor essential. Therefore we are entitled to expect that it reflects all the characteristic feature of economic life.' "[17]

In other words, Schumpeter saw science as an instrument to analyze reality. A theory was not so much true or false (provided, of course, that it was not logically flawed) but useful or useless.[18] But this in turn implies that all theoretical explanations should be designed to cope with facts that needed to be explained. On this point Schumpeter thought that "economists have got themselves into a hole by their effort, in itself meritorious, to refine the concepts of monopoly and competition so as to reduce them to mere logical schemes that have practically no application to real life."[19]

Beyond that, reality is enormously complicated, and any application of theory to reality had to be surrounded with the proper qualifications to be

---

[16] Ibid., 457. I will return to the concept of economic style and its relation to Schumpeter's analysis in the context of the analysis of time series in chapter 7. Spiethoff does point out, however that "Max Weber went too far, of course, when he denied that the essentials of a historic reality are reflected in an ideal type" (p. 456).

[17] Quoted from ibid. The original passage is found in the second and later edition (1926) of the *Theorie*, p. 77. As translated by Spiethoff's translator, Fritz Redlich.

[18] See on the instrumentalism most recently Shionoya (1990), 187–222, which is a more searching analysis than is possible here.

[19] Letter to George Stocking, dated September 19, 1949. In this letter, written in response to a letter from Stocking, Schumpeter also explained in more detail his attitude toward monopolies, large-scale industries, and government antitrust policy. In "Science and Ideology," Schumpeter used the attitude toward monopolies based on the pure-competition model of capitalism as an example of a questionable influence of ideology ("Science and Ideology," 279–80). Also see Nelson and Winter's analysis in chapter 6.

correct. Any theoretical analysis involved abstraction. But any policy analysis had to proceed in a particular historical context.

Finally, Schumpeter insisted that economic considerations were always only one of the necessary inputs into economic policy making, and at times not the most important one. In other words, the assumption of strict rationality was not usually appropriate. People might legitimately disagree about aims, but even where there was a consensus about those aims, other considerations might modify any conclusions reached on purely economic grounds. The application of theory to policy ceased to be wertfrei. This was acceptable as long as the *Wertfreiheit* of pure theory was preserved.[20]

Methodological and Political Individualism

The *Wesen* has been described as a methodological book and also as not very "original." There is truth in the first assertion, but a serious misunderstanding is involved in the second. Leaving aside the reading into the 1908 book results of later research, the fact remains that Schumpeter's major conclusions were rejected at the time.

The book was addressed to a German—not just a German-speaking—readership, which may explain in (small) part the attempt to establish a bridge to the dominant Historical School. Schumpeter had, of course, no doubt about the importance of the marginal approach. He himself stated that he felt closest to Walras and Wieser, but there are also flattering remarks about Alfred Marshall and particularly J. B. Clark.

For Schumpeter, as was explained, the basic assumptions for the analysis are to be derived from the observation of reality. Psychological insights had no place of pride in an equilibrium system; they were simply irrelevant. Wieser did not agree on that point.[21]

Second, analysis of equilibrium theory, whether Austrian or Walrasian, showed that it could not adequately explain certain phenomena which nevertheless were economic in nature, chief among them profit and productive interest and "crises."

Third, static theory did fit important parts of reality. There were long periods in history whose economic life was adequately described by equilibrium theory (*Wesen*, 564–65) and in which change was attributable to ex-

[20] In 1913, the Verein für Sozialpolitik had a meeting where this topic was discussed at length. Schumpeter's concise treatment was just two pages, "Joseph Schumpeter. Meinungsäusserung zur Frage des Werturteils." *Aeusserungen zur Werturteilsdiskussion im Ausschuss des Vereins für Sozialpolitik*. Als Manuskript gedruckt, 1913, 49–50. A copy was found in the library of the Institut für Weltwirtschaft, Kiel. The other and major discussant was Max Weber. Schumpeter's contribution is reproduced in Schumpeter (1993).

[21] This is an important basic difference to the approach of much of the Austrian school. Mises is credited with saying that if the facts (facts, not just statistics) do not agree with the theory, too bad for the facts. Though possibly apocryphal, Mises certainly defended this position to the end of his life.

traordinary events outside the economic system, such as wars, pestilence or the weather. But "in the last analysis, it is not the constancy of the data which is the essence of statics, but the kind of economic process which it describes."[22]

The point is that static theory dealt with processes of adaptation, but by itself could not explain how change arose from inside the economy. In strict logic, this limited the applicability of static theory very severely. In fact, however, if applied "with tact and sensitivity" it also might be useful to deal with small changes arising from inside the system.

Thus, the *Wesen* cleared the way for a dynamic analysis, which is, of course, the subject matter of all of Schumpeter's later writings, but of which important parts are already contained in the *Wesen*.

The term "dynamic" itself has a certain ambiguity.[23] How such a dynamic-evolutionary situation was to be analyzed was still unclear. Aprioristic prescriptions of how to deal with this problem seemed just nonsense to Schumpeter.[24] In any case, it was one of Schumpeter's major criticisms of Keynes's *General Theory* that it implied invariant production functions "[when]" on the contrary they are being incessantly revolutionized.[25]

But there is also the other limitation of the special case, of the special institutional and numerical assumptions that have to be made to arrive at useful results. This is not so much the important insight that the same general theory may yield substantially different results depending on the specific size of the parameters assumed. It is rather that in a book with theoretical intent it is the "besetting Ricardian sin" of making in the course of the analysis additional specific assumptions to reach the desired results and then pretending that those results were general.[26]

I shall not further deal with *Wertfreiheit* or the importance of facts and

[22] Although this formulation is from *Theorie* (1911), 465, it correctly states the point made in the *Wesen*. I am indebted to Professor Shionoya for directing my attention to this quotation, which I had overlooked.

[23] The older use of the term included both the modern usage, going back to Ragnar Frisch, Paul Samuelson, and Jan Tinbergen as referring to intertemporal relationships but with constant basic parameters, and the evolutionary view, which includes changes in these parameters in historic time.

[24] "In particular, preserve us from the blessing (Wohltat) to 'show us the way' a priori or to tell us what are the nature and methods of dynamics. What our paths are and where they will lead us we and our successors will see after we have gone them. Our starting point . . . is the existence of such facts which are outside our [static] system and yet are economic problems. Capital formation, interest on capital, entrepreneurs, profit and crises—these are phenomena with respect to which today's pure economics fails" (*Wesen*, 615; my translation).

[25] Review of J. M. Keynes, *General Theory*, *Journal of the American Statistical Association*. Reprinted in Clemence (1951), 155.

[26] Schumpeter remarked in conversation that the only thing wrong with the *General Theory* was its title. It was a very special theory. It might be added that Schumpeter also stated in 1908 that Böhm-Bawerks's interest theory relied on special assumptions rather than being general, but he evidently did not accuse or mean to accuse him of the "Ricardian sin." On the contrary: "I am concerned with the truth and not with the originality of my theory. In particular, I willingly base it upon that of Böhm-Bawerk as much as possible—however decidedly the latter has declined all communion" (*Theory*, paperback ed., 158).

institutions. There is, however, the further point of Schumpeter's methodological individualism. There is no ethical, political, or psychological judgment involved in this. Concepts like national income or gross investment are, of course, not inconsistent with that methodological individualism, although they are "social," that is, aggregative, applying to the economy as a whole, but involving interactions among individuals. To be meaningful, they must be based on individually observable facts. Gross domestic product (GDP) cannot be directly observed, and a figure of gross national product (GNP) cannot be properly interpreted unless it is known how the concept is actually measured and whether the prices at which it is calculated make economic sense.

Nobody doubts that individuals act in a social context. All economists investigate this, but as economists they are interested only in *how* individuals act and interact. "The deeper reasons [for their actions] may be interesting but do not affect our results. They belong to sociology, hence our point of view cannot be disproved by a proof that the events in an economy cannot be fully explained as being purely individualistic" (*Wesen*, 94–95).

In a 1909 article[27] Schumpeter discussed the concept of social value where it is not simply the result of the interactions of individual behavior. He takes the American "concept of social value" seriously. But he points out that while "our problem is a purely *methodological* one and has nothing to do with the great problems of individualism and collectivism" (ibid., 1; italics in original), the American concept makes sense, indeed is "indispensable in the study of a communist society" (ibid., 20). It is important, however, to realize that the "social" utility curves (or, to avoid this term, the demand curves for society as a whole) will differ in a communist and an individualistic society (ibid., 20).[28] The maxima that can be attained in the two types of society will differ as well.

The whole maximum principle is misunderstood in any case if it is treated as an absolute. It is only a maximum that can be achieved with given assumptions, among which is the initial distribution of wealth and what people are actually prepared to do.

In *Capitalism*, Schumpeter states explicitly that the maximum utility that can be achieved which competitive equilibrium describes is not entitled to be the standard by which all alternatives must be judged. All it says is—and it could be argued that this is perhaps more important than Schumpeter is willing to grant—that under the given assumptions some sort of maximum production (in the Paretian sense) will be reached. But it is *impossible* that *any* given circumstances are such that something better could not be achieved.

The point is important and it is basically made already in the *Wesen*: The maximization principle in the *Wesen* is restricted to very special and restrictive assumptions which severely limit the applicability of equilibrium theory. The point is developed in the much later discussion of Nelson and Winter, to which I will return in chapter 6. In fact, Schumpeter's reinterpretation of equilibrium theory as applicable only to adaptive processes also echoes

---

[27] "On the Concept of Social Value," reprinted in Clemence (1951).
[28] This will be expanded in the chapters on socialism.

Walras's perceived limitation of what theory could accomplish. And Schumpeter's extension of the limits of applicability to situations in which basic parameters have not changed significantly is a kind of salvage operation. Perhaps *Das Wesen* was more original than it was given credit for.

The whole discussion has gained new relevance with the introduction of "free markets" into formerly Soviet-style economies. Markets were for Schumpeter *not* a *definiens* of a capitalistic society. Markets just define what is scarce and how to economize scarce resources. But how the demands for resources are formed under capitalism and socialism (or for that matter feudalism) is quite different, and, more important, the effective demands and the achievable maxima will be quite different. Thus, the argument that market socialism will lead to the same results as an individualistic market economy is inherently flawed. In "Social Value," Schumpeter mentions explicitly the limitation in a non-Communist society that the initial distribution of wealth must be given, a limitation that does not apply to a communist society ("Social Value," 17). Of course, what takes the place of the initial distribution of wealth is the distribution of power. I shall return to these problems in Part II.

Schumpeter's own immediate thoughts evidently went in a somewhat different direction: the discussion of the importance and emergence of the modern State, that is, the emergence of a political individualism.[29] But even here methodological individualism is not dropped. *The Crisis* starts with developments in the "recent" past few hundred years. The problem of the individual versus society is, of course, age old and will never be resolved once-and-for-all. We have recently heard much about it in connection with the two hundredth anniversary of the French revolution and the universal declaration of the rights of man.

The French declaration of the rights of man of 1789 was conceived as a counterweight against the Rousseauan ideas underlying the basic concepts of the revolution, that is, as a protection of the individual against the power of the State, of society.[30]

It was Virginia, whose constitution had an explicit bill of rights in 1776 (more than twenty years before the French declaration) which became the model for the other states and for the French.[31] The conflict between the individual and society is, of course, ever present. The issue becomes whether

[29] *Die Krise des Steuerstaats*, first published in 1918, reprinted in Schneider and Spiethoff (1953). English translation by R. A. Musgrave and W. F. Stolper in *International Economic Papers* vol. 4 (1954) and reprinted in Swedberg (1991a). *Die Krise* will be more fully discussed in chapter 11.

[30] Jellinek (1919), 7 refers to Rousseau to the effect that "the idea of original rights which the individual (Mensch) takes over into society and which appears as a legal limit of he sovereign is explicitly excluded by Rousseau. There is no basic law which is binding on society (Gesamtheit), not even the *contrat social* itself" (my translation).

[31] Ibid., 18. The author of the bill of rights was the conservative George Mason. The dates of the individual bills of rights are: 1776 for Pennsylvania, Maryland, and North Carolina; 1777 for Vermont; 1780 for Massachusetts; and 1783–84 for New Hampshire. There was, of course, no U.S. Bill of Rights until after there was a U.S. Constitution. Other states, e.g., New York, had no appended bill of rights but corresponding articles in the bodies of the Constitutions. Jellinek

the State can do only what the individual allows it to do, or whether the individual can do only what the State permits. But the issue is also to what extent individuals may dictate the rights of other individuals.

These matters are not so extraneous as they might seem at first. Schumpeter considered himself a conservative, which meant precisely a high regard for the individual. In a letter to Redvers Opie he complained that he had given up all hope of ever seeing a civilized conservativism again.[32] In another letter in 1937 he stated that "no satisfactory exposition of the rationale of conservativism exists. . . . It is one of the humors of the situation that conservativism has never satisfactorily defined itself."[33]

By 1941, Schumpeter had arrived at a definition of conservativism which clearly derived from his developmental view of reality. In the last of the Lowell Lectures on *An Economic Interpretation of Our Time* given on March 28, 1941, Schumpeter analyzed the situation in terms of constant changes occurring in reality. The final paragraph of the last lecture summarizes in a pithy way Schumpeter's position about the relationship of accidents (i.e., unique events) and deterministic development:

> Mark the line of my argument. While I said that the fundamental lines [of development] are probably ineluctable and while I said, second, that much in the way in which the ever present change comes about depends on individuals and groups, abilities and conditions, I said, third, that no more can be achieved by individual or group coalitions than to perform transitions with a minimum of loss of human values. The latter, the bringing about of transitions from your social structure to other social structures with a minimum of loss of human values, that is how I should define conservativism.[34]

The matter so occupied Schumpeter that he planned to write a book on "The Meaning of Conservativism . . . that will be something different. Among other things I am pretty sure that no conservative that I ever met will recognize himself in the picture I am going to draw."[35]

(pp. 20–29) gives an article-by-article comparison in parallel columns of the same page between the declaration des droits de l'homme and du citoyen and the various states' bills of rights. He also points out that "the French have not only accepted the American ideas but also the form which the latter received on the other side of the ocean" (p. 29; my translation).

[32] "Still more bitterly I feel that there is no more and never will be any room on this earth for that cultivated conservativism which would command my allegiance." Letter from Schumpeter to Redvers Opie, dated "Saturday," probably 1933. The letter was made available through the courtesy of Loring Allen who in turn got it from Edward S. Mason.

[33] Letter to Albert Pratt, dated May 12, 1937. Reproduced in Swedberg (1991b), 222. This letter contains also several explicit comments on world politics which show Schumpeter as a conservative in favor of Generalissimo Franco, and stating that Chamberlain might have averted the First World War. The last statement is in keeping with Schumpeter's strongly held beliefs that war was a catastrophe and that capitalism was inherently pacific, perhaps even pacifistic.

[34] *An Economic Interpretation of Our Time.* Eight lectures given under the auspices of the Lowell Institute, March 4–28, 1941, reproduced in Swedberg (1991a), quotation on p. 399. My own definition, evidently derived from Schumpeter, is: change firmly rooted in the past.

[35] Letter to J. K. Galbraith, October 28, 1948. In the Harvard Archives.
In a similar situation in 1926 and in the context of fiscal policy, Schumpeter was quite explicit:

This whole discussion provides a nice illustration of the difference between an evolutionary and an equilibrium approach. Take the "ineluctability" of history. This is not nearly as deterministic as it looks. Of course, the course of history can be influenced, but any influence has to come years before the consequences of earlier actions become apparent.

Hayek protested "Why I am not a Conservative." He was a Whig, liked Whig philosophy, and hoped to preserve Whig society. He chastised British Conservatives for not opposing change more. But Schumpeter was a Tory. He admired how Whig society and policy looked, yet he had no illusion about the possibility of preserving it. He fought modern developments as much as Hayek, but not so much to preserve the past as to force the inevitable changes in a "humane" direction. The point is made explicitly in Schumpeter's critique of Hayek's *Road to Serfdom*. (See also Herbert Butterfield, *The Whig Interpretation of History*.)

Schumpeter also struggled with these problems, first in *The Crisis*, and later in *Capitalism* and a posthumously published speech in Montreal.[36] For the present purpose, certain remarks seem relevant which also link up with Schumpeter's ideas of the fundamentally developmental nature of all reality, not only of the economy. The second edition of the *Theorie* makes this abundantly clear:

> Both—rise and fall (Auftrieb und Deklassierung)—are theoretically and practically, economically and culturally, much more important than the existence of relatively constant property positions on whose functioning alone all analytical attention has been concentrated. And in their particular ways both are much more characteristic of the economy, the culture and the results of capitalism than any of the things that can be observed in the circular flow.[37]

In the Walrasian system, there is no State, and this is generally true for pure theory. The works of Wicksell, Musgrave, and Samuelson, to name a few, do link the theory of public finance to individual decisions. That is, these impor-

---

"We must know that we cannot reverse social developments and that a significant reduction in the sum total of the needs of the State is an illusion" ("Finanzpolitik," *Der Deutsche Volkswirt*, reprinted in Schumpeter 1985, 69; my translation). To which Schumpeter added the footnote: "This illusion is particularly dangerous for the very circles which love it. It leads to a dream life of fiscal policy (ein finanzpolitisches Traumleben), to a fiscal policy of basic lies (Lebenslügen)—to valueless apparent successes and to bad disappointments" (Ibid., note 2. A perfect description of the fiscal policies of the 1980s and their 1990s aftermath).

[36] "The Future of Private Enterprise in the Face of Modern Socialist Tendencies." Translation of a speech given in Montreal, November 19, 1945, "Comment sauve-guarder l'enterprise privée." Translated and with an introduction by Michael C. Prime and David D. Henderson, HOPE, 7, 5 (1975), under the title "Schumpeter on Preserving Private Enterprise." Reprinted in Swedberg (1991a), chapter 9.

[37] *Theorie* (1926), 369. This quotation is not translated. See also Y. Shionoya, "The Origin of the Schumpeterian Research Program. A Chapter Omitted from Schumpeter's *Theory of Economic Development*," *Journal of Institutional and Theoretical Economics* 146, 2 (June 1990), 314–27.

tant contributions to our understanding of the public economy, if I understand them correctly, base public decisions on individual decisions; in other words, these theories, too, are based on methodological individualism.

The modern State is precisely one that can be defined as being different from individuals, from a private sphere.[38] In a feudal society it is almost impossible to distinguish what is public and what is private, what is individual and what is societal.[39] *L'état c'est moi* is not a bon mot but an accurate description of the situation. So is the Communist claim that under communism the State will wither away, for under communism there will be—ideally—no difference between the individual and society.[40]

The communal and the individual demand curves will be identical under communism, as Schumpeter pointed out in *Social Value*, and not simply the addition of individual demand curves. The feudal State is run economically like an enterprise, with the king as the executive head, and various potentates as vice presidents in charge of particular "divisions" which, to be sure, may be quite well defined legally and perhaps also by tradition. The limits between them may and do, of course, change in the course of history, much as the divisions of General Motors are from time to time reorganized.

The modern State arose also because there was an increasing emergence of the individual, the citizen. In this view, the State becomes a necessary counterpart of the individual. Thus, it turns out that the modern State is an essential part precisely of a capitalist market economy based on individual decisions and a private economy even if it is considered a disturbance, even an enemy. There are now needs of the community distinct from the needs of the individual. The problem of limiting the power of the State vis-à-vis the individual really arises only in this context. There are tasks to be fulfilled for which the market solution is either not feasible or not desired; there are public goods and merit goods, to use Musgrave's terms.

Yet one has to be careful here. It is not at all clear just what a public good is. Private armies for hire were common in the Renaissance, and in fact William

---

[38] "The outstanding feature of commercial society is the division between the private and the public sphere—or if you prefer the fact that in commercial society there is a private sphere which contains so much more than either feudal of socialist society allocates it. This private sphere is distinct from the public sphere not only conceptually but also actually. The two are to a great extent manned by different people—the history of local self-government offering the most conspicuous exception—and organized as well as run on different and often conflicting principles, productive of different and often incompatible standards" (*Capitalism*, paperback ed., 197). Exceptions may have different causes. An important one is, as Schumpeter put it, that no period can be explained only out of itself. Exceptions may be remains of previous developments or foreshadowings of future ones. What is a flaw in a static context may be a virtue in an evolutionary one.

[39] In the 1920s there was a plebiscite in the Weimar Republic about *Fürstenenteignung* to decide what the Hohenzollern owned because their family had supplied the king of Prussia and the emperor in (not of!) Germany, and what they owned because they were a family called Hohenzollern, i.e., to sort out what was public and what was private.

[40] The relevance of this for Schumpeter's views about the transition to socialism will be discussed in chapters 8–10.

McNeill[41] shows that the prototypical public good, national defense, arose out of a sort of market transaction: the citizens of Florence gave up their Roman ideals when they found that it was cheaper to hire the marauding private armies and finance them with taxes than to continually interrupt their business to man the ramparts against the same hungry private armies, both parties being content with converting defense in this manner into a public good.[42]

Max Weber, on the other hand, points out that while private armies were accepted as normal, no self-respecting medieval or renaissance city would have entrusted its grain supply to the market.[43] "Society" might decide that certain goods or needs should be public, yet surely the Knights of Malta did not at the same time want to spend money unnecessarily to assure the grain supply of Valetta, and certainly could use the market mechanism to satisfy what they saw to be a public need.[44] This kind of reasoning becomes central to Schumpeter's discussion of socialism. It also highlights the difference between an equilibrium approach and seeing an economy in constant change.

"Society" must be set in quotes because someone must make decisions about what to do. The voting procedures and the precise limitations of the political versus the bureaucratic versus the individual spheres have to be constantly redefined, even after the basic decision has been made that there are indeed such different spheres. Hence, we find in *Capitalism* a theory of democracy which fairly must be called original and which is no less non-economic because it uses categories of economic theory for the analysis of a political process.

So we find in Schumpeter's insistence on methodological individualism in combination with a simultaneous discussion of development, how this development itself is likely to change society and with it the fundamental "value functions" that underlie basic economic theory. The "inevitable" rise of socialism must be understood in this context. The present tendencies are in this direction, but of, course, socialism itself will not be the end of history but will have its own tendencies for further change. *There is no such thing as a long-term equilibrium.*

---

[41] McNeill (1982).

[42] The fact that the idea arose in the Republic of Florence itself validates Schumpeter's analysis. The idea of national defense as a public good does not fit into the feudal picture of the world. There is an additional thought: A state which hires an army has to safeguard itself against being taken over by the army. That will happen, for instance, when wages due are not paid on time. To make the system work you need a sound fiscal policy which will generate adequate resources. Mutatis mutandis, this is also applicable to army takeovers in many an LDC. All these possibilities are easily explained in Schumpeterian terms. That such army takeovers as a rule make matters worse is no counter argument.

[43] Weber (1918).

[44] Musgrave, too, distinguishes between public and private goods and whether they should be supplied by the public or the private sector. The argument arises again in the context of the definition of capitalism and socialism, i.e., whether public goods should be provided by the public or the private sector. Battleships are public goods provided by private shipyards.

Pure equilibrium theory is completely untouched by these considerations. It is in principle time-less and applicable to the (partial) understanding of any momentary situation and its adaptive processes. But policy prescriptions for an evolutionary world following from purely static theory are made at great risk.

Perhaps one further comment might be made in this context. Röpke, in a critique of Schumpeter's *Capitalism*,[45] objects that with all the cleverness of Schumpeter's analysis he yet drew the wrong conclusions from his correct analysis (ibid., 280). Röpke does not accuse Schumpeter of logical errors but rather that he is "totally blind to the importance of the task to reform the economy and society of capitalism in a sense which in essential points corresponds to his own critique" (ibid., 280–81). This because "he has become a prisoner of his own deterministic social philosophy" (ibid.). This critique is, of course, quite mistaken. It is a textbook example of Schumpeter's warning not to mix policy prescriptions with scientific analysis. And in any case, Schumpeter was not a determinist—social, historical, or any other kind.[46]

Capitalism is a scholarly work which analyzes what is and what presently visible tendencies are, and it neither judges nor advocates. What Röpke wanted was certainly inconsistent with *Wertfreiheit*. E. B. Wilson's suggestion is quite a different matter:

> I should have been glad to see you make a little more than I detected in the book of such a notion as freedom. One can have freedom under any form of government and one may be without it under any form of government. So far as I can see what the world wants is more freedom. I have heard brakemen and conductors on the railroads wishing that instead of having to live within a second of time with their excellent watches they could be in a little place in the country and arrange their day most as they pleased. My neighbor across the way in Norwell has repeatedly said that he didn't make as good a living in dollars on the farm . . . as he made in Brockton at the factory but that he was his own boss and if he didn't want to work he didn't. . . . I don't know how widespread this attitude is but there is a good deal of it. I don't know but what our modern industrial efficiency is rather repulsive to many people. . . . If it is, that attitude may deserve a little more consideration than you seem to give it.[47]

Wilson suggested that Schumpeter was neglecting a possibly important set of *facts* in his analysis of the coming of socialism. Röpke suggested that Schumpeter was unconcerned about the political results of his analysis.

Of course, Schumpeter worried about where developments were taking

---

[45] Röpke (1948), 272–81; my translation. The quoted critique cannot really be taken seriously intellectually. This is not so for other points of disagreement of Röpke's such as that Schumpeter neglected international aspects. Schumpeter, however, did not neglect such aspects in his Lowell lectures, which Röpke could not know and he certainly did not neglect them as minister of finance.

[46] See chapter 4 on logic and determinism.

[47] Letter from E. B. Wilson to J. A. Schumpeter, dated Boston, November 4, 1943.

society—and he did not like it. In his posthumously published Montreal talk (which Röpke could not know), Schumpeter worried precisely about how the *actual* developments of *actual* capitalism were destroying its very basis—as analyzed in *Capitalism* and in part before. And as minister he actually was actively involved in combatting the bolshevik regime in Hungary. Capitalism would come to an end not because there was nothing more to do—as Keynes thought in the *General Theory*—but because changes in the environment inherent in capitalist development would not make it worthwhile to try to bring about further changes, and because such changes in the environment would bring about a state of things which it would be merely a matter of taste and terminology to call socialism or not.[48]

---

[48] "The Instability of Capitalism," reprinted in Clemence (1951), 72.

Most Interesting Things That Can Be Said about Factor Prices, Money, and Interest Are Dynamic

"Turbulence" and "Self-Organization" of Economic and Social Reality

In the *Wesen*, Schumpeter was mainly concerned with establishing the narrowness of the relevance of static equilibrium theory both in the analysis of and the applicability to real phenomena. The central point of all his analysis was that reality was, to use a modern term, "turbulent," that the capitalist economy was a system constantly in motion which never reached an equilibrium. "Capitalism in equilibrium" is a *contradictio in adjecto*.

Schumpeter's view of the economy was a new paradigm for which formal, that is, mathematical, analysis was not yet available. The development of nonlinear dynamics, in particular chaos theory, and the development of computers may in time allow a much better formulation of his ideas.[1] Equilibrium economics in Schumpeter's analysis includes also dynamics strictly defined as intertemporal relationships but without change in basic data.[2] So defined, the equilibrium process, Schumpeter's circular flow, may have movement and still be amenable to analysis by static theory. The theory may even be applied to small changes in the parameters as well as to conditions of less than perfect or "free" competition.[3]

Two major avenues of thought predominate in Schumpeter's ideas about the nature of the social and economic process. In a letter to Wesley C. Mitchell, Schumpeter described "the way in which that question puts itself to me" which basically amounts to the problem of how to separate the unique historical phenomena from the more systematic underlying "regularities," or, to put it differently, how to combine historic uniqueness and irreversibility with theoretical regularity and repetition.[4]

---

[1] For the following points I am specifically indebted to my friend and colleague Carl Simon, Professor of Mathematics and Economics.

[2] A standard example is the cobweb theorem which involves simple intertemporal relationships but no change in the basic data: the demand and supply curves stay the same.

[3] These ideas were expressed in the *Wesen* as mentioned before. The inclusion of imperfectly competitive situations is found already in 1928, "The Instability of Capitalism," reprinted in Clemence, (1951), before the appearance of Chamberlin's, Joan Robinson's, and Stackelberg's contributions. Schumpeter, however, refers to Chamberlin's unpublished manuscript, which he may have seen during his visit to Harvard in 1927.

[4] Letter dated May 6, 1937. This letter was written in response to Mitchell's request for Schumpeter's cyclical datings. Some of the points raised in this letter are further discussed in the section on cycles and the discussion of the analysis of time series (chapter 7).

First, logic and determinateness are not the same.[5] Second, unique solutions can be guaranteed basically only for linear systems. For example, every high school student knows that quadratic equations generally have two solutions, and the equations themselves do not tell you whether both, none, or which is relevant in a particular situation.

Third, nonlinearities of higher degree can lead to extreme sensitivity to initial conditions. While each initial condition of a dynamical system may yield a determined time path of the variables, very small changes in the initial conditions can lead to very different time paths. To the extent that this is so, the determinacy of each is not much help. Brian Arthur has shown that path dependency may be empirically important (Arthur 1990).

Fourth, and yet worse, since small differences in the initial conditions may have big effects in time, it can no longer be assumed that they will somehow average out, or that they will lead to optimal results (ibid.).

Turbulence is, however, not the whole story. Markets are highly complex systems which exhibit a power of self-organization and, at least for a time, stability. As in biological systems, self-organization of markets may be explicable by the interaction of individual elements as they receive signals from each other. These information aspects of markets have been emphasized particularly by Hayek.

In understanding economic reality as turbulent, economists may have anticipated later mathematical developments, an understanding which is likely to be improved by following the lead of mathematical ideas of "chaos" and "anti-chaos."[6]

The essence of the part of this approach which seems relevant to economics is that a system is seen as consisting of elements—genes in the case of biology, prices, and quantities in the case of the market—which interact with each other in that the state of any element in a given period is determined by the states of other elements in the previous period. The elements together with the manner in which they are linked and interact specify the system. For example, in economics we have given production functions, that is, a constant, possibly very complicated, rule about how the "input" elements affect the "output" elements and each other.[7]

In order to understand the working of a system we have to understand what its elements are and the precise interactions among them. The system itself

[5] Ekeland (1988) speaks of "Deterministic but Random," and "Unstable but Stable."

[6] Stuart A. Kauffman, "Anti-Chaos and Adaptation." *Scientific American*, August 1991, 78–94. Also Per Bak and Kan Chen, "Self-organizing Criticality," *Scientific American*, January 1991, 4693.

Professor Dieter Schmiedtchen of the Universität des Saarlandes (who is an admirer of Hayek) first drew my attention to the importance of self-organization of complex systems, but it was not until I read the Kauffman article that I got a glimpse of the relationship of chaos to self-organization, i.e., of a more precise way in which to think about the relationship of equilibrium and evolution. Once again my friend and colleague Carl Simon explained to me patiently and in some detail these ideas (see Schmiedtchen 1990).

[7] I have put "input" and "output" in quotes to indicate that these words do here not mean what they do in input-output analysis.

may change in two ways: (a) new elements may appear and old elements may disappear, and (b) the specific manner in which the elements interact may change. The first is analogous to product innovation, the second to process innovation and even more widely, to institutional changes, a point stressed by Schumpeter in a letter to Rostow.

In order to study the possibility of spontaneous self-organization in a complex system, it is necessary to specify precisely and in detail just how the system (market) is organized. This is, of course, one of the topics of the historical approach and it is also central to the New Institutional Economics.

In the discussion of self-organization, two points appear at the outset. There are a finite though very large number of "states" which the system can take. The market will settle into one of the states unless something new happens. It may reach an equilibrium or it may settle in repeating sequences of states. However, if anything does happen to disturb the network of elements and interactions, "its trajectory may change . . . into a new . . . recurrent pattern of structural behavior" (Kauffman 1991, 80).

This seems to describe well the Schumpeterian point concerning the relation between an inherently stable equilibrium and an evolutionary change that destroys that equilibrium irreversibly.

Some results of Kauffman's mathematical analysis fit the behavior of an evolutionary market surprisingly well. If the number of elements (prices and quantities) equals the number of interactions (all prices depend on each other), the system is chaotic in that it "exhibit[s] maximum sensitivity to initial conditions" (ibid., 81). Yet "the number of possible state [limit] cycles [i.e., equilibria] . . . is very small" (ibid.).

On the other hand, Kauffman's analysis shows that if there are only one or two inputs per element, that is, what happens to a price depends only on one or two "neighboring" prices, the influence of the rest being negligible, there is little sensitivity to initial conditions (ibid.). Instead of a chaotic system we have an ordered system where an equilibrium is reached fairly quickly. Physicists and mathematical researchers have found that "systems poised on [an intermediate state between chaos and order] seem to have the optimum capacity for evolution" (ibid., 82).

The analysis suggests the profundity of Schumpeter's insights. There are powerful forces which both destroy an existing equilibrium and work toward a new one that may never be reached. There seem to me two further points which are partly explicit, mostly implicit, in Schumpeter.

First, when evolution is rapid—both the number and kinds of elements change rapidly, and so do the "rules" by which the elements interact—we may not get a movement toward an equilibrium very quickly. Moreover, the eventual move toward an ordered equilibrium may be particularly painful. But since, second, the system seems in this case particularly open to evolutionary change, this might help to understand the structural changes in an economy which are intended to deal with such violent changes, in particular, institutional changes.

One such institutional change that is explicit in Schumpeter deals with the increasing emergence of large-scale enterprise which will—in Schumpeter's analysis—mitigate the severity of the cycle, that is, which will help the adaptation process. (On this point the analysis of Nelson and Winter 1982, chapter 6 is directly relevant.) But there are also other important changes, such as the emergence of the global economy, which makes the quite understandable "isolationist" and "protectionist" reactions seem both hopeless and dangerous.

All of this allows us to think more precisely about the relationship of what is unique and what is repeated, about what is random and what is determinate, and to think more clearly about the irreversibility of historic time in contrast to the reversibility of theoretic time. This manner of approaching the understanding of reality also explains why Schumpeter insists on great institutional and historical detail. And this is precisely what Schumpeter was concerned with in his analysis of the economic and the social process.

Schumpeter's most interesting examples deal with wages, money, savings, and interest. The wages problem illustrates better than anything else how Schumpeter envisions the relation of static theory to sociological and historical factors.

Wages and Unemployment

Schumpeter starts with Wieser's theory of imputation which subsumes all factor incomes to the theory of exchange—catallactics[8]—a name for which Bishop Whately is given credit. Wages are the price for one particular commodity, labor. The marginal product of labor explains its price.

So far so good. But that assumes that the services of labor are a homogeneous "commodity." They are not. To some extent, differences in inborn abilities of human beings exist. But to the extent that differences are not genetic the question is raised why labor does not move from worse to better paid occupations. To some degree, it does; however, there are also social and historical barriers to mobility. There is racial discrimination which effectively closes some jobs for particular groups. Schumpeter's example is Chinese labor in San Francisco. Even entrepreneurial positions are often inherited. Better qualities of a metal will—said Schumpeter—command a higher price. But this is manifestly not so for labor. Even within a category, the highest paid labor is not necessarily the "best" or the most suited. In other words, labor markets are imperfect.

[8] There is an entry under catallactics in *The New Palgrave* by Murray Rothbard. Rothbard states that "Schumpeter wished to purge economics of all concern about purposeful human motives or actions, and replace it with exclusive concentration on mechanistic alterations of economic quantities. Exchanges become thus "purely formal variations of economic quantities of goods" (Rothbard 1987, 1:378). This does less than justice to Schumpeter. Schumpeter did not *wish* to exclude purposeful human action but pointed out that the *logic of equilibrium* relationships did not require any such purposeful actions and was independent of any motivation. Purposeful action was a characteristic of an evolutionary economy. (See also Shionoya 1990 and Spiethoff as quoted in chapter 7.)

The issue is not simply to improve the workings of the labor market. In the *Wesen* we find a rudimentary discussion of the economics of education: Why not spend resources to increase mobility? This essentially sensible approach has severe limits. Not only is education in many cases not just a necessity for a job, it is demanded for itself. Besides, the income of large groups of people is not explicable on the marginal principle, from the civil list of kings to the salaries of civil servants. Moreover, the demand for education is frequently determined by one's social position, and some people not only cannot get a better education because of how they are positioned sociologically; they may not even want one.

In short, all really interesting problems of the theory of wages are outside purely competitive economics strictly defined as static general equilibrium theory. In his *Deutsche Volkswirt* articles on wage policy,[9] Schumpeter politely takes Gustav Cassell to task for deriving policy conclusions too glibly from equilibrium theory, specifically for seeing imperfect mobility as the main cause of unemployment, by pointing out particularly how little economic theory by itself, without further reference to specific facts and sociological and historical developments, has to offer. The classic argument is valid only on the assumption of free competition, a statement that is italicized in the original. Improving the market would certainly help. But while technical progress, or "*rationalization*," could not cause permanent unemployment under conditions of free competition, it could with the monopolistic tendencies that actually prevailed in Germany (ibid., 157).

However, the most important point undoubtedly is "that the equilibrium wage refers to a specific situation and its data and changes with every change in the data" (ibid., 190). Yes, wages have something to do with marginal productivity. But if they are too high, the policy implications may just as well be to raise productivity as to lower wages, which in fact would be the longer-term evolutionary approach. Yes, improved mobility would improve the situation, but this involves making obsolete labor competitive—by investment in education or improving the structure of the market—by retraining which, given the fact that people age in historic time, may not always be feasible. In the course of evolution, data necessarily change, and as they change, so does the equilibrium wage. From theory to application is in economics as long a way as is "the path from a theorem in pure mechanics to the construction of a bridge" (ibid., 188).

In short, all important problems and questions relating to unemployment and wages are evolutionary in character and their analysis requires attention to specific data. "Unemployment [is] not a uniform phenomenon but a mixture of quite different phenomena" (*Theorie* 1911, 510–11; my translation).

---

[9] Reprinted in Schumpeter (1985), 156. The specific reference to Gustav Cassell is in the first of the group of articles concerned with labor problems, "Die Arbeitslosigkeit" ("Unemployment") *Deutsche Volkswirt* (D.V.) vol. 1, 1926–27. A more detailed discussion of the limits of "competitive" wage theory is found in "Lohnpolitik und Wissenschaft" ("Wage Policy and Science") (D.V. 1928–1929) and "Grenzen der Lohnpolitik" ("Limits of Wage Policy"). Reprinted in Schumpeter (1985), 185ff. and 192ff., respectively.

MONEY

Money must initially be seen in the context of the discussion of pure equilibrium theory. In describing the Walrasian system, Schumpeter immediately points out that, although Walras was the first to see the need for a unit of account, he did not really follow through his own insight. Schumpeter's version of the "missing" equation is to substitute $\Sigma pq = MV$ for Walras's $pa = 1$, that is to relate MV, interpreted as expenditures, immediately to the prices and quantities of individual goods and services. The essential point here, however, is that in order to make the general competitive equilibrium determinate there must be one good which is demanded not for its own sake but only in order to be exchanged.

This point has now become so self-evident that its originality at the time is no longer evident. Menger still explained money genetically: on a market with many goods there would have to be indirect exchange. Indirect exchange in kind would be cumbersome. So gradually one or perhaps a few goods would emerge which it was convenient for everyone to use as money. "The mixing of the genetic and the analytic problem is characteristic for all monetary investigations (Geldforschung) including Menger" (*Das Wesen des Geldes* 1970, 18, note 5; my translation. Cited hereafter as *Geld*).

Schumpeter credits Wieser in the German literature rather than Menger or his successors Mises and Hayek with changing (from 1903 on) the basis of the theory of money by insisting "that the theory of money should grow out of the theory of the economic process" (ibid., 79; my translation).

It was, however, Walras who made "the desired cash holdings (encaisse desirée) [the] foundation of monetary theory," which is equivalent to "Wieser's principle of the relation between money income and real income."[10]

Thus, money is an essential part of the general equilibrium system for reasons of internal logic and not for reasons of convenience, and its value could not be explained on the basis of marginal utility of some good used as money (as does Mises).

Since the general equilibrium system can not do without money, there is really no sense to search for "neutral money," for the kind of money that will allow the "real" economy to behave as if there were no money. But there is also the analytical as well as policy-related point: "that analysis of the economic phenomena of any given period must proceed from the economic facts that produce them and not from the monetary aggregates that result from them" ("The Decade of the Twenties," in Clemence 1951, 208).

Schumpeter's version of the quantity equation was worked out in some detail in his "Sozialprodukt und die Rechenpfennige."[11] One most important

[10] Schumpeter (1970), 80. Schumpeter refers to Walras, *Theorie de la Monnaie*, 1886, "the essential còntents of which was incorporated in later editions of Walras' Elements (e.g., 1926) though the idea was already in the first editions of 1874 and 1879" (my translation).

[11] Originally 1918. Translated by Arthur Marget as "Money and the Social Product," *International Economic Papers* no. 6, 1956. The German original is reprinted in Schumpeter (1952).

point is that he changes the argument from a transactions to an income approach, with the velocity of circulation defined as income rather than transactions velocity, and all transactions not referring to newly created values being excluded. This MV is thus national income—das Sozialprodukt—and Σpq gets around the disagreeable problem of defining "the" price level.

In 1918, Schumpeter had already questioned whether the velocity of circulation was constant, and if not, just how useful the quantity theory (as distinct from the quantity equation) really was.[12] This led Schumpeter to develop the theory of credit creation which at the time was quite original. The important functions of money appear in the process of credit creation and how to control it. In connection with the English translation of the *Theorie*, Schumpeter wrote a letter with an appended page, both evidently intended to be used in the formulation of the publisher's blurb, in which he pointed out that in 1911 his message was " . . . so strikingly uncongenial and so far removed from traditional teaching that it met almost universal hostility. But since then both the general view and some of the individual theorems have been gaining considerable ground in contemporary work in Germany."[13]

And in the appended blurb Schumpeter wrote: "The third chapter contains the author's theory of credit creation and of capital, most of the results of which have been made familiar by later work of many authors, especially of the Cambridge School" (ibid.).

Schumpeter singled out D. H. Robertson, who developed views on money similar to his own—entirely independently as Schumpeter insisted. And of course, Keynes in the *Treatise* accepted "unreservedly" Schumpeter's explanation of the cycle. Keynes then added:

> [T]he pace at which the innovating entrepreneurs will be able to carry out their projects to execution at the cost of interest which is not deterrent to them will depend on the degree of complaisance of those responsible for the banking system. Thus whilst the stimulus to credit inflation comes from outside the Banking System, it remains a monetary phenomenon in the sense that it only occurs if the monetary machine is allowed to respond to the stimulus. (Keynes 1930, vol. 2, 96)

This is Schumpeter's point already made in 1911: credit creation—and monetary policy—had a function only in the context of a developmental economy and required the strictest attention of monetary authorities.[14]

---

[12] "*Severe depreciation is accompanied by a considerable increase in the velocity of circulation of money*. This conclusion was announced by Prof. Schumpeter as early as 1918 and at the end of 1923 it was restated by Mr. Keynes in a most original manner" (Walré de Bordes 1924, 162; italics in original). Walré bases his analysis explicitly on Schumpeter's "Sozialprodukt" and on Keynes's *Tract*. Until I came across this reference I was unaware of Schumpeter's claim to priority of much of modern monetary theory.

[13] Letter to David Pottinger, dated June 4, 1934. The reception particularly in the United States was much friendlier.

[14] Schumpeter's attitude toward actual monetary, fiscal, and tax policies will be taken up in the last part of this book.

However, the banking system was only a part of the monetary system, which included among many others credits given by businesses to each other, or by businesses to customers.[15] On the institutional level, businesses would always be able to get around regulations to finance their innovations. At the time, Schumpeter still had to argue that savings deposits were in fact part of the money supply!

Schumpeter's own attempt to write a book which, with a bow to Professor Rudolf Richter, might be titled *Money. Lectures on the Basis of Evolutionary Theory*, was given up around 1933.[16] We can only speculate why this was so, but we can rule out jealousy of Keynes's *Treatise on Money*.[17] The more important reason was, however, that money has a quite different function in an evolutionary than a stationary economy.

Money in the Process of Evolution

The two volumes of *Business Cycles* contain enough hints of just what Schumpeter was after.[18] The important point to remember was that what happened in the real economy always had first to be understood in order to make sense

[15] Schumpeter developed the institutional side of the problem in great detail in his posthumously published and unfinished *Wesen des Geldes*, to point out what an ambiguous concept the amount of money really was and how the process credit creation worked in detail.

[16] I may refer to Rudolf Richter, *Lectures on the Basis of General Equilibrium Theory and the Economics of Institutions*, (Berlin: Springer Verlag, 1989). Translated from idem, *Geldtheorie*. A book with the suggested title does not exist. Schumpeter's unfinished money book was posthumously published as *Das Wesen des Geldes*, edited and with an introduction by F. K. Mann (Schumpeter 1970). In 1990, an Italian translation appeared. On the history of the manuscript, see Bernd Kulla's and my own contributions in *Kyklos* 42, 3 (1989).

[17] Keynes had made several comments of agreement with Schumpeter in his *Treatise* of which I have quoted one. Schumpeter in turn spoke admiringly of the *Treatise* in his Bonn lectures. In the *Wesen des Geldes*, Keynes is referred to 8 times, always in agreement; Walras 9 times; and Irving Fisher 15 times.

Das Wesen des Geldes—the title is the editor's, not Schumpeter's—was intended to have a second volume (*Geld*, 211 or 243 refer to such a planned second volume). The existing volume starts with a chapter on monetary policy, followed by a chapter on the sociology of money, to formulate what the theory of money had to analyze. A major part of its contents is devoted to institutional analysis which is intended to explain how the monetary system works, and how it adapts to the needs of the real economy. This is the manner in which credit creation (and destruction) is analyzed and why expenditures rather than "money" or the "velocity of circulation" are the center of monetary theory.

Only the last, twelfth chapter (which ends in mid-sentence) connects the institutional pattern to the cyclical pattern and its cause, innovations. But, of course, Schumpeter had much to say about money, though it is distributed throughout *Business Cycles*. Nor is it at all illogical that this should be so.

[18] "The writer hopes to provide [the] background and to develop the theoretical structure of which these propositions are fragments in his treatise on money" (*Business Cycles*, 544 n.). In chapter 11 on *Expenditures, Wages, Customers' Balances* (vol. 2, 544ff), he refers specifically to chapters 3, 4, and 13 in addition to his discussion in chapter 11. There are also extended comments in chapters 6, 7, and 12, most of which deal with difficulties of measurement, given the inadequacy of the data.

of what happened in the monetary magnitudes. And the crux of the real economy always was the incessant change in its structure.

The first point is perhaps that money and credit creation are so crucial to the capitalist economy that they become its most important definitional criterion. Money exists in all economies in some form, but its function in the capitalist economy differs from that in, say, a socialist economy. The aim of all of Schumpeter's analyses is to analyze in the sense of an *histoire raisonnée* the whole capitalist process, which is much more than is usually meant by the analysis of business cycles: it really is the analysis of an individualistic economy in incessant change. The definition, which later reappears almost verbatim in *Capitalism, Socialism and Democracy*, reads:

> Excluding as we do noncapitalist change,[19] we have to define that word which good economists always try to avoid: capitalism is that form of private property economy in which innovations are carried out by means of borrowed money, which in general, though not by logical necessity, implies credit creation. A society, the economic life of which is characterized by private property and controlled by private initiative, is according to this definition not necessarily capitalist, even if there are, for instance, privately owned factories, salaried workers, and free exchange of goods and services, either in kind or through the medium of money. The entrepreneurial function itself is not confined to capitalist society since such economic leadership as it implies would be present, though in other forms, even in a primitive tribe or in a socialist community. (*Business Cycles*, 223)

This definition is not an arbitrary definitional privilege, but it is made for a specific purpose. Marx's and Sombart's uses of the term "capitalism" implicit in their analyses refer to certain "defining characteristics . . . of a definite historic phenomenon" (ibid.), and this is true also for Schumpeter's definition. But Schumpeter adds:

> [This definition will undoubtedly appear] strange at a first reading, but a little reflection will satisfy the reader that most of the features which are commonly associated with the concept of capitalism would be absent from the economic and from the cultural process of a society without credit creation. Our characteristic is not, however, intended to imply causal connotation. It should also be observed that, like most other definitions of capitalism, ours is institutional. But of course the institutions which, with very rare exceptions, we treat as data throughout, are themselves the results of and elements in the process which we wish to study. The only thing that could be controversial about this is our proposition that *the economic process of capitalist society is identical with the sequence*

[19] This is not a tautological statement. It refers to such events as wars and earthquakes, the last of which even the most ardent believer in the economic interpretation of history can not blame on capitalism. He might, however, blame some of its worst effects on the system: the devastating earthquake of Mexico City hit mostly the poor jerry-built sections, so the economic and political systems are partly at fault. But, then, what about the Armenian earthquake?

of events that gives rise to the business cycle. (*Business Cycles*, 223–24, italics added)[20]

Money, credit, and particularly credit creation for productive purposes is central to Schumpeter's analysis of the capitalist process.

Money need not be linked with a commodity. Indeed, as Milton Friedman has recently pointed out, since President Nixon's "closing of the gold window" on August 15, 1971, "every major country has accepted an inconvertible paper fiat standard, not as an emergency measure expected to be temporary, but as a system intended to be permanent. Such a world-wide fiat monetary system has no historic precedent."[21]

This does not mean that from an economic policy standpoint a link to a metal could not be, and indeed was, advocated by Schumpeter for reasons not too dissimilar from those advocated by the New Institutional Economics.

Now, because money is not a commodity "claims or titles to money (however defined) may serve the same purposes as money itself" (ibid., 545).

This is the first reason why the "quantity of money" is an ambiguous concept, and why the quantity theory (as distinct from the quantity equation, which is simply an identity) is not a theory of money at all. "*It is, in fact, impossible to speak of the quantity of "money" in the sense in which we speak of the quantity of a commodity*" (ibid., 546; italics in original).

As the quantity of money is an extremely elastic concept, so the velocity of money is a term covering a multiplicity of phenomena. Schumpeter in *Business Cycles* distinguishes three concepts, of which the income velocity is really the only meaningful one: "consumer expenditures divided by balances plus money in circulation."[22]

In a stationary economy, velocity is essentially defined "by the institutional arrangements within the period of account" (ibid., 545). Schumpeter refers to this velocity as "efficiency." But as soon as we deal with an evolutionary economy we find "a phenomenon which is entirely different from it, although it influences velocity figures similarly . . . the question whether or not to spend at any one moment becomes a question of policy for everyone" (ibid., 546).

It is this fact which underlies the measurement of "consumer confidence." These policy decisions are, of course, based on the real phenomena underlying

---

[20] The analysis of how the process itself affects the institutions is the major topic of Schumpeter's discussion of socialism. See Part II.

[21] Milton Friedman (1990), 87. Mr. Friedman can take some credit—or blame as the case may be—for this fact, since he was one of the first, perhaps even the first, to advocate flexible exchanges. Schumpeter's views on flexible exchanges were nevertheless less favorable. But, as is so often the case, what appears at first sight to be a sharp difference turns out on closer inspection to be much less so. Mr. Friedman substitutes for convertibility at a fixed rate other rules to keep the creation of money in check.

[22] Even so, the "distinction between velocity and quantity becomes blurred. K. Wicksell, for instance, treated the issue of bank notes as a means of increasing not the quantity but the velocity of money (the banks' reserves)" (*Business Cycles*, 546 note 1).

them, as Schumpeter stressed. Velocity in fact changes all the time and it is sometimes impossible to distinguish whether the quantity or the velocity has changed. Schumpeter goes further:

> We may, with some qualifications speak of a demand for money in the money market. . . . Demand for money carries, however, still another meaning; it may mean the wish to hold stocks of money or balances.
>
> [This] idea becomes misleading if we leave the stationary state. If we see someone displaying a wish for bread this is a clear-cut fact carrying its explanation in itself and fit to be used in order to deduce the explanation of other facts. But if someone displays a wish to hold cash, this itself means nothing at all. All the value of the observation lies in the circumstances that induce that wish . . . even if there is such a wish. But generally there is none. A man may, for example, hold a supernormal amount of cash, not because this is any good to him, but simply because his and other peoples' actions happen to produce that result, which in itself is not one of the objects he wishes to attain by those actions; it may even be a disagreeable by-product of them. All explanations which start with the famous adage: "if people choose to hold . . ." are *ipso facto* condemned.[23]

Now the crux of the empirical problem (which in Schumpeter is always related to and underlies his theoretical analysis) but equally the solution of the policy problems is that "in the sphere of money and credit . . . the surface [is] so entirely at variance with the processes below, that the first impression of the reader may well be fatal" (ibid., 109).

Schumpeter's footnote points out:

> At the time [i.e., 1911] criticism was mainly directed against certain points of credit creation which have become commonplace by now. The really controversial proposition which turns on the relation of credit creation to innovation was then not discussed at all. Nor has it really been discussed since, for the arguments from the classical theory of banking to the effect of what banks finance is precisely not innovation but current commodity transactions, miss the salient point entirely. (ibid., 109, note 1)

This reasoning also underlies the strong "sound money" tenor of his policy recommendations, which basically can be formulated thus: The basic function of bankers is to be producers of money, not financial intermediaries. The function of monetary policy must be to ensure that innovations can be financed as efficiently and as cheaply as possible—here is a strong affinity to Keynes's formulation in the *Treatise* quoted before—and to prevent credit creation from being used to finance increased consumption, which would interfere with resources being made available for investments to change the structure of the economy.

---

[23] *Business Cycles*, 547–48. Nothing illustrates the importance of this analysis so well as experiences in inflationary situations, and specifically in the Soviet-type economies where people held large amounts of cash simply because there was nothing to buy.

We can see once more the essential differences to as well as the frequent parallelisms with both the monetarist and the Keynesian approaches. Schumpeter is a great deal more interested in financing innovations and evolution than in stabilizing the price level, however defined, or in producing positive or negative offsets to aggregate spending. Yet he is very much committed to preventing even the threat of inflation or deflation, even though on the theoretical level "the" price level cannot be defined. The avoidance of "crowding out" is central in an evolutionary situation, not price stability. In any case, "neither prices of individual commodities, influenced as they must be by the particular conditions and policies prevailing in individual industries, nor the whole world of prices, however measured, can really be expected to keep a consistent relation to other series representing industrial conditions or to the processes that lie behind them" (ibid., 450).

Schumpeter explicitly rejects aggregative analysis for the purpose of analyzing the effects of an increase in spending. The effects of credit creation depend very much on the purpose for which the credits are given, and not on the quantity alone—even if "quantity" could be unambiguously defined.

In the context of analyzing the effects of the influx of gold from the New World, Schumpeter stressed:

> [T]he evolution of capitalism was indeed influenced, but in the end retarded rather than quickened, by that expansion of the circulating medium . . . below the glitter of the surface serious enterprise was thwarted by the dislocation of values and by social unrest. . . . All the durable achievements of English industry and commerce can be accounted for without reference to the plethora of precious metals, to which, however, we need not deny the modest role alluded to at the end of the preceding section. (*Business Cycles*, vol. 1, 232)

Inflation in modern times always, so Schumpeter, starts with the wage bill.[24] Inflation preempts resources which should be reserved for development and destroys the social fabric. Schumpeter did not favor orienting monetary policy around stabilizing the price level, however measured, because such a stabilization could not be achieved without affecting the structure of the price system, which has a basic function in a capitalistic economy.[25] He strongly opposed freely fluctuating exchanges—"Gold does not lie"[26]—and he would put little faith in the technical prescriptions to the Federal Reserve on how to handle the supply of money.

As with the monetarists, there is also with the Keynesians a fundamental difference despite many parallelisms. The similarities relate essentially to two aspects: interest is explained by a monetary, not a real theory. What matters are expenditures rather than the quantity and velocity of money. But con-

---

[24] This is, of course, quite consistent with linking inflation to budget deficits in war time.

[25] See chapter 22 on Schumpeter's criticism of Keynes's *Tract*.

[26] In a speech given to the Economics Club of Detroit on April 14, 1941 on "The Future of Gold." See chapter 22 for a detailed discussion.

sumption is a function, not indeed of some earned or past or expected income, but of a cyclical process whose real origins rest on innovations.

Schumpeter's emphasis on the continuous change in production functions resulted in a rejection of the consumption function and the marginal propensity to consume for purposes of evolutionary analysis, because they are by their very nature not stable even in the short run. With Schumpeter, demand is often "created" by innovational investments.

The crux is that in what Schumpeter defines as the secondary wave of his second approximation (see chapter 5), what firms pay out and what households receive is not identical, and it determines even less what households spend. Nothing illustrates the point better than a reference to "stability conditions" of the marginal propensity to consume.

I would like to interject here a brief autobiographical note. The "gospel according to Keynes" had been brought to Cambridge, Massachusetts in 1935 in the form of mimeographed lecture notes by Robert B. Bryce, then a Commonwealth Fellow. The excitement generated was so great that we could not await an American edition of the *General Theory*, but imported it on our own. We then had a seminar with the following participants: Paul A. Samuelson, Lloyd A. Metzler, Wassily W. Leontief, Edward S. Mason, Seymour E. Harris, John Kenneth Galbraith, Robert A. Gordon among them. Schumpeter did not participate.

We wondered what would happen if the marginal propensity to consume was greater than one. Paul Samuelson explained that any multiplier was really the solution of a system of equations, that there was such a solution only if one dealt with a converging infinite series, that income would be infinite, not negative, if alpha was greater than one, and that there were really as many multipliers as one could think of systems of equations. In other words, the multiplier is very much a child of equilibrium analysis.

But Schumpeter's point, made explicitly in *Business Cycles*, is precisely that consumption would in the course of the secondary wave expand by more than income, for example, by going into debt. This meant that it was not permissible in an evolutionary situation to apply stability conditions developed for an equilibrium system.

This problem is evidently not adequately handled by pointing out that the consumption function shifted upward in the long run. With Schumpeter, the "instability" of the consumption function is cyclical, but it is not unstable in the Samuelsonian sense.

SAVINGS AND CYCLES

Saving in a stationary economy and a static society would be quite small. It would amount to little more than the amounts of money which people hold, given the institutional framework, and if nothing else changes in the economy, there is really no reason to change one's holding of money. To derive his theory of savings, Schumpeter initially assumes "our economic subjects possess initially besides goods serving production and consumption, also savings funds (Sparfonds) which may, of course, be zero. They may consist of any good but we will immediately understand them as sums of money" (*Wesen*, 302; my translation).

This is really just saying that the amount of money which every individual holds in equilibrium is uniquely determined.

The relation of the theory of money to the theory of savings is based on facts as well as logic. It is a *fact* that savings out of income are relatively small. It is a *fact* that rich people do not save relatively as much as do the middle classes because their social position almost forces upon them conspicuous consumption. It is a *fact* that the great fortunes are not accumulated by savings but through innovations. It is these *facts* that persuade Schumpeter that a static theory of savings has not much to offer. And it is these *facts* that persuade him that the interesting part of monetary theory has to do with the creation of money for industrial purposes and that loans to businesspeople engaged in creating new industries are a totally different phenomenon from a loan to an unfortunate man who has broken his leg, or whose cow has fallen into the well. The similarity between the two is juridical and simply obscures totally different economic phenomena.

To create capital goods, to create new systems of production,[27] to change production functions, resources must be shifted from whatever they are doing—including doing nothing—to building new things capable of increasing the productive power of the economy.

While you can, theoretically speaking, use amortization funds to replace worn or buy additional machinery, the replacement or addition normally involves new kinds of machines rather than the old ones. The new processes require as a rule specific inputs different from the old ones. Except for raw materials, new inputs must first be created. In fact, this is usually true even for land or raw materials. You do replace an old factory by a more suitable one, a reason why even the process of capital maintenance is as a rule an evolutionary one and needs itself to be explained.[28] The existing stock of money is already allocated to keep the economy going in the old ways while the time-consuming process of creation of new things is going on. Yes, amortization quotas may be used, but they are quantitatively and theoretically uninteresting.[29]

---

[27] The word "capital" without qualifications is best avoided here, though it is obvious that the capital concept used here is closer to that of Böhm-Bawerk than that inherent in the Keynesian analysis of the *General Theory*. I have also chosen the term "system of production" to include agriculture or trade and the creation of new institutions.

[28] It should be observed that this theoretical statement itself is based on an assertion of facts. One of the troubles of the former Soviet-type economies was that technology lagged behind, that is, that replacement often did not involve sufficient new types, a fact which made my study of the East German economy possible.

[29] To the extent, however, that they become more important in the course of development they are one of the institutional changes on the "March into Socialism." See Part II.

As Schumpeter developed his ideas of the wavelike movements of the economy, there were also successive approximations to reality. In the first approximation, which must start from an equilibrium with full employment, the effect of credit creation must be a reduction in the standard of living. However, in the second approximation in which innovations may be initiated before the economy has reached the neighborhood of the equilibrium which corresponds to the preceding innovations, and which is therefore itself already evolutionary in nature, consumption and investments will rise hand-in-hand.

All this differs substantially from monetary theories of the cycle or from the proper role of money in the cycle. It differs also from the "Austrian" view of the structure of production and the shifts that occur in it. Neutral money becomes a chimera. It cannot exist in a developmental economy. Schumpeter considered Hayek's analysis of the 1930s in terms of undersavings and a change in the productive structure from investments to consumption unrealistic, though he added that the actual developments did in fact invite such an explanation.[30]

INTEREST

I finally come to Schumpeter's theory of interest which is generally considered wrong, or at least somewhat idiosyncratic, "ein Stein des Anstosses."

First, Schumpeter's interest theory is a monetary theory. There is no sense trying to pierce the "veil of money" to find some real phenomenon. There is nothing behind that veil. Interest is the price of money, and not a reward for something else.

The kind of loans possible in equilibrium strictly defined are inherently very small. They would be loans to replace barns struck by lightning or made in anticipation of an inheritance. Their common characteristic is that the underlying causes for such a loan lie outside the economy and the loans present an adaptive process which is in principle amenable to analysis by standard theory. It is also clear that replacing a burnt-out barn by means of a loan simply spreads out the loss over a number of years and must, ceteris paribus, lead to a temporarily smaller income of the borrower. But there would be no loans for the expansion of productive power.

For Schumpeter the answer was really quite simple. Of course interest exists in equilibrium.

> I can hardly understand the assertion that I denied it. [Of course it is a] premium on present over future purchasing power. This premium has several causes. Many of them constitute no problem. Interest on consumptive loans is a case in point. That anyone in unexpected distress . . . or in expectation of a future increase in income . . . values a hundred present more highly than a hundred future marks requires no explanation and it is self-evident that interest may exist in such cases.

[30] *Business Cycles,* 296 n.

All categories of government credit requirements belong here. . . . But they do not constitute the great social phenomenon that needs explaining. This consists of interest on productive loans (Produktivzins). It is to be found *everywhere* in the capitalist system and not only where it originates, that is in new enterprises. I merely want to show that productive interest has its source in profits, that it is by nature an offshoot of the latter, and that it . . . spreads from the profits incident to the successful carrying out of new combinations over the whole economic system and even forces its way into the sphere of old businesses, in whose life it would not be a necessary element if there were no development. This is all I mean by the statement "The 'static' economy knows no productive interest"—which is certainly fundamental to our insight into the structure and working of capitalism. (*Theory*, 157–58)

This quotation should really lay to rest that Schumpeter denies that some interest could exist in equilibrium. Obviously, if I decided to distribute my expected lifetime income differently, that is, if I exhibited some time preference, interest might arise and it might even be negative, which productive interest could never be. But on a strict definition of statics, barns are not struck by lightning, cows do not fall into wells, people do not break their legs, aged people are exactly offset by a younger generation taking their place, and old factories are replaced by new ones of exactly the same kind.

Schumpeter insists that quantitatively the only interesting phenomena in the real world are loans to finance new combinations; and those loans are given in the form of money, not of real goods and services.

The close relation between interest and money naturally raises the question whether changes in the quantity of money, that is, credit creation, do affect the rate of interest. "Static" money does not do so; it simply affects prices. But "dynamic" money definitely does.

That one gets wet when it rains is no more self-evident to the businessman than that interest falls when credit facilities increase, other things being equal. In reality, if a government were to print paper money and to lend it to entrepreneurs, would not interest fall? And would not the state be able to receive interest on it? Does not the connection of interest with rates of exchange and gold movements speak plainly enough? It is an extremely wide and significant range of everyday observations that supports us here. (*Theory*, 184–85)

The meaning is quite clear. "Static" money evidently refers to the function of money in equilibrium, which is simply that of a *numéraire*. This is really what monetarism, boiled down to its essence, is about: Inflation is a monetary phenomenon.

But "dynamic" money, credit creation undertaken to finance a change in production functions and the structure of the economy, is a different matter; and it is one about which monetarism is agnostic and which Keynesianism does not really consider.

Two final aspects should be stressed. In principle, only entrepreneurs need credit and are willing and able to pay productive interest out of an increased income which credit creation has made possible through the (successful) innovations it has financed. Interest becomes a steady stream because there are always innovations going on. Most important, interest is paid for money, which is not a veil hiding a real phenomenon. Static interest could be negative, but dynamic interest would simply disappear if the stream of innovations were permanently to cease. There is nothing in the static state which corresponds to Schumpeter's concept of capital, which is not Böhm-Bawerk's produced means of production, but sums of money used for productive purposes.

I want to conclude this section with a final quote. Unlike wages and rent which exist everywhere and at all times in some form, but also unlike entrepreneurial profits which are also a universal category in any developmental economy, interest is a truly *social* category in the sense that it appears only in an evolutionary society with private property. The reason for it being a capitalist phenomenon is linked to the function of credit creation as the lever which allows the entrepreneur to shift resources to do the new things he or she has in mind. In socialism—and this will be discussed fully later— entrepreneurs need no credit but get direct command over resources.

The German version makes the strong statement: "Man muss sich darüber klar sein, dass wir, *wenn wir vom Zinsproblem sprechen, an eine andere Erscheinung denken als die meisten Theoretiker*" (*Theorie* 1925 and later editions, 265; italics in original).

In the English translation this becomes somewhat muted:

> I should like to direct the reader's attention to the fact that our conception of the interest problem involves something different from the usual conception. (*Theory* 1934, 177)
>
> I have only one thing to add: I wished to explain the interest phenomenon but not to justify it. Interest is not, like profit for example, a direct fruit of development in the sense of a prize for achievements. It is on the contrary rather a brake—in an exchange economy a necessary brake—on development, a kind of "tax on entrepreneurial profits" . . . we may conclude that interest takes away something from the entrepreneur which would otherwise accrue to him, and not from other classes. Yet this fact, together with the fact that the interest phenomenon is not a necessary element in all economic organizations, will always result in the critic of social conditions finding more to object to in interest than in anything else. Therefore it is important to state that interest is only the consequence of a special method of carrying out new combinations, and that this method can be much more easily changed than the other fundamental institutions of the competitive system. (ibid., 210–11)

Cycles

CHAPTER 4 POINTED OUT that the mathematics of nonlinear systems and of self-organizations of complex systems seem to be just what Schumpeter was talking about. His "vision" was that the capitalistic process, which really encompassed all that was economic and social and even cultural in the history of the Western world at least as far back as the end of the twelfth and the beginning of the thirteenth century when banking started in southern Europe, was a process never at rest. Equilibrium described only a small part of reality. It never has been reached. Various temporary "equilibria" existed at discrete intervals. They were never maintained for long and never repeated exactly.

A comparison with Haberler's admirable *Prosperity and Depression* brings out the truly original nature of Schumpeter's approach. Haberler systematically analyzes all the extant business cycle theories by the same schema: how they treat the upswing, upper turning point, downswing, and lower turning point. There is no way to treat Schumpeter in this manner, and Haberler, who certainly quoted Schumpeter often enough, did not try to do so.

Schumpeter's theoretical problem was to explain how an equilibrium situation was disrupted, why adjustment processes did not lead back to the old equilibrium as described by the implied dynamics of supply–demand analysis; why it led to a dynamic process first away from equilibrium, then, as a wavelike process, to another higher equilibrium level. In the process of thinking about the process, the model became successively more complicated. But at all times it must not be forgotten that for Schumpeter any theory was, in Alfred Marshall's words, a machine to organize facts. It was an always changing reality that had to be explained.

In writing to McGraw-Hill, the publisher of *Business Cycles*, Schumpeter mulled over the title of the book and stuck to *Business Cycles* precisely because it was an accurate description of his vision of the capitalistic process.[1]

---

[1] "Funny enough I have still got to make up my mind as to the title. The difficulty is that all the titles that would naturally occur are already taken. At first I thought of Analysis of Business Cycles, Introductory Volume. It might also read Introduction to the Analysis of Business Cycles, or A Treatise on Business Cycles, but all this is not quite satisfactory.

Moreover, the hackneyed term 'business cycles' is not very happy, but unfortunately expresses exactly what the book is about as no other would. Economic fluctuations is too suggestive of Professor Pigou's treatise and moreover does not mean much to the general reader. Nor is Prosperity and Depression exactly the thing. Finally, I do not quite like: The Waves of Capitalist Evolution" (Letter to Hugh J. Kelly dated June 24, 1937).

THE THEORETICAL MODELS

The First Approximation

Schumpeter's first task was to show the limited nature of what general equilibrium theory could explain. This included a discussion of why such "events" as population growth could not account for cycles. Of course, all such events have an influence on evolution, *once evolution exists*. But in the interest of logic and in order not to assume what had to be proven, the strict equilibrium conditions and their logical implications had to be worked out. This work was essentially done in *Wesen*, and the first chapter of the *Theory* has a thoroughly rewritten summary version of the circular flow as it would work without shocks coming from outside or, for that matter, inside the system, with constant production functions and constant everything else.

What takes the system out of equilibrium is an innovation, a change in the production function, any change in the conditions of production. This innovation is carried out by someone called an entrepreneur, which initially is a technical term. An entrepreneur is someone who sees that things could be done differently and who actually *does* something about it, and as Schumpeter pointed out, such a person is not all that uncommon.

It is well to remember a few things here. First, as Schumpeter stressed, even in equilibrium the system is not in an optimal situation with respect to all possible alternatives. What is called a Pareto-optimum has a limited meaning. There is always something to be done differently. The issue is not that an optimum exists with respect to a particular set of circumstances but that the assumption that these circumstances themselves are the best possible ones is itself impossible. In the first (1911) edition of *Theorie*, we find the following statement:

> That those combinations are the best which the natural and technical circumstances permit is impossible. . . . Technical and commercial production can within a given state of technical-scientific knowledge be improved practically without limit. Never are all possibilities realized, and if they were new ones would immediately open up. Only with respect to a given mode of production is there a relatively best state, without such a mode of production, there is no such relatively best state. . . . The ideal method of utilization *itself* can not be reached because behind it there are necessarily still "more ideal" ones. . . . We are no nearer to the exhaustion of possibilities than at the stone age.[2]

So the initial model of the cycle must start with an equilibrium situation to make sure that it itself does *not* contain the seeds of evolution. It is not, as has

---

[2] *Theorie* (1911), 60–61; italics in original; my translation. In the 1920s, Schumpeter took Keynes gently to task for believing that technical progress itself was subject to diminishing returns. By the 1930s, this became, of course, the rejection of the secular stagnation thesis. The point made in the quotation is central to Nelson and Winter's analysis and foreshadows some of Alchian's analysis.

been occasionally said in criticism, a strange self-imposed limitation but a logically necessary starting point for what is really an *argumentum a contrario*.[3]

The first approximation gives only the barest bones, but it is already sufficiently powerful to integrate money as more than a numéraire and an explanation why the disturbance introduced by an innovation is self-limiting, that is, why the upswing comes to an end. There are only two phases in this model—an upswing, which is a movement away from an equilibrium, and a downswing, which is a return to a new equilibrium.

Since the competitive economy in equilibrium is rolling along nicely, all resources are fully employed. The mass of economic actors therefore has no reason to try to change dramatically. They may, of course, change by steps that are hardly noticeable. To break this circular flow requires borrowed money which in the most abstract model is manufactured for the purpose. In the English translation Schumpeter points out that "in a capitalist society, industrial development could in principle be carried out solely with credit means of payments. . . . [t]he great reservoirs of money which actually exist arise as a *consequence* of development and must therefore be left out of account at first" (*Theory* 1934, 195; italics added).

The German formulation makes the point more strongly by adding "that *all* economic development, wherever the leader has no power of disposition [over factors of production] on principle needs credit" (*Theorie* 1911, 212; 1926 and later editions, 151–52. Italics in original; my translation).

The point is central not only for Schumpeter's understanding of the capitalistic process but also for his policy prescriptions—in which, for example, the "great reservoirs of money" and what to do about them play a role—and for his discussion of the coming of socialism.

Why can there be no quick adjustment as envisaged by competitive equilibrium theory? The answer lies in the fact that the new processes occur while the old processes continue, that, in other words, we deal with historic time. In addition, if we start with a full employment equilibrium, money wages (and other factor prices) must rise, and prices must also rise as the innovators with newly created money bid away resources from their traditional uses.

The process comes to an end when the innovations begin to pour out the new goods, driving some out-of-date goods and/or processes from the market. Loans are repaid (and if nothing new happens to lead to new credits, destroyed); prices tend to fall, but money wages need not fall and real wages will rise.

Even at this level of abstraction a number of problems may be usefully discussed. The central question which is so often asked in criticism of the model—how can Schumpeter be so hostile to inflation when it plays such a

---

[3] It is, of course, conceivable that one day the chaotic nature of economic reality will become so commonly accepted that it will indeed be unnecessary to start with a discussion of the limitations of equilibrium analysis.

central role to explain the cycle—is really easily answered. The credit must be created for productive purposes; *you cannot divorce the discussion of credit creation from the purposes for which it is given.* And it remains absolutely essential to prevent consumption financing—which for all practical purposes includes budget deficits—from crowding out the needs of financing development.

Here is also the first clear statement of the need to establish a new structure of the economy by an *Einordnungsprozess,* a process of integration, later more dramatically called a process of creative destruction. The idea that this process could be smooth is unimaginable, illogical, and not simply unrealistic. The idea of balanced growth or its Communist equivalent, the law of proportional development, is a *contradictio in adjecto.*

Furthermore, once it is explained how new money enters into the economic process, it becomes easy to see why the auto-deflation might not lead to the old pre-credit-creation level, why the financing of all kinds of ongoing operations might become necessary.

The Second Approximation

It may now be more fruitful to go on to the second approximation, which has three major characteristics. First, once an evolutionary process has started, the new upswing might start *before* the neighborhood of equilibrium has actually been reached. To start with, possibilities exist all the time; hence, innovators—which includes the little fellow who sees an opportunity to make a buck—might venture and find financing even while there are still unemployed resources and even before prices have bottomed out.

Second, we now can have secondary repercussions: as the economy moves upward again and the auto-deflation has stopped, things ease also for noninnovators. They, too, begin to feel an increase in demand, may begin to make profits, expand and, of course, get credit. This credit, too, is given for "productive" purposes even though its original (in the sense of logical priority) impetus has come from the innovators. These secondary effects will, as a rule, swamp the "essential" original wave.

Third, the cycle is now envisaged as having four phases: two movements away from and two movements toward an equilibrium. There is the upswing initiated by innovations which break the existing neighborhood of equilibrium and move the system away from equilibrium. There is the recession initiated by the new goods coming on the market. The term "recession" in Schumpeter has a *theoretical,* not a statistical meaning. It is the period of creative destruction, of the *Einordnungsprozess.* It is not the meaning given by the National Bureau of Economic Research which is, in the United States, adopted by the press and the government to characterize a particular situation, nor does it simply mean a mild decline.

Because during the upswing mistakes are being made—some avoidable, others not avoidable in an uncertain situation—some, perhaps even most, innovations do not work out, some are overtaken by newer ones, consumer credit gets out of hand, good money is thrown after bad in an attempt to save a situation, not only antiquated production facilities may be eliminated. The adjustment process overshoots the new equilibrium and may in the absence of a careful economic policy take with it enterprises which otherwise may be viable: the Florida land boom of the 1920s, the savings and loan crisis of the 1980s, and the threatening banking crises of the 1990s are all vivid examples of what happens when insufficient care is exercised during the upswing.[4]

The point is that *depression* again has a *theoretical* meaning of a movement away from an equilibrium (or its neighborhood) which is not a necessary element of the capitalistic process. In fact, it could be avoided and its avoidance or mitigation would improve the capitalistic process. But it needs to be avoided already during the upswing. As Schumpeter had put it before, the influx of gold from the New World and the inflationary policies during the reign of the first Elizabeth in England retarded rather than helped development. Schumpeter agreed with Milton Friedman that the banking crisis during the Great Depression turned a retreat into a rout. And in *Capitalism* he pointed out that he was not so much against deficit financing during the depression once it had become necessary as against the policies which had made it necessary.

These secondary waves distort the process. There is little virtue in using— virtually unavoidably—the same words "inflation" and "deflation" for the Schumpeterian process of credit creation to finance innovations in the first approximation and the subsequent auto-deflation, and for the monetary processes of a secondary and (logically) entirely avoidable wave.

It is in this context that monetarist prescriptions of letting the amount of money grow at a certain rate, or the search for neutral money, becomes understandable. Neither can possibly provide a fundamental explanation of the cycle. Yet, because the secondary wave historically tends to swamp the underlying real core phenomenon, the monetarist prescriptions may, up to a point, be the best we have. But I must stress: up to a point, for it neglects the essential Schumpeterian qualification that it makes a difference just how the money is spent. Nothing at all can really be said for the idea of "neutral money."

All things come to an end, even a depression. Having done as much avoidable harm as it is allowed to do, it will turn into a recovery, the theoretical term for a movement to the new neighborhood of "equilibrium" which corresponds to the changed data. Without a depression, recovery would not exist.

The Third Approximation

The third approximation introduces Schumpeter's famous three-cycle scheme. The evidence is that Schumpeter came to this idea fairly early. He was impres-

---

[4] This is a rather bland way of describing what actually happened. In fact, matters are much worse because the boom of the 1980s was provably based predominantly on consumption rather than on an adequate increase in productive possibilities.

sed by the evidence which Kondratieff presented for the existence of long waves, also found by his friend and Bonn colleague, Arthur Spiethoff.

The idea of a multicycle scheme can be traced back at least to 1928.[5] In a talk in Münster, Schumpeter went to great lengths to explain that the popular impression that economists could not agree on anything was mostly due to the fact that most people pronouncing on economic matters were simply incompetent. Indeed, he had already much earlier pointed out that whereas in physics or chemistry people realized that some scientific training was needed, everyone thought himself to be an authority on economics. He mentioned that Keynes had told him in conversation that there were at most five people who understood anything about money! In business cycle theory, the surface chaos hid a really quite straightforward line of development in which the names of Juglar, Spiethoff, Kitchin, and the long wave are specifically mentioned.

This undoubtedly explains in part why in connection with the publication of the English translation of the *Theorie*, Schumpeter wrote that he felt "misgivings in submitting such a purely theoretical structure to the Anglo-American public in a form with which I have partly grown out of sympathy myself."[6]

This comparative lack of sympathy clearly refers both to the need for a more complicated theoretical schema and to the need to put the schema into a historical and empirical-statistical context.

As Schumpeter worked out the theory he had first formulated in 1911—but with significant insights at least as far back as 1908—it became clear to him that the reality he wished to explain was much more complicated than his first and even his second approximation could handle. There was in reality too much going on, with numerous feedbacks and shocks. This is how he explained his problem to Wesley C. Mitchell, who had asked him for his cyclical datings:

> Dear Mitchell:
>
> Many thanks for your letter. Of course, I am delighted to send you my datings. In fact I am very anxious to do so for many other reasons besides the desirability of cooperating in order if possible to settle a common list of phases for the sake of future work.
>
> In order to enable you to form a judgment and to make it possible for me to benefit fully from it, it is necessary to explain at some length the way in which the question puts itself to me and the purpose which guided me.
>
> To begin with, allow me to repeat that on principle I admit an indefinite number of fluctuations in the material which are due to a great variety of causes and of very different nature and which all interfere with each other in the most complicated ways. What is called my theory of fluctuations is really simple to the

---

[5] *Der neueste Stand des Konjunkturproblems*. Vortrag von Professor Dr. J. Schumpeter, Bonn, Münster, Saturday, Nov. 24. No year, but the perpetual calendar says it was 1928. In the Harvard Archives. This is not a manuscript of Schumpeter's talk but a not-too-reliable transcript of it.

[6] Letter to David T. Pottinger, Harvard University Press, June 4, 1934.

point of triteness: for it merely recognizes the action on the economic system of a very great number of factors external to it which are neither small or independent in the probability sense, and the presence of a process of change internal to the system which also produces fluctuations of a great variety of periods and amplitudes. We have thus two classes of fluctuations which are simultaneously present and to these must be added a third class: if any factor whatsoever so acts as to produce an "up" and a "down," for instance government expenditure financing a war and government deflation after that war, the system practically always adapts itself in a fluctuating way so that "waves" of a third kind arise which are simply due to the properties of the adaptive mechanism of capitalist economic life. This third kind is what Tinbergen calls the endogenous fluctuations.[7]

This formulation makes it abundantly clear that Schumpeter has a "turbulent" nature of economic reality in mind, with "positive feedbacks."

The three-cycle schema is thus to start with a compromise between what would be desirable to do and what in fact was practicable. When Schumpeter worked out his vision, he had neither the staff nor the money to do more than "to scratch the surface." But more importantly, the mathematical analysis of nonlinear systems and the development of the computer were still in the future. In fact, Schumpeter tried to work with a five-cycle schema, but it became too difficult to handle.[8]

The thoughts expressed in the letter to Mitchell appear again in *Business Cycles*.

[T]here is nothing in our theoretical scheme . . . why the cyclical process of evolution should give rise to just one wavelike movement. On the contrary, there are many reasons to expect that it will set into motion an indefinite number of fluctuations present in our material at any time. The word *present* meaning that there are real factors at work to produce them and *not merely that the material may be decomposed into them by formal methods*. . . . There are no particular virtues in the choice made of just three classes of cycles. Five would perhaps be better, although after some experimenting the writer came to the conclusion that the improvement in the picture would not warrant the increase in cumbersomeness. In particular, it cannot be emphasized too strongly that the three-cycle scheme does not follow from our scheme—although multiplicity of cycles does.[9]

The italicized sentence is indeed important. In a letter to D. H. Robertson, Schumpeter made gentle fun of mechanical decomposition of time series:

Much more important than the business situation, however, is the fact that one of my colleagues here has just discovered in the material we have between 1780 and

---

[7] Letter to W. C. Mitchell, May 6, 1937.

[8] The following account is based on an earlier paper. W. F. Stolper, "Aspects of Schumpeter's Theory of Evolution," in H. Frisch (1982), chapter 2, 28–48. In the *Wesen des Geldes*, Schumpeter included also "a wave of . . . in America between 15 and 22 years which was first investigated by Kuznets" (p. 121). The reference occurs in chapter 5; my translation.

[9] *Business Cycles*, 167–69; italics in original.

1930 no less than seventeen kinds of different waves. This he did by means of a formal application of periodogramme analysis which really has no earthly meaning but such is the human heart that I was nevertheless very pleased to discover that my own favorite cycles were all among the seventeen.[10]

Schumpeter had the habit, common in the natural sciences, to name phenomenona after their discoverer. Thus, he referred to the short or forty-month cycle as the Kitchin cycle. It is sometimes argued that the Kitchin cycle is due to or at least associated with fluctuations in inventory investments, the Juglar of 8–11 years, which is what is usually called *the* business cycle, with fluctuations in fixed investments and the Kondratieff, the Long Wave of 45–60 years with important investments that take more than one business cycle to carry through. This interpretation seems all right as far as it goes. But it does not seem to me to go to the heart of Schumpeter's meaning.

Schumpeter's three cycles are *real* phenomena and three cycles seem needed "to assure us that all of the three reasons for the multiplicity of cycles have the opportunity of coming into play—and not more" (*Business Cycles*, 170). Nevertheless, Schumpeter does *not* associate each cycle with a specific reason. Given the turbulent nature of historic reality, this would not make sense.

What seems at issue here is much more than a formal discussion of evolutionary events. It is really a view of history which, to repeat, tries to combine unique events (which are the stock in trade of historians) with a theoretical understanding in terms of a few principles (which is the stock in trade of economic theorists); to combine what is continuous and what is discrete in history. I shall come back to this problem in chapter 7.

In the present context something less ambitious is at issue. We understand anything by seeing it in relation to other things at the same time (the content of statics), to other things and to itself in time (the contents of dynamics), and as unique events (the specific parameters which can make all the difference of how the more general theory actually works out). This is a scheme made familiar by the work of Ragnar Frisch, Jan Tinbergen, and Paul A. Samuelson.

Schumpeter adds a fourth dimension in the interaction of the variables and the change in the basic parameters themselves. To see this, compare the static adjustment processes—defined as the adjustment process by which a small deviation from a stable equilibrium is brought back to this equilibrium—with the Schumpeterian evolutionary process. The long and the short run differ in traditional theory by what is assumed to be variable. Thus, output in the short run may vary only with given productive capacities; in the long run the capacities themselves become variable. This, too, plays a role in the Schumpeterian picture of the world. But in the Marshallian world the basic parameters remain the same[11] and there is no interaction between them.[12]

---

[10] Letter to D. H. Robertson, dated Cambridge, Mass., December 24, 1932.

[11] Any change in the basic parameters would come from outside the system and simply become a new item to which the system would adapt itself in the familiar way.

[12] Some interaction is allowed for by the analysis of external economies.

Compare this with Schumpeter: the construction of railways or the invention of the fractional horsepower electric motor or the prevalence of the automobile open up completely new vistas, leading to the possibility of further changes which as a rule are neither foreseen nor foreseeable.[13]

All of these innovations started small, a phenomenon familiar to everyone who has read reports of computer firms having started in garages. The German optical industry started in such a small workshop in the nineteenth century. All these first *became* big, only in *retrospect* can we identify a long wave with one or a few of them. In this view, all the smaller innovations and special events which feed into the long wave get lost to the casual observer (who in this instance might even be the practitioner of the usual statistical methods), and their contribution tends to be underestimated. Of course, one important Schumpeterian property is that the demand for many of these products did not exist before the product came on the market, but was created by the supply. This is a very different interdependence of supply and demand from the one that exists also in a general equilibrium system.

Schumpeter's approach puts a quite different perspective on the distinction between the short and the long run. There is, of course, the famous quip attributed to Keynes that "in the long run we are all dead." The counterquip is that Keynes is dead and we are living in his long run. But this counterquip misses the point. What is true in the Keynesian bon mot is that you cannot live to see the future if you do not survive today. This is particularly applicable to the many five-year plans in LDCs and elsewhere which paint a rosy picture of the future but do not show how to get from here to there.[14]

It is this aspect which makes the Keynesian quip so dangerous, for it leads to an overvaluation of the present to the point of obsession. In fact, it says: never mind the future. The true problem is that today's decision will have a significant effect on what happens tomorrow. The danger is that today's survival makes tomorrow's death rather than a better life likely. The problem is to make sure that today's decisions allow better and perhaps more decisions tomorrow.

---

[13] The real entrepreneurial achievement of Henry Ford seems to me to have been that he had the faith that people would buy simple, reliable, and cheap cars *before* there were any decent roads or networks of gas stations and garages. On the other hand there are failures of private business to foresee such demands: electric utilities hesitated to provide electricity to farms because they were so sure that all the farmers would use it for would be to light a 25 watt bulb. The Rural Electrification Authority of the New Deal taught them otherwise. And there is the not uninteresting case of the Canadian railway system built from coast to coast in anticipation of later needs which, it turned out, the airplane and the car would satisfy.

[14] In planning forward from the present to the future there may be no path from here to there, and planning from the future to the present one could not get to the starting point which, after all, is a datum for the planner. Few things illustrate to me better the dangers of dealing with an evolutionary problem by static means.

This criticism applies also to the so-called supply-side economics of the 1980s and 1990s which aim at growing out of what today is called structural budget deficits by a policy that depends on these deficits for growth.

To put it in terms of the ideas of nonlinear systems, the problem is this: The precise initial conditions may in time make an enormous difference to the way in which future developments work themselves out. But we have not only the problem of small random deviations from the initial conditions. We have in economics not only the problem of positive feedbacks. We have also the *fact* that all the time (I must avoid the word continuously in this context, because what happens *ex visu* of the current situation is discontinuous) innovations appear which impinge on that course of things which corresponds to the initial "initial" conditions. Some of these innovations work out, others do not, but it seems as if all the time new conditions arise.

I do not know to what extent the present state of the theory of nonlinear systems can deal with this problem. It is to my mind certainly what Schumpeter thought, if perhaps only vaguely.

Three Formal Models: A Digression

SCHUMPETER'S APPROACH to reality, for this is what his theory amounts to, has been criticized on several counts. In a way, the most serious criticism, by Jürg Niehans,[1] is that it was Schumpeter's tragedy that he never succeeded in developing a formal model.

W. W. Rostow, in his foreword to Robert Loring Allen's biography of Schumpeter, makes a similar point. "I believe Schumpeter's sense of failure derived in part from his inability to formulate his powerful, correct understanding of the significance of innovations into either an elegant mathematical formulation in the style of Walras or a neat historical pattern" (Allen 1990, xv).

There are several reasons for this. The mathematics did not exist. Neither was the historical detail available for a "neat historical pattern," a term which almost seems like an oxymoron once it is admitted that reality is essentially "turbulent."

But there were other criticisms, such as, that it was difficult to understand how small innovations could have such big effects. This point is formally cleared up by the mathematics of nonlinear systems and shown graphically by computers. But Schumpeter pointed out in a letter to Rostow:

> I have come to the conclusion that innovation was on a sufficient scale from 1786 to 1801 to account for what I mean it to account. You must never forget that I only claim "igniting" importance for innovations and that I do not deny that the bulk of the prosperity phenomenon comes about through processes not themselves of an innovatory character (see the postwar building boom in this country). And, second, that the innovations of that period did not simply consist of cotton textiles and in iron and steel development, but also in the further canal building and in *the spread of the factory system as such*. If this is properly taken into account, the thing is not as inadequate as those historians seem to think who always point out that the Watts engines were of small quantitative importance before 1820.[2] (italics added)

And in the same letter Schumpeter, answering Rostow's fifth query, wrote: "I do think that on the whole the long wave conception works rather well. In particular my partiality for it has increased by the fact that it clears up phe-

---

[1] Niehans (1981). I cannot accept Niehans' judgment in his *History of Economic Theory* (1990) of "vision without theory" as doing justice to Schumpeter.

[2] Letter to W. W. Rostow, March 12, 1940. This letter was written in response to a letter by W. W. Rostow of February 26, 1940, which raised five major problems. I have not found Rostow's letter to Schumpeter in the Archives.

nomena which otherwise would constitute unexplained problems, such as the Gibson [sic] paradox or the 'breaks in trends' which many students find in their series, for instance in the 90s of the nineteenth century." And "The long wave describes what I like to call the great recurrent industrial revolutions."

Criticisms such as "why should entrepreneurs appear in bunches?" or "why should cycles be so regular?" are hard to understand, except when one realizes how strong was the pull of thinking in terms of equilibrium and of linearities. The fact that innovations require after a while an Einordnungsprozess and that innovations appear simultaneously with, and not immediately instead of, the old methods of production, amply account for the former. The question really is why innovators have a chance only at discrete intervals. And there is Schumpeter's insistence that the *unavoidable* fluctuations need not affect most people seriously and need not constitute the social catastrophies of Great Depressions.

It is also hard to understand why a variation in the length of the Juglar of 8–11 years, or of the Kondratieff of 45–60 years, is called "regular." In fact, the conception of a multi-cycle scheme goes a long way to explain the variations in length and amplitudes of cycles.[3] But, of course, in no case is it sufficient to explain every detail, and sometimes not every important detail of reality.

There have in fact been a number of models to deal with some aspects of Schumpeterian theory. I shall deal briefly with three.

Ragnar Frisch's model, published in 1933, was I believe the first such formulation. The most recent one is by Richard Goodwin, who has the distinction of having been both a student and a teacher (of mathematics) of Schumpeter.[4] There were other important achievements, of which Erik Dahmén's book and articles, Nelson and Winter's book and articles, and the Swedish micro-macro model by Gunnar Eliasson are the most significant.[5] All of them acknowledge the inspiration of Schumpeter.

[3] Spiethoff, in his lectures, recounted that he came to the conception of his "Aufschwungsspanne" and "Stockungsspanne," his names for the upward and downward phase of long waves, by observing the business cycle and finding that, contrary to expectations, long upswings were followed by short downswings, and short prosperities by long depressions.

[4] Erich Schneider, too, first met Schumpeter to teach him mathematics and then became Schumpeter's protegé. Schneider was at the time a high school mathematics teacher, which in Germany, Austria, and Switzerland required university-level training in mathematics for a number of years. I remember Schneider's inaugural lecture. It dealt with some aspects of production theory. It was mathematical and seemed to the listeners a little like black magic.

[5] Space, and uneasiness about my competence to discuss it sensibly, have induced me not to describe the evidently very important Swedish micro-macro model developed by Gunnar Eliasson.

I am embarrassed to confess that Erik Dahmén's important work came too late to my attention to be included here. Dahmén is an economic historian, not a mathematician, and in that sense, but only in that sense, is his not a formal model. Being a very detailed study of Swedish evolution based on thousands of studies of enterprises and entrepreneurs, it is arguably the most Schumpeterian of all studies.

Dahmén considers himself a Schumpeterian. He has, however, developed his own theoretical constructs like development blocks, which are operational definitions of longer cyclical periods,

THE FRISCH MODEL

Ragnar Frisch published his famous model in 1933.[6] In this publication, he refers to a correspondence as well as to personal discussions with Schumpeter. The article has a section specifically referring to the Schumpeterian idea that the impulse setting the economy in motion might come from innovations. Frisch added that he felt he had modeled Schumpeter's ideas fairly.

Briefly, the model consists of a careful and novel analysis of the acceleration principle whose intellectual origins go back to Aftalion (1913) and J. M. Clark (1917). Frisch also reverts in part to Knut Wicksell's rocking horse analogy: any impulses to the economic system would lead to fluctuations as a push to a rocking horse would send it rocking. That is, there were waves which were due to "the properties of the adaptive mechanism of capitalist economic life," as Schumpeter had put it in his letter to Mitchell.

Frisch did not make any actual empirical studies. But by assuming reasonable "ballpark" estimates for the magnitudes of the various parameters, he could produce both Juglar and Kitchin cycles. In the article there is no mention of any long wave, but in his lecture notes he did also produce a fifty-year cycle.[7]

The acceleration principle, or the interaction of the multiplier and the acceleration principle à la Samuelson, could account satisfactorily for cycles of different length *once an impulse had started the system going*. Indeed, in his assessment of Frisch's contribution, Schumpeter made just this point. As far as he was concerned all these kinds of models had the "limitations . . . that they are nothing more than exact statements of possible aspects of repercussions within the adaptive apparatus of economic life ("propagations"). . . . This applies particularly to the only additional instance we are going to notice, the elegant model devised by Professor Frisch in his Cassel essay" (*Business Cycles*, 189).

Frisch had to solve two problems. The first was where the impulses keeping the system going were coming from. He solved this initially by making the reasonable assumption that there were always some random events happen-

---

including both upswings and downswings and tracing in detail the preconditions and spread of innovative behavior also to other industries. Because it has the microeconomic detail which in Schumpeter remained programmatic, it does at the very least complement Schumpeter's own discussion of historic periods. Although Schumpeter tried very hard to induce scholars to pursue this line of entrepreneurial history, I am not aware of any American or German equivalent to Dahmén's achievement.

  [6] Frisch (1933).

  [7] I owe this knowledge to Mr. Andvig of the University of Oslo. Mr. Andvig also told me that in his lecture notes Frisch had produced a fifty-year cycle, but that Swedish attempts to duplicate this result were unsuccessful. *Foreslesninger holdt 1933.II og 1934.I over Makrodynamik av Professor Ragnar Frisch*. Mimeo. I have been able to read these notes with the aid of Mrs. Frank Stafford and Mrs. Anna Mengia v. Albertini.

ing and that Slutzky had shown that such random shocks could cumulate to cyclical fluctuations.[8]

Schumpeter and Frisch had discussed this problem for some years. In a letter to Schumpeter, Frisch referred to a letter by Schumpeter from San Francisco, dated June 24, 1931, and to earlier discussions.[9] Frisch's letter is a model what a scientific discussion should be. Both Frisch and Schumpeter tried hard to accommodate their own views to those of their friend, but without compromising what each believed was the essential truth.

Stortg. 9 Oslo
July 5, 1931

Dear Schumpeter:

Thank you for your very kind letter of June 24. . . .

You say that you are not satisfied with my classification of the innovations as disturbances (part of the impulse problem), and I think I understand now why you are not satisfied, but I believe you will be so when you have read this letter.

Before I received your last letter (of June 24) I had started again pondering over your point of view, and I began to see clearer why you would not capitulate entirely to my pendulum. Let me tell you right away that I am glad you did not smooth out our difference in a more or less formalistic adoption of my pendulum analogy but took the trouble to attempt to convince me that there is something fundamental which is not represented in the picture of the pendulae [sic] as I gave it originally. We all have our peculiar way of working and I for one [here Frisch crossed out a few words] never understand a complicated economic relationship until I have succeeded in translating it either into a graphical representation or into some mechanical analogy. [sic] The reason why I did never under our conversation in Harvard or Cleveland seized your meaning exactly has been I suppose that I never was able to translate it into a mechanical analogy. I think I am able to do so now. Your San Francisco letter must have been working in my subconscience even after I sent to you my all to[o] simple answer classifying your innovations under the impulse heading. In fact, about two weeks ago (after I returned from Stockholm where I had given a talk on business cycle analysis) my thought got started along the following mechanical analogy:

Suppose you have a pendulum exposed to frictions so that its motion would die down if it were let to itself. Now build a container for water at the top of the pendulum (above the suspension point of the pendulum, and such that the weight of the water and the container does not rest on the pendulum but is supported independently). Further build a pipe down through the length of the pendulum and arrange an outlet for the water at the very lowest point of the pendulum. This

[8] Slutzky, (1933) In Russian with an English summary, as quoted by Frisch (1933). I do not read Russian.

[9] The letter to be quoted was found in the Harvard Archives. The Schumpeter-Frisch correspondence in the manuscript collection of the University of Oslo deals primarily with the business of the Econometric Society. I have found no letter by Schumpeter dated June 24, 1931.

outlet shall be of the following peculiar sort. Its opening points to the left and is equipped with a valve that is regulated by the *velocity* of the pendulum (for instance being influenced by the air-resistance or in some other way). The regulation of the valve is such that the opening is largest when the pendulum moves towards the right, and in particular the opening is largest when the speed of the pendulum (towards the right) is at its maximum. We can imagine that the opening is some simple function of the speed. When the pendulum moves towards the left the opening is nearly (but not entirely) closed, the opening being the smallest when the speed towards the left is the largest. This variation of the opening, both under the movement towards the left and the right can of course be represented by one and the same functional relationship. The only difference between the two movements is indeed that the variable on which the opening depends in one case is positive and in the other case negative. The amount of water flowing out of the valve will depend not only on the size of the opening as here discussed but also on the *pressure*, that is the level of the water in the container above the pendulum. Now let the container be alimented with water from some source which we may consider as a datum in the problem. In other words the stream flowing into the container we consider as a known function of time (for instance a constant).

If you now let the system loose it will evolve in cycles whose lengths will be determined partly by the length of the pendulum, partly by the friction and partly by the law that regulates the opening of the valve. Of course you understand already the whole analogy: The water represents the new ideas, inventions, etc. They are not utilized when they come, but are stored until the next period of prosperity (or even longer, some of the molecules in the container may rest there indefinitely). And when they are finally utilized they form the additional surplus of energy which is necessary to maintain the swings, to prevent them from dying down. The amount of energy which will thus be released depends on whether there is a large amount of *potential* innovations stored and also on the velocity of the upswing (which of course itself depends on the whole situation just in the way represented by this mechanical analogy).

This picture may now be completed by taking into account random disturbances of the type which I had originally in mind: Imagine a series of random impulses, working either to the right or to the left and being distributed in time and size according to some sort of chance law.

A thoroughgoing mathematical discussion of this sort of cyclical machine will I believe throw light on the economic cycle problem. It was on such a mathematical analysis I was engaged when your letter of June 24 arrived.

I hope you are more satisfied with this interpretation of the innovations. And you understand, of course, how much I owe you for being led into this avenue of approach, which I hope will be a fruitful one. As I see it now there are two aspects to the impulse (or "energy") problem: On the one hand the more or less random irregularity of inventions and progress in the arts. This idea can be followed back to Knut Wicksell's "Hack-teori." On the other hand the periodic release in the actual utilization of "stored" inventions, which is your idea.

Which one of the two that is actually the most important in the sense of representing the largest source of "energy" for the maintenance of the economic swings I think nobody can say today. This can only be found by painstaking studies that are *econometric* in the best sense of the word. I should be very much mistaken if such studies would not lead us to new Magellanic oceans in cycle theory. At any rate I think I see now the two-sidedness of the problem. One side I have seen long ago and the other I have finally realized through your patient explications.

Schumpeter's *Business Cycles*, even though not utilizing sophisticated econometric techniques, is precisely such an econometric study "in the best sense of the word." Tinbergen's important pioneering econometric studies of economic fluctuations in the United States and the United Kingdom appeared only in 1939, certainly after *Business Cycles* had gone to press. Large-scale computers were still in the future—the word "electronics" had not yet been coined—and large-scale econometric models for the development of which Lawrence Klein received the Nobel Prize were a development of the post–World War II decades.

A comparison of these large-scale attempts with Schumpeter's approach reveals his ambitiousness. Large-scale computers have reversed the relation between the availability of data and the ability to deal with them. This capacity has outstripped the availability of reliable facts. It has in fact restricted the use of econometric models to short-term analysis. In addition, past experience is an uncertain guide to the future. As Schumpeter had stressed, our parameters are not sufficiently constant.

This means that to this day Schumpeter's painstaking analysis has not been made obsolete by later theoretical and technological developments and it was in his grand attempt to deal with the economic history of the past centuries in which Schumpeter used intensively another of Frisch's suggestions, the method of normal points (see chapter 7).

Now I shall continue with the "impulse" problem. As far as the Frisch's first point was concerned, Schumpeter agreed: he had solved an important part of the impulse-cycle problem, but only a part:

> If this model had been associated by its author with a claim to representing the cyclical process, objections . . . would . . . have to be urged. But since it is not intended to be another *perpetuum mobile* theory of business cycles but the presentation of a piece of mechanism, we can not only enjoy its simplicity, but also use it to demonstrate the possibility of a distinct type of oscillation. (*Business Cycles*, 189)

There is a second difficulty to which Frisch's model does not address itself at all, which yet seems central to understanding Schumpeter's attempts to deal with the reality of capitalist evolution. In terms of Frisch's mechanical analogy, it is clear where the water is coming from: the stream of potential innovations may or may not be regular, but its release is determined essentially by the construction of the machine. Of course, if the stream of incoming water dries up, the mechanism ceases to work, the pendulum ceases to swing, the rocking horse ceases to rock. Schumpeter is worried about this possibility in his discussion of the Coming of Socialism, and it is the basic assumption of the thesis of secular stagnation. (See Part II).

Suppose that the stream of water does continue. What happens to the water after its release has re-energized the pendulum? One can imagine the whole machine floating in a pool of water, or being set in the earth. If it floats in a pool, the water will get higher and higher as the impulses keep making the pendulum swing anew. This might account for successive equilibria reaching ever higher levels.

At the same time, the water flowing into the pool would itself cause disturbances which might be the mechanical analogue for the generation of the long wave. This can be only a suggestion, for, to the best of my knowledge, the mathematical analysis of such a situation/possibility does not yet exist. (But see below the account of the latest Goodwin model.)

Suppose, alternatively, the machine that keeps the pendulum swinging is set on firm land. If it is built on rock, the outflowing water wil not further affect it—unless an earthquake dislodges it, of course. Neither, however, does it in this case permit successive equilibria to reach higher and higher levels. It seems that Schumpeter was right in seeing an important limitation to what precisely the Frisch model could model.

But suppose the machine was built on earth which the outflowing water would gradually soften, thereby threatening the very basis of the machine. Is this the mechanical analogue for the End of Capitalism? It is not the mechanism itself which is at fault but the inevitable change in its milieu.

In other words, the Frisch model as developed by 1933 could account for a multicycle scheme but not for any trend, linear or not. Some of Schumpeter's problems with the treatment of innovations remain.

THE NELSON-WINTER MODEL

Nelson and Winter's book is a consciously Schumpeterian model.[10] While Frisch and Goodwin are concerned with the cyclical aspects of Schumpeter's model, Nelson and Winter focus on the structural changes of the economy in the course of evolution.

Nelson's and Winter's thorough and long book can, of course, be described only "in desperate brevity," to use one of Schumpeter's favorite phrases. It has structural characteristics which Schumpeter certainly would have liked: it is not about equilibrium but about change. It does not center on maximization procedures, because real choices are not made from the set of *all* possible

[10] Nelson and Winter (1982). The authors acknowledge explicitly the inspiration they received from Schumpeter's work.

alternatives,[11] and the future is in any case unknowable. Concepts like bounded rationality are stressed. And, most important, Nelson and Winter begin with the microeconomic behavior of the firms. They draw analogies between what makes individuals and what makes firms tick—analogies which are plausible because they do *not* pretend that firms are real people. They also draw parallels to modern biology: firms will pass on what they have found to work. All of this reminds one of how Schumpeter described the sensible use of mathematics to E. B. Wilson. (See above, pp. 24–25.)

The first part develops in detail two key ideas: individual skills and organizational routines. "Routines" are important rationalizations through which individuals and institutions have learned to cope with an immense variety of facts, have learned to reduce—one has to resist the temptation to say "minimize"—the cost which the inevitable choices impose. "We propose that individual skills are the analogue of organizational routines, and that the understanding of the role that routinization plays in organizational functioning is therefore obtainable by considering the role of skill in individual functioning" (ibid., 73).

The most important aspect here is the idea of "tacit knowing" (ibid., 76): much important knowledge is impossible to acquire through books, is highly personal, and is transmitted through personal contact. It is a form of "learning by doing" and perhaps also by watching. And, it might be added, it can become a dangerous knowledge when it unconsciously and for that reason all the more strongly resists change. For, as Nelson and Winter point out, routines that in one situation work might in another become catastrophic.

Any real behavior must deal with specifics, and even imitation is not as easy as orthodox equilibrium theory at least implies.[12] The words "routine" and "imitation" are apt to mislead if they suggest "uncreative" or "hackwork." And no behavior is costless—the New Institutional Economics deals specifically with such cost and the name of Oliver Williamson is prominently mentioned.

Innovation plays an important role in Nelson and Winter's account especially with regard to organizational routines, but it does not just appear. There cannot be a perfect imitation either, because "the target routine is not in any substantial sense available as a template" (ibid., 155). There simply is "no set of blueprints that completely describes available production techniques" (ibid.) and there cannot be. The implication of the availability of such a set is

---

[11] Nelson and Winter refer in this connection to Alchian and Williamson. They are in general most generous in acknowledging their intellectual debts—another very Schumpeterian characteristic.

[12] For a century people have tried in vain to climb Mt. Everest. But when Hillary succeeded, there was suddenly a rash of successes. The fact that something can be done powerfully eases other successes, but that does not mean that later climbers do not have to be highly trained and watch the weather and other specific conditions most carefully. What gave the secret of the atom bomb away was that it was exploded. Once it is shown that something can be done, imitation is inevitable. The world is full of real examples.

not just unrealistic, it is impossible.[13] Too much knowledge is "personal," "tacit."[14] On the other hand:

> The broad ideas that shape the most critical high-level decisions of a business enterprise may also be viewed as heuristic—they are principles which are believed to shorten the average search to solutions of the problems of survival and profitability. Much discussion of heuristics of this sort has been carried out under the name of "corporate strategy."[15]
>
> In many ways our position is consistent with that of Whitehead (1938) who proposed that sometime during the nineteenth century man invented the art of inventing, and also consistent with the Schumpeter of *Capitalism, Socialism and Democracy* (1950) who proposed that sometime during the twentieth century the modern corporation "rationalized innovation." Neither Schumpeter nor Whitehead, we think, would deny the role of genius or luck, or argue that systematic differences in innovative competence do not exist. But their views are quite compatible with the proposition that organizations have well-defined routines for the support and direction of their innovative effort." (ibid., 133–34)

Imitation may shade into innovation: "imitation, though costly and imperfect in the individual instance, is a powerful mechanism by which new routines come to organize a larger fraction of the total activity of the system" (ibid., 135).

Nelson and Winter point out that standard orthodox static theory also knows selection processes and indeed, much recent discussion of the equilibrium problem is devoted precisely to the *process* by which the equilibrium is reached. Nelson and Winter quote Milton Friedman's proposition of an orthodox selection process:

> Let the immediate determinant of business behavior be anything at all— traditional reaction, random chance or what not. Whenever the determinant happens to lead to behavior consistent with rational and informed maximization of returns, the business will prosper and acquire resources with which to expand; whenever it does not, the business will tend to lose resources and can be kept in existence only by the addition of resources from the outside. The process of natural selection helps to validate the hypothesis [of maximization of returns (N-W)] or, rather, given natural selection, acceptance of the hypothesis can be based largely on the judgement that it summarizes appropriately the conditions for survival (Friedman 1953, 23). (As quoted by Nelson and Winter 1982, 139–40)

Against this, Alchian's questioning proposition is quoted that "What really counts is the various actions actually tried, for it is from these that success is selected and not from some set of perfect actions" (ibid., 140). This was precisely Schumpeter's point. The validity of a maximization hypothesis re-

---

[13] Here is the fundamental explanation why turnkey projects in LDCs almost never worked.

[14] The term is Michael Polanyi's, whose influence is expressly acknowledged. Polanyi (1962). Nelson and Winter list two other items by Michael Polanyi in their bibliography.

[15] McCraw (1991), 384, credits Schumpeter with having invented this term.

ally requires the rather strict assumption of pure competition and that the lapse of real time makes no difference. It becomes dubious when competition is imperfect and when a decision in real time, changes the conditions for further actions. In other words, survival by itself hardly proves that we have an optimum similar to the one that the maximization procedures of orthodox theory would have reached.

Evolution proceeds in real time, which is irreversible and which creates by its very nature ever new situations. Hence

> [A] historical process of evolutionary change cannot be expected to "test" all behavioral implications of a given set of routines, much less test them all repeatedly. It is only against the environmental conditions that persist for extended periods (and in this loose sense are equilibrium conditions) that routines are thoroughly tested. There is no reason to expect, therefore, that the surviving patterns of behavior of the historical selection process are well adapted to novel conditions not repeatedly encountered in that process. (ibid., 154)

There are interesting parallels between (modern) biology and evolutionary economics (ibid., 160–61), some of which bring out the difference between the Schumpeterian and the orthodox approaches.

> [N]o theory of long-run evolutionary change logically can take the environment of the individual species (collection of firms) as exogenous. Hence, the notion of fitness (profitability) contributes much less to the understanding of the long-run pattern of change than might at first glance appear. What does play a crucial though obscure role is the character of the whole evolving system's interactions with the truly exogenous features of the environment represented in the current model by product demand and factor supply curves. . . . A theory that omits to explain how significant properties of that interaction affect the changing requirements for fitness (profitability) over time cannot be regarded as an adequate explanation of the evolution of the system." (ibid., 160–61)

There is also a significant difference between this approach and neoclassical growth theory, which in a way culminated in Solow's 1954 achievement. The emphasis was on identifying the role of various macroeconomic inputs (labor, capital) in accounting for growth of observed GNP. The upshot of these efforts was that neither the growth of labor nor the growth of physical capital came anywhere near explaining what actually happened. There remained that big residual factor, which was blithely equated with the presence of technological change. But Nelson and Winter show that it is possible to interpret the observed growth in different and mutually exclusive ways (ibid., 199–201).

To summarize the argument to this point: In a static classical view as now formalized—an important characterization—there is only one best way to produce a good which a maximization procedure discovers. In an evolutionary economy there are several firms, each differing in their ingenuity to produce goods. The firms in evolutionary situations are run by people who acquire certain skills (which may be quite different for different people) which they develop into "routines" by which organizations make decisions.

The strategies of the firms may differ, but they all search for new ways of producing. Their search may be innovative or imitative, but it always proceeds in an environment in which knowledge is necessarily imperfect - the future is in principle unknowable—and the choice of what to do is not from the set of all possible alternatives but only from those that are known to them. They must make irrevocable choices in any given institutional environment, that is, a given market structure. At the same time, the market structure itself evolves as the result of the decisions made.

The analysis of these problems proceeds by means of simulation techniques, assuming a search model for individual firms in an industry, with search for better methods increasing (decreasing) as profitability declines (increases), with individual firms using different technologies and searching for new ways in the neighborhood of the old ones.

In the process, Nelson and Winter dispense with Alfred Marshall's notion of a representative firm which in an evolutionary environment would indeed be misleading. "The key ideas" are instead

> [F]irms at any time are viewed as possessing various capabilities, procedures and decision rules that determine what they do given external conditions. They also engage in various "search" operations whereby they discover, consider, and evaluate possible changes in their way of doing things. Firms whose decision rules are profitable given the market environment expand; those firms that are unprofitable contract. (ibid., 206–7)

In chapter 10, "Economic Growth as a Pure Selection Process," the assumptions of the simulation model are sufficiently simplified to present an analytical model which helps to understand certain aspects of the simulation model. But in chapter 11, the discussion is again expanded to show the wide variety of "search strategies and topographies [of the environment]. Technologies and industries have evolved in dramatically different ways. These differences in technical change at the macro level are presumably connected with the inter-industry differences in the rate of technical progress and productivity growth" (ibid., 247).

This fact underlies, of course, Schumpeter's vision of seeing both a historically identified cycle and the long-term development analyzed as a Kondratief wave, as being centered in specific firms and industries.

There are different decision rules, some of which concentrate to fill a perceived demand, others to reduce cost. Strangely enough, Nelson and Winter do not stress the importance of the Schumpeterian idea that demand itself is created by the innovation, though it seems implied. But they do stress that the "learning process" itself is not inevitable, and that it can be influenced by resources applied to it (ibid., 258).

An important reason for the decline of firms and industries is that the strategies employed in one era to make them great may not work in the next. Experience which in one context may work may actually be an obstacle to success in another.[16]

Nelson and Winter discuss major Schumpeterian aspects of competition. First, "a central aspect of dynamic competition is that some firms deliberately strive to be leaders in technological innovations while others attempt to keep up by imitating the successes of the leaders" (ibid., 275). Second, there are "connections among market structure, R&D spending and technical advance" (ibid.).

In the nonevolutionary view, the market is essentially an information system which tells you efficiently what people want, what resources are scarce, and how scarce they are. Moreover, the market is an efficient method to deal with imperfect information. "Perfect" knowledge is not necessary: you only have to know what you can know. With Nelson-Winter, on the other hand, we get a competition where "there is no choice that is clearly the best ex ante." "Firms facing the same market signals respond differently, and more so if the signals are relatively novel. . . . In this view the market system is [in part] a device for conducting and evaluating 'experiments of economic behavior and organization" (ibid., 276–77).

This is precisely Schumpeter's insistence that development was a process that came from *inside* the economic system, and also that it fundamentally (and not only in degree) differed from adaptive processes as analyzed by orthodox equilibrium theory in that it required *personal* action by what he called an entrepreneur. In dynamic circumstances imitative behavior, too, may constitute entrepreneurial action, but this does not in any way diminish the analytic importance of the distinction between innovative and adaptive behavior. There are profound policy implications in this view, which Schumpeter stressed to the discomfort of those economists who saw in the maintenance of the conditions of pure competition the real heart of capitalist economic policy.

Schumpeter's concept of innovation goes much beyond the usual emphasis on technological advance, and it includes the very institutional one of "the spread of the factory system itself."[17,18]

[16] Experience with old processes may not be much good in the development of new ones and may even be an obstacle. When the Chase Bank opened an office in Lagos, Nigeria, it preferred to train new people from scratch to hiring experienced tellers from Barkley's. I have also personally found that experience may be a handicap in learning new things.

[17] Letter to Walt Rostow, March 12, 1940. A longer excerpt of this letter is given above which also makes clear the context in which the remark is made.

[18] Many of Schumpeter's views on market structure and innovation are found in *Capitalism, Socialism and Democracy* which clearly is not just a work of *haute vulgarization*. To quote McCraw: "Although Schumpeter liked to disparage [*Capitalism* . . .] as a mere potboiler in comparison with his earlier work, it is in fact one of the best analyses of capitalism ever written, perhaps even *the* best" (McCraw 1991, 382).

Nelson and Winter do not immediately analyze the full range of Schumpeter's insights. Their model sticks initially to some of the competitive assumptions, for example, all firms produce "a homogeneous product. The industry faces a downward sloping demand curve. Factor supplies are perfectly elastic and factor prices are constant over the period in question."

However, other assumptions cannot, because of the evolutionary point of view, be reconciled with pure competition: "At any particular time each firm operates a single technique—the best it knows," which is not necessarily the best there is or the same as the one operated by its competitors.

There are, of course, a whole slew of additional and important simplifying assumptions which may be omitted in the present context so as to bring out clearly the evolutionary aspects of the model. They are primarily "A firm can discover a more productive technique . . . by two methods: by doing R&D that draws from a general fund of relevant technological knowledge or by imitating the production processes of other firms. Either method involves expenditures in R&D, and such expenditures yield uncertain returns. Firms may differ in their policies towards innovation and imitation" (ibid., 282).

The model is limited to "science based" technological changes (ibid., 283). However, market structure is not assumed but evolves endogenously (ibid.). Here the authors introduce a very important Schumpeterian aspect of evolution, the function of bank credit, in analyzing what difference it makes how much firms can borrow (ibid., 290).

Nelson and Winter point to "two key differences" of their model of Schumpeterian competition from other models:

> The strategies and policies of our firms are not derived from any maximizing calculations, and the industry is not assumed to be in equilibrium. (ibid., 268)
>
> An essential aspect of real Schumpeterian competition is that firms do not know *ex ante* whether it pays to try to be an innovator or an imitator, or what level of R&D expenditures might be appropriate. Indeed, the answer to this question for any single firm depends on the choices made by other firms, and reality does not contain any provision for firms to test out their policies before adopting them. Thus, there is little reason to expect equilibrium policy configurations to arise. Only the course of events over time will determine and reveal what strategies are the better ones. And even the verdict of hindsight may be less than clear, for differences in luck will make the same policies brilliantly successful for some firms and dismal failures for others.

The analysis of the model proceeds by simulation and makes further specific alternative assumptions for different runs to explore "the influence of initial market structure on the innovative and price performance of the industry and on the evolution of industry structure over time" (ibid., 289).

The effects of the initial concentration are consistent with the Schumpeterian hypothesis; however, I found it surprising that "best practice did not appear to depend upon initial concentration" (ibid., 291). Equally surprising to me (though not stressed by Nelson and Winter) was that it also did not seem to depend very much on how much a firm could borrow. Considering the importance which Schumpeter attaches to credit as a method of financing innovations, I would have expected a larger effect.

This result may perhaps be due to the fact that all models deal only with a single industry producing a homogeneous good, that entry into the industry is not formally analyzed, and in particular that the rise of industries producing competitive goods is not analyzed.[19]

All other results were very much Schumpeterian.

> [A]verage productivity towards the end of the run . . . was lower when there were many firms than when there were few. . . . Since the initial productivity levels of all firms were the same under all initial conditions, average productivity apparently rose more rapidly and average cost declined more rapidly in the small-numbers cases than in the large-numbers cases. (ibid., 292)

Why should average productivity be so sensitive to industry structure? (ibid., 294). Aside from purely statistical reasons, the answer lies in the concept of the firm and the advantages of being big. "Within the boundaries of a firm, technical information that is available for use with one unit of capital is equally and costlessly available to all other units" (ibid., 294).

> Thus, in this model a more competitively structured industry does lead to a poorer productivity performance than does an industry that is more concentrated. But the reason in not the one commonly associated with the Schumpeterian hypothesis: that best practice technology evolves more slowly in the many-firm case than in the few-firm case. It is that there is a much larger gap between best practice and average practice in the case where industry capital is fragmented than there is in the case where it is concentrated. (ibid., 295)

Starting with an unconcentrated industry subject to Schumpeterian competition, Nelson and Winter ask: "Under what conditions would one expect an industry to undergo a rapid increase in concentration? Alternatively, what conditions should be conducive to preserving the competitive structure?" (ibid., 311). These are questions the answers to which do go to the heart of the comparison of standard orthodox and Schumpeterian evolutionary theory.

If market structure was concentrated, "the most striking feature in the four-firm runs was that through thick and thin and in spite of the fact that long-run policies were noncooperative or even competitive, productivity levels of the firms tended to stay close and the initial division of the market tended to be preserved. . . ." (ibid., 315). "In the sixteen-firm runs, the structure was quite different" (ibid., 316).

As mentioned before, the model excludes entry of new firms, a significant potential limitation to its results. It is recognized explicitly that different entry

---

[19] This is, of course, not a criticism of Nelson and Winter's achievements. They themselves point to an extensive research program to deal with various open problems (407ff.). Besides, Winter has analyzed some aspects of the entry problem. Reasons of space preclude further consideration of this contribution.

conditions might affect their results. Nelson and Winter speculate briefly only on three: "(1) the scale at which entry occurs; (2) the technological progressiveness of entrants; and (3) . . . the nature of the calculations on which an entry decision is presumed to depend" (ibid., 327–28). The effect of the rise of new industries which might produce competitive goods, even "killer" inventions or goods—word processors versus manual typewriters, calculators and computers versus slide rules and logarithm tables—is not even speculated upon.

There arises, of course, the problem of a trade-off of static efficiency versus dynamic growth.[20] It is often assumed that the industry structure itself should be a policy target "and that structure should be chosen so as to optimize the trade-off" (ibid., 332). This description fits in particular the orthodox (but not Schumpeter's) view of the superiority of a purely competitive industrial structure.

Nelson and Winter proceed with their simulation experiments as follows: They "focus [on the] competitive struggle between firms with different R&D policies. There are three parameters in the model that can be interpreted as abstract counterparts of policy variables. They relate to the ease with which technology can be imitated, the extent to which large firms exert investment restraint, and the initial size distribution" (ibid., 333).

Initially, all firms are assumed to be the same size. There is an oligopolistic case with only four firms and a more competitive case with sixteen. Half of the firms do innovative R&D. Latent productivity growth is assumed at 2 percent for a slow growth, at 6 percent for a fast growth case, and there are two levels of difficulty of imitation assumed (ibid., 333–34).

The runs showed that an oligopolistic structure tended to preserve itself, while a competitive structure tended to change toward more concentration (ibid., 341).

Evolution with "cumulative technology" was somewhat different. Cumulative technology compared to "science-based technology" assumed an innovative R&D which involved only incremental improvements in prevailing techniques.

The consequences of cumulative technology run counter to orthodox expectations.

> [A]ggressive competitive behavior has a clear negative effect on both best-practice productivity and average productivity . . . aggressive competitive behavior tends to generate a structure in which there is at least one large competitor that is capable of quickly mimicking any new innovation and that operates with lower

---

[20] There is a corollary to this to which Nelson and Winter do not address themselves: the (supposed or real) conflict between equity and growth. Schumpeter envisages a short-term conflict, but a long-term complementary relationship. In the real world this conflict is, I believe, much exaggerated. A conflict really arises only in equilibrium situations. In the absence of equilibrium and with all-too-frequent miserable economic policies, growth and equity can often be improved substantially at the same time.

costs than the innovators. The result is "slower growth of best practice." (ibid., 345)

Preserving a competitive environment in order to preserve evolution is a rather tricky enterprise. Some of the difficulties are inherent in the complexity of the problem. But part of the problem is due to the fact that its solution has been attacked with the wrong model of reality (ibid., 248).

The policy implications of the evolutionary approach are relevant in this book, which concentrates on the policy aspects of Schumpeter's thought and activities. They lead to some results which have also been found by the theory of the second-best: there is no way to avoid analyzing specific individual cases and the evolutionary viewpoint may give different answers from a non-evolutionary one about how to achieve a commonly agreed-upon aim. This shifts the problem in part to an organizational level, which is a major concern of the New Institutional Economics. Indeed, "much of the organisational argument is implicitly evolutionary" (ibid., 356).

Nelson and Winter have three problems with past discussions of evolutionary policy that need to be remedied. First, every analysis unavoidably rests on certain "stylized" assumptions. Unfortunately, reality may not allow an immediate application. There is the problem of historical uniqueness.

Second, policy suggestions rest too often on a neglect of

[T]he most fundamental problems of economic organization [which] are either dispatched by assumption in those stylized arguments or are subsumed in a "minimal" list of government functions—the implication being that they could easily be handled if only the government would mind its own business. Here the problem involves the dubious linkage between the institutional assumptions of the theory and the range of institutions that could conceivably exist in a real system. (ibid.)

This is precisely what Schumpeter defined as ideological prejudice and what he defined as "Wertfreiheit": it "is merely the freedom . . . from judgments about how it would be *desirable* for the phenomena under study to behave."[21] And it is precisely why Schumpeter warned against too early an application of theory to policy. This is expressed by Nelson and Winter forcefully in their third objection: " . . . [T]hese advocates often have the tendency to apply general stylized arguments to real policy issues and hence to neglect the fact . . . that in real policy analysis the details of the situation and of the specific organizational alternatives under consideration often are of central importance" (ibid., 362).

This not only confirms the results of the theory of the second-best, but is also in agreement with the New Institutional Economics, by pointing out that

[21] "Rationality in the Social Sciences," in Swedberg (1991a), 318; italics in original.

neither property rights nor contracts nor their enforcement are "costlessly delineated in unambiguous terms and enforcement . . . is perfect and costless. . . . A real legal system that could approach the theoretical standards of clarity and perfection in the delineation and enforcement of entitlements would be an elaborate and expensive system indeed" (ibid., 363).

The specific entitlements mentioned are not social security and related matters, but pollution rights. I will return to this problem again in the discussion of Socialism as understood by Schumpeter. Here it is well to remember that Schumpeter stressed that legal concepts made sense only in a juridical framework,[22] and could do harm in an economic context. His very early example was that the law treated entrepreneurial and monopoly profit the same. The legal provision for "private enterprise" in agriculture "must be vastly different from the "private enterprise" in aircraft manufacturing." (ibid., 364).

All of Nelson and Winter's conclusions are consistent with the Schumpeterian views, and some are identical. For example:

> There is similarly an evolutionary view of the nature of the activities and of the goods and bads that society conceives as being of collective rather than private concern. Publicness is almost always a matter of degree. What is "public" depends in part on certain technological attributes of products and services and in part on what people think is important and valuable. (ibid., 368)

This is precisely Schumpeter's argument in his *Crisis of the Tax State* and it is also consistent with Musgrave's idea of merit goods and his analysis of whether public goods should be publicly or privately provided.[23]

Or consider Nelson and Winter's statement:

> Economists increasingly are coming to recognize that the income distribution problem is the inverse of the incentive problem. From the orthodox perspective, differences in income stem from differences in endowments; the transfer problem is to compensate for these without damping incentives. The evolutionary view emphasizes that a nontrivial part of the income distribution problem is associated with people who have been hurt, through no fault of their own, in the course of economic progress. . . . On the one hand, this implies that compensation and rehabilitation ought to be viewed as routine aspects of social policy in a world of rapid social change. But on the other hand, efficient economic performance in a

---

[22] Interestingly enough, Mises' arguments on this point are quite similar. See his discussion in Mises (1926).

[23] This point is probably more important than seems at first blush. Musgrave not only made much of the German and really general European tradition of *Finanzwissenschaft* available to English-speaking economists. More important is that he deviated from that tradition in one most important way: he put the theory on the basis of methodological individualism rather than on the collective notions of a general good or an "organic State." Here must also be mentioned Samuelson's "The Pure Theory of Public Expenditures" reprinted in *The Collected Scientific Papers of Paul A. Samuelson*, vol. 2 (1966), 1223–54.

dynamic world puts a high premium on job and locational mobility. The income distribution problem ought to be looked at more in terms of income security than in terms of transfers to compensate for initial lack of assets. (ibid., 369)

This is precisely how Schumpeter viewed the wage problem theoretically and politically in his criticism of Gustav Cassel discussed earlier.[24] And it is precisely the view expressed as maintaining incomes, not jobs.

THE GOODWIN MODEL

Richard M. Goodwin, who was also a student and friend of Schumpeter, has produced one of the first economic models of the Schumpeterian vision using chaos theory. The first of his two articles which will be considered here is more mathematical in character; the second goes more specifically into the economics to be modeled and Schumpeter's relation to Walras.[25]

At the beginning of his paper, Goodwin lists the goals his model is intended to achieve: "[It] must exhibit an unstable equilibrium; . . . must be globally stable; . . . must endogenously generate morphogenesis in the form of structural change; that it does so in cyclical form, albeit erratically or aperiodically; . . . generates both short and long waves . . . and finally, these waves are growth, not stationary waves" (Goodwin 1991, 30).

Goodwin's model involves five variables. The basic Schumpeterian notion is what Goodwin calls innovational capacity, k, modeled by a logistic equation which has been widely used in economics to model growth of individual industries and has the property that the growth starts small—as Schumpeter had put it in his letter to Rostow, his innovation has only an igniting role—that growth at first accelerates and then decelerates to reach asymptotically an upper limit. Goodwin, however, still proceeds to model successive streams of innovations by a single curve, a simplification he himself points out.

Next Goodwin introduces q, the gross product, v, the rate of employment, and u, the share of wages in gross product. It is variations in the last two variables—real wages rise as employment rises, thus putting a brake on specific developments—that helps generate the cycles which push the system to ever higher real income levels and unstable equilibria.

The complete model consists of five equations (ibid., 34) which I refrain from reproducing. Goodwin starts with a predator–prey model, which is easier for a layperson to understand, the model worked out by Lotka-Volterra. This ecological model has become familiar to laypersons. But it is a

---

[24] See also W. F. Stolper (1991), 189–205, where I have tried to integrate this view with the cyclical aspects of evolution, the conclusion being that social policy is a logical and necessary complement of evolutionary economic policy. See also W. F. Stolper (1984).

[25] Richard M. Goodwin (1991), 26–47. Idem, "Walras and Schumpeter: The Vision Reaffirmed," in Heertje and Perlman (1990). There was also a preliminary version.

periodic model: foxes eat hares. If they eat too many, their number falls, which soon leads to a fall in the number of foxes. When the number of foxes has fallen sufficiently, the number of hares will start to increase again and eventually so will the number of foxes. This model does not lead to a delicate ecological equilibrium between foxes and hares. It envisages the relation to be cyclical. For Goodwin, wages are the predator, and profits are the prey.

Thus far, the model is not yet chaotic. It follows the original Poincaré analysis of an area with an unstable equilibrium in the center of a region. Because of its instability, any deviation from the equilibrium will set the system going away from the equilibrium. If the dynamics far from the equilibrium pushes the motion back toward the equilibrium, some sort of cyclic behavior must occur between the equilibrium and the boundary of the region.[26] It models a kind of perpetuum mobile which underlies most business cycle theories. Evidently, theories which believe that development can proceed non-cyclically do not fall in this category.

To push the dynamics back toward the unstable equilibrium, Goodwin introduces as a fifth variable a control variable z, which is specified to provide negative feedback to the system but is not specified by any particular economic process. To make the system chaotic, Goodwin introduces one non-linearity to allow the "vastly more potent gyrations of chaotic motion."[27] Goodwin's final model is similar to the Rössler system, which, I understand, is a well-studied example of chaotic dynamics. What all this does is to switch from the simple notion of an equilibrium to the notion of strange attractors. At this point the mathematical layperson (which I am, of course) may profitably turn to Goodwin (1990). Goodwin starts with Schumpeter's basic two-phase cycle described before. "The problem then becomes how to formulate a two-cycle scheme in the context of innovation" (Goodwin 1990, 43).[28]

Here we meet again the logistic equation to produce the "life history of an innovation."[29] Yet:

> [C]omplicated as the model is, this model is still too simple: it omits the interdependence of the stock cycle and the short cycle, nor does it allow for the short wave in the logistic. And worst of all, it would have been rightly rejected by Schumpeter for the Keynesian sin of using aggregates which precisely conceal the source of the dynamics, i.e., the specific effects of technical change on relative prices and output. One can only say this sort of analysis helps us to understand a very complex process. (ibid., 44, 46)

[26] In two dimensions, this result is called the Poincaré-Bendicson Theorem. This phenomenon lies at the heart of Goodwin's 1951 model of the business cycle. I owe this knowledge to my colleague, Carl Simon, without whose help I could not have understood the Goodwin model.

[27] Goodwin (1991), 32. Goodwin admiringly acknowledges Rössler's work and help, but no specific bibliographic reference is given.

[28] The modeling of the third cycle, the Kitchin, is omitted as not involving (fixed) investments.

[29] The use of the logistic curve to model the life of a specific industry has a comparatively long history. Walther Hoffmann used it in his analysis of German long-term development; so did Schotte in his analysis of British industries.

Goodwin concludes:

> To me [the picture of] these time series look generically like economic statistics, though none of the parameters were derived from economics. I should say that this seems like the area where macrodynamics should be and probably always should have been. In my youth and innocence, I tried and failed to persuade Schumpeter to take linear cycle models seriously.[30] In retrospect, I think he was right to reject what did not fit his vision, but I think I could have sold this package to him. No exogenous shocks have been used and there is no identifiable periodicity, yet there is plain evidence of various waves. Accurate prediction is not possible, nor could one deduce the model I have used from the statistics it produced. Of course, if one knows the model, one can determine the future from the past, as is done in simulations like this. (ibid., 48–49; The pictures of the time series are reproduced in Goodwin 1990 and Goodwin 1991.)

Goodwin's is a true pioneering effort, and pioneers are permitted simplifying assumptions which epigones are expected gradually to eliminate. Or, to put it differently, Schumpeter would probably have bought this package, yet would have immediately raised questions for further work. For it is the enormous merit of the pioneer not to have given final answers but to have opened a fruitful way for inquiry.[31]

Schumpeter certainly would have raised some questions. Goodwin himself points to the aggregative nature of the model which has forced him into a number of ad hoc assumptions. The next generation of mathematical economists certainly has its work cut out in this direction. But there is another request to be made of future scholars.

Some of Goodwin's criticisms of Schumpeter seem to be the consequence of Goodwin's going directly from the first two-phase approximation to the third approximation involving multiple cycles. The second approximation of the four-phase cycle is skipped. This really explains the to Goodwin "baffling fact that [Schumpeter] totally rejected Keynes' *General Theory* . . . [written] to destroy the absurd assumption of full employment" (Goodwin 1990, 41). According to Goodwin, "Schumpeter in turn fell into the error of reasoning in neo-classical terms of full employment" (Goodwin 1991, 30).

But this is really not quite so. The real function of Schumpeter's initial discussion of the stationary state is to show how little relevant it is to the real world which is chaotic. The function of the first approximation involving two phases starting with the stationary neoclassical state is to show how the equilibrium is destroyed by an innovation and how, by an "Einordnungsprozess," a new (and higher) equilibrium is reached which has the

---

[30] Goodwin probably refers to his "Dynamical Coupling with especial Reference to Markets Having Production Lags" (1947).

[31] I repeat that I am not a mathematician, that I can understand mathematical articles involving calculus (though I can not write them, nor am I likely to catch any but the crudest mistakes), and I certainly need help to understand the mathematics of nonlinear systems. Fortunately I have this help in the person of my friend and colleague Carl Simon, an authority on chaos theory.

general characteristics of the old equilibrium (though with different parameters) and which needs a new innovation to be destroyed.

But once we get into the second approximation with its four phases, the full employment assumption is really subtly changed from one of full employment (which technically means less than it seems) to one of fluctuating employment and rising productivity.

Once you get to this approximation (which has already been discussed in detail), the puzzle of Schumpeter's rejection of the multiplier and the consumption function also disappears. For a multiplier really is simply the solution of a stable nonevolutionary linear system with interactions. Schumpeter takes care of these interactions in his discussion of money and by pointing out that in the second approximation any increases in income (initially caused by innovations financed by new money) would lead to a *larger* than proportionate increase in consumption. In the Kahn-Keynes multiplier such an assumption would have to be rejected as leading to an increase in income with no upper limit. Not so in Schumpeter.[32]

An advanced Schumpeterian-Goodwin model would have to introduce a control variable, like Goodwin's z but with a well-specified economic meaning. What prevents Schumpeter's model from being explosive is that, after a while, innovations pour new goods onto the market. This requires an Einordnungsprozess—a pause—before any new innovations can be introduced. It is this Einordnungsprozess that provides a natural negative feedback to push the system back toward an equilibrium. Modeling such an Einordnungsprozess also would differ from the wage-profit hunter-prey model, which really seems to me to be Marxist in nature. It models the function which the industrial reserve army has in the Marxist explanation.

Schumpeter actually defended Keynes against some Keynesians precisely on this point that, in Goodwin's words, "Keynes, . . . using Kahn's multiplier supplied the theory of effective demand-controlled output. This is crucial for realistic output and wage behavior" (Goodwin 1991, 30).

Not so in Schumpeter. Where in the *General Theory*, the notion of demand-controlled output has led to a strong anti-savings bias—long since abandoned by present-day and more sophisticated Keynesians[33]—Keynes himself rapidly changed with changing facts.

> We have heard from Washington the voice of several economists who, incredible
> though it sounds, stick to their anti-saving views and seem to be advocating loose
> spending as they had during the past decade. Keynes may be in error on a number

---

[32] In Keynesian language these problems are taken care of by shifts in the consumption function, as modeled, for example by Dusenberry or Modigliani. But these shifts are Schumpeterian, not Keynesian processes. Moreover, Schumpeter's analysis cannot entirely be translated into Keynesian language as discussed before.

[33] It is always dangerous to use such classifications by schools. As Schumpeter stressed, only fish swim in schools, economists are either good or bad. Most present-day Keynesians call themselves such to acknowledge an inspiration. The only simplistic Keynesian model is, of course, the so-called supply-side economics.

of points, but he is after all an able and responsible man. He recognized the complete change in scenery and has accordingly reversed his position.[34]

Goodwin is also "doubtful if Schumpeter fully appreciated the difficulties of analyzing a three-cycle scheme, since they are bound to be interdependent" (Goodwin 1991, 42). Schumpeter certainly did not know mathematical complications which as a matter of fact are still not fully worked out. But as the next chapter on the Analysis of Time Series will show, he was certainly fully aware of the interdependencies, treated the three-cycle scheme purely as a heuristic device to get a handle on historic reality, and insisted for this reason on detailed historical research.

Much remains to be done, and we must be deeply grateful to Goodwin for his pioneer effort and for opening to full view the complexity of the task ahead. In the meantime, one surely must agree with his judgment: "In my opinion . . . in the long run Schumpeter's work will stand with that of Walras[35] as a landmark in our discipline. . . . It is the perceptive choice of postulates, how the problem should be formulated, that determines the ultimate worth and power of analysis, and it is there that Schumpeter is outstanding" (Goodwin 1990, 42, 46).

Or, as Sidney Winter put it: "It is easy to admire Schumpeter's taste in problems" (Winter 1984, 287).

[34] Letter to Walter F. Spahr, dated February 1, 1941.

[35] It is perhaps misunderstood why Schumpeter thought Walras the greatest economist. In the *Wesen des Geldes* he gave the following explanation which perhaps also explains why he continued to consider equilibrium economics important.

> We consider . . . economic equilibrium in a closed area of investigation with pure competition. The first question which arises is whether such an equilibrium exists and is uniquely determined, i.e., whether and under what conditions the actions of households and firms result in a state of affairs in which the amounts of goods and services produced, bought and sold by households and firms, and the market prices determine each other in a manner that we can understand on the basis of purely economic considerations, why each of these quantities and each price is so and not different. Evidently that is the basic question of theoretical economics, as an analogous question is the basic question of any theoretical discipline. For, on the answer to this question depends whether we deal with a logically autonomous sytem or not. . . .
>
> Logically this really means . . . whether the facts which constitute our empirical knowledge, may be put into conditions or pieces of determinants (Bestimmungsstücke) which, first, are mutually compatible and secondly, for each of these magnitudes exclude all values except one. In our instance, it was already Walras who clearly saw this task and solved it in a first approximation. (*Wesen*, 214, 215; my translation)

History and the Theoretical Analysis of Capitalist Evolution

THE NATURE OF THE PROBLEM

For Schumpeter, the business cycle is identical with the life of capitalism. It is no accident that Schumpeter does not fit into the scheme of Haberler's classic analysis of *Prosperity and Depression*. It is fair, though perhaps somewhat oversimplified, to say that most cycle theories treat the cycle either as unnecessary, a mistake, frequently due to faulty monetary policy;[1] or as a perpetuum mobile, with prosperity necessarily following depression and depression prosperity.

As for the first view, with the proper monetary policy, for example, there need be no cycle. The extreme case is perhaps that of Hawtrey, but this description also fits the Hayekian approach where monetary policy is made responsible for the distortions in the structure of output as between investments and consumption. It is cheap money which is made responsible for overextending investments which in turn will be stopped by insufficient savings.

Alternatively, the cycle becomes a perpetuum mobile with ups following downs and downs following ups in perpetuity. The concept of (point) equilibrium has no logical place in this approach. Things move up until something happens to stop it—the upper turning point must be specially explained—and similarly with the downward movement. It is a world without friction and without any real "first cause" for the periodicity. There is a third strand of analysis exemplified by the historical approach and the—typically German—theory of stages. Schumpeter had considerable sympathy for the aims of the German historical school.[2] Econometrics might be considered a legitimate offspring of that approach.

Schumpeter by contrast aimed at an analysis of history that would allow both for the uniqueness of particular events and such underlying regularities as existed, and for discontinuities in the short and continuities in the long run.

Schumpeter had sketched to Mitchell that he envisaged reality to be what has since become known as "chaotic." There were external events, internal

---

[1] There was a German analysis of the cycle blaming it on faulty accounting: "Die Konjunktur: ein Rechenfehler?" ("Business cycles: a mistake in calculation?").

[2] See his friendly assessment in "Gustav v. Schmoller und die Probleme von heute," reprinted in Schneider and Spiethoff (1954).

shocks, and the modus operandi of the system itself: "It is my conviction that this situation must be faced and that an immensely laborious analysis of every historical pattern within the reach of our material must be undertaken,"[3] to which Schumpeter added a cry of despair: "It sometimes makes me quite melancholy to think that what I have really to say will have to remain unsaid forever."

> Now this bears on the carrying out of the three cycle scheme and on my datings in the following manner. What I am particularly interested in is the second group of fluctuations which I believe owe their existence to a process I can fully explain and roughly trace through the whole sketch of economic history that lies within the institutional framework of capitalist society. . . .
>
> [I]f from historical evidence I find that the industrial processes at a certain time are such that it is reasonably certain that if they had acted alone they would have produced, say, what I call prosperity, I date it as prosperity, even if other factors blotted it out, or introduced symptoms incompatible with the historical evidence on which it rests, I am prepared to accept any criticism on the score of incompleteness of my historical analysis. But what I do not admit is that such a proceeding is meaningless. If it were inadmissible, it would also be inadmissible for a doctor to say: "Organically this man is perfectly sound. If he is dying it is due to a brick which has fallen on his head."[4]
>
> I strongly feel that we must get rid of the prejudice that our phenomena are simple and can be directly handled by simple methods theoretical or statistical. . . .
>
> Now the first thing to observe is that such datings are only mere approximate estimates that are imperfectly determinate from the very nature of the material and the problem: for, owing to the presence of lags of different length in the different parts of the system, and owing to fortuitous conditions affecting some parts of the system and others not the system as a whole never does display strictly uniform characteristics in any given year, let alone month. This must be recognized and can, as I see it, not be remedied by simply counting from statistical peaks or troughs.[5]

Thus, a period might be classified as a prosperity even if specific and *provable* historic circumstances show it to have been a depressed period.

Schumpeter's is really a remarkable statement. It is his attempt to understand the course of history, but stressing that part which is within his special

---

[3] Letter to Mitchell, May 6, 1937, which has been quoted before.

[4] In the 1920s, Schumpeter also used this kind of analogy only the patient pronounced healthy by his doctor was run over by a car when he stepped out of the office.

[5] Letter to Mitchell, May 6, 1937. The last sentence refers to the method used by the National Bureau of Economic Research. Economists are not the only people suffering from an unwillingness to go beneath the surface. There are plenty of people who do not believe that smoking has something to do with lung cancer because there are smokers who do not succumb to cancer and nonsmokers who do. But economists seem particularly prone to stay at the surface.

competence, the part played by economic development, seen as a process of innovations and their consequences, and by the reactions which emanate from the structure of the economy.

Schumpeter's purpose, his ambition, is to go beneath the surface, to trace the underlying developments, to reconcile historic uniqueness with theoretic regularity; to combine the theoretic circularity with the one-directional historic changes, to combine what is circular and what is one-directional in reality. Schumpeter stresses that his argument about timing "runs in terms of historical and not theoretical conceptions." But because he is an economic theorist first of all, he is primarily interested in the second kind of fluctuations and he pays less attention to the kind of data which annals provide. Moreover, it is important for Schumpeter to date his fluctuations from the beginning of a new prosperity phase after the recovery phase has been finished, that is, after the adaptation to the preceding cycle has run its course. In Schumpeter's view, each cycle is an individual. Each cycle needs a new stimulus to get going. There is no such thing as a long-term secular trend, except as a sequence of short-term—in his case three—cycles. And this is, of course, why he is so interested in inflection points rather than peaks and troughs. Schumpeter stresses: "But I must repeat again, lest misunderstanding should arise, that I file no theoretical claims for the three-cycle scheme. It is primarily a descriptive device which I have found useful . . . nor [do I hold] that there is any mystical value about the regularities which reveal themselves as soon as this method is adopted" (Letter to Mitchell).[6]

Evidently Schumpeter was not wedded to the three-cycle scheme. If another theoretical scheme could in a simpler manner allow for both the underlying regularities and the uniqueness of historical reality, all the better. Perhaps "chaos" theory and the analysis of path dependency will turn out to be such a theory.

THE FRISCH METHOD OF NORMAL POINTS

The statistical method favored by Schumpeter was a successive free-hand smoothing of the available time series. Chapter 5 of *Business Cycles*, "Time Series and their Normal," has a survey of time series analysis from the standpoint of Schumpeter's theoretical approach. Schumpeter is interested in those "time series which reflect economic growth and the cyclical process of evolution as distorted by the influence of external factors" (*Business Cycles*, 193–94). Schumpeter insists: there exists no foolproof statistical method and no such method can possibly exist.[7]

---

[6] I have heard Schumpeter say several times that reality exhibited more regularity than his theory required.

[7] When *Business Cycles* went to press, the prevalent statistical methods were fitting (mostly linear) trends by least squares, harmonic and periodogramme analysis, the last two of which having apparently fallen out of fashion since.

Schumpeter's central concern is to find a statistical method which allows a theoretical interpretation, which does not impose regularities that do not exist or fails to find some that do. There is no objection to calculating a long-term trend as a descriptive device, but there is a serious question whether deviations from any such descriptive trend have any reality, that is, whether they can be given a meaning in theoretical or historical terms.

So, for Schumpeter, there is first his theoretical discussion outlined before, and his decision to limit himself to three cycles. But as there is no justification for assuming that successive cycles should have the same lengths—this is true for each of the three cycles—and there is no justification for believing that the three cycles are additively related to each other, a method recommends itself that does not require such regularities. As for the trend, it is "nothing but the result of the cyclical process or a property of it. . . . Real is only the cycle itself" (ibid., 206–7).

In Schumpeter's eyes the great thing about Frisch's approach is that it has "no difficulty in doing away with what are most obviously unacceptable properties . . . namely, the constant period, equality of expansions on both sides of the normal, and equal length of phases" (ibid., 210).

Finding by observation inflection points in time series is, of course, neither foolproof nor does it eliminate judgment of the analyst. But this is inevitable for many reasons. As Schumpeter put it:

> [W]e will emphasize once more that historical information about each individual case is the only means by which to reduce to bearable proportions the influence of external factors and that study and discussion of each situation which seems to have some claim to being called a neighborhood of equilibrium, and unavoidably rough estimates will be the surest way to reliable results, at least for some time to come. (ibid., 207)

Schumpeter's use of the method of free-hand smoothing has been ridiculed or at least viewed with some skepticism.[8] Certainly, statistical methods have improved and computers have allowed the handling of large systems of equations with any number of interactions and feedbacks. As the Goodwin model shows, "chaotic" systems can generate cycles of varying length. Still, one wonders how much of an improvement really has occurred, specifically, how much judgment really has been eliminated.

For example, the Michigan forecasting model, which is the direct descendant of the original Klein-Goldberger model also developed at the University of Michigan, has now grown to 220 equations. While the model is operating, new data are constantly fed into it as they become available, new equations and improved versions of existing equations are introduced. There is, of

---

[8] I plead guilty myself, having pointed out that when *Business Cycles* appeared the statistical and particularly the econometric methods began to change radically. See Stolper (1979). And there was some justification for this skepticism in Schumpeter's own qualification "for some time to come," and his own assessment of Tinbergen's contributions which were cited before. Still, I look upon the free hand method with considerably more tolerant eyes now than I did before.

course, much short-term inertia in such a system. Occasionally, the computer is overruled by the operator whenever the operator has reason to believe that he knows better than the computer.

Thus, the quality of the (short-term and frequently updated) forecasts depends on three things: the quality of the model; the quality of the data which are exogenous (and which introduce much short-term inertia into the system); and, not least, the quality of the operator. Of course, this leaves the system open to all kinds of arbitrarinesses and incompetence. But the point is that this is inevitable once we see reality as "turbulent," nonlinear, nonadditive, nondeterministic, and the future in principle unknowable.

Of course, this is not what people like me were brought up to think of as scientific method. The "scientific" procedure was to make your model and then to see what the model finally produced. Certainly, to interfere with the model while it was running was, to put it mildly, frowned upon. Yet the "turbulent" view of reality in fact makes such interference by the analyst-operator inevitable. Schumpeter's approach may or may not be the best way to handle this problem, but in itself there is nothing unscientific about it. On the contrary, models which sidestep this problem really do so by ignoring a central feature of reality.

Neither is this subject to the stricture which Schumpeter used against others, that he makes too many ad hoc assumptions to make the result come out right. For his more or less arbitrary assumptions deal with historic uniquenesses which are independently established, not ad hoc assumptions to produce theoretical regularities. And, of course, Schumpeter does not prejudge what he wants to find.

To be sure, Schumpeter's is a theoretical model designed to explain the past and *understand* the present and the future, not to forecast it. Still, it vindicates Schumpeter's insistence that there cannot be a foolproof statistical method. Schumpeter puts it even more strongly:

> [F]or the present, our material, being what it is, no formal method can replace common sense and experience with both theory and material. To call for such a method is as reasonable as it would be to call for a machine which will automatically perform surgical operations in an ideally foolproof way. And to smile in contempt on freehand methods is as reasonable as it would be to scorn the subjective judgment of the surgeon or the inexact working of his hand. It is therefore not derogatory to the Frisch method to say that it will issue, in very many cases, into freehand procedure, which alone can bring to bear on our work all we know historically and otherwise and which alone can, to some extent, cope with the fact that our material is distorted by external factors besides being internally irregular. (ibid., 211, note 1)

CONTINUITY AND DISCONTINUITY IN THE HISTORICAL PROCESS

There is one important question dear to Schumpeter's heart and close to the theoretical-historical approach: the question of the relation of aggregates to the underlying individual reality, the step from the microeconomic theory of individual consumers and firms to a macroeconomic theory of the economy they make up.

Schumpeter disliked and distrusted aggregative determinants unless they could be derived from underlying individual data, and even then, as his discussion of monetary aggregates shows, declined to consider many aggregative theories adequate for theoretical and hence policy use. It is possible for an "industry" to be in equilibrium, yet for any one member of that "industry" not to be. In his letter to Marschak, which I quote in extenso in chapter 25, Schumpeter raised this problem and asked for Marschak's help with it.

The whole approach of Nelson and Winter is based on this central *fact*. And in Nelson and Winter an "industry" can even be uniquely defined because all its member firms produce a homogeneous product. With monopolistic competition or other "imperfections" inherent in reality—that is, imperfections which are clearly not "noise"—the whole definition of an "industry" becomes arbitrary. But this means that the market in general becomes an imperfect signaling system, because product differentiation makes the experience of any one firm an unreliable guide for the reasonable actions of a possible competitor.

The "chaotic" approach to reality has been questioned. In their Survey article, Baumol and Benhabib raised the question to what extent reality is indeed chaotic. However, on the theoretical level, Brock[9] shows that the process of aggregation itself might convert an underlying chaotic nature of individual data into a nonchaotic appearance of the derived aggregates. But if this is so, the question seems legitimate to a non-mathematician what difference it makes whether the underlying data are chaotic or not. In the first place, path dependency has been shown to be very real in important cases (Arthur 1990). And the emergence of whole new industries speaks against this view. Individual decision makers react not to aggregative events but to individual views and events. I have mentioned the simple case of monopolistic competition. In general, the internalization of entrepreneurial action into economic theory is based on the assumption, suggested by reality, that the search for new things is inconsistent with any permanent repetitive (point or a circular) equilibrium.

---

[9] "An informal definition of chaos is this: A determinate dynamical system is chaotic if it displays sensitive dependence upon initial conditions in the sense that small differences in initial conditions are magnified by iteration of the dynamical system" (Brock 1992).

In his textbook on chaos, *An Introduction to Chaotic Determined Systems* (1989), Robert Devaney adds the condition that in the chaotic region, arbitrarily close to any initial condition, is an initial condition that has a periodic orbit.

Professor Carl Simon has pointed out in a letter "that a number of economists and statisticians are working presently on this problem. Given noisy data, first separate the noise from what matters, then use techniques of chaotic dynamics to say whether the "rest" is chaotic determined or random."

Schumpeter was certainly aware of the problem of "noise" in his reference, in his letter to Mitchell to "approximate estimates that are imperfectly determinate from the very nature of the data."

Hence, the apparent nonchaotic nature of aggregative data in the face of underlying chaotic individual data suggests that the continuity of historic processes prevents chaotic disturbances from having very quick effects. Yet we know that, while as a rule history moves slowly, there are sudden rapid changes and explosions.

For Schumpeter—and this can not be stressed too often—theory is an essential part of understanding history and vice versa. Indeed, the very first subheading of chapter 6, "Historical Outlines," is "The Fundamental Importance of the Historical Approach to the Problems of the Cyclical Process of Evolution" (*Business Cycles*, 220). It is the analysis of a process in historical, that is, irreversible, time that is Schumpeter's central contribution.

History has no beginning and—so far—no end. Schumpeter discusses at length the apparent inconsistency between his insistence that the basic phenomena of change are discontinuous and the fact that history at the same time reveals strong continuities (ibid., 226).

To some extent it is easier to get over this apparent inconsistency today than it was in Schumpeter's days, although even then physics provided evidence of basic constants and discontinuities, such as Planck's quantum physics. Even today the notion is still rampant that there is an unbridgeable gap between the ideas spawned by the natural and the social sciences.[10]

Schumpeter was concerned with "economic and generally social change" (*Business Cycles*, 226). There is also the principle of historic continuity (ibid.). The latter seems to say that the discontinuities of social change make themselves felt only in time, and only in—to us—rather long stretches of time. Of course, it makes no sense to draw earth-shaking conclusions from data which cover only one or two decades. Thus, Schumpeter declined to see the Great Depression as a unique phenomenon and a break in trend by pointing to historic parallels. He declined to see it as the beginning of the end of capitalism and considered talk of secular stagnation unhistoric nonsense.

Capitalism, as will be discussed in detail in chapters 8–10, was defined by Schumpeter by private property, an individualistic preference system, and the emergence of a banking system whose primary function was to finance innovations. On these criteria, the beginnings of capitalism are traced to southern Italy as far back as the eleventh or twelfth century. But there were, of course,

---

[10] Mises held to this view to the end. See Mises (1962). His strictures on mathematics are found on pp. 3–4, where Mises insists that "he who wants to achieve anything in praxeology must be conversant with mathematics, physics, biology, history and jurisprudence, lest he confuse the tasks and methods of the theory of human action with the tasks and methods of any of these other branches of knowledge" (p. 4). Mises also states: "The German language has developed a term that would have been expedient to denote the totality of the sciences dealing with human action as distinguished from the natural sciences, viz. *Geisteswissenschaften*" (p. 9). Mises suggested as the equivalent "the sciences of human action."

Contrast also "No competent mathematician can fail to see through the fundamental fallacies of all varieties of what is called mathematical economics and especially econometrics" (p. 4) with Schumpeter's attitude as expressed in his letter to E. B. Wilson and his willingness to learn from Tinbergen and to rethink earlier views.

important innovations before that time.[11] When innovations are introduced they start small. The development of capitalism can be understood as a small capitalist sector, embedded in a large noncapitalist economic and social system, growing in time to dominance, but growing *sub specie aeternitatis* by small discrete steps.

It should be remembered that an innovation simply means doing something differently and that the entrepreneurial act consists often in doing it against the more or less strong resistance of the environment. The facts and insights underlying an innovation may be quite well known and even generally available.[12] And, as the history of inventions or medicine or mathematics or anything else reveals, an innovation may be simply the last step in a long line of development. As Schumpeter put it: "The decisive step in bringing about a new thing or ultimate practical success is, in most cases, only the last straw and often relatively insignificant itself" (*Business Cycles*, 227).

This view of historic continuity leads to a view where small steps accumulate in time to large effects, but do so in a wavelike manner. It is a view which makes it unnecessary to assume the emergence of a special capitalist "spirit":

> Hence . . . there is no need to speak as Sombart and others did, of a new "spirit" (Geist) having come about somewhere in the stretch between 1400 and 1600 to make people think and behave differently or the rise of a new economic system fundamentally different from the preceding one. In particular there is no need to trace what that group of authors entirely unrealistically considers as a new rationalism on the one hand and as a new attitude towards profits on the other hand, to religious changes (M. Weber)—which is a way of arguing hardly superior to the economic interpretation of history which it was intended to improve or replace. (*Business Cycles*, 228)

This statement complements the earlier analysis that a stationary equilibrium economy needs no particular economic motivations at all, while an evolutionary economy needs people who *do* things and motivations to do them.

Those who work in underdeveloped countries run across precisely these problems. Schumpeter discusses these matters in the context of economic history and economic and social evolution. But they are very much alive problems of daily policy making. There is a literature on dual economies, one traditional, the other modern, and never the twain shall meet. On the other hand, Theodore Schultz among others pointed out that subsistence farmers behaved quite "rationally," of course, within the limitations of their environ-

[11] The wheel was, after all, invented rather early. And the invention of the harness increased the available horsepower enormously compared to the use of a yoke, and so on.

[12] A great deal of pernicious nonsense is these days being talked about the Japanese "stealing" American inventions, e.g., the transistor. But that is just the point: the general principles are openly available. The first application gives away that something is feasible. From then on it is a question of entrepreneurial activity, which depends on many things, of which economic policy is one. For a detailed study of such problems, see F. M. Scherer (1992).

ment. And anyone with eyes to see knew that the picture of stagnant traditional societies and subsistence sectors (as distinguished from subsistence production) simply did not fit reality in West Africa.[13] Of course, Schumpeter had stressed that there were long periods in history when equilibrium economics fitted reality fairly well. But this did not involve irrational behavior.

Even a revolution "never can be understood from itself, i.e. without reference to the developments that led up to it; it sums up rather than initiates" (*Business Cycles*, 227). These views will again become relevant in connection with the "coming" of socialism. Here the point is that Schumpeter's is a truly dynamic-evolutionary way of looking at history. He had no trouble going back to the eleventh century if he can get sufficient facts of sufficient quality. And he did not hesitate to speak of waves and even cycles, which to him are heuristic descriptive devices to deal with a turbulent reality. Of course

> Many students of the cycle, notably Professors Mitchell and Spiethoff, display a strong aversion to admitting that we may speak of cycles in that sense before the end of the eighteenth century, while others, historians among them, do not hesitate to go far beyond that . . . the question is whether there is any warrant to use the schema of the cyclical process as a heuristic hypothesis farther back. (ibid., 224)

Schumpeter did not hesitate to answer "yes, there is a warrant," even though noncapitalistic events like wars and crop failures were even as late as the eighteenth century much more important than the purely capitalistic events he analyzed. Schumpeter's is much more than just another business cycle theory. It is the analysis of long-term evolution which proceeds in a wavelike manner. It is really an analysis of (mostly economic) history which tries to explain in some detail how one gets from here to there, from today to tomorrow.

Of course, Schumpeter respects Mitchell's and Spiethoff's decision to stick to the observed changes from the eighteenth century on when the capitalist process was sufficiently robust not to be swamped by extra-capitalist happenings, and also when the quality of the data improved significantly.

But take the Protestant ethic. It is, of course, often perverted by people who view it as a witness to their own virtue.[14] Theologically speaking, no worldly success is "deserved," it is always a gift of God which should put the fear of God into the recipient of the favor. He has to "walk in the ways that please God," which in the specific economic case means that God's bounty has to be translated not so much into high living as into savings and investments, into doing something for the poor, for one's fellow man.

Only as the historian H. M. Robertson[15] has pointed out, the rise of eco-

---

13 Cocoa was introduced in West Africa by "traditional" farmers, often successfully ignoring the advice of "experts." See, e.g., Polly Hill (1970), and her many other studies.

14 Schumpeter protested explicitly against this perversion in the context of his discussion of the marginal productivity theory.

15 See H. M. Robertson (1959). Robertson put it in a way which could hardly be improved upon by Schumpeter: "That the countries in which the science of bookkeeping made the most

nomic liberalism substantially antedates the Protestant revolution, and good books had more to do with it than the Good Book. Both Catholics and Protestants had to come to terms with changes, and the responses were creative and adaptive. In theological terms—which are permissible in the context of this discussion—there is both a priestly-conservative (one is tempted to say: a bureaucratic) tradition which resists change and adapts reluctantly, and a prophetic (one is tempted to say: entrepreneurial) tradition which preaches it. The question may be pushed back even farther and it may be legitimately asked whether the Protestant reaction itself did not come about as a creative response to the new opportunities. "Within the whole of that social process that simultaneously produced free ownership of land, increase in population, agrarian and industrial revolutions, and, as an element of all this, enclosures, there is nothing but interaction. No argument that uses the words "depends upon" can have any meaning except for the most restricted purposes" (*Business Cycles*, 239). The specific quotation refers to a discussion of English development, but *mutatis mutandis* it applies to any period and to any argument.

In his view of the rise of capitalism and the Protestant ethic, Schumpeter certainly had the backing of professional historians. And here we again encounter his evolutionary views. In the 1940s, it was fashionable to condemn the "profit motive" and the "self-seeking" Protestant ethic. Thus, Archbishop Temple's *Christianity and the Social Order*[16] took issue particularly with Calvin and various ethical shortcomings of capitalism.

In a searching review of this book, the Cambridge (England) historian Herbert Butterfield took issue with this view on historical (i.e., not theological) grounds.[17] The issue was precisely that the attitude of the church(es) toward usury—the specific example chosen—gelled in an agrarian society, that there was now a development toward a more urban, bourgeois society, that it was not just Protestants but also Catholics in their opposition to Protestants who contributed to this development. In short, there was nothing but interaction.

> [W]ho shall say what man is to "blame" for capitalism? We might have stayed medieval and agrarian if we had been without cupidity. . . . If capitalism has the

---

progress were always those in which most economic progress was being made can no doubt best be explained as a mixture of cause and effect. But working on the same lines as Weber, it would be very easy to substitute systematic books for the Protestant ethic as the origin of the capitalist spirit. There is no doubt that reliance on good books meant more than reliance on the Good Book. As there is still less doubt that the rise of the capitalist spirit is the same as the rise of capitalist rationalism something which took place independently of Church teaching, on the basis of commercial experience. The great cause of the spirit of capitalism has been capitalism itself: and it has been conditioned by general cultural conditions, more particularly by developments in business technique and the governmental and legal institutions affecting commerce" (p. 56).

[16] Penguin Series, 1942.

[17] Butterfield (1942). Note that Butterfield inverted the more usual order of Protestantism and the Rise of Capitalism. I owe the reference to this review to Professor Thomas McIntire, Professor of History at the University of Toronto, who referred to it in his introduction to Butterfield (1979). Professor McIntire kindly made Butterfield's review available to me.

hated "profit motive," surely all these other things [i.e., private property, etc.] were organizations of man's cupidity too. Let us reform, as the Archbishop suggests. Let us say that the old order has had its day. Let us see that statesmen shall not sleep in their beds till they have used all imagination to overcome obstructions. But let us be sure that neither Calvin nor any other man sponsored capitalism. Given the cupidity of human beings, it was a mighty product of History herself—a work of Providence. (Butterfield 1942, 325)

Surely this expresses what Schumpeter talked about. But this is also the place to remind the reader again of the essential distinction between a stationary society whose chief preoccupation is how to adjust to changes which from its own standpoint are external, and a society which is evolutionary, that is, which creates the changes itself. "Usury" is a word which in an evolutionary society becomes a different animal. "Entrepreneurial profit" becomes not a moral category but simply the expression of the fact that as the result of a successful reallocation of resources you come out with more resources than you started with. The "profit motive" is common to all types of economy and society. It is not a nice motive, and while its importance must not be underestimated, creative urges and not profits are the major motive for innovation.[18] And in any case, is the desire to know better than your fellow men what is good for them, that is, to play God, not even less attractive and a great deal more dangerous than the profit motive?

It may bring out the true originality of Schumpeter's analysis, and perhaps help to define his place in intellectual history, to contrast his approach with the—typically German—theories of stages and Spiethoff's analysis of economic styles already discussed in chapter 3. The theories of stages can be understood as trying to classify economic history by certain criteria: the size of the market (from the autarkic farmstead or manor to the world economy), the structure of production (from hunters and gatherers to postindustrial society whatever the latter is supposed to mean), and so forth.

The central weakness of all these approaches—which seem to me ingenious and often learned ways to come to terms with economic development, but essentially with unsuitable means—is that on the one hand they claim to have established a sequence of stages that are at least logical and may even be necessary, but on the other hand that they neither do nor possibly can explain how one stage leads to the next. And this suggests that they try to explain the process of historic evolution essentially by a static approach.

Nor is this approach dead by any means, as the works of Colin Clark, Kuznets, Hollis Chenery, or Walt W. Rostow suggest.

Spiethoff's theory of economic styles is much closer to Schumpeter precisely because it is not intended as a theory of historic change at all. It is not

---

[18] There have been reports of the many millionaires among the employees of Microsoft Corporation which the success of their innovations created, who have not changed their lifestyles or cashed in their millions, simply because there is still so much to do. I do not know the religious preferences of those in question, but surely they are a beautiful example of the Protestant ethic and of what Schumpeter meant by an entrepreneur and the overpowering drive of creativity.

intended to deal with evolutionary change, and Spiethoff acknowledges Schumpeter's inspiration. Spiethoff lists sixteen characteristics grouped in five categories which among them are intended to encompass all important characteristics of an economy.

As discussed before, Spiethoff is interested in the relation between theory and specific historic situations. He is rather critical of historic stages and, somewhat surprising in a volume of essays in honor of Sombart, which Spiethoff himself edited, also of Sombart's approach. By contrast, he explicitly approved of Schumpeter's analysis. Interestingly, Spiethoff explicitly rejects the alternatives "traditional" and "rational."[19] He prefers as motivations for actions: whether there is a desire for profits or a fear of punishment. As for the former, Spiethoff stressed Schumpeter's originality in drawing attention to motivation as important only in dynamic situations. As to rational economic acting, it "is so general that it applies to all humanity," a point stressed by Schumpeter in his analysis of the static state.

Spiethoff's own work or that of Mitchell limits itself deliberately to the analysis of the capitalist era and neither asks, as does Schumpeter, how capitalist evolution itself affects its own institutions, its own working. There is not that kind of "feedback" in any economist except Schumpeter and possibly, though very differently, Marx. The economic historian Douglass North ends his book *Structure and Change in Economic History* with these thoughts: "Economic history conceived as a theory of evolution of constraints should not only explain past economic performance, but also provide the modern social scientist with the evolving contextual framework within which to explain the current performance of the political economic system. This task remains to be done" (1981, 209).

North himself pointed out earlier that "an explanation of this fundamental transformation in the structure of the economy is not to be found in the work of new economic historians. Looking elsewhere, we find that Joseph Schumpeter alone amongst the major economists of the twentieth century analyzed this transformation" (1978, 965).

This is not the place to enter into the important work of North. There are, of course, differences between his approach with its specific emphasis on the changes in institutions as defined by the New Institutional Economics, and Schumpeter's approach, which concentrates on the workings of and changes in capitalism. The two approaches seem to me quite compatible. They share the most important characteristic of Schumpeterian theory: the internalization of the entrepreneurial function into the capitalist system and its theory, and perhaps also of population changes. There remain differences about the exact role of relative price changes and changing power positions and structures, but they are of secondary importance in the present context.

Seen in such a context, Schumpeter appears as a major innovator in the field of the interpretation and analysis of historic change.

---

[19] Spiethoff (1933). The *Festgabe* was published as a book as well as a special issue of *Schmollers Jahrbuch*, vol. 56, no.6. Page references to the *Jahrbuch* in brackets. The specific reference is to p. 81, note 4 [p. 921].

PART II

Socialism

or

The Evolution of Capitalism

"No social system is ever going to survive when allowed to work out according to its own logic."

—J. A. Schumpeter, "Can Capitalism Survive?"

"Capitalism is essentially the framework of a process not only of economic but also of social change."

—Schumpeter, *Capitalism, Socialism and Democracy*

Prediction and the Interaction of Economic and Social Change

PRELIMINARY REMARKS

The belief is widespread that Schumpeter "prophesied" that capitalism would eventually turn into socialism, and also that it would do so for exactly the opposite reasons from those given by Marx. Schumpeter admired Marx for asking the right questions as well as for his theoretical acumen, but disagreed fundamentally with his analysis. Capitalism would die of its successes, not of its failures. Moreover, while Marx envisaged a cataclysmic end with the expropriated expropriating the expropriators, Schumpeter thought that the transition might be undramatic and gradual and, I might add, perhaps not even noticed.[1]

On the other hand, the belief is equally widespread that Schumpeter was "obviously" wrong. Capitalism is not only doing fine, it is actually expanding, and it is socialism which is dying. The events in Hungary, Poland, even China, and certainly in the Soviet Union are cited as proof for the correctness of this view.

In 1942, when *Capitalism, Socialism and Democracy* (cited hereafter as CSD) first appeared, Schumpeter suggested that capitalism had at least fifty more years to do its good work. That was at the time a rather courageous statement to make, even if the number fifty is taken literally instead of simply meaning a long time. The world was then in the throes of war economics with its widespread controls, as it had been during the First World War, which was both during the First and the Second World Wars widely, and according to Schumpeter's expressly stated belief quite wrongly, viewed as preparing the world for socialism. Moreover, the uncertainties of the future in Western countries (and even more so in the Soviet Union and the Eastern countries) may once again bring about a fundamental change in the perceptions of the direction which history is about to take. This is the more likely as most people think short term, while Schumpeter thought long term. At no time did he

---

[1] This is explicitly stated as early as 1928. "Capitalism, whilst economically stable, and even gaining in stability, creates, by rationalising the human mind a mentality and a style of life incompatible with its own fundamental conditions, motives and social institutions, and will be changed, although not by economic necessity and probably even at some sacrifice of economic welfare, into an order of things which it will be merely a matter of taste and terminology to call Socialism or not" (Schumpeter, "The Instability of Capitalism," reprinted in Clemence (1951), (71–72). This collection has been reissued by Transaction Publishers with a new introduction by Richard Swedberg.

share the widespread belief that the Great Depression or the First World War spelled the end of capitalist development, although he considered the attempts to deal with the Great Depression and the aftermath of war quite harmful and misguided. And he did, of course, speak of capitalism in an oxygen tent.

In one sense, the prediction of the end of capitalism—which incidentally is not automatically identical with the coming of socialism, however defined—is really trivial. Only God is eternal; everything else changes and eventually dies or turns into something else, as Herakleitos already pointed out. The fact that there is nothing deterministic about development does not mean that it is not logical or understandable, or that it is not subject to scientific inquiry.

This is a fundamental point that must be remembered. It distinguishes Schumpeter not only from Marx, but equally from Mises or Hayek with whom Schumpeter shared his love for individual freedom and the achievements of capitalism and the regrets at the attempts to supplant it with a less efficient system. It distinguishes him from Marx, because he was led into a faulty analysis by his inadequate theoretical bases; and from Mises and Hayek because they too were basically stationary in their approach. Like Schumpeter and unlike Marx, they believed that there is nothing in the economic system viewed in isolation, which must lead to a breakdown. But, as with Marx, and despite all statements about the dynamic nature of capitalism and development, their static approach is betrayed in their belief in the eternal youth of capitalism, if it only behaved reasonably. And in this, as in so many other things, they have a great deal more in common with Marx than with Schumpeter.

PREDICTIONS

Schumpeter's discussion of the coming of socialism, and indeed even its definition, is understandable only in the context of Schumpeter's view of economic development. His definitions of socialism and capitalism differ substantially from the generally accepted ones, which go back to Lenin and Stalin and to Hayek and Mises, whose discussion itself is a reaction to the monstrous events which converted Tsarist Russia first into Bolshevik Russia and eventually into the Soviet Union. It has already been stressed that the use or nonuse of the market mechanism is an inappropriate criterion for distinguishing between the two systems.

But first it is important to define what is meant by a prediction. This question is not trivial. It has been asserted that Schumpeter's predictions were as much falsified by the facts as were Marx's. Schumpeter, however, is explicit in that he does not assert flatly the end of capitalism, but that he analyzes what present trends, if unchecked or overcome by external events, imply for the future. It remains true that the future is largely unknowable—unless it has already happened.[2]

It may be worthwhile to quote his last expression on this point, among other reasons, because it shows an "instinctive" understanding of "chaotic" development:

> I do not "prophecy" or predict [socialism]. Any prediction is extrascientific prophecy that attempts to do more than to diagnose observable tendencies and to state what results would be, if these tendencies should work themselves out according to their logic. In itself, this does not amount to prognosis or prediction because factors external to the chosen range of observation may intervene to prevent that consummation; because with phenomena so far removed as social phenomena are from the comfortable situation that astronomers have the good fortune of facing, observable tendencies, even if allowed to work themselves out, may be compatible with more than one outcome, and because existing tendencies, battling with resistances; may fail to work themselves out completely and may eventually "stick" at some halfway house.[3]

It has been suggested that Schumpeter was perhaps a historic determinist.[4] In view of his explicit warnings about the restrictive meaning of "prediction," this is difficult to understand. Perhaps the inability of most people to take a long view, and the ingrained habit of thinking in terms of equilibrium even when talking about historic changes, may explain this.[5]

The solution of this apparent contradiction may perhaps be that (assuming reality to be chaotic) small changes may have big consequences in time, but that when the consequences become fully visible it may be too late to do

---

[2] As for the former: "Analysis, whether economic or other, never yields more than a statement about the tendencies present in an observable pattern. And these never tell us what *will* happen to the pattern, but only what *would* happen if they continued to act as they have been acting in the time interval covered by our observation and if no other factors intruded. "Inevitability" or "necessity" can never mean more than this" (CSD, paperback ed., 61; italics in original).
Schumpeter believed that wars were events external to capitalism, which was inherently pacifistic. To avoid criticism on this account, his favorite example of an external event was the 1906 San Francisco earthquake.
As for the latter: the number of physicians coming out of medical schools next year is fairly well known. Of course, even there, unforeseen events may wipe out a whole class in the manner in which, for example, an airplane accident wiped out the basketball fortunes of one college a few years past.

[3] CSD, 3d ed., 416. The quotation is from the posthumously published chapter on "The March into Socialism."

[4] See, e.g., Winterberger (1983).

[5] Thus, it is true that Mises' "Die Wirtschaftsrechnung im sozialistischen Gemeinwesen" (1920/1921), 88–121, talks about something always happening in the real economy, but there is no further analysis of the implications of this fact. The analysis is *always* one of adaptation to what is happening. Equilibrium is a necessary concept even though it cannot exist, which is true enough, but less than the whole truth. Schumpeter told of his conversation with Walras who also thought economics could never explain more than adaptation to external changes.

something about them. The impression of Schumpeter's historic determinism may thus be due to a number of facts. Critics may subconsciously fall into linear patterns of thought which tend indeed to be deterministic if they are logical.

In addition, Schumpeter argues on two quite different levels. On the level of economic theory he asserts that the capitalist machinery—to be defined presently—functions sufficiently well so that there is no purely economic reason to expect it to break down or even that it will exhaust all possibilities of development, that it will make itself "technologically unemployed." He thought ideas of secular stagnation absurd.[6]

There is, however, also the sociological-political-institutional level. Schumpeter's "pessimism" about the future of capitalism is based on the tendencies he sees and analyzes on that level, and on the effect which economic development with its steady increase in the standard of living of the masses (albeit bought at the price of constant upheaval) has on the "environmental" facts. Theory is the analysis of institutions. Evolutionary theory is the analysis of how institutions—firms, government, methods of finding and adapting to new things—change out of their own logic. The extension of the argument from the purely economic to the sociological-political-institutional level is the logical consequence of the analysis of the developing economy itself which necessarily produces constant change in its institutional and noneconomic bases. A stationary capitalism is a contradictio in adjecto; socialism may or may not become stationary.

SOCIAL AND ECONOMIC DEVELOPMENT

One of these environmental factors is, for example, "that the capitalist process produces a distribution of political power and a socio-psychological attitude—expressing itself in corresponding policies—that are hostile to it . . . so that they will eventually prevent the capitalist engine from working" (CSD, 112).

The fact that capitalism has made everyone so much better off that poverty, as it was known one hundred years ago, has practically vanished in the North Atlantic world and parts of the Pacific rim becomes irrelevant. It is not only that you cannot defend slavery on the grounds that the slaves were better off as slaves than as free workers (though this has been precisely the argument which repressive regimes have used in many LDCs or most recently the Soviet block). In general, political attacks do not come from economic grievances. Indeed, the very fact that it is possible to become better off breaks any fatalism about never being able to escape poverty that may have existed.

---

[6] "We are no closer to the exhaustion of possibilities than at the stone age" (*Theorie* 1911, 161; my translation). This statement is not found in the English edition. However, this does not mean that Schumpeter changed his mind on this point. It is simply the consequence of the idea expressed about what precisely optimality of equilibrium involves. See CSD chapter 10.

It is here that Schumpeter differs most from Hayek's *Road to Serfdom* (or for that matter from his later *Constitution of Liberty* which Schumpeter could, of course, not know), or the whole idea of constitutional economics or its German cousin of Ordnungspolitik of the Freiburg School. Their central question is: What do you have to do to preserve liberty, a question with which Schumpeter was certainly in complete sympathy. But this very question breathes the air of a stationary equilibrium approach.

The answer, that only in this atmosphere of freedom may an evolutionary society and economy thrive, may or may not be true. But the crux is that all the ideas which Hayek and Constitutional Economics "dislikes so much are the products of the social system which he does like . . . in this situation there is no point in appealing to Cicero or Pericles whose individualism blossomed in societies whose very basis was slavery."[7] In this sense this whole approach must be considered stationary, for it essentially tries to preserve a status quo which in the real world it is impossible to preserve. In Goethe's words, there is a nostalgia here which leads to damnation: "Verbleibe doch, Du bist so schön."[8]

[7] Schumpeter (1946), 269–70. Schumpeter might have gone further. After all, Pericles' Athens thrived on public works financed to a considerable extent on payments by the allies of Athens, i.e., the budget must have shown a considerable deficit.

[8] When Goethe's Faust signs his contract with the devil, he agrees that his soul will belong to the devil in the moment when Faust will say to a moment of reality: Stay, remain, you are so beautiful.

> If to the fleeting hour I say:
> Remain, so fair thou art, remain!
> Then bind me with your fatal chain,
> for I shall perish in that day."

(J. W. Goethe, *Faust*, Part 1. Translated by Philipp Wayne. Baltimore, MD: Penguin Books, 1949 and later, p. 87. Actually, in the original German, Faust says that he will *gladly* (gern) perish that day.)

Goethe's comment is to me the ultimate criticism of the Mises-Hayek-Lange-Lenin approach. Nor do I believe that linking these otherwise so disparate names is a nasty perversion on my part. It is precisely what Schumpeter points out in the last paragraph of his Hayek review.

The dying and almost blind Faust, in Part 2, utters the same words, mistaking the shadowy ghosts digging his grave for workers digging to execute his development project, a drainage ditch. This is what the dying Faust says (with apologies to Goethe for my clumsy translation):

> The last would be the highest achievement,
> if I open up space for many millions,
> to live, not safely, yet working-free.
> Green the land, and fertile. Man and herds
> comfortably on the newest land,
> comfortable on the mountain slope
> created by the bold-industrious people.
> Inside a paradisical land.
> Let outside floods rage against the edge. . . .
>
> common urge speeds to close the break.
> Yes! In this sense I am quite content,
> This is wisdom's last conclusion:

Possibly the most important environmental factor relating to capitalism is that it is inherently rationalistic and has difficulties in understanding other attitudes. It is an attitude which has brought ever-increasing welfare to most people and produced a great culture.[9] Yet "capitalist rationality does not do away with sub- or super-rational impulses. It merely makes them get out of hand by removing the restraint of sacred and semi-sacred tradition" (CSD, 144).

These ideas go back a long way. In April 1932, Schumpeter gave a talk to a social-philosophical workshop at the University of Bonn on "Social and economic development." The theme of this talk was that development was not to be interpreted normatively, but that it referred to changes in the whole social system of which the economy was a part, and that it proceeded in waves and discontinuously. The main task of economics was to explain these discontinuities after Walras had succeeded in describing the steady state (Zustand). The problem was a formal one: "How do things become different?"[10] Schumpeter's conclusion was: "Wenn fundamental Neues in der Welt geschieht, dann stehen wir vor einem Rätsel" ("When something fundamentally new occurs in the world we are confronted by an enigma").

> Only he who daily must conquer it
> earns for himself freedom and life. . . .
>
> Such activity I want to see,
> to stand with a free people on free soil.
> To such a moment I would say:
> Stay. You are so beautiful.

(Faust, Part 2, Act 5)

This is a beautiful description of the Hayekian, of the Whig, ideal. But its achievement spells its damnation. Goethe's happy ending relies, if the somewhat improper metaphor be permitted, on a deus ex machina. Mephistopheles gets cheated of Faust's soul, less by the logic of Faust's life than by love, a quite uneconomic emotion.

[9] Schumpeter has a chapter on the culture of capitalism, which also includes Shakespeare. The puzzlement about the timing which I once had dissolves in view of the previous discussion of the Analysis of an Evolutionary Economy. There are some obvious comments on the connection of capitalism and culture. Mozart could not have composed his piano concertos in the twelfth century because, among other reasons, the technology to build a piano for his concertos did not yet exist. Mozart also was a free artist, and he thought about moving to England, the most advanced Capitalist country. Goethe also thought about emigrating to America. Monet could not paint in *plein air* the way he did because the paint tube had to be invented first. Perhaps more telling than the growth of technology is that it took the bourgeois culture of Holland to produce pictures of burghers and the interiors of their houses, where before only saints and princes and churches and palaces could be painted, and religious and classic heroic themes. It was, I believe, the American Benjamin West who first painted princes not in classical but in modern garb. And it is doubtful whether Klee's idea of painting like nature, not after nature, could have been thought of in the past. Of course, the question whether Klee or Jackson Pollock were "good" or "bad" is not answered thereby. Schumpeter's point about the subconscious is verified by the great number of people who feel menaced by modern painting or music, and only time can tell whether they will be seen as liberating or destroying.

[10] Schumpeter (1932a).

In July 1932, Schumpeter spoke about tendency toward socialism.[11] He started with two questions: "First, to what extent is there a tendency towards socialism? And once this question is answered: Second, how does the present situation fit into this picture?" Schumpeter dealt with Marx in terms which he later worked out in *Capitalism*. "The greatness [of the Marxian theory] lies not in its content but in its form [and] in the fact that thousands find in it a substitute for religion." But its theoretical bases, the theory of accumulation and of the breakdown, are not tenable. "What really happened was, that the army of workers led by the entrepreneur has broken through the constraints (Hemmungen) which surround the individual."

Competitive capitalism would be stable, "except that we find that things developed differently. . . . Competitive capitalism has never existed by itself, but was always permeated by the preceding Herrenkultur, lordly culture." Because of this we find combinations, cartels, trusts, and so on, and the bourgeoisie (Bürgertum) socialized itself. The result is that though socialism is not inevitable it becomes more and more possible.

Since the talk was given in 1932, Schumpeter dealt with three contemporary problems, all of which have their present-day analogues. First, England's abandonment of the gold standard is a more important symptom of the way to socialism than anything "that happens in Russia." Second, the world crisis is not a verification of the move towards socialism. Quite the contrary: "it may radicalize the masses but it is a temporary setback which has made the chances for socialism smaller than ever before. As soon as one recognizes that the present situation is a [temporary] reversal, it becomes clear that the modern planned economy is not comparable to what will come but to what was. The analogy lies in the 18th century. Then, too, [there was a] crisis psychology with autarky etc. Then, too, there was bureaucracy" (1932b; translated from my notes).

Once one investigates the inherent possibilities of a system one can say something about the future, although there is, of course, nothing deterministic about this. But there is one thought which I do not recall being expressed later: once some disturbance occurs, the system gets additional degrees of freedom, and this allows development in different directions.

The third point of interest is what Schumpeter had to say about national socialism in 1932, half a year before the Nazis actually came to power. It is these additional degrees of freedom which make it inappropriate to "describe national socialism in categories which have been taken from the ideologies of a preceding period."

"The essential point about national socialism appears to Schumpeter to be that it is possible to take a group out of the population which, as it were, considers only the common good and the common weal which, because it is taken out, is not class-oriented but can at any one moment pursue that policy which benefits best the common ideal. This structural idea explains among

---

[11] Schumpeter (1932b); my lecture notes. Unfortunately I have forgotten what PAV stands for.

others the absence of a program so characteristic of the National Socialists. Such a party could pursue a capitalist or a socialist policy without logical contradiction" (translated from my notes).

This characterization of the National Socialist ideas does not, of course, prove that Schumpeter thought them correct. But it is in this general context that Schumpeter deals with intellectuals and sociology. In Schumpeter's view, the bourgeois stratum can survive only in symbiosis with something emotionally more uplifting than prices and products and production and economic well-being. Those of us who lived through the Great Depression remember the optimism that all would be well with the world if only mass unemployment were eliminated. Instead, the result seems to be, at least in the United States, what has been referred to as the now-now generation with a diminished sense of community and regard for future generations.[12]

I shall deal in the next chapters with the question of how developments in one direction are likely to produce societal reactions trying to counteract them. For the moment, the previously given definition must suffice. Here I want to limit myself to what Schumpeter's "prediction" really argues.

Capitalism is essentially rationalist and pacifist. It tends to destroy its own basis by constantly rationalizing more and more things, and questioning more and more former tabus, that is, matters about which there was a consensus that they should not be touched, and which may or may not be surrounded by a protective wall of sacredness. This need not be interpreted as meaning religious sanctions, whether from Church or State—that orthodox Marxism is a religion is hardly questionable. All that is necessary at the present level of the argument is to realize that "gentlemen just don't do such things." The Bill of Rights is such a limit, which is of course under constant attack, as was the Divine Right of Kings. The statements "one man one vote" or "rule by majority" say nothing about what the majority can do, and whether there are some things that must not be touched, that must remain "for ever" private, individual.[13]

It is one of Schumpeter's arguments that these protective walls get eroded by development itself, and I shall argue this later in more detail. But Schumpe-

---

[12] Perhaps we should have known better: I am sure that I read in Kierkegaard that the human problem would begin when the economic problem will have been solved—something very different from Keynes's optimism in this regard, and reminiscent of the problem E. B. Wilson, in the letter reproduced before, suggested that Schumpeter had not sufficiently stressed: that most people even in the United States did not really like capitalism, but preferred more personal freedom to a higher income attainable only at the cost of submitting to industrial discipline. Of course, this might just have been a romantic nostalgia, in Germany referred to by the intelligentsia of the right as the anticapitalist longing. The idea is also the reverse of Hayek's or Mises's that capitalism is the best guarantee of personal freedom. The strength of the anticapitalist longing does, of course, not prove that it is the right idea.

[13] Arrow's impossibility theorem has sometimes been interpreted to justify a dictatorship. But this is a nonsequitur (of which Arrow is, of course, quite innocent). I consider it proof that there are matters which are nobody's but the individual's business. This proves only that Arrow's impossibility theorem is politically and morally neutral.

ter worried very much about the process itself which had no inherent limits and could thus lead only to the dissolution of society. Thus, in his post-humously published Montreal speech,[14] Schumpeter looked for such a possible ethical basis in papal Encyclicals—he mentions *Quadragesimo Anno*—and ends by urging a "moral reform." This points to the true problem with most reform proposals or political reactions: they deal only with and are only reactions against the symptoms of the results of development without understanding how these symptoms have in fact arisen. Or to put it in terms directly related to Schumpeter's analysis: they are based on a static rather than an evolutionary view of the economy and society. Consequently, they are more often than not condemned to be hardly more than wishful thinking with the potential of making matters worse.[15]

On the political-sociological level, Schumpeter saw only a trahison des clercs and an erosion of capitalist motivations. But there was also an erosion of the capitalist concept of private property and of the perception of what was public and what was private. Politics is about power, economics is about welfare. Power is inherently a much more relative concept than welfare. If you are well-off it is not really a matter of great concern that someone else is better off, and much of competitive economic theory consists in showing that an increase in my welfare also implies an increase in yours. Of course, psychologists tell us that relative positions matter, and so they do, but being poorer still may leave you well off; being weaker is dangerous.

Intellectuals as discussed by Schumpeter do not fare well. They are "people who wield the power of the spoken and the written word, and one of the touches that distinguish them from other people who do the same is the absence of that direct responsibility for practical affairs. This touch in general

---

[14] "The Future of Private Enterprise in the Face of Modern Socialistic Tendencies," in Swedberg 1991a, chapter 9. Originally in HOPE 1975.

[15] Here perhaps lies the answer on the policy level to Röpke's accusation, mentioned before, that Schumpeter did not seem to care about the fate of the economy, and what had to be done to prevent it.

I personally find it very attractive that ordinary people who a hundred years ago had no chance can now live a reasonably decent life in many parts of the world. After all, the Peaceable Kingdom with swords being beaten into plowshares—today called the peace dividend—has always been considered a worthy ideal. But the real question is how it is best achieved. Goethe's Faust at the end of his life turned to economic development and built dams, not without cost to Baucis and Philemon. The irony with an income distribution felt to be unjust is that once the lowest income groups get a satisfactory income, inequality becomes at the same time morally less intolerable as it becomes also less necessary: for it would be possible within limits to reduce it without harm to the development process. Just the same, income redistribution would not make a real impact on the lowest income strata if it were limited to the amounts above what was necessary to maintain growth. Of course, whatever may be said for or against the behavior exemplified by Malcolm Forbes, who spent a reputed $2 million on a birthday party, it certainly is not what the Protestant ethic had in mind!

Schumpeter was not the first and certainly will not be the last to find that for the victory of your ideas it is not sufficient to be right and well-intentioned. But surely he is right to insist that wishful thinking and faulty analysis will not work.

accounts for another—the absence of first-hand knowledge of them which only actual experience can give" (CSD, 147).

That is, they have no "tacit" or "personal knowledge." The Schumpeterian prototype and Renaissance predecessor of modern intellectuals was Pietro Aretino, a blackmailer and pornographer. The final threat is summarized by Schumpeter:

> Intellectuals rarely enter professional politics and still more rarely conquer responsible office. But they staff political bureaus, write party pamphlets and speeches, act as secretaries and advisors, make the individual politician's newspaper reputation which, though it is not everything, few men can afford to neglect. In doing these things they to some extent impress their mentality on almost everything that is being done." (CSD, 154)

Now to return to the "prediction" of the coming of socialism. This requires a slight detour into the definition of a market failure exemplified by the existence of public goods. As was pointed out before, today's prototypical public good, national defense, arose to supplant a market transaction which was inefficient. For Schumpeter, the very emergence of a private sphere, or rather the clear distinction between a public and a private sphere, suggests not only that there may emerge some goods for which the market does not provide an adequate solution; there may also be some goods for which the market does so inefficiently in the perception of the political environment, national defense and primary education being two prominent examples. Much of the present discussion of privatization is relevant here.

There seem to me to be two issues here. The one (which is discussed in detail by Schumpeter in his *Crisis of the Tax State*; see chapter 11) is precisely how the modern State has arisen, a State that is different from what was called a State before. Of course, under feudalism, too, there is an interest in defense and education and there exist clearly defined duties of various lords, princes, burghers, and even lower types. Yet the idea, for example, of universal military service, present in ancient Greece, absent in feudalism, did not emerge until, I believe, the French Revolution. The defense of the realm was not the matter of everybody but of the various legal entities having various legal powers and duties. This really suggests that what is an external economy itself depends somewhat on the political and sociological surroundings.

A feudal peasant had objectively as much interest in peace and quiet as a modern one. He got as much or as little protection against war and aggression whether he had a duty to serve under his immediate feudal lord or not. He suffered if he was in the path of fighting. After the fighting he probably could not care less to whom he had to pay taxes or who oppressed him. Yet he could not withdraw his support from the lord, that is, there could be no free-rider problem for him. He might escape his lord by successfully fleeing to an independent town—"Stadtluft macht frei"—or find himself a better lord if he could get away with it. But such possibilities are signs of a breakdown of old relations, and they surely have nothing to do with the analysis of public goods or externalities.

In any case, how such public goods should be financed or produced is another question altogether. Public goods and public-budgetary financing and public production are different matters. Thus, many costs of the Swiss army are directly paid by the private sector. A man (now also a woman) called to service which until his or her forty-fifth year happens yearly for varying periods, keeps his or her job with full salary and the employer also pays a substitute if one is needed. Thus, the Swiss federal budget reflects only part of the cost of the army. Likewise, in the United States, war planes or naval vessels are not produced in government arsenals.

With education, there would be no inherent difficulty to provide education entirely by the private sector—you get it if you can pay for it, whether the money comes from yourself, your family, or some donors does not matter in this context. The prince needing civil servants or the church needing priests might provide the necessary funds. That was in fact how education was organized.[16]

What happens in these cases is a phenomenon quite familiar to anyone working in LDCs. When there are externalities it becomes necessary and often feasible to create entities which themselves are subject to market forces, such as large enterprises, which internalize external economies. This would even be possible in evaluating the reasonableness of some investments in a five-year plan where a waste of resources could only be avoided by specifically including in the evaluation all externalities that one can see, and only those.[17]

I will argue with Schumpeter that there are many developments in capitalism which tend to convert private into public and/or merit goods generally perceived as necessary. (Nelson and Winter gave some clear examples and reasons for this in their discussion.) This still leaves open many questions of just how goods should be provided and who should pay for them, questions which never—even in the case of armed services—can exclude the market mechanism. That, too, is in keeping with the Schumpeterian analysis of the universal (and neutral!) importance to have economically reasonably right prices and of what happens in a dynamic-developmental economy. It is correct that one cannot do without a market mechanism. But the conclusion that therefore only capitalism is feasible follows only if the market mechanism is given this restrictive political, sociological, and historical definition.[18]

Thus, Schumpeter's "pessimism" about the future of capitalism goes deeper than his "optimism" about its inherent viability. The survival of cap-

---

[16] The State and the Church might even have an interest in excluding the "masses" from education, since once able to read, they might get ideas of their own. In this case, propaganda also becomes necessary and feasible.

[17] "Specifically" means here that one does not simply assume that externalities of a particular size exist in general, but that they are specifically identified and themselves evaluated.

[18] On one level these developments have been analyzed by Mancur Olson in his discussion of how society's actions may change from income-creating to income-distributing policies. There possibly is a little more determinism in this analysis than I would accept, though it needs to be stressed that in Olson's analysis, too, there is definitely more than one possible future outcome. Of course, my anthropomorphic formulation must not be interpreted literally but merely as a shorthand (Olson 1982).

italism does depend on the symbiosis with other political groups, or at the very least with a political leadership whose convictions come from an earlier period, and which can take a long-term view. As I interpret Schumpeter, the end will come because those groups which should have a long-term view— such as those characterized in the present American political constellation as "conservative"—do not really understand how capitalism works.[19]

This interpretation can be supported by a direct quotation, uncanny for its present-day relevance. In 1926, Schumpeter wrote an article about *Finanzpolitik*, fiscal policy, which to him was above all economic policy writ large:

> 1. The immediate situation is not yet dangerous but only because we have *reserves*, particularly the turnover tax the mistaken reduction of which . . . it would be as ridiculous to argue against as it would be to argue against the extension of the tax on alcoholic beverages (Getränkesteuer) . . . Deficit financing . . . [or] inflation we cannot afford even as possibilities. . . .
>
> 3. We must know that *social development* can not be reversed and that a significant reduction in the total sum needed for Government purposes (Staatserfordernisse) is an illusion.* To be sure, we must save, but only to achieve as big a surplus above the cost of the Government machinery, a surplus which we need exactly as Colbert, but not for the Court and army, but for other purposes which correspond to the changed power relationships."[20]

> *The illusion is dangerous precisely for those groups which love it. It leads to a dream life of fiscal policy, to a fiscal policy of self-deception (Lebenslügen)[21]—to valueless apparent successes and serious disappointments.

A successful counteroffensive by capitalist interests is not excluded, but given the political and sociological circumstances emerging from economic development it becomes increasingly difficult to mount while preserving individual liberties.[22]

[19] An intellectual or analytical understanding would not be necessary. But it would be necessary that a policy that has short-term disagreeable consequences—say a tax increase—is not opposed if longer-term advantages are seen, and vice versa.

It is perhaps the function of a statesmanlike political leadership to understand the long-term consequences of a policy and to instill sufficient understanding and trust in the electorate to allow the necessary measures to be taken before a catastrophe occurs. These views can be documented to have been Schumpeter's. He was very much involved with attempts to balance and restructure the budget, first as minister of finance in Austria and later in the Weimar Republic as a publicist.

[20] Schumpeter, "Finanzpolitik," originally *Der Deutsche Volkswirt*, vol. 1 (1926/27). Reprinted in Schumpeter (1985), 69 ff; italics in original; my translation. It should be obvious that Schumpeter's mention of the sales tax only strengthens his argument as far as the present American situation is concerned. His position on the tax system will be discussed in Part 6.

[21] The term "Lebenslüge" comes from Ibsen's *Enemy of the People*. There it refers specifically to the belief that in a democracy the majority is always right even in scientific matters. In the drama, the issue is the discovery of pollution in a mineral spring which has been the basis of the welfare of the community, and to the problems of shutting down the spa for repairs of the pipes.

[22] This should not be interpreted to mean that a dictatorship would be any better. The neglect of this political and historical level is one of the major criticisms of Hayek's *Road to Serfdom* and

If capitalism has certain inherent developmental tendencies, so has socialism. In this context the major point is that socialism becomes a possibility though not a necessity only when capitalism has done its good work, when the conditions for it have become ripe. Schumpeter never tires to stress that this is also the only possible interpretation of Marx: there is a historical process which cannot be ignored.

Consequently, Schumpeter considered attempts to establish socialism before its time doomed to failure. He never saw in Soviet communism anything but an Asiatic despotism.[23] For him, attempts at establishing socialism before its time would be at best reversals to previous forms, kinds of feudalism.[24] After all, "scientific" socialism has changed its meaning substantially among the various groups that call themselves Marxist. At one time, the meaning of socialism was fairly clear: public ownership of the means of production; a political basis of an industrial proletariat; internationalism; and emergence in the industrially most advanced country.

Lenin adhered to the first three criteria, but decided that socialism/communism could also emerge in a backward country. Stalin gave up internationalism and decided socialism was possible in one country; subversive activities in other countries only served to protect his own brand of "socialism." And there never was any doubt that "fraternal" countries had to accept blindly Moscow's primacy. Mao decided that communism could also be based on the country side. And heaven only knows what a "Marxist-Leninist Peoples Republic of Benin" or Marxism in Ethiopia is supposed to mean, except to rationalize the monopoly of power by a particular group. This is in fact the result Schumpeter foresaw in the case of socialization before its time.[25]

---

it remains the major objection to his otherwise admirable *Constitution of Liberty*. In the *Constitution* Hayek has a chapter "Why I Am Not a Conservative," expanding his views first expressed in the *Road*. It is not likely that the expansion of the original arguments into a lengthy chapter was a reaction to Schumpeter's criticism. The weaknesses of both books basically stem from Hayek's remaining essentially wedded to a static framework despite all the dynamic trappings appended to it. As pointed out before, Schumpeter's dynamics is something very different from Hayek's or even Samuelson's. Dynamics really remains in Hayek a deus ex machina. See Schumpeter (1946), 269–70.

23 So in a letter to Redvers Opie, dated Cambridge, Mass. Saturday, but presumably 1933, kindly made available to me by Loring Allen. "I see nothing in Lenin but the bloodstained mongol despot, you nothing in Hitler than the stupid 'oriental' (?) demagogue. But for thousands of sophisticated and for millions of simpleminded both of them not only were leaders but saviors. Yes, Goebbels is the Trotzky of Hitlerism." Also see chapter 10.

24 Consider the following: The distinction between what is private and what is public is blurred. Instead of the Divine Right of Kings there is now the leading role of the party. There is a great suspicion of anything not approved: why should anyone really care whether you painted abstractly rather than in the approved "socialist realism"? Heretics are killed. The required Sunday attendance of church is supplanted by party rallies. And there is not even an exception made for dissidents corresponding to the *privilegium odiosum* of the Jews.

25 See also chapter 10. I am convinced that many nationalizations in LDCs are not so much based on ideology as on the absence of imagination. Nationalizing gives the appearance of action when in reality no new values have been created. It also shifts the distribution of wealth in favor of whoever controls the economy.

At the same time, the rediscovery, as yet quite incomplete, of the market mechanism can not on Schumpeterian grounds be interpreted as a reversal to capitalism, except to the extent that it recognizes that socialism's time has not yet come. The tendencies toward socialism may remain even if the tactics change. But Schumpeter correctly foresaw that Socialists would have to control the working class much more strictly than capitalism if they were really serious about establishing socialism. This, too, follows from seeing the course of economic events in the context of development. But I am running ahead of the story to be told.

The conclusions of the article *Finanzpolitik* quoted earlier point to two further views of Schumpeter on the relation between capitalist development and the possibility—I am avoiding the word "coming"—of socialism. The first is that the State has a very positive role precisely in an individualistic society, one of the major themes of the *Crisis of the Tax State*. Savings must mean that the State has the resources to do whatever "society" decided to do, but that the tasks of the State cannot be defined by a simple list. In his fiscal policy writings Schumpeter makes it clear that "available resources" means what is left over after maintaining an efficient government apparatus and maintaining the productive capacity of the economy—I avoid the word capital, which in Schumpeter does not mean "produced means of production"— and also what is needed to ensure economic development. Also, fiscal policy might be directed to stimulate savings and investments by the private sector.[26] Ensuring development becomes a central task of the government through strict fiscal policies and through monetary policies that avoid serious monetary disturbances.[27]

[26] This is why in LDCs it makes sense to distinguish a recurrent and a capital budget. It is not that recurrent expenditures may not be developmental—many like education or agricultural extension services obviously are—but that the recurrent budget helps to identify the presence, or more often the absence, of required savings.

[27] In his *Constitution of Liberty*, Hayek worries precisely about this problem, though from quite a different standpoint. In his chapter on "The Decline of Socialism and the Rise of the Welfare State," he points out that "unlike socialism the conception of the welfare state has no precise meaning" (1960, 257). Hayek's definition of socialism differs substantially from Schumpeter's in crucial respects and lacks, I believe, realism. Moreover, Hayek adds, "though a few theorists have demanded that the activities of government should be limited to the maintenance of law and order, such a statement cannot be justified by the principles of liberty. Only the coercive measures of government need to be restricted. We have already seen . . . that there is undeniably a wide field for non-coercive activities of government and that there is a clear need for financing them by taxation" (ibid.). "Our problem is not so much the aims as the methods of government action" (ibid., 258). And Hayek, reasonably I believe, refuses to "attempt to limit the functions of Government in terms of aims rather than methods" (ibid.), which is precisely what Nelson and Winter (and others before them) have argued. Eucken, the father of the Freiburg school of neoliberalism, could be quoted in the same sense and almost in the same words.

Expressed somewhat brutally, Schumpeter's and Hayek's approaches differ in two respects. Hayek's approach is essentially normative, while Schumpeter's is throughout strictly analytical. Hayek is interested in what is required to maintain individual freedom. Schumpeter is interested in explaining what makes capitalism tick and how economic policies engendered by the very capitalistic process might become inconsistent with further development. Both share a wide vision of social science and perhaps even of the kind of world they would like to see, but they differ

Advocating strict monetary policies decidedly does not make Schumpeter a deflationist, which he never was. The difference between Keynes and him is not that the former was for deficit financing under certain circumstances and the latter was not, as the following quotation from CSD shows. The difference is that Schumpeter at all times has a developmental view with its constantly changing production functions, while Keynes works essentially with constant production functions and envisages even secular stagnation.

> [W]e should agree with the advocates of government deficit spending so far as this: Whenever there is danger, either from causes inherent in the business cycle mechanism or from any other, of a "downward cumulative process," that is to say, whenever a situation threatens to emerge in which A's restriction of production induces B to restrict and so on throughout the economy, in which prices fall because they have fallen, in which unemployment feeds upon itself, government spending will stop this "vicious spiral," and therefore, if we chose to neglect all other considerations, may be justly called an efficient remedy. The true objection is not against income-generating government expenditures in emergencies once they have arisen but to policies that create the emergencies in which such expenditure imposes itself.[28] (CSD, 397–98)

Once the resources for development are safeguarded, the government is free to use resources on anything the body politic has decided on, and this includes definitely social policies—as long as they do not interfere with further development. Schumpeter has been rightly considered one of the intellectual fathers of what has later become known as the social market economy.[29]

Later I will take up the second question posed by this analysis: how will

---

not only in their strictly economic analysis, particularly of the business cycle, but I believe it is fair to say that only Schumpeter offers an integrated view of societal development in which account is taken of interactions of sociological, historical, technological, and economic factors (narrowly defined).

[28] Schumpeter added a footnote: "The wholesale condemnation of income-generating government expenditure under *any* circumstances . . . may be justifiable in people who think that once the use of this tool is granted, the door will be wide open for all kinds of legislative and administrative irresponsibilities. But it cannot be upheld on purely economic grounds" (297, footnote 29; italics in original). An example might be that the savings and loan crisis was allowed to develop as far as it did, quite aside from the fact that it was this easy spending and not so much investments which fueled the prosperity of the 1980s. It is nowadays customary to blame FDIC insurance of bank deposits up to $100,000 for this debacle. But it is evident that this can account for only a small part of it, if any. There was no FDIC insurance during the Florida land boom of the 1920s and similar excesses antecedent to the Great Depression. And it should be held against the criticism of the $100,000 insurance limit that the absence of this insurance caused a bank run, while its presence goes a long way to explain the maintenance of the money supply.

[29] Hayek really comes to the same conclusion. It is not possible here to develop the question of how many resources should be "reserved"—this is Schumpeter's term for what in the development literature is called the social discount rate—for further development. This is of course a central question for policy makers in LDCs and elsewhere. Here Schumpeter's interest theory and its relation to profits becomes crucial. The point has to be left at that in the present context except to say that here, too, Schumpeter is a much better guide to practical policy making in any economy whose primary goal is economic development than almost any other theorist. I have tried to work out some of these problems in W. Stolper (1991).

capitalism end and socialism come about? Schumpeter's analysis raises the possibility, indeed the likelihood, of gradualism in social developments which seems to differ somewhat from his analysis of discontinuous waves in economic life. But then one has always to remember Schumpeter's warning that legal forms make sense only in a legal context and have no bearing on economic theory,[30] and that what looks discontinuous in the small appears continuous in the large.

[30] Much of the New Institutional Economics analyzes the effects of specific legal forms on economic life, and vice versa. The validity and importance of this approach is, of course, not denied by Schumpeter. He does insist that all economic theory is an analysis of how institutions work, but also of how they change *out of their own logic*. I am referring back to the discussion of Nelson and Winter.

How the Definitions of Capitalism and Socialism Follow from Schumpeter's Analysis of the Development Process

DEFINITIONS ARE ARBITRARY. The only question is whether they are useful, whether they describe a set of facts which is interesting to analyze further. It may, therefore, not be trivial to treat Schumpeter's analysis of socialism and its possible coming initially as one of definition.

Like Marx, Schumpeter analyzes the development of capitalism. Unlike Marx, he also analyses the *possible* face of socialism in terms of the state of affairs toward which capitalism tends. Schumpeter's definitions follow logically from his analysis: first, of what equilibrium theory is and is not; second, from his analysis of an evolutionary economy; and third, from his analysis of social changes which may accompany the economic changes. Schumpeter's is the analysis of *presently visible tendencies, and only if these tendencies develop unchecked by deliberate action or external events.*

I shall discuss later possible societal reactions to such tendencies, which here means primarily political reactions based on individual wishes. It does not yet involve a deviation from methodological individualism. From what has been said before, it should be clear that the use or nonuse of the price mechanism cannot be a defining criterion of capitalism and socialism. Equilibrium theory applies to, and the price mechanism is characteristic of, any society in which exchanges take place, and they are socially, culturally, and economically neutral.[1] To show this was, after all, one of the basic purposes of the *Wesen*. The very universality of what general equilibrium theory says also severely limits its usefulness. Being neutral, it does not describe a social process in full bloom. To prove that socialism can or cannot work without a price mechanism really proves very little either way.[2]

---

[1] No complicated social structure can do without some decentralization, and this implies on the economic level a price mechanism. Neutrality means no more than that. Evidently, the ownership of factors of production and the manner in which the demands for goods are expressed is different and the results of the working of the price mechanism will thus differ. But it should immediately be pointed out that while central planners may be able to substitute their own ideas of what should be demanded for those of consumers, they cannot arbitrarily assume the scarcities of existing factors. I also refer back to Spiethoff's views given in chapter 7.

[2] Paul Sweezy stressed in a letter that he knew of no definition of socialism that required nonuse of the market mechanism. Mises at least may be excused when he originally made the use of the price mechanism the *definiens* of capitalism, and the nonuse for socialism, and for trying to show that economic calculation for factor prices (or as he put it for goods of higher order) was impossible under socialism because there could be no market for them. In his 1920 article "Die

This is why I believe Schumpeter's definitions to be superior to the alternatives. He simply dismisses as wishful thinking the idea that you can do without the market and that problems may just go away once you have "socialism."

Equilibrium theory is not only neutral; it also requires no special motivations. This is not so for a developmental economy. By Schumpeter's definition, capitalism never can be anything but developmental, whereas socialism could be stationary or developmental.[3]

This does require motivations for entrepreneurial activity. Most of these motivations *might* exist also under socialism. Where neutrality ceases is that in socialism, the motivations begin to have different roots: it may become possible to speak of *society's* wishes; it *could* be the end of methodological individualism. This was pointed out by Schumpeter already in 1909 in his discussion of "social value."

What really defines the nature of socialism is precisely this change to a conscious social rather than individual basis: "The meaning of socialization —this cannot be repeated too often—lies in the moment of a conscious economic plan for the whole economy and not in putting a planned cooperation in place of an anarchic chaos of the race for profits. For the economy of private property and of free competition is nothing less than anarchic" ("Sozialistische Möglichkeiten von heuter, in Schumpeter 1952, 460).

This change in the fundamental value system requires time and economic development. Attempting to introduce socialism before its time must be economically a failure and politically despotism. Yet, the disappearance of the

---

Wirtschaftsrechnung im sozialistischen Gemeinwesen," he had a Russia before him that even tried to abolish money, then to introduce money that systematically lost its value at regularly short intervals at a time when it was crystal clear that the central economic problem was capital formation and not spending.

But by 1926, in an article on "Interventionismus," Mises pronounced socialism dead because the New Economic Policy had been introduced: "Since the Bolsheviks have given up their attempt to realize the socialist ideal in Russia in one fell swoop and have put in place of their original economic policy the New Economic Policy (NEP), in the whole world there operates only one system of practical economic policy: the system if interventionism" (p. 610; my translation). Mises's basic argument in this article now becomes that interventions in the market which operate on the conditions of supply and demand are acceptable, but not direct interventions with prices. Mises deals directly with the American discussion of public utility pricing. The most interesting aspect of this discussion is the evident respect Mises has for his American colleagues even where he believes them to be wrong, which contrasts sharply with the tone he usually reserves for his German colleagues. In Spiethoff's view, Mises's 1920 article is really the analysis of a *future* economic style.

[3] "Capitalism, then, is by nature a form or method of economic change and not only never is but never can be stationary. . . . The fundamental impulse that sets and keeps the capitalist engine in motion comes from the new consumers' goods, the new methods of production, or transportation, the new markets, the new forms of industrial organization that capitalist enterprise creates" (CSD, 82–83). With all the chasms that separate Schumpeter and Mises, here is one agreement. Mises, too, considers "action" the basic element of reality. Hence, "praxeology."

Soviet Union shows only the failure of Leninism-Stalinism-Maoism. The leading role of the Communist party is understandable only as—to put it paradoxically—a counter-historic attempt to force history into a certain pattern before the time is ripe, with necessarily pathological results.[4]

For, as Schumpeter put it in 1920:

> The economic revolution must already have occurred if a political revolution is to be successful. For, the economic conditions for a different social system (soziales Anderssein) could thus far never be construed by conscious desire, they always had to evolve by the social things (Dingen) themselves over centuries. It is for this reason that peasant revolutions, for example, of the middle ages and the early modern times have almost totally failed. These were precisely attempts to change economic matters by political force, I know of no significant example where such attempts had longer-term success. (ibid., 455–456; my translation)[5]

Given that the time for socialism was evidently not yet ripe in 1920, Schumpeter found it not surprising

> [T]hat today when everybody speaks of socialization the concept of socialization has lost all clarity. . . . It is less understandable, though it is a fact, that the literature about socialization is so terrifyingly uninteresting. The ablest people have written the greatest banalities about the problem. Nowhere is there a real analysis of the difficulties, nowhere a satisfactory answer to the specific questions that will arise . . . That has many reasons: In particular one: . . . The courage is lacking for that ruthless frankness which would be necessary to face two facts . . . the fact that socialization inevitably would also lead to a fall in production and with it to a worsening of the misery of all groups of society, and the fact that a successful socialization would require a discipline and an unheard-of severity imposed precisely upon the working classes. (ibid., 457–58; my translation)

[4] "Although it must as a rule be very difficult to say whether socialization is possible at a particular time and can be successful for a particular people, the diagnosis in the case of Russia is nevertheless quite easy: a people where industrial workers are about 5% of the population, can at a time when most advanced industrial countries do not yet socialize, not be taken seriously when it tries to socialize. The problems which at present are relevant for Russia are exclusively with the peasants. Whoever satisfies the latter's wishes can for the rest do anything, even blast all cities into the air if he so desires: and among others also affect a migration of socialist ideas into Russia. This must be judged—and rests on exactly the same power bases—as the decree of Peter the Great which wanted to force west European cloths onto Russian society. As a matter of fact that comparison would be in favor of Peter, for he only tried to force upon Russia something which already existed elsewhere. Russian bolshevism can be understood only, but then totally, as the successor of Tsarism" ("Sozialistische Möglichkeiten," in Schumpeter 1952, 782, note 5; my translation).

[5] How this analysis translated into the political positions of 1919 when Schumpeter was a member of the German Socialization Commission and then Austrian minister of finance, will be discussed in Parts III and IV. I have heard a theory that the exodus from Egypt, which created a new nation out of dishomogeneous elements, was possibly the only successful slave/peasant revolt.

There is an irony of history which confirms Schumpeter's analysis. It may plausibly be argued that bolshevism in the Soviet Union has created a big educated middle class not only of apparatchiks but of technocrats who can function efficiently only in a freer economic environment. It is internal pressures which have been powerfully reinforced by the Western policy of containment that have been the most important reasons for the collapse of the Soviet empire.

The increasing inefficiencies of the Soviet system in the course of development have been documented and analyzed by numerous Soviet studies in the West. And one might here also refer to Amalrik's provocatively titled study "Will the Soviet Union survive until 1984?"[6]

But the question which this poses goes deeper and confirms even more Schumpeter's analysis of the course of history: was such a development "in the cards" anyway, or was it a cruel and unnecessary detour? Has the revolution of 1917 helped or hindered it?

Here again, two of Schumpeter's assessments turn out to be correct. As he put it in his Lowell Lectures, the grand lines of development are probably "ineluctable." Tsarist Russia before the First World War was one of the fastest developing economies. And an extrapolation of developments allows the plausible suggestion that without the war and without the subsequent revolution (which without the war would not have had the virulent form it had) it would have continued to develop faster than it did. This has, I believe, been the argument of Warren Nutter in various articles.

Given the fact that Schumpeter makes private property part of his definition of capitalism, while public *ownership* is not mentioned as part of the definition of socialism, two further points have to be made here. First, Schumpeter mentions that when the time is ripe it does make no substantive difference whether socialism is achieved in a legal or a revolutionary way: "The importance of legal continuity is very great from the standpoint of social psychology. Its disruption is so demoralizing that it leads to difficulties even for the leading people. But the importance goes no further" (ibid., 459; my translation).[7]

Second, what matters economically is not the legal form but its economic content. The legal concept of private property changes all the time. I will argue below that there is an erosion of this concept in the course of economic development. It is another instance of the gradual change away from methodological individualism toward social values. Central control over the means of production does not automatically involve the *legal* abolition of private property.

Interestingly enough, it was Hitler rather than Stalin who understood this perfectly. What mattered to Hitler was the socialization of people, not of factories. And he relied on his brown and black shirts to bring it about, not on

---

[6] Amalrik (1970).

[7] Hitler understood this perfectly and insisted on achieving power "legally."

the abolition of private ownership which could be made obsolete by other means, such as thoroughgoing exchange controls and foreign exchange allocations. Both Nazi Germany and Soviet Russia relied on terror in their attempts to change the nature of man. The results of their premature socialization attempts were equally disastrous.[8]

SCHUMPETER'S DEFINITIONS

Schumpeter's definition of capitalism includes the following elements:

1. private property
2. never-ending though discontinuous change in the conditions of production through entrepreneurial activity

---

[8] "The NSDAP always placed emphasis on the need for individual initiative and action. It tried to cut itself off from 'Marxism,' the SDP's socialism. Nazi collectivism was political, not economic, and left individuals as economic agents. The repeated and famous declaration of Nazi intention to socialize people rather than factories meant that far-reaching programmes of state control over the economy were unnecessary" (James 1986, 347).

Schumpeter has been, not entirely unjustly, criticized for not taking the Nazis more seriously in CSD. The references of James to Nazi policies are not from *Mein Kampf* but from Hitler's so-called *Second Book*, which came to light later and which Schumpeter could not know. Of course, Nazi reality differed from the ideal: the Nazis discovered that actual expropriation was unnecessary for central planning; exchange controls and foreign exchange allocations could do the trick.

Of course, the Nazis prepared for a war and Stalin built up a powerful war machine. James's extremely careful analysis leads him, however, to conclude that the end result of Nazi policy would not have been different had there been no war: "If we may speculate there had been no war, Nazi policy would have produced a society with low wages and high savings ratios, manufacturing ever cheaper and shoddier goods. The features of a low wage economy would in the end have endangered Germany's position on world export markets. . . . As a result of decisions taken in 1933, but principally later between 1934 and 1935, Germany had locked herself into a situation where increasing Government expenditure was not only politically desirable but also economically necessary" (ibid., 417–18). *Mutatis mutandis*, this applies also to the Soviet Union. The end of Hitler's Germany would have come with a whimper, not a bang. It did in fact so come in the Soviet Union in 1991.

On Hitler's economic (and other ideas), see also Zeitelmann (1987), particularly Part 5, pp. 195–336.

The case of Japan is also interesting. Many observers have been struck by how closely knit— and "ethnically homogeneous," to quote Schumpeter—Japan is. They have been struck not only by the legendary Ministry of International Trade and Industry (MITI) which supposedly was responsible for the successful investments in new industries, but perhaps even more by the close cooperation among the big Japanese industries. A recent article in the *New York Times Magazine* sheds some light on what Schumpeter saw as the socialization of demand and investment, except in the Japanese case it has its roots more in a feudal past than in socialist future: "There are, of course, Japanese who share an outsider's sardonic view of their homogeneity and singleness of purpose. These few dissenters question whether Japan is truly a democracy and wonder if it hasn't become a kind of Communist system that works" (Steven R. Weisman, "An American in Tokyo," *New York Times Magazine*, July 26, 1992, p. 27). The difficulties of the Japanese economy in 1993 have already produced radical changes and suggest that Japan too cannot escape the logic of history and of capitalist evolution.

3. a critical distinction between the entrepreneur as the locus of change, and the capitalist as the owner of resources

4. emphasis on the function of the banking system as the producer of purchasing power, and of the function of the newly created money to enable the entrepreneur to acquire and direct the resources into the channels desired by him.

The market is not mentioned as part of the definition because it is a universal and not just a capitalist phenomenon.

CSD provides a definition of what is called "commercial society," of which capitalism is a subform:

> Commercial society is defined by an institutional pattern of which we need to mention only two elements: private property in the means of production and regulation of the productive process by private contract (or management or initiative) . . . commercial society [is not] identical with capitalist society. The latter . . . is defined by the additional phenomenon of credit creation—by the practice, responsible for so many outstanding features of modern economic life, of financing enterprise by bank credit, i.e., by money . . . manufactured for the purpose. (CSD, 167)

In 1920, Schumpeter defined socialism as follows:

> We want to speak only of true socialization, i.e. of socialization in the sense of a change of an economy which rests on private property and private initiative into a socialist economy, i.e., an economy in which a social central organ has power over all means of production, works out and executes a social economic plan including the distribution of the final consumers' goods to the individual citizens. The word socialization could in this sense signify either a slow historic process or a conscious political action directed towards this aim. But such a political action can be successful only if a historic automatic process of socialization which is inherent in things themselves has already started, when the social development steers by itself towards socialism. We owe this insight primarily to Karl Marx. It distinguishes scientific from utopian socialism, i.e., that socialism which recognizes what it wishes to see as a necessary development and hence possible, from the other socialism which expresses nothing but human yearning for a paradise. ("Sozialistische Möglichkeiten," in Schumpeter 1952 p. 458–59; my translation)

In CSD, the definition of socialism is given without the process by which it may be achievable: "By socialist society we shall designate an institutional pattern in which the control over the means of production and over production itself is vested with a central authority—or as we may say, in which, as a matter of principle, the economic affairs of society belong to the public and not the private sphere" (CSD, 167).

Schumpeter adds one important point which has become quite apropos by the events in the former Soviet Union:

> [O]ur term is not intended to suggest centralism either in the sense that the central authority, which we shall alternatively call Central Board or Ministry of

Production, is necessarily absolute or in the sense that all the initiative that pertains to the executive proceeds from it alone. . . . some freedom of action must be left, and almost any amount of freedom might be left to "the men on the spot," say, the managers of the individual industries or plants. For the moment we will make the bold assumption that the rational amount of freedom is experimentally found and actually granted so that efficiency suffers neither from the unbridled ambitions of subordinates nor from the piling up on the desk of the minister of reports and unanswered questions—nor from the orders of the latter suggestive of Mark Twain's rules about the harvesting of potatoes. (ibid., 168)

The changes in the Communist bloc during the 1980s and 1990s suggest that the assumption made about the "rational amount of freedom" is indeed bold.[9] It will be more or less difficult to achieve it depending on the history of the society, the specific historic situation, and the time at which it is made. Hungarians, Czechs, and Poles or Balts have always felt Soviet rule to be an occupation. This should make the change to a new system easier. But it is also true that the harm done by a premature introduction of a Communist society may be so profound and the way out of it so painful, that the known evil may be preferred to the unknown good.[10]

It may be good to counter immediately one possible objection. It is in reality impossible to find a sharp divide between different types of economy because history—or for that matter, truly dynamic-evolutionary considerations—does not work that way.[11] There is in historic fact no other than a "mixed" economy, a term which I heartily dislike, pure types being strictly theoretical models of very limited applicability. One situation grows out of a previous one so that any specific historic situation always contains elements out of the past and a foreshadowing of the future.

Although it partly anticipates an argument to be expanded in chapter 10, it is worth quoting from a piece published in 1943. It is particularly relevant

[9] Indeed, Mises basically argues that without private property, no sensible market in "goods of higher order" is possible. See Mises (1920/21), 86ff.

[10] On the political level there is now an entrenched bureaucracy which would lose its power as well as its livelihood, and which may, therefore, be expected to fight against any changes. Of course, if the change occurs anyway, they may be expected to rush to the feed trough. But there is also the fact that the change from the existing to a sensible price system—i.e., one that reflects real scarcities of goods and factors—implies that most subsidies must be abolished and prices be allowed to rise substantially, with resulting unavoidable and substantial further reductions in the standards of living of most people and a substantial shift in the income distribution. This is naturally resisted—see Schumpeter's warning that precisely this would happen under socialism and hence would require a ruthless government to carry out—but the resistance might be supported by most people who might feel that price rises were profiteering and gauging. Is not Sartre's *No Exit* all about the Gates of Hell being wide open; that anyone can leave, but that most people prefer to stay for fear of what might be outside?

[11] Although Mises insists that there is no such thing as a mixed economy and the choice is harshly between a "free" market economy and socialism, he does in fact modify his opinion in his "Interventionismus" (1926), where he states, for example, that public ownership of a railroad is compatible with a free market economy. He does in fact talk quite sensibly about what kind of government interferences with the market are compatible with it and which are not. But it would go much too far to discuss Mises's position in this book, or to what extent he changed in his book.

because on the Socialist side there are arguments that look for "a third way," and the "capitalist" side attempts to prove that there is no such animal. Such arguments are reflections of political struggles for power and intellectually not serious if one accepts Schumpeter's analysis:

> No social system is ever pure either in its economic or in its political aspects. As regards the former, structural principles, such as, in the case of commercial society, private management of the process of production and free contracting, are never fully carried to their logical consequences. People were at no time allowed to do with their own quite as they pleased, and society at all times limited the range within which they might freely contract. In the epoch of intact capitalism, law, custom, public opinion, and public administration enforced a certain amount of public planning, while in a society that had adopted the structural principles of socialism, there was such a thing as Lenin's New Economic Policy that left room for a certain amount of *laissez-faire*. It follows that public management or planning being never either absent or complete, our question concerning the immediate future should not be couched in terms of "capitalism or socialism": there is a great variety of intermediate possibilities.
>
> Still more important for social diagnosis and prognosis is . . . the fact that no society is ever homogeneous. By this I do not merely mean that the political sector of every society grows out of, and hence reflects, all the different interests and attitudes of the various groups and classes that the prevailing social system produces. I mean something much more fundamental: every society contains, at any given time, elements that are the products of different social systems. . . . And this fact is not only, as one might think, responsible for frictions and other secondary phenomena. It is of the essence of the social process. A purely capitalist society—consisting of nothing but entrepreneurs, capitalists and proletarian workmen—would work in ways completely different from those we observe historically *if indeed it could exist at all.*[12]

The contrast between the definitions of capitalism and socialism is nevertheless of the essence. Capitalism can be understood only as an evolutionary process. Socialism, on the other hand, may or may not be evolutionary. Capitalist decision making is necessarily individualistic; its basis in true socialism becomes "social" in the true sense of the word.

ALTERNATIVE DEFINITIONS

Hayek's definition of socialism is at least on first reading very similar:

> [S]ocialism [once] had a fairly precise meaning and a definite program. The common aim of all socialist movements was the nationalization[13] of the "means

---

[12] "Capitalism in the Post-War World." Reprinted from *Postwar Economic Problems* in Clemence (1951), 170–83; quotations pp. 170, 172. Italics in original.

[13] But see below Otto Bauer's hostility toward nationalization as distinct from socialization.

of production, distribution and exchange" so that all economic activity might be directed according to a comprehensive plan toward some ideal of social justice. The various socialist schools differed mainly in the political methods by which they intended to bring about the reorganization of society." (Hayek 1960, 253–54)

There are, however, subtle differences to Schumpeter. The question of social justice really does not arise once socialism has been achieved, once "people are socialized." However, the question of social justice certainly arises in the process of achieving that state of affairs. And since socialism is certainly not the same as anarchism, the question of power distribution also remains. But in that case, the social democrats were as much afraid of the government as Hayek, as will be documented (see chapter 13). The differences among the various Socialist schools involved more than differences about the method of achieving socialism.

In fact, Hayek's position (in Schumpeter's time and shortly thereafter) is not quite clear in this quotation. He obviously considers the use of the price mechanism the only feasible economic system and, if I understand him correctly, he has argued not only that an exchange economy could not work without a market as an irreplaceable system of information, but that socialism could not introduce a working market in the absence of private property, the latter certainly being the position of Mises. Since the market as a criterion is not part of Schumpeter's definition, there is certainly a difference to Hayek/Mises here. Whether Hayek also believes, as does Schumpeter, that over the centuries there may be a true socialization of the value system I cannot say. I do not think that Hayek was interested in this kind of long view.[14]

At the extreme other end is the definition of Gustav Stolper which he formulated in his scathing review of Sombart's *Die Zukunft des Kapitalismus*: "[It is] well known [that] the capitalist economy orients its behavior on prices and the rate of interest. That—and not the problem of private property (Eigentumsverhältnisse)—is the essential feature of the capitalist system."[15]

[14] Professors Shionoya and Schmidtchen have pointed out to me that Hayek later moved in a direction which I should characterize as Schumpeterian. Since I have not gone as deeply into Hayek's thought as either of these two friends, I prefer to quote Professor Shionoya's letter, with his permission:

There is room for interpreting Hayek vs. Schumpeter differently, neither as static vs. dynamic, nor as normative vs. analytic, Hayek now insists on the evolution of culture and morals as a spontaneous order in the defense of the market and cannot be regarded simply a static and normative observer of the capitalist system. Both are in common in regarding a constructivist approach to [the] social system as the product of rationalization tendency under capitalism. Given this common notion, the alleged difference between a normative and an analytical approach is superficial.

[15] G. Stolper (1932c), 919; my translation. The differences in the definitions of Schumpeter and Gustav Stolper are not as great as may appear when it is considered that the concept of private property itself is not immutable, as will be discussed further on. Hayek's position is not quite clear. Obviously, socialism as a system without the price mechanism has collapsed (Hayek 1960,

Gustav Stolper also argued that the resurgence of the liberal economy—defined in the European sense as one oriented on prices and the rate of interest—was closer at hand than most observers thought who saw in the Great Depression the harbinger of the irreversible end of capitalism. And he thought so simply because the planned economy was at the end of its rope and just could not manage any more.

The identification of capitalism with the market and of socialism with its absence raises many questions. In one way it is a preferable definition to Schumpeter's because it is apparently clear-cut. It also identifies what has since become known as a Soviet-type economy in which the State gives instructions about everything in greatest detail and in which investments are allocated through the budget. It is also a system in which income distribution has no relation to the market: in particular, the *nomenklatura*, the privileged few, derive most of their income through direct allocations.

Schumpeter's definitions seem nevertheless preferable. Schumpeter talks about a developmental process in time, that is, about a process of "becoming," while a definition by private property and prices alone talks essentially about a situation that "is." The alternative views seem to me to rest on this difference in the way of looking at things, at history. (But see footnote 14 above.)

The State through its budgetary and other policies greatly influences the course of the economy. In the *Crisis of the Tax State*, Schumpeter uses such dramatic language that he who knows how to read the budget can hear the thunder of world history in it. And indeed the budget and the State are given a central role precisely in the capitalist and individualistic market economy. It is for Schumpeter not only the size of the budget but its detailed composition which becomes increasingly important as capitalism develops. The State takes on functions which in different circumstances used to be private, and it occasionally even sheds functions to the private sector.[16]

Yet this development toward increased involvement of the State, which for Max Weber is associated also with increasing bureaucratization of government and industry, is on the whole irreversible for sociological and political reasons and, as will be argued below, also because development produces problems which cannot be solved otherwise. In any case, it is not the legal form that matters but the economic content.[17]

254ff). But it has been replaced by the "conception of the welfare state which has no precise meaning" (ibid., 257).

[16] Max Weber (1918), points out that while in Renaissance times armies were private enterprises, businesses for hire, no city would have entrusted its grain supply to the private sector! (This pamphlet was the text of a lecture given by Max Weber during his tenure at the University of Vienna to officers of the "k.u.k." Austrian Army" als eine allgemeine einführende Orientiering über den Sozialismus.")

[17] Thus it does not matter whether the government itself provides universal health care or mandates employers to provide it to all employees and their families.

Interestingly enough, and contrary to popular misunderstanding, Hayek also accepts the growth of the role of the State at least in step with everything else:

> All modern governments have made provision for the indigent, unfortunate and disabled and have concerned themselves with questions of health and the dissemination of knowledge. There is no reason why the volume of these pure service activities should not increase with the general growth of wealth. There are common needs that can be satisfied only by collective action and which can thus be provided for without restricting individual liberty. It can hardly be denied that, as we grow richer, that minimum of sustenance which the community has always provided for those not able to look after themselves, and which can be provided outside the market, will gradually rise, or that government may, usefully and without doing any harm, assist and even lead in such endeavors. There is little reason why the government should not also play some role or *even take the initiative* in such cases as social insurance and education, or temporarily subsidize certain experimental developments. *Our problem here is not so much the aims as the methods of government action.* (Hayek 1960, 257–58; italics added).[18]

Clearly, Hayek does not see the welfare state as such a threat to individual liberty. But Schumpeter's first question is whether and when it may become a threat to economic development, and second, whether it engenders political and sociological changes that will lead not only to a threat to further economic development but perhaps to the individualistic basis of the economy.

One of the major questions remains the size of social expenditures which the capitalist, or more generally an evolutionary, economy can afford, as well as the specific methods of achieving agreed-upon aims. This inevitably allows for substantial disagreements at any one time even among people agreeing on the principles and aims.[19]

---

[18] The limitation to pure service activities is presumably intended to exclude public produciton.

[19] I have tried to work this out in some detail in the African context, though I believe it to be generally applicable, and specifically in the Schumpeterian context of development rather than the Hayekian context of preserving liberty. There is, of course, no conflict between the two. The difference is really whether the context remains essentially stationary or not. See W. F. Stolper, "Social Factors in Economic Planning," *The East African Economic Review* 1964 (originally a United Nations Conference Report, Addis Ababa). My chief argument is that the budget is the central document for economic policy making, not The Plan, that the amount of necessary domestic savings itself is defined by the social profitability of the proposed investments at undistorted world market prices. Once the necessary savings are forthcoming and safeguarded— necessary being defined by what could be profitably invested at undistorted interest rates and prices—social expenditures could be expanded without harm as far as any surplus resources permitted. This is a strictly Schumpeterian standpoint, clearly expressed in his article on "Finanzpolitik." At the conference in Addis Ababa, the participating economists were quite unhappy with my arguments. The only person who supported me was the representative of WHO— who was a physician!

Authentic Socialist Views Are Not Too Different from Hayek or Schumpeter

It is important to note that undoubted Socialists and even Communists also thought the market essential and were as worried about the dangers to individual liberties coming from an all-powerful State as was Hayek. Indeed, the generally accepted definition of socialism as central planning without a market fits more the Leninist-Stalinist version than that of Marx, and it is unfortunately the definition that Mises accepted in 1920.

Thus, Otto Bauer, an authentic Marxist and antagonist of Schumpeter, in the second Renner cabinet in 1919 wanted to improve not to abolish, the price mechanism and in the best Hayekian manner wanted to keep socialized industries out of the hands of the government. Austro-Marxists wanted to socialize (vergesellschaften), not nationalize (verstaatlichen):

> Who should run the socialized industries? The Government? By no means. If the Government dominates all possible plants, it would become too powerful vis-à-vis the people and parliament; such an increase in the powers of the Government would be dangerous for democracy. At the same time, Government would run the socialized industries badly; no one runs industrial plants worse than the State. For this reason we social democrats have never demanded nationalization, only socialization" (Bauer 1921, 10; my translation)

What the difference between nationalization and socialization meant at the time will be discussed in the context of Schumpeter's role in the German Socialization Commission and his policies as minister of finance. Any more abstract meaning is probably best interpreted as what Schumpeter discussed as a value system based on individual as distinct from one based on true social values.

In any case, this is not so different from Hayek's position. It shows the same concern for individual liberties and the same dislike of an overwhelming power of the State. Hayek might consider it naive, but neither stupid nor unsympathetic.

Bauer wrote during the uncertainties of revolution and the disasters of the lost war. His was necessarily an abstraction. More astonishing—among other reasons because he sees the market also as an information system in circumstances where all information is inherently unavailable (another contact with Hayekian thought)—is, therefore, Trotzky's testimony, written in 1932 as a specific criticism of Stalinist central planning:

> If there existed the universal mind that projected itself into the scientific fancy of Laplace, a mind that would register simultaneously all the processes of nature and society, that could measure the dynamics of their motion, that could forecast the results of their interactions, such a mind could, of course, draw up a priori a faultless and exhaustive economic plan, beginning with the number of hectares of wheat and down to the last button for a vest. In truth, the bureaucracy often

conceives that just such a mind is at its disposal; that is why it so easily frees itself from the control of the market and of soviet democracy. But in reality the bureaucracy errs frightfully in the appraisal of its spiritual resources. . . .

The innumerable living participants of economy, state as well as private, collective as well as individual, must give notice of their needs and of their relative strength not only through the statistical determination of plan commissions but by the direct pressure of supply and demand. *The plan is checked and to a considerable measure realized through the market.* The regulation of the market itself must depend upon the tendencies that are brought out through its medium. The blueprints brought out by the offices must demonstrate their economic expediency through commercial accounting. . . . Without a firm monetary unit, commercial accounting can only increase the chaos.[20]

Bauer wrote before there was any Socialist country, barring the future Soviet Union and the abortive Bolshevik attempts in Budapest and Munich. Trotzky wrote in opposition. The final quote comes from an impeccable Communist source in an established Communist state supported by the Soviet Union: Le Duan, first secretary of the North Vietnamese Communist party. Le Duan's speech, made during the Vietnam War, consisted of a political part in which the American bombing came in for a severe scolding. But in the part dealing with the economic problems, American bombing is not mentioned once. Instead, all the blame for the failures is put on the incompetence of North Vietnamese cadres who think that ideology can take the place of honest work![21]

[B]eaucoup de nos camarades . . . n'ont pas vue toute l'importance de la gestion économique. . . . n'ont pas approfondi suffisament les problèmes d'organisation économique.

Gérer l'économie, c'est gérer un organism vivant qui se développe selon les lois objectives . . . Né de la necessité objective, changeant constammant avec la conjuncture économique, il ne tolère ni fantaisie, ni schématism, ni bureaucratism. . . . (Le Duan 1970, 136)

Le problème qui se pose a l'heure actuelle est de savoir comment nous allons pouvoir et devoir planifier. Dans quelle mesure utiliser les rapports de marché et les leviers du crédit, des prix, des salaires, du profit? . . . (p. 137)

A l'heure actuelle . . . l'Etat sache *habilement coordiner le plan avec le marche* . . . La pratique dans l'édification économique de notre pays comme des

---

[20] Leon Trotsky, *Soviet Economy in Danger*, New York: Pioneer Publishers (1932), 29–30, as quoted by Sweezy (1935), 78–79; italics added. Leontief (1971) makes the neglect of the market a central point of his criticism of Cuban socialism. Of course, the neglect of the price mechanism by the Stalinist central planners really has a much simpler explanation than that the planners thought they knew better than the market: it is really a power play by a few to dominate the many. But it would go too far to pursue that thought here. In any case, Trotsky would agree with Mises: Stalinism was *Planned Chaos* (The Foundation for Economic Education, Irvington-on-Hudson, New York, 1947).

[21] Le Duan (1970).

pays socialistes frères a prouvé que dans la question économique, nous devons savoir *utiliser correctement ces leviers* qui constituent les prix, les salaires, le profit et le crédit, appliquer rigoureusement la comptabilisation. . . . (p. 140; italics in original)

[M]any of our comrades . . . have not seen the importance of economic manage-ment . . . have not gone sufficiently deeply into the problems of economic organization.

To manage the economy is to manage a living organism which develops ac-cording to its own objective laws. . . . born of objective necessity, changing constantly with the economic situation it tolerates neither phantasy not schema-tism nor bureaucratism. . . .

The problem of the day is to know how we can and must plan. To what extent use the signals of the market and the levers of credit, prices, wages and profit? . . .

At present . . . the State knows *skillfully to coordinate the plan with the market.* . . . The practice of economic construction of our country, as of the socialist brother countries, has proven that in the economic question we must know how to *use correctly the levers* which prices, wages, profits and credit constitute, that we must rigorously apply accounting [accountability?] . . .

It seems that Mises's "proof" that socialism cannot work because—or perhaps if—it does not use the market mechanism runs in open doors. The market is, to repeat, a socially, culturally, and politically neutral concept and not characteristic of any particular system. It is also, according to Schumpe-ter, feasible in socialism and a most democratic phenomenon. And price-less planning does indeed interfere with individual liberty and democracy, as not only Hayek argues. It also interferes with the efficiency of factor allocation.[22]

Schumpeter reasonably insists that anyone, including Socialists, can use the market mechanism for their purposes, and indeed that they better do so in their own interest. The real contrast is between an all-encompassing or a limited public sphere—sphere, not sector. This is to a large extent identical with Hayek's distinction between individual freedom and government coer-cion. Hayek's approach did not really investigate the tendencies within the capitalist system which may change capitalism into something else, including the most important problem of how value systems change in the course of

[22] This does somewhat less than justice to Mises's argumentation which, if I understand him correctly (which is sometimes hard to do) really is that no market in factors of production is possible without private property. I will come back to the point in the context of the erosion of the concept of property. Here only two comments seem in order. What seems necessary is really legal security, Rechtssicherheit, and a complete separation of economic decision making from State control, which essentially means no budgetary subsidies for productive purposes, or as I was fond of telling my African friends, the introduction of the concept of bankruptcy into socialist think-ing. Second, central planning, being antidemocratic, must appear to bureaucracies an ideal system of keeping things under their control. Of course, there is a contradiction here. For unless the economy generates sufficient resources, which it has more or less spectacularly failed to do in most LDCs, but seems to be able to do in Mainland China, there is not much point to control it. But then power has its own logic.

economic development. Hence, the approach did not really deal effectively with the problem where any remedial action must be applied if it is so desired, and indeed whether it will be desired when it should and could still be applied.[23]

[23] In an interview with Marion Gräfin Dönhof, Adolf Löwe pointed out that in 1918–19 the contrast between "Free Economy" and "Planning" was not yet a contrast between the political right and the political left (Dönhof 1988). Löwe credits Mises and Hayek with having made this identification.

Implications of Schumpeter's Analysis and Societal Reactions against the March into Socialism

EROSION OF THE CONCEPT OF PRIVATE PROPERTY

A number of institutional changes are likely, and in many cases inherent in the process of development as analyzed by Schumpeter. There is only one certainty: Capitalism will *not* end because of a shortage of investment opportunities. It is not merely that Schumpeter does not see secular stagnation as an economic problem. It would be true even if there was such a stagnation, because people would adjust their savings patterns to the available investment opportunities. In Keynesian language, the consumption function would shift upward to the full employment level.

It also follows from his definition of equilibrium and his denial that even under competitive conditions general equilibrium represents an optimum optimorum, simply because there cannot be such a thing.

This point of view, never abandoned, is most forcefully formulated in the 1911 edition of the *Theorie*:

> Technical and commercial production is within a given state of technical-scientific knowledge improvable practically without limit. Never are "all" possibilities realized, and if they were new ones would immediately arise. Only with respect to a given method of production is there a relatively best method, without it, however, not. . . . The ideal method *itself* cannot be reached because beyond it there are necessarily even "more ideal" ones . . . within given combinations there is a limit to every amount of goods. The combinations themselves, however, have no such limits. We are no nearer to the exhaustion of possibilities than during the stone age. (*Theorie* 1911, 160–61. Italics in original; my translation)[1]

To develop the next point I start with population increases which for Schumpeter are not external factors that might explain development but, as also for Marx, its consequences. In this Schumpeter agrees with much of modern population theory which analyzes economic determinants of population changes. Schumpeter quotes with approval Marx's "lapidary" statement that capitalism has brought about enormous population increases. Population would not have increased as much as it did if the economic space for it had

---

[1] This basic aspect of Schumpeterian reality is modeled by Nelson and Winter. When Schumpeter chided Keynes in the 1920s for believing that technical change itself was subject to diminishing returns, he then thought the only thing you could know about the future was that you could not know it, and that in fact, in the past there always had been such change.

not been created first. Thus, population increases cannot explain development, nor can decreases explain stagnation.[2]

The difference between developments in the capitalistic and the underdeveloped world is immediately understandable in Schumpeterian terms. In the capitalistic world, population changes are consequences of developments coming from the inside. In the underdeveloped world, they are responses to developments coming from the outside. Coming from inside the system, there are reasons to believe that the changes themselves might trigger limiting responses. Coming in LDCs from the outside, there are no such reasons. The explanatory problem of development remains. There may or may not be reasons to fear population increases also in the developed world, but there certainly are such reasons in LDCs.[3]

In capitalistic countries there are also institutional changes which become inherent with rapid population increases and which necessarily enlarge the governmental sphere. There is need for more schools and health care which, whether privately or publicly supplied, eat into the necessary savings which otherwise might have been used to finance economic development. Of course there is such a thing as investment in education. But this does not change the fact that while an educated labor force becomes more essential than ever, so does the need for resources to employ that labor force when it reaches the labor market after a considerable and possibly increasing lag.[4]

Of more direct concern are the environmental effects which scientific and population changes produce. Nature cleans itself up to a certain point, beyond which that self-cleaning property ceases. It inevitably becomes a social concern to make sure that these limits are not passed. These are basically the external economies which are also the basic reasons for the existence of public goods.[5]

[2] Of course, population changes have a big impact on development, but these are matters of the second approximation. August Lösch, *Was ist vom Geburtenrückgang zu halten*, Selbstverlag 1932, argued that a declining population would be economically advantageous, even from a military standpoint.

[3] I believe that there are also reasons to fear rapid population increases in the developed world, but not primarily in an economic sense. Rapid changes strain the adaptive abilities of any system once a certain level is passed.

[4] The increased tax burden, about which Americans so vociferously complain, has essentially two sources: the cold war and the population increases. Most increases in public civilian employment have not been on the federal but on the state and local level: school teachers and police protection, and health care. The attempts to escape these problems by moving elsewhere can have only temporary success. Social security raises different problems, because it is mainly an attempt at a different intertemporal structure of one's income, and only secondarily an income redistribution problem. But this itself raises questions about financing, and all of it raises the need for a Schumpeterian policy of increasing productivity and output.

How confusing and generally inconsistent these problems have become is shown by the fact that the American people will elect a president because he promises no tax increases, while voting for representatives who promise to deliver increasing governmental services. This is not a perversion, but the logical consequence of fundamental institutional changes which Schumpeter discussed in his Mexico lectures, and about which something will be said below.

[5] The statement implies that earlier generations care for the welfare of future generations.

But, as pointed out before, not all externalities are necessarily of public concern, though most are likely to be. A case can be made, I believe, that armed forces become a public good only when democratic development has proceeded for some time, that is, when ordinary people begin to be interested in being protected by a particular group. If the fight is just between overlords while taxes paid and services due remain unchanged regardless of who wins, the ordinary man in the field—hardly in the street—may have only a limited interest.

Clean water and air pollution in all its forms necessarily become of public interest with development and population increases which themselves are a consequence of development. Air pollution and acid rain are no respecters of political boundaries, and the immediate interest of a particular group of people may have more to do with the direction of the prevailing winds than any high principle of individual freedom.[6]

The particular form in which the public interest is safeguarded will vary with circumstances. It always makes sense to use the market as far as possible and it always makes sense to allow people as far as possible to decide how to meet certain standards, but this has nothing to do with whether the public sphere itself is expanding. This even applies to the control of individual safety in cars, or bicyclists being required by law to wear crash helmets. The idea that it is really no concern to anyone except myself whether I want to kill or maim myself is not convincing if at the same time others are expected to pay increased taxes for police and hospital costs. Generally, the argument that environmental protection costs too much is not convincing—provided the proposed standards are scientifically, technically, and economically soundly based—because environmental destruction is really capital consumption.

The growth of large-scale enterprise can be partly understood as an economic reaction to external economies which might be more efficiently handled by internalizing them. (The fact that even experienced managers frequently make mistakes in this regard does not change the principle.)

[6] Since I have quoted Hayek at length before, it is only proper to add that he would not disagree in principle. He specifically mentions difficulties "where property in land is concerned. The effect which the use of land often has on neighboring land clearly makes it undesirable to give the owner unlimited power to use or abuse his property" (Hayek 1960, 229). More generally, therefore, the existence of externalities justifies societal regulation. It is only fair to state that Mises seems to ignore external effects, which vitiates much of his analysis, as does his assertion in *Gemeinwirtschaft* that the income distribution arising from the workings of the market is somehow optimal without considering that there is an infinite number of such competitive income distributions depending on the initial distribution of wealth—a point quite well known since Wicksell.

There is, of course, no such thing as an unlimited property right. It is always legally defined. It is also proper to add that Hayek is concerned mainly with the desirability of rules vs. discretion. But a rule of law frequently still requires judicial or in any case executive interpretation because no rule can be all-inclusive and applicable to all cases that might arise. This raises questions which were discussed by Hayek, John Stuart Mill, Georg Jellinek, and Wilhelm v. Humboldt, to name just a few recent authors. I refer back to Nelson and Winter's discussion of pollution controls as entitlements.

Schumpeter has been accused of singing the praises of large-scale enterprises and monopolistic structures as the sources—perhaps better the loci—of innovations. He did indeed do so. But in the developmental context the meaning is not necessarily glorification, but a statement of fact: Enterprises *become* big by successful innovation; and they lose out not only to imitators, as stationary theory and the onset of the cyclical downturn quite correctly analyze, but essentially to emerging innovations forcing them either to innovate further themselves or die.[7]

Schumpeter foresaw a growing importance of large-scale enterprise, but it should be remembered that he never predicted anything but only stated what the existing trends implied if left unchecked. In fact, the verdict on this point is not yet in. At the present time, computers, whose ultimate effects cannot be foreseen, seem to have a decentralizing effect, allowing the growth of many small enterprises—but also the emergence of such giants as Hewlett-Packard, Apple Computers, or Microsoft Corporation. Schumpeter is not a determinist and nothing is inevitable in his analysis.

There are other points relevant to the erosion of the concept of private property. Some of them have been discussed for a long time under the heading of the separation of ownership and control. On the purely economic level the difference between equity and debt is only a legal fiction: the risks of loss and gains are distributed differently. The legal difference remains a useful, perhaps even a necessary, fiction. If I own one hundred shares of IBM, I am legally something like an owner of IBM, though it is really IBM which owns the physical assets, but that does not seem to make too much difference—except that Schumpeter stresses that owning shares is not the same thing as owning and controlling a factory outright.

Going public with ownership is an erosion of private property. It changes the relationship to the employees, and to the community in which the plant is located. It is difficult to imagine that an entrepreneur-owner of a single plant in a town does not also take an interest in what happens in the community, that he feels that he owes allegiance only to himself. With absentee ownership, there are only profits, and many executives are understandably bewildered by demands that they should behave "responsibly."

But problems do not go away, and they become increasingly public concerns. When Minneapolis wanted to attract its famous theater, Pillsbury helped. When a local brewery in the West was purchased out-of-town, the *New York Times* reported concern that the cultural life of the town would suffer when some fellow in Chicago would have to make decisions which before were made quickly and on the spot.

The latter is precisely a form in which the interest of the public is consid-

---

[7] I refer back to the discussion of Nelson and Winter in chapter 6. F. M. Scherer has devoted his research to the analysis of evolutionary aspects of industrial structure. Space limitations prevent a discussion of these important contributions. I now refer to a forthcoming paper by Scherer on "Schumpeter and Plausible Capitalism."

ered; it represents an inevitable increase in the public sphere. It also means that the executive is motivated by subtly different considerations and that these motivations are consistent with socialism as defined by Schumpeter.

None of this is as farfetched as it may sound at first. Consider what has been happening in the course of development in the rust belt. Industries based on coal and iron are becoming increasingly less important. Coal and iron, as well as many natural resources, are becoming less important as locational factors. The most important locational factors are becoming clean water, clean air, and the quality of life. Firms want good schools to attract good people who are concerned about good schools for their children and not only to supply the skilled labor force they need. They expect the public sector to supply the need—as is in the best American tradition, at least as far as schools are concerned. They also expect the cities to create an environment in which the executives and their families will feel comfortable. Schumpeter, in his discussion of German public finance during the Weimar period, thought that what was considered a waste of municipal funds was a justified expression of public pride and a lively public cultural life.[8] But he also thought, if only in a footnote, that during the Gladstonian era low taxation allowed the accumulation of large fortunes which were then spent on cultural pursuits; and this, too, is in the best American tradition.

This is, I believe, also the context in which the "bureaucratization" of the entrepreneurial function must be seen. The change in the concept of "private" allows entrepreneurship to become—you choose the word: bureaucratized, routinized, professionalized. And with this there is no further reason why it should not exist also in the public sphere—as historically it very often has on the European continent. The German Socialization Commission or the Austro-Marxist Otto Bauer wanted to abolish the capitalist but to nurture the entrepreneur. (See chapter 13.)

Increasing Independence from Bank Financing

There is a final point inherent in Schumpeter's analysis of savings and the rate of interest. Savings in equilibrium are of minor importance and they are made for purposes unrelated to the founding of enterprises.[9] Interest on consumption loans may exist, and may be positive, zero, or negative. But this is not a phenomenon that interests Schumpeter or that requires extended analysis.

The distinction between the entrepreneur and the capitalist is crucial. The

---

[8] There is no question that municipalities borrowed too much abroad during the Weimar period. But this is a question of how to finance public pride. See chapter 24.

[9] The absence of net savings in equilibrium is generally agreed to. The discussion relates only to whether this may be compatible with less than full employment—the Keynesian view—and whether it requires a positive rate of interest to prevent capital consumption—the classical view. I accept Schumpeter's argument in toto that neither will be the case under purely competitive assumptions. This has been described in some detail in chapter 4.

entrepreneur can initially—in the first approximation before development has started—get funds to start development only from the banker who creates them ad hoc. If successful, this will allow the entrepreneur to make profits which he must split with the banker-capitalist in the form of interest.

The characteristic of socialism is the direct command over resources. In the socialism which has collapsed, the investment resources come from the budget and are allocated according to a central plan. The resources which an individual plant may retain out of any profits it makes are insignificant and cannot, as a rule, be used to enlarge the productive capacity of the plant except within very narrow limits.[10]

If a capitalistic enterprise is successful it may retain increasing amounts of profits. Self-financing for expansion becomes increasingly possible. The major source of societal savings are successful innovations; that is, significant amounts of savings are themselves the result of development. In the course of successful development entrepreneurs may become increasingly independent of bankers. This is a kind of surplus value theory of interest, but one not based on exploitation but on creative activity and growth. In fact, business savings have become the major part of available savings.

Interest on productive loans to create enterprises—the only kind of loans Schumpeter is interested in—would fall to zero in the absence of a stream of innovations and in fact approaches zero during the depression phase of the cycle. Also, to the extent to which business becomes independent of the capital market it not only does not have to pay interest—as stated explicitly in Schumpeter—but it also changes significantly the institutional framework of capitalism.

There is an important literature showing empirically that observed growth over the past century or so cannot to any significant extent be explained by increases in the labor force and in capital equipment of the economy. The names of Abramovitz, Dennison, Kendrick, and Robert Solow, who received the Nobel prize for his work in this area come to mind.[11] There is also the path-breaking work of von Neumann linking the rate of interest and the rate of growth of an economy under certain strict assumptions.

This process of making the entrepreneur increasingly independent of the capitalist is inherent in capitalist development. How fast it will proceed is a matter of fact and cannot be foreseen. It will depend also on the speed with which emerging innovators require funds beyond those made available from savings out of old innovations. But there is such a possibly irreversible process.

There is nothing equivalent to this analysis in Hayek or Keynes. For Hayek, growth takes place as the natural result of freedom, and the business cycle

[10] The reconstruction of the banking system to finance investments and cutting the umbilical cord between enterprises and the budget at least as far as investment allocations are concerned are in this view crucial tests for the change from the (actual) planned economy to a "free" market system.

[11] See R. M. Solow's Nobel lecture "Growth Theory and Thereafter," *American Economic Review*, June 1988, for a convenient summary.

could be avoided by proper monetary policies without harming growth. The Keynes of the *Treatise on Money* accepted Schumpeter's explanation of the cycle *in toto*, but the Keynes of the *General Theory* really was quite uninterested in the cycle, or for that matter growth, as such, but only in how various cycle theories fitted into his approach.[12]

This process explains in large part Schumpeter's assertion not only that larger firms and temporary monopolies may begin to dominate the economies, but also that innovative activities may become increasingly bureaucratized. Large firms become both the sources of innovative ideas and the funds to finance their execution.

Schumpeter indeed makes the startling assertion not only that entrepreneurs do not have to pay interest in such a case, but that Socialist production becomes "kapitallos"; that there is no interest in socialism because there will be no one to receive it, and that there will be no need for further indepenedent credit creation. All of this is quite logical in the context of the institutional changes envisaged and the definition of capital as a sum of money to be used for productive purposes.

Of course this emphatically does not mean that Socialist enterprises or Socialist planners could consider investment funds a free good. They may even call what they charge themselves "interest." But again, this is a case where two quite different social and economic phenomena are called by the same name, where a legal fiction may obscure economic and social reality.

A few words must be said here of what Schumpeter considers the gravest danger to capitalism: the danger of inflation. "[O]ne of the most powerful

---

[12] This assertion requires further justification since it has been challenged by a friendly reader. In chapter 21 of the *General Theory*, Keynes argues first that the proper distinction is between what is now referred to as macro and micro theory. Second, "the importance of money follows from its being a link between the present and the future" (1935, 293; italics in original). This would be accepted by Schumpeter only with qualifications. For Schumpeter, the central importance of money is its function of financing innovations. The important effect of an increase in the quantity of money is in the short run the effect on the rate of interest. With this Schumpeter agrees. But in his view, the rate of interest tends toward zero in the short run in any case. His explanation is not any liquidity preference, but the cyclical disappearance of the marginal efficiency of capital schedule, to use Keynesian language. There is also the (Keynesian) implication that micro theory comes into its own only when full employment is created.

In the explanation of *The Trade Cycle* (chapter 22), Keynes thinks that one has to explain the crisis by a sudden collapse of the marginal efficiency of capital because expectations of the future yield of capital goods suddenly change (p. 315). Keynes discusses all kinds of theories, including overinvestment and agricultural fluctuations, but not the one he had accepted in toto in the *Treatise*. This seems odd particularly as he might have linked the increased output of new enterprises coming on stream competing with the older ones to explain the changes in expectations.

Keynes also thought that investment opportunities would diminish and there might be reason to socialize investments. Neither would be acceptable to Schumpeter. But Keynes also thought that this state of affairs would not be just around the corner.

It would go too far here to make a detailed comparison of the explanations of these two great men, but on careful rereading of the relevant chapters, I see no reason to do more than somewhat to modify my judgment.

factors that make for acceleration of social change is inflation" (CSD, 421). It makes the proper monetary and fiscal policies essential. Schumpeter's detailed opinions will be examined in Part 6. For Schumpeter the fact that on the one hand inflationary pressures are accepted as the lesser evil to unemployment and bankruptcies, but that changes in the real economy have already gone so far that "credit restriction would at present achieve little beyond increasing difficulties of business" (CSD, 423) suggests how far the transition away from traditional capitalism has already gone. I shall deal with these aspects at the end of this book.[13]

Societal Reactions against "The March into Socialism"

As this section is rewritten for the seventh time, all over the world communism is in retreat and capitalism as well as democracy seem to be breaking out everywhere. Does this prove that Schumpeter's "prediction" was wrong? More specifically, does it prove that Schumpeter's analysis of the tendencies inherent in capitalism have turned out to be faulty? Does it not show that capitalism is a healthy organism that has produced enough antibodies to confound Schumpeter's analysis of "visible inherent tendencies"?

To start answering these questions it must be recalled that the price mechanism itself is socially, politically, and culturally neutral. Right prices are important for the efficient allocation of resources. The fact that Communist countries rediscover the superiority of the market over the inefficiencies of centralized administrative economic decision making in itself only proves that Communist countries are trying to learn from their mistakes.[14] That does not

[13] The quotations are from "The March into Socialism." It is here necessary to add only that Schumpeter considered the monetary solution of fluctuating exchange rates with a steady growth of the money supply a sign of how far capitalism had moved from its old ideal. Hayek would probably not agree with this. Yet he agrees with Schumpeter that even conservatives have been and are now subscribers to policies inconsistent with capitalist development. Hayek explains this in the chapter in the *Constitution* "Why I Am not a Conservative." Yet there is again an enormous difference to Schumpeter in that Hayek evidently thinks there is a way back to paradise, while Schumpeter's evolutionary view is that "As soon as we take account of [the political structure of our time] we shall think more kindly toward those English conservatives who incur Hayek's displeasure" (Schumpeter 1946, 182). "Perhaps they are the only group in the world that, as a group, combines frank recognition of the data of the situation with an adequate appreciation of our responsibility toward mankind's cultural inheritance—in the best Beaconsfield inheritance" (ibid., 270).

Of course, Hayek prefers Gladstone to Disraeli, as does Schumpeter in "Wage and Tax Policies in Transitional States of Society" (Swedberg 1991a, 491ff). The difference is again Schumpeter's evolutionary and Hayek's stationary view. For Schumpeter, history moves only in one direction; for Hayek's *Constitution*, historic time is not considered.

Schumpeter's failure at currency reform as minister of finance (see Part IV), but even more the failures of post-Communist Poland and the Soviet Union to have thorough currency reforms *before* privatizing suggests that the problem of inflation is not unique to capitalism or democracy.

[14] Trying is not the same as being successful. Any situation which lasts for some time creates vested interests which will do what they can to preserve their positions. In the Soviet Union the

in itself make them capitalist. As long as we stick to equilibrium situations—
which in Schumpeter's analysis also includes adaptive processes to small
changes coming from outside the economic system—they can use the market
mechanism without ceasing to be socialistic. In the argument between Mises
and Hayek on the one hand, and Barone in the other, Barone surely wins
hands down for an equilibrium situation. But this is something of an empty
victory. After all, Hayek too has pronounced dead and of no further interest a
socialism defined as not using the market.[15]

Leninist-Stalinist heirs of Tsarism have had 70 years to entrench their power, and that in an
environment that was not unfavorable to centralized decision making to start with. In China, on
the other hand, the cultural revolution may have had the paradoxical effect of destroying the
power of the party. (See most recently Roderick MacFarquar, "The Anatomy of Collapse," *The
New York Review of Books*, Sept. 26, 1991.)

The situation in the East European countries is different. For them Russia was a conqueror, a
fact that all the rhetoric about fraternal Socialist countries could not eradicate. It is no accident
that reform movements are strongest in Poland and Hungary, weakest in the former East Germany and Czechoslovakia. Poland and Hungary have long histories as independent nations. In
both countries, all eradications of their national existence—in Poland two divisions, in Hungary
conquest by the Ottoman Turks and then attachment to the Double Monarchy—have not
succeeded in killing their national memories.

Czechoslovakia on the other hand was an artificial creation of the Entente in 1919. The
historic unit is the kingdom of Bohemia. For the rest, it was carved out of defeated Austria and
Hungary. But historic memories are long: there was a time—not so long ago as historic developments go—when Prague was the cultural center and capital of the Holy Roman Empire and
Vienna its inferior. The (German) University of Prague is older than that of Vienna and among the
oldest in the world. Mozart's operas had their premieres in Prague. Even here, the legitimacy of
national leadership rests on somewhat shaky foundations, as evidenced by the political infighting
between Czechs and Slovaks.

East Germany had no legitimacy as an independent organism at all—except for one historic
fact which also seems generally forgotten: Until 1871, Germany was never united. It always
consisted of a multitude of principalities which were quite independent. Even the founding of the
German Empire in 1871 did not unite all Germans. It excluded Austria which had run the show as
it were until 1806 when the HRE was officially dissolved; and the Hungary as constituted before
the Second World War also was not a historic unit.

The facile interpretation of events in the former East bloc suffers from an almost total lack of
historic knowledge of that part of the world. And it seems ironic that the non-Marxist West seems
to resort to a crude kind of materialistic interpretation of history! The basic fact seems to be that
nationalism caught up with the Soviet Union to destroy an empire which with reasonable economic policies might nevertheless have survived at least for a while and might have been in a
better position to change. But I must leave it to professional historians to give more subtle (and
hence more correct) answers to the problems of the interactions of nationalism, historic and
political trends, and economic policies.

[15] Mises, "Wirtschaftsrechnung" has tried to show that Barone (whom he does not mention!)
cannot be right because without private property in "goods of higher order" there cannot be a
market for them, and without a market there can be no rational pricing. I cannot accept the
arguments as they stand. One of them is that the concept of private property is not defined. It takes
a legal rather than an economic definition of "Sondereigentum." But what is required is only a
decentralization of the power to dispose within legal limits and "Rechtssicherheit," i.e., a guarantee that the legal rules will not be arbitrarily changed or enforced. To repeat, by the Schumpeterian definition, socialism would be quite compatible with private property, though capitalism
would not be compatible with its absence.

I have tried to show that Schumpeter's definitions are not arbitrary but follow from his analysis of the developmental process. Schumpeter's central argument is that *in the course of economic development the sphere of societal decision making will increase irreversibly though not necessarily at an even pace or without temporary reversals, but does so mainly for sociological and political reasons which themselves are favored by economic development.* (So does Hayek, though by a different route.) The real issue is what is considered to be the proper role of the State and the individual.

What are some of the present tendencies in the United States? The core of Schumpeter's argument of tendencies toward socialism is that more and more matters become a public concern. In this respect the definition of what government is expected and allowed to do becomes crucial. It involves the view of democracy primarily as the rule of the majority as against the protection of minorities and individuals. The "conservative" appointments to the Supreme Court have tended to widen the government's role compared to that of the individual. Previously I argued that the Bill of Rights is *the* American contribution to the establishment and preservation of individual liberty, and a very conservative contribution it was. Any erosion of the Bill of Rights must be considered an erosion of the private sphere. The fact that this erosion comes from the "conservative" side strengthens Schumpeter's analysis and cannot, I believe, be interpreted as a reaction against the March into Socialism.

It is not irrelevant that Hayek, too, in his *Constitution* makes the point that Conservatives have more in common with Socialists than with their own past. Liberals, in the old-fashioned European sense of the term, distrust government which they nevertheless see as necessary under all circumstances. Liberals are neither anarchists nor "libertarians."

There is also far-reaching agreement between Schumpeter and Hayek, certainly also myself, of what is desirable. On Schumpeter's side this can be documented by his posthumously published Montreal talk in which he referred to the papal encyclical *Quadragesimo Anno* and worried about the moral basis of capitalism.[16] On Hayek's side it is documented by the lengthy quotation given before about legitimate extensions of government functions with increasing wealth.

Given this wide agreement about what *is*, it therefore becomes important to

---

[16] Mises, too, mentions this papal encyclical. But the only thing he finds in it to his liking is the sanctification of private property, though it is too much hedged for his taste. "The evolution toward Socialism is common to all denominations. In Catholicism, Leo XIII's encyclical "Rerum Novarum" of 1891 has recognized the origins of private property in natural law; but simultaneously the Church laid down a series of fundamental ethical principles for the distribution of incomes, which could be put into practice only under State Socialism. On this basis stands also Pius XI's encyclical 'Quadragesimo Anno' of 1931. In German Protestantism the Christian Socialist idea is so tied up with State Socialism that the two can hardly be distinguished" (Mises 1951, 255 note 1). It is amazing that "all denominations" are Socialistic. Apparently only a secular atheism of a particularly ridiculous kind will do. See also the previous discussion of Archbishop Temple's view and Butterfield's criticism which is, *mutatis mutandis*, also applicable to Mises.

analyze how that ever-increasing wealth is generated, and what it implies about the common needs that it allows to be increasingly satisfied. Hayek clearly allows for both public and merit goods. But Schumpeter's argument goes much deeper. It is really that capitalist development brings about a gradual change in the whole value system of individuals and society. There is nothing in present developments to suggest that he was wrong in this, that conservative governments everywhere and specifically in the United States present a societal reaction. It is after all beginning to be generally recognized that the economic policies of the 1980s have in fact meant—although not yet irreversibly—that the next American generation will be the first to see a lower standard of living than the present one because the prosperity of the 1980s has depended in the best Keynesian manner on consumption and not on investment. The true conflict is, as Schumpeter never ceased to stress, between the present and the future, and at present it is the future which is being sacrificed. The fact that this is due not to "laborism" as Schumpeter expected but to the highest income receivers adds another "joke in poor taste" of history.

Private property being a legal, not an economic category, its precise contents depends on the historical situation as expressed by the laws and customs of the time, and the interpretation of these laws. Certainly, even under communism slavery is likely to be outlawed at least formally; the deprivation of personal liberty for criminal actions depends on law and is, or should be in civilized society, very strictly interpreted. Civilized society, certainly ever since the establishment of Roman law, does not know retroactive criminal law or lynch justice. There was private property under feudalism with a different content given it now, and even private businesses staffed by owners and their family members have been allowed under communism. Not so long ago, prohibition outlawed alcoholic drinks, and what will happen to drug legislation is not certain.

So private property neither is nor ever has been an absolute right. In the United States you own subsoil rights, but this is not generally true in Europe. Even in the United States you cannot under all circumstances prevent a plane from flying over your property. There is a catch in Shakespeare's *Merchant of Venice*: Shylock has a right to his pound of flesh but not to the blood that is inevitably spilled. Yet it is conceivable that a modern judge would rule that, since you can't cut out flesh without spilling blood, the latter is implicit in the contract. But another might with some reason argue that since you can't cut out the flesh without spilling the blood, the contract is unenforceable, perhaps even null and void. Gambling debts and cartel agreements have been treated differently in different countries. Prostitution is treated differently in the various states within the United States, and foreign countries do not consider insider trading an offense. The enclosures changed common into private property. But even before that, the content of private property was changed when the poor were prevented from gathering fire wood. The list can be lengthened ad libitum.

The point is that real controls are more important than legal definitions.

The concept of private property has changed, sometimes to allow for more societal concerns, sometimes also to protect vested interests, sometimes with more, sometimes with less justice. That is, even the latter may be more an expression of power relationships than of official concerns about externalities, or both. In the *Codex Justinianus* there is a case of a man complaining about the smells coming from a neighboring cheese factory. Modern equivalents abound: ecological concerns and acid rain, and zoning in particular. These are all cases of external effects which Hayek, too, recognizes as legitimate concerns of society and which Nelson and Winter discuss in great detail.[17]

Zoning laws offer particularly instructive examples. In some parts of Germany, even the angle of the roof of your house is prescribed not for reasons of safety or health—as may be the height of buildings—but for esthetic reasons which themselves may be defended on grounds of preserving the character of a town, presumably as a tourist attraction, or perhaps more often to keep out undesirables with different tastes. One wonders how this kind of problem is to be handled under the rules-versus-discretion category.

The example is instructive for a particular point of Schumpeter's. The issue is not only that external effects may, and probably do, become more and more important with economic development as well as with increased scientific understanding, in which case there would in principle be general agreement at least about the purpose of appropriate action. The point is rather that more and more things are felt to be of public rather than of private concern, including how a neighborhood looks esthetically.

The last point may seem rather trivial, but most of the changes from an individual to a societal perception may be the direct result of population increases, which are at least in the Western world the result rather than the cause of development. As long as we deal with a small community in which everyone knows everyone else and/or is related, my neighbor's welfare automatically becomes part of my welfare function. In such cases the social behavior is integrated into the individual behavior. This becomes increasingly impossible as the community increases in size and complexity. In this case the best, perhaps the only, way to become your brother's keeper is through social action.[18]

---

[17] Hayek specifically mentions difficulties "where property in land is concerned" (see footnote 6 above). The use of "land" surely is not limited to agriculture, or starting a fire on your property which might endanger your neighbor. In the Alps the cutting of trees has for centuries been strictly regulated to prevent avalanches from destroying villages. The point has perhaps been somewhat labored but it really says that it is impossible to define the legitimate realm of government by a list of functions. Hayek is mainly concerned about the problem of rules vs. discretion, but even rules require detailed judicial or administrative interpretations which are ex ante not obvious and which may have to be changed with changing circumstances.

[18] I am sure that the idea of my neighbor's welfare being part of my welfare function as long as society is small comes from N. Georgescu-Roegen. But as I have been unable to trace my memory to a specific quotation, I must take responsibility. Of course, my neighbor's welfare may not always be generously conceived. And family twists are also well known. The idea that your neighbor is anyone in need is already clearly present in the New Testament (e.g., Matthew 25:

More important in the present context are the policies pursued in the 1980s and in part before. Deregulation itself is a reasonable aim. But the real sin has been the fiscal policy of the 1980s—and Fiscal Policy writ large was for Schumpeter primarily economic policy—which is incompatible with counteracting the March into Socialism.[19]

On the problem of societal reactions Schumpeter's analysis seems to me essentially correct. Political developments in the course of economic developments seem to have been such that government policies have only accelerated the dangers to capitalist development, regardless of whether they have come from the right or the left. That these dangers have recently come primarily from the political right, which is intent to defend capitalism and despises socialism, is ironic but perhaps not so surprising. The policies do indeed hurt most the people who love them most, and the victories are illusory, as Schumpeter pointed out more than fifty years ago.

This section may read like a partisan attack. It is not meant so. It is meant to continue the arguments and examples Schumpeter gave in his "March into Socialism." As he stated at the end of this last lecture, "I do not pretend to prophecy. I merely recognize facts and point out the tendencies which the facts indicate" (CSD, 424). The facts have continued to point in the same direction.

THE END OF CAPITALISM

The presently visible tendencies, so Schumpeter stated, were moving in the direction of laborism,[20] that is, "that stage in which the labor interest is predominant." That, and not imperialism, was to lead the way to socialism.

31–46) as well as in the Old. From his standpoint, Mises is quite right to consider all religion Socialist.

The interaction between the function and the size of cities is on the economic side discussed by location theory and has become a separate field of urban economics. It is also a major difference that in a developed economy the structure of a city changes with its size while it seems to change but little in LDCs. The problems of urbanization are therefore quite different. In developed countries, big cities are not simply larger small cities. The whole problem of the role government is expected to play changes with the problems to be handled.

[19] It is not possible to enter into a detailed analysis of American economic policies since the New Deal. Personal savings rates have never been very high in the United States in the post-war years. They declined precipitously in the 1980s, and fiscal policy continues to be directed toward stimulating consumption. That the fiscal policies of the 1980s have seriously hampered government to deal with the problems of the 1990s seems to me beyond dispute.

[20] This is explicitly said in a lecture on Capitalism, Socialism and Democracy given by Schumpeter on August 29, 1949 to the Institute of World Affairs in Twin Lakes, CT. The contents of this lecture have been preserved in the form of notes by a student of Schumpeter's, Mr. Peter K. Obglobin, further identified as "1950 Harvard. Ideologies Commission Chairman." Discussants were Arthur Smithies, who deposited the notes in the Schumpeter papers in Harvard University, and William Yandel Elliott, both of Harvard; and Stuart Cole, Yale. Smithies prefaced his gift to Harvard with the words "So far as I know this lecture presents the fullest exposition of [Schumpeter's] ideas on capitalism." Reproduced in Schumpeter (1993), 249–54.

The laborist society has these characteristic features: (1) labor market control, (2) capital market control (cheap money), (3) public finance has a purpose in the budgets of laborist states. Greater sums are spent for food subsidies than for defense, and the working class has the luxury of services which include the famous gratis wigs of England. . . . (Schumpeter 1993, 251)

[T]he dominant interest (i.e. the labor class) *doesn't want* eternal economic progress. Take the dictum of Keynes, "in the long run, we shall all be dead"—if you accept this, why build for the future? . . . The laborist world would not have the phenomenon of economic progress, but it would be perfectly workable for the rest. Objective problems are one thing, attitudes toward them are another; if you don't want progress, you don't want it. The laborist society has a ruling group, too, and their attitudes are important. Democracy, however, will be muzzled in the process. (ibid., 252)

There would, of course, be ups and downs in the movements, felt to be setbacks, since all reality moved in wavelike patterns. But the long-term political pattern would be in favor of the working classes and their interests essentially would be in a larger present share of the social product and a smaller regard for the future. Schumpeter always reverts to this as the true conflict.

Schumpeter gave a set of lectures in Mexico City in June 1948 on "Wage and Tax Policy in Transitional States of Society" of which an outline exists.[21] It is in some respects a skeleton of the arguments advanced in CSD.

Schumpeter starts with an all-encompassing concept: the civilization of an age.[22] An intact society is one in which all aspects fit together. Each society may have a class structure, but the preeminence of a dominating class and its values is generally accepted. When society is whole, all domestic and foreign policies fit together. But "[i]t happens frequently that the class structure of society and its civilization or different parts of a nation's civilization cease to correspond to each other" (Swedberg 1991a, 429). This is a transitional society.

Schumpeter does not say so—possibly because he thought it self-evident— that *intact* societies *cannot* be the rule in a world whose chief characteristics are both spontaneous self-organization—the equilibrating and adaptive tendencies—and chaotic evolution. Schumpeter's sense of history and of the time it takes for God's mills to grind involve a long horizon—fifty or one hundred years—before conditions will have turned Socialist *if* they ever do so. For in the course of decades many unforeseen and unforeseeable events might occur to deflect the course of history from its presently visible course. The normal state must be transitional; and

---

[21] Reprinted in Swedberg (1991a), 429—37.

[22] German usage distinguishes between "Zivilisation" and "Kultur," the former being restricted to the more "worldly," the latter to the more "spiritual, higher" aspects of reality. No such distinction is made in English, and for Schumpeter it certainly would make no sense. He did consider Shakespeare part of the civilization of capitalism.

The fact to which I want to call attention particularly is that in such a state policies are no longer consistent with each other and with the existing economic conditions. They cannot be any longer described by such general principles as laissez-faire or socialism. And individual policies do not any longer produce the effects which they would produce in a pure or intact system. (ibid., 430)

The crucial economic policies relate to wages and taxes which are economically and politically closely related. Yet the policies tend to make the working of the capitalist system difficult if not impossible, while at the same time sticking to the institutional framework of the capitalist economy. "[P]olitically, policies that aim at high wages and high taxes go together; but economically they conflict with each other because with certain exceptions, it is generally true that high wages are more easy to obtain with low taxation and high taxes with low wages" (ibid., 431).

In a dictatorship, full employment is possible.[23] Not so in a free society where workers may accept or reject employment at a given rate (Swedberg 1991a, 436). Schumpeter could have added the German example where employers cannot refuse Government orders to employ workers at a given rate whether the workers can be employed profitably or not, as was the case under pre-war Hitler economics or in Socialist countries. "What is really meant by a full employment policy is a policy which regulates government expenditures in such a way as to prevent mass unemployment beyond given limits" (ibid.). All of which leads to "the fundamental question" of the present versus the future.

In Part 6, Schumpeter's analysis of the Weimar Republic will be discussed further. Here it is perhaps useful to stress the close interdependence of monetary, fiscal, and wage policies. In the present context I quote just one sentence from Schumpeter's "Limits of Wage Policy" which related to the proposed solution of the dilemma raised by transient societies: "It must *and it will* sooner or later come to this, that employers and employees will sit down together in order then to consult *uno actu about wages, capital formation and tax burden.*"[24]

The historical period embodying the liberal spirit in the Hayekian-European sense was the Gladstone era. In the Mexican lectures Schumpeter devoted one page to it, but in his *History of Economic Analysis*, he treated it in greater detail.

The greatest feature of Gladstonian finance—the feature that it shares with and that may be said to define all "great finance"—was that it expressed with ideal adequacy both the whole civilization and the needs of the time, *ex visu* of the

[23] James (1986) considers achievement of full employment the *only* economic achievement of Hitlerism, and it certainly was *not* achieved by market methods but by direct interventions enforced by terrorist threats.

[24] Schumpeter, "Grenzen der Lohnpolitik," originally *Der Deutsche Volkswirt* vol. 3 (1928–29), 847–51. Reprinted in Schumpeter (1985); quotation on p. 196; my translation, italics in original.

conditions of the country to which it was to apply, or to put it slightly differently, that it translated a social, political, and economic vision, which was comprehensive as well as historically correct, into the clauses of a set of co-ordinated fiscal measures.[25]

To reflect the liberal view, "the most important thing was to remove fiscal obstruction to private activity" (*History*, 403). This meant reducing the functions of government and keeping those maintained, such as military expenditures, as small as possible.[26] Schumpeter always insisted that capitalism was inherently pacific.

Germans in particular always ridiculed this "Night Watchman State" whose only function seemed to be to guarantee law and order for the petit bourgeois. Experience in LDCs shows that in the presence of what Myrdal has called the "soft State," even this "minimalist" State was impossible to achieve.[27] In any case it was the ideal policy for the England of 1853 and *not a matter "of timeless general principles"* (*History*, 404; italics added).

The third principle was to raise revenue by taxes which distorted businessmen's behavior as little as possible, and there had to be a balanced budget, or even a surplus (ibid., 405). The "automatic gold standard also belonged to this syndrome, and there should be only "the regulatory power of the central bank [as] . . . a 'lender of last resort' " (ibid.).

In full centralist socialism—here defined as "(a) all physical means of production are public property; and (b) production and distribution are controlled by a single authority" (Swedberg 1991a, 432–33)—consistent policies are also possible. Russia explicitly does not qualify as a Socialist state. In fact, there exists no such state, so the discussion remains hypothetical, "utopian" in Spiethoff's terminology.

Schumpeter distinguishes two Socialist cases. It is centrally decided how much every citizen must work and what kind of work he is to do, and how much of the total product is to be available for consumption and how much for investment. In such a case, neither wage nor tax policy exist.

[25] Schumpeter (*History* 1954), 403. Some aspects of the ideas of how a society fits together and develops are expanded in *The Crisis of the Tax State*, to be further discussed in chapter 11. And of course, Schumpeter's own activities as minister of finance reflect his sensitivity both to all aspects of society and to the specific historical situation. (See chapters 14–17.)

[26] The inconsistency of the Reagan concept of economics was that it believed in removing obstacles to private enterprise while simultaneously maximizing military expenditures. That it may have been forced into this inconsistency only strengthens Schumpeter's analysis.

[27] I have always thought that LDCs' ambitions for socialism were absurd. No one has been able to construct a picture of the whole public sector in Nigeria even in 1963, shortly after the English left. Since then matters have deteriorated. Budgets now hardly exist even where they did in colonial times. No one really knows what goes on in the public sector, let alone in the economy. The idea that, because markets are very imperfect, planning becomes necessary is the opposite of the truth. Which is why I called my book *Planning without Facts* (Harvard University Press, 1966). But if a viable budget can be established, much would be gained and the government in fact could have a very beneficial influence on development. The budget is the most important planning, i.e., economic policy, instrument.

But there is a second case, where citizens get a money income and are free to choose, and the citizens decide how much to save, which the Ministry will then invest (ibid., 433). This simply would reproduce a capitalist society and there would be the same "problems of wage, interest and tax policy of capitalist society" (p. 434).

Well, not quite, if it is remembered how Schumpeter actually defines socialism in CSD: preferences are developed in a truly "social" manner. Schumpeter expresses this here by requiring that "the large majority of the people" accept it (ibid., 434). And, of course, the end result would thus be different from one based on individual preferences as has been developed before.

Transitional societies accept budgetary deficits as a matter of principle, a maximum of public services, and redistribution of wealth "particularly . . . by means of income and inheritance taxes" (ibid., 434). In particular, wages and hours of work are neither fixed nor free, nor completely left to private contract, but flexible within limits." Wage rates and hours become political questions" (ibid., 435).

Since Schumpeter dealt with the then current situations resulting from the Second World War, specifically with England, I feel justified to consider American policies of the 1980s in the context of Schumpeter's analysis of transitional societies. He had not liked English policies in the 1920s and saw in the post–Second World War policies no reason to change his analysis of the March into Socialism.

He also was very unhappy with New Deal policies, which will be recounted in the last part of this book. The basic unhappiness had been that New Deal policies changed from the careful fiscal policies of the preceding administration to loose fiscal policies which would become irreversible.

A brief speculation about Schumpeter's views of the policies of the 1980s seems justifiable. He certainly would sympathize with the aim of reducing the size of government. He certainly would question the manner in which otherwise defensible, even necessary, policies were actually translated into reality. But given his views of the irreversibility of historic developments, he would consider the proposed aims of reducing the size of government hankering after a lost paradise. Being a Tory rather than a Whig, he would regretfully accept the inconsistencies that increasingly manifest themselves in the American situation. Yet policies to restore the past could only cause damage and disillusionment. He had said so explicitly in his criticism of German Weimar fiscal policy.

He would point to fluctuating exchanges as a permanent system as a symptom of the extent to which capitalism had already strayed from its true nature. After all, he considered England's abandonment of the gold standard in 1931 a more significant portent of what he later described as the "March into Socialism" than anything that happened in Russia.

Schumpeter actually discusses two possible scenarios for the transition to socialism (CSD, chapter 19). To start with, Schumpeter summarizes what he has said before: "Most of the argument . . . may be summed up in the Marxian proposition that the economic process tends to socialize *itself*—and also the human soul. By this we mean that the technological, organizational, commercial, administrative and psychological prerequisites of socialism tend to be fulfilled more and more" (CSD, 219; italics in original).

There is one more point to remember: the purely economic aspects of a capitalist society are inherently viable. Therefore, even "in the limiting case . . . the capitalist order would not of itself turn into a socialist order; such a final step, the official adoption of socialism as the community's law of life, would still have to be taken, say, in the form of a constitutional amendment" (CSD, 220).

Evidently, since history involves discontinuous small steps which, seen at a distance, look like a continuum, all manner of intermediate states are conceivable. Schumpeter discusses only two such states: "Socialization in a State of Maturity" (CSD, 221) and "Socialization in a State of Immaturity" (ibid., 223).

When the time is ripe, there need be no revolution. There will be competent bureaucracies in government and business "which are in the habit of accepting orders from the legal authority whatever it is and who are not very partial to capitalist interests anyway" (CSD, 221). If farmers are left alone this would even get political support for socialization "for nobody hates large-scale industry . . . as the farmer does" (ibid.).[28] The interests of capitalists would be quantitatively of minor importance, be just stock and bond holders who could be easily pacified by being paid interest. The structure of demand would not change very much "unless egalitarian ideas assert themselves much more strongly than I have assumed" (ibid., 223). Some transfers of labor might cause trouble, such as of lawyers who in a Socialist economy would lose many functions, but on the whole nothing much would have to change. There would be continued rationalization of industries into more efficient larger units. "Of socialism of this type it may without absurdity be expected that it would in time realize all the possibilities of superior performance inherent in the blue print" (ibid.).

It should be stressed that Schumpeter does not lay out a time table for when this state of affairs will be reached. There are countries which have approximated the preconditions for successful socialization and possibly even reached it: Sweden (which claims it) and Switzerland (which pictures itself as the epitome of capitalism, perhaps Japan).[29] All have reached levels of efficiency, productivity and, on the level of daily life, standards which would

[28] Schumpeter evidently did not foresee the speed with which the relative importance of the farming sector would decline and itself become a large-scale industrial business, and with it lose its political clout. The family farm still exists, but numerically it has declined and has itself become rather large scale. The Great Depression slogan "Five acres and independence" would hardly be a viable alternative today. Similar developments are also observed with mom-and-pop stores and the growth of supermarkets and shopping malls. But not having foreseen this does not invalidate the arguments; on the contrary, by eliminating even these last vestiges of private enterprise they strengthen the conclusions.

[29] As J. K. Galbraith put it: The Swiss have an infinite capacity to do the socialist thing and call it Capitalist. I cannot give the precise reference or guarantee the precise quotation, however. And there has been a political reaction in Sweden—out of boredom?

satisfy the proverbial man on the street. But both, particularly Sweden, show signs of tiredness of it all, feelings of discomfort and of being oppressed as complaints about the tax burden show. This suggests that the "socialization of the soul" may be the real obstacle to reach a Socialist state of affairs in a peaceful manner. Envy even about small income differences are only symptoms. No one has, as far as I know, made the calculation, but I should not be surprised if personal income after taxes is higher in Sweden than it would be if taxes were lowered and Swedes had to pay for health, education, and housing out of that income. Swedish industry has achieved international competitiveness, so this problem can also evidently be solved even if more than half the GNP goes through the public sector. The "high" tax burden may well be just a front for the feeling of reduced personal freedom.

Events in Eastern Europe and the former Soviet Union also suggest that the assertion, heard particularly in LDCs, that people do not really care about freedom if they are hungry or that democracy is a luxury of the rich, cannot be true. In any case, neither Stalin nor Hitler ever really succeeded in socializing man, though both countries had comparatively favorable conditions for success: in the case of the Soviet Union, the historical absence of widespread individualism, in Germany the approximate "ethnic" homogeneity and high level of economic development. But in both cases, these preconditions were historically really quite inadequate. There were considerable developments in pre–First World War Tsarist Russia toward greater liberalism, and in the last free election in 1932, Hitler lost two million votes, and even in the first controlled one in 1933 got a smaller percentage of the vote than the Communists in Italy got after World War II! Both tried to force a pace on history which reality did not warrant.

In fact, a case could be made that the the failure of the Soviet Union proved that Marx was right, that you could not arbitrarily skip a stage of development, and that having created successfully not Soviet man but rather a large educated work force, the preconditions for successful capitalist development were created!

Schumpeter's prognosis for premature socialization is less happy, even if absurd attempts (like in Germany in 1918–1919) are avoided.[30] The trouble is that there will still be too many small and medium sized firms and "the development of big business . . . [has] not gone far enough to make it safe and easy to apply our method of socialization" (CSD, 224). "Souls [are] still more unprepared than things" (ibid.).

This is the scenario Schumpeter develops for this case:

Suppose . . . that the Revolutionary People . . . have conquered the central office of the government, the non-socialist parties, the non-socialist press, etc. and installed their men. The personnel of these offices as well as the personnel of the

---

[30] Schumpeter thought there was in 1919 a brief moment when socialism might have had general support in Austria, but the moment passed quickly. Schumpeter's account of the German Socialization Commission (see chapter 13) describes it essentially as a rearguard action against ideas of premature socialization (CSD, 300).

industrial and commercial concerns is partly goaded into—*ex hypothesi*—unwilling cooperation and partly replaced by the labor leaders and by the intellectuals who rush from the café to these offices. To the new central board we shall concede two things: a red army strong enough to quell open resistance and to repress excesses—wild socialization in particular—by firing impartially to right and left, and sense enough to leave peasants or farmers alone. (CSD, 225–26)

Allowing for the slight lapse of referring to the café which in Germany, unlike in Vienna, played no significant social role, this is a realistic description of the Nazi take-over in 1933. In 1932, when the Nazis became the largest party in Prussia, Göring, in keeping with parliamentary rules, took over as president of the Prussian parliament, immediately and deliberately creating havoc. No sooner had Hindenburg died, than the "conservative" coalition partners were eliminated from all power. "Shooting to the right" Hugenberg, the leader of the Conservatives, was quickly dropped as minister of economics; and "shooting to the left" Roehm, the boss of the Brown Shirts (SA) and a "Duz-Freund" of Hitler, together with a very large number of his associates, were murdered by the more elite black shirts (SS).

Since a political takeover by more or less polite methods could not solve the problems of the transition, Schumpeter envisaged a deliberate policy of inflation for two reasons. The first was to break the back of the remaining bourgeois resistance. This correctly foresaw what would happen in Hungary after 1945. It seems at odds with what happened in Hitler Germany. But reality is closer to what Schumpeter envisaged than appearances suggest. Consider the following analysis:

> The first thing which must be done is to bring about inflation. The banks must be seized and combined or coordinated with the treasury, and the board or ministry must create deposits and banknotes using traditional methods as much as possible. I believe inflation to be unavoidable because I have still to meet the socialist who denies that in the case under discussion the socialist revolution would at least temporarily paralyze the economic process or that in consequence the treasury and the financial centers would for the moment be short of ready means. The socialist system of bookkeeping and income units not being as yet in working order, nothing remains except a policy analogous to that of Germany during and after the First World War or that of France during and after the revolution of 1789, notwithstanding the fact that in those cases it was precisely the unwillingness to break with the system of private property and with the methods of commercial society that enforced inflation for so considerable a time; for "the day after the socialist revolution" when nothing would be in shape, this difference does not matter. (CSD, 226)

Hitler was more clever than this. Banks were not nationalized, but the Reichsbank, which had been able to deny the Weimar government financing of deficits,[31] was hardly in a position to do the same with Hitler. With price

---

[31] It was not so much any perverse deflationary ideas which made a "reflationary" policy in Weimar Germany impossible, but the inability to finance expenditures domestically or by foreign loans. On this see the detailed discussion of James (1986).

and wage controls strictly enforced and a detailed allocation of foreign ex-change, the economy was socialized in the sense that it was brought under control of Hitler and his apparatchiks and inflation remained suppressed.

But Schumpeter stresses in addition that "[i]nflation is in itself an excellent means of smoothing certain transitional difficulties and of effecting partial expropriation. As regards the first, it is for instance evident that a drastic increase in money wage rates will for a time avail to ward off possible out-breaks of rage at the fall in real wage rates that, temporarily at least, would have to be imposed" (CSD, 226–27).

This statement is reminiscent of Schumpeter's claim as minister of finance that Vienna, by not trying to eliminate the deficit immediately, at least avoided social unrest "between Budapest and Munich." As far as expropriation by inflation was concerned, Schumpeter through his capital levy tried to limit it to what the war had already caused. The statement just made also explains to some extent his failure to do so.

Regarding the actual socialization, in a transitional society "gradual social-ization *within the framework of capitalism* is not only possible but even the most obvious thing to expect" (CSD, 227; italics in original). But that would be difficult, because it would be impossible to leave smaller industries alone. They would cease to work properly because the system would not allow them to do so—this is quite different with socialization in a mature state. The conclusion, worth quoting in full, is a picture of what happened in Eastern Europe:

> [S]ocialization in any situation immature enough to require revolution not only in the sense of a break in legal continuity but also in the sense of a subsequent reign of terror cannot benefit, either in the short or in the long run anyone except those who engineer it. To work up enthusiasm about it and glorify the courage of risking all that it might entail may be one of the less edifying duties of the professional agitator. But as regards the academic intellectual, the only courage that can possibly reflect any credit on him is the courage to criticize, to caution and to restrain. (CSD, 228)

PART III

Political Activities of the Outsider

or

Coping with Nationalism

The Crisis of the Tax State

NATIONALISM AND RATIONAL EXPECTATIONS

Schumpeter's ambition to be a success in politics can be traced back to around 1916 when the until recently unknown and then secret memoranda were written.[1] Just what Schumpeter thought he could accomplish in 1916 or in 1919 is in retrospect difficult to imagine. He had a clear notion of what had to be done to save not only the Double Monarchy from destruction, or, later, the new republic from inflation and further decay, and he felt that what he wanted to do was also in the interest of the Entente. He believed the First World War was insanity, and he said so.

Schumpeter's sympathy for the Entente, particularly for the British, was well known. So was his distrust of the German Reich. He did not favor the proposed closer economic relationship with the German Reich during the war, in which he saw a danger to the continuing existence of the Double Monarchy. And he opposed the Anschluss in 1919, which was official policy of the very government of which he was a prominent member. In 1916, he wanted a separate peace with the Entente, and in 1919 he even proposed a monetary union with the French.[2] He was, or at least believed himself to be, on good terms with the foreign diplomats in 1919, and the French ambassador is mentioned prominently among the audience of at least some of the speeches he made as minister of finance.

It is perhaps permissible to speculate about Schumpeter's failures in light of the present discussion of rational expectations and the theory of games.

I believe that Schumpeter's analysis of likely long-term developments was correct. Recent developments in Eastern Europe bear out some of his analysis and political aims. His fiscal program would have solved the Austrian problem within the four years he had thought it would take. This is one instance where world history has repeated itself sufficiently to consider this proposition provable even in the absence of deliberate laboratory experiments, which economics cannot, of course, make. (But this is not so different from astronomy, which cannot do so either.)

---

[1] The memoranda have been discovered by Professor Christian Seidl, then of the University of Graz, now of Kiel, and are reprinted in Schumpeter 1985. They will be discussed in chapter 12.

[2] "Bauer told me that Schumpeter, minister of finance, had proposed to Allizé [the French Ambassador to Vienna]: 'Austria would renounce the Anschluss, a monetary union should be established between Austria and France; South Tyrol should not be separated from Austria.'" Richard Schüller, *Memoirs*, typewritten, p. 28; in English. In the Haus-, Hof- u. Staatsarchiv, Vienna. I owe this reference to Dr. Gertrud Enderle-Burcel.

The problem was not economic analysis but the assumption that both the Austro-Hungarians in 1916 and the Entente in 1919 would have the same long-term horizon he had. The 1916 peace offensive might have been doomed anyway. More important, the central powers' successes on the Eastern front leading to the collapse of the Tsarist empire—aided by Lenin's arrival in Russia by sealed train—seemed to make peace less urgent.

In 1919, on the other hand, Schumpeter remained convinced that the Austrian problem could be solved if only the world would remain sensible and see its interest in a stable peace decades ahead. He was a free trader as long as possible, arguing that what nowadays is called inward-looking economic policies made no sense not only for rump-Austria but also for the richest and industrially most advanced successor state, Czechoslovakia: 10 million people were just not a sufficient base for reasonable economic development.

Schumpeter's desire to preserve Vienna as the financial center of the successor states was thus much more than the desire to help German-Austria, which was the official name of the new republic until the Entente forbade it. His statement that it made no difference whether the coal Austria needed was located in German-Austria or Czechoslovakia made perfectly good sense when there was free trade and a common currency or at least convertible currencies, though it drew an outraged response from Renner as hurting his efforts in Paris to modify the peace conditions. So was Schumpeter's reluctance to back the creation of a new Austrian central bank as a local successor to the old Austro-Hungarian bank until the basic economic problems were solved.[3]

It was equally rational to expect the Treaty of St. Germain to provide conditions for the economic survival of the new republic. When it did not, Schumpeter pronounced the peace conditions a death sentence on German-Austria—but tried to carry on anyway.

Schumpeter may thus be faulted on misjudging the short-term world political situation, but not that his arguments were illogical. When it became obvious that the basic facts had changed, Schumpeter changed his policy recommendations. There may be, but need not be, an inconsistency between two apparently contradictory policy pronouncements. All of his switches in policy positions, which will be related further on, can be explained in this manner. (I believe this is also true for Keynes.)

This, however, raises the question of Schumpeter's sense of historical developments. On the one hand, all of Schumpeter's policy positions rest on his analysis of what makes an economy a *developing* economy. On the purely analytical level I believe his analysis to be unexceptionable: the economy is in constant flux, there is a constant change of production functions which transforms the economy to ever higher levels of productivity and living. The economic process also involves sociological and social changes which may also

---

[3] Renner's cable from Paris to Vienna in response to Schumpeter's speeches is reprinted in Schumpeter (1993).

change fundamentally the individual participants' preference functions. In the short run, attention to current prices of goods and factors is important but pure equilibrium theory sooner or later loses its explanatory value.

From the policy point of view, two matters become important: to safeguard the resources needed for development, and to safeguard a social and political environment which allows growth. Neither of these preconditions is uniquely determined a priori or even at the particular moment, when decisions have to be made. The second precondition is almost entirely subject to political judgment. For Schumpeter it was clear that it is a legitimate function of the State to take care of the latter, and Schumpeter has not without reason been considered one of the fathers of the so-called social market economy.

But there are further problems. For analytical purposes it suffices to say that development entails changes in the individuals' preference functions. From a policy standpoint, however, it is necessary to be more specific. There, judgments may legitimately differ and some people may have better political feel about what is likely to happen in the near and medium term than others. Ultimately, all judgments about the future are made with a great amount of hope, and being right involves a great deal of luck.

It is important to make sure that present decisions do not foreclose better decisions in the future. This was one of Schumpeter's basic objections to much Keynesian policy. It certainly would be his objection to present supply-side economics. Immediate successes are bought at the cost of future troubles. The long-run tendencies would still come through, but only after a period of quite unnecessary suffering.

The dissolution of the British and French empires at the end of the Second World War was foreseen, though it was not foreseen that the French would devolve their empire in Africa more quickly than the British.[4] The rapid dissolution of the Soviet empire is the expected result of the Kennan policy of containment decades ago, and of Willie Brandt's Ost Politik, the Carter policy of human rights, all of which was made believable by a strong defense policy. But neither the timing nor the suddenness with which events occurred was or could be foreseen, nor that it would also reflect Russian desires to get rid of their costly empire as the British had desired.[5]

The timetable is only one problem. What I believe to be more immediately important is the whole problem of rationality in decision making. Schumpe-

---

[4] An argument can, however, be made that the French devolvement was initially more apparent than real.

[5] I have always thought, and only half jokingly, that anticolonialism was a British invention when it became apparent that colonialism just did not pay any more. In the 1920s there was already a heated debate in Great Britain that too much was invested abroad and not enough at home. Of course, the fundamental historic tide is the tide of nationalism, which is now gripping the Soviet Empire and which also has affected internal Russian developments. The really frightening aspect of the present changes to me is the dissolution of the Soviet Union itself, which reminds one of what happened in the Austro-Hungarian Monarchy (although the Russian Republic is still a very big chunk of the Russian Empire, while German-Austria was a small minority). But it is good to remember that history never, or almost never, repeats itself precisely.

ter wanted peace but the Entente wanted victory and, when victory was within grasp, revenge. Depending on the length of the time horizon there need not be an inconsistency. But in the medium run there is. Thus, Schumpeter expected quite different reactions from the French than were actually forthcoming, and he probably underestimated the virulence of Italian hatred. He did not expect a death sentence on Austria. Keynes after all also protested in writing the Treaty of Versailles as mischievous and as causing a lot of trouble without doing any good!

Schumpeter's assumptions about the reasonableness of the reactions on the side of the Entente or the successor states turned out to be quite unrealistic. The Entente or the Czechs had quite a different set of—from their standpoint equally "rational"—reactions. If two negotiating parties play by different rules and have radically different aims, it is difficult to see how the short-term outcome can be sensible. This quite aside from the fact that "when everyone is foolish, 'tis foolish to be wise."[6]

What seemed to Schumpeter quite rational to expect was seen by others as an incredible optimism, an incredible faith in the possibility of free trade in 1919, or just an incredible pose. There is a "rational" and quite honorable explanation of Schumpeter's behavior and propositions in his political period. His long-run analysis is in fact vindicated by developments after the Second World War, which avoided many pitfalls of the peace settlement after the First World War. Also, the nationality problem which was not settled satisfactorily in Eastern Europe or Asia continues to haunt us.[7] The long-term logic has triumphed over the short-term solutions. Unfortunately, there is no way to get from here to there without going through somewhere between, or going from 1989 to 2000 without going through many tomorrows.

It seems essential to start this discussion with Schumpeter's analysis of the rise of the modern "tax state." This seems essential to do since even now there is so little sensible analysis of what government should and can usefully do.

This will be followed by an account of Schumpeter's "secret" memoranda which are Schumpeter's first documented entry into active politics, if only behind the scenes. This will be followed by his role as a member of the German Coal Socialization Commission, and finally, his policies as minister of finance.

---

[6] I am certain that I did not invent this quote, but I have so far been unable to trace its source.

After this was written, the fifth volume of Samuelson's *Collected Scientific Papers* arrived, from which I take the following quotation about rational expectations: "What I am now asserting is that the whole consensus crowd can be expected to be wrong, and to stay wrong for long periods of time, on what is going to happen to the macro data of the economy. Even if God told me in advance that the crowd was wrong, there is no way to make money in the short run by betting against the crowd and setting it right" (Samuelson 1986, 907).

The quotation is taken from "Evaluating Reaganomics," originally in *Challenge*, November-December 1984. Personally I consider the effect of Reaganomics a major disaster for the future of America.

[7] Some of the nationality problems were brutally solved by the Stalinist policy of expelling Germans by the millions. Yet the dissolution of the Soviet Union has not been sufficient to solve this problem. (This was written before the Bosnian disaster.)

THE EMERGENCE OF THE TAX STATE

Though published after the secret memoranda were written, the *Crisis of the Tax State* (cited hereafter as *Crisis*) will be discussed first.[8] The *Crisis* gives the fundamental analytical ideas about the emergence and proper functions of the modern State on an individualistic-commercial-capitalist basis. It was meant as a scholarly publication, but it is one in which it is unusually easy to see the connection between scholarly analysis and policy application.[9]

The *Crisis* is also an implicit criticism, later made explicit, of views of a capitalist market economy essentially as a stationary system. For the emphasis is on how the tax state *arose* and where it was going.[10]

The *Crisis* is the expanded version of a talk given to the *Wiener Soziologische Gesellschaft* before the collapse of the Monarchy. It addressed itself to the day when the imminent collapse of the Monarchy would occur. It asked the specific question whether the exhaustion of the economy would also involve a collapse of the economic methods to deal with the economic situation.

The discussion is the application of developmental ideas to historic situations. You must understand how things have *become* if you want to understand what they are or where they are going. Economic policy has "up to the turn of the century been motivated primarily by fiscal considerations" (*Crisis*, in Swedberg 1991a, 11). "Fiscal measures have created and destroyed industries" (ibid.), though historians are often inclined to overestimate the influence of the State on the formation of the economy. At no time have economy and budget formed a really uniform "state economy," never has the state been able to create something lasting which the free economy would not have created (Swedberg 1991a, note 3).

Here we also find the dramatic statement which I have been fond of quoting and which seems to have a frightening relevance today: "The spirit of a people, its cultural level, its social structure, the deeds its policy may prepare—all this and more is written in its fiscal history stripped of all phrases" (ibid., 111)

Some saw in the war economy a progress toward a Socialist economy, but "Marx himself . . . would laugh grimly at those of his disciples who welcome

[8] All quotations from the reprint of the English translation in *International Economic Papers*, vol. 4, in Swedberg (1991a), 99–140.

[9] It is also the first warning, later made more explicit, that it is dangerous to draw world-shattering conclusions from the experience of short periods: the war changed much, and catastrophically so for the Double Monarchy, but it spelled no more the end of the Tax State or of capitalism than the Great Depression did later.

[10] See Schumpeter's criticism of Hayek's *Road to Serfdom*: "The author deals with ideas and principles as if they floated in the air. If he had gone into the historical conditions from which the ideas arose which he dislikes so much, he could not have helped discovering that they are the product of the social system which he does like" (Schumpeter 1946, 270). One cannot criticize Schumpeter on such grounds.

the present administrative economy as the dawn of socialism" (ibid., 130). There was in 1918 the general notion that the existing situation was beyond the existing means to remedy and required a radical new ordering.

Schumpeter disagreed firmly. He started with a discussion of how the prewar State itself had arisen out of its feudal predecessor. The *Crisis*, being of scholarly intent, then proceeded to analyze the actual situation of 1918, to estimate quantitatively the budgetary problems to be faced—the quantification, too, was part of Schumpeter's general methodology which was always based on facts—and to outline steps that could deal effectively with the problems. It concluded that the "tax state" was perfectly capable of putting the exhausted economy back on its feet. Obviously, the plan of action outlined in the *Crisis* is the same that the future minister of finance would propose and whose centerpiece was the great capital levy, clearly conceived not as a budgetary but as a monetary measure of currency reform and as an essential part of a wider program.

It may be good to be clear about one of Schumpeter's central methodological points: a term may be unchanged for centuries while its contents changes drastically. And a concept gets its meaning from the purpose it is to serve. Legal concepts have meaning only in a legal context. Economic concepts belong to an economic way of analysis. The example offered for the latter was the distinction between owners and creditors, which is not as sharp economically as it is legally. The concept of investments in Communist and capitalist surroundings means different things and even carries entirely different meanings for an individual and for the economy as a whole.

Thus, for Schumpeter the State as the term is understood today did not exist in medieval days. There were bundles of rights and duties for the king or the nobility or even the cities and burghers; there were even "taxes," but not taxes that had to be paid whether you agreed to them or not. Schumpeter's examples all deal with the Holy Roman Empire, specifically the lands of the Hapsburgs, but developments were not too different elsewhere. Sometimes the barons got the upper hand as in England, or the king as in France, both of which eventually became nation states, but sometimes the nobility could defy the emperor sufficiently to become virtually independent sovereigns as in Germany.

The issue here is that in all cases needs arose for which the existing system could not supply the means. In the German case, there was the threat of the Turkish conquests (which had last reached the gates of Vienna in 1683 and which had gobbled up all of Hungary) which simply could not be met with the traditional sources available to the affected kings and princes.

The mercenary army was also an expression of this process and so were the fiscal needs thereby created. These in turn became the driving forces for further development. Around A.D. 1500 the normal income of the electorate of Cologne was, for example, 110,000 Rhenish guilders, that of Mayence 80,000, that of Treves 60,000, and that of Brandenburg 40,000. The house of Hapsburg towered over them with 300,000 guilders received from its hereditary Austrian territories alone. But even this sum would have paid for only 6,000 foot soldiers or 2,500 "armored horses" during a year. And with these 6,000 foot soldiers or 2,500 knights the prince would have been free to oppose the 250,000 Turks whom the Sublime Porte could have sent into the field at any time. Here we have with the clarity of a textbook example what we mean by the crisis of the fiscal *system*: obvious, ineluctable, continuous failure due to unalterable social change. (ibid., 106; italics in original)

The point is simply that

[T]here is nothing which *could* not be a "general" or "public" affair, once the state exists; and nothing which *must* fall within the "public" or "state" sphere in the sense that we could not otherwise speak of the state. As long as the state does not exist as a separate and real power, the distinction of public and private law has simply no meaning. The statement that during the middle ages public law was shot through with aspects of private law or that there existed only private law is as illegitimate a projection of *our* modes of thought into the past as is the opposite assertion. The concept of the state is inapplicable to the circumstances then existing, but not in the sense that what we see today within the sphere of the state was absent and that only the private sphere remained: instead the organizational forms of that time combined both what we nowadays call the public and the private sphere in one essentially different unity. (ibid., 103–4; italics in original)

In other words, "no border exists [between the private and the public spheres] unless one is content to say that "public is whatever is considered 'public' at a particular time. . . . [i]t is hopeless to . . . define the state by means of certain necessary public functions. . . . In particular the 'common purpose' is not the same as the "purpose of the state" (134, note 10).

Thus, the nature of the tax state is that there are distinct public and private spheres though, to repeat, the borders between the two are neither sharp nor unchanging. After all, as Max Weber had pointed out, at a time when armies were for hire, the grain supply of a city was "socialized." The same idea is already found in Schumpeter's pre–First World War article on *Social Value* and is at the heart of Schumpeter's ideas of the coming of socialism. Neither precapitalist feudalism nor postcapitalist socialism makes this clear distinction between what is private and what is public. The difference is that there has been much economic development in the intervening centuries.

If socialism truly became a reality,[11] the distinction would once again vanish and the state would indeed "wither away," a scientific statement with a

---

[11] Schumpeter made it quite clear that he did not consider Soviet Russia true socialism. (Also see *Crisis*, 117–18.) Indeed, he would argue that Lenin stood Marx on his head as Marx had stood Hegel on his head. For Marx, ideology is a superstructure on the basis of productive relationships. Lenin evidently believed that he could make productive organizations the superstructure of ideology, an idea Schumpeter considered absurd. Also, Russian communism actually delayed the day when socialism might become feasible, as did in Schumpeter's view the Great Depression.

specific content which would, of course, still allow the existence of criminal law or the private possession of toothbrushes, etc. Socialism is, after all, not identical with anarchy.

Once the modern state has arisen from fiscal needs, it soon "turns into something the nature of which can no longer be understood merely from the fiscal standpoint, and for which the finances become a serving tool. If the finances have created and partly formed the modern state, so now the state on its part forms them and enlarges them—deep into the flesh of the private economy" (ibid., 110–11).

Given the origin and methods of the "tax state" it has definite limits which, however, are "not conceptually definable limits of its field of social action but limits of its fiscal potential" (ibid., 111). In an essentially individualistic society, the state remains

> [P]eripheral, something alien to the proper purpose of the private economy, even something hostile, in any case something derived.
>
> Here we have arrived at the fact which can become the leading principle for the theoretical understanding of the economic capacity of the tax state. In the bourgeois society . . . the state lives as an economic parasite. It can withdraw from the private economy only as much as is consistent with the continued existence of this individual interest in every particular socio-psychological situation. In other words, the tax state must not demand from the people so much that they lose financial interest in production or at any rate cease to use their best energies for it. (ibid., 112)

Again, this limit may vary widely with historic circumstances, but it exists nevertheless.

This is the context in which Schumpeter explains the general effect of taxes, starting with indirect taxes. There is a brief statement of what nowadays is called the "Laffer curve" which even in Schumpeter's days was considered old hat. Unlike Laffer, Schumpeter, while agreeing that such a limit undoubtedly existed beyond which no power could increase tax revenues, nevertheless did not consider this particularly interesting. He pointed to two "great practical difficulties" in defining these limits. The first is that "every significant indirect tax enforces technical and commercial changes in the productive apparatus, the consequences of which are most difficult to follow" (ibid., 112–13). This involves more than the usual discussion of tax shifting, of precisely who bears the taxes; it refers to the indirect effects on taxable capacity itself. But, second, "the situation in which the tax was imposed does not remain unchanged in other respects" (ibid., 113).

As for direct taxes, the situation differs with the specific tax base. Entrepreneurial profits are "the premium which capitalism attaches to innovation" (ibid.). "Here the limits of taxation are reached fairly quickly because it would soon damage or even destroy the tax object" (ibid., 114).

Not so for monopoly profit, such as of a cartel, or ground rent, or windfall profits. (Inheritance taxes do not quite fall into this category—and this fact later becomes an issue between Otto Bauer and Schumpeter in the socialization policy of the German-Austrian government.) Though difficult to identify in practice, such taxes would be the ideal tax objects.

On the other hand, taxes on interest and wages (including management income other than entrepreneurial profits) meet such limits. The theoretical points made are that such taxes have two contradictory effects. On the one hand, such taxes tend to lower production because they tend to raise cost. On the other hand, they might raise savings and worker efforts (but do not necessarily do so).

For purposes of the discussion in the *Crisis*, which is after all not a technical treatise on taxation, "what matters to us is that the possible tax yield is limited not only by the size of the taxable object less the subsistence minimum of the taxable subject but also by the nature of the driving forces of the free economy" (ibid., 115).

Of course, the State need not limit itself to taxation and may become an entrepreneur itself within the world of capitalism, (ibid., 116) but here:

> The decisive criterion is whether, apart from any monopoly position which it might secure for itself, the state does or does not continue to work within the framework of a free economy whose data and methods it has to accept in its own enterprises. If it does and thus works in a capitalistic spirit towards as high a money profit as possible, then its possible profits are limited by the laws of capitalistic production. And these limits are narrower than the layman believes. (ibid.)

This is akin to Eucken's very similar statement that it is not the size of the public sector that matters but how it behaves.

These are the true fiscal limits of the tax state and not the rather trite limits of the Laffer curve.

> If the will of the people demands higher and higher public expenditures, if more and more means are used for purposes for which private individuals have not produced them, if more and more power stands behind this will, and if finally all parts of the people are gripped by entirely new ideas about private property and the forms of life—then the tax state will have run its course and society will have to depend on other motive forces for its economy than self-interest. This limit, and with it the crisis which the tax state could not survive, can certainly be reached. Without doubt, the tax state can collapse. (ibid.)

Thus, the *systemic* limits to the tax state, that is, capitalism, come from social expenditures. Of course, the tax state could break down for non-systemic reasons. The real threat in 1918 was war expenditures. Capitalism is inherently pacific and not imperialist. This contrasts as much with Marxist and particularly Leninist and Trotskist doctrine as his view of the nature and eventual end of the development process. For Schumpeter, the last phase of capitalism was laborism, not imperialism. Schumpeter was speaking then of Austria, not even of Austria-Hungary. But even in the Austria of 1918 the tax state need *not* collapse.

This is the immediate background for the analysis of what needs to be done to meet the problems of the imminent collapse of the Monarchy. Schumpeter is quite explicit: the tax state *can* successfully meet all challenges of the postwar world even in Austria, the worst of all possible cases—Russia being a special case. "If [*Austria's*] tax state can stand the test, the others can do so a fortiori" (ibid., 118).

Schumpeter clearly distinguishes between the *monetary* problem and the real problem of reconstruction. The *monetary* problem is really very simple—logically simple, that is, not politically simple. "What is needed is simply an adjustment of money values which would return them to harmony with the world of goods, that is to say, a large-scale writing-down of book values" (ibid., 119).

The fact that military service was the only payment in kind to finance the war while otherwise it was financed "as an enterprise through the purchase of goods and credit operations" (ibid.) guarantees that the problem is soluble.

The really difficult problems arise with reconstruction, which requires real goods. The "real" problem is universal and not a problem of the tax state alone. The solution of the monetary problem is a characteristic tax state problem.

In order to answer the original question of whether the tax state can handle the problems of the postwar world, Schumpeter attempts a rough quantification of the budgetary problem as it will present itself after the end of the war "when the murderous insanity that devastates Europe will end" (ibid.). Obviously no precise estimate can be expected. Schumpeter estimates the capitalized value of the cost of demobilization, payments for wounded veterans, etc., at a minimum of K100 billion with an assumed interest rate of 5 percent. Adding necessary civil service salary increases, necessary subsidies and the rest, he arrived at a minimum estimate for government expenditures of K15 billion (compared to K25 billion of the last war budget). Assuming K5 billion tax revenues, this leaves a prospective deficit of K10 billion.

How to cover this deficit? Schumpeter rejects further inflation as a solution. There is a way out via restoring both the fiscal and the monetary order (ibid., 122). Schumpeter mentions first a capital levy so large that it would actually lead to a substantial decline in prices, avoid the need to raise civil service salaries, etc. In such a case a budget of K6—7 billion might be sufficient.

Schumpeter considered this "mode of saving the situation . . . correct in principle" (ibid.) but not politically feasible. It would require "a government on the broadest political base" and a man with the "brilliance of will power and words that nations trust" (ibid., 123), a statement which has led to speculation of whether Schumpeter thought himself to be that man.[12] The interesting thing is that this solution was in fact more or less the solution of the German currency reform of 1949 which simply wiped out the war debt and led to a new beginning. It is perhaps also relevant to note that this radical

---

[12] Since Schumpeter considered this solution not feasible, he evidently did not think of himself as brilliant enough. This is one more example where a sentence, taken out of context, has misled people to unjustified speculations.

solution would perhaps not have been possible in 1949 without the Allied occupation which could provide the protection for the German authorities to execute such an unpopular and painful step. Nor would it have been feasible without a basic goodwill of the Allied, clearly absent in 1919. It is perhaps also relevant to note that the absence of such a protection has prevented this essential step in the Eastern countries.

Schumpeter is also quite explicit, more so than when he actually proposed the capital levy as minister of finance: "*The levy is not to hand over any goods to the state but only money and claims.* And it is to do so only in order that this money and these claims may be destroyed, not in order to finance expenditures" (ibid., 123. Italics in original; footnote omitted).

This is emphasized so as to distinguish his proposal from a capital levy that would hand over to the state "sources of income such as land, factories etc" (ibid., 124), that would use it as a tax measure or as a means for socialization. Practical difficulties result from the fact "that not all private fortunes contain the same percentage of war bonds" (ibid., 125) but this means only that the success would be incomplete. After the Second World War this fact was in Germany the basis for the equalization-of-burden law. "The operation ends in the furnace" (ibid., 126). Of course, there would still have to be tax increases, even government monopolies (ibid.). But the point is that the capital levy— conceived as a currency reform—would solve the monetary problem.

This leaves reconstruction, and this means that the "free economy"—the quotes are in the original—which "is the complement of the tax state, by its very nature must leave reconstruction to the market no less than normal economic activity" (ibid.).

Is it feasible? Can the "competitive economy at present in our concrete historical situation bring about reconstruction without delay—as compared to the only practical alternative, a far-reaching administrative economy of the state" (ibid.).

Of course, the state must play a big role in the "liquidation of abnormal war developments." "This is, however, self-evident. The decisive question is whether the motive force can remain that of the free economy, or whether the state has to take its place; and whether the *essential* task can be solved only by state intervention. The essential task is "recapitalization" (ibid., 127; italics in original).

The first task is to switch from war to peace time needs, a switch that will "bring home our poverty to its full extent" (ibid.; words in different order), which involves replacement of worn-out machinery and the like, and which "will at first make the shortage of consumer goods even more acute" (ibid.).[13]

It is precisely the competitive economy which can produce reconstruction most effectively, which can provide "the desperate energy" needed.

[13] This was eased in the German currency reform of 1949 by the fact that the currency reform itself brought goods onto the market which had been hoarded during the preceding system of rationing and controlled prices or which moved very inefficiently through the black market, goods which, however, already existed as they did not in 1918.

[T]here has been no difference of opinion on this point among economists of all schools since the middle of the eighteenth century, the socialists not excluded. . . . [t]he organizational form of the competitive economy can reconstruct the economy after the war exactly as it has created the modern economy in its essence . . . and therefore its public counterpart the tax state. . . . It is indeed a highlight of the Communist Manifesto to have demonstrated the effectiveness of this method with such classical precision. The tax state can further the reconstruction most effectively, if in its tax policy it makes allowances for this necessity to save and generally refrains from disturbance. (ibid., 128–29)

The other big task is to organize capital imports. Here, too, the private economy can do much better than the state: "Anyone who has the slightest idea about these things knows that any good bank has better access to foreign credits and will be accommodated much more readily abroad than the state" (ibid., 129).

In 1948 this problem was solved so brilliantly by the Marshall Plan. But it is worth recalling another crisis period in Germany: the Great Depression, when the government could not raise any more foreign loans and the Reichsbahn asked the government *not* to guarantee its foreign loans because such a guarantee would make raising the loans abroad *more* difficult!

This general analysis underlies Schumpeter's proposals as minister of finance where, of course, they are also fleshed out to deal with the existing economic and political situation. I will deal with this in a later chapter and also with the reasons for the failure, inevitable in light of the fact that all preconditions for success abroad and at home were absent. But I must first deal with the first known Schumpeterian foray into actual politics as distinct from scholarly policy analysis. This leads us back to 1916.

Political Activities behind the Scenes

The Historical Background

Schumpeter's first documented activity dates from the beginning of 1916 in letters to Count Harrach and to Professor Heinrich Lammasch, Schumpeter's revered teacher and friend.[1] Lammasch (1853–1920) was

[S]ince 1899 member of the Permanent International Court of Justice in The Hague . . . in 1899, Emperor Franz Joseph had appointed Lammasch to the House of Lords [Herrenhaus]; Archduke and Heir-Apparent Franz Ferdinand and his military office . . . had time and again requested Lammasch's presence for consultations. In a memorandum of November 1912 Lammasch warned Franz Ferdinand against interfering in the Balkan wars, and as late as July 28, 1914, in an article in the "Neues Wiener Tagblatt," he suggested to limit the punitive action against Serbia after the assassination of the Heir-Apparent— perhaps to the occupation of Belgrade as a mortgage. Lammasch was by no means a Utopian pacifist . . . but he loved peace and considered the war . . . a misfortune for the Danube Monarchy and for Europe.[2]

Verosta states that Schumpeter was in constant contact with Lammasch by letter and personal meetings. The here relevant correspondence begins in 1915 when the German Mitteleuropa plans started. *Mitteleuropa* was a book by the German liberal pastor and Member of the Reichstag Friedrich Naumann. It certainly did not have the overtones and ulterior motives for which it was soon abused.[3]

Schumpeter had strong reservations about Mitteleuropa, whereas Gustav Stolper voiced strong support. But in fact the two writers (who were to become friends) were not all that far apart. Schumpeter's memoranda are entirely political with economic considerations hardly touched on explicitly. Such as they were they had a general free trade bias.

Gustav Stolper's book, on the other hand, is strictly economic. Where

---

[1] The three known memoranda are reprinted in Schumpeter (1985). This section relies for historical background of the memoranda on Verosta (1978), 373–404; Gustav Stolper (1918); Alois Brussati (1967), 127–42. The letters to Count Harrach are reprinted in Schumpeter (1992).

It is relevant to note that the introduction to the first edition of Gustav Stolper's book is dated January 1917, and to the second and third editions November 1917, both dates before America declared war on Austria-Hungary on December 7, 1917. Stolper could therefore assume that the Double Monarchy was at peace with the United States.

[2] Verosta (1978); my translation.

[3] The first part of this section is based on the important article of Verosta (1978); Gustav Stolper (1918); and on the Introduction to Schumpeter (1985).

Schumpeter's economic aim, mostly implicit, is to restore a worldwide economy and to prevent the establishment of trading blocs, Stolper starts with the assumption that the war would leave all participants with major budgetary problems and that the world would be organized in trading blocs with only the few neutrals staying out of them, an assumption based on analysis of the then visible trends.

Both agreed on the necessity to preserve the political independence of Austria-Hungary and also the freedom to make any desired domestic economic policies.

When the alliance between Germany and Austria-Hungary was signed in 1879, Bismarck had wanted to make it part of the constitution of the three states—Hungary was an independent state—a suggestion which was rejected by the Austro-Hungarian side. However, as Verosta points out, what had been essentially defensive treaty against Russia[4] was expanded "on the occasion of the extremely dangerous international tension brought about by the annexation of Bosnia-Herzegovina[5] by a secret agreement between the German and Austro-Hungarian General Staffs (1909) for an offensive case which the German side considered given in July 1914" (Verosta 1978, 376; my translation).

The First World War was anticipated by the Central Powers, but with the German defeat at the Marne the then Chief of the German General Staff Falkenhayn, Moltke's successor, proposed "already in November 1914 the earliest possible start of peace negotiations which was rejected by the political leadership, particularly Reichschancellor v. Bethmann-Hollweg" (ibid., 376–77).[6]

These facts were certainly not generally known. Yet it puts in a different light the pressures Schumpeter expressed in his memoranda for peace with the Entente, and in particular for doing everything to prevent a state of war between the Monarchy and America. Schumpeter stressed that trying to achieve peace in order to avoid the destruction of the Monarchy was not treason to the alliance with Germany; he pointed out that Austria-Hungary had no differences of interest with England and France and he tried to prevent the hatred of the Reich from being extended to his beloved Monarchy. For he saw clearly that, unlike for all other warring parties, a lost war would spell the death of the Double Monarchy.

The crux of the matter, however, which explains Schumpeter's alarmed reaction against the Mitteleuropa plans, is found in a lengthy memorandum by the German Foreign Minister dated November 13, 1915 which suggested

---

[4] Verosta (1978), 379, quoting a German memorandum of November 13, 1915.

[5] Bosnia-Herzegovina had been administered by Austria-Hungary since the Congress of Berlin of 1878 before the annexation and definite incorporation into the Monarchy in October 1908. The occasion for the annexation appears to have been the revolt of the Young Turks in Turkey. The year 1908 was also the sixteenth anniversary of Emperor Franz Joseph's ascension to the throne.

[6] This was not quite as pacifistic as it sounds. Falkenhayn wanted to make peace either with Russia or with the Entente. In November 1914, neither the United States nor Italy were participants in the war. For documented details, see Fischer (1961), and later editions.

expanding the Treaty of 1879 to a long-term treaty of thirty years or so. This German memorandum was secret, as was a lengthy annex which Verosta published in full (ibid., 381–84). Verosta surmises that Schumpeter knew of this memorandum through his friend, Arthur Spiethoff, then professor in Prague who in 1925 was instrumental in bringing Schumpeter to the University of Bonn.[7]

The passages that were offensive to the Austrian-Hungarian government personally relate to the interpretation of the 1879 treaty as intending to guarantee the dominance of the Magyar element in Hungary (which included among others Slovakia and Croatia without Dalmatia) and of the German element in Austria (which referred to everything that was not Hungarian). But "while in Hungary this principle was allowed to become dominant, in Austria this principle of the dominance of the German element lost influence" (ibid., 380). The Austrian government should therefore undertake "proper measures which would prevent the 'Slawisierung' of Austria and once more give the Germanic elements the leading position in the interest of Austria as the East German March" (ibid.). This led Schumpeter to write to Lammasch on 21 February 1916:

> [T]he statements of my truly highly esteemed colleague (except for his role as a Prussian garrison among Austrian economists) Arthur Spiethoff in Prague are symptomatically too interesting to keep from you. The points which jumped at me are the following: Most importantly, for the first time . . . it is clearly said that it is the political purpose, i.e., our political chaining (Fesselung) to Prussia and not the economic usefulness which is the crux of the matter (des Pudels Kern). . . . To this extent my supposition (for Spiethoff is certainly an expositor of the Berlin *Diktat*) would be confirmed that the conquest of Austria is the most important German war aim—which would explain the fact that Germany seems to be quite flexible in other matters, e.g., in Belgium. . . . .
>
> [C]onsider what all this means: A Prussian-Lutheran-militaristic Mitteleuropa would from now on confront the rest of the world like a predatory animal fletching its teeth. *That* Austria which we know and love would cease to exist. I cannot convert myself to the view that it is so entirely without cultural value. . . . it is likely to be the policy of Berlin to bring matters to a head as long as there is no one but Count Tisza who has even a modicum of authority or talent, as long as in particular all Slavs are silenced. Without and against their will decisions are made about the peoples of Austria. (ibid., 384–85)

There is no need to go into the details of this lengthy appendix, particularly as Schumpeter does not go into economic details. However, it is appropriate to point out that Schumpeter was very pro-Slav and anti-Hungarian and that

---

[7] Professor Verosta is in possession of the Lammasch papers. I went through the Spiethoff papers in the manuscript collection of the University of Basel, Switzerland. Though it contains material on Mitteleuropa, all of it publicly available, there is nothing to suggest that Schumpeter was informed by Spiethoff of any confidential matters. I have been unable to determine just what Schumpeter refers to.

he was quite prepared to extend the Slavic influence by a coronation in Prague, thus converting the Double into a Triple Monarchy.[8]

To understand Schumpeter's alarm, one has to remember the history of the preceding fifty or sixty years.[9] Indeed, as one reader of this manuscript pointed out, it is difficult to understand what Schumpeter expected to achieve after the disasters of 1859 and 1866. The second half of the nineteenth century saw the emergence of two major national states, first Italy, then Germany, the former at the expense of the papal states and Austria, the latter at the expense of the Double Monarchy in two ways: the continuous strengthening of the Hungarian half, and the exclusion of the Austrian half from German affairs.

The background of the disaster of 1859 when Austria lost Milan and Lombardy was a secret treaty between the Kingdom of Piedmont and Napoleon III in 1858, according to which France would come to the aid of Piedmont in the conquest of upper Italy provided that Austria would provoke a war. In return, Piedmont would cede to France Savoy (which it had lost in the aftermath of the Napoleonic Wars) and if necessary the totally Italian Nice. There were other provisions about the Kingdom of Sardinia, of lower and of middle Italy. The papal possessions were to be restricted to Rome, and there would be an Italian confederation with the Pope as its honorary head.[10]

Cavour, the Piedmontese foreign minister, did his best to provoke the Aus-

---

[8] On the other side of the fence, the Bohemians wanted precisely the coronation in Prague and the establishment of a triple monarchy as Schumpeter suggested. Schumpeter apparently also wrote a memorandum on the Bohemian question which presumably dealt with such problems as what to do with the substantial German minorities involved in Bohemia, Moravia, and the Sudeten area. This memorandum, however, has so far not been found. But the Harrach letters give a clue to their probable content. The present mistreatment of Hungarian minorities in countries like Romania is explicable in part by the history of past policies of forced Magyarisation. So are the troubles between the Czechs (who were Austrian) and the Slovaks (who were part of backward Hungary). The Balkans are not an easy area to deal with. It is not possible and fortunately also unnecessary in the present context to describe the complicated relations among the different ethnic groups. (This was written a long time before the explosion in Yugoslavia, which makes all of Schumpeter's discussions quite apropos.)

[9] Since Austria was a multinational state, there arose inevitably a nationalities problem. A concise discussion of political developments from Maria Theresia is found in Josef A. Tzöbl, "Vorgeschichte des Österreichisch-Ungarischen Ausgleichs 1713–1867," in Brussati (1967), 9–32. Decisions such as making German the official language for all of Austria-Hungary under Emperor Joseph II, the son of Maria Theresa, did not help.

[10] This and the next paragraph are based on Omodeo (1951), particularly chapters 16 and 17. In his *Weltgeschichtliche Betrachtungen*, Jakob Burckhardt also criticized Napoleon III for his pro-Piedmontese policy which he pursued out of vanity, precisely because it could not but weaken Austria, his natural ally against Prussia. I owe these references to the help of Professor Rudolf v. Albertini, Professor Emeritus of History at the University of Zürich.

Schumpeter's distrust of Hungary was based on a long history of Hungarian troublemaking for the Double Monarchy. The Common Customs area had been established in 1850, mostly on the insistence of the Hungarians (Brussati 1967, 128). At first there were no problems because economic liberalism was the ruling ideology of the day, and in any case the economically much less developed Hungary with large grain exports was interested in maintaining free trade.

trians to attack—just as they were in fact provoked by the assassination of Franz Ferdinand in 1914 in Sarajevo. And thanks to the incompetence of the Austrian generals they lost the war disastrously. Peace was made; Austria ceded Lombardy to Napoleon III, who in turn handed it over to Piedmont, in the process pocketing both Savoy and Nice.[11]

The Double Monarchy really was born in 1867 after the defeat at Königsgrätz by Prussia. The so-called "Ausgleich" was negotiated in 1867 between what was thenceforth referred to as the "two parts of the Reich," "die beiden Reichsteile." Army, Finances and Foreign Policy were to be common: "k. k." = kaiserlich - königlich, the rest were left to each part "k.u.k." "kaiserlich and königlich." Bicameral systems were established in both parts, but in Austria reforms led to universal franchise[12] while Hungary maintained a qualified electoral system.

On the other hand, the Austrian parliament hardly had any hand in the Austrian-Hungarian negotiations: the Hungarian law had already been agreed to by Kaiser Franz Joseph before the Austrian law was submitted to the House of Lords (Brussati 1967, 127). The Ausgleich was to be renegotiated every ten years. The major initial problems were how to pay for the common tasks. As customs receipts were not sufficient, the residual costs were to be borne in the ratio of 70:30 by Austria and Hungary, respectively. A similar solution was found for the public debt.

The Hungarians never ceased to work for complete independence. The first real troubles arose with regard to protection. Hungarian agrarian interests lost interest in free trade when overseas competition threatened their exports to Germany, and Romanian competition threatened their domestic market. Indeed, the Hungarian minister President Tisza (the father of Tisza of 1914) actually gave notice of the dissolution ("kündigte") of the common customs and trade agreement as of 1877 (ibid., 132), and during the renewal negotiations of 1877 the words "Monarchie auf Kündigung" (Monarchy on Sufferance) became a continuous phrase.

In 1878, the name of the Austrian National Bank had to be changed to the "Austrian-Hungarian Bank" (which name it kept until 1923, long after the Hungarians had established their own central bank) to satisfy the first desires for a special Hungarian money and bank. In 1907, a compromise was reached in that there would be two equal and independent agencies with a common policy.

The protectionist policy created sour relations with Serbia. "Since the mid-

---

[11] The war was highly unpopular in France, both because the conservatives did not like the emergence at their southern border of another big power, and because the weakening of Austria could not help but strengthen Prussia on France's eastern border. But the Catholic party, including the empress, also feared the coming Italian unification because it necessarily would be at the expense of the Pope. And, indeed, the Pope was not reconciled to the loss of his territories until the 1920s. In fact, at one time the Pope excommunicated the various Italian princes involved.

[12] On the other hand, while everyone could vote, there really was not much everyone could vote upon!

dle of the eighties, the Hungarian agricultural interests increasingly dominated foreign policy in their attempts to restrict as far as possible agricultural
imports from South-Eastern Europe," a policy which led to the "poor view of
the Monarchy in South East Europe" (ibid., 135). Ever since 1887 the Hungarians had unsuccessfully pressed for their own army. But their policy of
Magyarization "led already in the seventies to disavowals of German civil
servants. . . . And a unilateral policy of railway tariffs as well as petty bureaucratic obstacles were laid onto the exports of Austrian goods into Hungary"
(ibid.). The effects of the Magyarization policy in Slovakia and Transylvania
still plague us in the 1990s.

Relations between Austria and Hungary had deteriorated to such an extent
that the Ausgleich of 1897 was not ratified by the Austrian parliament but
required an imperial decree.[13]

Hungary also wanted customs tariffs against Austria, a concession which it
did not achieve, but it did prepare for future such demands by changing the
name of the common customs area to "Vertragszollgebiet der beiden Staaten
der Österreichisch-ungarischen Monarchie" (contractual customs area of the
two states of the Austro-Hungarian Monarchy).

Now we can return to the Austro-German exchange of notes. Verosta
quotes the Austro-Hungarian answer of November 24, 1915 in full (Verosta
1978, 386–89). It stresses that the German interpretation of the Andrassy
Note (a Magyar) rests on a misunderstanding and would in any case be
unconstitutional. "The dominant position of the Germans in Austria rests on
their numerical . . . weight. The increasing importance of the other ethnic
elements (Völkerelemente) is a result of their increasing culture and cannot be
reversed and on the contrary must be greeted with satisfaction" (ibid., 388).
"All subjects are equal under the law."

Verosta believes that Schumpeter did not know this Austrian answer. It is
also most unlikely that Gustav Stolper knew the details of the note exchange,
though it is conceivable that both had some inkling. In any case, in a letter to
Lammasch dated February 21, 1916 (published by Verosta 1978, 389–90),
Schumpeter suggested that Lammasch use his connections[14] to present to the
emperor the dangers to the Monarchy. The Hungarian minister President
Tisza had already expressed misgivings about the idea of Mitteleuropa.
Schumpeter wanted Slawic voices to be added, and someone like Prince Liechtenstein with his impeccable conservative credentials to see the emperor "with
the subsequent formation of a small select cabinet" (ibid.).

Schumpeter suggested a well-researched, concise, understandably written
memorandum around which a group of like-minded persons could rally and
work out a program. "Would you not do so? It would be a historic task."
Lammasch seems to have responded immediately, requesting such a mem-

[13] There exists a vivid description of the parliament session of 1897 in "Stirring Times in
Austria," by Mark Twain, reprinted in Twain (1904), 200–49.
[14] Schumpeter suggested that he would have undertaken this task himself if he had the
necessary connections. But this consideration "does not apply to you" (Verosta 1978, 390).

orandum. Schumpeter described it in a letter of March 5, 1916. This is the first memorandum, not found in Lammasch's papers, which are in the possession of Professor Verosta, but reprinted in Schumpeter (1985). This memo is dated Graz, in the spring 1916.

THE MEMORANDA

The first memorandum deals primarily with the political consequences of the proposed customs union and the general rapprochement (Annäherung). Schumpeter allows that there may be some economic benefits of a customs union. But his concern is strictly the political consequences which are the central point and they are shaped by the realization that the real war aim of Germany was "the conquest of Austria."[15] Of course, an agreement with England would be welcome. There were no political conflicts of interest between Austria and England (or France for that matter, though only England is mentioned).[16]

Schumpeter was anxious to stress the consequences of closer association with Germany. While Austria would become totally dependent on Germany, the reverse was not true.

> These consequences hit the innermost essence of the Monarchy. The position of the All-Highest (Ah) Imperial House, the relative strength of the Austrian peoples, the freedom of action of the State in foreign affairs, the interests of the Austrian Society, the position of the catholic church in the State and vis-à-vis Protestantism,[17] all forms of life, the whole future of Austria. This, however, is mostly not understood. For the agitation [for the common market] would have made itself impossible . . . if it had tried a public discussion in these directions. (Schumpeter 1985, 252)
>
> It may, therefore, be permissible to expand on the great importance of even purely economic aims outside the economic sphere, that all the aims which

[15] See the letter of February 21, 1916 to Lammasch.

[16] "If we dealt with a customs union with any other state . . . which could not threaten Austria-Hungary politically, e.g., England, there would be much to be said for it. But it is precisely vis-à-vis Germany that the economic problem . . . is complicated by the further problem that it is a superior, the whole of the remaining Europe hostilely confronting, for an attack extremely well-positioned military power led by an unlimited energy" (Schumpeter 1985, 254).

"Capital imports from any other country, e.g., England, would not be dangerous, even very useful. Only German bank capital signifies a danger" (ibid., 257).

[17] The references to Catholicism and the position of the Church have, I believe, a political rather than a religious-theological meaning. There is evidence that Schumpeter was a closet Christian (see on this R. Loring Allen 1990). But he certainly was wedded neither to the Catholic hierarchy nor the Church. He did in fact become a Lutheran in 1925.

I believe, the meaning of these comments lies, elsewhere. Catholicism was part of the *national* (rather than religious) consciousness of Austria, much as it is in Poland, or as Islam is in so many countries of the Near East, or as Judaism is in Israel. This aspect of the religion of the area is shared by believers and unbelievers alike.

German nationalism may desire would be necessary consequences of an economic alliance. (ibid., 253)

The weaknesses of Austria—and it must be kept in mind that Austria referred to everything that was not Hungary—reappear later in Schumpeter's policies as minister of finance, both politically as remaining opposed to the Anschluss, and economically when he tried to keep at least the economic and financial ties of the Monarchy intact in the face of the rising nationalist tide. It was also this analysis which evidently kept up his hopes that the victorious Entente would see where their long-term political self-interest lay, until the Treaty of St. Germain dashed those hopes.

The consequences of the customs union would make Hungary totally independent, a development which many observers already viewed as virtually inevitable before the outbreak of the war. Even without the war and a customs union, many observers feared the renegotiations of the Ausgleich due in 1916–17 as the final and complete break-up of the Double Monarchy. Schumpeter certainly shared these fears: "It is precisely these facts—the merger of the Austrian economic area with the German and the absorption of Austrian finance capital by the German—which would make Hungary economically entirely independent of Cisleithania,[18] for the same [bank] connections which presently tie Hungary to Austria would now be tied in Berlin" (ibid., 257).

As of the date of the memorandum, separatist tendencies were firmly counteracted by business and the leading personalities. This would cease to be the case. German bank capital would dominate in the Balkans (Schumpeter 1985, 258). The customs union would most likely lead to further organizational forms such as common consular services, perhaps even a common parliament in fact if not in name (ibid., 259). Any common representation (gemeinsames Auftreten) would mean German, specifically Prussian dominance (ibid.) by a Prussia which was universally hated. It is precisely the present international circumstances which make the customs union politically so dangerous. "If in the Sandwich Islands a German consular official commits a tactlessness we shall feel the repercussions. The whole unpopularity of German diplomacy will reflect back on us" (ibid., 260).

I resist quoting in more detail. But there is one further point which relates to a specific Austrian weakness and is the background of one of Schumpeter's major recommendations: because the Austrian parliament had not been kept in session (by the Minister President Count Stürgkh who preferred to rule by decree) there existed no public opinion which could back any Austrian negotiators (ibid., 259).[19]

---

[18] The river Leitha formed the pre–1918 border between Austria and Hungary. The Burgenland on the Hungarian side of the Leitha was detached from Hungary and given to Austria by the Peace Treaty. This was the only territorial change in favor of a defeated nation, but then Hungary was also a former enemy.

[19] As recounted above, the Austrian parliament had already been excluded in 1867 when the Ausgleich was originally negotiated. Mark Twain (1904) expressed outraged shock at the manner

Austria would thus lose all independence, a process which had already begun in 1890 when Austrian relations with Russia and England began to change as the result of the German changes. The worst is that both in Austria and in Germany these changes were *wanted*. In Austria, the major reason for this fact is that "people even in circles and positions of whom this would have seemed impossible only a short time ago have lost all Austrian feelings . . . only because they were left to themselves and without any leadership in Austria and found nothing and no-one on whom they could lean" (ibid., 264).

Given this analysis, something should and could be done to counteract these developments. The fiscal difficulties were for the time being considered as given. Not so the possibility to create the preconditions for an effective independent policy: "Only an Austria that knows what it wants can in the present situation exercise any influence. To achieve this two things are essential: the reconvening of Parliament[20] and the creation of a strong political position of the Government in domestic policy" (Schumpeter 1985, 266).

The reasons for the former are interesting in view of the later problem of the great capital levy: only parliament can authorize the issue of long-term debt. Without it the war must be financed by inflationary means. Politically, "there must be a parliamentary expression of loyalty to the Ah Imperial House and of attachment to the State (Staatsgedanke). Austria is the only warring country which has not done so . . . which is an unending source of weakness vis-à-vis Hungary, Prussia, enemy states and particularly the neutrals" (ibid., 267).[21]

Schumpeter thought there would be some difficulties in parliament: criticism of the government, unfulfillable social demands. Still it was essential to try.

Parliament needs leadership, in this case a government that could lead and that is represented by more than a civil service.[22] Only a man with a historic name could lead such a government effectively, only he could rally the historic families. Only they could develop and carry through a program of action which could save the State they had helped to create. "The management (the English word is used) of public opinion and Parliament . . . is a task whose importance and difficulty is frequently underestimated" (ibid., 270).

The analysis here also gives a clue to Schumpeter's activity as a frequent

---

in which parliament was treated by the government in 1897, as well as by the total chaos prevailing in parliament.

[20] The Austrian parliament had been adjourned prior to the outbreak of the war. The Minister President Count Stürgkh refused to call it back, insisting on ruling (unconstitutionally) by decree. Stürgkh was assassinated on October 21, 1916, by Victor Adler, an idealistic Socialist.

[21] When parliament finally was reconvened in May 1917, it was too late. Chaos reigned. Schumpeter had actually anticipated that the problems would be getting increasingly worse by waiting.

[22] Thus, Böhm-Bawerk was a highly successful minister of finance. Wieser, too, was a minister. As professors both had civil service status. Austria was an absolute, not a constitutional or parliamentary monarchy. It was in these circumstances quite reasonable for Schumpeter to think that he might be a minister. What Schumpeter eventually wanted was the gradual conversion of an absolute into a constitutional monarchy.

speaker during his Finanzminister days, his constant striving to keep himself and his ideas in the public consciousness and to influence public opinion. In the very manner in which the government appears in public it must occupy the public, impress it, fascinate it, make it abundantly clear

[T]hat it deals not with conscientious chefs of departmental matters (Ressortangelegenheiten) but with statesmen who have firm political aims and personal weight. The importance of a systematic domination of the press[23] is clear, a loyal and intimate cooperation of the administrative apparatus . . . in a word, that technique of public life which has been perfected in England and which even in periods of sharpest democratic tendencies has preserved the influence of the aristocracy and generally of conservative interests: The technique of tory democracy. (ibid., 271)[24]

The crucial and difficult problems of life and death of the Monarchy would remain: the nationalities problems, Hungary, and in particular, "the serious fiscal difficulties hiding beneath the smooth surface of the modern credit system" (ibid., 271). But only such a government could even begin to deal with them.

Verosta surmises that Emperor Franz Joseph saw the memorandum and in any case it became later known that he "was very much put off by the German impertinence (Zumutung)" (Verosta 1978, 391).[25]

The second memorandum is dated Graz, December 1, 1916. A letter of Schumpeter's to Lammasch on August 21, 1916 gives some background to it. Verosta gives only a summary. Schumpeter wants action, repeats that the center of Austrian patriotism must be an aristocrat. And then comes almost a sigh of resignation, an expression of hope against hope: "Once in the water, our high aristocracy will eventually learn to swim and evolve people suitable for leading roles—but until then! In the meantime we will be economically conquered by Germany and politically dominated by Hungary" (ibid., 391).

The second memorandum was intended to take care of new facts and to clarify and supplement the reasoning of the first. Schumpeter's central interest remains, as he had put it in the first memorandum, to safeguard that

[U]nique political entity (Gebilde) which is Austria [in whose nature it is] that it cannot be ruled without those factors which are but a small minority [i.e., the

---

[23] This is *not* an advocacy of press censorship. It is what is commonly known in the United States: the president dominates the news.

[24] Again, the English words "Tory democracy" are used, and indeed it is almost a terminus technicus. The *Encyclopedia Britannica*, 11th ed. (pp. 346–47), states in an entry under "Churchill, Lord Randolph Spencer" that by 1885 "he had definitely formulated the policy of progressive conservativism which was known as 'Tory Democracy.' He declared that the Conservatives ought to adopt rather than to oppose, reforms of a popular character and to challenge the claims of the Liberals as the champions of the masses. . . . In 1884, the struggle between stationary and progressive Toryism came to a head and terminated in favour of the latter."

These ideas are also essential to understand the differences between Hayek and Schumpeter, expressed in Schumpeter's review of Hayek's *Road to Serfdom*.

[25] We do know that Count Czernin, the foreign minister, saw them. See Schumpeter's letters to Count Harrach.

imperial house and the historic families] and that it cannot exist [without them], as that Austria which we know and love. If this central authority is paralyzed what remains are only nationalities without bonds, a mixture without sense and will, which can become prey to any energetically and not too unskillfully presented will. (Schumpeter 1985, 262)

Thus a State which a hundred years ago was the center of European politics would have to follow in all things an "ally" of overpowering strength. (ibid.)

As the first, the second memorandum "is based on the position of the dynastic interests in which the interests of all peoples of Austria are concentrated and in the preservation of all existing obligations of the Monarchy which must be taken as facts that cannot be changed" (ibid., 272–73).

By the end of 1916, Schumpeter considered it "fairly certain" that the war would leave the borders and relative power positions of all major powers unchanged. Only the Monarchy was threatened in its very existence by the changing relation to Germany. The most important political consequences are rather drastically expressed:

[L]oss of the possibility of an independent Balkan policy; a precarious position vis-à-vis Russia; total uncertainty in the position towards Italy; permanent enmity of the Western powers; forced participation in all actions and changes of German policies; orientation of domestic policy according to German points of view; Hungary's growing out of the Monarchy. (ibid., 274)

Yet Schumpeter stresses that his insistence on developing a specifically Austrian program is not based on hostility to the Ally. But

[N]o obligation of an Ally goes so far that one would have to forego asking about the direction of the path one is jointly walking. (Ibid.)

The Monarchy must, should and always will consider its Ally, but this goes also for the Ally. Faithfulness to the alliance can not mean giving up one's own existence, action against one's own vital interests. (ibid., 275)[26]

So Schumpeter saw himself as a kind of "loyal opposition."

Everything had become more dangerous; even a favorable military situation could not hide this fact. No one talked about a customs union, only about a customs agreement. But Schumpeter notes that even the Christian Social Party (a conservative Catholic party which Schumpeter had counted among the pillars of the Monarchy) now demanded a close political, military, and economic affiliation (Anschluss).[27] In September 1917, nine months after the second memorandum was written and about six months after the third, Schumpeter praised the Socialists: "Truly, the socialists are the only party in Austria with whom one can deal" (Verosta 1978, 392).

In his second memorandum, Schumpeter notes that the role of German Finanzkapital in Hungary has progressed very much faster than he had antici-

---

[26] Actually much of school boy indoctrination was directed at teaching precisely this kind of "faithfulness until death" called "Nibelungentreue."

[27] In a party meeting (Tagung) of November 9, 1916.

pated (Schumpeter 1985, 275) which in turn had increased Hungarian support for Germany within the Monarchy against Austria. Worse, the German army high command had practically absorbed the Austrian one and that, too, had the backing of the Christian Social Party! (ibid., 276). Germany kept "advising" Austria in this and in such matters as that "any Austrian delegation would at least have to have a German majority" (ibid.). Still worse, "the Western powers have ceased to consider Austria-Hungary as an independent factor in world politics and have changed to a much more hostile attitude than only a short time ago. . . . Russian politics . . . is difficult to judge, but that much is sure that Russia feels very much closer to Germany than to the Monarchy. As for the neutrals . . . they remain strangers and cool" (Ibid., 277).

As for the other allies, Turkey had become a German dependency. Only Bulgaria was an uncertain exception. For Austria there simply were no other states in the world which would allow an independent foreign policy.

By the end of 1916, Schumpeter evidently believed that Austria-Hungary could still be preserved as a major world power with independence of action. Specifically Austria should aim to become equally friendly with Germany and Russia, "two overwhelmingly powerful neighbors." This should be possible because there really were no unbridgeable conflicts of interest between Russia and Germany, but "whenever this is not possible [by] joining the side on which the Western powers are" (ibid., 281).

Schumpeter never deviated from this essentially Western European orientation. But peace with Russia should nevertheless be possible because Russia's basic interests as a thinly populated and capital-poor country were its domestic development which would limit its expansionary tendencies (ibid., 282). All of this sounds rather modern, though just after the Second World War Russia was a wildly expansionary power, as it had been in the earlier decades of the nineteenth century.

As far as the German element in Austria was concerned, "the majority of Germans can as of today still be won over to a policy—it is, however, a question how much longer—which is neither German nor Slawic but Austrian which corresponds to the national structure of Austria and whose aim it is to embed the Monarchy into a system of ententes which assure it peace and an honored position in world politics" (ibid., 283).

This was not true of Hungary, whose policy harmed several of its peoples. A "German-centered policy is impossible in Austria. . . . [The only feasible policy] for Austria is a policy of national accommodation (Ausgleich), the freeing of the Idea of the State from any nationalistic tinges whatsoever" (ibid., 285).

A policy hostile to the Slavs was impossible in Austria. But this does not mean that such a policy was hostile to the Germans; it is compatible with maintaining German as the common language of business.[28]

---

[28] In the 1920s it was said that the nonpublic meetings of the Little Entente were conducted in German rather than in French. I recall that when as a teenager I went by railroad from Berlin to Vienna via Prague, the most direct route, the Czech passport control refused to talk German until

Schumpeter realized that the solution of the nationalities problem was virtually impossible during the war. Yet a policy of national accommodation was the only durable one and much could be done to prepare such an eventual policy. In particular, Schumpeter argued for an accommodating policy toward the Czechs. The policy actually pursued practically forced the Czechs into a disloyal opposition (ibid., 286–87).

Reconvening of parliament had in the meantime become a well-neigh universal demand. But to be successful, a government was essential which knew what it wanted and which was able to lead (ibid., 288) To be effective, the government program had to include effective popular points: civil liberties, a determination to meet all fiscal obligations and to restore the currency, and a "bouquet of social measures" (ibid.).

> But indispensable is primarily one thing: that the determination to achieve peace and a clear war aim of the Monarchy brightly shines out of the program. . . . Nothing damages the respect for a Government and the prospects for domestic and foreign success so much as that the Hungarian Minister President and the German Reichs Chancellor are made speakers and guardians; and that the impression arose that Austria neither had nor could have any will of its own. (ibid., 288–89).

The third memorandum is dated Graz, April 1917. Unlike the preceding memoranda, it had a title: "The Political Situation and the Interests of the Monarchy." It is a stark analysis. Schumpeter starts with making a strong case for immediate peace negotiations to save the Monarchy. The war will leave all warring powers exhausted; Austria alone is threatened in its very existence. None of the Entente powers need fear its allies. Not so Austria. "Austria-Hungary can live by itself and for its great tasks, can preserve its traditional position in the world, only if it is fiscally independent and lives in economically orderly circumstances" (Schumpeter 1985, 290).

For all other states, exhaustion would be a temporary matter. For Austria it is a death sentence. For all countries, the war will end in social disorganization. The Russian Revolution will not spread; it is due to special circumstances not found in the West. But conservative forces everywhere will be weakened, nowhere more so than in Austria (ibid., 291). "[O]ur workers are almost in their entirety . . . socialist; in some areas our peasants give up their traditional conservative views so that presently we can find socialist peasants in the Tyrol; finally the situation is made more difficult by nationality conflicts exacerbated by the war" (ibid.).

Austrian war aims could be defense and preservation. Territorial gains would cause trouble. Furthermore, "The complete defeat of any of the Great Powers is either impossible—as for example a really annihilating defeat of

---

I tried to use the officially demanded French, which he could not understand. In the 1950s in Yugoslavia, I got along well with German while Evsey Domar had trouble with his Russian! Nowadays the most commonly used business language is English, often even in France. Schumpeter asked for no more than that.

Russia—or from the standpoint of the Monarchy not desirable—such as a defeat of the Western powers from whom no conflicts of interest separate the Monarchy and which would possibly rob the latter of important support in the future" (ibid.).

Schumpeter hammered at this theme: even though the military situation may be favorable, even the "most brilliant military successes become illusory if at the same time the political and economic situation deteriorates and the enemy can with equanimity look at all defeats whose importance can only be local and temporary. It is a fact that the political and economic means of the Entente are still continuously growing" (ibid., 292).

The entry of the United States[29] was "even militarily not useless, financially enormously important" (ibid., 292). The unlimited U-boat war could not possibly achieve its aim and was a political mistake "in whose consequences the Monarchy . . . has unfortunately become entangled." The Monarchy must make peace a "political role for which . . . only the Monarchy seems . . . predestined" (ibid., 293) and thereby restore its days of glory.

The chance was unique precisely because the United States was not yet at war with the Monarchy and the Monarchy itself enjoyed considerable sympathy with the Western powers (ibid., 294). Schumpeter even points out that the Entente could initially only present unacceptable peace terms which Germany nevertheless would have to accept but could not herself formulate (ibid.).[30]

Peace would be in the interest of the conservative parties, the Monarchy, the Historic Families (ibid., 295). It would rally the nationalities around the Monarchy. For the Monarchy, the benefits would cumulate. Here we find again one of the few sentences specifically referring to economic benefits:

> It would give the Monarchy . . . increasing advantages. To start with, the sympathy of the world, a moment whose importance is most insufficiently appreciated for the outcome of the peace negotiations and for the organization (Gestaltung) particularly of economic relationships after the war (loans, raw material supplies, etc.). . . . The Monarchy would escape an eminent danger . . . that peace would be concluded at its expense. . . . Furthermore, any treaty limitations on armaments would ease the economic pressure. (ibid., 295).

[29] The break was with the German Reich but not yet with Austria-Hungary and the other of its allies. The United States declared war against Germany on April 6, 1917, against Austria-Hungary on December 7, 1917.

There were peace efforts in 1916. The trouble was that though Germany agreed to peace feelers of Americans, the Entente presented a number of peace conditions which proposed to reorder Europe on the nationality principle which would, of course, have involved the dismemberment of the Austro-Hungarian Monarchy. The real trouble became, however, the fact that on January 9, 1917, the German government decided on the unlimited U-boat war and so notified the United States on January 31, 1917, which led to a break of diplomatic relations with Germany on February 3, 1917.

[30] As it happened, when the German Army High Command recognized that the war was lost, it was Ludendorf who insisted on an immediate armistice, while the Social Democrats and the last Imperial Reichs Chancellor Prince Max of Baden implored the army in vain to continue fighting until acceptable armistice terms could be negotiated. This did not prevent Ludendorf and the right from inventing the stab-in-the-back legend.

Schumpeter argued that only the Monarchy could initially propose a reasonable peace settlement. He proposed emphasizing any peaceful utterances by Germany but always going one step further, to avoid at all cost a break with the United States and to nurture relations with the Holy See. This would allow the Monarchy to grow into the role of peace advocate, first with the Entente, then on the world stage. Faithfulness to the German ally did not prohibit a more conciliatory attitude toward the United States and thus undo the mistakes of German policy (ibid., 298).[31]

The Monarchy would always have to depend on West European capital and trade. English trade and capital were greatly to be preferred to German. The world would be preserved from a trade war and the world's resources could be freed for reconstruction if the Monarchy were free of any economic vasselage. "It is practically a question of existence that there will be no customs treaty. To conclude such a treaty would mean to perpetuate economic warfare and to abdicate as a major power. It is high time to recognize the significance and aims of the customs treaty and to oppose it" (ibid., 301).

The precondition for a strong foreign policy was a strong "corresponding and complementary domestic policy" (ibid.). This was particularly true for Austria, where the failure to convene parliament allowed the Entente to use such phraseology as to liberate the Austrian Slaws. The central task was to bring back to the center the Idea of the Austrian State (den österreichischen Staatsgedanken) which was practically synonymous and identical with the interests of the Monarchy.

The first problem Schumpeter analyzes is how much centralism really was required to keep the State intact. "The concerns of a modern community are a much smaller part of its tasks than is generally assumed" (ibid.). Too much centralization can only be a source of friction, not to say danger, for the State. Without a maximum of federalism it is impossible to secure the necessary measure of centralization. Dominance by any one of the Austrian nationalities is numerically and politically impossible (ibid.).

The trouble was that there was no strong conservative party, and particularly that the *common conservative interests* (italics in original) of the propertied classes and of industry were insufficient to prevent either of them from making common cause with their enemies, such as on tax policy (ibid., 302–3). If such conflicts could be avoided there would be a basis for a big conservative party which automatically would be led by the high aristocracy. Such a party would become a strong parliamentary basis for the State.

---

[31] Schumpeter adds: "It would go beyond the scope of this Memorandum if the author were to show how badly the policy of the United States was misunderstood by us . . . if desired further comments on this point could be made available. Here it must only be emphasized that the maintenance of, if possible, official, but at least unofficial, relations with the Union will be of greatest importance for peace negotiations and the position of the Monarchy. . . . No faithfulness to the Ally can prohibit cooperation with the Holy See. . . . [o]pens possibilities to represent particular wishes of the Holy See at the peace negotiations which itself will strengthen the position of the Monarchy" (Schumpeter 1985, 298). How badly American policy was misunderstood in Germany is documented by Fischer (1961).

Such a party, however, would need a viable program and freedom of action. Interestingly, Schumpeter mentions first of all the idea of a loyal opposition. Without it, any disagreement is immediately considered disloyalty to dynasty and the State and thus becomes stultifying to the best men. What would be otherwise conciliatory would be interpreted as weakness and treated with contempt.

This was the right time to create such a party, when Austria had rejected the German demand for predominance of the German element.[32] Unfortunately, it was likely that when parliament finally reconvened, the parties will "certainly prove that they have learned nothing and forgotten nothing" (ibid., 304). Schumpeter mentions chaotic circumstances in the German National Association, uncertainty in the Polish Club and with the Ukrainians, conflicts in the South-Slavic camp (ibid.).[33] This left only the Christian Socialists, the Social Democrats, and the Cesky Vaz (Czech Club) capable of action. These three groups might be the basis for effective parliamentary action, and this might attract other groups.

Under no circumstances was this the time for "big measures" (ibid., 304). Aside from the opportunities for sheer demagogy this would open up, the postwar conditions are simply not known. Besides "the Austrian problem can not be solved with one stroke—whoever thinks so misjudges the complications and sensibilities of the structure of Austria" (ibid., 305). Just the same, the various peoples must be offered quite a bit.

The first point Schumpeter mentions is a coronation in Prague, the first since Emperor Charles VI, the father of Maria Theresa, was crowned. This was more than symbolism. It meant constitutional reform, the conversion of the Double Monarchy into a Triple Monarchy, and changing the Austrian unitary State into a federal State. Again there is a statement of considerable insight: "[T]his might present an occasion to make the legalization of German as the business language acceptable to the Czech people—though the author does not really understand the necessity of this" (ibid.).

In any case, the Czech-German problem would be the easiest to solve— provided the all-German element would be controlled. The Polish problem was prejudged by imperial action which must be taken as a datum (Schumpeter obviously thought it a mistake). The Southern Slavs also presented difficulties. But most of all it was the relation to Hungary that radically changed.

The Magyar element had become dominant and Hungary had grown out of the Monarchy. Yet the change to universal suffrage in Hungary would become inevitable and so would the change in the whole social and political structure of Hungary. In short, the present was not a favorable time to renegotiate the Ausgleich with Hungary. Of course, the Hungarians wanted, the Ausgleich and were even presenting this willingness as a concession on their part. In fact,

[32] See the account given by Verosta discussed above.

[33] In fact, when parliament reconvened in May 1917, chaotic scenes resulted. "Associations" or "clubs" were the names for what in the United States are referred to as Democratic or Republican caucuses.

however, a change in the electoral system would make Hungary a "dying regime" (ibid., 308).

As for fiscal policy, the essential point "for the Government and Parliament and every serious party is to stress the determination to fulfill all Government obligations and at the very least to preserve the currency from further deterioration" (ibid.).

A further deterioration of the currency would create a situation whose "effect would be as bad as a social revolution" (ibid.).

> This, however, does not mean that all economic activity is crushed by taxes, that all security of property is annihilated by confiscatory measures. . . . The socialists may not care about the public debt and the currency—they can only like it if the State is discredited . . . nor are they afraid of crushing taxes or confiscatory measures. A conservative party can never wish to avoid difficulties in this manner. It would give itself up if it did so. (ibid., 308–9)

Nevertheless, a definitive fiscal program could be developed only after the war. The criticism of the actual fiscal measures of the government reads frighteningly contemporary; all that can be done at the present time (i.e., 1917) are credit operations; it was a mistake not to raise indirect taxes together with direct ones.

And here is the first hint of how Schumpeter was proposing to solve the postwar fiscal problem:

> It will have to allow for the developmental conditions of the economy and must crush neither individual initiative nor capital formation. It will have to become part of the policy of reconstruction, will have to complement it as it is complemented by it. It will disappoint many popular demands and nevertheless impose heavy sacrifices on all circles. The greatest insight and skill will be necessary to carry it through. But now all chances for success are ruined if one imposes one wrong measure after the other without any connection, exasperates all interests and yet does not satisfy anyone" (ibid., 309)
>
> Nevertheless much must and can be done. An extension of social security to include also the problems of veterans is without doubt necessary. So are labor offices and youth programs (Jugendfürsorge). And in all these areas much can be achieved . . . [by] better organization and better utilization of existing resources. (ibid.)

It was too late. Verosta quotes a letter of Schumpeter's to Lammasch on September 19, 1917, in which he mentions the difficulties in safeguarding German interests under the Crown of St. Wenceslas: "analogy: the Ulster question in a Home rule—Ireland" (Verosta 1978, 392), and calls a public meeting for reconciliation convened by the German(-speaking) social democrats of Bohemia prächtig, magnificent. But America did declare war on Austria on December 7, 1917. Lammasch gave a third peace speech in the House of Lords on February 20, 1918, which was badly attacked. (ibid., 393). On April 10, 1918, Schumpeter wrote Lammasch a letter of support and a completely pessimistic assessment of the political situation. "The further development is very clear. The appeasement of Hungary by far-reaching concessions which Berlin guarantees, an economic alliance (Wirtschaftsbündnis)—and for Cisleithania there remains a position similar to that of Kurland" (ibid., 394).

Actually, Emperor Karl I had upon his accession to the throne dismissed all ministers that had in any way been party to the beginning of the war. Verosta also says that the German General Staff had ready plans for the occupation of the centers of the Monarchy (ibid.) and quotes Otto Bauer—whom we will meet again in connection with Schumpeter's ministerial days—to the effect that the Austrian social democrats "knew how serious was the danger of a German invasion. We knew that only the fear of a German invasion kept the Viennese Court from making a separate peace. We knew that the Czech revolutionaries feared the German invasion" (ibid., 394–95).[34]

On September 29, 1918, the German Supreme Army Command demanded from the government an immediate armistice and peace (only to invent shortly after the stab-in-the-back legend). On October 16, 1918, Karl I promulgated his so-called Völkermanifest, which invited the individual nationalities to form their own parliaments, which would have transformed the unitary into a federal state. There was also a change of government. Lammasch became the last prime minister of the Monarchy. The armistice with the Western powers was concluded on November 3, 1918, by the (common) Austro-Hungarian chief of the General Staff. The individual nationalities went their own ways. Power devolved upon them in a peaceful manner.

The Harrach Letters, the Bohemian Question, and Other Foreign and Domestic Policy Issues

The three memoranda discussed are the only ones that have been found so far. However, early in March 1991, Professor Seidl and I discovered ten letters from Schumpeter to Count Harrach written between January 25, 1916 and February 19, 1918, which indicate that Schumpeter wrote at least four other memoranda.[35] The letters give additional evidence of Schumpeter's thoughts about solving the nationalities problem, specifically the Bohemian question, and they bring out an eagerness to play a more active political role in conservative circles.

Count Harrach was a scion of an old noble family of German-Bohemian origin. In the early nineteenth century, the counts were permitted to be addressed as "Erlaucht," which in its adjective form means illustrious. And in 1861, the counts became hereditary members of the House of Lords, the

---

[34] Lest this sounds far-fetched, it is, of course, precisely what happened when Italy made peace with the Western powers during the Second World War. Or what happened later when Soviet tanks rolled into Budapest and Prague.

[35] The letters are reprinted in Schumpeter (1992).

Herrenhaus. Count Harrach was thus well connected, evidently intelligent, and evidently more or less on the "same wavelength" as Schumpeter, though inclined to be more authoritarian than Schumpeter. Unfortunately, Harrach's letters to Schumpeter have not been found. It is probable that they were in the boxes stored in Jülich which were burned during the war.

From the first letter which it seems worthwhile to reproduce (in translation) in full, it is evident that there were earlier letters as well as at least two memoranda. This letter is the longest of the ten, and it contains some matters not elsewhere touched upon. The translation of the beginning and the end of the letter is somewhat stilted, intentionally so, to give a flavor of how the lower-class Schumpeter addressed the higher-class count. But the body of the letter(s) is polite and straightforward and does not hide disapproval.[36]

Graz
Parkstrasse 17
25. Jan. 1916

Your Erlaucht

is asked to accept my most devoted (ergebenster) thanks for the kind letter which I received after a hunting and skiing absence of several days, and which pleased me as much as I found its content interesting and instructive. The agreement of Erlaucht fills me with true satisfaction and I feel myself extraordinarily obligated that you deemed the two memoranda worthy of such thorough a study. Unfortunately, Erlaucht is only all too correct with the comments about the Graz milieu. I am here pretty much isolated and see myself totally cut off from any possibility of being effective by my lack of sympathy for German-national beer-house phrases.

I follow with pleasure the kind invitation to respond to your arguments (Ausführungen). Nothing is more stimulating and productive than, sure of the common basis in principle, to discuss the usefulness (Zweckmässigkeitsfragen) of the individual case. To start with, as to the question of the position of the Monarchy towards its ally, it is clear that the task is, on the one hand, to remain faithful to the existing obligation and a powerful military support, and, that on the other hand, to stick to independent war aims, which requires the utmost tact. Diplomatically we labor (laborieren) in this under the disadvantage that the enemy and neutral countries begin to view the Monarchy not as an independent power, but as an annex of Prussia, and, domestically, under a disorganization of Austrian feeling for the State (Staatsgefühl) brought about by an all-too-great "Connivenz"[37] to Prussia, with the result that Austria's Germans begin to feel as protegées of Germany, and the non-German Austrians quite logically begin to feel hostile towards this new German-centralistic Austria. To this comes the danger that Austria might become the object of compensation for some of the belligerent powers.

This danger could, in my opinion, be met if the government succeeded to rally

---

[36] Schumpeter (1992), 361–62.

[37] A legal term meaning a punishable agreement, conspiracy.

public opinion around specifically Austrian war aims: this would have a very favorable effect abroad and would immediately direct the world's attention to Austria, and this would domestically create the basis for a collaboration of all parties with the exception of the German-radicals (Deutschradikale). For this, hardly *more* would be required than a happily formulated pronouncement of the Government and, on the basis of it, a boldly executed (durchgeführte) session of Parliament, which, however, would in the specifics require good tactical skills. And I believe that this would be quite compatible with the decision—and a corresponding pronouncement—to go through thick and thin with Germany: The example of the Entente powers is instructive in this respect; they, too, declare individually, to stand by their allies to the very end—yet none of them foregoes to discuss their own aims and to create an enthusiasm of their own people for them, thus safeguarding their own individuality. For the Monarchy matters are still more favorable. She has no part in the great confrontation between Germany and England. She could—precisely now—speak an authoritative word of reconciliation, which would find an echo and create a favorable diplomatic situation, which in turn would strengthen the domestic authority of the Government and at once give conservative circles a basis among the mass of voters.

I must freely confess that I have no arguments against the accusation of Erlaucht concerning my estimation of the chances of the Monarchy in Asia Minor and Mesopotamia—it is very correct, and I can also see (es leuchtet mir sehr ein) that the Monarchy, for a number of reasons, has every right, to compete successfully with Germany both with the Balkan Slaws and Asiatic Turkey (the former would, however, require a change in the nationality policy of the Magyars). The question how the Monarchy could best find a footing in Asia Minor is indeed worth studying there, and action in this respect by the Government would indeed be meritorious.[38]

The most useful behavior, from the standpoint of the Monarchy, towards the Bohemian people is a problem with regard to which I gladly submit to the more thorough knowledge and experience of your Erlaucht. I had the feeling that an injustice towards it [i.e., the Bohemian people] was done in several respects, in particular, however, that misdemeanors of individuals and of all minorities were politically exploited by the German-radical side, in order to embitter the nationalities struggle, to stigmatize the entire Bohemian people as subversive (staatsfeindlich) and therewith to work towards the realization of the plan for a German majority in the Reichsrat. The best means (Gegenmittel) against such plans, which, even disregarding everything else, are politically impracticable, seemed to me to be the active political collaboration of the Bohemian people in the service of the Staatsgedanke.[39]

And in order to make this possible for the more thoughtful leaders without

[38] This evidently refers to a response, suggested by Harrach, to the German plan for a Berlin-to-Baghdad railroad. Schumpeter's policy clearly suggests that he considered the suggested Austrian action unimportant, if not impossible. Schumpeter apparently never reverted to this subject matter.

[39] This really untranslatable expression refers to the conception of the Monarchy as a multinational state with greater freedom of its individual nationalities.

them having to fear to be swept away in elections by the radical elements, it seemed to me that the greatest possible mildness and readiness for reconciliation on the side of the Government—particularly avoidance of the creation of "Martyrs"—was most in the interest of the Dynasty and the State, particularly as it seemed to me that many Bohemian politicians would gladly grasp the opportunity to put themselves at the disposal of the Government, if they could do so without humiliation which would cost them their authority with the masses. However, I admit, that this train of thought might have mistakes which became visible from the height of the knowledge and experience of your Erlaucht, and that possibly another course of action would be preferable. I fear, however, that the experiences of the seventies and even more the subsequent period prove, how little a Government can count on the political ability and reliability of the parties which today are united in the German National Union, and how little the bureaucracy, too, exhibits those political instincts and prestige which are required for the solution of our problems—and these are the two elements on which the Government would have to lean which would want to win over our Slavs to the Austrian Staatsgedanke by other means than by patient and reconciling attempts at reconciliation.

I must apologize for this long letter. The great kindness (Entgegenkommen) of your Erlaucht has seduced me to this quite inexcusable length—and I almost would have touched upon—Accommodation (Ausgleichs) and financial questions which have so great an importance for the future position of the Monarchy and the conservative parties that one may perhaps say that whenever in the past foreign or domestic matters went wrong, this had in the last analysis financial reasons.

I thank your Erlaucht from the bottom of my heart for the willingness to show my memoranda also to other gentlemen, and ask your Erlaucht to be convinced that I shall always consider myself fortunate to be allowed to participate in the political ideas of your Erlaucht.

Receive your Erlaucht the expression of my particular respect (Verehrung).

Always (ergebener) respectfully,
Joseph Schumpeter)

There is only one other letter from 1916, dated Graz February 1, 1916. Schumpeter approvingly mentions attempts by neutrals to make peace which are not sufficiently known in Austria. The letter cites what is also said in the memoranda, that "none of the belligerents has so much the calling as Austria to cooperate with such an action emanating from a neutral side" (Schumpeter 1992, 364).

The letter bemoans the total ignorance of the United States, as well as the American ignorance of the peculiarity of the Austrian State.[40] The letter continues:

---

[40] The mentioned report by Mark Twain starts, however, with a quite accurate description of the Monarchy, which in Twain's view had no right to exist, but which had in the past emerged from successive crises stronger than before!

It is therefore to be regretted that, e.g., the relations to the United States have so far received so little care that, on the one hand, the political individuality of the Monarchy is there unknown, and, on the other hand, the political structure of the United States and her leading circles is so little known here. Financially and politically the United States could have the greatest importance for us, and it fills me again and again with sadness to see the lack of understanding—in diplomatic circles and in circles of the Ministry of Finance (finanzministeriellen Kreisen) of the pecularity (Eigenart) of that state and its leading persons which four years ago, on the occasion of a longer visit, were the subject of my study.[41]

The increased U-boat warfare could not help but alienate the United States and strengthen English war sentiments, and it must lead to a further erosion of such sympathy which the Monarchy still enjoyed in western Europe, sympathies which might become quite important in peace negotiations.

The next letter is dated January 14, 1917. Schumpeter sent a copy of the two memoranda written in 1916, stating that Prince Jaroslav Thun had shown them to "about twelve" other gentlemen. Schumpeter hoped his Erlaucht would also send it on. In the next letter, dated February 9, 1917, Schumpeter bemoaned the fact that Parliament had not been convened at the beginning of the war, causing irreparable damage. And the government was simply incapable of bringing the right people into the right position, or to inspire and lead the voters. "This is true for special questions, e.g., fiscal policy, even more so for great questions of life and death for the Monarchy" (Schumpeter 1992, 366). But then the letter reverts again to the questions that evidently seemed more central to Schumpeter, the conversion of the Double into a Triple Monarchy and the formation of a truly popular conservative party.

> The great idea of Trialism (plus a special position of the Länder of the Bohemian crown) has touched me greatly. This must be boldly said from an authoritative side . . . and it is surely true that the decisive word must be spoken already now. This would break the core of all anti-Austrian tendencies at home and abroad, and a problem of European importance would be solved in a manner which *could* and *would* satisfy Russia. That would have to be a plank in a platform of a great conservative party whose organization should urgently (endlich) be begun. . . . I get to the plans of a conservative paper. It is with pleasure that I make myself available to your Erlaucht whenever you believe that I—despite the total isolation in which I live here—may serve the great cause. The task is difficult. . . . But what is possible elsewhere, e.g., in England, must also be possible with us, and if a staff . . . is won which can compete with the savoir faire of the Jewish press[42]

---

[41] The extent of this ignorance also in Germany is documented by Fischer (1961), who reports that it was contemplated—how seriously I do not know—to offer Canada to the United States in exchange for a pro-German policy!

[42] This is one of the few remarks that could possibly be interpreted to be anti-Semitic. The reference is probably primarily to the *Neue Freie Presse*, a paper of international standards which had a Jewish editor-in-chief. So had other Viennese papers.

it . . . might be made into Austria's leading paper and give us a paper of world standards (Höhe der Zeit) and which can fulfill the great task to make the modern political technique of dominating public opinion serve old Austrian ideas and interests. However, there must first be an agreement about a definite program which would be pursued by every Government. Without such a program, . . . must lack all elan and influence . . . very great means, excellent work (Leistung) and finally also continuous effort are needed to attract if possible all good pens even if they come from the enemy camp. The readers, and with it the influence of the paper would have to extend from the Prince of the Church to the businessman. The paper would have to offer all of them as many news as any other in order to master the task to carry conservative views gradually into circles which were thus far strangers to them and thus to spread the basis of conservative thought and feelings. The strictly catholic character and the specifically catholic point of view would everywhere have to be brought out, which could only help the success of the paper, for this point of view is frequently latent in the consciousness of the Austrian even where it is not apparent. And the paper could smoothe the path to successful government policy if it does not simply identify with *every* government. Finally, the aim of all political activity must be practical work and to this end the achievement of political power. (Schumpeter 1992, 366–67; emphasis in original)

Evidently, Schumpeter had in mind a paper, such as the *Wall Street Journal* or the *New York Times* (or the *Neue Zürcher Zeitung*), conservative in its editorials, but *really* bringing "all the news that's fit to print."

On May 7, 1917, Schumpeter alerted Harrach to another memorandum he had sent by separate mail. Austria's independent position—evidently referring to the peace feelers—had aroused German sensibilities. Also, the strength of the Social Democrats had increased, which would present the domestic danger that the peace talks would be taken over by them. And this "would just be an occasion of reviving an international revolutionary spirit."[43]

Schumpeter toyed with the idea of peace negotiations by private diplomacy. It was advisable to inform oneself unofficially about a number of points and quickly for the coming peace negotiations.

I had the idea to travel in June to Sweden—strictly as a scholar who wished once again to talk to foreign colleagues about purely scientific matters—to discuss

---

[43] All of this sounds a great deal more far-fetched than it is unless it is remembered that Tsar Nicholas II had resigned on March 15, 1917, but the Kerenski regime continued to support the Entente, thus leaving the peace issue to the Bolsheviks. Shortly thereafter, Lenin was spirited to Russia in a sealed railroad car. On November 28, 1917, Lenin and Trotsky offered peace negotiations, and on December 15, 1917 the armistice of Brest-Litovsk was signed. Within a year Soviet regimes were installed in Munich and Budapest. I have found no clue to how Schumpeter felt toward the Kerenski regime, but he was actively involved in activities against the Bela Kun regime, and in one of his parliamentary speeches he pointed out that government policy in Vienna had succeeded in preventing a Communist takeover. It should be stressed that the Austro-Marxists, too, were anti-Soviet.

privately essential questions of the day and thus perhaps to gain valuable information. This would easily be possible precisely in Sweden, and something might be achieved which neither official diplomacy nor just any (irgendwelche) faiseurs might be able to do. However, further thought showed me that such an undertaking would be possible only with the support of the Foreign Office. . . . I venture to ask your Erlaucht to show [the Minister of Foreign Affairs] this memo provided it has the approval of Erlaucht, and perhaps to make an entrance to him possible, in which I could explain the usefulness (Opportunität) of such a visit to Sweden. (Schumpeter 1992, 368)

Erlaucht had indeed forwarded the memo to Count Czernin, the foreign minister, who had written an approving letter to Schumpeter, but regretted that pressure of work made it impossible to see Schumpeter in person (Letter, June 4, 1917; Schumpeter 1992, 378).

On June 25, 1917, Schumpeter sent yet another memorandum to Harrach. He argued the government's failure in parliament did not prove that the advice to convene parliament was wrong. But what really was on Schumpeter's mind was again the Bohemian question.

[I]t is urgently necessary just now in the eleventh hour, to make an effective attempt at a reconciliation with the Slavic parties and at the solution of our difficulties, if the position of the Monarchy vis-à-vis the enemy countries is not to be endangered in the extreme, and the domestic situation is not to become untenable. Instead we have received a Cabinet of civil servants which has neither authority nor a will of its own and which will entirely give in to the German-national Diktat at a time when the trade negotiations with Germany, the Ausgleichsnegotiations with Hungary and the serious . . . food situation demand, . . . a government which knows what it wants (zielbewusst). In my modest (unmassgeblich) view, only a coronation in Prague, sufficient concessions towards the Southern Slavs, and a determined position vis-à-vis the German Reich can save the situation, and the initiative for this can come only from a conservative party or a conservative Government. The alternative—to rule centralistically without Parliament, or even only a delay in forming a final Cabinet—make the possibility of a catastrophe immediate (bringt die Möglichkeit einer Katastrophe in greifbare Nähe). May God give that I am wrong, but *this* is how I see matters." (Letter, June 25, 1917; italics in original. Schumpeter 1992, 370–71)

It is quite clear that Schumpeter's optimism that it was still possible to save the situation was hard to sustain. He kept reverting to the Bohemian question as the central problem.

I, too, see the Thema probandum and the core of the matter in the fact that our constitution resembles for the Slawic people a too sharply pulled martingale, as a result of which, if I may be permitted to pursue the simile, the horses are overworked on the carriage of the Monarchy. I, too, believe that it explains about everything in the dualism which appears to be wrong, and that a reconstruction is unavoidable. Your Erlaucht is absolutely right: we do not suffer a lack of democracy, one could rather say that the social structure of Austria cannot stand *so much* democracy—and in particular so much giving in to every slogan of the day—that it does not correspond to its nature, and that it was imposed artificially: to guide and dominate such a far-reaching democracy with us is a very difficult task for which our government unfortunately is totally incapable. And because we have created so democratic institutions which, however, we—unlike English society—are unable to handle, these organs, in particular Parliament and the Press, get so easily out of hand. . . . [t]here remains still the hope, as your Erlaucht stresses, to continue the Ausgleichswork of the late Prince Thun and thus come to a good end. But if at all possible, it would seem to be desirable without pressure of the Crown to make yet another attempt. The . . . attempts of the last Government seem to me too inadequate to consider it proof that the lack of success must be interpreted as its impossibility. . . .

In the meantime valuable time is irretrievably lost. The negotiations with Germany, which are in the hands of nationally oriented civil servants continue quietly. And if agreements are reached which touch the independence of the Monarchy, the Slavs will really become what their majority certainly is not yet— enemies of the State. (Letter, July 6, 1917; Schumpeter 1992, 372–73)

Schumpeter agreed with Harrach. The Germans of Austria had the same ambitions as the Magyars (i.e., to make the German element dominant) but without the latter's political power or talent (Letter, July 16, 1917; ibid., 372).

I draw from this the conclusion: Because without an understanding with the Slavs the Monarchy never will find domestic rest, this understanding must be made as easy as possible. I share the outrage about illegal acts and words, and I, too, believe an expression of loyalty to the State essential. But after this, one should forgive and forget. A close attachment to the German Reich would have many advantages, but it might drive the Slavs to extreme measures and necessarily would raise other dangers for the Monarchy, particularly damage to its position vis-à-vis third countries. (ibid., 373)

There are no letters in the files for half a year. But on February 7, 1918, Schumpeter sent yet another memorandum to Harrach with a request for criticism. The letter is a cry of desperation:

All national groups have so radicalized themselves in the recent past, and all of them have adopted such an unacceptable (unqualifizierbar) language that it is difficult to maintain earlier sympathies. And yet it is necessary to find a modus which satisfies them and eliminates the most important frictions. Otherwise the Monarchy will die of it. The news of a military convention with Germany has saddened me greatly. I cannot confirm the news. But I confess that I would never have considered it possible that Austria would capitulate before Prussia.

But just for this reason, a strong Government which knows what it wants seems to me necessary for Austria. And the possibility of such a Government from the conservative standpoint I have tried to discuss in the third part of the memo. The second discusses the cause of the parliamentary misère, and the first the foreign policy problem. (Letter, February 7, 1918; ibid.)

The last letter in the files is dated February 19, 1918. Schumpeter again reverts to the Bohemian question:

The decisive standpoint before my eyes was that in *form* one should concede as much as possible. To be sure, I should not like simply to hand over German-Bohemia to the Czechs [Schumpeter wrote "Cechen"]. But if it is entirely autonomous, and if a Reichs Court watches over its rights—couldn't it then remain under the Crown of St. Wenceslas?[44] Language and administration of its own affairs remain safeguarded—one would thus fulfill precisely a *German* desire if this were the solution. That it would nevertheless be a province of the *Crown of St. Wenceslas* would be a concession to the *idea* on which the heart of the Czech people hangs. German as the official language in other directions might perhaps be conceded by the Czechs. (Letter, February 19, 1918; ibid., 374–75; italics in original)

Of course, this letter was much too late. On October 27, 1918, Emperor Karl I sued for a separate peace which in effect spelled the end of the Monarchy—if the Völkermanifest had not already done so. On November 11, 1918, the armistice between Germany and the Entente was signed. Schumpeter soon thereafter became a member of the German Socialization Commission, and Austrian minister of finance on March 17, 1919.

AN ASSESSMENT OF SCHUMPETER'S ANALYSES

I have gone into considerable detail of Schumpeter's memoranda and his letters to Count Harrach because they are the only detailed instance of Schumpeter as a political analyst and policy prescriber, not with a scholarly intent or audience in mind, but with the intent of influencing policy makers in a specific situation and of bringing about specific policy changes. The memoranda reveal Schumpeter in a role whose modern American equivalent would be that of the president's or at least a political party's domestic and foreign policy adviser.

Schumpeter considered himself a conservative, a term which in the meantime has lost all even halfway precise meaning.[45] He also identified himself unequivocally with the Monarchy, that "unique structure which we know and love," the characteristic of which was its multinationality with freedom for everyone in as many respects as was consistent with maintaining the State. That was what he defined as the Austrian Idea of the State, der österreichische

---

[44] This was in fact similar to the solution of German-speaking South Tyrol in 1945.

[45] Schumpeter's definition found in the Lowell Lectures was to facilitate change with a minimum damage to human values.

Staatsgedanke. It is relevant to note that he wanted to strengthen the Monarchy by converting it from an absolute into a constitutional Monarchy and to strengthen parliament by introducing a Tory democracy. But it made him an enemy of all kinds of nationalisms and intolerances which lived by suppressing other "different" people. This attitude is clearly consistent with his views of capitalism as an individualistic versus socialism or feudalism as a "social" structure, or with his analysis of methodological individualism recounted before.

He unequivocally opposed the war from the beginning, seeing clearly that it threatened that "civilized conservatism" which in a letter to Redvers Opie he mourned as lost forever. His conservativism was not reactionary, and it had a strong sense of social responsibility which to him was obviously quite consistent with individualism. It was a conservativism open to the needs of other nationalities, particularly the Czechs (who in the kingdom of Bohemia could look back to a distinguished past of national existence), and generally to all Slavic groups in the Monarchy. If it excluded the Hungarians it was only because Hungary wanted out of the Double Monarchy and because of the suppression of all non-Magyar elements, a policy which to this day has led to violent suppression of Hungarians in turn, and to the troubles between the formerly Hungarian Slowaks and Czechs.

Again, his opposition to war is not merely pacifism. It is also rooted in the analysis of imperialism which he saw as a precapitalist atavism rather than as a characteristic of late capitalism. Here, too, he took a position diametrically opposed to that of Marx and certainly of Trotsky, for whom imperialism was the last stage of capitalism. For Schumpeter, capitalism was by its very nature peaceful and certainly did not make war for war's sake. He was not alone in seeing the war as a major tragedy—see the famous remark of Earl Grey to the effect that the light had gone out over Europe, or, in France, Jean Jaurès's attempt to mobilize international socialism in opposition to the war. His attitude, too, was part of his world view, and what is remarkable is that he preserved a cool analytic head at a time of high emotional tensions. He was just as unhappy about the outbreak of the Second World War, and wrote in a letter that Chamberlain might have succeeded in averting the First World War.

I believe that Schumpeter's discussion and policy analysis have considerable interest in themselves, for the knowledge of pre–1914 Austria-Hungary, which, after all, was a major power, is practically nonexistent even in present-day Austria. It is not often that a theorist of highest caliber applies his analysis to a specific historic situation to formulate policies for achieving aims subject to specific historic limitations. In modern analytic terms he tried to formulate behavioral equations, tried to change some of them as much as possible, tried to find and influence as many policy variables as possible, set out clear target variables; that is, he did in greatest detail what Tinbergen later formalized. Thus, to refer constantly to Germany and Prussia as practically synonymous also reflected real constitutional situations. Prussia was based on its army in a way in which Austria—which to remind the reader did not exist in the present sense—was not. To be sure, Austria, too, had its share of past military glory. Yet there was a Latin hexameter which we as schoolboys learned: "Bella gerant alii! tu felix Austria nube" (Let others wage war, you happy Austria marry), which continued: "Nam quae Mars aliis, dat tibi regina Venus" (What Mars gives others, queen Venus gives you). This, too, was a fact which in 1919, for example, explained considerable separatist movements in all the Länder and the very modified loyalty to the Vienna of the republic. Why, after all, should Tyrol be all that loyal to Vienna only because in the fourteenth century, after the death of her second husband, Margarete Maultasch left it to the House of Hapsburg?

Yet questions must arise. As Schumpeter certainly was aware, the switches for the future policy were wrongly set in 1859 and 1866, long before the First World War. Schumpeter believed he knew how to set the switches right so that Austria could get back to its glorious past of providing, again in modern terms, a Commonwealth of Nations, and he evidently believed that this was still possible, though urgent. In 1814, at the Congress of Vienna, Austria had been the arbiter among the Great Powers. He saw the flood of nationalism unleashed by the French Revolution. But by 1914, it may well have been impossible to contain it, once the war had broken out—any more than colonialism, which incidentally Bismarck opposed, could withstand it, or in the 1980s and 1990s the Soviet Union. And who knows who will be next?

Schumpeter saw that to hold together a multinational State you had to, on the one hand, be able to satisfy what for want of a better term is called their national ambitions (that is, to make sure that they were not suppressed by other nationalities), while at the same time preventing them from doing unto others what they would not like to have done to them. But you also had to provide a central idea to hold them all together.

In Austria he saw this central magnet in the Hapsburg dynasty and the Historic Families of the high aristocracy, related by marriage and a common Catholic faith. Closer relations with the German Reich, which held no such substantial minorities would threaten the Monarchy and destroy it. During the war, Schumpeter, saw no alternative central idea which could hold a multination State together, at least not without suppressing its minorities.

But Schumpeter's analysis has its relevance to the present situation, nowhere more so than in Europe and the former Soviet Union. To take the latter first: with all the differences to the Double Monarchy, the Soviet Union succumbed to the same problems which plagued Austria (or for that matter which made Ottoman Turkey the Sick Man of Europe before). It is comparatively easy for Gorbachev to set East European countries free. They were never incorporated constitutionally into the Soviet Union. And there are precedences for it.[46]

---

[46] The Russian provisional government recognized Finland's autonomy within a Russian federation on March 21, 1917. On July 20, 1917 Finland declared itself independent. War followed. But on October 14, 1920, Finland became independent in the Treaty of Dorpat. Before, in 1899, there had been massive petitions in Finland reminiscent of the 1989 demonstrations in

But for the Soviet Union, once dynastic interests with their marriages and covenants are no longer considered legitimate anywhere in the world (except possibly in Japan), there remains only an idea, a Staatsgedanke. That idea was communism of the Leninist and later Leninist-Stalinist variety. This idea failed thoroughly and not only because of economic inefficiencies. In Schumpeter's view and on the basis of his long-term analysis, it necessarily failed.[47] The Soviet regime could never overcome its self-imposed ideological and historically inherited limitations of a totalitarian system which in fact vitiated even such successes as it had.

With the breakdown of this unifying Staatsgedanke of communism-Marxism-Leninism-Stalinism, this central idea vanishes as it did in the Monarchy, and nothing is left except raw power and unrelated nationalities. What is happening in the Soviet Union has frightening similarities to the dissolution of the Hapsburg Monarchy. Mutatis mutandis Schumpeter's analysis and prescriptions have gained considerable current interest.

There is then his political argument against the customs pact. Although based entirely on political grounds rather than on a strictly economic analysis, the two are in fact linked and Schumpeter's position is also economically vindicated to a considerable extent by the much later developments of customs union theory.

The issue was in a different form debated when the Treaty of Rome was signed in 1956 by the six original members of the Common Market. At that time, two question complexes were raised. One was that the treaty made sense only as a preliminary to closer political ties; otherwise free trade was an easier and more efficient means of achieving the same economic ends. The second was related: the treaty would benefit the participating countries only if it reduced general trade barriers, if it did not lead to a high-protectionist trade bloc. In 1916, Schumpeter foresaw the emergence of such a trade bloc as the result of an Austro-German customs pact, high-protectionist and hostile to the rest of the world, potential trade and economic war, and a continuous disturbance of world peace.

Schumpeter obviously lost on this point. The high-protectionist pest overwhelmed everyone after the First World War. It was one lesson well learned after the Second. Yet it may be questioned whether Schumpeter's arguments still had any realistic chance. In 1916, Schumpeter thought so and he evidently thought in 1919 that they were still possible in a modified form when he was minister of finance, when he hoped to preserve Vienna as the financial

---

the former Baltic states against Russian violations of its autonomy. Finland and the Aland Island had been ceded to Russia by Sweden in 1809, with the support of Napoleon.

[47] See the previously quoted assessment by Schumpeter to the effect that one could not understand the Russian revolution without knowing something of the Tsarist past, and that any comparison with Peter the Great would be favorable to the Tsar, who after all tried to introduce into Russia only something that existed already elsewhere, while Lenin tried to introduce something completely new. See also Schumpeter's insistence of the impossibility of socialism if it was introduced before its time (chapter 10 of this volume).

center of the successor states with a modicum of economic cooperation among them.

What Schumpeter wanted was to establish a situation in which nationalities could live together, in which general reduction of armaments to a purely defensive level could occur and in which, to coin a phrase, borders are not so much abolished as made irrelevant. Individual freedom and fulfillment of national ambitions together with mutual economic integration, that is, a free trading world, are precisely what Schumpeter and like-minded persons wished for.

All this would surely be made much easier if it were based on the idea of a liberal democracy. It basically requires only that nationalities achieve their ambitions if freer trade, the free movement of goods, persons, and capital could be achieved. This idea requires greater use of the market which in Schumpeter's analysis is after all culturally and socially quite neutral. It does not necessarily require giving up all State ownership of enterprises. But it does require strict budgetary policies, no subsidies for production (or at most only such subsidies as can be financed with local resources), a cutting of the umbilical cord between production and the budget, but also a willingness of people to adapt to their host country in language and customs—as is taken for granted in Switzerland with its four national languages, its large producing public sector, and its virtually all-pervasive local government.

This is how Schumpeter saw the solution of the Austrian problems. There is one further problem which is basic. The American version of democracy is based on a short Constitution which is constantly reinterpreted by the courts as new problems arise. The wisdom of the founding fathers was that they did not trust anyone, not the government, not the churches, but not the people either. There is in the Bill of Rights—and I have documented this in as much detail as seemed necessary for the understanding of Schumpeter—a prohibition in principle of what government can do. The Bill of Rights in principle should be interpreted that if in doubt, the powers of government, whether the legislative or the executive branch, must be restricted whenever there is a conflict between the claims of the individual and society.

If this interpretation is correct, Schumpeter's analysis of the problems of the Monarchy was brilliantly perceptive. It was not heeded partly because Kassandras are never heeded. His analyses have at the present time regained an unexpected actuality.

But Schumpeter was in part also not heeded because the mills of God grind exceedingly slowly. Hence, considerable lags are involved between the time when decisions are made and the time when their effects become manifest. While corrective actions are probably possible to the last—no one can be sure about that—they get more difficult to make as time progresses. Seventy years of mismanagement in the Soviet Union or forty in Poland and the former East Germany cannot be wiped out in a short time with the best of will and the best of policies. To anticipate, even Schumpeter's analysis as minister of finance turned out to have been quite realistic in its time table—and for that reason not acceptable.

Present times are perhaps more hopeful. For one thing, everyone realizes that a major war is no longer a viable alternative to solve any, even the largest, problems. Gradually the recognition also sinks in that military gains become quickly illusory if too great an economic damage results—which Schumpeter said in so many words. But this in itself is not sufficient to be sure that the right decisions will be made, that the necessary patience will prevail which the long lags require.

The German Coal Socialization Commission

MEMBERSHIP IN THE German Socialization Commission was Schumpeter's entry into the public arena, no longer only as an academic trying to bring his ideas to the notice of the people who might actually be able to do something, but still not with full political responsibilities. It was rather like being a member of a Royal Commission.[1] The burden of actual responsibility came a few months later when Schumpeter became minister of finance.

Calls for socialization were in the air and some people even saw in wartime agencies prototypes of things to come. However, it remained vague what was to be understood by socialization. In fact, the only thing clear seemed to have been that socialization was not to be the same as nationalization, and the particular form it was to take was left open.[2] There were several socialization commission reports dealing with specific sectors[3] but only the coal socialization commission produced an intellectually substantial report. The *Preliminary Report on the Socialization of High Sea Fisheries* has a more general discussion of the economics of high sea fishing, but states explicitly that

> The Socialization Commission—some of its members were absent during the crucial deliberations in Berlin—did not deal with the question whether High Sea Fishing should or could be socialized, of its own accord. Rather, the question was posed to the Commission from the outside. It arose as the result of the following circumstances: Presumably numerous enterprises on the German High Sea Coast connected with the navy will lose their reason for existence. It is therefore important, to find new employment opportunities for the population.[4]

A letter by Theodor W. Vogelstein to Professor Haberler gives us a clear idea of the workings of the Coal Socialization Commission and the circumstances under which Schumpeter became a member.[5] Schumpeter was not among the

---

[1] This was the phrase used by Theodor Vogelstein; see footnote 5.

[2] Oscar Simon (1919). The specific reference is found on p. 13, and refers more specifically to the justification of the proposed Law concerning the Communalization of Economic Enterprises.

[3] There was one on Municipal Enterprises, Ship Building, Housing and High Sea Fisheries.

[4] Socialization Commission (1919), quotation on p. 1. No members of the Commission participating or absent are mentioned.

[5] The information is contained in a memorandum by Vogelstein (1950), 7, which Professor Haberler kindly made available to me. The accompanying letter of Vogelstein to Haberler states that "I am forwarding a copy of this letter to Staudinger of the New School of Social Research in New York. I am also sending a copy the Hans Schaeffer, at present in Sweden." The letter also states: "I leave it to you to make whatever use you may wish of my remarks." Letter dated Hotel San Regis, Rue Jean Goujon, Paris, December 4, 1950. Professor Haberler's acknowledgment and comments are dated December 20, 1950.

original members who were presumably selected by the Ministry of Economics. Vogelstein recounts that Emil Lederer and Rudolf Hilferding, both original members,[6] agreed with him before the first meeting that they "wanted the Commission entirely independent of government influence. Kautsky and the other members agreed with us" (Vogelstein 1950, 1).

On the other hand, in his welcoming address the ministry spokesman wanted the commission to be "closely attached to the Ministry of Economic Affairs" which "would put certain problems before us and ask for detailed plans regarding their legislative and administrative execution" (ibid.).

This was rejected by Vogelstein with the concurrence of all members of the commission; Lederer and Hilferding are, however, specifically mentioned. The Ministry grudgingly accepted, but with the result of an outspoken distrust and enmity of the Ministry (ibid., 2). Schumpeter was brought in later at the suggestion of Lederer and Hilferding (ibid., 4), who had already made sure that Schumpeter would accept if asked.

There was in fact constant friction between the Commission and the government, particularly the Reich Economics Ministry, and the independence insisted upon by the Commission led to its practical irrelevance. Schumpeter resigned from the Commission on March 15 to become minister of finance. At the beginning of April 1919, all members of the commission resigned. Kautsky and Francke complained in a letter, dated April 7, 1919, that from the very beginning they had met with open or hidden obstruction from the Reich Economics Ministry. Thus, the Ministry had held back the publication of the preliminary report about coal socialization until it had pushed through its own proposals in the National Assembly, proposals that had not be shown to the Commission. And on March 26, the Ministry requested from the Commission proposals about the communalization of mortgage banks, telling it at the same time that the Ministry had already examined the question and made its decision. The Kautsky-Francke letter concluded that in the unanimous view of the Commission, no bureaucratic Ministry with a membership consisting entirely of members of the old regime could possibly develop a consistent, economically justifiable program for a new organization of the economy.[7]

It is worth mentioning that Vogelstein was asked to write the General Report, signed by all members, as well as the Majority Report, signed by all members of the Commission except Vogelstein and Francke, both opposed to socialization, who signed a separate Minority Report. In Kautsky's frequent

---

[6] Both Lederer and Hilferding were friends of Schumpeter. Both were Marxists, though pragmatic. Lederer became director of the scientific section of the Austrian Socialization Commission and thus senior adviser of Otto Bauer in 1919 as the head of the Austrian Socialization Commission. In 1931, he was appointed to the chair for Economic Theory at the University of Berlin. Hilferding became a social democratic minister of finance during the Weimar Republic. As refugee in France, he was handed over to the Nazis, and after being tortured, succeeded in committing suicide.

[7] Oscar Simon (1919), 7, 8, where a paraphrase of the Kautsky-Francke letter is given.

absence, Francke, a non-Socialist, was the chairman. "There was never any idea that membership of the Sozialisierungskommission implied a preference for socialism" (ibid., 2).

Since the hearings were held *in camera* there are no records of its deliberations. There are a few printed accounts of some hearings, but Schumpeter asked only very few and rather uninteresting questions.

Vogelstein also mentions that he, Lederer, Hilferding and Schumpeter contemplated writing "a platonic dialogue of the principal problems of socialism—without a Socrates who dominates the scene and brings the others to accept his views" (ibid., 6), but this came to nothing, among other reasons because "Schumpeter was in a hurry to leave" (ibid., 5) to become minister of finance in the second Renner Cabinet, also at Hilferding's suggestion.[8]

Vogelstein, however, believed that at that time Schumpeter was inclined toward socialism, and that he sided more often with Lederer "as against Hilferding who—as always in practical matters—was more compromising and willing to yield to the arguments of his opponents" (ibid., 5).

Haberler cites Schumpeter's bon mot that he gave as a standard answer how he, a non-Socialist, could be a member of a socialization commission: "If someone wants to commit suicide it is good for a doctor to be present," a somewhat obscure saying whose only meaning one can sense is that perhaps the doctor could keep the suicide from dying should he change his mind at the last moment.

Vogelstein, on the other hand, mentions Schumpeter as saying: "Ich weiss nicht, ob Sozialismus möglich ist. Aber wenn, dann nur integral. Wenigstens wäre es ein interessantes Experiment, es einmal zu probieren. [I do not know whether socialism is possible. But if it is, only totally. It would at least be an interesting experiment to try it for once.]" (Handwritten addition to Vogelstein's letter).

This remark has the mark of authenticity. There is the playfulness, felt by Wieser to be irresponsibility, of talking in desperate times of making a major social experiment. But in fact, Schumpeter, in one of his many speeches, makes quite clear that there was an either-or here, that you either stuck to the socialist principle—never closely defined—or to capitalist principles, but that in any case no one, socialist or capitalist, could possibly have an interest in ruining the economy. And in a speech of March 21, 1919, Schumpeter did state that in the Majority Report he went as far as he could.

It is certainly true that in 1918–1919 noone had any set ideas of what precisely socialism should mean. To be sure, Lenin had established (though not yet consolidated) a Soviet regime in Russia, and there were short-lived

[8] See letter by Gustav Stolper to Dr. Kurt Singer, Schriftleitung des Wirtschaftsdienstes, Hamburg, dated Vienna, December 5, 1919. "Schumpeter who was brought into the Government by Otto Bauer on the recommendation of Hilferding." The letter is found in a Stolper Nachlass deposited with the Bundesarchiv, Koblenz. The letter is reprinted in full in Schumpeter (1985).

attempts at a Bolshevik revolution in Hungary and Bavaria. But certainly these ideas made no headway in Austria. The small Austrian Communist party flirted with Hungary, but it had an ulterior motive in the hope that Hungary would ship grain to Austria, assistance the Hungarian comrades declined to provide.

Mises had not yet published his *Gemeinwirtschaft*, and Schumpeter had not yet published anything specifically to do with the problem of socialization. On the other hand, Otto Bauer had in 1918 published his *Der Weg zum Sozialismus*[9] whose ideas are in many respects remarkably similar to those held by the authors of the Majority Report of the Coal Socialization Commission.

To start with, no one, not even Lenin, thought in 1918–1919 of socializing the whole economy at once— and noone had any very clear idea what to do. As Bauer had pointed out:

[T]he political revolution can be the work of *one* day. . . . The political revolution was the work of force; the social revolution can only be the work of constructive organizing labor. The political revolution was the work of a few hours; the social revolution will be the result of daring, but also of thoughtful labor of many years. (Bauer 1921, 7, 9; italics in original; my translation).

Certainly Bauer was aware that the specifics of socialization had to be determined by the specifics of the historical situation. He also made quite clear that many of the Austrian industries were not yet ripe for socialization and that socialization would have to take different forms in different industries (ibid., 12). It is therefore clear that what was meant by socialization in 1919 is not what under the influence of later writings, particularly by Mises, and of events particularly in Russia, is understood by it now, and that one has to guard against judging the past by present standards.

The Preliminary Report of the Socialization Commission[10] is a remarkable document for several reasons. It saw the socialization of the coal industry mainly as a problem of productivity and getting the economy going again, and it was signed by Marxists and non-Marxists alike. This was also explicitly stated by Bauer:

---

[9] Otto Bauer (1921).

[10] *Vorläufiger Bericht der Sozialisierungskommission über die Frage der Sozialisierung des Kohlenbergbaus*. Abgeschlossen am 15. Februar 1919. R.v.Decker Verlag. G. Schenk, Berlin SW 19. Members were Ballod, Cunow, Hilferding, Lederer, Schumpeter, Umbreit, Francke, Vogelstein and Wilbrandt. Kautsky, though chairman, did not sign the Reports due to frequent absences.

The Preliminary Report was also reprinted as an annex to the Final Report, *Bericht der Sozialisierungskommission über die Frage der Sozialisierung des Kohlenbergbaues vom 31. Juli 1920*, Verlag Hans Robert Engelmann, Berlin W. 15, 1920. Schumpeter was no longer a member. On the other hand, Hilferding and Lederer as well as Kautsky signed various parts of it, and among the greatly enlarged membership were Rathenau, Siemens, and Kuczinski. (No first names are given.)

We have become terribly poor. . . . In such times we must be very careful not to do anything which would destroy our productive apparatus even more, which makes raw material imports even more difficult . . . which would reduce the total result of our labor even more. Our poverty forces us to make the distribution of goods more just; but it forces us also to make this change so that the production of goods does not suffer. (ibid., 8; my translation)

On this count there was no difference of opinion. Also, all agreed that socialization should mean a more democratic and not a dictatorial organization. The Austro-Marxists and the German Social Democrats were democrats. So they made a careful distinction between nationalization and socialization, in German between "Sozialisierung" and "Vergesellschaftung," "societization" if such a word is permitted. It was the latter not the former which was the true socialist principle.

In fact, the social democrats distrusted government intensely. The distrust was partly political, partly moral, but also quite practical. Bauer has this remarkable statement:

Who should administer the socialized industry? Government? Certainly not! If the Government were to dominate all possible plants, it would be all too powerful vis-à-vis the people and the representatives of the people. Such an increase in the power of the Government would be dangerous for democracy. And besides, the Government would administer the socialized industry badly; nobody manages industrial enterprises worse than the State. For this reason, we social democrats have never demanded nationalization (Verstaatlichung) always only socialization (Vergesellschaftung) of industry. (ibid., 10; my translation)

The introduction to the Commission Report points out how much industry was already in the hands of the (Prussian) State. However, the real justification for socialization—the term will from now on always be used to denote Vergesellschaftung—of industry was that it enjoyed regional monopoly power, being based on a cartelized organization. The potential monopoly power is considered "to make evident that it is necessary to abolish it altogether" (Socialization Commission 1919, 2). The existence of monopoly power gives both the moral and the economic justification for socialization. The Commission stressed that the existing organization of the mines conflicted with economic necessities and therefore had to be thoroughly changed:

[The Commission] is unanimous that the whole organization of the authority, of employment, promotion, salaries, budgeting and accounting, in short the whole order of the normal Government enterprise with its bureaucratic point of view constitute severe obstacles to the economic exploitation of the mines. Any extension of Government enterprises is uneconomic and therefore to be rejected as long as the economic activity of the State is not completely separated from its political and administrative traditions, as long as there is not a complete break with the bureaucratic traditions of the enterprises of the State. The hearings of the Commission have produced such striking examples of the inadequacy of this slow

Government organism that there can be no doubt whatever about the necessity of the complete reorganization of the existing Government mines. (ibid., 4–5)

Examples given for the slow operation included most strikingly a dependence on parliament for decisions and "negotiations over years about questions which in private industry would be settled in hours, in short, control upon control instead of trust and incentives for independent action are the characteristics of this organization" (ibid., 5).

Socialization of isolated enterprises would merely substitute many for a few owners and change nothing.

There is here a real difference from the Communist practice in which enterprises get their capital through the budget. The insistence on cutting the umbilical cord between the enterprises and the budget is central, and during the finance minister days it is the real issue between Schumpeter and Bauer. It is also the real trouble in the present (1990) turmoil in the Eastern bloc countries: who should run the industries, how they should be run, and how they can be weaned off budgetary subsidies.

The Commission considered several alternatives. A return to the free market was considered impossible, partly for political reasons: "socialization" was in the air and some rather weird (verschrobenste) ideas floated around. Liquidation of the war would require continuing regulation, at least for a while, and the war had increased the degree of cartelization.

A simple nationalization of the industry, that is, what is usually understood by socialization, "a universal organization of capital under public ownership" (ibid., 8), was also rejected as State capitalism:

> Such plans which derive from wartime organization want to organize the supply of goods uniformly so as to meet more effectively the needs of the State and to syphon off or even increase capital rents, such plans of a gigantic compulsory organization with merely technical internal mobility are nowadays economically as well as politically impossible. In truth, such intentions . . . are simply an intensification of the capitalist system. (ibid.)

There remains socialization, which "given the present difficult situation is resolutely based on the socialist principle" (ibid.). The arguments were both economic and moral:

> The present situation demands the strictest adherence to economic points of view . . . the unnecessary frictional losses of capitalist competition must be avoided by organization . . . with the . . . cooperation of the workers. . . . But this involves the danger that the workers of each plant may claim the ownership of the means of production. Against this, the need for uniformity of procedure can not be stressed enough. Democracy within the plant with uniform direction of the industry as a whole, elimination of the dominating role of capital, nurturing (Aufbau) of entrepreneurial and economic activity on the basis of creative personalities—this is the content of the reconstruction which the wishes of the workers desire. This means the socialization of the production of goods. A com-

plete socialization (Vergesellschaftung) is therefore also what the majority of the Commission proposes. . . . The entire German coal mining [activity] is to be transformed into an efficient uniform economic body. Private and Government enterprises become the property of this [new] organization. A public (gemein-wirtschaftlich) coal organization is formed, run by the workers, management and the general public. The majority of the Commission rejects therefore the creation of a bureaucratic State enterprise. It also rejects the maintenance of the private capitalist system and merely to subject it to stringent control. Such a solution would hit private initiative in its vital nerve without at the same time the advantages of the social idea. Rather our ideas amount to creating an organization in which the initiatives of the managers and the work morale of the workers have the widest possible play. The organization would therefore not only allow the fullest development of *those* forces which produce the richest results of the private-capitalist (privatkapitalistisch) system, but also stimulate the personal interest of the last worker in the success of the enterprise and would thus realize the principle of socialism. (ibid., 8, 9; my translation)

This vision may have been politically naive, but if so it was also shared by the authentic Marxist members and basically also by the two non-Marxist "liberal"—in the European sense of the word—signers of the Minority Report. The Minority Report went in one respect further than the majority in insisting that, as diminishing returns (for geological reasons) created substantial differential rents, these differential rents should be taxed away.

The vision also very much corresponded to what Bauer proposed for Austria. The Soviet model was rejected as undemocratic internally—Soviet-type economies certainly never permitted any union power but used unions as means of controlling the workers. It also rejected what later became the so-called Yugoslav model of worker management. The ownership of workers as shareholders as exists in the United States is, of course, simply a capitalist form. But the Commission also rejected the public utility model.

The State was in fact also seen as something of an enemy by Socialists, with its expected bureaucratization and what has since become known by the Soviet epithet "nomenclatura." Socialization—Vergesellschaftung—was seen as working for society as a whole, not for the State. It was the capitalist who was to be eliminated, but not the entrepreneur.

This certainly was very much in keeping with the Scbumpeterian analysis which I have recounted before. Rejecting the State as the repository of the "Common Good" is probably also in agreement with Marxist as well as Schumpeterian sociology with roots apparently going back to Engels. Marxist sociology always asked the question in whose interest the State would be run, and for the Marxist it was run in the interest of the bourgeoisie, self-denying philosopher-kings being rather rare. Bureaucratization involved not only being "slow," "cumbersome," and "inefficient," but also run in the interest of the bureaucracy (or in the case of Leninism in the interest of the party).

There is thus a clear line to later discussions of bureaucracy and democracy from the Socialization Commission via *Capitalism, Socialism and Democracy* to Downs, Niskanen, and others, with the roots of the discussion certainly going much further back. The distinction between nationalization and socialization is thus not an empty one.

The proposed German Coal Community (GCC) was to be a totally independent legal person, in particular independent of the government. The government owned the mines "only in a formal sense" since it could exploit neither the workers nor the consumers. Schumpeter had always distinguished sharply between the legal forms and the economic content of an institution.

In 1911, Schumpeter had already pointed out that unfortunate legal definitions could have harmful economic results.[11] The legal and administrative organization of the proposed GCC therefore required careful attention.

> It would be no progress but a regress to transfer property rights of the present owners—following syndicalist or production-cooperative ideas—to the workers and in every enterprise and to put into the place of *one* entrepreneur a few hundred or thousand in form of the former workers whose interests would correspond to the interest of the private capitalists, but whose ability to run the business would be less. The organization to be sketched is *objectively* as much a break with the system of private property in coal mining—as distinct from the mere transfer of ownership to different legal subjects—as it means a break in principle with the system of wage labor since the purpose of production is no longer capitalist profit even though the legal form of wages is to continue for the time being. (ibid., 10–11; italics in original; my translation)

On this point the majority and the minority of the Commission agreed almost completely. The GCC should be as independent as possible in its decisions. Its powers would be not less than that of existing private corporations. All technical and economic decisions were to be made by the GCC

---

[11] "Gründungsgewinn in Recht und Wirtschaft", *Zeitschrift für Notariat Osterreich* (1911), vol. 4, 31. This is a report about a speech given by Schumpeter before the Wiener Juristische Gesellschaft on January 11, 1911. Reprinted in Schumpeter 1993. In this speech Schumpeter refers to entrepreneurial profits as founder's profit. After analyzing its nature, Schumpeter concludes:

> The economic nature of the founder's profit does thus not agree with its treatment by the legal system. With us, the founder will get the profit which rests on his own labor only with great difficulties. Here we have one of the reasons for the backwardness of our corporate law (Aktienwesen). The dislike of the founder which shows itself also elsewhere is, however, not explained by abuses but has deeper reasons. The legal system . . . does not agree with the economic nature of the founders' profit but it does agree with the *legal consciousness* (Rechtsbewusstsein), *of the people*. The legal consciousness of the people and its legal picture in the legal system rests thus on earlier economic facts. Those facts change under our feet and we confront them with the standards of earlier days. Hence the anticapitalist excesses (Ausschreitungen). Moral views change only slowly and it takes a long time until one is conscious that one deals with ghosts. In other fields, too, we see that the dead rule the living. (italics in original)

including borrowing from banks and the capital market. Only the sale of mines (but not of subsidiary enterprises) was to be forbidden.

The Reich had certain tasks. The price policy of the GCC was to be subject to approval (Genehmigung); and mortgaging required the consent of the Reich. But the budget and auditing of the GCC were to be legally and economically independent of the Reich. Only the final profits were to be transferred to the Reich after due allowance for reserves. Interestingly, or perhaps characteristically, losses are not mentioned. Yet the burdening of the budget by expected losses was precisely Minister of Finance Schumpeter's objection to Bauer's later proposals.

The internal organization of the GCC was to follow the principle of economic democracy. *But*

> [N]ot so self-evident but equally important is that the leadership of the GCC must have adequate power and mobility. The Commission puts the greatest possible emphasis on this point, for one of the worst dangers threatening the planned organization would be the elimination of the initiative and individual readiness to accept responsibility. If that shifting to collegiate decision or agreement of control organs occurred, if every decision would be the result of long consultations and a cumbersome movement of files, if no one were identified with success or failure of a measure . . . even the best will of all participants would not prevent the cessation of economic development. But this would from the very onset discredit the basic idea of socialization for a long time to come. If the Commission is in complete agreement to stress the importance of leadership in economic life . . . it does so in the conviction that this does not contradict the basic principles of democracy. For, democracy surely requires that every action of the leading personalities is supported by the trust and will of all concerned. But it requires also that the leading personalities have complete freedom to decide and to move as long as they have this trust. (ibid., 12–13; my translation)

So we meet again the problem of decision making and leadership which is central to Schumpeter's distinction between statics and dynamics-evolution, which concerned him in the Secret Memoranda and again in his *Deutsche Volkswirt* articles and in *Capitalism, Socialism and Democracy*. It is clear that Schumpeter, but also Lederer, Hilferding, and really also the earlier Otto Bauer, meant by socialization essentially a public corporation which—like a university—owns itself, but unlike a university is run for profit, with internal democracy but without monopoly power.

Of course, there is no detailed consideration of what the interest of society as a whole could mean. Schumpeter always questioned what the general welfare could mean—except perhaps in a besieged fortress.[12] The GCC would behave like a (more or less) competitive firm with internal democracy with respect to working conditions, but with the Reich ensuring that no monopolistic abuses of market power occurred nor any exploitation by its

---

[12] See the article of 1911 on "Social Value."

workers which might be disguised as "social necessities," a favorite ploy in LDCs. But the Commission cannot be faulted for not seeing the problems such an organization would have to solve in order to remain a dynamic actor in development.

To achieve these aims the GCC would be supervised by a Coal Council of one hundred members, consisting of elected members of the workers, management, consumers, and the Reich, meeting every three months. Ten of the Reich representatives were to be named by parliament, the rest by the Reichspräsident personally. Any influence of a "responsible Ministry"—le ministère tutelle, as the French call it—is explicitly excluded to ensure that the economic and the political activities of the State were strictly divorced from each other. Not more than a third of the Reich representatives were to be civil servants.

The Coal Council was responsible for the business of the GCC including the determination of the tonnages to be mined, the extent and methods of operations of individual mines, prices, and the basic documentation (Unterlagen) for fixing wages and the distribution of coal. "The wages agreed upon by the workers' representatives and management must be transmitted to the Coal Council for its information" (ibid., 14).

Executive power was vested in the Reich Coal Directorate elected by the Council for five years and operating on the basis of an annual budget. The executive was, however, to be free to authorize unforeseen expenditures and if necessary to borrow money. "It is above all the organ through which the GCC adapts itself to changes in the market, in particular in international trade" (ibid., 14).

There was unanimity that this freedom of decision making had to be supported by good pay so "that the greatest possible effort be achieved by combining a social sense of responsibility and a professional (sachlich) pleasure in the work with an economic interest in the productive success" (ibid., 15).

I forego a further description of how the democratic principles of nonexploitation of both the workers and the public was to be ensured; also the discussion of the economic extent of the GCC. The section concerning "Expropriation and Compensation" contains the remarkable sentence that the State, too, should be expropriated in favor of the GCC and compensation be paid on the basis of the average return of a "ten year prewar period" payable in fixed interest bearing convertible bonds, a proposition which the subsequent rampant inflation would have made largely irrelevant.

The final section of the report (pp. 36–39) signed by all members of the Commission dealt with the internal organization of the workplace. It comes closest to defining what is meant by the socialist principle:

[The Commission] supports unanimously the widest possible say of the workers and employees in the determination of the organization of work, safety measures, wages . . . and safeguards against personal and political abuses by superiors. In the workplace the principle of democracy must be applied. But this does not require to withhold the technical leadership from the management. *The workers themselves have made no such demands.* Nor can the hiring and firing of management be subject of the vote of the workers. . . . not only the interest of the workers but of society as a whole depend on the correct selection of the manager. This selection must ensure that the productive forces are expertly administered. *Hence the choice of the leading personalities can not be entrusted only to the workers. Nor have the representatives of the workers expressed such demands.* (ibid., 36–37; italics added)

There was also unanimity that "the material interest of all" should determine the wage structure. For workers, productivity premia were to be instituted but "a good average effort" should account for the major portion of the wage which thus "should not depend on fortunate accidents or extraordinary effort." No Maoist equality,[13] but also no Stakhanovism. Nor a standard-of-living determined wage so commonly proposed by wage commissions in LDCs. Middle management should be paid on the same principles but with the premium element playing a bigger role. Top management, however, would receive bonuses in addition to their salaries comparable to those prevailing in private industry: the GCC was to be competitive with private industry.

SOME COMMENTS

Thus, in 1919 socialization meant something quite different from what, under the influence on the one hand of Mises and on the other of Soviet propaganda, it has come to mean since. It was neither the transfer of ownership of the factors of production to the State, nor the Soviet model of the leading role of the party, nor the Yougoslav model of worker management, and certainly not the Maoist one. Nor was it the model of public utility regulations.

There is only the barest hint of how such enterprises should be run. The *Final Report* is somewhat more specific but mainly by stressing even more the indispensability of true entrepreneurs and expert managers. There is no discussion of how prices should actually be set and supervised by the government, but this is quite understandable: the coal industry was an export industry, subject to international competition—or rules of an international cartel. Socialization would improve efficiency, presumably through increased worker morale, but also by eliminating monopolistic practices. How to deal with possible losses is nowhere mentioned, but the clear implication of the discussion is that they certainly should not be met by budgetary subsidies. The emphasis is on efficient, profitable, and above all independent and dynamic enterprises.

The independence from government was expressed through the manner of

---

[13] This was incidentally also Bauer's position who was quite aware of the free rider problem (Bauer 1921, 7–8).

vesting and raising its capital. Unlike in the typical Soviet-type—or LDC-type—enterprise, the necessary capital should not come from the budget, but the enterprise was expected to generate the needed investment funds internally but *without* using its monopoly power to charge high prices, or to raise them on the capital market including by borrowing from banks. The bonds for the compensation of the expropriated owners were also not to burden the budget, though this is not stated explicitly in the report.[14] The bonds were evidently to be issued by the Corporation without government guarantees, and interest payments were expected to be made out of operating income, though again this is not explicitly stated. The principles stated by the Commission were exactly the principles which Schumpeter later defended against Bauer in the actual Austrian case as it later developed, though not as it was originally conceived.

The second comment is the optimism, perhaps even naiveté, coming through the recommendations. How could you be sure that people would in fact behave as they were supposed to? Marxist critics would, of course, stress that the bourgeoisie would never permit a transfer of profitable enterprises to the public sector—except that in fact no one at least in Austria opposed such a transfer and that Hilferding and Lederer were Marxists in good standing. Bourgeois critics on their part stress that the workers would exploit the enterprises in the interest of those employed in the plant, though again in fact the workers were quite sensible and considered the "Yougoslav model" guild socialism, not "scientific socialism." And, again in fact, in the 1980s worker-owned factories follow the recommendation of the Commission as far as management is concerned: management salaries of $300,000 were reported for the Wierton Steel Company bought by the workers.

In fact, the political situation described before was such that the unions distrusted the State intensely and feared the loss of their hard-won gains. But the real issue was the abuse of power by whoever happens to have it. References to the general good or the supervision by the Coal Council remain somewhat unconvincing to us. In theological terms you have to solve the problem arising out of original sin. This is the real content of Hayek's *Constitution of Liberty*, of constitutional economics. Milovan Djilas had already rediscovered it in his *Unperfect Society*[15] and it was not exactly unknown to Lord Acton.

The third comment is, in the context of Schumpeter's views of socialism, perhaps the most relevant. How could Schumpeter, the high priest of entrepreneurial genius, support socialism when he obviously was not a Socialist? The answer has been given, in part at least, in the discussion of the meaning of an evolutionary economy. Entrepreneurs were the moving force of development, but not necessarily of capitalist development only. They *could* be pres-

---

[14] From Lederer's advice to Bauer to be quoted below it is however evident that this was certainly the intention.

[15] Milovan Djilas (1969).

ent also in socialism, they *had* to be present in capitalism if capitalism were to continue to be capitalism. Capitalism was defined by constant change. Socialism was defined by how preferences were formed, not by specific legal property rights.

The entrepreneurial function is exercised by different people at different times. We need banks—which surprisingly most Socialists did not want to socialize immediately—but strictly speaking we do not need capitalists unless they behave like entrepreneurs.

In chapter 7 of the first (1911) edition of the *Theorie*, Schumpeter points out how little capital—as he defined it—really was needed in a capitalist economy, how little it really takes to make such a society work. He points out how quickly economies can recover from devastating wars— this was written before the First World War, but the Thirty Years War or the Napoleonic wars were also traumatic experiences—if only the entrepreneurial drive is given its head unless totally stupid domestic or foreign policies are made. When the Coal Socialization Report was written, Schumpeter evidently believed that this could also happen in Austria. The success of the European Recovery Program after the Second World War proves that on an analytical level he was right.

There was thus no theoretical or political contradiction in supporting *this* kind of socialization which the Coal Socialization Commission outlined and which the Austro-Marxists also endorsed. *That* kind of socialism had a chance as long as sound principles of economic behavior were safeguarded.

The Minister of Finance

or

Coping with Disaster

Initial Problems

THE PRELIMINARY REPORT of the German Coal Socialization Commission was finished on February 15. There was an item in the press regarding negotiations with Schumpeter about his becoming minister of finance while he was still in Berlin. Schumpeter became minister on March 15, 1919. He lasted until October 17, almost exactly seven months.

It was a period of extraordinary activity for Schumpeter, both in the cabinet and as a public speaker. As already noted, he was brought into the cabinet at the suggestion of his friends Hilferding, Lederer, and Bauer, but he was brought in as a technical minister without a party affiliation, which also meant without a power base of his own.

His conservative leanings could not have been unknown,[1] but this did not seem to matter at a time when everyone really was in favor of socialization, though everyone probably had something different in mind. His final resignation occurred in circumstances which the *Neue Freie Presse* (NFP) chastised as a political execution. At the end, Schumpeter joined the Christian Social Party. But he was not trusted by them either, because he was considered a friend of the Jews—ein Judenfreund—and he had the tough luck that a former colleague of his in Graz, Gürtler, whose promotion to full professor he had prevented when dean, was the Christian Social Whip (Fraktionsvorsitzende) in parliament.

But wanting to become a minister in two situations which at least in retrospect seemed hopeless raises questions. Schumpeter certainly thought he knew what had to be done to save the situation, and the analysis of his proposals certainly suggests that he was right. He had in the *Crisis of the Tax State* characterized the man who could save the situation as a man who could fascinate the people and rally them behind him. He developed an intense political activity in many speeches and interviews. These speeches were certainly intended to do just that and to build a power base of his own.[2]

But there were from the beginning objective as well as personal reasons why he had to fail in the end.[3] Schumpeter's analytical acumen was not matched by

---

[1] When Wieser heard of Schumpeter's appointment as minister, he made the following entry in his diary: "Schumpeter as 'bourgeois whipping boy' in the new government, he, the monarchist, arch conservative, England's friend and German hater, the enemy of social democracy!" (Schumpeter 1992, 10).

[2] See the Wieser diary (1919), partly reproduced in Schumpeter (1992), already quoted in chapter 2.

[3] "He makes no bones about his opinion of the Cabinet in which he sits. The only person of intellectual standing (Kapazität) is Otto Bauer, who in turn respects him. (His words make it

a political sense of what in fact turned out to be realistic. He came to grief also because he expected a "rational" behavior on the side of the Entente, his beloved English and his respected French, as well as of the successor states, that simply was not in the cards. In other words, he lacked the requisite political know-how.

Yet the question is legitimate whether even a Metternich could possibly have succeeded in a situation in which a bitter war had left the belligerents exhausted and the atmosphere poisoned.

During the imperial period he thought that Austria could still be saved by being converted into a true multinational state. In 1919, he thought that the Entente and the successor states would see that inward-looking policies made no economic sense for the latter and that the Entente would see that preserving a non-German dominated Central Europe was in their interest. Thus, he had proposed to Allizé, the French ambassador, a monetary union with France.[4]

Schumpeter evidently held on to this opinion as late as July 1919, and he may have been misled by the French ambassador to believe that this was a serious possibility. Bauer did not think so and insisted on resigning as foreign minister. Bauer thought that

> [I]t would be impossible to change the general lines of the peace terms and that we should concentrate on particular points as otherwise we would achieve nothing at all. We believed that the big powers tried to establish their influence in Prague, Belgrade and Bucharest, and would, therefore, not quarrel with these countries on our account. Schumpeter, the Minister of Finance, was opposed to this opinion, because the French minister Allizé had told him that the Allied powers waited for our counter-proposals from St. Germain and would then change the terms fundamentally, if we renounced the Anschluss. Schumpeter believed that small concessions would make it impossible to avoid Austria's bankruptcy.[5]

Bauer and Schüller were right about the realistic chances of Allizé's encouraging words. But it also shows that Schumpeter did not oppose the Anschluss just out of gut feelings or behind the Bauer's back, and it explains the other-

---

quite clear that with all differences of opinion they esteem each other highly as personalities while they think little of the others around them.) Of Renner he says that he "cowers" when Otto Bauer just begins to take the word. Of course, Schumpeter is against the Anschluss with Germany. He gives for this economic-financial considerations, but it is more likely based on gut feeling of his soul. When taking my leave I told him openly, after having let him speak without interruption, that I am for the Anschluss and why" (ibid., 1919; Schumpeter 1992, 10–11).

[4] "Bauer told me that Schumpeter, Minister of Finance, had proposed to Allizé: Austria would renounce the Anschluss, a monetary union should be established between Austria and France; South Tirol should not be separated from Austria. I believed such a plan to be very advantageous for Austria if it could be realized, and thought it would be worth the establishment of a government friendly to the Entente. Bauer agreed but did not believe the plan could succeed. . . ." Richard Schüller, Typewritten manuscript in the Haus- Hof- und Staatsarchiv, Vienna, 28. I owe this reference to Dr. Gertrud Enderle-Burcel. The Schüller account is in English.

[5] Ibid., 44. Refers to a meeting of the Austrian Cabinet in Feldkirch, July 21, 1919.

wise quite inexplicable optimism of many of Schumpeter's initial speeches. In any case, Schumpeter's sympathy for the Entente and his love for England were general knowledge.

The interview with *Le Temps*[6] is not quite what has been commonly believed. It is true that Schumpeter makes very strong statements about Germany's interest in the Anschluss with a rather remarkable analytical foresight:

> The German Reich has a great interest to absorb Austria, for, if successful, it would encircle Czecho-Slovakia which would sooner or later be reduced to capitulate first economically, later politically; it would assure a very strong position vis-à-vis the Yugoslavs against whom one day she hopes to come to an understanding with Italy to reopen a road to Trieste. Hence, Germany, despite suggestions of some of its representatives about the "bad business it would be with Austria" is quite ready to make considerable sacrifices to favor the union. Germany offers us one billion marks per year, an assimilation by monetary cooperation of the krone to the mark, to take over our war debt. We prefer, however, the advantages and inconveniences of independence, *provided* this independence lets us live. (italics added; my translation)

The interview otherwise strongly repeats what Schumpeter also said in his domestic speeches and interviews. It starts with a lengthy description of the magnificent office in the Palais built by Prince Eugene of Savoy[7] and designed by the great Fischer von Erlach in the Himmelpfortgasse—the Street of the Gate of Heaven—and the impression le Docteur Schumpeter made on an outsider:

> Le docteur Schumpeter, Minister of Finance, is the youngest member of the present cabinet, not forty years old. His clean shaven face, animated by very lively brown eyes, is pale and a little tired though energetic. Le docteur Schumpeter whom informed circles consider an important delegate to St. Germain now that the real negotiations begin, was professor of political economy in Graz and his previous work in economic history and particularly on tax questions make him on the morning after the dismemberment of the Monarchy the right man [the English words are in the original] in the ministry of finance, one might almost say the ministry of the financial liquidation of the ex-Empire. His works are inspired by the political and social ideas of a very advanced liberalism. He is, however, not a socialist, being in a ministry of coalition [*sic*] one of the technicians without political label to whom the delicate portfolios have been entrusted. Some even blame him with a certain bitterness for the impeccable cut of his morning coat,

---

[6] "Entretien avec le Docteur Schumpeter." De notre enyoye special. Vienne, Mai." No day is given. *Le Temps*, June 2, 1919, 2. My translation. Reprinted in German translation in Schumpeter (1992).

[7] The prince was the Austrian general who defeated the Turks. One of the rooms is decorated with numerous battle scenes of the Prince's victories. In one, a nineteenth century restorer painted in an anachronistic dispatch rider on a bicycle. Savoy was Sardinian at the time and ceded to France only in 1859.

and I must say that if he is a very "pure" republican, he has nothing of a sans-culotte. His international experience (he was exchange professor in England [sic] and America), his personal culture, partly French, partly Anglo-Saxon, have opened his eyes for a long time to the dangers of German imperialism and have led him in the face of it to a fairly clear pacifist position.

Marcel Dunan, the special correspondent signing the dispatch, also makes very perceptive remarks about Schumpeter's problems. Aside from the general uncertainties of the situation,

> there is a general silence for reasons of domestic politics, which hamper all ministers of the coalition and the civil servants, whose personal ideas and political attachments diverge greatly. Ministerial solidarity, however, binds them and it would be very difficult for any of them to express entirely his own view of any subject matter without tearing up at some point the compromise which constitutes the actual program adopted. The minister of finance nevertheless was happy to resume in the following brief declarations our first conversation.[8]

Except for the already quoted paragraph on German intentions, the interview strongly repeats what Schumpeter said publicly in his speeches. There are two preconditions for Austria to survive and to avoid bankruptcy and complete collapse. The first is an equitable distribution of the burden left by the Monarchy to the successor states: "My whole fiscal policy rests on the assumption that such an equitable distribution of the burden could be obtained; no reasonable policy could otherwise be achieved in Austria on other conditions. *If our legitimate hope is realized I am not pessimistic about the future of the new Austria.*"[9]

As the correspondent pointed out, the difficulty was how to define equity. Schumpeter actually had some comments on this. There were two conditions to assure a future for Austria: first, Austrian assets in the successor states were not to be confiscated; the second was the already mentioned equitable distribution of the burden left by the Monarchy.

As to the first point, Schumpeter stressed that the old Austria had been an economic unit. Practically all mines and factories were outside the borders of the new Austria. Austria had the headquarters of the firms and the only banks of international reputation which financed the firms in the Nationalstaaten. "Now our State has only a few paper factories, wagons, electrical goods, etc., its territory is covered with picturesque but unproductive mountains and we could not survive if the neighboring States confiscated under one pretext or another. . . . Their loss, even with a rather problematic compensation would for our people mean the loss of all means to work and live."

The equitable distribution of the debt burden is equally important. Austrian industry could not revive, and any otherwise so desirable rapprochement among the Danube states would become impossible, with Austria be-

---

[8] I have found no record of a previous conversation. The interview also states that the correspondent was unable to secure an interview with the foreign minister, Otto Bauer.

[9] Italicized in the original, which suggests that Schumpeter stressed it in speaking.

coming a dead weight. Schumpeter in particular argued against a distribution according to prewar tax revenues which would unduly burden Austria as the seat of prewar private-sector headquarters, or a distribution according to territory.

> This would be inevitable bankruptcy. And bankruptcy means bolshevism: financial collapse brings on a collapse of the social order. To avoid such a catastrophe Austria should not deliver itself to Germany. The most desirable arrangement for the peace of the world is not this attachment (i.e., the Anschluss) but an economic agreement with the other States of the monarchy under conditions which permit the resumption of work and life.

This ends the literal transcription of the interview, presumably given in French, which Schumpeter spoke fluently, and which is marked by quotation marks.

The correspondent added a postscript which sheds light on the problems. No one in Vienna doubted, so he reports, that the French position would carry the day. Italy, however, caused trouble. Italy was afraid of the reemergence of a dangerous Austria. The correspondent quoted the *Tribune de Lausanne*: "France wants a free Austria, but Italy wants this free Austria to be unable to live. (Unabhängig und lebensunfähig.)" And in the interest of French-Italian friendship the Italian view would prevail. When the peace terms actually became known, Schumpeter pronounced them a death sentence.[10]

SEPARATIST TENDENCIES

Still, the optimism in 1916 or in 1919 is at least in retrospect difficult to understand. This is particularly true for 1916. The problem of the Double Monarchy was the nationality problem, which made its constitutional structure a hopeless anachronism. When parliament was finally reconvened during the war as Schumpeter had wanted, the session was chaotic, but this was really nothing new. It had also been chaotic in 1897: There is a remarkable reportage by Mark Twain who pointed out that Austria really was no country, that every ten years (when the Ausgleich had to be renegotiated) it was in danger of becoming two countries, and that it was a collection of twenty or so states speaking twelve languages, who hated each other, but who were held together because they also all hated the government and Jews.[11]

But in 1919 there were also strong separatist tendencies within what was to become German-Austria. The difficulties under which Schumpeter labored were indeed formidable.

[10] *Wiener Zeitung*, June 26, 1919.

[11] Twain (1904), 200–249. An excerpt of this piece was published in Mark Twain, *Concerning Jews*, Philadelphia: Running Press, 1985. This essay is also reprinted in the mentioned collection, pp. 250–75. Mark Twain also characterized Austrian policy as one of keeping things quiet. As the Viennese dialect has it: "Da muss was g'schen. Da kamma nix machen." ("Something's got to be done. Nothing can be done.")

In the first place, until the Treaty of St. Germain was signed on September 2, 1919, the borders of the new State were not known. It was generally assumed that the borders would be along linguistic lines. This meant that South Tyrol, parts of Bohemia and Moravia, possibly even parts of the Sudeten area, would remain Austrian. As foreign minister, Otto Bauer had tried very hard and unsuccessfully to convince the Italians to leave the South Tyrol with Austria.

Since most of Austria's industrial capacity as well as of its better coal deposits were in the later Czech areas, it was not illogical (though totally unrealistic) for Schumpeter to insist that with free trade it made no difference where coal came from.

In fact, Schumpeter apologized to parliament for presenting his budget late, because he had trouble getting the necessary data from the various Länder.

There were really only two solutions to the Austrian problem: Anschluss or economic integration into a relatively free-trading world economy, starting with the maintenance of the old economic relations with the successor states. The post–1945 success of Austria is based on this integration into an economically liberal world economy. In 1919, the Austrian socialists hoped to get help from their German colleagues. In 1919, all parties were overoptimistic.

The separatist tendencies within German-Austria were, however, no less severe. Vorarlberg voted overwhelmingly to join Switzerland, which the Swiss declined. By the end of 1919, Tyrol considered joining Germany,[12] partly to get credits for food imports, partly in the vain hope of saving the South Tyrol. Similar separatist tendencies were reported for Salzburg.

As the chaos spread, individual Länder tried to safeguard their food supplies not only by interfering with food shipments to Vienna but by refusing to accept tourists from other Länder, which really meant specifically Vienna, and even kicking out "foreigners" who were already there vacationing.

It is not an exaggeration to say that the new Austria was a creature of the Treaty of St. Germain. On September 17, 1919, there was a Länderkonferenz. The report of the conference in *The Reichspost*, the Christian-Social paper, of September 16, 1919,[13] introduced its detailed report with a long editorial which pointed out that until "the iron clamps of St. Germain which presented Austria with unchangeable facts there simply was no governmentally organized unit." It compared the new creation to a forced marriage which might perhaps sometime in the future become a love match. It also stated that the "Länder are more sharply separated from each other by laws promulgated by themselves, Mautsperren and controls of travel than by barbed wire."[14]

The conference, chaired by Chancellor Renner and attended by all provin-

---

[12] *NFP*, December 12, 1919.

[13] *Die Reichspost* No. 398, 16. September 1919. "Staat und Länder."

[14] Actually, the separatist economic tendencies had already begun during the war:

Hungary . . . had taken steps, very soon after the commencement of the war, to restrict the movement of food supplies to Vienna. . . . ; Bohemia and Galicia, though otherwise under the Government of Vienna, endeavoured to do likewise. In the winter of 1917–18 the

cial governors as well as by many high officials and some elected representatives, first heard a report by the chancellor on the Peace Treaty. At the end of the morning session Schumpeter explained the "state of the preparatory work concerning the Federal (Staat) and State (Länder) finances." Renner pointed out that a new constitution was urgently needed, probably as a federation of autonomous towns and regions. In any case, a thorough administrative reform was necessary: "We live with an administrative anarchy, which is much worse than in the times of the former bureaucratic Governments" (ibid.).

The report on Schumpeter's remarks consists of only one paragraph of eighteen lines. It is the earliest report of Schumpeter's ideas about intergovernmental fiscal relations. He pleaded for cooperation with Vienna, stating that economic and fiscal independence of each Land was "technically impossible." He wanted uniform consumption and income taxes throughout the whole area, but "real taxes" (Realsteuern), that is, property taxes, could be suitably transferred to the Länder.

"For the time being the fiscal system must essentially remain intact. In two, perhaps in 1 1/2 years fiscal authorities could be divided. In the interim there might be transfers from the Federal to the State budgets" (ibid.), and the Länder might also borrow to a minor extent.

Most discussants agreed that intra-Austrian barriers should be abolished, though, needless to say, everyone wanted exceptions of special interest to his Land. Thus, Salzburg considered a strict control of postal and freight traffic necessary for the time being "in the interest of combatting the black market," a point to which Tyrol agreed. Styria and Carinthia would not forego taxing their wood exports, and Lower Austria pointed out that 3,000 of its 11,000 hospital beds were occupied by "foreigners."

All of this meant that the authority of the Viennese government was in fact severely limited, and this was one of the major constraints facing Schumpeter.

---

authority of the Viennese Government had become so enfeebled that it could no longer defend itself against such treatment. The Slav portions of the Monarchy prevented the fuel and foodstuffs produced in their territory from being transported to the German-Austrian manufacturing districts. . . .

Vienna was . . . forced to rely exclusively on the remaining provinces of German Austria; but even here the doors were barred to her, for the provinces were themselves short of the barest necessities and were indisposed to meet the demands of the capital. The Workmen's Councils prevented the export of food-stuffs from the provincial districts and their organs picketed the railways. The peasants . . . supported this policy of exclusiveness. . . . Customs and passport offices were accordingly established on the provincial frontiers, and the free passage of travellers and goods was restricted. . . . Restrictions were even placed on transit traffic; the Styrian authorities prohibited the transit of cattle from Yugoslavia to Vienna, in the hope that the Yugoslav peasants would thus be compelled to sell their cattle at lower prices in the market of Graz. . . . Vienna . . . was only saved from [starvation] by American and Allied Relief Missions. . . . Traffic in Central Europe had come to a standstill. Only if escorted by officers of the *Entente* could the rare food trains from Trieste to Vienna win their way through the unbelievable obstacles raised at the frontier.

To enable a single train-load of coal to pass through Czechoslovak territory five separate diplomatic communications had to be exchanged with the Government of that country. (van Walré de Bordes 1924, 6, 7, 9)

As Max Adler of the radical wing of the social democratic party put it: A Soviet-Austrian Republic would in the West end in Hütteldorf, a suburb in the Viennese woods! It was also a constraint which made accusations against Schumpeter in the Alpine affair simply irrelevant (see below).

"Krone ist Krone"

Before discussing the Finanzplan, it is necessary to account at least briefly for the first of the many executive orders (Verordnungen) which Schumpeter signed alone or together with other ministers. His very first Verordnung became known as *The* Schumpeter executive order. In 1924, it became the basis of a court decision which denied any revaluation claims similar to the claims honored in Germany, where debts repaid with valueless money were allowed to be revalued up to 20 percent, depending on when the debts were incurred and when they were repaid. It was this later court decision and not the original Verordnung which made Schumpeter the best-hated man in Austria.

The Verordnung was dated March 25, 1919, about a week after Schumpeter became minister, and issued the following day as "1919 No. 61." In a sense it was routine. The successor states had stamped old Austro-Hungarian money for their purposes and Austria had to decide what to do about note circulation in the absence of its own central bank. The following is a translation of the title and the first paragraph of the executive order.

Vollzugsanweisung of the Ministry of Finance in Agreement with the Ministry of Justice of March 25, 1919, concerning the Circulation of Bank Notes in German-Austria and the Regulation of the relevant legal Circumstances.
Based on the law of 24 July 1917 R.G.Bl. No 307 it is ordered provisionally until the legal regulation as follows:

Para. 1

(1) Beginning with the day when this Vollzugsanweisung becomes valid and unless it is otherwise determined, only such notes of the Austro-Hungarian Bank are legal tender which have been officially stamped with a "guillodierte" frame containing in red color the word Deutschösterreich.

(2) The notes, marked for circulation in Deutschösterreich are—subject to the exceptions enumerated in the following paragraphs—sole legal tender which must be accepted for all payments denominated in crowns unless these are payable by law, contractual obligation or other private declaration in actual coin (klingender Münze) or in particular means of payment (Zahlungsmitteln). They must be accepted to their full nominal value by everybody, as well as by all public authorities.

Para. 2

The Minister of Finance can, in agreement with other concerned Ministers, permit the acceptance by Government and other public authorities and institutions (Kassen und Ämtern) of notes of the Austro-Hungarian bank stamped by other national states and determine the conditions therefor.

Suits concerning the constitutionality of the order had been lodged with four lower district courts which had referred them to the Constitutional Court (Verfassungsgericht) to declare the Schumpeter Verordnung unconstitutional. The courtroom was packed with an excited public consisting mainly of small pensioners who "participated" in the hearings to an extent which induced the presiding judge to threaten the clearance of his courtroom. One particular outburst was occasioned by the revelation that the file of the Schumpeter Verordnung had disappeared.[15]

The arguments turned around the alleged illegality of the Verordnung because only two ministers instead of the whole cabinet had signed it, because the government had neglected to submit the Verordnung to parliament for ratification in time, and because it was based on an imperial law which the revolution had voided. In any case, so argued one plaintiff, it was not a question of a 100 percent revaluation which indeed would mean chaos, but a reasonable (massvolle) one.

The representative of the Ministry of Finance argued against ruling the Verordnung unconstitutional. The courts had already set precedents which gave the government the right to change a Verordnung "to limit economic damage." As for the Zwangskurs, that is, the nature as legal tender, it existed ever since 1848—Austria-Hungary was one of the few countries on a gold exchange instead of a pure gold coin standard. And as far as the requested interrogation of Schumpeter as the responsible minister was concerned, it would be better to hear Dr. Than, presently the vice president of the Austrian National Bank, who had actually worked out the Verordnung and knew more about it than the minister who merely signed it—a comment that elicited amusement among the audience.

There were odd questions. Had the cabinet actually discussed whether an Austro-Hungarian krone was actually equal to a stamped German-Austrian one? After reading the then still confidential cabinet protocol, the judge read aloud the one paragraph dealing with Schumpeter's precise role.

> Secretary of State Schumpeter states as an introduction that he does not consider the monetary policy measures of the preceding Government appropriate and that he could therefore not identify himself with them, that, however, he would as the successor to the position [as Minister of Finance] be ready to uphold the position if the Cabinet continued to take the same standpoint that only bank notes stamped as German-Austrian should be legal tender. The vote called for by the Chairman of the Council unanimously voted to stick with the decision of the previous Cabinet. Minister Dr. Schumpeter points out that the period for the exchange of notes had to be prolonged. He will submit a proposed legislation to Parliament about the note circulation in Austria and about the monetary order in Austria.

[15] Based on an account of the hearings in the NFP of December 16, 1924.

The Verordnung was promulgated and the "Akt" (law? file?) was published in 1920 but has since disappeared.

The representative of the Ministry of Finance then replied to various arguments of the plaintiffs to the effect that the Constitutional Court had already decided that a delay in submitting legislation to parliament did not make the Verordnung illegal but only the minister responsible. The plaintiffs had also argued that when the currency was changed from that of the Monarchy to that of the republic, the exchange rate of the old for the new money was not determined.

The judgment of the Constitutional Court was pronounced on December 23, 1924, and published in full in the *Neue Freie Presse*.[16] It decided the only way it could: the Verordnung was juridically valid and not unconstitutional. The legal basis of the Verordnung was valid. The government issued the Verordnung to prevent worse damage to the economy. It was for the government and parliament to decide whether this was the best way to do so.

The Constitutional Court rejected the arguments of the plaintiffs that the new notes meant—or were meant—to have the same gold content as those of 1914 which they replaced. The argument of the Court was that only when it was agreed that payment should be made "in klingender Münze," that is, in actual gold coins, was there a right to be paid back in gold coins.[17] The Court also rejected the argument that repayment in valueless paper money amounted legally to "expropriation."

The public in the court room reacted to the reading of the judgment with agitation. One member of the public yelled "Even among the lowest Albanians there are no such criminals as the Austrian Government," which led to his expulsion from the room and his subsequent arrest. And when a lady pensioner asked the presiding judge what she who had lost everything could do, he declared: "It was the duty of the court to arrive at this judgment. It has concluded that the Verordnung was legal, but it has nothing to do with further procedures at revaluation."[18]

As the editorial introduction of the *Arbeiterzeitung* to its reproduction of the judgment stated: The Verordnung created no new legal facts and neither

[16] "Das Urteil über die Rechtsgültigkeit der Schumpeter Verordnung," NFP No. 21652, December 23, 1924.

[17] The court would therefore not have declared the gold clause invalid as did the U.S. Supreme Court in 1934. This account is based on the following newspaper articles found in the *Archiv der Arbeiterkammer*, Vienna: (a) "Die Valorisierunsgfrage vor them Verfassungsgerichtshof. Gegenschrift des Finanzministeriums gegen die Anträge auf Aufhebung der Schumpeter Verordnung," NFP No. 21639, December 10, 1924. (b) "Die Schumpeter Verordnung vor dem Verfassungsgerichtshofe. Das Urteil wird erst am 23. Dezember bekannt gegeben," NFP December 16, 1924. (c) "Krone ist Krone. Die heutige Entscheidung des Verfassungsgerichtshofes," NFP No. 21652, December 13, 1914. This is an editorial rather than a report. (d) "Die Erkenntnis des Verfassungsgerichtshofes über die Banknoten Verordnung," *Arbeiterzeitung* No. 352, December 24, 1924. (e) "Gerichtssaal," *Wiener Zeitung* No. 285, December 27, 1924. (This is another reproduction of the Court's judgment.)

[18] "Krone ist Krone," ibid.

would its invalidation. But the editorial of the *Neue Freie Presse* insisted that although other and wealthier countries than Austria did not master this extremely difficult problem—the return of the British pound sterling to pre-war parity was still in the future—parliament should do something. "To do nothing is the worst possible policy" (ibid.).

The famous dictum "Krone ist Krone" always attributed to Schumpeter was not his but the heading of the editorial of the NFP. Here once again Schumpeter is blamed for miseries not of his making.

In popular opinion, Schumpeter remained responsible for the ensuing opinion, and the "Krone ist Krone" Verordnung responsible for the loss of their personal fortunes. A letter in the Harvard Archive written in a semi-educated high sounding style and combining almost cringing politeness with crude "demands [that] Schumpeter help . . . his son after having lost his whole wealth because of Schumpeter." And an obituary written in 1950 is headed, "Schumpeter, the father of inflation."

CAPITAL LEVY

The analysis of *The Crisis of the Tax State* had made it quite clear that the precondition for, if not even the centerpiece of, a fiscal program to rebuild the economy was a sound monetary system, a currency reform.[19] In 1919, this meant a capital levy which Schumpeter conceived entirely as a currency reform, as a method of getting rid of the monetary overhang and nothing else.

In his first *Deutsche Volkswirt* article, Schumpeter stressed that a capital levy could save a situation at one time and at another time under different circumstances would be catastrophic.[20] And in 1948, he thought a capital levy in the United States unwise.[21]

In his letter to Gulick, Schumpeter pointed out that the capital levy made sense only as long as the incipient inflation had not actually begun to work its way through the economy. Once the inflationary process was under way, a capital levy could only do harm, as a tax measure or a measure which would destroy the needed working capital. Gulick did not make use of this comment, of Schumpeter, and indeed made rather selective use of the other parts of the letter.[22]

The idea and indeed necessity of a capital levy was in the air and bruited

---

[19] The soundness of Schumpeter's approach is attested by the difficulties experienced in all the ex-Soviet bloc countries including the successor states of the Soviet Union itself. You cannot have a working price system until money is worth something. To rely on "free" markets without a preceding currency reform invites trouble.

[20] "A capital levy may at the beginning of an inflation under certain circumstances save a currency and a year later kill it for good" (Schumpeter 1985, 64).

[21] "There is still time to stop inflation." *The Nation's Business*, June 1948, reprinted in Clemence (1951), 236–47.

[22] The letter is reproduced in Schumpeter (1993).

about before Schumpeter became minister. In fact, many of his Verordnungen dealt with preparations for a capital levy which never came during his tenure as minister.[23] But the levy was understood also, if not primarily, as a tax measure to balance the budget, which was precisely what Schumpeter rejected as unacceptable. There was therefore widespread lack of understanding in the cabinet of what Schumpeter was trying to do. But there was also a quite understandable political dread of recognizing the depth of the catastrophe that had befallen the monarchy and with which the new republic had to cope.

The first necessary action of course had been to define a new monetary unit, which the stamping Verordnung related in the preceding section was intended to do. Without it there would have been a limitless supply of money coming from outside of Austria to buy up what few goods were still available.[24] In the first months in office Schumpeter evidently had to deal with one emergency after another.

The first detailed discussion of the "principles which in [the Minister's] opinion had to underlie the once-and-for-all capital levy" were discussed in cabinet on July 16, 1919.[25] The confidential part of the protocol was but a single page stating who was present and who was absent—the chancellor himself was absent—and that the discussion lasted from 3:00 PM until 6:30 PM. The discussion itself was to be reported in a special top secret appendix of thirty-four (unnumbered) pages, of which Schumpeter's initial presentation took fifteen.

To start with, Schumpeter pointed out, the government could not present its plans for the capital levy to parliament until there was clarity about the borders of the new Austria. Schumpeter dismissed any analogies with what was being discussed in Germany as reported in the press and in particular insisted that Austria could not consider spreading the levy over thirty years but had to accomplish it at most within three years. The reason was that "in Germany . . . the note inflation has not gone anywhere near as far as in German-Austria" (ibid., 2–3).

It was essential—and to this there was general agreement in cabinet—that it was not permissible "*to use the capital levy for current expenditures*. The law had to guarantee that the capital levy would be used only for reducing the war burden (Abbürdung der Kriegslast) and for socialization" (ibid., 3; emphasis in original). The Länder wanted to keep the proceeds of a capital levy to apply only to their own debt and this was not acceptable. Or even worse, they just wanted to keep a fraction of the levy for their own use. If the levy was to be used for purposes of socialization, this should be explicitly stated in the law. But as a matter of fact the socialization commission (of which Otto Bauer was

---

[23] There was a capital levy in 1921, but it was conceived as a tax measure pure and simple.

[24] Something like this happened in 1945 in Germany when the American Forces issued scrip redeemable into dollars which for a while the Russians also printed. In this case the ultimate sufferers were the United States, which redeemed all scrip into dollars. Needless to say, this possibility was quickly abolished.

[25] Kabinettsprotokol No. 89 vom 16. Juli 1919, marked "vertraulich" as were all Kabinettsprotokolle. Unpublished. Typewritten.

the head) did not expect the direct use of government monies. (This point came up again later and will be discussed in the context of socialization and the Alpine affair.) In any case, whatever final decision cabinet made about explicitly including or excluding "socialization" in the law—this was purely a technical-political question—there was one decision to which Schumpeter could not submit: that the proceeds of the capital levy should be used for any purpose other than to lower the burden of the war debt" (ibid., 5).

There was an "objective" and a "subjective" method of executing the levy. The difference was that with the former the object itself was the basis for the levy. With the latter it was the owner. Though the "objective" method was economically the correct one, it would be considered unjust because it did not permit a progressive taxation except at the expense of its great advantage of simplicity, an advantage which was not to be underestimated given the demoralized state of public administration. Hence, Schumpeter pleaded for the "subjective" method.

The tax rates would have to be high and the tax base low, starting at 10 percent with assets of K15,000 and rising to 55.83 percent (the base not being given in the document). Assets (Vermögen) are defined as "the sum of in money expressed objects and rights (Vermögensgegenstände und Vermögensrechte) of the tax subject regardless of whether they have a yield or not, after deducting debts and charges (Lasten)" (ibid., 9), including insurance claims of all kinds. However, ordinary household goods, to some extent jewelry and under certain circumstances cash and deposits, were to be exempted.

The levy was to apply only to physical, not to legal persons. Corporations were to be taxed only at the level of the owner to avoid double taxation. Taxation of corporations by the issue of gratis shares to the government would be technically very simple but complicated by the fact that there were "practically no purely German-Austrian corporations" (ibid., 10). In fact, many corporations had their head offices in Vienna but their operating assets in the successor states.

All objects had to be valued at their market value rather than at their prewar price (ibid., 11) and the capital levy had to yield about K15 billion if it had to have any effect at all.

Real concessions would have to be made to the farmers in that their land tax (Grundsteuer) would be kept unchanged. In any case, the necessary operating capital would be kept intact, and, besides, a successful capital levy would keep the value of money approximately constant. Schumpeter's presentation ended with the already mentioned insistence on taxing bank notes and deposits.

The first, and longest, speech was given by Otto Bauer (ibid., 16–20). He thought Schumpeter much too optimistic and did not see how government bankruptcy could be avoided. The only question was how to find the proper form for it. Given the fact that the war debt alone was K25 billion[26] to which

[26] It is not clear how Bauer arrived at this figure. No one really knew at the time how the debts of the Monarchy were to be apportioned among the successor states. But Schumpeter and everyone else proved to be too optimistic also on this account. Walré de Bordes (1924) 48, gives a figure of K41.4 billion for the total circulation of the notes of the Austro-Hungarian Bank as of

would have to be added sums for reparations, the purchase of government estates of the old State, and the whole indebtedness of communities and Länder, he just did not see how bankruptcy could be avoided. An alternative would be a further use of note issue which only would reduce the foreign value of the krone still further.

Schumpeter, he continued, simply wanted to reduce the war debt by three-fifths and by nothing at all of any additional debts. There was no objective value of money which could be used to value assets. For the "objective" method this did not matter, and the issue of gratis shares to government had the inestimable advantage that they would leave the working capital of corporations intact. Bauer argued that issuance of gratis shares not only would aid socialization but also serve the purpose of getting foreign credit "particularly as German-Austrian capacities could by the issue of gratis shares be partly bought abroad." The inconsistency of these two purposes was not stressed, of course. It would also be unjust, Bauer continued, to treat only bank notes by the objective method. However, the problem of small industrial and agricultural businesses would be left unsolved by the objective method" (ibid., 19), really a fatal flaw of Bauer's argument, since these small businesses were by far the bulk of German-Austrian enterprises. As far as Bauer was concerned, the "objective" method was the proper one to use; it could be made progressive by excess taxation of the wealthier classes, though unfortunately no concessions could be made to the small property owners. But a concession could be made by distributing the burden of the small owners over several years and by making the whole exercise a socialization measure in a grand manner. "If this question is not solved in the indicated manner [we] will head towards Government bankruptcy in the most brutal form" (ibid., 20).

Schumpeter answered immediately. In his reply he stressed Bauer's political courage, for Bauer's proposal was the toughest political test for the government. Schumpeter said that he had worked out a capital levy according to the objective method but had not submitted it to cabinet. Also, the printing of new bank notes to take the place of the old stamped ones, suggested by Bauer, was in preparation, and evidently Schumpeter and Bauer used the term "bankruptcy" in different senses. To tax only large enterprises was impractical since there were too few of them. Besides, the small workshops in the cities had recently done rather well.

Bauer's opening remarks in the discussion were the only extended and systematic ones. There were comments and questions by several other ministers, and also repeatedly by Bauer, and Schumpeter answered each of them immediately. There was agreement on the need to treat farmers carefully; the

July 15, 1919, of which K7.6 billion circulated in the German-Austrian Republic. By comparison, total bank note circulation in the monarchy in August 1914 was K3.7 billion which had risen to K37.6 billion by February 28, 1919, the last date for which only a total circulation is given (ibid., 46, 48). When Schumpeter came into office on March 17, German-Austrian note circulation was given as K2.446 billion as of March 15, 1919. When he left office it had risen to K10.076 billion by October 15 (ibid.).

impression of the discussion is that this was not only a matter of political caution but a sincere concern. Most discussants asked questions or made suggestions concerning their special responsibilities, which was after all their job.

The only discussion which came from Vice Chancellor Fink—Chancellor Renner was absent—dealt also with the farmers' problems. But it is worth mentioning mainly because it undoubtedly reflected a general belief that "a few years after the war the value [of land] would once again fall because in more orderly circumstances the prices for agricultural products would once more be determined by supply and demand."

The impression which the discussion leaves is that with the exception of Bauer, Schumpeter was not really understood, and Bauer, too, was not really convinced. The fact that Bauer preferred the "objective" method at least suggests that even he did not really see the importance of the capital levy as a method of getting rid of the monetary overhang, as a currency reform. So Bauer's proposal at the end of the meeting was accepted by the Cabinet Council that "to give the discussion a positive (greifbares) result the Secretary of State for Finances is requested to work out a proposed law about the capital levy both according the subjective and the objective method so that the Cabinet Council could swiftly decide which of the two proposals should be submitted to the National Assembly once the economic situation of German-Austria was clarified" (ibid., 34).

In his letter to Gulick, Schumpeter pointed out that the practical exemption of peasants really gutted the capital levy.

Public Speeches and Activities in Parliament

PUBLIC SPEECHES

Schumpeter could not present his proposals for a capital levy or his Finanzplan to parliament on September 29 and 30. But, of course, at least the general ideas of his program were known. There had already been its forerunner, *The Crisis of the Tax State*. But Schumpeter gave one speech after another in public, outlining his ideas and relating them to and commenting on current political events.[1] Schumpeter was trying to drum up public support for his program. And, as Wieser's quoted diary shows, he was quite aware of having to do this.

Schumpeter lost no time presenting his ideas. In a speech to the civil servants of his ministry on March 19, 1919, he proceeded to outline his program as was the custom of a new minister (Schumpeter 1992, 36). First, the people had to be told of the seriousness of the situation. Everyone knew that there were three obstacles to recovery which could be overcome: the war, the foreign exchanges, and the budget (referred to as autonomous finances).

The war debt had to be eliminated (italicized in the original report) without breaking faith with the foreign creditors in Germany, and particularly The Netherlands and Switzerland. And this had to be done "without brutality and without destroying any existence."

A return to the prewar parity of the krone was out of the question. Austria would have its hands full just to prevent a further deterioration.

A radical change of the fiscal system was out of the question for the next two years. The idea that each land might order its own finances would, whatever the political wishes, lead to a situation to which people would "react bloodily within two years." The immediate problem was the once-and-for-all capital levy. The rest had to wait. The longer-term prospects were not unfavorable if only the obstacles to renewed economic activity were removed. The consequences of the war could be removed relatively quickly and orderly circumstances could return.

"Everyone actually realizes the need for the capital levy and it is self-evident that special consideration has to be given to the needs of the farmers (Bauernstand) who have most to gain from the effect of the capital levy." Indirect taxes would have to be raised. But "an unsystematic consideration of one tax after another, to raise one, or to change another," would make any calculations

---

[1] All public speeches as reported in the press are published in three volumes edited by Christian Seidl and Wolfgang F. Stolper, 1985, 1992, 1993, cited hereafter as Schumpeter (1985, 1992, 1993), respectively.

impossible and would have unhappy repercussions on wages and employment. The property tax was most easily handled. But "the objective problems are one thing, the political possibilities another." How those stacked up was uncertain, but Schumpeter was "in any case determined to try and lead public opinion along the path which I consider the only possible one and not to deviate from this path in any essential point" (ibid., 40).

At the beginning of his speech Schumpeter mentioned that the will of the people went at this time in the direction of "Great Socialization." But except to say that he would cooperate "with the eminent men responsible for this operation," he neither expressed great enthusiasm for nor great objections against it.

The *Oesterreichische Volkswirt* (Oe.V.) approved of this speech, though not of his next one on March 20. Perhaps Schumpeter underestimated the political, sociological, and historical obstacles of the time (though he had clearly foreseen the great hatred against the Monarchy in his Memoranda of 1916). But then he had Versailles and St. Germain to deal with, which were still in the future, rather than the Marshall Plan. He can perhaps be forgiven for believing that the Austrians and the Entente were capable of more farsighted actions.

In an interview in the *Neue Freie Presse* (NFP) given the same day but published three days later, Schumpeter suggested that the "preparations for the Anschluss as well as for socialization of the economy "presuppose orderly, finances." Of course, "a state which does not even know its own borders must be particularly careful what it does." Socialization of monopolies is especially mentioned. For the rest, it is the capital levy, stabilization of the value of money and of the foreign exchanges. Economy in administration is essential, but not too much should be expected from this side.

Schumpeter's second statement came at a press conference on March 20, where he spoke on the economic tasks of the future (ibid., 19). Schumpeter exuded optimism. To start with, Vienna was the heart of a larger area. It was easier to establish political than economic independence—as Bauer also had stressed. Vienna would remain the financial center of a larger area. This, it turned out, was not quite unrealistic though in a different manner from Schumpeter's intentions.[2] Some modus vivendi would have to be found with the successor states. Unfortunately, what happened was, as one wag put it, that the Czechs inherited the industry, the Hungarians the agriculture, and the German-Austrians the landscape, bureaucracy, and the debt.

Schumpeter continued to point out the problems of the world economy, the universal capital shortage with its high interest rates once interest rates were decontrolled and nothing could be done to prevent this.

However, for the rest, matters did not look so bad. There would undoubtedly be credits for imports of the necessary foodstuffs and raw materials.

---

[2] In the 1920s, much Western capital flowed to the Balkans through Vienna, which borrowed short in the West to lend long in the Balkans. This was one of the contributing causes to the collapse of the Austrian banking system.

There is an interesting political aside: Austria never had as good a credit in Paris as the Republic of São Paulo which two weeks before its bankruptcy could get a credit in Paris under much more favorable conditions than Austria could have gotten. "The political contrasts (Gegensätze, i.e., to the West) would never have been so large if we had had credit relations with foreign countries. If Austria had been a big debtor of Western Europe, the latter would hardly have pursued the Balkan policy which has always crossed us, for it would have endangered so-and-so-many millions" (ibid., 95). Here we have another contrast to any possible Marxist interpretation which even now talks of foreign lending as imperialism.

The rate of exchange had to be stabilized, domestic savings increased, and the entrepreneurial spirit liberated.

There is a lengthy paragraph on the problems of socialization. In a remarkable political phrase, he pointed out that "we must go in this respect so far that, so to speak, nothing is possible to the left of us" (ibid., 96). But what is not socialized must have complete freedom:

> One has to choose between socialism and free enterprise. Both simultaneously is impossible. Both principles may liberate good forces and are conceivable. Which principle is preferable I do not wish to discuss at present. However, I must insist that moving between the principles is pernicious. *One can socialize industry but one must not ruin it*. It can, of course, be ruined by tax policy. (ibid.; italics added)

Schumpeter left no doubt about his views of socialization:

> The Secretary of State refers to his collaboration with the German Socialization Commission where he is one of the authors of the Majority Report of the Coal Commission. The Report goes as far as possible in the question of a democratization. What, however, is not possible is to bring down all personalities to the same level. One must not close oneself to outstanding success and outstanding personalities, and one has to be ready to pay the leading persons in case of socialization almost as much as they earn now. The workers, too, must learn that this is necessary under socialism—as Lenin has already understood. With socialism, too, an organization is conceivable which shows the same promptness as does capitalism. When the time for this has come it will be possible to do it. If the time for it has not come, the economy must be handled with care. This is the alternative which requires decision. (ibid., 96)

It is difficult to understand how Schumpeter could have been accused of having suddenly changed his mind about socialization. And Schumpeter was equally clear about the ultimate chances of success: "If we keep these principles in mind, the economy will recover rather quickly, but only if it has a wider economic area than the present German-Austria, and only if within the wider area the economy has the corresponding freedom" (ibid.).

Walter Federn found this second programmatic statement much too optimistic (Oe.V., March 19, 1919, 457). He questioned whether the fact that

Vienna had been the financial center of the Monarchy was an asset, and he turned out to be right. Schumpeter underestimated the implications of what he himself had stressed, namely that interest rates would remain high as the whole Western world except the United States would be busy reconstructing its own economies. And the omission of Germany from the list was objectively wrong and politically dangerous. A Danube Federation was an illusion and the omission of the Anschluss (which the Oe.V. as well as Bauer advocated as the only possible economic solution at the time) was dangerous.

Besides, what mattered was not what the minister said but what he did. The capital levy remained the most important immediate task. And there Schumpeter could build on the work of his predecessors.

Two weeks later, Federn expressed dismay that the capital levy still had not sufficiently progressed (Oe.V., April 12, 1919, 404–6). Federn thought that Schumpeter might have changed his ideas and was to blame for the delay. Actually, Schumpeter expressed the same dismay in parliament and blamed the delay on people's neglect to register their assets. In fact, the delay reflected government rather than Schumpeter's indecision.

Schumpeter's next statement was an article under his signature in the NFP, April 6 (but dated April 5) dealing with the need to safeguard Austrian assets in Hungary. Austria had no desire to interfere with Hungary's desires to socialize, but had to insist that Austrian banks be free to dispose of their Hungarian accounts and that German-Austrian owners or shareholders of enterprises to be socialized had to be compensated. "We are quite conscious that claims on capital in Hungary are valuable assets of the German-Austrian economy and that we cannot forego our claims without collapsing."[3] The regulations for the registration of assets for the capital levy were in the meantime issued and reported in detail.

Aside from these tasks, Schumpeter worried about the direction the world was taking. In a speech before the Liga für den Völkerbund he rejected speculation that economic reasons had led to the war, which always was a crime and a bloody insanity (Schumpeter 1992, 99f). He nevertheless pointed out that mercantilistic tendencies, including colonies, created friction among nations. There was now a danger which only free trade could fight. Protective tariffs would lead to trusts, dumping, economic warfare, and perhaps even conflicts which might lead to war. To trade freely was really not all that difficult.

Having made this point, Schumpeter reverted de facto to his problems and proposals as minister of finance. By this time, his audience—which included the prince-archbishop of Vienna, the French ambassador, and a large number of conservative big shots whom the NFP listed, titles and all—must have been not unfamiliar with his ideas.

He first talked about socialism for which, "I must confess, I have consider-

---

[3] As the account of the Cabinet Council debate of July 16 revealed, the Hungarian assets were lost, and it was added there that the chaos in the Hungarian economy would have made them worthless in any case.

able professional sympathy" (ibid., 101). But then, Schumpeter went on, partial socialization—which really was what was being proposed by everyone including Bauer—would not work in the face of the overwhelming need for foreign capital. "*You can socialize industry but you must not ruin it if we are not all to starve to death* (Applause)" (ibid., 102; italics in original). In Austria, only entrepreneurs and merchants save, though not enough.

Second, we must have raw materials, machinery, and food. "The problem is to get a million here, a ship there, a machine here, or some raw material in the most hidden corners of the world, at the most impossible addresses. Only the *merchant* (lively applause) can do this task, and it would be absurd to use any other method. It is obvious, that this would be true also for a socialist economy" (ibid.; italics in original).

The State, on the other hand, had to ensure that industry, which could not get liquid funds on the market despite inflation, would get the needed credit and that taxes to stimulate production would be lowered. But all this would work only if industry were free to respond, and this included the abolition of import and export controls. The objection that the depreciation of the krone did not allow that was inadequate since the cause of the depreciation was "the pressure of our bank notes." Free trade was the only possible policy aim even then.

All of this was equally true of the national states. It would be in their interest to live in peace. "No one doubts the independence of these Part-States (Teilstaaten) but to create economic customs areas of 6 to 10 million people was not only a crime and a mistake but worst of all it was ridiculous" (ibid., 103–4), which did not, of course, prevent it from happening then as now. "We have to find a reasonable agreement about the burden of the Austro-Hungarian Monarchy, about international payments etc. which will prevent that each payment from one country to another will become a tragi-comedy. Worldwide integration is essential" (ibid.).

It all sounds reasonable and logical. So what was so utterly wrong with it? For one thing, the Peace Treaty and the conditions it imposed were as yet in the future, including the borders of the new state. Much of Schumpeter's vision turned out to be whistling in the dark. The Oe.V. pointed out that the omission of Germany was perhaps unintentional before an audience of known opponents of the Anschluss from the French ambassador down (May 31, 1919). Nevertheless, to talk about free trade was incomprehensible at a moment when the government was preparing a law for the forced cartelization of industry and when Schumpeter—"much too subtle a brain not to notice the confusion he causes"—means something totally different by free trade than those persons who revolted against any kind of forced economic organization. Free trade to the audience meant freedom from any government interference. It meant the freedom to develop their own interferences with the market.

Both Schumpeter and Bauer were wrong, the Oe.V. continued, because they did not seem to understand Austrian realities. The Socialists may have thought that they had allies in the peasants, "the rest of the country." The fact is, however, that no one was for a modern capitalist society and that the peasants and the Christian Socialists were no more "bourgeois" than the Socialists. They were for socialization as long as they were not affected by it, particularly as they associated capitalism with "big capitalists," "millionaires," "war profiteers," all imagined to be Jews. Indeed, in a parliamentary debate of April 4, 1919, Stöckler, in speaking against the bread tax, "the most unpopular law conceivable," and against Schumpeter's preliminary tax proposals, violently objected to any of them and suggested that none of it was any concern of the peasantry, the Bauernstand.

> The Government should intervene where the cancer really lies: in the black market, in the controlled economy, in this usurious economy. . . . I know much better methods for the Government and the Secretary of State for Finances to improve substantially the fiscal situation of the state. (Hear! Hear! Hear!) I recommend to them to dismantle as fast as possible the Zentralen. (Agreement.) I would also recommend to the Government to deal energetically with the black market which deals in enormous usurious prices. (Agreement. Representative Leuthner: How expensively does the peasant sell his grain to the black market?) Whose fault is it? The city people are themselves to blame, for they run down the doors of the peasants. (Because they don't want to starve to death without a struggle!). . . . I want to recommend furthermore: severely tax the war profiteers, people before the war still ran around with a Binkel [a dialect word for a small package, here evidently referring to house-to-house soliciting] and who are now millionaires. They should first of all be taxed. (Agreement). But now all others should suffer first, and only last the big capitalists and Jewish big capitalists.[4]

To understand Bauer's illusions, the Oe.V. continued, one had only to compare Austria with Germany. Germany had many big cities. If the spartakists succeeded in Berlin, they could count on similar reactions in Hamburg, Munich, Stuttgart, etc. In Austria by contrast there was only Vienna (which at the time had over 2 million inhabitants out of a total of about 6 million). "Vienna will always remain isolated, its economic form, its social needs as well as its whole political and cultural spirit."[5]

The Oe.V. certainly saw the situation much more realistically. Schumpeter's audience heard what it wanted to hear, as Otto Bauer believed what he wanted to believe—or perhaps more charitably what he was forced to believe by the pressure of his more radical followers. And after all, the Anschluss

---

[4] *Stenographic Protocol of the Sessions of the Constituent National Assembly of the Republic Austria*, 1919, vol. 1, Sessions 146, pp. 11290. Vienna: Austrian Government Printer, 9th Session, April 4, 1919, 222–23.

[5] The Socialists themselves were not unaware of this fact. See Gerlich (1980), 14, who quotes the left-wing Socialist Friedrich Adler: "There is a possibility to establish the rule of the proletariat in Vienna where it is in the majority, but the borders of such a socialist republic in the West are not much farther than Hütteldorf," a suburb of Vienna in the Viennese woods.

which Bauer and the Oe.V. supported turned out to be just as illusory. Still, in a more rational world without hatred overwhelming reason, Schumpeter would have been correct. And hatred, of course, breeds its own destruction. Schumpeter expressed this frustration:

> The primitive truth is simply not accepted that the welfare of every individual depends primarily on orderly finances and a rational fiscal policy, that everything else in the State, however little idealistic it may sound, is of subordinate importance compared to a rational fiscal policy. (Agreement) And when I thought about the task before me I hesitated not so much before the objective difficulty of my task: the objective problem seems to me indeed difficult but not insoluble. I have often been accused of official *optimism*. I have always answered that this optimism is not just official. If we get down to business in a calm manner, if we don't commit outstanding blunders, our *situation is not hopeless*. . . . But even though the objective side of the problem does not seem to be unconquerable— there is always one matter that fills me with worries: the small public understanding for the fiscal necessities and for a sound fiscal policy.[6]

Unfortunately, the optimism related also to former fellow-citizens and enemies. On May 12, the Austrian delegation left for St. Germain to negotiate a peace treaty, again a not hopeless task. (Schumpeter used many double negatives at the time, itself a clue to the state of his mind.) There was after all a community of nations in which Austria could find its place. There was hope that the debts of the Double Monarchy would be apportioned among the successor states according to population, that assets in newly foreign countries would be preserved, that Austria would remain the financial center of the successor states, as after all England would remain the center of the Commonwealth. But all that required first of all the solution of the problem of the war debt, its just distribution, the avoidance of State bankruptcy. All of this required the great capital levy which is "only solvable by a large once-and-for-all high percentage levy which will come in a very short time. The law will be submitted to the public in 8 to 14 days."

And the levy must under no circumstances be used to cover current expenditures. This would be a catastrophe.

> The fiscal situation . . . *is still salvageable*. If . . . the levy is used only to reduce the burden of the war debt, we have a clear financial field. Don't be afraid that I declare again and again that the capital levy serves the reduction of the burden and of socialization. This means only that if one wishes, certain receipts may be used so as to serve both purposes. . . . The capital levy will be a very hard measure and it will be very oppressive in the highest brackets. The measure is . . . *very strongly progressive*. (Applause) . . . I would be dishonest if I told

---

[6] NFP, May 13, 1919, speech to the *Verein für Währungspolitik*. The current American debate about the deficit shows that not much has changed in this respect. Reprinted in Schumpeter (1992), 104ff; quotation on 105–6; italics in original.

you that the *small fortunes* could be spared. This would be a popular success . . . but it would be worth nothing . . . simply because we are a backward
country and there are just not enough big fortunes. . . . If we undertake this
operation it must be done quickly and in such a manner that it saves the situation.
I do not feel that I take anything from the people; I only feel that I *save them the
rest*. Obviously, the law concerning the capital levy must be formulated as simply
as possible. *Only a few weeks, then everything is over, then our State is financially
in order and the productive work can begin*. (Schumpeter 1992, 110–11; italics
in original)

Two weeks later on May 31, 1919, before the *Handels- und Industrieverein*,
a certain desperation is discernible beneath the optimism:

I believe in our future, but, of course only under certain conditions . . . only on
condition of a *reasonable* peace, and only if we do not make irresponsible mistakes. . . . All fiscal policy is in vain as long as the public and our politicians stick
to their peculiar childish mentality which amounts in the last analysis to the
belief that the whole population can live off the State. . . . Both the direct subsidies to the incomes of non-Government employees and the subsidies to the cost
of food *can not be maintained forever*. . . . Even two weeks, four weeks, ago the
situation was somewhat different. Then we could say that we were between
Munich and Budapest . . . [where] Bolshevism was at its peak . . . [our] expenditure policy could be justified on the grounds that peace would be maintained in
Vienna without bloodshed, without use of force. . . . It was an exceptional period. Once we are past it we must make a different fiscal policy . . . *if the peace
conditions are unreasonable it is in vain even to think of a correct fiscal policy,
and it would be better not to carry out the capital levy*. If we are not overburdened
then I can guarantee as an expert that every penny of the debt will be repaid.
(ibid., 112–13; italics except for the last in original)

If a normal fiscal policy would become possible, the deficit would disappear
in perhaps five years. The [internal] war burden had to be reduced, savings
had to be made in the budget. Production would then increase. The monetary
situation had to be reordered, perhaps by the introduction of a new currency.
The States of the Danube basin depended undoubtedly on a common currency whether they liked it or not. "There must be customs and currency
agreements among them" (ibid.).

Schumpeter's ideas were logical but he (as everyone else) overestimated just
how "reasonable" the world would in fact turn out to be. In a press conference
on June 24, he commented on the peace conditions which in the meantime
had become known. They were

[U]ndoubtedly ruinous. . . . they cannot be fulfilled as they are . . . their motivation can only be to *destroy* German-Austria The expropriation of assets abroad
and in the newly-foreign areas creates a totally impossible situation. The capital
levy can not be presented to Parliament in these circumstances until the exact

conditions of the peace treaty are known. It obviously can not be made if it is undertaken for the [enemy] in which case it would have to be made according to new bases and principles. (ibid., 122–32; quotations run together)

Three days later all optimism was gone. The known peace conditions were an economic death sentence. Once again "it is not easy to kill a people. In general, it is impossible. But here we have one of the few cases in which it is possible."

It would have been one of the greatest achievements of fiscal history if under the most favorable imaginable peace conditions we would have avoided a collapse. . . . As surely as one could count on reconstruction and a better future before the publication of the peace conditions, just as surely no orderly fiscal economy is possible without a *modification* of these conditions. . . . This is the more serious as the fiscal collapse inevitably brings with it social collapse. If the public (Staats) finances cease to work, the motives for a Bolshevik experiment will become unsurmountable. (ibid., 137–38)

On June 27, 1919, Schumpeter spoke to the *Volkswirtschaftliche Gesellschaft*, pointing out that though the peace had not yet been signed, what was already known was an economic death sentence on Austria unless there were substantial changes and that whatever lay in store made no difference economically. There were "three points which no fiscal policy could overcome: the liquidation and confiscation of our foreign assets; the rate of exchange at which our foreign obligations are calculated; and the subsidization of emigration of our intelligentsia and capital of German-Austria" (ibid., 135–36).

Schumpeter added, foreseeing the consequences of the peace as clearly as Keynes:

[T]he characteristics of all economic decisions of the peace treaty overshoot the aim so much that the consequences hit no longer just ourselves. For, the necessary consequences of the procedure against our socalled "old-foreign" assets must naturally be that our obligations toward foreign countries must default. . . . [T]his is a procedure which may have its political reason, but which economically is totally senseless. With this, Austria has lost all possibility to live. No credit institution, no bank, no savings institution could survive if this decision becomes effective. The masses of Vienna must become poorer and poorer (verelenden). (ibid.)

The treaty also provided that debts denominated in kronen had to be paid to the successor states at the guaranteed average rate of the krone in Geneva during October 1918 in Swiss francs, which Schumpeter characterized as simply adventurous. "Without modification of [the peace] conditions an orderly policy is totally impossible."

A speech in Graz on July 9, 1919, made two new points (ibid., 167ff). Schumpeter rejected the notion that he had spent too much money because "all these expenditures were made in the context of a policy which had maintained social order in Vienna while Bolshevism had taken over in Budapest." He also rejected the accusation of optimism.

In the meantime, Schumpeter had presented his first "regular" budget on July 1 with a speech that won the full approval of the Oe.V. (Oe.V., July 12, 1919, 767ff). Federn pointed to the difficulties under which Schumpeter had to work. Austria had no central bank and no control over the emission of bank notes. Schumpeter kept hammering at the need for the capital levy and preparation for orderly finances within five years. But, as Federn pointed out, in the old days fiscal policy had a strong influence on the economy. "Today it works the other way 'round, and even the greatest genius of a Minister of Finance could not put our finances in order as long as our economic life is dying." Which was, of course, precisely Schumpeter's point.

After the final peace conditions were handed to the Austrians, Schumpeter spoke to the Constituent Assembly on July 28, 1919.[7] There was certainly no optimism left. Schumpeter stressed that the law required him to submit a budget for 1919–1920. But the second sentence was: "You, ladies and gentlemen, know as well as I that in the *meantime the budget has lost all meaning*. . . . If I nevertheless bring the budget before the House it is basically because I consider it important that the House should know . . . where German-Austria would stand except for the peace conditions" (Schumpeter 1992, 65).

Schumpeter sketched the outlines of the budget, the expected deficit, the loss of purchasing power of the krone. But when he talked about the "annihilating (vernichtende) peace conditions," he pointed out the *"peace conditions had made [his proposals] totally impossible"* (ibid.; italics in original).

The peace conditions included a fixed exchange rate for the conversion of the debt owed to the successor states

which always was absurd. In the whole world the creditor bears the *exchange risk*, only we should pay *hidden reparations* for which there is no basis, no reason. We are to pay an exchange guarantee for the new-foreigners . . . at the same time everyone is free to declare himself a citizen of another country. . . . There are suddenly lots and lots of Czechoslowaks etc. (es wimmelt von) who a short while ago were no such thing. (ibid., 71)

Stocker interrupted: "Polish Jews!" And someone shouted "and Hungarian." To which Rep. Stricker objected: "But you have refused them citizenship!" which could be done because Czechs had been Austrians, but Hungarians were from a separate country. Schumpeter ended the speech:

Since the situation is thus I have refrained from going into the details of the budget, in particular from developing the details of the *plans* for the next three years. . . . In the meantime I want to say that the budget as presented—and I

---

[7] The speech was reproduced in full in NFP, July 29, 1919. For some reason, the index of the *Stenographic Protocols* has no reference to this budget speech. It is reprinted in Schumpeter (1992), 65ff.

want to tell this to the whole world if I could—would not have been a reason for despair, that the reason we have to despair does not lie with us but outside." (Lively and prolonged agreement and clapping of hands. The Secretary of State is being congratulated.) (ibid., 72–73)

Of course, Schumpeter continued to work and finally did present the Finanzplan in cabinet. But by that time it was too late for him and the government.

The Oe.V. had chided the Socialists for their ambiguity toward the Soviet system as "not yet" suitable when they knew perfectly well that it would be a catastrophe. But the most scornful words were reserved for the bourgeois parties which, coming from a bourgeois and anti-Socialist weekly, was particularly telling.

> The real sabotage of economic reconstruction comes from the bourgeois parties which are ready for any criticism of the Government in which the biggest of them is represented, but which are not ready to fulfil their duty towards the State and the people . . . they have poisoned the atmosphere towards the Anschluss. . . . They want to carry the particularism of the Länder to the point of complete separation from Vienna. They increase our food misery by refusing to deliver anything at all or only at exorbitant prices . . . they collaborate in the destruction of the economy by collecting gold and foreign exchange on the black market. They agitate against the capital levy and against any burden on the only group presently able to pay, the large landowners. (Oe.V., July 12, 1919, 769)

This is a very serious indictment and it is reinforced by the stenographic record of the discussion of Schumpeter's fiscal program in Cabinet Council.

After his resignation from cabinet, Schumpeter wrote a letter to the press to correct a statement made by Schumpeter's successor Reisch on January 16, 1920, which could be "misunderstood" (Schumpeter 1992, 286). No doubt Reisch's statement was an inadvertent misrepresentation, but it is but one of the many which dogged Schumpeter all his life.[8] The issue was Schumpeter's attempt to link the capital levy with making foreign credit available. He explicitly wanted the favors given only to persons who could make available to the government foreign credit *abroad*, while *explicitly* excluding making foreign currencies available in Austria (ibid.; italics in original).

> I want to state this because the manner of argumentation of the Secretary of State for Finances might give rise to the erroneous opinion that I have recommended something which I have explicitely excluded.
>
> Since I did not have the opportunity to defend my fiscal program in public and could formulate the program only in a confidential memorandum which could

---

[8] There are many such misunderstandings even of his carefully stated theoretical positions. One such is that he believed that the less government the better, which in this unqualified form is at least misleading. Another is that he was a deflationist during the Great Depression, which is not true.

hardly have remained unknown to the Secretary of State for Finances, I feel compelled to make this public correction. (ibid.)

ACTIVITIES IN PARLIAMENT

All of Schumpeter's speeches in parliament were relatively brief. He answered eight parliamentary inquiries, all concerning relatively minor matters and some revealing the petty nature of the bourgeois and peasant sensitivities, which must have confirmed his comments that it was not his habit to sing the praises of the bourgeoisie.

In his first important speech to parliament on April 2, 1919, Schumpeter asked parliament to vote for a money bill. He apologized and explained why he could not submit a regular budget: it simply had been impossible to get proper figures under the chaotic conditions of the time. Thus, in the absence of firm data, the requirements of government were calculated to be 36 percent of the requirements of the late Monarchy, which corresponded to the ethnic German population. The figures thus indicate that Schumpeter in common with everyone else assumed that the new Austria would include all ethnic Germans.

Schumpeter promised a budget that would rest on a firmer foundation for June. Indeed, on July 4, he made such a budget speech even though no definite figures were yet available to put the budget on a firmer basis, even without the problems of a rapid inflation and the lack of knowledge of peace conditions.

But on April 2, Schumpeter had pointed out that German Austria had inherited a debt of about K80 billion. "But this is the least of it. For [the war] has bequeathed us a complete disorganization, unrest everywhere, unemployment, a misery with which the young freedom has to struggle. In this situation it is obviously essential to return immediately to orderly ways."[9]

The return to orderly ways demanded that the "great work of the capital levy" be carried out within a few weeks. But there simply was no way to present a balanced budget. Schumpeter estimated the deficit at K2.4 billion, without subsidies for food, flour and bread, clothing, invalids, concessions to the railway workers and others, which would bring the deficit to K5–6 billion.

> The first of these sacrifices is the Great Capital Levy which must be quickly and energetically undertaken, which must serve the reduction of the war burden and the spirit of the times, socialization. For, once the war debt is substantially reduced, once a number of essentially temporary tasks is finished, then—say in

---

[9] Seventh Session of the Constituent National Assembly, April 2, 1919, 140. Seven of the parliamentary speeches are reprinted in Schumpeter (1985) where the quotation is found p. 314; my translation. The last major speech is reprinted in Schumpeter (1992). It was reported in full in the press.

three of four years—we will have returned to orderly circumstances, if you, ladies and gentlemen cooperate. (Schumpeter 1985, 314)

As it turned out, the inflation had run its course in four years and stabilization was undertaken along the lines outlined by Schumpeter. Schumpeter repeated again and again that the only task of fiscal policy had to be to provide bread for the population and to serve reconstruction.

Two days later, on April 4, 1919, and also in connection with the money bill, Schumpeter pleaded not to change his proposals further in favor of this or that special interest, mainly in favor of the farmers. Schumpeter pleaded that in the situation there was only a "least bad way." The law was simply an expression of the misery of the times.

Bread and flour taxes had to be raised as the krone depreciated. If the bread price had been raised as proposed in January, the necessary subsidies would have been K115 million instead of the present K351 million. Obviously, the budget could not stand these subsidies (Schumpeter 1985, 316–17).

To mitigate the shock of higher bread prices, Schumpeter proposed an increase of flour rations. He stressed the social nature of the measures taken by pointing out that a rich man with an income of K150,000 would pay K750 for a loaf of bread. "This is acting socially (Applause)" (ibid., 317). Unfortunately, Austria was a country of small businesses and it simply was not possible to squeeze out the necessary sums by taxing only the rich.

The issue under debate was the taxation of landowners against the objections of the peasant party. Schumpeter insisted that not only were peasants better off than urban dwellers because they produced their own food, but that owners of forests in particular were much better off since wood prices brought a good return.

He pleaded that Austria was at the edge of the abyss and it simply was impossible to worry about a few kronen here and there. He pleaded that the increase in the bread price and the increase in the bread tax were essential to save consumers and farmers alike. He kept insisting that even the smallest landowner was by no means the poorest (ibid., 318), and there, too, the progression of taxation would be energetically applied. It was impossible to accede to other modifications of the law in favor of the farmers. Schumpeter ended with the plea:

> I would be a traitor to my duty if I conceded anywhere near as much as the proposed changes in the law demand.
>
> Ladies and gentlemen, do not leave my appeal unheard. Changes have practically no effect. . . . Should you really misjudge your own interests so completely? However this may be, I must do my duty. My path is clear. I must reject the amendment and must ask the High House to accept the Government bill. (Lively applause and clapping of hands) (ibid., 319–20)

This speech certainly does not agree with the so frequently heard characterization of Schumpeter as being "all things to all men."

The next speaker was Stöckler, and he simply said that the farmers would never accept the law. It was technically flawed. Moreover, the peasant had already paid during the war when he delivered grain at maximum prices of K40–50. If flour prices were three times that amount in the cities, that was not the fault of the peasant. The peasant delivered at K2–3½. It was none of the peasant's business if city dwellers paid a multiple. The trouble was the black market, the Zentralen, usury, etc.

The minister of finance called this petty. Farmers worked hard to grow grain, and would never understand, and rightly so, why they should pay a high bread tax. It would ruin any incentive to work. If the government wanted to do something it should get rid of the Zentralen (i.e., price controls), tax large capitalists, Jewish large capital, get rid of the useless army.

There had been increasing interruptions from the floor as the speech proceeded, and at this point the presiding officer of the House had to ask for order.

Three weeks later, on April 25, there was a formal parliamentary question to Schumpeter, this time concerning the blockage of bank accounts in connection with the proposed capital levy, a blockage that was interfering with economic life.

Schumpeter answered immediately. First, he did not ask for anything that was not essential. "All that is necessary is to go and register the account, and it is immediately unblocked . . . I have personally added this point to the proposed legislation" (ibid., 321).

On May 6, Schumpeter had to answer questions concerning the blockage by representative Schumacher, who had had the courtesy to give the questions to Schumpeter ahead of time, for which Schumpeter thanked him from the floor.

"Is the Minister prepared to extend the period for registration?" The answer: In principle, no. "If you must mistreat the people, let it be done as briefly as possible." Until the registration is completed, the capital levy, which should come as soon as possible, could not be carried out.

Schumpeter also answered immediately an unrelated inquiry asking for a two-month extension. The answer was a rather exasperated "this is out of the question . . . I would have to postpone the capital levy by two months" (ibid., 322–24).

All of this discussion was comparatively optimistic. "All" that Schumpeter had to deal with was starvation, total disorganization, and inflation. But by July, when the interim budget for the second half of 1919 was submitted to parliament, the situation had badly deteriorated further in every respect. Inflation was worse, the exchange rate had dropped from 16½ centimes to about 10. Starvation had become worse. The first preliminary peace conditions had become known, pouring cold water though not yet completely dashing any hope that domestic policy measures might get the economy going so that in three to four years it might have mastered the misery.

Actually, at the time there were simultaneously two laws before parliament:

the proposed budget and a foreign loan to be negotiated by the Austrian delegation to St. Germain to finance food import to deal with the worst emergencies.

There was a slight delay in the discussion of the budget because the budget committee of parliament had not quite finished its report. The committee chairman then reported to the House, explaining first a number of changes compared to the earlier budget for January 1–June 30, and he gave some of the highlights. There was the data problem which Schumpeter had stressed before. But a really meaningful budget simply could not be submitted. The most urgent task was to reduce prices (!) and to improve the exchange rate and the credit of the State. Without stopping inflationary finance, the economy and the social situation would totally collapse. The time to act was now.

Schumpeter's speech filled only five pages[10]—short for a budget speech. It was to the point and sober. He stressed the data problem and hoped to submit a final budget in about two weeks. But this was not the real problem. The real difficulties were twofold. First, new demands were made on government daily. He used harsh words "in den Rücken fallen," "a stab in the back" for the constant and too frequently successful breaches of agreed-upon budget ceilings. There was no way to proceed with "correct" budgeting with such successful special pleading.

Second, it was really "monstrous to present a budget before peace negotiations have been concluded" (Schumpeter 1985, 325). Hence, everything would probably have to be totally changed once peace conditions would become known. The reasons why the passage of the provisional budget were urgent were to end the period in which there was no legal authorization to spend money, and to allow Austrian delegates at St. Germain to negotiate a food loan.

There was just one point that required discussion: the proposed deficit of K2 billion, which certainly would become much bigger than forecast. There were continuous attacks against government expenditures and the use of the printing press to pay for them. Schumpeter fought the expenditures daily, nay hourly, but at least "one thing is clear that we in Vienna, between Munich and Budapest, have maintained a not useless policy of social peace. We have maintained a united front . . . and I would like to ask all who get so excited about our fiscal policy, all capitalists and other [special] interests what they prefer: our policy or a total collapse which would be irremediable" (ibid., 326).

Using a "strong man" was a totally unacceptable policy. To meet the wishes of the people with force, even if it were available, would be a shortsighted policy even from the standpoint of special interests! "It would be sheer madness to base Government policy on bullets."[11]

---

[10] A little more as reprinted in Schumpeter (1985), 324–30.

[11] Schumpeter actually used the idiomatic expression "blue beans," "Blaue Bohnen," for bullets. There was agreement from the listeners.

Schumpeter then turned to the impending peace treaty: "A peace which forces us fiscally on our knees we cannot survive either fiscally or socially. The peace conditions which have become known thus far need only be ratified to make a catastrophe inevitable" (ibid., 327).

Schumpeter then addressed the issue of government expenditures. No one talked about tax increases, nor did he have to mention that enterprises had deficits and hence nothing to offer the State. He explained how the credit mechanism had inflationary results: The government issued $2^{1}/_{2}$ percent (!) Treasury bills, which were sold for notes of the Austro-Hungarian National Bank which had already been issued. This was indeed inflationary, but not in the malicious manner which the successor states had accused Austria of pursuing.

The inflationary situation was nevertheless serious. The note issue of what was still the Austro-Hungarian Central Bank would continue to increase even under the best of circumstances without covering government needs. It, and not usury, was the reason for the inflation. Everyone has pockets full of money. Here also was the reason for the decay in the exchange rate.

> This, and not lack of social conscience, is the reason why I so desperately fight against increases in salaries and wages etc. This thought is so obvious that everybody must accept it who thinks about this matter at all: for the increases in money incomes due to note inflation have the effect that we get our foodstuffs under increasingly worse conditions. This causes the *circulus vitiosus* which we cannot immediately escape. (ibid., 328; italics in original)

A big long-term government loan is impossible. The conditions would be

> [I]mpossibly hard. . . . This was possible when I took over my office. . . . But in the meantime Hungary has happened and has endangered our credit at home and abroad. I know, these circumstances endanger the position of the working masses, they endanger the future of our wives and children, they endanger the food supply (Ernährungszustand) of the whole population, but we just do not have the means to change them immediately. We have arrived at the most serious point of our fiscal policy. If the credit mechanism works through the next few weeks and months, if we come though all of this, then we can, together with the capital levy, undertake larger credit operations at home and abroad. At the moment we can not get any credit even abroad because foreigners have no faith in our future. This is what I have to say about the two billion [deficit] and their coverage. (ibid., 329)

But first must come the peace conditions, because until then all obligations remain unknown.

> But there is another point: The capital levy makes sense only . . . and people will put up with it only if one can say: Pay! It is hard, but if you pay you will be saved. If this is not so, if the capital levy is merely a preliminary to a payment to the enemy, then I will not carry it out, then we can not defend it in conscience, then

there is nothing but the collapse. (Right!) First, reason towards us must be shown, first we must be shown that we will at least be allowed to live, then we can come with the measure which will bring order into the value of money together with the interest burden, the public debt burden.

These are the few points which I have to say today. . . . Fiscal policy is possible only if it is supported by the whole people. I have no use for force or secrecy. . . . Let us work together . . . that we can get over the most urgent matters which the next few weeks will demand of us. If we get over this then my old and so often criticized optimism may yet turn out to be right. (ibid., 329–30)

The budget speech was greeted with "great applause and clapping of hands" (Lebhafter Beifall und Händeklatschen). Despite the "optimistic" end, it could hardly be called thus. And it certainly did not lack realism.

In the subsequent debate, Schumpeter intervened only briefly, to answer fairly trivial questions. This was the last time Schumpeter spoke in parliament. The date was July 28, and it is also after July that the public speeches of Schumpeter which he had been making almost every week became exceedingly rare. The peace conditions evidently had a sobering effect. As he himself pointed out in his budget speech, they made any rational solution of his problems impossible. But it was not in his nature to give up, so he kept on fighting against impossible odds.

The Finanzplan

SCHUMPETER HAD SUBMITTED a preliminary budget to parliament on July 1, 1919, as required by law, but everyone including Schumpeter knew that it hung in the air. It was produced before the peace conditions were known; it assumed that the borders of German-Austria would be along linguistic lines; it was expected that German-Austria would be saddled with about one-fourth of the imperial war debt corresponding to the importance of the German-speaking population. Instead, it was saddled with three-fourths. There was complete administrative chaos and the separatist tendencies recounted before. Even under these "optimistic" assumptions, the deficit was estimated at over 60 percent of expenditures.

Schumpeter's Finanzplan was the culmination of his ministerial activity. The outlines of his thinking were known through his *Crisis of the Tax State*, and all his parliamentary activities, public speeches and discussions in Cabinet Council were, of course, formed or colored by his concerns about finances.

Schumpeter did submit his Finanzplan to cabinet on September 27, 1919, shortly after the peace treaty was signed. It was 33 octavo pages. The plan discussed in cabinet in detail on October 1, 1919.[1] The published version of the Finanzplan was printed by the Government Printing Office (Staatsdruckerei) in 1919, but no date is given.[2]

The original version is considerably more outspoken than the published version, which is "cleaned up" and changed in style from the first person singular "I have shown . . ." to a more formal grammar. The present account is based on the typewritten rather than the printed version. The typewritten version is a thoroughly pessimistic document.

The general attitude of hopelessness was illustrated by an expected budget deficit of K6 billion, of which K2 billion were overruns of the original expenditures projected. Much worse, the government simply could not borrow either at home or abroad, and to buy food abroad the government had to sell art objects. The deficit had to be financed by printing money.

Bankruptcy of the government had to be avoided at all cost. Bauer thought what happened *was* bankruptcy, but Schumpeter insisted that there was a difference between paying and repudiating one's debts. A repudiation of the

---

[1] *Finanzplan*. Streng vertraulicher Anhang zum Kabinettsprotokoll No. 110 vom 29. September 1919. Typewritten, pp. 33. For an unknown reason, this Protokoll was not available, when I first searched the *Finanzarchiv* and the *Staatsarchiv*. I found the document only in 1990. The various versions of the Finanzplan are discussed in Schumpeter 1992, 302–23.

[2] Reprinted in Schumpeter (1985).

debt would tear the whole fabric of the economy and the State apart without doing anyone any good.

The real problem was restoring a sound fiscal policy, which Schumpeter discussed in two steps: the longer term problem of restoring a (more or less) balanced budget in four to five years, and the immediate problem of how to get from here to there. The discussion of the first step, which constitutes two-thirds of the plan, is really a discussion of how the structure of the budget should look to deal with the longer-term problem of the growth of the economy and to increase the well-being of the economy after the immediate problems of survival were dealt with.

To start with, Schumpeter rejected as pernicious as well as "impossible to solve the problem by raising the value of money to its pre-war level. . . . [e]xcluded is also any attempt to restore the monetary system by a reduction of expenditures or a substantial reduction of the circulation of bank notes" (Schumpeter 1992, 304). To do so would require a reduction of [money] wages. "A particular reason is that an increase in the value of money would take a long time and would mean a lengthy period of depression" (ibid.).

Schumpeter further felt it necessary to accept the devaluation of the crown by 90 percent, maintain workers' incomes but limit or even eliminate increases in pensioners' incomes, and have no reduction of notes in circulation but also no further use of the printing press.

"We must imagine an economy with a price level ten times that of prewar" (ibid., 305) which would also raise government revenues tenfold. There is a detailed discussion of what this would mean for civil service salaries including wages of railroad and other workers employed by the government.

Price rises would make small businesses quickly profitable again. Large enterprises would remain unprofitable for a while because of social payments and foreign debts, but this would not matter for a few years. Agriculture, too, would quickly become profitable. But nothing could be done for rent recipients and owners of old houses, and dividend recipients also would suffer.

The decisive point is that Schumpeter *at no time* was a deflationist. He was nevertheless overoptimistic in believing that a further devaluation of the krone was not likely.

The expected deficit had to be eliminated by raising taxes rather than cutting expenditures. Rising prices would raise budgetary revenue, but not sufficiently. Tax rates had to be increased selectively. Property taxes should evidently be raised but not at the same time as the capital levy. Of the direct taxes, the income and inheritance taxes had to be raised.

The income tax had to be raised substantially with a strong progression and larger tax brackets. Inheritance taxes also could be further raised—contrary to the opinion of the relevant government office. The tax rates voted in February 1919 were to be doubled. Moreover, with the inheritance taxes the decrease in the value of money had not yet become effective because it had been impossible to reassess all properties. There was, therefore, quite a bit expected from these two taxes toward reducing the deficit.

But it was indirect taxes which had to be raised substantially. Of all the warring parties, only the Monarchy had not raised indirect taxes—"for lack of moral courage, and the courage which absolutism lacked must now be shown by the Republic" (ibid., 311).

Schumpeter laid down the following principles for indirect taxation:

1. Taxes had to be raised gradually so that consumption would not fall drastically. "[b]ut the population has to be told how high the rates would eventually be if only not to shatter any confidence in the Government. Such information about future tax rates have not been known in fiscal history, but it will be inevitable for the Government to do so now" (ibid., 311–12). This seems to be the first instance for phasing in new tax rates.

2. Schumpeter refers to the English example of taxing only a few important goods rather than employing a general sales tax. Taxation should be limited to luxury items including luxuries of the lowest income groups such as beer. Only goods with an inelastic demand should be taxed—this term is not used but the fact is described. Beer, spirits (Branntwein), and tobacco are mentioned first. But so are meat and sugar, and for the top income groups, housing (ibid., 312). Beer taxes were to be raised with the alcohol content which would rise from a war time 3–4 percent to the normal 11 percent. Wine taxes were to be raised proportionally.

Tobacco was already a monopoly, yet its price had to be raised tenfold, the monopoly having failed to raise prices during the war because it considered high wages and the depreciation of the krone temporary phenomena! (ibid., 313).

Railroad rates had to be raised, though there was no necessity to eliminate the railroad deficits altogether given the difficult terrain of Austria. Postal rates had to be quadrupled. Meat taxes could remain low and a sugar monopoly might be considered. All of these were taxed goods which were not strict necessities.

But there also are *luxury* taxes proper. Schumpeter refers to the French *grand luxe* as distinct from merely pleasant comfort. Schumpeter proposed a very high taxation for "luxury foods, luxury entertainment, luxury textiles, luxury stores, servants, luxury clothing etc" (ibid., 315). "I lay great stress on the fact of luxury taxation, it is the means to tax conspicuous consumption in a manner which calms the public conscience" (ibid., 315).

With a tax on houses and apartments "we cannot afford even small comfort" (ibid.). Old houses should be taxed but rents controlled "because an increased profit would not induce [the landlord] to increase his activity." An increase in rents by a factor of 4 to 5 would suffice, given a tenfold increase in the general price level. The house tax could be restricted to old houses; if it were applied also to new structures it could be used to divert supply from large structures to small apartments (ibid., 316).

After four years the budget deficit would have shrunk to K1.8 billion. "We will have to show a deficit. For a perfectly balanced budget is not desirable for reasons of foreign policy" (ibid.). About 20 percent (K1.8 billion) of the planned expenditures would be "serious but not hopeless. Hence I say that the Government which carries out such measures may claim that it has produced order and this is the essential point. The individual measures can not be carried out in isolation. But carried out in the context of a total plan they are not impossible" (ibid.).

This then was Schumpeter's vision of the future. The use of the double negatives indicates that he was quite aware of the problems. But to get to this future there had to be an "Economic Plan for the Next three Years" (ibid., 316–23). In a sense this is the heart of the proposals. The first two-thirds of the Finanzplan really are a picture of how Schumpeter envisaged the eventual structure of the budget with which he could live and with which the country would have to live.

The problem was how to arrive at that point. The decisive problem was to get the credit machinery going again to furnish the necessary resources to get the real economy going again. The decisive fact was that the government had no credit at home or abroad. The sale of art work and similar sales of national wealth were necessary but were in fact quite inadequate. The immediate need was for at least 1 billion Swiss francs just to get production and with it exports rolling again (ibid., 324). In addition, there was a need for K10 billion (at the then existing domestic prices) of internal credit. "Any Finanzplan for the next three years is a failure if it does not show how we can get foreign exchange, and domestically, how we can get along without additional bank notes" (ibid., 317–18).

Without private credit made available to the State there was no hope: "The problem is to force the citizens to make their credit relations abroad available to the State" (ibid., 318).

To this end Schumpeter made a number of technical proposals, including the issue of interest-bearing government paper which could circulate like money.

The Treaty of St. Germain mandated the dissolution of the Austro-Hungarian Bank. This implied the creation of an Austrian central bank. But, of course, no serious monetary and exchange rate policy could be pursued unless and until the bank had some foreign exchange reserves. In any case, the new Austrian Central Bank must under no circumstances be permitted to give credit to the government. The bank should be endowed with some gold whose function would be a certain readiness to make [international] payments. "But as we cannot afford this, a gold treasure would just be solace for the eyes (Augentrost). The basis of our note emission would have to be Government paper money which is what future bank notes will be" (ibid., 319).

Schumpeter's monetary theory as first expounded in the *Sozialprodukt und die Rechenpfennige* is based precisely on this assumption.

The remaining pages of the plan were devoted to a discussion of the capital levy. A distinction was to be made between productive and unproductive assets. For the latter, the actual present value was to be the basis, for the former the capitalized value of the yield. Schumpeter refers to the cabinet discussion of July 16, to Bauer's suggestion to allow farmers more time for the payment of the levy, to the wishes of the Länder to keep 20 percent of the levy for their own uses, and to the cabinet decision to work out a proposal for a capital levy according to the objective and the subjective method. There were, so Schumpeter, now three drafts for a levy according to the subjective method with numerous additions of objective elements, and a fourth draft according to the objective method (ibid., 328).[3]

Schumpeter repeated his earlier assertion: the objective compared to the subjective method had technical difficulties. More generally, Goldscheid's idea of giving the State more influence over the economy by the direct possession of physical assets became irrelevant because these assets would have to be sold abroad. "To use the objective method would be only an apparent success (Scheinerfolg) with enormous disadvantages, for by giving assets to the State we "destroy the private credit [abroad] on which our life depends without creating [foreign] credit for the State" (ibid., 321).

Here Schumpeter makes the strongest statement concerning socialization:

> I favor an orderly socialization, but such is possible only with an orderly budget. The gentlemen (Die Herren) will find me on the path to socialization when the preconditions for it are given. At the present moment when we so urgently need foreign credits through private connections I consider a measure like the objective capital levy impractical. With these sentences I support the most radical measure which conscientiously can be defended. (ibid.)

Since the government has no domestic credit, the capital levy must be used as a means to force the Capitalists to give credit to the government and particularly to save flight capital. Austria had much more capital abroad than normal for a country of its size. "Capital has not fled abroad only since the war; rather the big capital flight began already in 1906 when the structure of the Reich showed more and more cracks and the trade and payments balance became more and more passive" (ibid.).[4]

This flight capital had to be mobilized by such measures as the exclusion from the capital levy of such foreign assets as in fact were made available to the government.

As a rule, the capital levy was to be paid over three years. For assets of up to K1 million, the levy could be spread over thirty years provided at least one-fourth consisted of government paper. For assets of more than K1 million, the conditions were more stringent.

At this point Schumpeter also makes a realistic concession. The capital levy

---

[3] I have not found these drafts.

[4] In 1906, the Ausgleich had to be renegotiated. The statement shows that Schumpeter was quite aware of the seriousness of the problems which his political memoranda had been intended to solve.

should in principle not be used to finance current budgetary expenditures, but he would agree to use part of it to cover current expenditures rather than print new money.

In some respects the final version was even stronger than the version cabinet discussed. It is evident that Schumpeter was allowed to write as he wanted since cabinet had made no decisions and washed its hands of it. It is also evident that Schumpeter was on the way out and no one cared if he made himself unpopular.

The printed version starts with the uncompromising italicized statement that "no new bank note or Government note must be issued which directly or indirectly serves to finance the needs of the State" (Schumpeter 1985, 344). It ends with the equally blunt statement:

> The preceding pages have described the fundamentals of the tax policy for the next years. To be sure, the immediate need is only to decide on the capital levy since for the time being we cannot count on tax revenues which would greatly ease the need. But it is absolutely essential to decide already today seriously and decisively about the fundamentals of tax policy and to cease vague hints and the piling up of dead files. It is necessary that today not only the capital levy and its connection with raising credits be decided upon but that at least the most important and most difficult indirect taxes, particularly the taxation of alcoholic beverages, be fixed *already today to the full extent*" (ibid., 368; italics in original)

In between, the facts are laid out without any euphemisms or embellishments. The summary sentences, many of them italicized, paint a grim task:

> The relevant calculations show that the State will need K20 billion for the next three to four years until the economy is reconstructed and an orderly budget is produced which *must be financed without paper money* (ibid., 345). . . . *The present credit problem is the problem of fiscal policy. The whole fiscal policy must be the servant of credit*" (ibid.). We must get foreign credit but must not use our capital for current needs. Not to do so, would mean "the total dispossession of our people in their own country and a capital import not to fructify our economy but to dispossess our people. . . . The debt *burden must be borne. It is a credit-destroying breach of one's word if we reduce for whatever reason unilaterally . . . our obligations* (ibid., 347). . . . *Only private enterprise and assets are at present a possible basis for foreign credit. As of today there is only one basis for credit to save the fatherland: not that of the State, not that of socialized capital but only that of private wealth.* . . . The only thing left to Austria of the labor of many centuries is the credit of its old honorable firms and citizens. It is the last thing. *This last thing must save us*" (ibid., 348; italics in original)

This is an appeal to reason and patriotism. It was doomed because no one wanted to hear "blood, sweat, and tears" at the exhausted end of a terrible war, but also because there was no such thing as Austria except in the articles of the Peace Treaty. What fatherland?

An Assessment

The "cleaned-up" version by no means lacked punch or embellished any problems or their inescapably harsh solutions. But it also explains to a large extent why the plan or even the capital levy were never accepted by government which, it should be remembered, was a coalition government. Schumpeter in fact joined the Christian-Social (conservative) party and tried, unsuccessfully, to sell the party his plan. There were, therefore, powerful political factors which Schumpeter could not overcome while in the cabinet or after.

But there is also another reason for the failure. Schumpeter's ideas were ahead of their time, and nobody in the cabinet, with the partial exception of Otto Bauer, understood what he was talking about. Recognizing the definite devaluation of the exchange rate or, in essence, advocating flexible exchanges until the domestic economy could be put in order was simply not considered realistic—"immoral" is perhaps not too strong a word to characterize how such propositions were seen.

The plan is vintage Schumpeter. It recognizes facts as they are, not as he would like them to be: there is no ideological bias in his solutions as he defined the term later. The solutions of the problems are adjusted to the specific irreversible facts of the historic situation with which it is senseless to quarrel. But remembering that there is no determinism but still a choice—in this case not of Schumpeter and Austria but of the Entente and the successor states—one might still quarrel with his hope that the rest of the world would be sufficiently rational to allow, for example, free trade.

The plan is vintage Schumpeter also in taking a developmental view based on a long-term analysis; the long term matters for immediate decisions. Schumpeter is conscious of the lags in an economy which require immediate actions for long-term effects.

The plan stresses the need for fluctuating exchanges—a term not then in use—until the domestic conditions for stable exchanges are given, though it evidently prefers stable exchanges as a permanent solution which only a responsible domestic policy can produce. In fact, we must turn to Schumpeter's economic policy writings for his views on international economic matters; they are not discussed in his purely theoretical writings.

The plan stresses the intimate connection between fiscal and monetary policy which at the time was certainly not common. It stresses the importance of a tighter fiscal policy to permit a looser monetary policy, which is real "supply side" economics proper. The analysis of the *Tax State* shows, and the plan confirms, that this is not because Schumpeter was in principle anti-State, but because the achievements of all government purposes require increasing real resources which only a developing economy can provide.

The plan emphasizes the importance of freeing the economy from price and exchange controls, using the market to the full extent. The Finanzplan is worth studying today for its relevance in dealing with present problems, mutatis mutandis, of course.

The plan stresses that Socialist solutions were out of the question. It must, however, be remembered that Schumpeter's definition and analysis discussed before differ from the usual ones in that they do not make use of the market the definiens of capitalism. The rejection of the Socialist solutions has nothing to do with Schumpeter's personal preferences but with his analysis of a historical process: the time was not ripe. This also explains in part the necessity of an independent central bank which is essential for a working Capitalist system and the central role given to monetary policy, with fiscal policy becoming an essential servant of the former.

Was Schumpeter's analysis right? To reduce his proposed solution for 1919 to the barest bones, it consisted of (i) a capital levy conceived as a currency reform; (ii) the immediate freeing of the domestic and international economy with price controls limited to a few cases in which higher prices would not elicit larger supplies; (iii) a fiscal policy to encourage increased savings; and (iv) large-scale capital imports which would also be in the best long-term interest of the lenders. It was also based on the assumption that the former enemies would allow rump-Austria to survive and that they and the successor states would pursue a sufficiently rational policy to allow the world economy to recover.

History has, of course, falsified these assumptions. And there is every evidence that Schumpeter really hoped against hope. Yet, unless he was to throw in the towel from the beginning and declare the situation beyond hope, it is really difficult to see what else he could have done.

It happens that history has repeated itself sufficiently to strongly suggest if not prove that Schumpeter's prescriptions were right. After the Second World War, which at least in Germany was as devastating and demoralizing as the First World War had been in Austria, these steps were taken which produced the various economic "miracles": Currency reforms which removed the monetary overhang; the speedy end of price and exchange controls; free trade in the world; and large-scale capital movements initially made available by and to governments through the Marshall Plan—Schumpeter's stabilization of the exchange rate through government balances abroad rather than through the foreign exchange market. There was also an absence of reparations and interallied debts, which did not allow many problems to arise in the first place. Fiscal policies were savings-directed. Even the timing was approximately right: it took about three to five years until the Marshall Plan became unnecessary, though American capital movements to Europe lasted on a commercial basis much longer.

Yes, Schumpeter was right and the plan the only one which could possibly have saved the situation.

Cabinet Discussion of the Finanzplan

THE WHOLE CABINET discussed the Finanzplan on October 1.[1] The meeting ended with the defeat of Schumpeter, which made inevitable his final demise from the cabinet two weeks later.

Schumpeter started the proceedings by proposing an outline for the discussion which followed the plan: (1) absolute avoidance of bankruptcy; (2) no issuance of new bank notes; (3) accepting the devaluation of the krone and adjusting incomes, prices, and wages as well as the budget to it; (4) the problem of how to get foreign credit. Following the outline of the plan, Schumpeter also suggested first discussing the budget four years hence and then the immediate urgent needs: "I have tried hard to present a politically feasible plan." Since the capital levy had been discussed in detail in cabinet on July 16, no separate discussion of the levy was proposed.

Renner opened the discussion. He thought the plan less a plan than a set of instructions with the devaluation of money a *deus ex machina*. He objected that the existing devaluation of the krone "could not be relevant to the internal value of the krone because the balance of payments is an accident which changes with changing economic conditions." He objected—somewhat strangely for a Socialist—that private credit was expected to come to the rescue of the State instead the other way around. He would have preferred a systematic treatment of the sicknesses of the economy and a frank statement of what had to be done about it. This was a rather puzzling statement because Schumpeter did exactly this, so Schumpeter made no immediate response to Renner's remark.

The first discussant proper was Otto Bauer, former foreign minister and still head of the socialization commission with cabinet rank. Bauer was also a renowned Austro-Marxist whom the literature usually depicts as a friend and fellow student of Schumpeter, the man who brought him into the cabinet and the antagonist who was ultimately responsible for his dismissal. Maybe so. The cabinet discussion, however, brings some surprises. For, in this discussion, Bauer, though with some serious reservations, essentially backed Schumpeter. It is no exaggeration to say that he was the only one who understood what Schumpeter was trying to do.

Bauer agreed with Schumpeter in accepting the devaluation of the krone, though he thought that the existing value in Geneva was perhaps too low. Any attempt to raise the external value of the krone would lead to unbearable

---

[1] The "streng vertraulich" appendix to cabinet protocol No. 112, October 1, 1919, on which this chapter is based, is now reproduced in full in Schumpeter (1992), 323–57.

domestic burdens. Perhaps the correct value of the krone was 15 instead of $7^1/_2$ centimes. On this point the difference between the two was minute. The devaluation of the krone would act to stabilize the price level.

But then Bauer thought raising the external value of the krone would make Austrian government paper a welcome object of speculation which would serve the urgent purpose of getting foreign exchange, a point which Schumpeter had dismissed as a waste of scarce foreign reserves.

Schumpeter had estimated the immediate need for foreign exchange at 1 billion Swiss francs, which Bauer thought too low, without giving an estimate himself. Bauer also questioned, reasonably, whether the capital levy would mobilize Austrian funds abroad.[2] Nevertheless the objection did not touch Schumpeter's central concern: to cut down the domestic monetary overhang by means of the levy. Bauer referred to the Kola-Alpine Montangesellschaft affair.[3]

Bauer weakened his case substantially by recognizing that "a country which can pay its foreign debt only in part with its labor must pay with its capital, hence our natural resources and enterprises must fall into foreign hands. But the way this happens nowadays is insufferable" (Schumpeter 1992, 327).

Bauer next insisted that the problem really consisted of creating Austrian titles that would be attractive to foreign buyers and that required the expectation of an appreciation of the krone. He considered it an "error of the public to believe that the capital levy had to be used only to reduce the war debt. This is due to the mistaken assumption that the war debt is the most oppressive issue" (ibid., 328).

This, of course, misinterpreted Schumpeter on several counts. First, Bauer evidently saw the major effects of the debt reduction in the reduction of future interest payments. But Schumpeter wanted to get rid of excess money *before* the monetary overhang had time to work its way through the economy.[4] Second, Bauer continued, Schumpeter did not believe that government had any credit abroad or at home. And third, Schumpeter was adamantly opposed to *any* increase in the foreign value of the krone, to any, even a slight deflationary policy, a point he also repeatedly stressed later, such as in 1924 in connection with the stabilization of the Austrian schilling.

Bauer then reverted to his earlier point made in July that the "purely subjective method" would not fulfil the purpose to make available to the state

[2] Obviously only funds in neutral countries and Germany. The others had been confiscated by the terms of the peace treaty. Poland and Hungary, too, had confiscated German-Austrian assets in their territories.

[3] This affair will be discussed below in some detail. Schumpeter rejected this accusation categorically in a letter to Gulick, who quotes it in Gulick (1945), 140–41. As will be shown below, this accusation can be proved wrong, and Bauer knew it.

[4] Schumpeter, in his letter to Gulick, drew attention to this point, though Gulick did not reproduce it.

real assets."[5] "For me," Bauer continued, "the first decisive point is that the Finanzplan of Secretary of State Schumpeter does not at all show the means to get foreign credit in adequate amounts and that he refuses to apply the only suitable means to make available to foreigners part of the results of the capital levy in titles based upon it" (ibid.).

Bauer rejected Schumpeter's objection that such titles might be sequestered as possible reparations. Again, he missed the whole point of Schumpeter's argument that, to repeat ad nauseam, the capital levy was to establish sound monetary conditions as a precondition for making a sane fiscal policy. On this issue Schumpeter surely was more realistic than Bauer, who expected to sell to foreigners such government titles denominated in kronen, which he of course preferred to obligations denominated in gold imposed by the peace treaty.[6] "If we get a chance at such a solution we should grasp it, for if we get over the next two years we will be alright. I consider the fulfillment of this purpose of the capital levy more important than the reduction of the war debt. A reduction of 2½ billion [kronen] will not put us on a sound footing, a foreign credit of 2 bill francs will" (ibid., 328–29).

Bauer next turned to the problem of the budget. He agreed with the basic idea that inflation had increased the [nominal] GNP and wealth tenfold. But as to the details, he objected that Schumpeter depended entirely on increases in indirect taxes "The increase in indirect taxes and even the introduction of new ones seems to me, in view of the reduced value of money, completely unacceptable. But we have to be clear that a budget which puts all the burden on indirect taxes is politically impossible" (ibid., 329).

To be sure, Bauer continued, Schumpeter did refer to the sacrifices of the propertied classes, but the capital levy would hardly contribute to reducing the budget deficit and he felt that Schumpeter had greatly overestimated how much it could save. And Bauer added that all problems would be greatly eased if the external value of the krone could be substantially raised.

Bauer then reverted to the problem of socialization. People had the notion that socialization would come about by government using "the capital levy to buy all sorts of enterprises. This was, of course, absurd" (ibid., 330). However, there would be enterprises which the capital levy would force to convert to corporations, and this would allow the government to acquire shares which should then be used to reduce the debt and to fund the titles to be sold to foreigners. But some such shares "in certain enterprises which the state considers particularly important ought to remain in Government hands . . . e.g. if one wants to avoid that certain enterprises should fall into foreign hands" (ibid., 330–31), a fairly clear allusion to the Alpine. "A capital levy which

---

[5] Someone—not Schumpeter—had put a question mark against this passage in the copy of the protocol in the files of the *Staatsarchiv*. Penciled additions by the unknown reader will be pointed out in footnotes.

[6] This remark was underlined by someone in the copy of the *Staatsarchiv*.

makes such an eventuality totally impossible would in my opinion (lose) an important function" (ibid.).

Bauer rejected Schumpeter's assertion that the credit worthiness of enterprises would be diminished by socialization. If the government got gratis shares, shareholders would lose something, but not the enterprises. "Socialization as a slogan creates disquiet abroad. . . . As much as I believe that it is impossible to say that we forego socialization . . . as much do I believe that it is possible to say that we will bring about socialization not through expropriation but in connection with the capital levy" (ibid., 331).

Bauer reverted to his earlier assertion that the external value of the krone could easily be raised (ohne weiteres) by 50 percent. After some remarks about the burden placed on agriculture, Bauer summarized: "This Finanzplan of Secretary of State Schumpeter puts indirect taxes too much into the center, gives too little function to the capital levy, and is therefore not the way to prevent the catastrophe" (ibid., 332).

Bauer's remarks take about one-fourth of the transcript of the discussion. As Schumpeter was quick to point out, there were really only few disagreements in principle though some differences not only in details but in the magnitudes involved. Of course, there are also serious differences about what is feasible at any one moment, and whether certain theoretical choices exist in a given historical situation.[7]

Schumpeter responded immediately and at length. He agreed that there were many details still to be worked out. But at that particular time there were fundamentals at stake and he was pleased to note agreement. To start with, "since the old parity of the krone cannot and should not be achieved," the differences were only at what level the krone should be stabilized. Schumpeter only wanted the krone to find its own level. He did not agree that a 90 percent devaluation would raise prices very much except for subsidized food and rents, since domestic prices were in fact much higher than the tenfold increases implied in the 90 percent devaluation. Obviously, foreign capital would be more easily available if the exchange rate improved, but this would be "cut out of our economic body" (ibid., 333). An improved exchange rate implied a tremendous sacrifice. It is clear that no one understood the harm an overvalued exchange rate could do—and on this issue there has not been all that much progress.

Both agreed that putting the financial house in order was the crux of the problem. Schumpeter also agreed that a foreign loan of 1 billion Swiss francs was insufficient, but then Schumpeter gave five ways to get additional capital. "Once we have the first billion we will also get the others" (ibid., 334),

---

[7] "The difficulty of making practical recommendations—ex post—as to 'what should have been done about it' at any point of time consists entirely in the fact that, unlike doctors, we hopelessly differ on aims, preferences, valuations. So as soon as people sincerely tell us what they really want we can tell them . . . what should have been done at any moment in the past, or, for that matter, what should be done now" (Schumpeter 1951, 215).

particularly as the first billion would be used to get the economy going and would be rolled over for further raw material imports.

Schumpeter next turned to the proposal of giving the state shares of existing or yet to be created corporations or to an as yet to be created trust company which would in turn issue obligations denominated mainly in foreign currencies to be offered to foreigners. The establishment of such a trust company was in fact worked on in the treasury and by several independent groups for some time. But here Schumpeter disagreed with Bauer. While this method might make foreign exchange available to the State, it was unnecessary for the government to actually acquire shares—unless other aims than getting credit were involved (which of course they were in Bauer's mind).

However, Schumpeter denied that this method would make it easier to get foreign credit except at exorbitant rates of interest. Bauer implied that a devalued krone would permit foreigners to acquire Austrian assets at distress prices. Schumpeter pointed out that this would cease to be so once the krone was stabilized at its own level.

Schumpeter expressed pleasure to find Bauer's agreement that the decisive task of the capital levy was to raise credit. But "it is not correct to say that in the final budget all incomes will have been mechanically multiplied by ten. The basic idea underlying the budget is to shift the burden of the reduction of the war debt onto the rentiers since it seems unjust particularly in times like these to protect precisely unearned incomes against the effects of a loss of the value of money."[8]

Nor, Schumpeter continued, was it correct that the Finanzplan rested entirely on indirect taxes. He refused to speak of taxes on alcoholic beverages as unjust. And though beer prices would rise, that was hardly a tragedy in present circumstances, particularly when agricultural prices would have to rise to world market levels.

Schumpeter denied that he put the whole burden on the masses of the population, pointing to the sums he expected to raise by luxury taxes and the like. But he also had his reasons for not raising income taxes at present. "Government finances will . . . rest essentially on income taxes whose progression will be increased, however not now but as a reserve for future income needs" (ibid., 336).

A tax on shares would prevent industrial development. A tax on buildings would make rent controls untenable. The land tax was to be reserved for the Länder. Business income taxes (Erwerbssteuern) were low "but I must reserve such receipts as might be achieved by an increase as a reserve for further improvement in the finances (Sanierung)" (ibid.). The capital levy had been been thoroughly discussed by cabinet on July 16. It certainly was not ne-

---

[8] Ibid., 335. Someone had put a question mark against the line containing "rentiers" and underlined the line speaking of protection with an exclamation point! Shades of Keynes's death of the rentier?

glected in the Finanzplan, whose very heart it was. Schumpeter would agree to higher taxation of large landholdings including forest latifundia—a term actually used by Schumpeter.

Schumpeter finally objected to Bauer's proposed use of the capital levy for purposes of socialization. It would without any doubt reduce the credit worthiness abroad of enterprises which would first have to prove over some years that they would be as efficient as private enterprises had been. (After all, every public enterprise at the time had losses.) The issue of gratis shares to government was also damaging since once used, everyone would wonder whether it would be repeated. To be sure, foreign bankers were frequently reactionary (rückschrittlich), but this was not the time for experiments.

> I cannot see that the Finanzplan has the disadvantage of resting entirely on indirect taxes. The major burden is borne by the propertied people, only their sacrifice is insufficient. But it is certain that the proposed taxes are the least oppressive, less than would be a turnover tax or a tax on grain milling. . . . Government income is more or less a given datum and must be raised. I admit that many details require improvement, but the great lines can not be changed, not because I would not like to do so but because no one can change the situation. (ibid., 337)

I have presented the discussion between Schumpeter and Bauer in some detail because of the eminence of both discussants and because of their basic agreement. One cannot help but feel that Bauer was basically convinced of the justice of Schumpeter's case, yet had to make points dear to his political convictions. Both of them turned out to be overoptimistic about their fellow Austrians and about the Entente. But both saw the internal situation essentially as it was, disagreeing about specific magnitudes, and of course how far and in what manner to proceed with socialization.

Still, Bauer's and Schumpeter's discussion was on a respectable intellectual level. This, alas, can not be said of the other cabinet members.

Chancellor Renner reentered the discussion. Pleading limited time and competence in economic matters he objected—mildly and in a most gentlemanly manner—to both Schumpeter's and Bauer's readiness to accept devaluation as a datum.

> To express [their] error rather candidly: we are told to accept the devaluation of the krone as a fact and adapt the whole economy to it. . . . It is as if a bad barometer had to be corrected by changing the universe. We should turn everything upside-down only because we must avoid to change the foreign exchange rate. The problem is, however, the reverse, how to save the exchange rate . . . in order to avoid economic shocks and the revolution of the entire budget. For the Finanzplan of Secretary of State Schumpeter is a plan to revolutionize the whole budget and would astonish people. The question would have to be: can the exchange rate be so changed that it corresponds best to economic interests and requires the least revolution in taxes and wages, and is it not easier to help in this

manner than to accept the low level as permanent and to change everything else. (ibid., 338)

Schumpeter, so Renner continued, said last time: "There is no help for the rentier. Someone has to pay for the war." But many war bonds are held by social institutions. The problem is how to hit everybody equally. "The task of the reorganization measures would have to be to avoid the danger that the owners of war bonds and bank notes alone pay. . . . You will think this a strange argument from a socialist, but I know that we have to deal with an existing social order" (ibid., 339).

Renner objected to the proportion of indirect and direct taxes in the budget as impossible.

We have already agreed . . . on the principle that direct and indirect taxes must always be raised *pari passu*. Such a proportion of taxes as the Finanzplan wants would be intolerable for our parties and Parliament, even on the bourgeois side. I do not believe that any political party could dare to go before the voters with such a project. I am not quite accustomed to the final multiplication [of everything] but a tax of K250 for the hectoliter of beer. (ibid.)[9]

Even Renner! This statement really spelled the death of the plan and of Schumpeter, who was not even to be allowed to present his plan to parliament.

Next the Undersecretary for Social Administration Resch objected to the lowered exchange rate of the krone as the equivalent of government bankruptcy. He wanted to raise the exchange rate by a foreign loan, thought Schumpeter's budget had no original ideas (while Renner had thought it revolutionary!), and that the parties would not accept such a "tax bouquet" with its high indirect taxes.

Stöckler, the minister of agriculture, spoke at length. The problem is that the exchange rate is to be the basis of fiscal reconstruction. "We can not change the exchange rate, but I was astonished to hear that we have to reconstruct the economy on the basis of this rate" (ibid., 342). He therefore preferred Bauer's suggestion as did Renner, though neither of them suggested how it was to be done, nor why an 85 percent devaluation was so much better than an 89 percent one.

Stöckler referred to the Alpine affair which would be repeated on the basis of the peace conditions which, for example, would allow the Italians to buy wood at domestic prices, which they succeeded to depress by various tricks.[10]

---

[9] I am reminded of a column by the local equivalent of Art Buchwald on austerity measures in a Nigerian paper in 1962: Ministers' salaries should be cut; whoever had two wives should give up one; and the price of beer should be halved. The Nigerian was probably joking. Schumpeter's cabinet colleagues were dead serious. Schumpeter must have thought of this cabinet discussion when in the 1920s he made the "cynical" remark in connection with his tax proposals to save the finances of the Weimar Republic: "but, then, what is the future of the nation compared with the well-being of the restaurant trade!"

[10] The peace terms actually did impose wood exports at unfavorable prices, an important matter since wood was just about the only export product available to Austria.

He agreed with Bauer to use the capital levy for purposes of socialization. He objected to the too high proportion of indirect taxes. He agreed that large land holdings should be treated like industrial enterprises but wanted small farmers to receive help to get more capital and to be forced by law to ameliorate their land and to fertilize it and improve production.

Eldersch, minister of education, objected to accepting the devaluation of the krone at either 10 or 15 centimes. He could not imagine that every price and wage had to be raised tenfold. He warned that it might be difficult to maintain the exchange rate at so low a level and if it rose it would hurt the export chances of industry. Then comes the real point. The plan gives the impression of putting a one-sided burden on the urban population.

> [Five] billion are to be raised by the taxation of beer, spirit and other consumption goods. The project is not original but its generosity I cannot deny, for it proposes taxes which the great majority of the population will consider insane. The rates are so high that the people will stop consuming. . . . The tax on spirits and sugar is monstrous, particularly as we produce no sugar and must pay tribute to the Czechs in buying sugar. . . . Such a tax plan which forces the urban population alone to bear the deficit will not be taken seriously by the public and we, too, cannot agree to such a one-sided increase in taxes to the disadvantage of the urban population. (ibid., 345)

Bauer accused Schumpeter of having changed his mind within two days about how to execute the capital levy, an accusation difficult to understand. Eldersch doubted whether much flight capital could be repatriated by the methods proposed by Schumpeter because Austrians who had got their capital abroad were profiteers and swindlers. And Eldersch ended with bitter words against Schumpeter, which presaged his demise from the cabinet.

> In my opinion, the first matter is to get clear notions and a clearer presentation of the intentions of the Secretary of State for Finances. For in the present debate the opposing views have become so blurred that one does not know any more what is the issue. One knows that Dr. Schumpeter wants to go in other directions, but in decisive points he has shown such flexibility that one does not know anymore what is what. (ibid.)

Hanusch, minister of social affairs, professed horror at the omissions from the budget. Social security payments to invalids would rise to K1.5 billion, all insurance institutes would have to be reorganized, everything would rise ten times. "The present circumstances are considered bearable because they were considered temporary and so no adjustment seems needed" (ibid., 346). The tenfold increase of wages was so unappealing to the minister that he asked under no circumstances to inform the public about it. "It would be a catastrophe and would smash our whole economy without increasing the tax yield of the capital levy" (ibid., 347). For industry an objective capital levy is not even to be considered.[11] Thus far, Hanusch had accepted the misery because he

---

[11] The anonymous commentator wrote on the margin: "Also was dann?"—so what else can be done?

considered it temporary, but eventually prices would fall again and the exchange rise. "If the present Finanzplan is presented [to Parliament] there is no more salvation. It is the end" (ibid.).

Bauer intervened once more and at greater length. He voiced his pleasant agreement with Stöckler about raising the productivity of agriculture and wanted immediately to use the capital levy as an incentive system to raise that productivity, for example, by reducing the levy by the part used for raising productivity—another agreement with Schumpeter who had made the same point more forcefully. Besides, increased agricultural production would affect the exchange rate favorably.

Bauer then returned to the issue of the exchange rate. It depended on the balance of payments. But he took issue with Renner's simile of the barometer. At the cost of an enormous deflation, one could raise the exchange rate to 100 percent. One had to accept the devaluation of the krone which meant that the rentiers, that is, the owners of savings deposits, had to pay for the war.

Bauer then pointed out that the "subjective" method of the capital levy had really much the same effect as the issuance of gratis shares. Only the legal form differed. And bankruptcy, which Bauer did not like either, was really the same thing. All the capital levy would do is to declare an orderly bankruptcy, because the population still did not really believe that it had to pay for the war. He admitted that with respect to foreign loans it would be worse, which had been exactly Schumpeter's point. So, "if political parties could agree on a program with adequate sacrifice, bankruptcy could be avoided" (ibid., 350).

Bauer then warned that he disagreed more with Schumpeter than the latter believed. There was perhaps agreement in the large. But "the proposals made are inadequate. . . . The need for foreign credit must get priority over the mere reduction of the internal debt. I have no desire to construct an insurmountable gap and if Secretary of State Schumpeter feels we will come to an agreement in the detailed execution, I shall be very content" (ibid., 351).

As for socialization, he disagreed with Eldersch and Resch who had not recognized his proposal as socialization. What he wanted was for the state to ensure itself an influence on certain economic branches.

Löwenfeld-Russ, minister of food (Volksernährung), worried about the next months, about which the Finanzplan said nothing. He urgently needed foreign exchange for food purchases. In the meantime Upper Austria was making itself practically independent. He worried about the price increase in the wake of the deteriorated exchange rate and about taxes on sugar and spirits, which were not produced in Austria so that the tax was really a fiscal tariff. And he worried in general about the choice of goods selected for taxation: tobacco, alcohol, and sugar, which seemed to him particularly unfortunate.

The other taxes I consider to be grotesque and . . . the calculations are totally wrong particularly for beer. Strange as it may sound I consider a tax on flour milling in the form of a grain monopoly far more bearable. It could be administered more easily. The price of flour could then, the world market price permitting, be restrained by the state and the development of prices could then be slowed down. The same is true for coal. I would prefer a trade monopoly to an enormous increase in taxes. (ibid., 352)

Miklas, of the Ministry of the Interior, who was also responsible for religious affairs (Kultus), spoke next. To stabilize the krone at the existing level seemed politically impossible. There ought to be simpler procedures, but he did not specify.

The minister of transport was depressed because he did not understand anything. And if he did not, how did anyone expect the people to understand? He breathed easier at the exposition of Bauer, but then Schumpeter and the other participants brought back his depression. He was particularly depressed because everyone was so upset about the beer tax, and if the cabinet was upset, what about the people? The railroad workers were told that matters would improve if the exchange rate improved.

All of German-Austria expects a Finanzplan which lays out exactly what happens from week to week, everything with the aim to raise the value of the krone and there we get a Finanzplan which wants to stabilize the krone at the present level but raises wage. The workers will say: we accept the wage increases, but the other consequences of the Finanzplan we'll reject. I don't see how we can best tell the public that we don't really have a Finanzplan. (ibid., 354)

The minister was an honest man: no one understood what Schumpeter was talking about. And he quite accurately characterized what everyone—even today—understood a plan to be.

In his final reply, Schumpeter pointed out that any other Finanzplan would be worse. His plan was less burdensome than any other. As for the chancellor's remarks, they could either accept the value of money and try to stop a further decline, or stamp the money. But this would only change nominal, not real values. He agreed with Hanusch that rents had to be raised but not tenfold, perhaps twofold, particularly as they were not based on prewar but on higher wartime wages. The insurance institutions had to be reconstructed. The export premium existed only as long as the value of money was declining; once stabilized it ceased to exist. It is impossible to raise the international competitiveness and the value of the krone simultaneously. One should get rid once and for all of the idea that prices might decline. "We will then see that our path is much less difficult than any other" (ibid.).

As for Eldersch's comments that it would be a pity to adapt the domestic value of the krone to its foreign value, this would happen anyway despite all regulations and price controls. Trade would equalize domestic [and foreign] prices at a much higher level than the present. "I must reject the suggestion that my Finanzplan implies any excess burden on the broad masses. The consumption taxes do not hit only the broad strata, and do not forget that the capital levy with a top rate of 60% takes from the propertied classes every available means. An increase in direct taxes simultaneously with the capital levy is impossible" (ibid., 355).

The capital levy should yield everything possible. The objective method would not make this easier. Its details would have to be made so complicated as to be technically too troublesome. His proposal preferred the subjective method, but he would have no objection to including elements of the objective method if, for example, the government were to receive specific objects.

It was obviously impossible to talk about next week's measures, as Löwenfeld-Russ wanted. Furthermore, the radical socialization which a few months earlier might have been politically feasible, had ceased to be so now.[12] "As matters stand now the proposed Finanzplan is the only possibility. The choice is between it and collapse. In any case I ask for the opportunity to answer all objections. The seriousness we miss in public must be found in ourselves" (ibid., 356).

Renner made the concluding remarks. Unfortunately the discussion had concerned only basic principles rather than concrete details. There ought to have been enough specifics to prepare a law for submission to parliament. Renner stated that the discussion had brought cabinet much closer to an agreement despite understandable differences in detail. As Bauer had indicated, the capital levy should be designed in a different manner depending on what kind of economy one wants. "For this reason clarification demands a prior decision about general economic policy of the Cabinet, e.g. concerning the grain problem, the Zentralen, prices and wages etc. We must first clarify our economic policy which Cabinet will do soon. In the final analysis, Parliament must decide" (ibid., 357).

With this disastrous statement, the meeting closed. It is quite clear that with the exception of Bauer nobody understood what Schumpeter or any Finanzplan was about. It was less the Socialists than the bourgeois parties which doomed Schumpeter, as Water Federn had also pointed out. It is rather amazing to find that a representative of the bourgeois party would have preferred a grain monopoly to a higher beer tax.

And Schumpeter was right: the alternative was total collapse. The krone devalued to one 14,000th of its prewar value. The inflationary episode ended in 1923 with a new currency. Unlike in Germany, there was no partial revaluation of debts repaid with worthless money. Schumpeter was blamed for this, too, because of his alleged saying "Krone ist Krone" which he never said. Schumpeter came out of this discussion much better than is always depicted: a serious man, who worked hard to save his country. His trouble was that there was no country to be saved.

[12] During the term of the second Renner cabinet, of which Schumpeter was a member, the Social Democrats had 69 and the Christian Social party had 63 members in the Constituent National Assembly, with other parties having 27 representatives. By October 17, 1920, the Social Democrats still had 69 seats, but the Christian Social party now had 85 seats, with other parties having 29 representatives (Walré de Bordes, 16, note 1).

The Kola Affair and the Socialization of the Alpine-Montan-Gesellschaft

THE BACKGROUND

The Kola affair was the first of two major scandals which pursued Schumpeter throughout his life and tried to cast a shadow on his honor (although he was certainly completely exonerated in both cases). In the first case, he was in particular accused of having instigated sales of shares of the Alpine-Montan-Gesellschaft (AMG) to Italian interests in order to sabotage Bauer's attempt to socialize the apparently biggest Austrian enterprise which was scheduled to be the first to be socialized. In a cabinet meeting of July 15, Bauer made the serious accusation that Schumpeter had "jeopardized the interests of the State, for the chances of socialization were annihilated thereby,"[1] a comment which was only the beginning of a bitter attack.

By this time Bauer had already resigned as foreign minister, but remained president of the Socialization Commission with cabinet rank. He gave as reason for his resignation his failure to persuade the Italians to leave South Tyrol with Austria, and also his failure to persuade the French to modify some peace conditions. "The French, as already Marx sneeringly remarked, seemed to consider the disintegration (Zerissenheit) of the German people a right of their own nation."[2] In effect, Bauer had lost his fight for the Anschluss, of which he remained a stout advocate, as did the Social Democrats or the *Oesterreichische Volkswirt.*[3] It now looked as if he would also lose his fight for socialization.

---

[1] Top secret annex to Cabinet Protocol No. 88 of July 15, 1919. Typewritten. The cabinet meeting lasted from 9:00 PM to 1:00 AM and was in the absence of Chancellor Renner chaired by Vice Chancellor Fink. Renner's absence may explain why Schumpeter found it necessary to send the long explanatory letter to Renner, appealing to the latter's sense of fairness. The letter is reproduced in Schumpeter (1985), 337–43. This Protocol, as most of the documents quoted in this chapter, has now been reproduced in Schumpeter (1992), 176–93.

[2] In a letter to President Seitz that is quoted in a newspaper clipping, which can be found in the Protocols of the Social Democratic Club. In the Parliament Archive.

[3] There is considerable misunderstanding about the issue of the Anschluss, who was for and who was against it, and why. From 1919 to 1932, the pro-Anschluss groups were the social democrats and all non-Catholic groups (including of course many nominal catholics), but also many communicants, e.g., the already mentioned Wieser, who would have felt comfortable in a country with more Socialists and Protestants. Also Catholics in Germany, being a minority, were considerably more liberal than in Austria, where they comprised 97 percent of the population. It was precisely the Socialists and Catholics in Germany who favored the Anschluss, while the conservatives and what one might call the professional Protestants who were against it.

With the advent of Hitler this changed completely. The Social Democrats wanted to preserve

The cabinet protocol of July 15 listed twelve matters for discussion, several of which required Schumpeter's intervention. A more serious one dealt with "economic demands of German-Austrian military authorities" (Item #5). It was one of the many attempts to break budget discipline which was, of course, not limited to the army.

Schumpeter made no further comments, not even to the report that the Poles had asked on July 15 to amend a compensation agreement of July 5 according to which the Poles were to pay 10 million marks and deliver 4,500 railroad cars of potatoes. The Poles wanted instead to deliver additional petroleum products worth K55 million. Secretary of State Zerdick thought this most advantageous, particularly as the potatoes were probably spoiled by now because of the shortage of railroad cars and the advanced season. Since July 5, substantial amounts of petroleum products had already arrived in Vienna. There was also to be some change in the composition of the goods Austria was to deliver. The Cabinet Council agreed to the amendment.

The top secret annex has one peculiarity. It had four annexes to the annex, all concerning Schumpeter. Annexes A to C are typed with the usual typewriter for the cabinet protocols, but the last annex is not further identified, is typed on a different typewriter, and all have handwritten corrections and comments not in Schumpeter's hand. Bauer objected to all four, though his objections to annexes A and C were quickly cleared up to his satisfaction. All annexes are written in the first person singular. All annexes deal with rumors about Schumpeter's supposedly shady behavior.

The attacks originated in the press impugning Schumpeter's character as well as his supposed attempts to sabotage socialization. The rumors attacking his character very probably started on the right, specifically the big banks. But they were cheerfully taken up by the social democratic press.

The Ministry of Finance wanted to reorganize the Creditinstitut für Transportunternehmen (Bank for Transport Enterprises) into a semi-public bank to finance socialization and the capital levy.[4] The accusation, this time coming from the right, was that Schumpeter simply wanted to subsidize an otherwise bankrupt institution. The attacks from the left concerned on the one hand the kind of person who was to represent the government on the board, and on the other hand the supposedly excessive salaries to be paid to them.[5]

Austria as a free German country. The Austro-Fascists in turn were using the occasion to suppress the Socialists, and also hoped to gain Mussolini's support against Hitler, as did also many nonfascist groups. I remember, for example, that Oskar Morgenstern, at that time visiting Cambridge, Massachusetts, assured me in a conversation a few days before the Anschluss when it seemed obvious that there would be an Anschluss shortly that there would be no Anschluss because Mussolini would never allow it. Whether he really believed this I do not know. Löwith (1989), recounts how widespread this belief was in Vienna during the Schuschnigg regime.

[4] Schumpeter gave an account of this proposal in an annex to the top secret Annex to Protocol 86, Cabinet Meeting of July 8, 1919, "Report concerning the Preparations for the financing of the Capital Levy, Socialization and Industrial Production." Schumpeter (1992), 176ff.

[5] *Streng vertraulicher Anhang zum Kabinettsprotokol no. 88 vom 15. Juli 1919.* According to custom not always followed, however, page numbers refer to double pages, or Bogen. Schumpeter (1985), 175ff.

Schumpeter had laid out his reasons in annexes A and C, and he had an easy time refuting all accusations. Oberfinanzrat Dr. Mosing of the Ministry of Finance pointed out that the old institute had issued K163 million which were overwhelmingly in the hands of German-Austrian savings banks. The cabinet accepted Mosing's explanations.

In Annex A, Schumpeter pointed out that the big banks naturally would not like the creation of a semi-public bank which would compete with them in the placing of new issues. On the other hand, he stressed that the creation of a purely public bank was simply not feasible at the time. He had in any case left eight board positions to be filled by those private banks which in fact would be useful for various financings to be undertaken.

To succeed, all preparations had to be kept confidential, and only the deputy secretary of state for socialization and Bauer were notified beforehand, the latter only orally. The accusation of aiding an otherwise bankrupt bank could be easily disposed of because the balance sheet and profit and loss statements of the bank were particularly simple.

Schumpeter also pointed out that all obligations were *old* government debts "which must be repaid by all States of the former Austria according to a particular key. If the presently unlikely case happens that some or all successor states can not fulfil their obligations this would affect all banks of German-Austria equally."[6]

The assets of the bank were practically all first-class obligations of local railroads, some in German-Austria, some elsewhere. It was likely that the successor states would find these first-class titles desirable, and indeed several Czechoslovak and Yugoslav titles had been sold advantageously (Schumpeter 1992, 182). Also, the Land Bukowina had already remitted interest on an advance for August 1, 1919.

Schumpeter ended this report by insisting that "I have no intention of excluding the existing private banks from the financing of the capital levy and socialization although this has been strongly suggested to me." On the other hand, it is self-evident "that I must insist that all actions of the financing consortium to be created must be supervised by an authority organized according to banking principles. A purely bureaucratic supervision, e.g., by a delegated State Commissar, is completely excluded considering the novelty and complicatedness of the relevant agenda" (ibid., 183).

Obviously feelings would be ruffled no matter what the government did. However, if one were to give in to all these sensibilities, nothing could ever be done and one "would have to watch resignedly (mit verschränkten Armen) the so-called 'play of free economic forces.' But this can most definitely not be our task at the present time when in a number of areas the Government first must popularize new ideas" (ibid.).

Thus, Schumpeter asked for leadership by the government which he did not get for the simple reason that the government itself held together only by not exercising such a leadership—as the reporter of *Le Temps* had pointed out.

[6] Ibid., 181.

Appendix C dealt with two problems: who the government board representatives were to be and how were they going to be paid. Here Schumpeter went against two bureaucratic traditions. Traditionally such positions were held by retired civil servants. Schumpeter wanted active civil servants because the tasks to be fulfilled would be far from routine and thus also deserved higher pay.[7]

I forego telling Schumpeter's detailed arguments for paying civil servants something extra for their "business" activities and turn to the much more serious Kola affair. The attacks against Schumpeter in this matter were vicious and were more or less accepted by Gulick, who evidently was not satisfied with Schumpeter's explanations.[8] The press, particularly the *Arbeiterzeitung*, continued its attacks after the cabinet discussion of July 15, 1919, which Schumpeter answered by letters to the press, which in turn led to further attacks. Cabinet established a special investigating committee to look into the affair, the conclusions of which were presented to cabinet on October 14, 1919, three days before Schumpeter resigned. Schumpeter's inability to stop the attacks in the Socialist press led to a long and detailed letter to Chancellor Renner, appealing to the latter's sense of justice.[9]

The untitled and unnumbered annex of eight pages seems to be an account of Schumpeter's introductory statement to the discussion of Appendix B, "Report about the Government Communiqué Concerning the Alpine Hausse." Schumpeter wanted to say a few words about "the confidential tasks which the firm of Kola had to execute for the Ministry of Finance during May and June" (Schumpeter 1992, 191).

Schumpeter's overriding concern was to get foreign exchange; second, he wanted to strengthen the Zürich exchange rate of the krone. To that end he wanted to absorb some of the plentiful foreign exchange circulating on the Vienna black market, a task for which official authorities were obviously unsuitable since the black market was fed by export transactions which had escaped these very same authorities.

---

[7] One of the government representatives suggested was Dr. Adolf Drucker, the father of Peter Drucker of management consulting fame. Schumpeter also added that "the break with tradition to name only retired civil servants to such positions has also found favor with one of the severest critics of the finance ministry, the editor Walter Federn, who in the last issue of the *Volkswirt* has extensively commented on the issue" (ibid., 188).

[8] See Gulick (1948). Gulick summarizes Bauer's 1923 account of the Kola affair as follows: "According to Bauer, the socialization of the *Alpine* was rendered impossible by his colleague in the Government, the minister of finance, Professor Joseph A. Schumpeter; that is, Schumpeter authorized the banker Richard Kola to make an arrangement with Italian interests whereby they would buy up large quantities of *Alpine* shares." Bauer continued: "Schumpeter supported this action although he knew we had planned the socialization of the *Alpine Montan Gesellschaft*. He supported it without informing the other members of the cabinet of it. . . . This procedure on the part of Schumpeter led to violent conflict within the coalition government in which Schumpeter sought and secured the support of the Vienna Christian Socials." The upshot of the affair, according to Bauer, was that the socialization plan had to be dropped, particularly after Italian intervention. (Gulick 1948, vol. 1, 139).

[9] Renner had not been present at the Cabinet Council meeting. Schumpeter's letter is reproduced in Schumpeter (1985), 337–43.

Kola did indeed succeed in buying substantial amounts of foreign exchange on the black market which he duly handed over to the Ministry of Finance. The Ministry in turn used some of it for the purposes of the Foreign Exchange Authority (Devisenzentrale), but used the rest to ask Kola to "organize an action for the support of our exchange in Zürich" (ibid.).

Schumpeter explained why in these abnormal times it was necessary to "organize" the foreign exchange market: to establish some faith in the krone so as to prevent holders of substantial amounts of bank notes from either hoarding them or selling them in a panic. He considered such an organization at that moment "a most essential and urgent task. . . . The preventive measures allowed us in the moment when the peace conditions became known to prevent a panic" (Schumpeter 1992, 192).

While engaged in Zürich in this task for the Ministry of Finance, Kola used his visit to start the purchase by Swiss firms of a parcel of Alpine-Montan-Gesellschaft shares, the foreign exchange for which he duly handed over to the Ministry of Finance at the official rate of exchange. "This transaction had no connection whatever with the officially executed task" (ibid.).

Was this purchase by foreign interests also advantageous for German-Austria?

> I consider it favorable, subject, of course, to the proviso that not such a big parcel of shares of this most important enterprise goes abroad as to endanger in any way the majority relations and the dominance of domestic ownership. Since this was not the case and only a relatively small portion of such shares which were not in firm hands were involved I consider the whole transaction to be advantageous for our economy. (ibid.)

Of course, foreigners acquired these shares relatively cheaply because of the unfavorable exchange rate.

It would be advantageous for German-Austria, so Schumpeter continued, if more foreigners would invest now when Austria's shares were not in demand at home or abroad, to create a foreign exchange fund for the payment of imports. Once the economy got going again, these shares could be repurchased.

Schumpeter made it quite clear that

> The preconditions, of course, are that to the extent to which the peace treaty permits we remain *masters in our own country* with all our enterprises, that not so many shares of any enterprise go abroad that foreigners could influence the majority relations or that our freedom to dispose, and particularly the freedom to socialize *could in any way be touched. Domestic enterprises must remain domestic enterprises.*
>
> Another precondition is that the foreign exchange resulting from such sales of shares . . . is used only for economically necessary purchases. *The Government* must watch such transactions like a hawk (ein strenges Auge haben) but it should use, not prevent, them.

> That is, foreign exchange must flow in and of our enterprises not so much must flow abroad that the domestic control of an enterprise becomes in any way questionable. (ibid., 193; italics in original)

The Alpine Hausse led to the demand for other shares, and since there had been a lot of uncovered short selling, the Hausse was reinforced. Moreover, low share prices were disadvantageous for the proposed capital levy. The Hausse was a fiscal advantage.

There are other points made, the retelling of which I forego.

Otto Bauer was not satisfied. Why did Schumpeter not use a more reputable firm than Kola for his purposes? The fact was that the Communiqué of the Ministry of Finance seemed to imply a total identification of the Ministry with the "bulls" (Hausse Partei) which led to considerable distrust. But the decisive point was that "the interest of the State was damaged, for it had annihilated all chances for a socialization of the Alpine." The Hausse had raised the cost to the State of buying the shares and Italy in particular would try to get control of more Austrian industries.

Bauer admitted that some sales of shares were inevitable to pay for raw materials and foodstuffs, but he wanted to sell first shares of enterprises located in the successor states. The suggestion was, of course, totally unrealistic. The real assets were in the successor states and any attempt of Vienna to sell shares was nullified by confiscation of the real assets. Bauer wanted assurances against a takeover of Austrian businesses by foreigners.

Schumpeter replied vigorously. First, the Alpine shares were sold without the knowledge of the Ministry of Finance. It is this point which the continuing defamation of Schumpeter's character more or less explicitly chose to disbelieve. Second, only K40–50 million were deposited with the Giro und Kassenverein, not K100 million as reported in the press, and that solely to pay for foreign exchange. The choice of Kola was determined by the latter's Styrian connections: the relevance of this point will become clear presently.

Third, the government communiqué implied not favoritism toward the "bulls" but only a statement that the foreign purchases of the Alpine shares were not the only reason for the Hausse. Fourth, higher Alpine prices would also raise other share prices, and socialization should not be considered isolated from the capital levy. Seen together, the bull market was advantageous for the State. Fifth, preventing takeovers by foreign interests required a law, but the Ministry of Trade had objections against such a law which in any case could be frustrated by the ease with which Austro-Hungarian citizens could become citizens of a successor state.

Eldersch (a Social Democrat) thought that at the very least the Ministry of Finance should have informed the Socialization Commission of its intentions, and both he and Bauer thought that a law against capital flight should be enacted. With these final comments, the Cabinet Council agreed to take note of Schumpeter's statement.

THE INVESTIGATION

The newspaper attacks continued and became more scurrilous. On August 20, Bauer raised questions in cabinet: "It is quite impossible for Government to keep quiet about these matters . . . because they touch the personal honor of its members. . . . I am considering whether matters are not so grave that we should even (geradezu) constitute an enquête. . . . If this would be ineffective there would have to be judicial steps."[10]

Schumpeter responded to Bauer's comments at length.

> I confess that I am outraged about the attitude of the Press and the financial community. The only difficulty . . . is not the Alpine matter. . . . [T]he only difficult problems are] the foreign exchange policy aspects.
>
> At a time when the Ministry of Food comes to me daily with requests for foreign exchange to buy food, I have used a few private firms in Zürich for foreign exchange purchases. Several Ministers have made their own foreign exchange policy. I have used the private firms for kronen sales abroad because individual Cabinet members requested it. However, I have now abandoned this practice. I have now used the local house of Kola. . . . All of this is entirely above board, but it is totally untenable if the Entente found out that we have, for example, an account with the firm Blanquard [in Zürich]. This is precisely what makes it so difficult to talk about it in an enquête.
>
> As for the intrigues of the Big Bankers, they are definitely made *mala fides*. All Big Bank directors and all economic editors speculated à la baisse. But the stock market rose, the short sales had to be covered, and this drove quotations still higher. . . .
>
> My policy was the only correct one.
>
> Hoover does not want to supply more [food]. I had to prepare for the future, and since the amount which I got is a mere drop, I shall continue this policy. . . .
>
> I do not believe it possible to discuss foreign exchange policy in an enquête. [These are] matters which could be discussed only in Cabinet. (Schumpeter 1992, 200–1)

Eldersch wanted to know whether Kola had in fact delivered the foreign exchange. (Yes, he had.) And what about the slush fund? Schumpeter stated: "I know nothing about negotiations to create a *Dispositionsfond*, I ask Secretary of State Eldersch to name the source (Gewährsmann)," to which Eldersch only replied: "We shall see." (It turned out later that Bauer did know the name but never revealed it.)

Bauer agreed that a public enquête was impossible and suggested an informal meeting of a few respected persons. Vice Chancellor Fink took up this suggestion and proposed a Cabinet Commission. This was agreed upon on August 20. The commission, also referred to as an enquête, held its first

---

[10] Document in the Finanzarchiv (now in the Archiv der Republik) File FA 63.239—14 A/1919. Schumpeter (1992), 200.

session on August 28 under the chairmanship of the Minister of Justice Bratusch.

Before Kola, the first witness, was questioned, Schumpeter made a statement to the enquête members. For weeks, ever-new insinuations were circulating which attacked his personal honor, even though he was confronted with the biggest task any finance minister ever had. The Alpine business of Kola had no connection with the foreign exchange policy task. The verbatim transcript then continues:

> When I took over the Ministry, the Exchange Control Office (Devisenzentrale) worked poorly. Great amounts of foreign exchange were floating around and traded on the black market and thus escaped Governmental purposes. It was necessary to collect them. It was impossible to command them because they were precisely the amounts which escaped central disposition. Under these circumstances there was only one means: absorbing them through purchase.
>
> This collecting is not the same as when someone else does it, e.g., a Land authority or a private person. For I got the foreign exchange in order to make it available for central disposition (Bewirtschaftung). The Federal Administration engages in such business on its own account, it pursues the same aim as the Exchange Control Office, namely to ensure the available foreign exchange for the State. The fiscal authority supplements the effectiveness of the Devisenzentrale. I could not start the action through the Devisenzentrale, because by its very structure it is unable to undertake this task, neither could I use any of the Big Banks because there everything leaks out. It had to be done in secret because if you announce that you buy foreign exchange, the exchange rate jumps upward. The choice of the firm of Kola was determined by the fact that I needed a versed stock exchange technician and Kola is. . . . Kola, who was very highly recommended to me, had also to investigate the foreign exchange market in Zürich. He has come up to expectations and has solved his task brilliantly. Of course, the foreign exchange had to be bought above the official daily rate.
>
> This action was necessary because we had to create . . . a foreign exchange reserve . . . [which] is in any case necessary for proper economizing (budgeting?). It is even possible that other countries will require immediate interest payment for any loan. I also wanted to prepare an intervention to prop up our exchange (eine Valutastützungsaktion). . . .
>
> I have contributed nothing to the sale of the Alpine. (ibid., 203–4)

Schumpeter then explained when Kola had first told him of the purchase of Alpine shares, the foreign exchange proceeds for which were duly deposited. Schumpeter then continued:

> When the bull market continued I took notice of it but saw no reason to do anything. I have, rather, looked favorably on it. One day, the editor-in-chief of the Arbeiterzeitung told me over the phone that the matter had to be cleared up.
>
> I have published a communiqué to the effect that the increase in the Alpine quotations and generally the bull market . . . was not merely (ohne weiteres) the

result of foreign purchases, but the result of short selling which had to be covered (Kontermine). This was blown up as favoritism. The bull market is for us precisely the means to get as much bread as possible for any shares. (ibid., 204)

Here Vice Governor Wimmer interjected: "The sale of shares to foreigners is nothing bad" (ibid.).

The Arbeiterzeitung of August 20 had in the last paragraph of its article talked about "stock market orgies." On this Schumpeter commented:

There is now an investigation of the Deutsche Bodenbank because of black market activities in foreign exchange.[11]

The Ministry has not given Kola any permission to sell Shares abroad. He needed no permission. The sale is not forbidden or punishable. . . .

The assertion that the Big Banks were to make a slush fund available to the Ministry of Finance is entirely and totally (ganz und gar) untrue. (ibid., 205)

Here Eldersch interrupted again: "A source which shall remain unnamed said that Secretary of State Schumpeter had called on a bank lawyer (Bankjurist) and requested him to intervene with the Big Banks to make available a slush fund because of the uncertain attitude of President Seitz and Secretary of State Bauer."[12] Eldersch kept hammering away at the various accusations (i) that the ministry had frequently permitted the free disposition of assets which would better have been kept in government hands;[13] and (ii) that the ministry had in a few instances instructed the tax authorities not to question certain tax returns. Schumpeter rejected these defamatory accusations "with contempt." The case of Wittgenstein will be mentioned in greater detail further on. Here needs to be stated only one point which will not come up again: "At the time, Art. 49 of the peace conditions was not yet eliminated[14] and there was a danger that the State had to make good (presumably for any expropriation of Wittgenstein by the Entente). Wittgenstein could perhaps save [his assets in New York]. (The German sentence is very clumsy.)

The second session of the enquête was on September 1. The witness was Kola. There is one matter to be mentioned immediately because it is a direct corroboration of Gerlich's account of the involvement of the Styrian land government (see below).

Vice Governor Wimmer: Did you also buy for the Government?

Kola: The Deutsche Bodenbank also turned to me. Any kind of foreign exchange was to be bought for 10 million kronen at the best possible prices. I first made some objections. In order to prevent a stormy (stürmisch) demand during my

[11] These activities are mentioned by Gerlich. See below.

[12] Both Seitz and Bauer were Social Democrats.

[13] One such matter turned out to be that the Ministry had permitted a lady who had duly handed over her jewelry to the authorities to borrow it for one day to wear at a party!

[14] Article 49 of the Draft Treaty had provided for the confiscation of all Austrian assets in the successor states.

purchases for Government, I finally accepted the order of the Bodenbank, particularly as I seemed to be covered by an order of Representative Wutte. (ibid., 211–12)

Kola's testimony starts with April 1919:

Kola: [T]he stock exchange was in a deep depression. . . . As the only banker with connections abroad I had thought that it might perhaps be possible to interest foreigners in our stocks. . . . I gave a list of papers which in my opinion were worth buying to a visiting Dutch friend. . . . After a few weeks he appeared again and told me that he could not sell the Alpine in Holland but elsewhere. I should buy 50,000 shares on his order (in seinem Auftrag). . . . At that time I did not know the identity of the buyer . . . [until I got] a purchase order from Rome and the purchase price was deposited.

   . . . When the quotation was 620 there were rumors that the Alpine was bought for Switzerland . . . because at the time I was in Switzerland. When I returned to Vienna I had already bought 45,000 shares.

SS Dr. Schumpeter: Did you need any credit?

Kola: No. (continuing) . . . By the end of June I had bought 70,000 Alpine shares. At the beginning of July the matter was finished as far as I was concerned. (ibid., 206–7)

The next topic was the short selling of the Alpine shares (Kontermine).

Kola: When my Dutch friend asked me about the Alpine I went to Director Krasny of the Escompte-Gesellschaft to ask him whether he wished to sell Alpine. He went into great detail how bad the shares were, and that the Escompte-Gesellschaft could not sell such bad paper abroad. This opinion might have spread and led to short sales (Kontermine).

   I bought Alpine up to 1,125. Then there was a pause and the shares fell to 900. Then the Italians reappeared and we agreed on 40,000 shares. (ibid., 207–8)

So much for Kola's testimony on the Alpine. According to his testimony, he bought 110,000 shares.[15]

At Schumpeter's request, the lire received from the last transaction were delivered to the Director of the Devisenzentrale Sztankovits who had been very pleased. In answer to a question by Schumpeter, Kola stated that the Devisenzentrale still owed him some money. Sztankovits then told Kola he needed French francs for which he was ready to pay 6K. "I got the Francs at K5.98." Kola had to pay immediately. Sztankovits paid only after "the Francs had been deposited in his name with the firm of Blanquard in Zürich" (ibid., 209).

Again in response to a question by Schumpeter, Kola stated that he charged

---

[15] See W. F. Stolper (1985) for März and the *Oesterreichische Volkswirt*'s estimates of the number of shares bought.

a fee of only 1 percent compared to 5 percent on the free market, and sometimes even 10 percent. Now something quite extraordinary happened which was not mentioned in the report to cabinet. Kola continued:

> This . . . was the origin of the attack. When the well-known notice was published in the *Neues Wiener Tagblatt*—as it turned out at the inspiration of a bank director who appeared in the middle of the night at the editorial office—I went to Director Sztankovits to demand a dementi. He promised an official dementi. When such a dementi was not published I went again to Director Sztankovits who told me that the editor of the *Neues Wiener Tagblatt* had urgently begged him, not to publish a correction. (ibid., 209–10)

Schumpeter then wondered why a bank director should have wished to visit the editorial office in the middle of the night: "[y]ou must have supposed that he belongs to a group which did not like the Ministry of Finance. Did you know who it was?" Kola replied, "A director of the Escompte-Gesellschaft. I was not told the name."

Kola then testified that he knew nothing about any relation of the Escompte-Gesellschaft to any political party and the latter probably resented that it lost its shirt (depossediert) "with the Alpine and wanted to discredit the thing." Sztankovits also wanted Kola to get him more foreign exchange. "He might have mentioned this at the next meeting of the Advisory Board of the Devisenzentrale which probably annoyed the Big Banks" (ibid., 210).

Next Kola went into his relations with the Ministry of Finance. He mentioned that the Ministry had asked him in May to get foreign exchange in Zürich to be used to stabilize the krone.

Kola's testimony was corroborated in every detail by all the other witnesses. He certainly behaved above reproach in the Alpine matter and was content with a smaller profit than the big banks would have been or the black market normally demanded. The name of Wutte appeared again as well as a transaction with the Deutsche Bodenbank. There was perhaps one difference of opinion: Director Kux of the Escompte-Gesellschaft stated flatly that the short selling of Alpine shares was perhaps 20,000–25,000 shares, but the stock exchange commissioner Mosing insisted that it was substantial. Sztankovits gave Kola a good reputation, while Kux expressed disdain that the government had dealing with a man of his reputation, an opinion which incidentally the *Oesterreichische Volkswirt* shared.

Sztankovits also stated that Kola sold his foreign exchange at the foreign quotation and that this could hardly be called a "black market rate." The Styrian land government came up again. Kola had after some hesitation told Sztankovits that he had bought foreign exchange "for a certain personage who had assured him that everything was perfectly legal" (ibid., 211). The personage was Representative Wutte. Kola added that never again would he undertake such business. (But he did.)

Schumpeter then asked: "Has the fact that Kola bought floating material for the Ministry of Finance caused anger among the bank representatives?" to which Sztankovits replied: "By his own confession of a bank representative this was due to professional jealousy [Brotneid]" (ibid., 213).

Schumpeter kept asking and Sztankovits again told the enquête that he had asked the editor to retract the story but the editor had asked him not to deny it. There never was an explanation just why not. Stankovits thought perhaps the Ministry of Finance would deny it.

This story never found its way into the official report to cabinet. There were two other items which did not find their way into the final exoneration of Schumpeter, this time for legitimate reasons. In both cases Schumpeter made a statement to the enquête after having asked the witnesses to leave the room.

One concerned the Wittgenstein matter.[16] Schumpeter wanted to reduce the Austrian assets that might be subject to reparations payments. On the other hand, Wittgenstein tried to get his American assets decontrolled. If Wittgenstein were successful, first, in separating his own account from that of his Austrian bank, and then, through his many American connections, get the American authorities to free it, the Austrian State would also benefit. Evidently this could not be accomplished as a general rule, and equally obviously the matter had to be kept secret because if it became known, it would be interpreted by the Entente as mala fides (the Latin phrase is used).

The second matter had a similar motivation. Schumpeter considered setting up front firms in the "Neuausland," the newly foreign countries, which would buy up Austrian securities, thereby nominally making them Polish or Czech and thus saving them for Austria.

Nothing happened in the Wittgenstein matter because the Escompte-Gesellschaft refused to execute Wittgenstein's order. I do not know what happened to the plan to establish front businesses.

THE REPORT TO CABINET

The findings of this investigation were presented to cabinet on October 14, 1919, three days before Schumpeter's resignation from cabinet. The report is given in a top secret appendix to the Cabinet Protocol No. 114 of October 14, 1919.[17] It is difficult to understand, and there is no hint in the protocol itself, why this report which totally exonerated Schumpeter should have been kept top secret. The enquête, as it referred to itself, had no subpoena power, nor did the witnesses testify under oath.

After listing the members of the investigating committee—Vice Chancellor Fink, Ministers Eldersch, Schumpeter, Bratusch, and the Vice Governor of the Austro-Hungarian Bank Wimmer—the persons interviewed, and the documents and press clippings read, Bratusch listed the accusations against Schumpeter as follows:

---

[16] I believe the father of the philosopher and the left-handed pianist.
[17] This Cabinet Protocol with its annex has been published in Schumpeter (1992), 195ff.

1. that the Ministry of Finance had originated or at least approved the sale of Alpine shares, stressing the fact that the Alpine was one of those industrial enterprises which were among the first to be socialized;

2. that the Ministry of Finance had given the Firm of Kola the necessary means for this purchase;

3. that the foreign exchange proceeds had not been handed over to the Ministry of Finance;

4. that it was handed over not at the official but the black market rate;

5. that the Ministry of Finance had chosen the speculative and not very rigorous firm of Kola which already had had difficulties, instead of a more respectable firm.

Further

6. the Ministry of Finance was accused to have approached the banks to create a slush fund (Dispositionsfond) for the Government. (Schumpeter 1992, 197–98).

The results of the investigation were unequivocal. To start with, the investigation found "that the affair did not touch the personal honor of SS Dr. Schumpeter." Moreover, the investigation could not even find any evidence that the shares were actually handed over to a foreign power! Specifically "ad 1. that the Ministry of Finance did not know of the purchase of the Alpine shares beforehand and even less originated it. Secretary of State Schumpeter explicitly told Kola that he does not wish this transaction" (ibid., 198).

On this point, Eldersch had stated at the very end of the last session that in his opinion the secretary of state for finances had seriously damaged the socialization of the Alpine-Montan-Gesellschaft, "practically the only enterprise that could be socialized," and that he should have taken every measure to prevent further purchases of Alpine shares as soon as he got knowledge of the big purchases by Kola.

Schumpeter immediately replied that he was not persuaded that he had in fact damaged the socialization since there were evidently other problems with socialization when the share prices were at their lowest, problems which in the meantime certainly had not become smaller. Besides, the bull market had also had other reasons and the purchase price of the Alpine for purposes of socialization was not necessarily determined by the price of the shares. This exchange in the enquête made at the very end of its last session was not transmitted to cabinet.

Ad 2. When Kola bought the Alpine shares he had only K118,229,331 on hand.

Ad 3. and 4. Kola did indeed hand over the foreign exchange at the official rate of exchange.

Ad 5. Schumpeter stressed that the minister of finance needed a skilful stock exchange technician, which Kola was. Kola was asked to investigate the foreign exchange market in Zürich, a task he had solved brilliantly. As for the reputation of his firm, the Director of the Foreign Exchange Authority Sztankovits called him one of the smartest (gerissenste) bankers whom other bank directors used to execute their own transactions. Oberfinanzrat Mosing, the stock exchange commissioner, explained that Kola was the only private banker active on the foreign exchange market. Both he and Sztankovits thought that the hostility of the big banks was simply due to envy—Brotneid. Moreover, all banks had orders to sell Alpine shares and thus were suddenly caught by the bull market as it did, of course, all short sellers. Moreover, the firm of Kola was a thorn in the flesh of the stock exchange which did not like that a private banker played the leading role on the exchange (den Ton angebe).

Schumpeter added the quite correct point that Kola needed no permission for any transactions and hence Schumpeter had no reason to start proceedings against him. This point was and is continuously overlooked: It accused Schumpeter of not doing what he had no power to do. There was confusion about the law in the mind of Director Kux of the Escompte-Gesellschaft. The law did indeed forbid the export of Austrian shares, but explicitly only to the successor states, the "Neuausland."

The sixth point is perhaps the most absurd. The rumor about a slush fund started with a Bankdirektor Kux who had overheard a remark by the "Kommittent der Eskomptgesellschaft Ludwig Wittgenstein" on the occasion of the negotiations to free his dollar assets which the Ministry of Finance supported that the "Volkswehr gets 2 million." According to Kux this remark could be interpreted as the creation of a slush fund. However, the word "Dispositionsfond" was not actually used. During the hearings, Eldersch casually mentioned that he knew who had told Bauer about the Dispositionsfonds, and said that he would try to get permission from his source to reveal his name! Schumpeter was thus denied the opportunity to face his accuser, and this happened again when his possible appointment to the University of Berlin was considered. The name was never revealed.

All this makes the characterization of the *Neue Freie Presse* that Schumpeter was politically assassinated quite an apt description.

Schumpeter was thus exonerated in every respect, his honor as well as his reasoning vindicated. It is not clear why this report had to be kept top secret. As a result, the accusations against Schumpeter never ceased, even to this day, despite all evidence that they were totally false.

WHY THE ALPINE WAS NOT SOCIALIZED IMMEDIATELY

The question naturally arises why the Alpine (AMG), if it was that important, was not immediately socialized. By May, its stock had fallen to an all-time low, itself in need of explanation in an inflationary situation. Actually the Alpine was completely run down, the government having preferred to maintain other plants during the war. "Prominent industrialists believed at that time that the socialization of the works with adequate compensation would, under the existing miserable circumstances, be welcomed by the shareholders" (Gerlich 1980, 201, and note 817; my translation).

A socialization plan for the AMG had actually been worked out by Lederer, now the research director of the Socialization Commission, with the specific duty to work out such socialization plans. Lederer's plan was sent to Rintelen, the governor (Landeshauptmann) of Styria, and Professor Steinwender, Schumpeter's predecessor as minister of finance. Both of them objected that socialization was a matter for the Länder, as did the Styrian social democrats. Naturally Bauer objected, as had Schumpeter, when similar claims were put forward in the context of the capital levy. Obviously, when the *Oesterreichische Volkswirt* had talked about "probably" it was not speculating.[18]

In fact, the Styrian government had not even deigned to answer repeated letters from the Socialization Commission on July 16 and again on August 25 asking it to state its position (ibid.). Besides, it was totally irrelevant what Schumpeter wanted or did not want:

> A few weeks before the Alpine transaction, Kola had transacted foreign exchange business, evading the foreign exchange regulations, for the Deutsche Bodenbank which the Styrian Government used to buy foreign exchange. In particular, Rintelen and Wutte were in close contact with the Bank so that one cannot dismiss the suspicions that the sale of the Alpine shares was a deliberate manoeuvre to block the socialization plans in which Rintelen and Wutte used Kola. (ibid., 204; my translation)[19]

I interpret the Styrian action as thumbing its nose at the Vienna authorities. Schumpeter surely was right that it was not the sale of the shares which prevented socialization but the lack of power of the central government. And surely the *Oesterreichische Volkswirt* was also right when it surmised that the causal nexus ran the other way around, that the Italians would not have bought the shares if they had believed that socialization was imminent; or perhaps, would not have cared one way or another. As victors they could count on adequate compensation or impose their will.

Actually, on August 8, 1919, Bauer admitted that sales of domestic industries to foreigners were unavoidable but did not like the manner in which it was done:

> It would be inevitable that our industries would fall into foreign hands but it is just as true that it would be most dangerous if this transfer were to proceed in an unregulated fashion in the style of the stock exchange. We cannot wait with such a regulation: would it not be better to declare openly that of all enterprises which we compulsorily change into corporations we offer foreigners a fifth instead of waiting until, as was the case with the Alpine and the forests, they have fallen into foreign hands.[20]

[18] See the previous discussion about separatist tendencies.
[19] See the preceding section for Kola's account.
[20] Cabinet Protocol No. 96, August 8, 1919. So far unpublished.

It is difficult to see how such a procedure could have attracted any foreign capital except under the most onerous conditions. But then Bauer probably cared only about the implied socialization.

And in 1920, Bauer, in a talk to the Social Democratic shop stewards (Vertrauensmänner), admitted that in the last analysis the sale of the Alpine shares had been unavoidable.

> Our balance of payments is passive. We could not get the foreign exchange we needed to import bread and coal. There was only one method . . . the method of the liquidation sale (Ausverkauf). . . . Without that none of us would be alive. . . . If the shares of the AMG went into foreign hands this was bad, but we have lived off it. If you knew that you couldn't socialize. For if we had socialized a single plant, no foreign capitalist would have bought another share. (ibid., my translation)[21]

As matters developed in 1919 it was Bauer, not Schumpeter, who changed his position and went against government policy. And he did so in a somewhat underhanded manner.

A letter from the Socialization Commission to the Ministry of Finance seems to be the first suggestion of using the capital levy for purposes of socialization: a special financing institution was to be created. Lederer is mentioned as having seen this letter.[22] The proposed legislation went through five typewritten versions before being sent to the printer.[23] An accompanying memo states "after a few changes requested by the Secretary of State [Bauer]." There was also a meeting of the Parliamentary Socialization Committee to be called for July 3.

However, a letter from the Ministry of Finance of July 9 stated that no such meeting had taken place. "On the other hand Secretary of State Dr. Bauer remarked yesterday evening that the last version of the proposed legislation contained a few changes compared with the relevant proposals of the Ministry of Finance. I know of no such proposals by the Ministry of Finance or of the changes decided upon."[24] The letter then continued:

> We wouldn't dream (es fällt uns gar nicht ein) to interfere in any manner whatsoever with the sphere of competence of the Socialization Commission. . . . However, as soon as the proposed law . . . will have been enacted it is certain that not the Socialization Commission but the Ministry of Finance will be made responsible if the actual socialization procedures would be delayed for lack of the provision of financing. And it is only self-evident that financial matters and the particular matter of a financing institute would have to be worked out and solved

---

[21] This did not keep Bauer from repeating his accusations against Schumpeter as late as 1923, as quoted in E. März, "Joseph A. Schumpeter as Minister of Finance of the First Republic of Austria, March 1919–October 1919," in H. Frisch (1982), 174. Actually, the Alpine later offered to sell some shares to the government, an offer which Reisch, Schumpeter's successor, reasonably declined.

[22] Socialization Commission, File 8004 No. 371. My translation.

[23] Ibid., No. 390, on July 2.

[24] File 8004, No. 390. Signed Hosing.

by the Ministry of Finance. . . . Dr. Bauer seems particularly concerned that pharmaceutical and leather firms be socialized and financed. I would be extraordinarily gratified if you . . . could send me the necessary details for a serious financing plan. (ibid.)

More seriously, on June 26, the Ministry had written that the day before it had found out that the Socialization Commission had prepared statutes for a credit institution to issue debentures of socialized enterprises and was contemplating the organization of yet another such institution.

The Ministry has thus far not had any knowledge of these facts even though the proposed law concerning socialized enterprises which the Commission itself has drafted and which was approved by Cabinet Council gives all authority about financing including the working out of and changes in the statutes exclusively to the Ministry of Finance. The Ministry of Finance must point out that any suggestion not initiated by it concerning these questions will be invalid and only suitable to endanger or at least seriously delay in a regrettable manner the necessary uniform treatment of these matters.[25]

In an answer of June 27, the Socialization Commission soft-pedaled the whole matter by stressing that it was just working out proposals to be discussed later (ibid.).

But even before, on May 9, long before the Kola business, Bauer had written a brief and seemingly innocuous letter to the Ministry of Finance, suggesting that, since socialization would require substantial budgetary funds, the Ministry of Finance should consider a substantial increase in the inheritance tax in the form of an obligatory government share (Pflichtanteil) similar to the obligatory shares of children and widow(er)s. Bauer must have been uneasy about it because he did not show the letter to Lederer, who was after all responsible for the actual working out of proposals. When he got wind of this letter, Lederer was obviously upset and considered the proposal unfortunate. In a handwritten note to Bauer dated May 21, which I reproduce in full, Lederer wrote:

I consider the preceding proposal (Eingabe) of which I had no knowledge, for several reasons unfortunate (unzweckmässig): in particular the status of the socialized enterprises would thereby become too favorable and as a result an ownership free of any obligations would permit a wasteful management. Moreover, it would become impossible to compare the results with those of private industry.

The emphasis that socialization would require very significant funds from the Treasury (Staatsschatz) does not agree with the views which the State Commission for Socialization has thus far taken. The socialized enterprises should really *at the very least* be able to maintain themselves economically, in particular to pay interest and to amortize their debentures.

[25] Ibid., No. 394, June 26, 1919.

The idea to link the inheritance tax organically with socialization may perhaps be realized in the following manner:

Payment of the inheritance tax may be made in the form of debentures of the socialized enterprises or such payments may be given preferential treatment. In this manner the Government acquires possession of the debentures. They continue, however, to remain a debt of the enterprises. This would create a market for the debentures and raise their price.

An increase in the inheritance tax to the extent here envisaged (obligatory share of the State to the extent of that of a child) I consider at present impracticable (undurchführbar) at the same time as the capital levy.[26]

Schumpeter's letter is dated July 17, and is ten typewritten pages long. Schumpeter had, of course, not seen Lederer's memorandum. The letter is addressed to Bauer personally. I reproduce the first three and a half pages in toto:[27]

From the notes of the State Commission for Socialization of May 9, 1919. XI, 198 and 199, the Ministry of Finance has seen that in the execution of the law of March 14, 1919 St.G.Bl. No 181 considerable demands on the Treasury would arise in the opinion of the State Commission for Socialization.

This communication was for the Ministry of Finance all the less expected as during the preparatory discussion about the socialization law it had energetically rejected any demands on the Treasury arising out of this action. Moreover, the justification for the proposed legislation on socialized enterprises (No 166 of the supplement to the stenographic protocol of the Constituent National Assembly) stresses explicitly that all legal persons serving socialization action must not request Government subsidies.

Already now, some regulations (Bestimmungen) concerning already passed socialization laws contradict the principle which the Commission for Socialization itself has enunciated, deviations which despite the objections of the representatives of the Ministry of Finance during the discussions nevertheless were incorporated into the laws, which, however, are not of sufficient importance for the Ministry of Finance to oppose decisively.

Concerning the needs for Governmental means announced in the mentioned note, the Ministry of Finance requests information about the justification for and extent of the demands on the Treasury. It must state already now that in view of the extremely sad state of Government finances, not only the existing but also the resources yet to be opened up must be dedicated to the presently most important task of the fiscal administration—gradual restoration of an orderly budget.

The earmarking of particular sources for specific purposes contradicts all principles of rational budget and fiscal policy and hence could not be agreed to.

---

[26] File 8006, No. 565; my translation; italics in original. I believe it important to reproduce the whole letter to remove any doubt about my interpretation of the respective roles of Bauer and Schumpeter.

[27] The whole letter is reproduced in Schumpeter (1985), 337–43, quotation on 330–32. I have occasionally broken up excessively long sentences.

The suggestion of the State Commission for Socialization to use the proposed new revenues exclusively to amortize the debentures which arise from socialization with the guarantee of the State must, however, raise the most lively amazement.

A law which would provide public payments for this purpose would have the effect of completely discrediting the whole socialization action a priori and in one fell swoop. Our industry which is at present virtually at a standstill and sees in socialization already an absolute obstacle to the reconstruction, which for economic and fiscal as well as for political reasons is essential. A law of this kind would give it a decisive argument against socialization. Who should have any confidence in the management (Gebahren) and prosperity of the socialized institutions if the legislature itself thought it necessary to provide for the payment of interest and amortization by additional sources of revenue? Who could welcome socialization as economic progress if the Government itself formally provided the basis for the belief, propagated by the enemies of socialization, that the socialized enterprises would be unable to maintain themselves as independent bodies? How could the Ministry of Finance which has the enormous task to create order in the budget through the use of all possible revenues and the elimination of all not absolutely necessary expenditures, have the joint responsibility of creating socialized enterprises, if it had to finance not only their creation but also current expenses of running the enterprises whose extent could in the final analysis not be estimated? By taking over such obligations, the fiscal administration would undermine the core of the State and with it destroy the only foundation on which the reconstruction of the fiscal and general economy (Staats- und Volkswirtschaft) could possibly proceed. The Ministry of Finance could, therefore, under no circumstances agree to such a law if it wants to keep the trust of domestic and foreign sources in its will to restore orderly finances. The Ministry, however, is also of the firm opinion that such a law could not be defended in the interests of socialization itself. If the Commission should really mean that the socialized enterprises would be unable not only to maintain themselves (sich aktiv zu gebahren) but in addition would be unable to transfer their surpluses from current operations to the budget, the Ministry of Finance, which has so far assumed the opposite to be the case and which so far has accompanied the socialization with the greatest benevolence despite individual second thoughts (Bedenken), would have to revise its position on the question of socialization most thoroughly and as the responsible guardian of Government finances and the credit of the State would have to veto all measures energetically (entschieden) which would could make its task more difficult or prevent it.

Most of the rest of the letter dealt with the inheritance tax, which was already very high and which in effect already had the Pflichtteil in the form of a high transfer tax.[28]

---

[28] In his *Weg zum Sozialismus*, Bauer had ingeniously suggested using the inheritance tax to compensate socialized capitalists at the expense of the those not yet socialized, the argument being that it was unfair to punish just a few capitalists while letting the others go scot free, and also to make the capitalists pay for their own expropriation. The proposal was, however, entirely

Bauer does not seem to have answered this letter or its arguments. There is, however, a six half-line comment attached to the letter, signed Krasny and initialed B with instructions to file the letter for the time being (Zunächst ad acta) and leaving the date of the answer open as Vienna . . . Oct 1919. The comment reads in full: "The question of change of inheritance laws and the increase in inheritance taxes is now being treated within the framework of the whole financial and economic plan, and it is there that the existing opposing views will be resolved." The Ministry of Justice had been sent an identical letter by the Socialization Commission on May 9. In an answer dated August 26, it too raised strong objections to Bauer's proposals.

Bauer did not seem to give up. On August 23, he requested the ministry of finance to find out how many government papers the banks held (File 8006, No. 580, initialed B). On August 29, the ministry of finance responded to a different letter from the Socialization Commission of August 22, which had invited it to a meeting on September 2, to discuss questions raised by the Socialization Commission relating to the increased capitalization of public and private corporations and the cost arising thereof to the budget. Item 3 of the proposed agenda related to "competence to request authorization from the Cabinet or the National Assembly concerning the cost to the State arising from participation in such corporations." The answer was unequivocal: "[T]he Chief of the Budget Section of the Ministry of Finance (Budgetreferent) declared that no credit existed for participations by the State in private corporations. It will, therefore, be necessary that each case will be discussed with the Ministry of Finance or, if the sums involved are large to request them from the National Assembly as recently decided by Cabinet Council" (File 8006, No. 608). Bauer initialed this account of the meeting to be filed.

This pattern of behavior of the Socialization Commission was not just a feud between Schumpeter and Bauer. Thus, on November 17, Schumpeter's successor Reisch sent a long memorandum to the chancellor, a copy of which Renner forwarded to Bauer on November 26. The memorandum refers to a Cabinet Council meeting in which a proposed law concerning power development was discussed. Reisch complained that this important item had not been on the proposed agenda so that he had to speak (against it) completely unprepared.

The Ministry of Finance objected to just about everything in the proposed law. Power development would require a maximum of foreign capital, which would need guarantees against socialization for many years. The law proposed an administrative guardianship and police control(!), a compulsory monopoly, and expropriation at prewar cost. The Ministry of Finance also questioned the assumption that the Länder could be forced or for that matter had the executive capacity to do anything (File 8006, Item 803).

---

out of context of any budgetary or economic problems of the time. Bauer thought of course that socialized enterprises would be profitable, in which case they would contribute to the budget.

It has been necessary to go into the details of the day-to-day working of the Ministry of Finance and the Socialization Commission to show that all the accusations against Schumpeter were not true. Bauer's accusations in 1923 blaming Schumpeter for the failure to socialize are incorrect at best and in any case irrelevant. Schumpeter, with considerable more charity than Bauer (or Gulick), absolved Bauer of any deliberate falsification. And Wieser turned out to be more correct than he could have thought, when he explained Schumpeter's role in the Second Renner cabinet as that of a whipping boy.

It is also strange that the question has never been raised whether Schumpeter's opposition to socialization at any price, his insistence that there was no sense in ruining industries, was not the right thing to do in any case and that loyalty to Bauer's fatally flawed ideas would have been irrational—as if reality was not impossible enough.

Schumpeter never talked about this period in his life. It is quite clear that the reason was not that he was somehow embarrassed by his "failures." But he was put into a position where the other participants in the history of this period had written their memoirs while he had no access to document what really happened. When he had tried to set the record straight in his letter to Gulick, Gulick had obviously not believed him. Besides, Schumpeter was a proud man.

There are questions for which any answer, any defense, only makes matters worse. "Have you stopped beating your wife" is a prototype for questions that cannot be answered truthfully in one sentence or two. The detailed account should lay matters to rest. Requiescat in Pace.

The Final Days

SCHUMPETER MUST HAVE been aware that his days in cabinet were numbered. With the partial exception of Bauer no one understood, much less accepted, anything he proposed. It was a personal as well as a political defeat, for the Finanzplan was his personal work in a literal sense. On October 8, 1919, the NFP reported under the heading "How the Finanzplan came about (entstand)" that "the Finanzplan is a personal work of Doctor Schumpeter who in writing the draft did not consult the section chiefs and ministerial councillors (Ministerialräte). The chiefs of the relevant sections and departments were not in a position to comment or present materials" (Schumpeter 1992, 268).

In retrospect, Schumpeter evidently did not entirely trust his subordinates. In any case, his ideas differed radically from either his predecessor's or his successors' so that the comments and materials would most probably have consisted of telling him "you can't do this" or "this is politically just impossible."

On September 17, Schumpeter had talked to a meeting of the Peasants' Association under the chairmanship of his cabinet colleague Stöckler. He laid out clearly what could be achieved: "that after years of suffering and heavy sacrifice we will finally be able to say that those who will come after us and for whom we want to work will be better off than we" (ibid., 249).

No sector of the economy could permanently work with a deficit. Farmers, too, had to bear their share of the misery, but they also had to get cheap credit. Schumpeter then explained briefly the basic ideas of the Finanzplan. At the end, "Secretary of State Stöckler thanks Dr. Schumpeter for his words and assures him that his views about the war debt and the capital levy find complete approval of the meeting. Furthermore he assures him of the warmest support in the Cabinet Council and the National Assembly" (ibid., 251).

So less than two weeks before Schumpeter actually submitted his plan to cabinet on September 29, he could feel that he would have at least some support in cabinet. Stöckler, however, did not support him when it came to the crunch.

By September 26, Schumpeter had to defend himself against the accusation that he had dawdled about reform of the civil service. Not so; but this depended on a new regulation concerning civil service salaries. In the forthcoming Finanzplan he had included substantial salary increases. (ibid., 251–52).

But the same issue reported also the approaching crisis in the coalition. Monsignor Dr. Seipel, later to become Christian Socialist chancellor, talked at length about a party rally on September 25. There was urgency about a new constitution, production had to be started up again, and he stressed that "the population will not be ready to make this big sacrifice . . . only to socialize at all cost but I will demand that the socialization lists will always consider whether the economy as a whole is being promoted or not. I have recently demanded that it is high time to stop theoretical discussions about the concept of socialization if only to calm our economic life. My opponents have badly attacked [me] because I have made this demand but I have not noted that they could muster any objective arguments against me" (ibid.). Hence, Schumpeter had reason to believe that he would also get support from this side.

The first public sign of trouble was a semi-official (offiziös) report of the Christian Social party correspondence that the Finanzplan was to be discussed in cabinet that same day. (ibid., 260). The first impression of the plan was "not unfavorable, one might even say that the boldness and the thoroughly worked out structure of Schumpeter's ideas were indeed surprising since the members of cabinet had hardly expected such a radical approach of the decisive (einschneidend) importance and probable effects from the secretary of state. But one could not speak of fiscal proposals of the government until after the plan was adopted" (ibid.). The party correspondence reported some reactions of Bauer and hoped the Cabinet Council would stick to Schumpeter's proposals. In any case, there was no reason why the Finanzplan should be kept secret, particularly as it was now certain that the main committee of parliament would meet and among other things hear the plan.

The same issue of the NFP (ibid., 258–59, but with dateline September 30) reported that the members of parliament did not understand why the plan was kept secret and they did not like the precedent it set. The government on its side explained that so far the Cabinet Council had only taken note of the plan. "With this alone the Plan has not yet been adopted." Secretary of State Dr. Bauer in particular desired some changes. "Only when the Finanzplan has been adopted by Cabinet does it receive its definite form and becomes the Finanzplan of the Government."

On October 2, the paper reported that the chancellor explained that there was fundamental agreement in cabinet. The radical socialist Bauer, who had wanted to buy the Alpine Montangesellschaft for the State, and the proponent of the opposite view (i.e., Schumpeter) that the sale of the shares had acquired the necessary foreign exchange for the government, agreed on the basic principles of the Plan. "The Government does not state that the Finanzplan is its own but it wants to negotiate about it with the parties and bring it before Parliament for final decision" (ibid., 264–65). There were also some hints about the contents of the plan.

By October 8, the NFP reported under heading "Possibility of a Resignation of Secretary of State Dr. Schumpeter" that the Finanzplan should have come before the main committee of parliament on October 8, but did not because of serious differences of opinion in cabinet (ibid., 265–66). The whole process of dealing with the Finanzplan was felt to be unusual. The parties were not informed about the details of the Plan "since the Secretary of State has not received permission to develop his Plan before the Parties." In fact, Schumpeter's successor Dr. Reisch had already explained his ideas to the

Social Democratic club and was about to do so before the Christian Socialists. Though the bourgeois parties were divided, Schumpeter still had some support among the Christian Socialists.

In the evening edition of the same day, the NFP reported that the cabinet would resign only after the ratification of the peace treaty. "However, in today's meeting of the Main Committee there occurred an incident which presumably will result in a crisis in the Ministry of Finance" (ibid., 266–67). Schumpeter had recovered from a two day's cold and was ready to develop his plan before the main committee, but he had been told that it was inopportune for him to do so. In fact, he did not even get an invitation to attend the meeting. But "Dr. Schumpeter considers it his right to go with the Finanzplan before the Main Committee. The fact that he can not do so shows that he has no political backing" (ibid., 267). The cabinet did not wish to have the plan discussed to avoid taking a position on the plan.

On October 9, it was rumored that the cabinet would resign the following week, to be reconstituted without Schumpeter. Reisch would become minister of finance.[1] Reisch announced that not the whole of the capital levy would be used to reduce the war debt "which might even have some undesirable effects." The most important task was to stabilize the foreign exchange rate and the value of money. He thought there might be a period of an improved exchange rate that might stabilize the krone at 20 percent or at most at 25 percent of its par value. Taxes and prices of public utilities would have to go up, but it was even more important to increase the tax base.

In the same issue, the NFP also reported that Stöckler had not backed Schumpeter as he had indicated he would at the farm association meeting. A cabinet meeting scheduled for October 9 had to be cancelled because the Social Democrats had to meet, a meeting in which the Arbeiterräte were reported to have used some strong language and to have put the social democratic members of parliament on the defensive.

That same evening, the NFP expressed dismay at the political manners of German-Austria which lacked the equivalent of the American congressional courtesy. It said that Schumpeter had been "assassinated," that there was no reason why his case should have been treated separately since the whole cabinet was to resign a week later anyway.

> The public which Dr. Schumpeter had not succeeded in rallying behind him despite all his attempts to be accommodating had the correct feeling that he was to be politically assassinated. This procedure has been the subject of lively discussion and the effect was that despite the dislike of Dr. Schumpeter's methods there was a not permissible injustice done him. The pretense that the Plan had to be kept secret and could not be presented to the Main Committee is too absurd to be taken seriously. (ibid., 274)

---

[1] Schumpeter (1992), 269–72. Reisch was at that time president of the Bodenkreditanstalt. He had been the civil servant in the Ministry of Finance responsible for direct taxes under Böhm-Bawerk and his successor, and later section chief of the Tax Division. He became president of the Austrian National Bank in 1923–1924.

Schumpeter last appeared before the Finance Committee of parliament on October 15 to defend the government proposal to sell or mortgage government-owned art treasures.[2] There was, he was reported to have said, a foreign exchange and a budgetary problem. The bread price had to be raised since the budget simply could not support a monthly subsidy of K300 million just for grain imports. Moreover, the payment for grain imports had been possible only by a number of "temporary tricks of the fiscal administration." The public saw only what was not achieved, not what was achieved. "The Secretary of State had to state that when he took over the Ministry there was no foreign exchange at all" (ibid.). There were some export earnings, but that source was about to dry up. There was the sale of assets, but there was the danger of selling the future of the nation for a mess of pottage.

But he had also established a foreign exchange fund. One reason for doing so was to have a nest egg for an "absolute emergency. This emergency is now upon us and we must now make this fund available to the Government and it will therefore be used up quickly."

The Ministry had taken pains to get foreign credit, to a small extent even for purposes of consumption, but it is obvious now that we need more credit to get producing again. Hence we must sell "immortal works of art" to get us through the winter.

All this is bearable if we can have the hope that matters will improve. "The greatest problem for the State would be to get through the next three years without Government bankruptcy and without the issue of new notes" (ibid.). "The Secretary of State finally begs to pass the law as quickly as possible since the whole action was useful only if it is taken immediately and a sale of productive assets is avoided which would annihilate the strength of the State and the people to rebuild production."

On October 17, the "former Secretary of State Dr. Schumpeter" explained his plan to the Christian Social Association (ibid., 274–75).

On October 19, the NFP reported a farewell speech of Schumpeter's to his officials. After Schumpeter had left the room, the new Secretary of State Dr. Reisch entered the reception hall to be greeted by the officials, who expressed particular pleasure that Dr. Reisch had once been one of their own.[3]

AFTERMATH

There were discussions between the Social Democrats and the Christian Socialists about forming a new coalition government once more under Renner as chancellor. The compromise decided that the capital levy should be used primarily to get foreign exchange, second, to reduce the war debt and to cover current budget deficits, and also to ensure governmental influence on partic-

---

[2] NFP, no. 19807 (October 16, 1919): 4. Not reprinted in Schumpeter (1992).

[3] NFP, no. 19810 (October 19, 1919): dateline October 18. Not reprinted in Schumpeter (1992).

ularly economically important enterprises. As for socialization, "it remained valid [whatever that was supposed to mean] but it is recognized that the time and circumstances of its realization must be determined by fiscal and monetary (kreditpolitische) considerations." The Social Democratic negotiators were Renner, Bauer, Seitz, Adler, and Eldersch.

There is no point in going into detail about the new policy. It was wrong, but perhaps no other policy was possible under the circumstances. Hyperinflation and misery followed for another four years.

The idea, sometimes found in the literature, that Schumpeter made a mess of things is not supported by the facts. Quite the contrary; he formulated the only policy that could have saved the situation. But he did apparently intrigue against Bauer in the matter of the Anschluss, which after all had been official government policy, and this was considered improper.[4] In the end no one trusted him, but once again it remains a question to what extent it was his behavior and to what extent nobody really wanted to hear the truth: that the Austro-Hungarian monarchy had lost the war disastrously, that German-Austria did not yet exist except as an imposition of the Entente, and that the new Austria was totally exhausted, morally, psychologically, and economically.

Walter Federn commented on Reisch's Finanzplan that to use the capital levy as if it were an ordinary tax revenue spoke for his sense of realism, but he still preferred Schumpeter's ideas.

So Schumpeter became again professor in Graz. His first reported public speech was about "The United Sates of America in Politics and Culture."[5] It is a very positive assessment of recent American tendencies. It is characteristic Schumpeter in stressing developmental tendencies in the structure of the American economy, but also toward an independent culture and science "with a rapidity which is almost shaming for us who needed so long for these achievements."

But the last paragraph asks the question: "What was it, then, that induced this people to the crusade which gave victory to the Entente?" Certainly not economic considerations. It would have been to the economic interest of the United States to stay out of the war. It could not have been the fear of an all powerful Germany.

> There was something else which not only the professional politician but the Central European in general is used to overlook: the fact that moral strengths (Kräfte) are real powers in the life of a people. Right or wrong, for the American people the world war is seen as an illegal invasion (Ueberfall) which to resist is a matter for all civilized people. (Schumpeter 1993, 131–32)

---

[4] Letter by Gustav Stolper to Kurt Singer, December 5, 1919, in the Stolper Nachlass, Federal German Archives, Koblentz. See chapter 2, where some of Schumpeter's intrigues have been detailed.

[5] "Die Vereinigten Staaten von Amerika in Politik und Kultur," *NFP* October 21, 1919, No. 19812, p. 6. Speech given before the Association of Journalists and Writers "Concordia" on October 20, 1919. Reprinted in Schumpeter (1993), 128–32.

Publicist and Investment Banker

or

Making the Best of It

Participant in Economic Policy Discussions

AFTER HIS DISMISSAL from cabinet, Schumpeter returned after a leave of one semester to the University of Graz. Nature took its course as predicted: inflation worsened; the value of the krone declined so much that there was apparently even a threat that it would no longer be quoted abroad. No one had the political will or ability to tackle the problems at their root. During this period and until his move to Germany in 1925, Schumpeter developed an intensive journalistic activity in which he spoke out on questions of the day. These articles have considerable interest for understanding his views on how money fitted into an evolutionary economy, as his later articles in the *Deutsche Volkswirt* expand on his views of public finance in an evolutionary context.

Schumpeter never cried—at least in public—about spilled milk, and he at least fought to prevent unfortunate consequences whenever action at the right moment could help. In private, and after the death of mother, wife, and child, it was perhaps somewhat different. In a letter to Redvers Opie he wrote that he had given up all hope ever to see a civilized conservativism again.[1] But just as his theoretical analysis remained wertfrei, so his policy analysis did not quarrel with the initial conditions in which it had to be applied.

Of course, Schumpeter was aware of the political conditions needed to apply economic policy in the first place. Economic policy had to apply to a country as a whole and had to fit into a world economy. In a speech before the Civil Servant Association he pointed out that while in the old Monarchy he had been a federalist, the new Austria had to be a single economic area; it was simply impossible for each land to make its own economic policy.[2] Put more generally: fiscal and economic policy autonomy of small economic units is an illusion, though one which many an LDC cherishes.

The international equivalent to this proposition was a fixed exchange rate and free trade. But this required in turn a fiscal, monetary, and economic policy which allowed individual economies to work efficiently. Fluctuating

---

[1] "Still more bitterly I feel that there is no more and never will be any room on this earth for that cultivated conservativism which would command my allegiance. It boils down to a choice between the right of nationalism and the might of socialism. . . . I see nothing in Lenin but a blood-stained mongol despot, you nothing in Hitler than a stupid oriental(?) demagogue; and for thousands of sophisticated, for millions of simple minded, both of them not only were leaders, but saviors. Yes—Göbbels is the Trotzky of Hitlerism . . . ." Letter, dated Cambridge, Mass., Saturday, probably 1933. This letter was made available by Loring Allen.

[2] Speech before the Zentralverband der Österreichischen Beamtenvereine, reported (but not verbatim) in the *Neue Freie Presse*, March 11, 1920, under the heading "Staatssekretär a. D. Dr. Schumpeter über die Rückwirkung der Verfassungsreform auf die Staatsbeamten."

exchange rates were preferable to fixed rates as long as the conditions for the maintenance of fixed rates could not be achieved.

Of course, fluctuating exchanges were not really the problem at the time, but rather the steady and catastrophic deterioration of the external value of the krone. And that certainly was not a desirable state of affairs. But it was hopeless to tackle the stabilization of the foreign value of the currency without first establishing the domestic conditions for its success. This was not a universally held opinion: "order in the foreign exchanges is the last and not the first step for the recovery (Genesung) of the economy."[3] This formulation appears again and again.

When the interview was given, there were rumors that Schumpeter would join the government once again. The editorial introduction to the interview stated that "Dr. Schumpeter did indeed participate in the discussions about the formulation of the new Government program."

The krone had fallen to five centimes in Geneva. The interviewer asked about a possible improvement in the exchange rate. Schumpeter answered categorically that he did not believe it to be imminent or desirable. Any substantial increase in the external value of the krone would lead to a crisis with substantial unemployment. Austrian tax policy came in for the substantial criticism that it virtually forced a transfer of Austrian wealth to the successor states. The krone could not be stabilized until exports got going again. Those arguments are familiar now. They were not then.[4]

The answers to privatization of industries are in keeping with the views expressed in the preliminary report of the German Coal Socialization Commission. Privatization is certainly the first step to renewed health of government industries. But the problems of the industries were due primarily to the fact that "with us, all economic questions are political questions." Because of this fact an industry becomes not viable. The result of the political treatment of agricultural policy is that "we must import wheat at highest prices while wheat land is converted to pasture." And with "government industries we have carried on a system of incredible waste for two years, as if our deficit were not big enough."

Two months later, *Die Börse* published a long excerpt of a speech which Schumpeter had given on "World Economic Crisis?" (Schumpeter 1993, 22f). Schumpeter started with the Austrian situation which could be explained entirely by domestic factors and/or such special factors as the shortage of coal. Too many people lived off the state, which could not afford it. Inflation had progressed to such an extent that money was scarce for industry but abundant for the stock exchange. "Our policy drives money out of the

---

[3] "Unterredung mit Staatssekretar a.D. Dr. Schumpeter über die nächste Zukunft der Krone, Einführung der Goldkrone, Übertragung der Staatsindustrien an das Privatkapital, und Möglichkeiten des wirtschaftlichen Wiederaufbaus." *Die Börse*, November 11, 1920, 3–4. All articles in *Die Börse* are reprinted in Schumpeter (1993). The interview is found on pp. 20–22.

[4] One should remember the horror in cabinet when Schumpeter made the same points there— or Keynes's futile efforts to prevent the return of Sterling to the old parity.

banks, makes productive investment more and more difficult and condemns it to profiteering (Schiebergeschäft), and when this becomes impossible, to idleness, gambling or consumption" (ibid., 23).

Abroad these factors applied only to a minor extent. Normally, a peace inflation based on an enormous pent-up investment demand for reconstruction would have followed the war inflation. Prices, wages, and interest rates would have risen, all phenomena of a healthy process of healing. High wages as the result of market forces would not have caused trouble. This was in fact what happened in the United States when price controls were abolished after the Second World War.

The immediate cause why countries with orderly circumstances had economic troubles is "the behavior of the banks which prefer to refuse credit at low interest rates to giving credit at high rates" (ibid., 25) a phenomenon, incidentally, which also caused trouble during the Great Depression in Weimar, Germany (H. James 1986). In short there was a faulty, deflationary economic policy. Unlike in Austria, where a restrictive policy was forced by a deficit-fed inflation, this was not the case abroad.

Schumpeter discussed briefly the reasons for such a perverse policy in Switzerland and the United States. Switzerland had been a haven for flight capital. But it did not have a war boom proper. The United States, on the other hand, had a real war boom. The necessary restructuring of industry from war to peace was easy. There were problems, "but basically the situation is sound and if the peace boom does not show clearly, this is due to external reasons."

Schumpeter then turns to the question of "Socialism, Capitalism and Economic Depression"[5] (Schumpeter 1993, 27). The purpose is to dismiss false explanations of the origins of the depression and with them misguided attempts to deal with the situation. This discussion has a frightening actuality.

Schumpeter rejects both the Socialist and the anti-Socialist explanations. The demands of the workers are not the *cause* of the economic troubles; they are their consequence. Productivity is the problem, not wages.

But the Socialists are equally wrong. The economic crisis is *not* a crisis of capitalism and private enterprise. "Even a year ago it took a good deal of imagination to interpret the military and economic collapse and its consequences as a breakdown of the economic system. . . . The actual socializations were and had to be a miserable affair in every conceivable respect." The system did not change as the result of the war.

The consequences Schumpeter draws are equally applicable today. First, a return to normal conditions is even under the best of circumstances a lengthy affair. "To look for measures that could heal the situation of a people in one fell swoop is dilettantism or charlatanry." Monetary experiments are particularly dangerous. Laymen feel the domestic and foreign troubles first. But they are a symptom. Specifically: "Order in the foreign exchange situation is not the first, but the last achievement of the process of healing."

[5] It is not clear whether the subheadings are in Schumpeter's text or an editorial addition.

This policy discussion defines Schumpeter's relation to monetarist prescriptions with which he—up to a point—agrees. When the situation is ripe, credit is essential and credit crunches can hurt a hopeful situation. But the underlying situation must be allowed to heal. Flexible exchange rates are preferable to fixed rates as long as the real situation is all fouled up. But they are evidently not desirable in themselves. They are unavoidably a second-best when the real situation is bad and requires a change from financing consumption to financing investments. But once this is achieved flexible rates cease to be desirable—points which Schumpeter later elaborated theoretically in his "Goldene Bremse."[6]

Second, "The essence of an economy does not lie in accumulations of goods and the apparatus of technical production but in the psychic relationship among people and in the psychic disposition of the individual."[7] For this reason:

> [T]he credit needs of an economy are not simply statistically measurable sums which organization of States[8] could raise but the sum of huge and very variable items whose justification rests in the individual case on means, possibilities, abilities, personal behavior, views, decisions (Willensdispositionen), etc., in the most perfect as well as the most economical manner. This problem can be solved in Europe only by individual initiative. Not he who . . . works for large intergovernmental capital movements works at its solution, but the industrialist or merchant who in the individual case works to get his own little ship afloat. (ibid., 28–29)

In a theoretical context, *Business Cycles* made the point abundantly clear:

> For it must never be forgotten that the theory of credit creation as, for that matter, the theory of saving, entirely turns on the purpose for which the created—or saved—means of payment are used and on the success which attends that purpose. The quantity-theory aspects or, as we might also say, the aggregative aspect of the practice is entirely secondary. The trouble with John Law was not that he created means of payment *in vacuo* but that he used them for purposes which failed to succeed. (Schumpeter 1939, 113–14)

About a year later, Schumpeter wrote an article on "Austrian Credit Prob-

---

[6] This argumentation differs from today's arguments for flexible exchanges. It is essentially a microeconomic argument, not a macroeconomic argument of dealing with differing growth rates. "Die goldene Bremse der Kreditmaschine, die Goldwährung und der Bankkredit." Originally *Kölner Vorträge*, vol. l, 1927. Reprinted in Schumpeter (1952).

[7] Schumpeter (1993), 28. It should be noted that Schumpeter does not use the term "psychological." For at no time did he deviate from his position that economics was quite independent of any particular psychological theory. The point is again to stress the importance of economic policies which can send the right or wrong signals, and which really should get people to react so as to make the economy work properly. In the Schumpeterian sense this means so as to achieve proper evolution. There are also social contexts of this proposition, but it would go too far to repeat them here.

[8] This formulation refers to the efforts to organize international consortia to supply credit to Austria.

lem" (Schumpeter 1993, 29–32). Again the problem discussed is the relation between—specifically foreign—credit and domestic policy. Schumpeter pointed out that it was unreasonable for Austria to expect extensive foreign help without actual changes in Austrian policy. To start with, agricultural policy had been ideally designed to reduce production to a minimum. There were the bureaucratic obstacles—and it should be emphasized that they were due to the policies of the bourgeois, not the social-democratic parties—and there were still enormous problems with intra-Austrian communications—"as long as intrigues and fights are needed to get a single oxen to Vienna, our production can not approximately be what it could be" (ibid., 30).

It was evidently unreasonable to expect foreigners to "pay the cost of our policy. Nor should it be overlooked that States which themselves lived with austerity must look at our policy as wasteful."

> Almost more important than credits seems to me to link any potential credits with the condition of effective economies and an effective freeing of economic forces. (ibid.)

This sounds like prescriptions of the IMF in LDCs, or the cutting of Soviet subsidies to East Bloc countries, or what to do with the economies of East Bloc countries struggling to rescue their economies from the morass in which 40–70 years of terrible economic policy has landed them. But it also is a warning of the inevitable results which present economic policies in some Capitalist countries will have without drastic changes.

Credits are needed for two quite distinct purposes. First and less important are credits to mitigate the hardships which the transition to a productive economy inevitably involves, including a loan to stabilize—but *not* to raise—the foreign value of the krone.

> Much more important . . . are those credits which the *economy* and specially *industry* needs. Here I believe the only sound and correct way seems to *me*, *foregoing any attempt at organized and Governmentally controlled inflow (Auftretens)*, one lets *foreign capital trickle into the country slowly and in the normal course of events*. As is well known, this is not the general opinion. It is said that this will direct capital not into the best purposes but only to businessmen of inferior class, who only want to make a good profit here and there. *But just this is the correct way. . . .* This is indeed the way which praxis has actually taken. Politics can do no better that to make sure that *foreign capital feels safe and well with us*. If we had done this right after the collapse we would already be over the worst. In reality, our policy does exactly *the opposite*. It invites foreign capital and when it comes it cries "Ueberfremdung" (undue influence of foreign capital). . . . This explains the astonishing fact that foreign capital wants to come only with special guarantees. (ibid.; italics in original)

It would take only very few changes in wording to apply all this to present problems in Eastern Europe or LDCs. Thus, East Germans fear that West Germans might buy up their industries at bargain prices, as if they were worth even that much. Or the United States—which really should know better—is worried about Japanese purchases of American properties and industries while expecting Japan to continue to finance forever the budget deficit. It makes rather depressing reading to see how little things have changed.

The subject matter of the next few articles changes subtly, yet always comes back to the importance of short- and long-term fiscal policy. On December 15, 1921, *Die Börse* published a long interview with Schumpeter, asking three questions which agitated the financially interested public (ibid., 35–39).

The first referred to the value of shares on the stock exchange. Shares were being bought on the basis that they represented "real" values, regardless of whether they produced any return or not. Schumpeter's answer was fairly long. Given the domestic inflation and the continuing decline in the foreign value of the krone, shares were indeed cheap, provided that under more normal circumstances the enterprises would produce some return. If they would not, the shares were evidently worthless no matter how many bricks and mortar they represented.[9]

More interesting is the response to a statement by the then Minister of Finance Gürtler (the same whose promotion Schumpeter as dean had blocked in Graz and who then caused difficulties in parliament as Christian-Social whip) which insisted that industrial bills of exchange used as collateral by the Austro-Hungarian Bank were not inflationary. Of course, this was nonsense, and Schumpeter politely said so. But perhaps the minister did not quite mean what he seemed to say because he did not have the time to make himself absolutely clear. It did after all make a difference whether government or private industry guaranteed the bill of exchange because the State would use the money to finance consumption directly, while private industry would first finance some production before the paid-out money would enter the consumption sphere and raise prices.

And perhaps the minister had thought of the fact that if the Central Bank stopped to print money, a sharp deflation could not be avoided. Even in England with its highly developed sense of social cohesion, a deflationary policy caused the structure of society to creak—"in allen Fugen zu krachen."

---

[9] This problem is coming up with the privatization of East German enterprises. The Treuhandgesellschaft, the agency charged with privatization, cannot even give the biggest and previously world renowned chemical plants away!

"After taking a close look at East German chemical plants West German chemical firms have been reluctant to buy on any terms. One exception is BSAF which says it is willing to acquire Synthesewerk Schwarzheide, a poly-urethane maker with yearly sales thought to be equivalent to DM 600m ($360 m). BASF has promised to invest up to DM 400m in the business over the next few years. However, Mr. Max Dietrich Kley, the company's financial director, has delivered an ultimatum: BSAF will only take over Schwarzheide if it has to pay nothing (yes, nothing), if it is protected against the company's liability for past pollution, and if it receives ownership of the company before the end of September. Otherwise, says Mr. Kley, forget it.

"This is quite a bargaining position. But the Treuhandgesellschaft may count itself lucky that BASF is bothering taking Schwarzheide for free." *The Economist*, London, September 8, 1990, 75.

In Austria, without the discipline and national consciousness of England, there would be the much worse unemployment riots. Unemployment and bankruptcies could be avoided during the period of transition to a stable currency by substantial Central Bank credit to industry. This was so because the exchange rate was much below what corresponded to the rate of inflation. Hence, there was room to grow somewhat, provided the krone was not allowed to rise.

Schumpeter's attitude toward the continuously falling exchange rates was once more explained. Terrible as it is, at least it kept the economy from feeling the world depression which in England, Switzerland, and Northern Europe had produced unemployment and instabilities in society. But once the foreign exchanges stabilized, a painful new process of adaptation would become inevitable.

For the time being, a crisis in Austria could be avoided only if the Central Bank made more credit available to banks and industry.

> In general, there is nothing more immoral and wrong from the business standpoint than to preach easy credit. But for the next few months it is likely to be the means of salvation: granting credit at the highest possible rate of interest to deter requests of less than absolute needs. But then there is one means, though I fear exactly the opposite will be done: *to free private initiative from excessive burdens . . .* and the chains and tutelage which prevent it from working. (Schumpeter 1993, 38–39; italics in original)

Schumpeter advocated lower taxes on business and higher taxes on consumption. All his life he liked sales taxes and the kind of personal income tax generally known as an expenditure tax.

He advocated flexible exchanges essentially to gain time for fundamental reforms and only if combined with high interest rates. He wanted the time so bought to be used to create the conditions for stability in the exchanges and growth in the economy, and thus reserve capital imports for increasing the productive apparatus of the economy rather than financing consumption in the form of the budgetary deficit. Monetary policy becomes essential not merely to stop inflation but—at high interest rates—to allocate funds to where they had a chance to finance viable enterprises, rather than consumption.

Most of Schumpeter's theoretical as well as his policy writings are in the context of an isolated economy—a small and desperately poor one in the case of Austria, a large and rich one in the case of the United States. But it is at the same time never forgotten that individual countries are part of the world economy. Schumpeter was a free trader, and domestic policies at home and abroad had profound economic and political consequences.

Some of these issues are discussed in a speech which Schumpeter gave before the Austrian League for the League of Nations.[10] The central point of Schumpeter's analysis is made at the very beginning:

[10] "Finanzpolitik und Völkerbund." Speech before the General Assembly of the Austrian League for the League of Nations, March 22, 1922, reported in NFP, March 23, 1922. Reprinted in Schumpeter (1993), 39–42.

Fiscal and economic questions were at all times extremely important (massgebend) for the behavior of States towards each other. That they are today almost exclusively so is due to the general impoverishment of the world which has pushed economic factors into the foreground. . . . The layman believes that the present fiscal problems are easily solved by foreign exchange credits and cancellation of debts. . . . [b]ut this is not so; the problems of fiscal and exchange rate policy are only symptoms (äussere Einflüsse) of deep economic problems. (ibid., 39)

The English attempts to return to a "normal," that is, pre–1914, state of affairs "without regard to the consequences for the economy" simply produced 2 million unemployed. In Germany, on the other hand, an inflationary policy led to a breakdown of the normal capitalistic methods insofar as the connection between the amount of money and the rate of interest was cut. But it was also accompanied by an enormous burst of economic energy (Kraftanstrengung). In Austria, inflation was not the cause of all evil but the consequence of political apathy which lead to capital consumption.

Actually, the liquidation of the consequences of the war had become more difficult because of a new element: "*The aggression of the countries with damaged currencies*" (ibid., 40; italics in original) which apparently was the then current phrase of what later was called "beggar-my-neighbor policies." The decline of the German mark had almost become a greater worry for England than for Germany.

Yet the basic causes are domestic, not external. International credits will not solve the problem but make it worse. "The first precondition for any removal of national antagonisms is that each country finds its place in the automatic development (Gang) of things, eliminates the fear of threats to its existence (ibid., 41).

A reasonable fiscal and economic policy at home will remove the danger of international economic antagonisms. A wrong policy leads to protectionism which, as Schumpeter sees it, has not simply damaging welfare effects but introduces uncertainties into the legal framework which causes international political troubles.

Somewhat later Schumpeter gave his views on a possible cartel of central banks to solve the problems of currency stability (ibid., 42–47). The plan was, of course, unworkable, besides being quite old-fashioned. It was proposed at the time of bimetallism, and before 1914 there had been proposals to split the Austro-Hungarian Central Bank into two autonomous institutes which would then form a cartel. Austria had energetically refused to participate, as did England in 1922. These plans inevitably require the strongest partner to underwrite and subsidize the economic follies of the weaker.

To get international coordination, each country had first to solve its own specific problems, and had to do so not at the expense of each other. There was talk of an international clearing system and a "World Check Bank" and indeed if the war had not interfered this probably really would have been the next step on the road of the world economy. But such matters must grow organically, they cannot arbitrarily be erected. The first task is a sensible domestic economic policy. "Again and again I come to the result that the problems of the day can in no country be solved from the foreign exchange side."

In short, for most countries something like a cartel of central banks would just be a gimmick; it could not solve but only postpone unavoidable decisions.

In June, 1922, Schumpeter gave an extraordinarily interesting speech about "Should the Government Pursue a Policy of Scarce Money?"[11] The answer was: No, not in the actual abnormal circumstances. Even in England the policy achieved its desirable ends only at the cost of enormous unemployment and bankruptcies. Austrian circumstances were totally different.

To start with, there was no idle money, as shown by the fact that prices adapted immediately to the changes in the exchange rate. "But, the producer has still another alternative . . . he can simply stop to produce. . . . A reduction in credit possibilities without a simultaneous reduction in Government expenditures would simply result in productive activity being hampered by new claims."

> It is hardly an exaggeration to say that at present a policy of credit restriction is the opposite of what could be useful. At the moment, State and economy need a liquid money market as a brake on the steep descent of our capital consumption. If it is beyond our will to deal with the true sickness of inflation for consumption purposes, then it is probably more correct to allow the much milder form of inflation to be followed by credit inflation of productive business in which case there are at least new values facing new means of circulation. (ibid., 48)

This is, of course, a cry of desperation, not a defense of inflation, certainly not of inflation for consumption purposes. But it is important evidence that Schumpeter always considered the economy, growth, capital formation important, and not merely price stability—with important qualifications—or even exchange rate stability, both of which were, of course, highly desirable and even essential for a healthy economy.

---

[11] "Soll der Staat eine Politik der Geldknappheit betreiben?" *Deutsches Volksblatt*, June 14, 1922. Reprinted in Schumpeter (1993), 47–49. Unfortunately this speech is not reported in extenso. The talk, which was given in the rooms of the Handelskammer, probably was given the day before. I have not found a report on this speech in the *Neue Freie Presse*.

Bank President and Investment Activities

THE BIEDERMANN BANK

The Biedermann Bank went public on July 16, 1921.[1] The founding took place in the rooms of the old private Bank M. L. Biedermann & Co. Its share capital was given as 600,000 shares of K400 value, which was paid in cash. Schumpeter was elected president, Artur Klein was elected one of the two vice presidents. Among the original shareholders and member of the Verwaltungsrat were prominently Dr. Gottfried Kunwald—and, not mentioned in the newspaper dispatch, also Dr. Braun-Stammfels, who was the source of most of Schumpeter's later troubles.[2] Kunwald was prominently connected with the Christian Social Party.

The Biedermann Bank was the first private bank founded in Vienna in 1792 by M. L. Biedermann. In the nineteenth century it had been prominent together with the Rothschilds in financing the construction of the Austrian Railways. The motif to go public was to replenish the private means which war and inflation had eroded.

The Verwaltungsrat consisted of thirteen members. Among the original shareholders was prominently the Anglo-Austrian Bank which was de facto a subsidiary of the Bank of England. There was also an executive committee of four. Schumpeter presided over all meetings and was ex officio a member of all of them.

According to Rudolf Klein, Schumpeter got into the Bank because he had

[1] So briefly reported in the NFP of July 23, 1921. My account of this episode in Schumpeter's life is based on newspaper reports, two letters to Professor Robert Loring Allen by Rudolf Klein, the son of Artur Klein, the last owner of the Biedermann Bank before it went public, and a vice president actively involved in running the bank after it went public, and on the files of the Banking Commission concerning the Biedermann Bank in the Staatsarchiv, Vienna. The files are unfortunately incomplete. They contain the annual reports of the stockholders' meetings, but the protocols of the, theoretically monthly, meetings of the board of directors (Verwaltungsrat) start only with No. 6 of May 24, 1922, and only three of the protocols of the meetings of the executive committee of four.

In addition there are two important documents not previously known. One is a long letter written by Schumpeter to the Ministry of Education in Berlin in 1932, a copy of which is found in the papers of Gustav Stolper in the Bundesarchiv, Koblentz, and Schumpeter's statement about his investment activities before the investigating judge in connection with the Braun-Stammfels affair in 1925.

[2] The founding document shows Braun-Stammfels as a member of the Verwaltungsrat. In this respect, Dr. Rudolf Klein's memory has been faulty. Klein wrote to Professor Allen that his father Artur Klein had prevented Braun-Stammfels from getting into the firm as Schumpeter had suggested.

received a banking license in lieu of a pension when he was eased out of the cabinet. Banking concessions were hard to come by at the time. Also his share capital was, according to Klein, given to him in return for his providing the license, although the annual reports and the available protocols mention only that all shares were paid in full with cash. But this does not necessarily prove that Klein is wrong.[3]

Klein stresses that Schumpeter had nothing to do with the actual running of the bank, but dedicated himself entirely to his private investment activities which eventually cost him his fortune, plunged him into heavy debt, and threatened to cost him his good name which only such good friends as Arthur Spiethoff and Gustav Stolper helped him to rescue. The documents certainly bear Klein out in this. Schumpeter just presided over the Verwaltungsrat meetings, nothing more. Among the few available protocols of the executive committee meetings over which Schumpeter also presided, there is only one where Schumpeter actually made a suggestion on his own.

The records also show that Braun-Stammfels was actually present at only one of the Verwaltungsrat meetings, and represented at the others only by proxy. Rudolf Klein also states that Artur Klein prevented Braun-Stammfels from getting a loan from the bank, which is certainly correct since in the later Braun-Stammfels trial no such bank connection is asserted. But the available bank records do not show any application. Nor do they show any debts by Schumpeter to the bank. Klein states that Schumpeter did borrow a large sum which was still outstanding when the bank was liquidated. Klein recounts that this debt to the bank was canceled to avoid a scandal which might have embarrassed the government. But it was not entirely hidden from the public. Indeed, one paper speculated that the cancellation was in lieu of a "retirement" payment, was, in modern parlance, Schumpeter's golden parachute.

The bank was eventually liquidated in 1926, two years after Schumpeter resigned. It did *not* go bankrupt, the difference being that all creditors were eventually paid in full. All of Schumpeter's troubles arose out of his private investment activities.

Schumpeter's resignation was announced by Artur Klein at the Verwaltungsrat meeting No. XIX on July 6, 1925, and accepted with thanks for his past services. In the stockholders' meeting it was stated that Schumpeter had decided to devote himself entirely to his scientific work. Braun-Stammfels had resigned earlier, giving overburdening with work as his reason. Protocol

---

[3] The list of shares represented at the stockholders' meeting of 1923 states that 769,000 of the 778,555 shares outstanding were actually represented either in person by the owner or by a representative. The Anglo-Austrian Bank with 85,000 shares was the third largest shareholder after Kunwald with 95,000 shares and Schumpeter, 90,000 shares, of which he acquired 65,000 in the second and third placement. This is not likely to have been a gratis distribution to him for providing the license. Artur Klein was the fourth biggest stockholder with 75,928 shares. The total number of shareholders given by name was 32. Among them was also Johann Prince Liechtenstein (20,000 shares) and A. Spitzmüller (20,000 shares) who was also the rapporteur of the Verwaltungsrat meetings. Braun-Stammfels is not among the shareholders, though he was in the Verwaltungsrat.

No. XVII of the Verwaltungsrat meeting of June 18 (1924? no year is actually given) no longer listed his name. His resignation was announced in this meeting and accepted with the usual regrets and thanks. The protocol of meeting No. XIII is not in the files.

Protocol No. XVII also contains two other items which directly or indirectly touched upon Schumpeter's troubles. Kunwald reported that Biedermann had come to an arrangement with Morgan-Livermore of New York. The hopes put in this New York connection about placing Austrian fixed-interest bearing securities in the New York market later turned to ashes.

More important for Schumpeter were the accusations of improper behavior against the bank made with great publicity in the press. The protocol has a rather disappointing lack of information. Kunwald admits only that the bank did not have any legally required Verwaltungsrat meeting since the summer of the preceding year, and explains this with his own extended illness which had induced the bank to postpone any meetings. For the rest, the protocol states only that he read a draft of a reply to the chancellor's office which refuted point by point the accusations made also by the vice president of the Banking Commission, Hofrat Stern.

The portrait which Rudolf Klein paints of Schumpeter shows the split personality of which most people knew only the one or the other. Rudolf Klein knew Schumpeter from his banker's side, but also as a serious student of economics. He thus is one of the few people who knew Schumpeter both in his private persona as a scholar and teacher, and in his public persona as a man of the world, a would-be aristocrat, the universal genius.[4] The scholar was interested in his students, would spend time with those he felt were truly interested in economics, invite them to tea, discourse on his ideas, listen, give freely of himself. He was the kind of person his friends and students knew and loved, fascinating, kind, demanding, open-minded, helpful, with personal quirks—his famous yellow slips, his cape, his hat—which were accepted with loving amusement. These were accepted as it were as characteristic side conditions of genius, of which a certain eccentricity is expected. There were also his comments on others which occasionally could be biting.[5]

His public persona was considerably less attractive. Klein describes him as a social climber who wanted to succeed in high society (which, however, did not mean that he snubbed his lower-class friends). He wanted to be accepted by the aristocracy with which he felt, or so he thought, some empathy. The empathy had after all found expression in his secret memoranda which cer-

---

[4] The use of the Latin *persona* seems particularly appropriate. The word means "mask." The real Schumpeter is still hidden in all his complexity, though he probably has some, and in his scholarly side probably considerable, resemblance to the mask. In any case, these were two masks he chose, so they evidently must have presented something important to him, perhaps of him.

[5] I have been personally a recipient of Schumpeter's generosity. I probably was the only tutee he ever had in Bonn, when I still was a beginner. But even there he lived well above his means in the villa which had been the Emperor's when he was a student in Bonn. I have recounted these memories in my memoir in *Challenge* (1979).

tainly must have been known in the circles to whose company he aspired. He was evidently not accepted[6] even though he adopted their lifestyle and lived well above his means. He lived in Strudlhofgasse,[7] where he had rented half of the palais of the late Austro-Hungarian Foreign Minister Count Berchthold. And he kept a race horse in addition to a horse for personal use during the revolution while he was a cabinet member. Though not an aristocrat, he certainly had nothing of the bourgeois in him.

His behavior also showed a certain insensitivity toward his surroundings and a certain recklessness. Not being Jewish meant that he was not accused of sinister machinations but "merely" of being corrupt. This together with his evident brilliance which he made no attempt to downplay, as an Anglo-Saxon would have, made him almost a predestined target for scurrilous attacks. The company he kept included well-known anti-Semites as well as Jews, which made some conclude that he was anti-Semitic (which he certainly was not) while others distrusted him as a "Judenfreund," friend of the Jews.

According to Klein he was paid the very generous salary of öS100,000–120,000, between $14,000 and $15,000,[8] corresponding to easily fifteen times that amount in present dollars.

In any case, Schumpeter devoted himself to his private investment activities, which he backed with his own money and all of which failed. In the end a guarantee to another bank given to bail out his schoolmate Braun-Stammfels kept him in bondage for most of the rest of his life. He actually repaid all his debts to his friends with money he earned as professor in Bonn and later in Harvard and from his numerous speeches and articles.[9]

---

[6] Erich Streissler, "Schumpeter's Vienna and the Role of Credit Creation," in Frisch, (1982), 60–83, gives an amusing account of the social stratification in Schumpeter's time.

[7] There is a long novel by Heimito von Doderer, *Die Strudlhofstiege.*

[8] There is something wrong with this figure, since the Austrian Schilling was introduced only much later in 1924.

[9] The Schumpeter papers in the Harvard Archives contain a correspondence with Karl Schlesinger, in which the latter asked Schumpeter for an early repayment. Schumpeter immediately complied. There is also a brief accounting on a separate sheet of paper of money still owed to Schlesinger. This is the only direct evidence of a debt or a repayment I have found.

The Stolper papers in the Archive of the Federal German Republic, Koblentz, have the copy of a long letter by Schumpeter to Ministerialrat Richter in the Prussian Ministry of Education dealing with the appointment of Schumpeter to the Berlin Chair of Economic Theory. The original letter, if it still exists, is in the files of the Ministry of Education in Merseburg, in the former GDR, but so far I have not been able to locate them.

The letter in the Stolper files in Koblentz is not a true copy. It is a typewritten letter, evidently typed by Schumpeter personally, written from stenographic notes of what he had dictated to his secretary. The last page states that the letter to the ministry was written by hand by his secretary, and Schumpeter had to reconstruct the last page from memory. This rather extraordinary procedure indicates how seriously Schumpeter took this matter, and how anxious he was to keep it from becoming public. It seems that besides Richter only Gustav Stolper and Arthur Spiethoff were informed of the details of the proceedings, both close friends who did what they could to clear Schumpeter's name and whom Schumpeter consulted about further steps to be taken in this matter.

SCHUMPETER'S ANSWERS TO HIS ACCUSERS

Rumors about Schumpeter's supposed questionable behavior continued to circulate. They threatened to block his appointment to Bonn, and it was essentially Spiethoff's honorable insistence on facts which overcame the rumors in this instance. On August 14, 1925, Spiethoff had written to Gustav Stolper for information: "Some rumors about Professor Schumpeter are circulating here which I need not specify in detail which have caused some disquiet among some faculty members and which have produced the wish to investigate the matter."[10]

These rumors are likely to refer primarily to Schumpeter's ministerial days. But Gustav Stolper's detailed answer sheds considerable light on the Viennese atmosphere and its vindictiveness, as well as on Schumpeter's flouting of convention which went much beyond the wish later exhibited to liven up a lagging conversation with the desire to épater les bourgeois. Gustav Stolper's answer is dated August 22, 1925.

> I am aware of the rumors about Schumpeter, for they did not start yesterday. I have several times been consulted about them, and time and again I am at a loss how to answer them. For years—ever since Schumpeter's ministerial days—I have tried to find out what concrete facts lie behind these rumors. And although I know almost everyone who might be helpful, and although I know some of them sufficiently well that they would at least give me some confidential hints of any knowledge on their part, I have never been able to get any concrete answer. I have some idea how this talk might have arisen. Schumpeter has always had many enemies. This is due not only to his meteoric rise, but also to the fact that his whole life style is un-Austrian, if you wish, un-bourgeois. And Schumpeter was careless enough not to hide this but to stress it in a manner that can be explained only by inadequate knowledge of human nature (Menschenkenntnis) or lack or experience of life. That a University Professor does not go to the local pub, or repeats unthinkingly (nachbetet) current political slogans left or right, that a bourgeois Minister in a Government consisting of petty bourgeois wears silken handkerchiefs and shirts, or even keeps a riding horse—this cannot, given the horizon of these people, be quite above board (mit rechten Dingen zugehen). I know how all this has been held against him. Of course, this life style could not be financed with his professorial or ministerial salary. Hence—so Fama continued—it had to come from shady income sources. In reality Schumpeter probably lived off his capital. And as this was insufficient to pay for his needs at the time, he was after his Minister episode forced to accept a position which gave him a large income and the possibility of quickly accumulating a large fortune. As inexperienced as a politician who thought he could navigate (lavieren) between the parties and in reality made enemies of all of them, he proved to be equally so in

[10] Spiethoff's handwritten letter and a copy of Stolper's typed reply are in the Bundesarchiv, Koblentz. They have been reproduced in Schumpeter (1985), 33–34. Copy is also found in the Spiethoff papers in the Handschriften Sammlung of the University of Basel, Switzerland.

the field of practical business which was even more foreign to him. Long before last year's crash I told him to resign from the Bank and to return where alone he belonged: to science. That Spann kept him from the University of Vienna burdens in my eyes most heavily the already badly burdened scientific debit account of this man. I believe it simply to be a matter of honor of German Universities to right this wrong, and I am pleased that it is you who has taken the initiative.[11] It would be a crime if German Universities would let malicious gossip of malevolent people alienate such a person who has already to his credit so great scientific and pedagogical achievements and who can produce more such achievements in the future. (Schumpeter 1985, 33–34)

In 1931–1932, it was the Berlin faculty which successfully blocked Schumpeter's appointment to a chair which he himself had not sought[12] and which Ministerialdirektor Richter of the Prussian Ministry of Education had suggested. In fact, the Protocols of the Berlin faculty showed that it had hired a CPA (Treuhänder) to analyze the printed parliamentary report concerning the role which Minister Mataja had possibly played in the affairs of the Biedermann Bank. The attack in the Berlin faculty against Schumpeter was led by Sombart and Jastrow, both of whom were already retired.[13]

The faculty decided also to delete the names of the Viennese gentlemen who had drawn the attention of the Berlin faculty to Schumpeter's old problems, thereby in fact depriving him of being able to face his accusers. Indeed, Schumpeter had wanted to sue the rumor mongers, thus smoking them out, but Gustav Stolper had advised against this because the Berlin faculty could hide behind the official secrecy of the faculty meetings.

The faculty also strongly impugned Schumpeter's honor, suggesting that he had never taken any steps to clear his name, and it simply disbelieved his claim that he did not know of the Parliamentary Report. Of course, there really was

---

[11] This was not just politeness. When I was a student, my father told me not to attend any lectures on economics in Berlin "because they don't know anything. You wait until you go to Bonn to Spiethoff and Schumpeter. Die können was."

[12] The following is an extract of Schumpeter's letter to G. Stolper, Bonn, May 8, 1931:

> Dear Friend, . . . Your lively interest in my appointment to Berlin gives me great pleasure and I owe you for this not only thanks but an honest account (Aufrichtigkeit). To start with, I want to assure you that my appointment in Berlin is for me personally certainly not unimportant, because it would mean a substantially wider circle of students. But I ask you to believe me that I am beyond any other motives to want Berlin. and that even this motive loses by the fact that, as you know, such a wider circle is mine at any time and in a milieu in which scientific competence rather than political party membership counts. . . . The interview with Ministerialdirektor Richter of which you write was at the beginning of 1929. To the concessions then made to me [The University of Bonn, being in Prussia, was also under the tutelage of the Prussian Ministry of Education—W.F.St.] Ministerialdirektor Richter added on his own initiative the prospect of one of the two Berlin chairs which would soon become free.

[13] The Protocols were found by Ms. Christa Schulze-Kranz in the Archive of Humboldt University of (formerly East) Berlin. I am most grateful to Ms. Schulze-Kranz for her help in this and other archival matters involving the former GDR.

no reason for Schumpeter to have known anything, since the parliamentary committee of inquiry was interested in bringing down the former Minister and then Representative Mataja and Dr. Gottfried Kunwald, and Schumpeter never was either interrogated or otherwise called to testify.

Beyond that, the faculty with the exception of Lederer decided that Schumpeter not only was not quite honorable, but had scientifically nothing to offer, a view particularly expressed by Sombart and Jastrow, and that the faculty in any case did not need another theorist but an agricultural economist (as successor of Sering) or a statistician (as successor of v. Bortkiewitz), and no one had ever claimed that Schumpeter was an authority in either of these fields. This "out" led Schumpeter in a letter to Gustav Stolper to express his first admiration for the Berlin faculty. Emil Lederer in a nine-page letter defended both Schumpeter's honor and his scientific importance, to no avail.

Richter, who wanted to make good on his promise—to which Schumpeter explicitly did not wish to hold him—evidently wrote to Schumpeter requesting him to deal with the various accusations and insinuations made, and he sent him an article which had appeared in the *Arbeiter Zeitung* and a report of an investigating committee established by parliament to look into these matters. Schumpeter's detailed letter of March 26, 1932, is the point-by-point answer to the accusations and insinuations made.[14]

Schumpeter started the letter by thanking the Ministry of Education for allowing him "finally to counter the rumors circulating in the dark while thus far no-one who has attacked my honor has given me the opportunity to answer."

He explained that he had seen neither the article in the *Arbeiter Zeitung* nor the *Report*. He had stopped reading Viennese papers when he left Vienna. Also, he had never been interrogated by the Investigating Committee, nor had he received the report nor had he been aware that his name was mentioned in it.

The printed Report is ninty-five pages long.[15] It starts with reproducing the publicly made accusations by the Arbeiter Zeitung, the organ of the Social

[14] The handwritten letter sent to Richter has so far not been found in the files of the ministry. The letter sent to Gustav Stolper is in the Stolper papers in the Bundesarchiv, Koblentz.

[15] *Bericht* des in der Sitzung des Nationalrates vom 29. Oktober 1925 gemäss Artikel 53 B.-V.G. beziehungsweise para. 15 des Geschäftsordnungsgesetzes eingesetzten Untersuchungsausss-schusses, *betreffend die Untersuchung der öffentlich aufgestellten Behauptungen, dass die Biedermann-Bank Begünstigungen durch Organe der Bundesverwaltung erfahren hat, ferner zur Feststellung, ob dem Abgeordneten Dr. Heinrich Mataja von der Biedermann-Bank Begünstigungen zugebilligt worden sind.* 473 der Beilagen. Nationalrat. II. Gesetzgebungsperiode.

[Report of the Investigating Committee established according to Article 53 B-VG and para 15 respectively of the Law on Business Organization in the Session of the Nationalrat of October 29, 1925 *concerning the Investigation of the publicly made claims that the Biedermann Bank has been shown Favoritism by Organs of the Federal Administration, also to determine whether Representative Dr. Heinrich Mataja received favored treatment by the Biedermann Bank.* 473 of the Annexes. Nationalrat. II, legislative Period.]

Democratic party.[16] More specifically it dealt with two questions: whether the Biedermann Bank had received favored treatment by the government in the form of large deposits by various government monopolies under favorable conditions; and whether the Member of Parliament and former Minister Mataja had received favored treatment. It is fairly clear that the real object of the investigation was Mataja, that the bank was a convenient vehicle to this end, and that Schumpeter just got in the way, which was sort of an extra bonus.

The article in the *Arbeiter Zeitung* made essentially three accusations. The government had kept the bank afloat by depositing large sums of money with it. The Ministry of Finance had permitted an increase in capital "under the most astonishing conditions." It had permitted the shareholders and members of the syndicate organized to place the shares to purchase the shares at the price of K11,000 and K14,000 respectively at a time when the shares were quoted on the stock exchange at K35,000. "One can see: the State has treated the Biedermann Bank particularly well."

The Biedermann Bank in turn, so the article continued, had treated Dr. Mataja particularly well by letting him buy 10,000 shares at a price much below the current stock market quotations.

Schumpeter did not know Mataja personally, and asked Kunwald who was a friend of Mataja's what the matter was all about. Kunwald explained the matter to Schumpeter exactly as he stated under oath to the investigating committee (*Report*, p. 15). There were two orders to buy shares at two different dates with the share price of K14,000 at the first and K27,000 at the second date. The entry in the books was for K27,000 which was wrong and had to be corrected. There was no special treatment of Mataja. "I believed Kunwald then, and I still do."

What about the large government deposits with the bank? The Austrian State had always kept temporary surplus funds with trustworthy banks, "and that *was* the Biedermann Bank." Interestingly, however, Schumpeter added in the letter that when he was minister he did not allow this practice, no reason given, but then there could not have been any such funds anyway. In any case the Biedermann Bank owed the deposits exclusively to the fact that it paid a higher rate of interest, and as Kunwald testified under oath, it was his business to solicit deposits; there was nothing wrong with that. The majority of the investigating committee of four accepted this explanation, the minority of three did not. It also referred to the Biedermann Bank as "undoubtedly a dubious enterprise" (*Report*, p. 19).

Neither Schumpeter nor the Investigating Committee could know a year later that the twenty-third meeting of the Verwaltungsrat of the Biedermann Bank would meet on November 14, 1926, under the new President Robert von Schöller, in which it was stated:

[16] "Unsauberes, Unappetitliches . . ." [Something unclean, something unappetizing . . .]. *Arbeiter Zeitung*, October 16, 1925. Unsigned article.

As the members of the Verwaltungsrat know, we hold on the basis of old business relations deposits of public authorities the repayment of which has severely strained our liquid assets and, together with the public awareness (Aufrollung) of the question at the end of last year has damaged our development severely. We have negotiated for many months with the relevant public authorities with a view to agree on a repayment schedule that is feasible in our situation, and we are in the pleasant position to report that, thanks to a friendly understanding of these authorities we have come to an agreement which adjusts our repayments automatically to our liquidity so that no embarrassment can arise for us from this side.[17]

What about the accusation that the Biedermann Bank was allowed to issue shares substantially below the current stock market quotation? Banks required permission from the Ministry of Finance to issue new shares, and it was both legal and efficient to send someone to the Ministry of Finance beforehand to find out what the Ministry of Finance wanted to know. Moreover, there obviously was nothing wrong with offering present shareholders a chance to buy them before offering the shares to the general public. It would, of course, have been incorrect to offer new shareholders the shares at a lower price; this would indeed have meant a defrauding of the existing shareholders. But this did not happen.

It was also misleading to state that members of the syndicate had received gratis shares.[18] The bank was founded without many assets except its good name, and a syndicate had indeed been formed to place the shares. The activities of the syndicate had resulted in a profit and the remaining shares which the syndicate had bought under less favorable conditions than those offered to the present stockholders were distributed among the members of the syndicate. But they were entered into the books as zero.

Schumpeter discussed the next accusation in some detail. The relevant paragraph of the Report reads as follows:

The main point concerns the syndicate. In this respect we have noted that there did not really exist any syndicate members [sic].[19] Dr. Kunwald has stated that he has no notes about the syndicate members, neither does the Biedermann Bank. Dr. Kunwald had only a piece of paper (einen Zettel) according to which an attempt was made on May 3, 1923 to form a syndicate which, however, did not materialize. After this there was a so-called Four-Man and a Five-Man syndicate. With the Four-Man Syndicate there were serious irregularities. Of the six billion

[17] *Protokoll der 23. Verwaltungsratssitzung . . . .am 14 Oktober 1926 . . .* Typewritten. Transmitted to the Banking Commission December 14, 1926, as shown by letter of transmission. In the files of the Banking Commission, Archiv der Republik, Vienna. My translation.

[18] Hofrat Stern testified: "I have pointed out that at the third emission there was a distribution at which Messrs Schumpeter, Kunwald, Anhauch, Treischel, Halpern each received 30,000 or 16,000 gratis shares respectively. . . . This was not the case with the fourth emission" (*Report*, 23). My translation.

[19] The German is precisely that peculiar: "dass eigentlich keine Syndikatsmitglieder bestanden."

[kronen] the Bank received only two billion. However, the four billion were later used to make good the losses of the Five-Man Syndicate. (*Report*, p. 93)

Schumpeter's outraged comments on this insinuation were as follows:

Just as wrong is (p.93) the picture of the profits of another such syndicate whose figures expressed in terms of the deteriorated currency read most impressively.[20] This is a purely temporary book keeping excess value of the shares still held by the syndicate created by the uncontrollable fluctuations of the stock market quotations and which—and this is the decisive criterion—was never given to the syndicate members. This is indeed admitted on the mentioned page but only as an afterthought (Nachsatz, secondary clause) which the layman must read as if this were an irrelevancy and the accusation would nevertheless stand.

Characteristic indeed for the birth of rumors.

Schumpeter notes the same kind of insinuation without real foundation on other pages of the Report. The insinuations expressed in the Report gave Schumpeter the opportunity to clear up two matters which have remained unclear so far. Schumpeter quotes the testimony of Hofrat Stern as follows: "[The second line which I pursued was how the Biedermann Bank came] into such a situation. Here I came upon the line Braun-Stammfels with which (!) Schumpeter was connected and where I have noted that the manipulations were more than incorrect."[21]

Again Schumpeter had to deal with the insinuation that the troubles of the Biedermann Bank had anything to do with Braun-Stammfels. At least, so Schumpeter thought, an unprejudiced reader of the Report had to understand the passage in this manner. The facts were that the Biedermann Bank never held any shares of any of Braun-Stammfels' enterprises, nor had it financed them or given them a single penny credit.

Braun-Stammfels was never an active member of the Verwaltungsrat of the Biedermann Bank—the protocols of the Verwaltungsrat meetings bear this out. Neither was he a shareholder. Braun-Stammfels had requested financing from the bank, which the Executive Committee (which Schumpeter chaired) unanimously rejected.[22]

The second insinuation was the suggestion that Schumpeter had something to do "with or without connection with the Biedermann Bank [with the] more

[20] During 1923, the krone was de facto stabilized and fluctuated around K71,000 for the US$, compared to about 5 K/$ in 1914. K6 billion are thus about $84,500, not a very impressive sum.

[21] The whole quotation is in the letter. The words in square brackets are Schumpeter's paraphrase of the *Report*, the others are direct quotations from the *Report*.

[22] None of the three protocols of the executive committee meetings in the files of the Banking Commission mention Braun-Stammfels. Schumpeter's statement that the rejection was unanimous indicates that Braun-Stammfels applied on his own and not at the suggestion of Schumpeter. Schumpeter, being a man with an almost feudal sense of honor, would have considered this a conflict of interest and probably would have challenged any one making such a suggestion to a duel.

than incorrect manipulations." "That, too, is not said explicitly, but so that a reader had to understand it in this manner."

Schumpeter explained that as Braun-Stammfels' classmate in high school they naturally used the familiar "Du." But there were no further close relations between them.[23] It was in 1922, Schumpeter explained, that Braun-Stammfels approached the Biedermann Bank for possible financing, which the bank declined to do. This led Schumpeter to purchase shares. Schumpeter added that he could fairly be accused of bad business judgment, but hardly of anything worse, particularly as he had kept the shares to the end and had not sold them when they had risen on the stock exchange. Stern had admitted all this, though falsely stating that Schumpeter had founded the enterprises.

Actually, as will be detailed in the next section, Schumpeter was interrogated by a judge in connection with the Braun-Stammfels trial and exonerated of all wrongdoing.

Besides, Schumpeter added, a member of the Aufsichtsrat hardly could influence matters in the short run. And when the collapse was imminent, he gave a guarantee for one of the enterprises, an unfinished glass factory "which meant for me complete financial ruin. Whoever expresses moral qualms about my behavior should do this himself before I take his behavior seriously."[24]

---

[23] *Der Abend*, a not overly serious Viennese paper had a long article dealing with the Braun-Stammfels scandal which had recently broken. The headline was in inch-high letters "Herr Schumpeters Duzfreund." And a little less screaming in the next line: "Die Lösung des Rätsels Braun-Stammfels." (Mr. Schumpeter's bosom friend. The solution of the puzzle of Braun-Stammfels.) *Der Abend*, August 4, 1924. The article also had strong attacks against Dr. Kunwald. It stated categorically that Schumpeter had strongly recommended Braun-Stammfels to the Bank and that he was in this supported by Kunwald "the almost legendary figure, the lawyer who lies crippled in his bed, whom the Chancellor visits, as well as today's and former Ministers, without whom in Austria no large financial transaction is carried out, from whom the Chancellor and the Ministers seek council as with a mysterious oracle, this Dr. Kunwald has also spread his blessing hands over Dr. Braun-Stammfels." The only truth in all of this was that Kunwald was a friend of the Chancellor and was consulted. The rest was made up of whole cloth. But the quotation gives a flavor of the atmosphere and the reckless abandon with which reputations were attacked.

[24] The story of this guarantee is told in the following report of a trial about this matter, published in the NFP, July 11, 1925 (Schumpeter 1993, 95–96). It reads in full:

Vienna, July 11. (*Lawsuit against the former Minister of Finance Dr. Schumpeter.*) After repeated hearings (Verhandlungen) the judgment was handed down in writing in the law suit which the *Wiener Kaufmannsbank* through Dr. Joseph *Stein* had brought against the former Secretary of State for Finance Dr. Joseph *Schumpeter* and Dr. Joseph Maria *Braun-Stammfels*. In April 1922, the Glass Industry "Rudolfshütte" Inc. had intended to increase its capital and to this purpose a syndicate was formed of which Doktor Schumpeter and Dr. Braun-Stammfels were members. The latter informed the Wiener Kaufmannsbank that Doktor Schumpeter *did not have the sum of K1, 890,000,000* for the purchase of the shares and would try to *lend* him this sum. On April 10, Dr. Schumpeter handed over a signed letter with the payment obligations and got the money. Since this amount with interest had not been repaid, Dr. Schumpeter and Dr. Braun-Stammfels were sued. The proceedings against Dr. Braun-Stammfels are in abeyance for the time being. Dr. Pressburger representing Doktor Schumpeter objected that Dr. Schumpeter was of the opinion, on the basis of internal

In the testimony reproduced in the Report, Hofrat Stern stated further: "Dr. Kunwald is a lawyer, Vice President of the Biedermann Bank, and there he was the leader. During the auditing I noticed in particular the Schumpeter account because he owed a lot of money and because his foundations were the collateral."

Schumpeter agreed but added that until the beginning of 1924, everything "was perfectly in order" and that his account "was covered to a higher degree by marketable securities than any other customer's." It was only when the stock market crash reduced the value of the collateral by three-fourths that the problem arose. To cover the deficit, Schumpeter sold the better securities but was still left with an uncovered debt of M300,000. "The debt to the Biedermann bank was at first paid with the help of friends and then by my own labors in the course of a period of time which to live through I would not wish on any one of my enemies, but to which in moral respects I nevertheless look back with complete satisfaction."

Schumpeter's explanations were candid and obviously completely satisfactory to the Ministry of Education, which continued to press for Schumpeter's appointment. But before turning to the court interrogation in connection with the Braun-Stammfels trial, it must be stated that the whole Report and particularly the testimony of Hofrat Stern, one of the expert witnesses, was, to use his own insinuations, somewhat peculiar. Stern even found it suspicious that the Biedermann Bank was an investment bank, particularly as it was so small and insignificant.

Yet this was precisely what the *Oesterreichische Volkswirt*, which was famous for its annual reports analyses, liked. In its long analysis of the Annual Report for 1923, the *Oesterreichische Volkswirt* even suggested that the stockholders' report was written by Schumpeter himself.[25] It was precisely that the Biedermann Bank was not just another bank.

---

agreements with the syndicate members, to have been freed from all guarantee obligations; his guarantee were to apply only for the case that the Wiener Kaufmannsbank would give further credits to the "Rudolfshütte" for the expansion of facilities which, however, were not given so that Schumpeter's responsibility did not apply. During the last negotiations, Dr. Stein limited the suit to 194,963 S[chillings] with 8 percent interest which sum Dr. Pressburger recognized but whose objective relevance (dem Grund nach) he denied as Dr. Schumpeter had no reason to pay the debt of the syndicate since he had left the syndicate long before. Dr. Stein denied that there ever was an agreement that Dr. Schumpeter was responsible only for new deposits for the "Rudolfshütte" and insisted that the Letter of Guarantee explicitly stated that the guarantee applied to the sum which was intended for the payments of the previous advances to the "Rudolshütte." The judgment of the senate under the chairmanship of *Hofrat Dr. Fränkel went against Dr. Schumpeter for the payment of about 199,000 S* on the basis of the guarantee of the syndicate contract. (Italics in original; my translation. I do not know why Schumpeter's title was sometimes spelled out in full.)

[25] "[O]ne notices in each phrase that the author is a man who commands the heights of theoretical knowledge and is endowed with brilliant stylistic qualities." M. L. Biedermann & Co., Bank-Aktiengesellschaft. *Der Oesterreichische Volkswirt* vol. 15 no. 52, September 29, 1923. *Supplement Die Bilanzen*. This phrase suggests that the balance sheet analysis was written by Gustav Stolper.

When we changed the Banking House M. L. Biedermann & Co. into a Corporation we did not intend to add to the many young banks in Austria yet another younger one. What our founders, among them the unforgotten Dr. Wilhelm Rosenberg, intended was not to found yet another bank but a Bankhaus auf Aktien (i.e., an investment bank), a corporation which was to take over the 130 year old confidence in the Biedermann Bank as its most valuable asset and which was carefully to protect and develop in its new form as administrator of other peoples' wealth and as a valuable intermediary on the capital market which could not be bypassed."[26]

Schumpeter tried to get the secret reports of Hofrat Stern but was told that they no longer existed. Gustav Stolper tried to get information and wrote to Kunwald about the matter.[27] From Kunwald's answer, the following facts emerge. Hofrat Stern was "the social-democratic vice president and spiritus rector of the Banking Commission. . . . [t]he whole attack was originally directed against Minister Mataja, then, because the attacks against Mataja, who never had intervened for the Biedermann Bank and never received favors from the Biedermann Bank, proved to be false, against me personally because the socialists did not want to come out of this with empty hands." The rest of the letter deals with the unfair, unprovable attacks against Kunwald. The letter starts: "Sehr geehrter Herr Doktor, immediately after receiving your letter I tried to get the desired report of the Banking Commission. I do not have a copy. They are secret and I do not believe that I can get them. I myself have never seen them."

Gustav Stolper also sent a copy of Kunwald's letter to Ministerialdirektor Richter.[28] The covering letter states that Stolper, too, had written to Hofrat Stern, but had not received an answer.

The original Report and the Protocols of the Investigating Committee of which it was a part were found in the Archive of Parliament.[29]

The letter of transmission, dated November 14, 1925, when Schumpeter had already left for Bonn, was addressed to the Chairman of the Parliamentary Investigating Committee, President of the Nationalrat Dr. Franz Dinghofer. It is on the stationery of the Banking Commission, but with its normal address exed out and "Parliament" substituted.

[26] Stockholders Report for the 2. Stockholders Meeting. *Vorlagen zur II. ordentlichen Generalversammlung der M.L. Biedermann & Co Bankaktiengesellschaft. 4.August 1923. Geschäftsjahr 1. Jänner—31 Dezember 1922.* Selbstverlag der Gesellschaft, p. 9. Copy in the files of the Banking Commission, in the Archiv der Republic, Vienna.

[27] Letter of Gustav Stolper to G. Kunwald, dated January 21, 1932. Letter of G. Kunwald to Gustav Stolper, dated Vienna, January 27, 1932. Both in the Gustav Stolper papers in the Bundesarchiv, Koblentz.

[28] Letter dated January 29, 1932, in the Gustav Stolper papers in the Bundesarchiv, Koblentz.

[29] Austrian documents are preserved in various archives. Before thinking of looking for the Archive of Parliament I looked into the Archive of the Republik and the Verwaltungsarchiv (both of which are housed in the same building) and the Archive of the City and Land Vienna. The files of the Ministry of Justice are in the Verwaltungsarchiv, but the files of the court case are in the Archive of the City and Land Vienna in the Vienna City Hall.

The secret Report contains more detail than the printed investigation (see footnote 15 for precise reference), but the part dealing "with all relevant observations and conclusions which forced themselves on Hofrat Stern at an earlier audit and whose accuracy (Zutreffen) later events have completely confirmed is signed only by Hofrat Stern because they are based on inquiries undertaken by Hofrat Stern alone." This itself is peculiar. The other member (presumably Christian Social) refused to identify himself with Stern's report.

The letter of transmittal then continues: "Some of the collected detail might have undesirable effects if they were to be made public. The publication of the entire content of this [typewritten] document should, therefore, not be considered, particularly as the collection is intended solely to complete the information of Your Honor."

The Protocols of the Investigating Committee also suggest that many suspicions heaped on Schumpeter were based on hearsay. For example:

Representative Dr. Eisler: Did Dr. Schumpeter visit you in this matter?

Dr. Odehnal: I do not know Dr. Schumpeter at all (überhaupt nicht). I have never spoken a single word with him.

And perhaps characteristic of the whole atmosphere is the following exchange:

Rep. Dr. Eisler: How did the Department [in the Ministry of Finance] assure itself of the safety and worthiness of these Banks as depositories of public funds?

Ministerialrat Dr. Frank: For this there was a special Department IV, at the time under Ministerialrat Huber.

Rep. Dr. Eisler: . . . You told us yesterday that you got an order (Auftrag) from Sektionschef Hirth, and today you tell us that you believed the Biedermann Bank suitable because of its connection with the Anglo-Bank. Yesterday you said you did not think the Biedermann Bank suitable because . . .

M. R. Dr. Frank: I have not said "that it seemed not suitable." . . .

Rep. Dr. Eisler: You said you believe that Dr. Schumpeter made representation with Dr. Hirth, whereupon Dr. Hirth gave you an order. You were concerned and finally said: okay, let's see to it, but not more than a few hundred million kronen; and there was talk among the civil servants: well, this time one has also taken on a Christian establishment.

M. R. Dr. Frank: Yes. This was also said at the Zentralbank of German Savings Banks, because one believed the two to be Aryan.

Chairman: Dr. Hirth says he does not know Schumpeter.

M. R. Dr. Frank: It is now some years ago. I remember that I certainly have discussed this matter with Dr. Hirth. . . . I thought Schumpeter as President and former Secretary of State for Finances, Sektionschef Hirth as Chief of the Fiscal Section (Finanzabteilung), they probably did work together in the past—this was my combination (Kombination), thus this was very probably an influence of Schumpeter. That he made a personal representation, that was just my impression. There can be no question of certain knowledge.

Chairman: Since the file is not here at present . . . I have in the meantime taken the liberty to call upon Sektionschef Schwarzwald. . . .

M. R. Dr. Frank: I do not remember who approached me. I supposed that there was a community of interest (Interessengemeinschaft) between Schumpeter and Hirth.

Rep. Dr. Gürtler: Because of this supposition you went to see Schumpeter?

M. R. Dr. Frank: No. To deposit a few hundred million in a bank was something rather unimportant for me . . . I only know Schumpeter was mentioned to me and I was told: please notify him.

Rep. Dr. Gürtler: Who told you to notify the Schumpeter?

M. R. Dr. Frank: There was a submission from the Biedermann Bank. It was a question of freight business. To save endless correspondence I went there and told him: there are in Vienna 20–30 banks of your importance. If I give this credit business to all these banks, then I have to deal with the accounts of all 20 banks, and this won't do (geht nicht). Proof, that an undue influence on me by the Minister or a higher personality was certainly not exercised.

Rep. Dr. Gürtler: This deposition of a connection (Verkehr) of the former Minister Schumpeter with Minister Odehnal and Sektionschef Hirth is what vulgarly is called Civil Service Gossip.[30]

This extended excerpt from the secret hearings gives an idea of the atmosphere prevailing in Vienna at the time. It explains, I believe, why Schumpeter wanted to get away from it all, and why it is quite believable that he refused to follow Viennese newspapers—to which Karl Kraus referred contemptuously as "journaille."

Schumpeter was, of course, innocent but rumors continued and are not quite dead even today.

SCHUMPETER AS INVESTOR: THE JUDICIAL INTERROGATION

On March 10, 1928, the district attorney of Vienna (Staatsanwaltschaft Wien I) sent

[T]he files concerning Dr. Braun-Stammfels and others, and sends at the same time the indictment (Anklageschrift) against Dr. R. Braun-Stammfels and Franz Haller.

For the prosecution of the following:

Dr. Josef Schumpeter, Dr. Max Borowsky (and thirteen other names)

No reason has been found.[31]

The accusations were that Braun-Stammfels had "(a) in the years 1923 and 1924 negligently caused the insolvency of the three corporations mentioned

---

[30] Protokolle des Untersuchungsausschusses, pp. 219ff. of the file.

[31] The whole file is found in the court archives of the City and Land Vienna, in the City Hall of Vienna. The file number is S XVI 5689/24/27. The later file of Braun-Stammfels' appeal for clemency on the other hand is found in the Verwaltungsarchiv of the Republik.

[in the indictment] particularly by using credit frivolously and excessively; (b) that he has negligently damaged the creditors of the three mentioned corporations by incurring debts despite a knowledge of an inability to pay . . . and not started negotiations with his creditors (Ausgleichsverfahren) in time." The District Attorney presented a long justification for the indictment in which Schumpeter's name appeared several times.

Braun-Stammfels stated that he had been a wealthy man as the result of two inheritances and a prosperous law practice, a wealth still intact in 1920 and 1921. "During 1920 he decided" so the indictment "because of his relationship with the former Secretary of State for Finances Dr. Joseph Schumpeter to found industries in Austria which in view of the change in the domestic economic situation brought about by the peace treaty were to make Austria in important industries independent of foreign countries. This idea was undoubtedly correct."

The district attorney then turned to Braun-Stammfels' behavior in three industries, starting with particulars about the glassworks Rudolfshütte. When the completion of the factory was threatened, it was decided to double the capital. "For this purpose a guarantee syndicate was formed consisting of Dr. Braun-Stammfels, M. Gerstbauer, M. R. Meisels and Dr. J. Schumpeter. . . . Except for Dr. Schumpeter, the guarantee syndicate failed to fullfil its obligations to take over all shares which sealed the fate of the enterprise." Then follow several pages of justification in which Schumpeter's name does not appear. Then the district attorney continues:

> Now [Braun-Stammfels] had in the summer of 1922 made the acquaintance of Friedrich Mayer-Winterhalde, a young man from a good family who succeeded in bamboozling (an der Nase herumführen) the very much older Dr. Braun-Stammfels. . . . The continued procrastination (Zuwarten) of the accused Dr. Braun-Stammfels is the less explicable as he was practically warned against Mayer-Winterhalde by the former Secretary of State Dr. J. Schumpeter.

The Court File records that the court received the indictment on April 12, 1928. A document also in the files dated May 2, 1928 stated that Braun-Stammfels had already on November 14, 1927 requested to see the files to give him a chance to answer the accusations in detail, but that the court (Landesgericht) had not reacted. (Das Gesuch wurde nicht erledigt) "so that I did not even have the opportunity of a lawyer." The court proceedings started in June 1929. Braun-Stammfels was found guilty. He made an appeal for clemency in which he stated that he, who had been used to a comfortable life, was now totally ruined and reduced to emergency snow shoveling in the city. It seems at least in part a case of justice delayed is justice denied.

This is the background of Schumpeter's interrogation which started on April 24, 1925 and lasted for a few days, that is, before he had lost his fortune through the already mentioned guarantee to the Kaufmannsbank for the Rudolfshütte. Shortly after the interrogation he left for Bonn. The brief CV with which the document starts lists Schumpeter as Catholic, bank president by profession, wealthy (vermögend, propertied) and unmarried rather than divorced. The interrogation starts with general principles of Schumpeter's attitude toward the new companies, then goes into some specifics, and ends with answers to specific testimonies by Braun-Stammfels involving Schumpeter.

Schumpeter was a member of the founding syndicate of only two firms, the Wels Porzellan factory and the Glass Industry Rudolfshütte. He was also in the Verwaltungsrat of three other firms. He owned, however, shares in all firms, some of which he was forced to sell in 1924. He stated categorically that Braun-Stammfels had the general direction of the companies. "As far as I remember I was not on the executive committee of any of the companies, nor have I exercised a decisive influence on the activities of any of the firms. There were no founders profits and the like."

Schumpeter speaks rather gently of Braun-Stammfels, as he had earlier of Otto Bauer, although in both cases it would have been understandable if he had felt betrayed.[32] "Braun-Stammfels devoted his entire energy to his industries, and his industries were his whole raison d'être." But Schumpeter gave also more objective reasons for getting involved in Braun-Stammfels' companies than his schoolboy friendship.

> Above all, I consider all enterprises which he has founded economically correctly conceived, even independently of the fact that they would have produced real values, there was also a strong demand for the products which had to be satisfied by imports so that I considered the industries viable. I also liked the idea to finance industries without a close connection with a bank which is the usual method in Austria, a bank which normally receives a large part of the profits, particularly as this method of financing is usual in other countries, e.g., England.
>
> I also liked that as far as I know the founders made no initial profits as is frequently the case, but made the purchased objects available to the industries at the purchase price. That the industries did not flourish despite this sound basis was in my opinion caused by the absence of a firm capitalistic [sic] basis such as a bank connection provides, which was particularly felt by so young enterprises during the crisis at the beginning of 1924, since no money was available to help over the bad period, and that the industries, however well equipped technically, suffered from the absence of a good marketing direction since the Chief Executive Officer (Leiter) Dr. Braun-Stammfels just was not a merchant and hence was not very lucky in the practical execution of his in principle correct ideas and in the choice of the executive organs, etc.

The Welser Porzellan AG should have done well. With the rapid depreciation of the krone, however, more capital was needed. Braun-Stammfels made personal advances which were repaid in depreciated money. There was a syndicate in 1922 whose small profit consisted of a few gratis shares. The industry had the usual childhood diseases which were being overcome. One of

---

[32] Indeed, in a letter published by E. März he wrote that Braun-Stammfels had been lying to him about the state of the enterprises.

the problems was—as is the case in many an LDC—that foreign technical labor had to be hired for lack of domestic skills which required in turn provision for their housing. Another capital increase became necessary. Braun-Stammfels firmly believed in the future of his enterprises and refused to sell his shares at a profit.

The same import substitution ideas played a—in Schumpeter's view correct—role in the founding of the Glassindustrie Rudolfshütte. But one difficulty arose. The Ministry demanded cash financing and delayed permission to increase capital. Also, the inflation caused suppliers to refuse to fulfill their contracts without price increases. The progressive inflation had made the paid-in capital insufficient. So Braun-Stammfels got a credit from the Kaufmannsbank. This is where Schumpeter's troubles, detailed in the preceding section, had their origin. At the end of 1923, a new guarantee syndicate was organized but the Ministry did not like a capital increase for an as yet not working industry and dawdled over giving permission to issue shares. The shares were to be issued at a nominal value of K2,400, a sum on the basis of which the syndicate contract was made. The crux of Schumpeter's description was as follows (as it appears in the report of the Judicial Interrogation; see note 31):

> Now Dr. Braun-Stammfels, without consulting the syndicate, got the Ministry to permit a reduction of the share value to K1,500. He later presented this to the syndicate members, me included, . . . who considered the syndicate dissolved because its most important condition had fallen by the wayside and Dr. Braun-Stammfels had not got the consent of the syndicate members.
>
> I do not know the terms to which he has come with the other syndicate members. I myself, in order to contribute something, have at his request taken over a guarantee of about K1,800 million vis-à-vis the Kaufmannsbank, provided the latter would provide new means to that extent towards the completion of the Rudolfshütte. Dr. Braun stated to me that the Kaufmannsbank had obligated itself to actually make this sum available to the Rudolfshütte on the basis of my guarantee. I myself have not dealt with the Kaufmannsbank directly. Dr. Braun undertook in turn a countersecurity (Rückbürgschaft) towards myself.
>
> The Kaufmannsbank however has not made any sums available and has sued me for the sum in question. The proceedings are still under way.

Schumpeter then summarized why the Rudolfshütte got into difficulties. "The first was the progressive hyperinflation. The second was the failure of Mayer-Winterhalde to come up with the promised funds, which also prevented alternative financing. The consequence was a slowdown in construction, then a sudden need for funds which in the absence of bank connections necessitated taking credit under onerous conditions.

Third, "the ministry delayed its permission to raise capital for months. . . ."

Fourth, ". . . the Kaufmannsbank did not keep its promise for further credit though the expectation that it would grant further credit was justified since it would have been in its own interest to finish the enterprise. . . ."

"Finally, the onset of the crisis which temporarily considerably reduced all real values and disquieted all creditors so that no further credit could be got."

The interrogating judge asked why Braun-Stammfels had not immediately started negotiations with the creditors (Ausgleich). Schumpeter explained that he personally had been against trying to raise more capital at that time "since I considered it hopeless given the situation on the market," though he could not propose an alternative solution. But he also pointed out that the enterprise did not have an excessive debt burden if times had been more normal—it was valued at the time at K14 billion—and that it actually was a small creditor who threatened foreclosure. Schumpeter also pointed out that he had resigned from the Verwaltungsrat in May 1924.

The porcelain and glass factories were Schumpeter's two major investments, but there were also problems with other factories. Braun-Stammfels had put Schumpeter on the Verwaltungsrat without his knowledge. He also did not know, as Braun-Stammfels had stated, that he was on the executive committee of the Rudolfshütte, "in any case I have not received a single invitation to any meeting of the executive committee." He specifically denied that he had intervened at the Ministry of Finance. "Dr. Braun-Stammfels must be mistaken."

The interrogating judge showed Schumpeter further testimony of Braun-Stammfels. Schumpeter's answer was the sharpest denial he gave:

> The statement that Dr. Braun-Stammfels informed me almost daily about any important incidents in the factories and consulted me on all actions is false. I have visited him only about every week, he has consulted me essentially only about questions of tax law and increases in capital, given me always calming explanations about the state of the industries, but he has always left me in the dark (im Unklaren gelassen) about the peculiar bookkeeping entries, particularly that the monies were always moved from one industry to the next, also that credits given to the industries went through his account. Neither has he, with the exception of the profiteering loans (Schieberdarlehen) . . . consulted me about the conditions of the loans or informed me about them nor consulted me whether the loans should be accepted under the, as I later found out, very onerous conditions. Thus I thought until today that the credits of the Kaufmannsbank were perhaps 30–40%. That the cost was more than 100% I have not known.

Schumpeter's comment may serve as a fitting conclusion to this section: "I have always considered this refusal of further credit [by the Kaufmannsbank] the cause of the collapse since in my opinion none of the enterprises was excessively in debt considering the real value of the plants, and only the capital for the completion was unavailable."

The interrogating judge asked Schumpeter about other industries about which Braun-Stammfels had testified. Schumpeter again and again categorically denied having been consulted, and even more, having suggested a number of dubious uses of funds; and finally, denied the facts underlying his lawsuit with the Kaufmannsbank. Schumpeter explained:

> Dr. Braun has insisted to me that the Kaufmannsbank had obliged itself to finish the Rudolfshütte. Whether it really has done so I do not know. I have never been informed that Dr. Braun withdrew K2.7 billion from the Kaufmannsbank after I gave the guarantee and on the basis of it. Neither did I know that the sum was not used in its entirety for the Rudolsfshütte.

The picture that emerges from this account is quite clear. First, the court believed Schumpeter's testimony, his explanation of his industries as well as his version of events when they conflicted with Dr. Braun-Stammfels's testimony.

Second, on the theoretical level the justification for the industries was based on the kind of import substitution that was later made plausible by, for example, Arthur Lewis's famous *Report on the Industrialization of the Gold Coast*, or Albert Hirschmann's *The Strategy of Economic Growth*. The existence and size of imports is used as a substitute for market research, as proof of potential demand, not of course as justification for protection. There is therefore, third, nothing inconsistent with Schumpeter's general position as a free trader. Given the unreasonableness of the rest of the world and the impossibility of maintaining the old Monarchy as a kind of free trade area, this unreasonableness becomes a datum that must be accepted and decisions made on it.

It was the hyperinflation and the final denouement of the terrible situation in which Austria found itself after the lost war and the complete destruction of its capital which Schumpeter had tried unsuccessfully to prevent as minister of finance which did him in.

PART VI

The Theoretical Analysis
of Current Policies

or

Trying to Prevent Another Failure

I almost would have touched upon . . . fiscal questions which
have so great an importance . . . that one might almost say
that wherever things abroad and at home have not gone as
desired the ultimate reasons have been financial.

—*Schumpeter letter to Count Harrach, January 25, 1916*
(my translation)

Monetary Policies: The 1920s

THE THEORETICAL ROLE of money in an evolutionary environment has been described in chapter 4. Briefly, Schumpeter attached to money in a stationary economy only a role as a numéraire. In an evolutionary economy the function of money changed from a harmless muméraire to a not so harmless method of reallocating resources into new channels, and this meant—"as a matter of fact though not of logical necessity"—credit creation.

Schumpeter's policy observations in this context were made essentially in three periods. In the aftermath of the First World War, the problem was to reach monetary stability. This was not seen as merely stopping inflation but establishing the conditions which made stable money possible without undue cost.

This linked up immediately with fiscal and other economic policies and it found its climax, as it were, in the discussion when it made sense to establish a new central bank in postwar Austria, when to return to fixed foreign exchanges, and at what exchange rate. Schumpeter advocated fixed exchange rates and urged the return to the gold standard but only when the time was ripe and in the context of establishing general conditions favorable to evolution.

The second context was the Great Depression, mostly in the American context. The third was the Second World War and its immediate aftermath. Obviously, what he had to suggest is related by the same underlying theory.

POSTWAR STABILIZATION IN AUSTRIA

I have stressed before Schumpeter's view of the capital levy in 1919 as currency reform, as wiping out the monetary overhang before it could affect prices and distort the economy. Failure to wipe out the monetary overhang would also postpone reestablishing a fixed exchange rate.

The basic policy, once the monetary overhang was wiped out, had to be to reestablish the economy by increased savings and investments, and the formulation of a balanced budget by methods that would not crush all business initiative. Price and exchange rate stability was desirable but not at the cost of evolution.

This is not an argument for fluctuating exchanges. Fluctuating exchanges are part of what Schumpeter described as "capitalism in an oxygen tent." They are the result of ceasing to believe that the political will or the understanding of how a capitalist economy works exist to establish the conditions necessary for fixed exchanged rates. Schumpeter opposed deflationary policies and stressed the importance of proper fiscal policies.[1]

It remains to add four expressions of Schumpeter on the proper monetary and fiscal policies and their relation to growth, two of them made when he was already in Harvard. Two of them relate specifically to the Austrian situation, the other two are on a general level.

The first is contained in the already mentioned letter to Gulick. Schumpeter added a long paragraph about the capital levy which seemed to him much more interesting than the matter of the Alpine, and the political reasons for its failure, confirming that he saw it as a currency reform.

> In conditions of advanced inflation, which has, however, not yet taken full effect on prices, there is an argument for a capital levy which does not apply in other circumstances. For a few weeks I thought it possible to break the spiral of inflation by such a measure, but the idea had to be given up for two reasons. First, owing to the political alliance between socialists and Christian socialists, the agrarian sector would have to be practically exempted from its proper share in the burden. Secondly, socialist opinion was in favor in using the capital levy as a means of socialization. For both reasons the measure would have been futile as a means of combatting inflation. (Schumpeter 1992, 357–58)

Gulick made no use of this information.

TESTIMONY FOR THE U.S. SENATE IN 1924

The second comment is in a written testimony before the U.S. Senate.[2] Schumpeter is identified as "formerly Minister of Finance, president Biedermann Bank. Vienna," indicating that he had submitted the memorandum before his resignation as president in 1924. At the same time, Richard Reisch, Schumpeter's successor as minister of finance and identified as "formerly Minister of Finance, president of the Austrian National Bank (Oesterreichische Nationalbank)" also submitted a memorandum on "The Return to the Gold Standard in Austria."[3]

The contrast of the two memoranda is instructive. Reisch's submission is that of a technician; Schumpeter's is that of an economist and economic policy maker. Reisch explained that Austria-Hungary had been on a gold exchange standard. He explained the course of inflation, the "reorganization of Austria inaugurated by the League of Nations" (ibid.) and stressed that "[i]t was of vital importance to the Austrian economy that the prevailing gold

[1] See the detailed discussion in chapters 14, 15, and 20.

[2] J. A. Schumpeter, "The Currency Situation in Austria." United States Senate, Commission of Gold and Silver Inquiry, pursuant to S. Res. 469, 67th Congress, 4th Session, creating the Commission of Gold and Silver Inquiry. *European Currency and Finance. Foreign Currency and Exchange Investigation*. Serial 9. By John Parke Young Ph.D., 2 vols. Washington D.C. 1925. Testimony in vol. 2, 225–31. Reproduced in Schumpeter (1993), 63–70.

[3] Senate Document, 221–24.

value of the crown was permanently maintained." He explained the success of the stabilization action in 1923 and then added: "The development of the Austrian national bank in 1924 was also quite satisfactory, although it is true that the Austrian economy had to pass through a serious crisis in this year" (ibid., 223).

This is all about economic consequences. Reisch's testimony ends with a statement that "The Austrian National Bank is able to continue to maintain the present exchange rate for dollars. . . . We therefore are justified in hoping that the Austrian crown, if inflation of uncovered notes can be avoided in the future as it has up to the present, will remain at the present rate of exchange with the dollar and thus with gold" (ibid., 224).

Schumpeter, too, started with the background, but pointed out that the pre–1914 Austro-Hungarian bank "was expressly forbidden to grant any credit to the government" (Schumpeter 1993, 63).

He then briefly referred to what was later called *the* Schumpeter Order. There were actually two relevant Orders, the first issued shortly before Schumpeter became minister.

> Soon after the breakdown of the Monarchy in 1918 the Succession States proceeded . . . to construct monetary systems of their own. The new Austrian state had to follow suit. This was done by the orders of February 27 and March 25, 1919, according to which the notes then in the hands of the public in Austria were marked with a stamp. (ibid., 63–64)

In the lawsuit mentioned in chapter 14, the circumstances which made the orders necessary had not been mentioned, an instance of Schumpeter's insistence that legal categories really made sense only in a legal framework.

By 1922, the situation had deteriorated so much that

> [T]he government could submit to foreign control. . . . The program of reconstruction was essentially a program of economic liberalism. . . . Not to raise the value of the crown. . . . Not to delay stabilization until the budget could be balanced, [and to stabilize] at nearly the lowest point the crown had ever dropped to . . . since November 18, 1922 no more notes have been issued against Government securities. (ibid., 64–65)

This was essentially Schumpeter's program as minister, which he could not press through, perhaps "because the situation had not yet sufficiently deteriorated." The legal stabilization of the crown came only later.

What was the outlook for the economy? As far as the monetary system was concerned, only the technical matter of defining the value of the crown in terms of gold remained, "whilst everything that is essential has already been completed" (ibid., 68). Convertibility with gold "barring a new international catastrophe, would very soon be perfectly feasible."

> But, of course, the problem lies deeper, and the real question is whether the economic conditions of Austria are such as would justify a reasonable hope that, given the absence of serious disturbance in central Europe, a sound currency

system based on gold, when once established, will not be upset again, but continue to function by its own momentum and without further extraneous help.
There need be no danger from the side of the federal budget. (ibid., 68)

This economic and not merely technical question was not asked by Reisch. Schumpeter proceeded to estimate the wealth of the new Austria at no more than a fourth of prewar Austria (ibid.). Given this fact, the budget authorized by the League of Nations representative was quite reasonable.

But "the system of taxation has been thus far very harmful to saving and enterprise" (ibid., 69), and Austria was in a severe depression, with the bank rate having been raised from 12 to 15% (ibid.). The foreign capital inflow had been essential, yet "only a fraction . . . went for productive purposes . . . consumption was to a considerable extent financed out of capital in 1923" (ibid.).

Then comes the conclusion of the last paragraph which, though optimistically formulated, is in fact deeply pessimistic in its assessment of the Austrian economy. There is not a hint of this in Reisch's submission.

> Conditions in Austrian trade, industry, and finance are, of course, unfavorable, owing to the crisis; bankruptcies are frequent, and the figures of unemployment are on the increase. But it is difficult to say to what extent these troubles are only of a temporary nature . . . and to what extent, though brought on by the crisis, they are due to the consequences, in their nature lasting, of the breaking up of the great economic unit covered by the old monarchy. Industry hampered by want of capital, by heavy or clumsy taxation, in many instances by the backwardness of methods of production, by the level of wages, not high if taken absolutely but too high considering the low efficiency of the workmen, hampered also by the comparative insignificance of the home market, by the strongly nationalistic policy of some of its most important customers and by the superiority of German competition, must necessarily go through a difficult process of adaptation, in some respects of reduction. Vienna's position as a financial and commercial center, although impaired, is still an asset of great importance, but exactly to what extent Vienna will be able to hold her own it is too early to say. Much will depend both as regards its industrial as well as its financial position on the success or failure in securing the cooperation of foreign capital, In this respect chances seem to be fair. The stability of the crown, the quiet social atmosphere, the balanced state of parties, excluding any dangers of violent political experiments in either direction, the absence of foreign ambitions, and the high rate of interest should prove sufficiently attractive to foreign capital, the immigration of which would automatically solve many of the problems mentioned. (ibid., 70)

Already in 1924 Schumpeter had raised alarms about the Austrian situation.[4] The budgetary situation as sketched by the financial experts of the League of Nations was in the aggregate realistic, but its structure was all wrong, with the result "that the burden [of taxation] appears much more

---

[4] "Der Weg zur stabilen Wirtschaft," Schumpeter (1993), 58–60.

oppressive than the same revenues need be. *In particular, all scholars agree that a reduction of the corporation income tax would probably not reduce its returns*" (ibid. Italics in original; my translation).

The real danger came from the balance of payments, which would impose severe restrictions on consumption. The ultimate root of the situation was the low productivity of the Austrian economy, particularly of agriculture, "where there were areas in which agriculture was still on the level of Roman times" (ibid., 59).

In addition, fiscal policy was bad. And new investment into existing enterprises was hampered because a possible revaluation of old debts (which parliament never enacted) would relegate new investments to a secondary status.

Many of the questions raised by Schumpeter have a frightening relevance to the American conditions of the 1980s and 1990s. Schumpeter, in 1924, might have said: "I told you so in 1919." But it was, of course, only half of Schumpeter's proposed policies. The inflation was halted by the drastic step of ceasing to provide any credit to the government. But an easier monetary policy was still not possible because the budget was balanced without enacting the proper tax structure. In other words, it was an anti-inflationary but not a pro-growth policy.

The opinions about stabilization policies were expressed much more strongly in Schumpeter's critical discussion of Keynes's *Tract on Monetary Reform*, which also appeared in 1925. In this discussion Schumpeter's assessment of the Austrian problem is really quite brutal: "[In Austria] one has first of all established sound money, i.e. one has stabilized the krone in the hope that everything else would right itself as a result. The result was a crisis of such vehemence that the successful stabilization of the monetary system ex post almost seemed a failure" (Schumpeter 1993, 84 note 1).

KEYNES'S TRACT ON MONETARY REFORM AND THE RETURN TO A CAPITALIST ECONOMY

Some time in 1924 or 1925, Schumpeter gave a lecture in Rotterdam on "Old and New Bank Policy" which afterwards was published in Dutch. Professor Wagener dates the speech before April 28, 1925, the date when England and several other countries returned to the gold standard, while Schumpeter's talk still pleaded for such a return.[5]

Schumpeter worked out in detail what at first appears as a sharp disagreement on monetary theory and policy but which is in effect a strong plea for the reestablishment of a working capitalist economy. He stressed that he did not

[5] "Oude en nieuwe bankpolitiek. I, II, III" *Economisch-Statistische Berichten* 10, 1925. Schumpeter must have given the speech in German or in English since he could read Dutch only slowly with a dictionary, as he wrote to Redvers Opie. A German translation is printed in Schumpeter (1993), 70–93. An introduction by Prof. Wagener, "Schumpeters Keynes Attacke und die Niederländischen Monetaristen," is found in ibid., 12–17.

disagree with Keynes's theory of money, but with his theory of the business cycle:

> [I]n his talk to the Annual Meeting of the Royal Economic Society in June 1924, Keynes challenged his opponents to state precisely to what extent they could agree with his diagnosis.
>
> I consider it wrong, not because I doubt that cyclical fluctuations could be prevented with measures of credit policy. Nor because I deny the assertion that the increase of the price level during the prosperity phase and the decline during the depression must have their immediate cause in monetary events. But simply because I believe that both the prosperity and the depression period have an essential function and that in this the expansion and contraction of credit plays an essential role which is difficult to replace. In other words, I do not consider Keynes' monetary but his business cycle theory wrong. (ibid., 86–87)[6]

Schumpeter starts agreeing with Keynes on monetary theory: no metallic base is necessary for money, the gold standard works quite imperfectly and is up to a point also a managed currency. However, for Keynes the stabilization of the price level rather than of the exchange rate should be the aim of monetary policy. But

> [T]he basic idea of the reform goes much further and deeper and does not depend on any particular objective: the idea to develop bank policy as a general therapy of the economy, to develop it as an instrument by means of which the economy may be regulated consciously and according to a particular scheme. . . . [This, as well as] Keynes' scientific motivation, put his proposals sky high above other reform proposals. Besides the basic ideas and methods are original. (ibid., 80)

The new policy would use the same instruments as the old one had. But under the old policy, they were mere instruments to allow an automatic working of the monetary system.

> Under the new regime on the other hand the interventions become the principle. The automatism is abolished in principle. In this manner the capitalist society gets a central organ which decides consciously and according to a fixed schema what has to be done and whose nervous system (Nervenstränge) are precisely the

---

[6] My translation. In his *Treatise on Money* (1930), Keynes wrote:

Apart from the many minor reasons why [fixed investments] should fluctuate in a changing world, Professor Schumpeter's explanation of the major movements may be unreservedly accepted. . . . It is only necessary to add to this that the pace at which the innovating entrepreneurs will be able to carry their projects into execution at a cost in interest which is not deterrent to them will depend on the degree of complaisance of those responsible for the banking system. Thus whilst the stimulus for a Credit Inflation comes from outside the Banking System, it remains a monetary phenomenon in the sense that it only occurs if the monetary machine is allowed to respond to the stimulus. (Keynes 1930, vol. 2, 95, 96)

This almost sounds like a response to Schumpeter's comments in 1925, except that it is very unlikely that Keynes read the Dutch version. He may however have been informed about it. In any case, Keynes quoted Mitchell's summary of Schumpeter's theory, not Schumpeter himself.

instruments of bank policy. Keynes wishes in addition to strengthen the effect by an adaptation of note circulation according to a fixed schema. (ibid., 81)

This startling characterization of Keynes's position reads like the monetarist prescription to let the circulation of money—say M2—change at a constant rate, which would make Keynes a "premature" monetarist! Schumpeter sounds optimistic about the possibility to do everything Keynes—or for that matter today's monetarists—want. "If bank policy gets the form which [Keynes] wishes one can change any prosperity into a depression and any depression into a prosperity" (ibid.). Of course, Schumpeter later became considerably less sanguine on this score when he characterized the notion of the powers of the Federal Reserve "ludicrously" exaggerated (Clemence 1951, 206–15). And the monetarists keep criticizing the Federal Reserve for missing their monetary targets when perhaps it was not really possible to do so except in a completely socialized economy (whose actual track record, however, on this as on every other score was worse).

There is in the final analysis no particular aim, not even the aim of aiding individual industries or even firms which could not be made the target of monetary policy. "This is no longer management of the monetary system, it is management of the whole economy without any one being able to draw the line. It means a considerable restriction of private initiative on principle (wesentlich) and a strong deviation from the principles of private property and free competition" (Schumpeter 1993, 83).

It is in fact part of "The March into Socialism" where the same points are made as an ineluctable development of capitalist society. However, in the Dutch talk Schumpeter limited himself to following the ideas of the *Tract* to their ultimate logical consequences, specifically, to the discussion of price policy. There are two points: there are many reasons for inflation or deflation—which a "credit policy directed towards specific aims could mitigate. But then the danger arises that the adaptation to a new situation becomes more difficult" (ibid., 84).

Schumpeter was quite sure that depressions of the future would become milder—that is, provided policy or war did not interfere. There was increased statistical knowledge and theoretical understanding of the economy which allowed businesspeople to make better decisions.[7] But the growth of large-scale enterprise would also mitigate the severity of cycles because it could afford to and would in fact make investment decisions on the basis of longer-term considerations.

The kind of price movements later analyzed in Schumpeter's second ap-

---

[7] This point is also developed in two newspaper articles on "Konjunkturforschung," *Berliner Börsen-Courier*, April 4 and 7, 1925, on the occasion of the founding of the Deutsche Institut für Konjunkturforschung, whose first director was Ernst Wagemann. Schumpeter pointed out that the business world had as so often preceded academia by recognizing that it needed better information about the surroundings in which it had to operate and which it could not directly control (Schumpeter 1993, 163–73).

proximation could be profitably eliminated, but not other price fluctuations which had essential functions for the workings of the capitalist economy. Schumpeter proceeded to outline his cyclical theory and the role of money which played an essential role therein.

It is this context in which Schumpeter's advocacy of a quick return to the gold standard must be seen, and of course only after the preconditions for a stable exchange rate have been established. Maintaining fluctuating exchanges in this context meant avoidance of the necessary adaptive processes. "The return to the gold standard has nothing to do with deflation, for the relation at which this return is to happen is in principle arbitrary" (ibid., 91).

People were scared that too much gold had accumulated in the United States which might monetize it and drag other countries into its inflation. Schumpeter thought this an unrealistic misunderstanding of American policy. But even if it happened, a small rise of American prices would lead to a flow of goods to the United States, and the *real* danger was that the Americans would not let this happen and become protectionistic.[8]

The real problem with fluctuating exchanges was not that they might allow an economy to make a policy that was exclusively determined by domestic needs—I do believe that this possibility is, in Schumpeter's later words, ludicrously exaggerated; the real point is quite different:

> Looking at our argumentation as a whole one observes at every step that the return to gold is not a measure which is meaningful exclusively from a monetary standpoint. Gold and its movements are precisely to the extent that they are automatic or at least tend to become automatic the very mechanism . . . to solve a number of non-monetary economic, political and social problems. The free gold standard can help Europe to master its crisis, it can facilitate America's growing into its new role, it can bring peoples closer to each other, it can enforce peaceful cooperation with the penalty of immediately felt disadvantages, it can help disadvantaged groups of workers to improve their living conditions and much more. Even though the gold standard by itself is no ideal, how can one condemn it in the very moment in which it can provide for mankind an enormous—perhaps its last—service? (ibid., 93)

So there it is. The problem is seen in a very wide context of preserving a world of private decision making to ensure continuing growth of the economy and with it continuing improvements of the lot of the poor. And it brings out also the radical difference to monetarists among whom the Keynes of the *Tract* must be counted. Substituting a rate of growth of the supply of money however defined, trying to make this a "rule" is itself probably not only not very realistic, it is in fact weakening the role of rules in favor of more discretion, of a central control of the economy. This leads inevitably to further radical "rules"

---

[8] Keynes made the same analysis of the post–Second World War situation in his posthumous article on the American balance of payments.

like amending the Constitution to prevent federal budget deficits, which, of course, would do nothing of the kind. It would be circumvented as was the Gramm-Rudman-Hollings budget agreement by all the exceptions which in a "turbulent" world would necessarily have to be made. Monetarism and fluctuating exchanges may be the best that can be done. But even if it were feasible, it also shows how far even the American economy has proceeded on its March into socialism.

"Gold Does Not Lie"

Lest this be seen as an exaggeration, it is precisely what Schumpeter said in 1941 had happened.[9] Schumpeter even stated that he would have preferred a greenback inflation to one printed on gold, which was possible because of the enormous gold influx into the United States, for then "every one would know what is happening" (ibid., 72).

The issue was not that the gold standard worked only imperfectly. The real point was that it had "one particular property which characterized it and which fitted the social systems that prevailed [before 1914]."

> As long as you had money in . . . your bank, through which you could acquire . . . a quantity of gold, as long as banks and government were in dutybound to redeem their obligations in gold, that puts a frame on their behavior. . . . In this particular restriction . . . lies the whole importance of the gold standard as far as domestic affairs of a nation go. But gold had also . . . an important international function. It equalized balances of payments and brought price levels of different countries in relation to each other, the price levels and also the interest rates.
>
> Again, if a banking system or a government or a country did something that, *looked at from the standards of the time,* was unsound, this would have caused an outflow of gold, and as long as a government respected its promise to redeem gold, that would have had the consequence to stop the offending practice. And this is the true meaning of the international gold standard. . . . like Supreme Courts and Constitutions, gold was a restriction on the freedom of action of government. It was in that sense, though in no other, a safeguard of the freedom of a nation, of individual freedom.
>
> [P]recisely because of this role that gold played and precisely because of its implications that that role carries, gold was an element of capitalist society, of contract capitalism.
>
> What now has changed since 1914 is that these things are precisely no longer recognized either by government or by a large sector of public opinion. . . . In a planned economy, therefore, the essential functions of gold are no longer filled.
>
> I have told you that gold has had a bad breath among many economists and

[9] "The Future of Gold" address given to the Detroit Economic Club, April 14, 1941. Reprinted in Schumpeter (1993), 70–78.

politicians all along, but it had that bad breath less because of the various shortcomings that it displayed in its working; it had that bad breath precisely because *it always tells the truth* . . . about the state of finances and fiscal organism of the country in question, *and that is precisely, in a planned economy, what it is not allowed to do*. (ibid., 72–74; italics added)

When the Second World War ended, Bretton Woods tried to reconstruct a pre–1914 world. The International Monetary Fund (IMF) was supposed to establish monetary stability, with rules for divergent behavior. The International Bank for Reconstruction and Development (IBRD) was supposed to regulate international capital movements. The Havanna Charter was supposed to establish free trade. Though the Havanna Charter did not become reality, the General Agreement on Trade and Tariffs (GATT) did fulfill this role for a long time. But as soon as real problems arose, the system broke down. The fact that it was the conservative President Nixon who closed the gold window (with the overwhelming approval of the economics profession) and that it is conservative economists like Milton Friedman who advocate fluctuating exchanges, or conservative (in the American sense of the word, though in his own eyes he is a liberal) economists like Hayek who even want to abolish central banks, prove to what extent Schumpeter's prediction of the coming of socialism has already been fulfilled. Whether he would criticize Friedman for it, as he did Hayek, or would praise him as a man who recognizes what cannot be changed and tries to preserve as much individual freedom and as many human values as possible may remain open.

Monetary Policy: The Great Depression and the Post–Second World War Inflation

WRITING AND TALKING are linear processes. But reality, certainly economic reality, is circular as well. Things are interrelated in time, and any purely linear account of necessity requires that "other things" are kept temporarily equal but certainly not forgotten. All of Schumpeter's policy discussions are characterized by seeing them in the developmental context.

The discussion of Keynes's *Tract* seems to deal with relatively harmless distinctions as compared to what happened during the Great Depression or the post–Second World War boom. Yet the fundamental framework is always the same: the underlying view of how the real capitalist economy works.

During the Great Depression Schumpeter always stressed the developmental framework, including the incipient three-cycle scheme, to deal with *facts* as they had developed over the last 100–150 years, and not, let it be repeated, as a theoretical explanation. Schumpeter was concerned at all times that monetary policy had to be seen simultaneously in the context of cyclical developments and fiscal policies.

At the Christmas meetings of the American Economic Association in 1930, Schumpeter talked about "The Present World Depression: A Tentative Diagnosis" (reprinted in Clemence 1951). Schumpeter there raised the question "whether the present world depression can . . . be attributed to a number of unfortunate events which interrupted what otherwise would have been continued prosperity or at least an even flow of economic life" (ibid., 96). There were, of course, special factors of which Schumpeter mentions the severity of the agricultural depression. In 1930, he brought the latter into the context, on the one hand, of the changed agricultural production functions (and to that extent they were part of the normal industrial cycle), but also into the context of protectionist European agricultural policies which from the American standpoint were "unfortunate events."

But, while it was "easy to exaggerate the influence of monetary policy . . . [y]et it is obvious that if a monetary system exactly equal in all particulars to the pre-war system were introduced, prices would have to come down to a level lower than that of 1913." England's return to gold at the prewar parity with its subsequent necessary deflationary policies is cited as proof (ibid., 97). In other words, there was some contributing and unnecessary deflationary policy.

In 1930, Schumpeter still blamed the depression—which in retrospect was still a pretty mild affair compared with what came later—on changes in the economy, some of which were by his standards pathological (a word he did not use) like sticky wages, rigid prices, and long-term interest rates which did not fall immediately with short-term rates.

Nevertheless, the importance of these factors, particularly the last one, should not be exaggerated (ibid., 98). There was also the stock exchange crash, the difficulties with installment debt and protectionist tariff policy. In 1930, Schumpeter thought "that there is no difficulty to devise on the basis of this diagnosis remedies both for the situation in general and for any particular feature of it" (ibid., 99). But he did not spell out the measures he had in mind. At the time, Schumpeter was as yet only a guest in the United States.

In early 1932, Schumpeter discussed "Crisis Policy in America by Means of Credit Therapy."[1] The *Deutsche Volkswirt* had published a number of articles on the American situation by Gottfried Haberler and George Katona to which Schumpeter referred. As was his habit, Schumpeter started with the actual situation and why the earlier forecasts of a rapid return to prosperity— "prosperity is just around the corner"—were disproved by events.

Schumpeter thought that "in retrospect . . . the known characteristics of the situation at the end of 1930 justified this prognosis" (Schumpeter 1985, 212). Two things were overlooked: the seriousness of extra-economic sources of disturbances,[2] and "a period of abnormal and temporary prosperity which made an abnormally high level of prosperity seem normal. The optimism based on both these circumstances crippled the will to therapy and particularly to prophylaxis. This was not the case in any other threatened country" (ibid., 211).

Schumpeter referred to the 1880s for similar developments. The 1980s would do as well: in both cases, excessive real estate and land speculation, excessive expansion of consumer and business indebtedness. There was also the absence of any substantial aid to help the broad masses or specially threatened sectors—except, as everywhere, agriculture.

> Even more important is that the firing of workers when the cycle turns down occurs with much fewer qualms (unbedenklich) than with us with the consequence that because of the absence of any kind of unemployment insurance of our type, aside from moral and social consequences . . . the continuity of demand for goods is much more severely interrupted than with us and that so more firings of workers follow the first. (ibid., 211–12)

Schumpeter referred to the "firm belief in the all-powerfulness of credit policy" (ibid., 213), for which the 1990s present a recent example. And, of

---

[1] "Kreditpolitische Krisentherapie." *Der Deutsche Volkswirt* vol. 6 (1931–32). Reprinted in Schumpeter (1985), 210–18. Page references in the text are to the reprint. My translations.

[2] Schumpeter mentions none. However, I remember that the so-called Hoover moratorium temporarily suspending German reparations payments, which came to nought because of French objections, was at the time considered a statesman's successful measure to deal with one of these major disturbances, and that its failure was felt to have pushed the world further into the abyss. Reparations were, of course, only one disturbing element.

course, there had been a stock market crash in 1929. In such a situation, what can credit policy do?

> Essentially three things: It can mitigate symptoms and momentary unbearable suffering. This is most easily achieved if the resources set free by business are directed into the hands of State and communities whose expenditures will partly take the place of the decreased private expenditures. Secondly, it can try to prevent panics, bankruptcies and losses for credit-technical or foreign exchange-technical reasons which would make the inevitable even worse. But thirdly, and this is the most important achievement, it can keep the credit system itself in working order. (ibid., 215)

Thus there is a proposition of some budget deficits and social policy, which is old Schumpeterianism, provided they were handled carefully and temporarily when the need arose. But Schumpeter also talked about the danger to the dollar by an outflow of foreign funds—which was of major concern in Germany and is or should be of major concern in the United States of the 1990s. A danger to the banking system was successfully averted by the Glass-Steagall bill which had improved the liquidity of the banks. But there was also the important matter of limiting the effect of the bill in time. In other words, Schumpeter approved of the use of government securities as a basis for issuing money, but wanted eventually to return to a purer gold standard.

> It is in this context that the opposition of the President [Hoover] becomes understandable that the elimination of the budget deficit was the precondition for an extensive action of help. By themselves, savings measures and tax increases in the middle of a crisis are, of course, nonsensical. But consideration of the literally incalculable consequences which would lead to a breakdown of the faith in the financial stability of the Federal Government and a panic of the foreign exchanges let both appear in a different light, particularly as the stupid (talentlos) and demagogic reach to an income tax of, in the highest brackets, absurd height must not be laid at the door of the Administration. (ibid., 216–17)

The basic characteristics of this analysis have, I believe, mutatis mutandis, direct applicability to present-day problems. Thus, Schumpeter stated that "*the outflow of foreign deposits has come to an end*" (ibid., 217; italics in original), so that foreign liabilities were now substantially smaller than foreign assets (which is the reverse of the situation in 1990) while member banks could continue to accumulate reserves. "This has largely justified the credit policy which must be considered successful" (ibid.). There was a substantial process of healing "which yet may mean little in the face of all domestic or foreign dangers which may stop and even destroy all that has been achieved (ibid.).

Thus, this is a careful analysis of what credit policy can and cannot do, a policy that must also be seen in the context of budgetary policy. Deficits are fine provided they do not become policy themselves. It is in effect advocating substantial improvements in the institutional framework of banking to allow an easier monetary policy while pursuing a stricter budgetary policy—which is exactly the opposite of American policy in the 1980s. It is a policy which would have preserved the foreign value of the dollar, which was sacrificed under President Nixon.

On October 22, 1932, Schumpeter wrote to Carl Snyder in the same vein:

> My dear Snyder,
>
> [I] . . . confess that I should be sorry to see the weight of your name added to the long list of theorists who have sinned by overestimating the monetary approach to things. I very much feel that we are in these questions very much in the same position as modern physics in that we are confronted by facts which admit of many explanations, the choice between which must rest on other criteria as our experimental findings will not speak clearly. (Harvard University Archive)

Schumpeter had written to Hawtry that the enormous expansion of bank reserves without effect on the cyclical situation showed the limited power of monetary phenomena. But, of course, the large reserves allowed an enormous monetary expansion once business improved again and presented an inflationary danger. It was this danger which was the basis of Schumpeter's criticism of much New Deal policy. Schumpeter had referred to this danger *before* the New Deal in the letter to Irving Fisher of February 10, 1933, of which I quoted the beginning earlier and the continuation of which I want to quote in extenso.

> I would first start from the assumption that the stage is set for a revival and that the only difficulty now lies in the fact that the shrinkage of prices and volumes has by this time become an automatic process. If this be true, then all business wants is a small fillip, and I think that this could be given to it without any inflation in the sense of increasing the sum total of deposits already existing simply by getting them to move. This could be done by the issue of Federal loans, the proceeds of which could be spent for additional unemployment relief, a measure from which almost immediate effects might be expected provided business knew that a certain amount of expenditure for unemployment relief would be forthcoming during, say, the next six months.
>
> But now I come to the danger which I fear much more than any protraction of the present situation: I think that as soon as the slightest upturn shows itself, as soon as business people feel that this upturn is going to last for some time, as it would necessarily in a case like this, all the rest of the inactive deposits together with all the credit made possible by the surplus reserves of banks and by the hoarded money in the pockets of the people, would throw itself on stocks and commodities, and we should have an inflation the results of which would be liquidated by a similar crisis again as the present one. Now in order to prevent that I should think it necessary to provide at the time of the issue of the Federal loan, for increased revenue sufficient to pay back that loan in, say, four to five years. The best means to do it would be, I think, by a sales tax. And now you see my difficulty. You see, first, that I quite agree with you on the necessity of a fillip to

business and to some measure of reflation. Yet I could not support it without some such measure as the sales tax and without some guarantee that the reflation started would be kept in hand.

When I saw you in New Haven you spoke about raising the price level to about mid-way between now and 1929. I have no objection to this. My reluctance of saying so comes only from the practical difficulty of making sure that the thing would stop at this point. With this proviso, however, I do think that I have the satisfaction of agreeing with you. I may add that a measure of reflation such as that outlined above would be possible without going off the gold standard and disturbing the exchanges and that German experience leads me to believe that raising revenue by a sales tax to the requisite amount would not be felt by anyone whilst the raising of the same amount by a progressive income tax would seriously interfere with the accumulation of funds necessary for reconstruction.

Schumpeter always saw policy prescription in a historic context. In his contribution to *The Economics of the Recovery Program* he gave a brief account of past "crises" of 1825 in England and 1873 in the United States (Clemence 1951). They really first formulate Schumpeter's cyclical explanation of the course of history. I forego repeating what has been said before except for the following: "[i]t is of utmost importance to realize that the only distinctive characteristic of the present world crisis . . . which makes it *fundamentally* and not only quantitatively differ from such crises as those of 1825 and 1873 is the fact that non-economic causes play the dominant role in the drama" (ibid., 114; italics in original).

So what can be done?

First, removal of extraeconomic injuries to the economic organism: mostly impossible on political grounds.

Second, relief: not only imperative on moral and social grounds, but also an important means to keep up the current of economic life and to steady demand, although no cure for fundamental causes.

Third, remedies: The chief difficulty . . . lies in the fact that depressions are not simply evils which we might attempt to suppress but—perhaps undesirable— forms of something which has to be done, mainly adjustment to previous economic change.

Fourth, reform of institutions not intended to *remedy* the situation but *suggested* by the moral and economic evils of both booms and depressions. (ibid., 115; italics in original)[3]

The crux of all this analysis is that

[O]ur story provides a *presumption* against remedial measures which work through money and credit. For the trouble is fundamentally *not* with money and

---

[3] Schumpeter recounted how during the 1920s it was impossible to get one's teeth filled without a discussion of the stock market boom, and how all decent discussion languished in the faculty club for the same reason. In these respects he only spoke of the "beneficial depression."

credit, and policies are particularly apt to keep up and add to maladjustments and to produce additional trouble in the future.

Finally . . . it is . . . wrong to believe that the evils of depressions are all of them inevitable and that the only sound policy consists in doing nothing. There is no single and simple remedy. The numerous problems . . . must be dealt with individually and patiently. The kind of activity which is clamored for in such situations is likely to make matters worse. But all those features of depressions which spell widespread suffering and needless waste can be taken care of. Especially if a country has steadily improved its public finances during prosperity as the United States did in the decade which preceded the present crisis, enough means are available, and other means can be procured, for an expenditure which will blot out the worst things without injury to the economic organism, *provided only* that action on this line is taken promptly and followed up by equally sound fiscal habits as soon as recovery gets under way. (ibid., 117; italics in original)

It would burst the limits of space to quote all the letters and writings which expound on these matters. Thus, in a letter to Gilbert Walker of May 19, 1937, which dealt mostly with the problems of measuring the volume of savings, Schumpeter proposed "a dear money policy whilst the boom lasts and public works when recession comes. . . . [This] would go a long way to mitigate fluctuations whilst the process itself should not be fought as a matter of principle."

During the Great Depression, Schumpeter was mainly concerned with remedial measures. By the time of the Second World War, his thoughts turned mainly to prevention. In a letter to Irving Fisher of December 6, 1940, Schumpeter explained to his friend why he could not support his reform proposals:

I see, of course the force of your argument. So far as that goes there are only two points which would induce me to qualify assent. First, I do not attach to monetary reform the same importance as you do and I am hence always apprehensive of the danger that monetary issues may obscure more fundamental ones. Do not misunderstand me. National disaster may occasionally come from the monetary side. But such disaster mostly comes from the irresponsible handling of the existing monetary machine itself. Secondly, like Robertson, I do not believe that the alternating expansions and contractions in the credit structure as far as they proceed from business transactions only are without function.

But my real objection is my frank and unqualified distrust in the monetary authority that according to your plan would control the nation's monetary supply. I realize that according to your idea it would function automatically. As a matter of fact, however, it would be an organ of the government and under political influence and hence could not be expected to function according to the principles which you have traced out for it. To put it bluntly, I think it would simply turn out to be a huge engine of inflation.

I am awfully sorry to have to take this stand. You must know how much I would prefer to agree with you. (Harvard University Archives)

And in a letter to Fisher of March 17, 1942, Schumpeter concisely formulated his objections to New Deal policy as one of confiscating savings and pursuing an anti-saving policy:

I am frankly concerned to gather from your letter that you have been almost ignoring the oversaving theories of depressions. The anti-savings humor of the country which was not created by Keynes but on the contrary created the success of his book, will necessarily stand in the way of your argument unless you make a frontal attack on it. The New Deal tendency to confiscate savings as much as possible has, of course, its roots in a wish to make industry entirely dependent upon state controlled credit during the reconstruction period after the war and thus to open the road for a permanent system of state socialism. This is the only explanation I have to offer for the persistent anti-saving humor in Washington which on the face of it is perfectly irrational. For it should be obvious to everyone (it has become so to Keynes since the outbreak of the war) that at present saving should be fostered and that in fact intensive saving is under the present circumstances the only means of avoiding wild inflation. Observe that this should be obvious even to those who during the world depression advocated measures hostile to saving. Myself, I should at present advocate a fiscal policy favorable not only to saving but to hoarding. The taxation of corporations I should confine to dividends paid out so that undistributed profits would go entirely free. And, of course, I am a strong advocate of the sales tax. But this is precisely what the Washington set-up wishes to avoid by hook and by crook. So the sponsors of Keynesian views are going on preaching the policy which Keynes espoused during and after the depression though for the situation that mow exists, Keynes' teaching does no longer lend any support to a policy hostile to saving: witness his plan of paying wage increases in claims on the future.

I do not think I have modified my views in this matter. . . . If I were you I should not so much attack the oversavings view itself as emphasize that, the situation being changed into its very opposite, the anti-savings views do no longer apply even if we concede that there is a certain measure of truth in them for situations of underemployment of labor and real capital. (Harvard University Archives)

Indeed, Schumpeter refused to join an anti-Keynes expression in a letter to Walter F. Spahr of February 1, 1941, although Schumpeter approved of and indeed belonged to the Economists' National Committee on Monetary Policy which urged return to "sound money." The letter dealt also with some current justification of the "loose financial methods of the past decade."

The loose financial methods of the past decade need only to be extended over a prolonged war, and national failure will follow.

Now in this argument there is one element of truth. If expenditure were rigorously kept in hand and if everything were most responsibly managed, in particular if wage costs were kept down and the working day extended, if agrarian subsidies were discontinued, and if the anti-saving policy were replaced by a pro-saving policy—for instance, exempting from taxation undivided profits of corporations—it would in fact be possible to keep war inflation within bounds and to avoid economic and social disorganization. But one need only look at those conditions in order to realize how little likelihood there is for their being fulfilled.

But there is more to this. We have heard from Washington the voice of several economists who, incredible though it sounds, stick to their anti-saving views and seem to be advocating loose spending as they did during the past decade. Keynes may be in error on a number of points but he is after all an able and responsible man. He recognized the complete change of scenery and has accordingly reversed his position. But his followers on this side of the water go on with the slogans they once learned and the chance that they will prevail is considerable because what they are preaching is after all the line of least resistance that will appeal to the politician. (Harvard University Archives)

Richard A. Musgrave confirms that Keynes during his wartime Washington visits argued that the postwar problem would be a capital shortage.[4] And Gottfried Haberler remembers that there were attempts to prevent the publication of Keynes's posthumous paper on the American Balance of Payments.

Schumpeter's main concern about money was always that it might not be allowed to fulfill its function to finance growth but, through financing primarily consumption, would lead to inflationary conditions which certainly were not desirable. So the last discussion I want to expound is his 1948 essay, "There Is Still Time to Stop Inflation" (Clemence 1951, 236–47).

The first point made is that the post–First World War inflations were simply processes. "All of them were the result of war finance and could have been stopped within a year or two. But they were not stopped because the people who counted politically did not *want* to stop them" (ibid., 236; italics in original).

Now Schumpeter distinguishes for argument's sake three phases. "*Incipient inflation*: Newly created money in the hands of government will be spent immediately. But in the hands of the private sector will first be used to repay debts and strengthen the cash position" (ibid., 238). This is a phase of latent inflation. Even government expenditures in an underemployed situation will raise output, and inflation may make thus little impression.

Advanced inflation starts when the first phase is finished. Money will be spent and thus leads to further borrowing. Schumpeter stresses that the analysis of what happens during this phase "is not peculiar to any group of economists but the common property of all" (ibid., 239).

When *wild inflation* starts, habits of handling money change and "increasing paper profits are paralleled by real losses" (ibid., 240). The United States is far from a wild inflation. "Yet two characteristics of this behavior are observable: the race between wages and prices has started; and the Federal Reserve

___

[4] In a thus far unpublished paper given in Stuttgart, Germany, in September 1991.

system has had to meet a growing demand for redemption of maturing government issues" (ibid.). This monetization of debt is still normal, but a definite danger signal.

Now Schumpeter repeats what he had stressed before: Measures that promise success at a given moment may be futile a few months later.

Schumpeter groups the measures to combat advanced inflation, that is, a phase in which there is increased spending of newly created money rather than a strengthening of cash positions and a repayment of debts, under four headings. But two things should be kept in mind. First, there is no single remedy for the disease. Second, it is not possible to stop advanced inflation without producing some symptoms of depression (ibid., 241).

To start with, there should be no rollback of prices.

1. *Direct control of prices, consumption, and production* deals with symptoms, not causes. It has never worked. But in individual cases such controls "may do more good than harm" (ibid.). . . .

3. *Credit Restrictions*: Those of us who believe that return to the principles of private enterprise will most speedily repair the ravages of the war realize, of course, that this implies the re-establishment of a normal money market. Accordingly some advocate that cheap-money policies should be abandoned, that interest rates should be allowed to find their level, and that the Federal Reserve system should rely on discount policy, open market operations, and the other methods of traditional money-market control. . . .

[No] serious economist has ever denied that such regulative powers are necessary if excesses of lending and the consequent breakdowns are to be avoided (ibid., 242).

But at present these regulative powers of the Federal Reserve system are paralyzed. Moderate increases in discount rates have little effect in inflation" (ibid., 243). Commercial banks hold a huge amount of Government paper which could be monetized which means that there is a large measure of latent inflation. "The poorest credit restriction scheme is in such circumstances better than none. Most of the proposed schemes . . . would do something to improve the situation" although all such restrictive measures carry disadvantages and dangers" (ibid.). Evidently it would be undesirable to restrict industry's ability to borrow for plant improvement "which could sacrifice the future to the present" (ibid.). However, credit restrictions could be directed toward consumer and mortgage credit.

This would mitigate inflation and at the same time take account of the truth that the best remedy for inflation is increase in production" (ibid.). But this requires that production increase by more than credit which would require a larger supply of labor which in the face of full employment would mean "more hours and better quality of work" (ibid., 244).

But Schumpeter placed in these circumstances most emphasis on the fourth point, *Public Finance*, which leads to Schumpeter's views of fiscal policy for growth, the final aspect of Schumpeter's policy views. His articles in the *Deutsche Volkswirt*, which will be considered after this analysis of the situation in 1948 (see chapter 24), may be described precisely as tax policy from an evolutionary standpoint.

In 1948, Schumpeter pointed out that "curtailment of public expenditures sufficient to produce a substantial budgetary surplus is the most orthodox of all means to fight inflation. But ordinarily it is also the most difficult to adopt" (ibid., 244). And indeed he had already pointed out in the 1920s that changed social situations make such a reduction for civilian demand impossible. Of course, a changed political situation may lead to what nowadays is called a peace dividend. He certainly would in the 1990s vigorously defend severe cuts in defence spending, and in 1948 he was doubtful about Marshall Plan expenditures.[5]

Schumpeter's central point, however, was that the structure of taxes had to be changed: "As a rule, effective retrenchment involves rationalization of the whole apparatus of the federal, state, and local governments and restriction of many government activities, both of which are sure to be resisted" (ibid.).

There should be tax relief, but to have an anti-inflationary effect it would have to be so as to induce saving and investment. If it induced further consumption, it would, of course, not be anti-inflationary. The first is "an old proposal . . . to exempt savings from income taxes" (ibid., 245). An expenditure tax would do so; exemption of undistributed corporate profits would do so. And there should be a reduction of corporate and individual income taxes (ibid.).

"To sum up" Schumpeter's position on anti-inflationary policy:

> It is not possible to stop inflation in its tracks without creating a depression that may be too much for our political system to withstand. But it *is* possible to make the process die out, and in such a way as to avoid a depression of unbearable proportions.
>
> Direct controls are futile except as temporary measures in individual cases.
>
> Reduction of the mass of money by Stalin's method or by a capital levy is out of the question.
>
> Credit restriction is necessary to the extent indicated but not sufficient by itself. It must be supplemented by a pro-saving fiscal policy and by an attitude to public expenditures that is prepared to fight for every dollar.
>
> If we add the proviso "except for emergencies" then all we shall achieve is that politicians will style any occasion to spend as an emergency. (ibid., 246)

[5] It might be recalled that at the time such authors as Thomas (later Lord) Balogh believed that Marshall Plan expenditures were required to maintain American prosperity, and that in the face of the only budgetary surpluses which the post–Second World War period ever produced!

Fiscal Policy

In 1926–27, Schumpeter wrote six articles on fiscal policy in the *Deutsche Volkswirt*. His friend Gustav Stolper had informed him of and asked for his advice in the founding of the new weekly, and he wanted Schumpeter to contribute twice a month, mentioning that he wished him to do for the *Volkswirt* what Keynes did for *The Nation*.

Schumpeter, who had already contributed to the *Berliner Börsencourier* at Stolper's request, had been enthusiastic: "I wish such a sphere of activity (Wirkungskreis) and what I really want is to teach a large audience economic thinking, which . . . in my opinion is best done in the form of dealing with the questions of the day and their analysis with always the same basic principles."[1]

Gustav Stolper offered Schumpeter the choice of any subject matter, including sociological problems and the review of important books.

"Fiscal Policy Is Economic Policy"

So, starting with the first issue, Schumpeter wrote six articles on fiscal policy in the *Deutsche Volkswirt*, followed by eight articles two years later. The second of these articles stressed Schumpeter's overarching vision: "Above all, fiscal policy is economic policy. The two cannot be separated. It is as impossible to make a successful fiscal policy without clarity about one's economic policy aims, as it is impossible to make a successful economic policy without regard to the public finances" (Schumpeter 1985, 63–70).

Thus, the first set of articles does not so much discuss individual taxes as the proper tax system for growth which is accepted as the primary policy aim rather than equity or fairness. However, in Schumpeter's view the two are not incompatible. In fact, as he never ceased to point out, the real conflict was not between labor and capital, but between the present and the future. And it should really be evident that a conflict between growth and equity could arise only in equilibrium situations under conditions of perfect competition. In a suboptimal situation, no such conflict need arise.

In important cases, however, growth of the economy will hurt a particular factor. This raises the problem of compensation. It is not sufficient to argue

---

[1] Letter dated May 28, 1926, in the Stolper papers in the Bundesarchiv, Koblentz. The first issue of the *Deutsche Volkswirt* appeared on October 1, 1926, and it included the first of Schumpeter's articles. Schumpeter's and Stolper's letters are reprinted in Schumpeter (1985), 34. All quotations are my translations.

that because total income has grown it is possible for the gainers to compensate the losers and still be better off. It is also necessary to show that in fact a method exists which will allow such a redistribution without reducing the total to be redistributed. Without such a method, the new situation cannot automatically be considered to be "better." If it does exist, it is a political question whether in fact such a redistribution should take place.[2]

Evolution introduces the further complication of intergenerational comparisons in historical, that is, irreversible time. People age, become more difficult to reemploy at the old wages, and so on. In Schumpeter's first approximation (see chapter 5), evolution will temporarily reduce total consumption. Not so in the second and third approximations. Who specifically will be hurt depends theoretically on further assumptions as to the original situation and in reality on the specifics of evolution and the structure of the economy. In such a case, some redistribution which, for example, is implied in the so-called social market economy becomes necessary, among other reasons also to maintain incomes when new goods enter the market. This was certainly Schumpeter's position.

There is the important additional point that only a productive economy can afford a decent social policy and only an evolutionary economy can produce substantially increasing incomes. In any case, after the devastations of the First World War and the hyperinflation capital formation and growth were evidently needed just to get back to pre–1914 levels. But even from a fairness-equity standpoint, it is the total system of revenues and expenditures which matters and not the effect of taxes seen in isolation—a point also stressed in the 1950s by Musgrave.

> [Fiscal policy] is never a specialty like veterinary legislation . . . but—and this is its fascination and difficulty without which fiscal policy is simply bumbling of civil servants (Referentenstümperei) and the academic discipline of public finance the most boring thing on God's earth—it is always the resumé of all social, political, cultural, economic and foreign situations (Lebensverhältnisse) and relations of a people, and its success or failure, its correctness or falsity, and its greatness or inadequacy depends upon whether it is based on correct diagnoses of all these things and whether it translates the diagnoses correctly into fiscal policy.[3]

There is also the Schumpeterian characteristic to recognize the existing political and economic situation, of how it has become what it is, where decisions about future aims are possible, and where reversals simply are not feasible. It seems quite clear that these articles were conceived as a unity: as fiscal policy for development.

The first of these articles ("Taxable Capacity and National Future," Schumpeter 1985, 57–63) tried to define the limits of taxing power, but not in the

---

[2] This is my own view, one that is not shared by many competent economists whom I respect, who insist that there must be an actual compensation.

[3] Ibid., 63. I have made no attempt to break up this exceedingly long sentence to make it more readable in English in order to give the flavor of some aspects of Schumpeter's German style, which was as good as his English.

profoundly superficial (if this oxomoronic formulation be permitted) of what has since become known as the Laffer curve. The argument of the so-called Laffer curve is twofold: lower (income) tax rates would yield the same or higher revenue. This limit to taxing power was relegated by Schumpeter to a footnote in the *Crisis*, and dismissed as old hat and unimportant.

But the second aspect was that lower tax rates would stimulate investments to such an extent that the resulting growth would increase tax yields and the tax cuts would be self-financing. It should be noted that the discussion is entirely in terms of aggregates. But this was not what Schumpeter talked about. At the time the German budget showed surpluses. In fact, Schumpeter wrote that the situation was *not yet* dangerous but would become so without fiscal reform: "Among the questions which not only are wrongly answered but even incorrectly posed is also the question of the fiscal possibilities, the question what fiscal effort (Leistung) can be demanded of a people without endangering the possibility of that effort over time (auf die Dauer), the question of taxable capacity" (ibid., 56). The Schumpeterian prescription is not to cut expenditures—this is explicitly stated—but *actually* to change the *structure* of taxation, to favor savings instead of consumption.

So the first of the six articles starts with an estimate of required capital formation, then develops, on the example of reparations payments, the concept of the dead weight loss of taxation—the word itself is not used though the concept is abundantly clear. This went beyond the discussion of the so-called secondary burden of reparations, that is, the price changes that were necessary to actually transfer the payments. But Schumpeter's point is that it is quite inadequate to discuss the burden of any tax—or anything else—simply by considering only its size. The limit of taxation, that is, the size of the taxable capacity, is determined by the moment in which taxation affects adversely the savings necessary to finance expansion of productive capacity. And that leads quite naturally to a consideration of the structure of taxation.

There was, Schumpeter thought, no sense in advocating a substantial reduction of expenditures since it was obvious that the German people wanted all the government services (ibid., 62). It was trite simply to *council* a savings policy. What counted was to implement such a policy. The best individual measure would be a gentle treatment of savings, if possible the complete exemption from taxation of savings. And this was technically and politically quite feasible. (ibid., 62; italics in original).

But this will not be enough. There was already a dangerous movement away from a capitalistic economy. The tax burden of the time was incompatible with capitalistic motives. There was no sense to hope for a return to the nineteenth century. The trouble was that it was *impossible* to reduce the total tax burden, and this would lead to a situation in which people did not even *want* to do so. Hence, new forms of taxation had to be found which would solve these problems.[4]

---

[4] This is a paraphrase of the last paragraph (pp. 62–63), but the underlined words are italicized in the original.

These ideas are developed in the second article of the series on fiscal policy. The problem is clearly posed at the beginning and the end of the article: How can we *"restructure the fiscal system so that it is changed from a leaden weight to a motor?"* (ibid., 64; italics in original). To illustrate the political problems as well as the achievements of good fiscal policies, Schumpeter briefly described Colbert's and Poincaré's successes in France, the Prussian policies in the nineteenth century, and Gladstone's policy, a version of which in the *History* I reported on before.

The greatness of all these policies lay not in new ideas and new measures, but in developing a fiscal policy which expressed the needs of the existing social system (ibid., 66). All fiscal measures got their meaning from this recognition. The point seems important because it so distinguishes Schumpeter's analysis from even Hayek's and certainly Mises': There is the awareness of a historical situation, of given data. There is regret that the past is gone but no vain desire to get back to it. And here is perhaps also the explanation of Schumpeter's hatred—the word seems not too strong—for New Deal policies and what he would have felt about the actual Reaganomics (as distinct from the rhetoric) which must have seemed to him to start a process from which there would be no return.

Here we also meet Schumpeter's praise for the income tax—"the great tax idea of the liberal era" (ibid., 67)—*provided* it is kept low. But to apply it to modern times with its high rates is totally inadequate. It would be analogous to a physician who applied a successful treatment for cancer to tuberculosis (ibid.).[5] The precise aims of the political situation must be understood before a successful fiscal policy can be made.

The next question to be settled was the degree of federalism desired. This was at the time a hotly debated topic, and there was a strong movement to convert the federal into a unitary State. The situation was (and Schumpeter discussed this in the same article) that the Reich of 1871 was born with a wrong tax system which did not give enough tax sources to the Reich. This flaw was corrected in 1919 by the so-called Erzberger Reforms which allocated the income tax to the central government. But this reform had the crucial flaw that its structure was all wrong.

Schumpeter's last two comments are central to his views and also give a clue to his later American discomfort about New Deal policy:

> 3. We must know that we cannot reverse *social developments* and that a significant reduction of total demands on Government is an illusion.* To be sure we must save, but only to produce as big a surplus over the cost of the governmental machine as possible which we need just as much as Colbert, but not for court and army but, in keeping with the changed power structure, for other purposes.
>
> 4. Finally we must know that we do not have a *competitive economy* whose fiscal-policy child was the income tax, but a *more and more thoroughly organized planned economy* in which it would be more sensible (zweckmässig) for the

---

[5] The specific discussion of the income tax appeared two years later.

State to take its yield directly instead of letting it be paid out as incomes in order to run after it with great cost to the State and unbearable chicanery to the citizens.

---

*This illusion is dangerous precisely to those circles that love them. It leads to a dream life of fiscal policy and a fiscal policy of basic lies, (Lebenslügen)[6]—to valueless apparent successes and bad disappointments. (ibid., 69–70; italics in original)

This analysis gives, I believe, a clue to Schumpeter's happiness in the United States in the 1920s which turned into dismay under the New Deal that struck many observers and friends as almost irrational. It went much beyond his lifelong preference for a sales tax and his dislike of "unsound" monetary policy. He saw in the 1920s and early 1930s in America a country which, in his view, had entered the First World War as a moral duty and not for economic gain, slid through effects of the stock market boom, excessive land and other speculations and other faulty policies into a depression, and became what Europe already was.

But it is equally evident that while he would have understood the yearning for the past in what passes in the United States as supply-side economics, he would also in some desperation have pointed out that this was a *Lebenslüge* and not the way to go. "There is still time to" change direction, but it was rapidly running out, then as it is now.

The ideas expressed in the Secret Memoranda about the need for strong leadership and public support are developed for the German situation of the 1920s by comparing the English Cabinet with the American presidential system. The basic conclusion is that the two differ more in form than in substance. There must be a "strong and free executive power" (ibid., 70) but that comes from public support and can only indirectly be safeguarded by legal provisions. And there is an accusation against academic economics, reminiscent of Keynes's observation of the power of long dead scribblers: "German [economic] science shares the guilt in this matter, for it trains the lobbyists who make the opinion of the [political] parties from whose mouths come the wrong arguments.[7] The science has other great achievements but it does not adequately teach the technique of economic thinking" (ibid., 74).

The article on "Spirit and Technique of Fiscal Administration" (ibid., 77–83) draws the administrative consequences from the changed situation. As long as income tax rates were low it had made sense, in case of disputes between the tax authorities and the citizen, to make disputed payments and settle the case later. But such a procedure becomes a serious burden on the taxpayer and objectively harms the economy which is still based on private

---

[6] The term "Lebenslüge" is not in Langenscheidt's Encyclopaedic Dictionary. It comes from Ibsen's *Enemy of the People*. It means a big self-deception necessary to go on living. In Ibsen it refers to the democratic Lebenslüge that the majority is always right, even in scientific matters.

[7] Here we meet perhaps for the first time the "intellectuals" for whom Schumpeter expressed such distaste in *Capitalism*.

property and private enterprise. Schumpeter's main suggestion is to apply civil rather than criminal law procedures to tax disputes.[8]

Schumpeter considered his two articles on intergovernmental fiscal relations (Finanzausgleich) the best then existing treatment of the problem, "objectively . . . certainly the most really thought-through discussion of the problem"[9] though he still thought it not quite satisfactory. It was also a big success: The German Städtetag (Mayors' Conference?) ordered 1,000 reprints for distribution to its members.[10]

There is one overarching idea: the problem of intergovernmental fiscal relations is unavoidable regardless of constitutional arrangements except in a city state. Hence, the principle should be that whoever is responsible for a task should also have the fiscal means and the responsibility for the execution of the task.

But there are some caveats: the fiscal needs of the central government must always be adequately considered. Most important, any task mandated by the Reich must be financed by the Reich. This refers particularly to unemployment relief.

At the time, the question of tax oases was very much debated. Schumpeter was unequivocally in favor of them. They were part of communal autonomy. They were a safeguard against fiscal demagoguery. The argument is political competition:

> One community will try to be attractive by low taxation, the *other* will just then offer great communal services; each of them will be forced . . . to consider the point of view of the other. . . . Not only the legal *possibility* of oases is essential but also their *real* existence, because only the actual existence of tax oases . . . [puts] an automatic brake for tax demagogic excesses. (ibid., 89; italics in original)

Schumpeter was from the first concerned with certain abuses. Given the strong progression of the federal income tax, he was against piggy-back income taxes and even more against lowering the taxable minimum. One of the sections which even breathes a certain amount of positive passion is Schumpeter's defense of "wasteful" municipal spending on beautifying their cities. The "waste" of cities in this direction is questioned: these cultural activities were an expression of municipal pride, dangerous only if they provably "destroy an otherwise existing equilibrium" (ibid., 91). In 1927, Schumpeter did not find any such case, though he looked for them. This, however, was hardly the case

---

[8] It is clear that Schumpeter would consider the emphasis on strengthening enforcement of income tax laws and easier criminal prosecution of offenders as a method of raising tax revenues in most cases a symptom of policy failure.

[9] Letter to Gustav Stolper, March 15, 1927. In the Stolper papers in the Bundesarchiv, Koblentz.

[10] Letter from Gustav Stolper to Schumpeter, August 12, 1927. In the Bundesarchiv, Koblentz.

later when municipalities were rightly chastised for excessive foreign borrowing to finance stadia and the like.[11]

The first of the two articles on intergovernmental fiscal relations deals with principles. In the second Schumpeter turns to specifics. He starts repeating: How can expressions of a desirable city culture best be fulfilled? So it is logical that Schumpeter first lists the conditions for a proper municipal fiscal system.

Of course, any reform must start from the *existing* situation. The Reich, and this was said before, must finance the activities which it mandates. Transfers from the Reich to the Länder and municipalities are limited to cases where re-sponsibility for the tasks are not unambiguously formulated. Municipal finances must not damage the fiscal system of the Reich. The revenues of the municipalities must increase substantially. Municipalities must have several taxes at their disposal; they must have substantial freedom to chose.

The last condition is an adaptation of Schumpeter's views of a developing economy. For private households and businesses the money to be spent must first be gotten hold of. To translate this into public finances means that "a tax increase [should not be a] pure pleasure for the politician" (ibid., 92).

Schumpeter next turns to particulars. Schumpeter favored consumption taxes, particularly luxury taxes and taxes on alcoholic beverages. These were the only taxes which he without hesitation considered suitable for simultaneous exploitation by all levels of government. Since Schumpeter smoked and drank, kept an excellent wine cellar, and liked to live a comfortable and elegant life, any suggestions that these proposals were expressions of a puritan sourpuss are quite off the mark.

Among the direct taxes Schumpeter favored the exclusive use for municipalities of the tax on house rents (Hauszinssteuer, Schumpeter 1985, 94) assuming at the same time the gradual elimination of rent controls. The discussion of this tax has three aspects: the tax object is more than any other part of the life of the community (ibid., 95). It is at least partly shifted to ground rents, the consequences of which for growth were in Schumpeter's opinion at that time less serious than that of any other tax. At the same time he favored "a privileged treatment of housing for the poor" and " . . . also for families with many children within the framework of the total tax load on the yield of houses" (ibid.). This was an argument for some progressivity.

Schumpeter had argued early on that taxing ground rents did not interfere

---

[11] Schumpeter refers in the text to Pericles and Eubolus in whose budgets the cultural expressions played a much bigger role and whose methods of financing "particularly of the latter" were substantially more disagreeable than those of today's municipalities. Schumpeter adds in a footnote: "Nevertheless Eubolus would have to be called a conservative in today's terminology. This is just how a conservativism would look like which can live politically—and create Athens." Eubolus in 355 B.C. de facto dissolved the Attic Naval League. He was the representative of the peace party in Athens. (My wisdom comes from Karl Plötz, *Auszug aus der Geschichte*, 1928 edition. I do not myself know anything else. The classic reference to Eubolus would, however, have been readily understood in the 1920s when the Humanmistische Gymnasium still flourished.)

with development. So the reference to shifting was relevant. He also saw no irreconcilable conflict between development and equity objectives except in equilibrium situations. So his point that the structure of this particular tax could serve social purposes is also relevant.

The only necessary control of municipal behavior Schumpeter saw in an independent monitoring organization which would report not to the Reich but to the public.

Unlike his discussion of municipalities, the discussion of the Länder finances lacks much passion, perhaps even sympathy. Much of this ambiguity was due to the already mentioned fact that at the time there was a serious debate about a unitary versus a federal state and more immediately, if a federal state was maintained, just what the rights and duties of the individual Länder should be.

Schumpeter saw the existing system of Länder finances untenable in the longer run. Except for the tax on alcoholic beverages already mentioned, there is virtually no discussion of the problem of Länder finances and it is quite clear that this was due to the existing uncertainties about the future political organization of the Reich.

GROWTH EFFECTS OF INDIVIDUAL TAXES

Because of his visit in America, there is a hiatus in Schumpeter's contributions to the *Deutsche Volkswirt*. But late in 1928, he returned to the discussion of individual taxes starting with the inheritance tax.

When the second series of articles dealing with individual taxes appeared at the end of 1928, the German economic situation had ominously deteriorated. The expansion of 1925 had more or less stopped by 1927, Federal budget surpluses of 1924 and 1925 had disappeared, and it was the *Socialist* Minister of Finance Hilferding who desperately tried to undo the harm the bourgeois parties had done. This fact was "particularly shameful for the nonsocialist parties whose force and ability fell short of the simplest expectations" (ibid., 100), a criticism which Schumpeter and the *Oesterreichische Volkswirt* had made before in Austria.

About the same time Gustav Stolper had published his proposal for fiscal reform which was an expression of the Schumpeterian views.[12] Schumpeter's criticisms of his beloved England were relevant to the German situation: there were a million unemployed in England. Gradually the insight had gained

[12] G. Stolper, *Ein Finanzplan. Vorschläge zur Deutschen Finanzreform*, 1929. Its nine chapters appeared originally in the *Deutsche Volkswirt* between June 21 and August 30, 1929. Schumpeter's first articles appeared before the publication of Stolper's Plan, but the last ones commented on and identified with the Plan. Schumpeter and Gustav Stolper agreed on economic matters, theoretical and policy, but had at times strong disagreements about political matters. For example, Schumpeter opposed, Stolper supported, the Anschluss. Later Schumpeter opposed New Deal policies, while Stolper largely supported them.

acceptance there that perhaps the wage level had something to do with this. But gradually the insight would have to dawn upon people that

> [T]he stubbornness with which the number of unemployed remains so high for so long has something to do with the tax system, and particularly with the income and inheritance tax. The astonishingly high capital exports despite the reduced total of savings would most regrettably fit this picture.
>
> In *Germany there cannot be the slightest doubt from any standpoint—and particularly not from the socialist point of view—that accelerated capital formation is not only the basic necessity but, considering the drying up of foreign credits which must be expected, also the immediate practical necessity.* (ibid., 102; italics in original)

Capital formation is *"the economically decisive standpoint for judging today's fiscal policy"* (ibid.; italics in original). In an article on "Limits of Wage Policy" ["Grenzen der Lohnpolitik"], Schumpeter had also stressed that the real conflict was not between labor and capital—a formulation which he repeated several times—but between the present and the future (ibid., 192). Workers had as much interest in the future as capital. And in this article we find out how strongly Schumpeter viewed the existing economy already an organized one, "durchorganisiert":

> [The] sacrifice is, however, not where it is usually looked for, namely, a cut in wages, but in the circumstance that, because the reserves are typically used to expand the productive apparatus, the supply of consumption goods is temporarily smaller *than it otherwise would or could be: It must and it will* eventually be the case that employers and employees will "sit together" in order then to consult *uno actu about wages, capital formation and tax burden.* (ibid., 195–96. Italics in original; my translation)

It is logical that Schumpeter should start with a consideration of the inheritance tax, for the primary effect of a good tax should be to support savings and capital formation.

The inheritance tax can affect existing capital, as well as the motivation for future capital formation. Both are serious drawbacks of the tax which do not apply to a current (laufend) tax on wealth. The difference is that while the tax object is the same, an inheritance tax is usually paid out of capital while a wealth tax is paid out of income.

> As long as an inheritance tax remains a true inheritance tax it always involves a conversion of capital into income, hence an act of economic waste which is damaging to all. If it is structured so that it does not do so more than any other tax it ceases to be an inheritance tax but is a current wealth tax, in which case there is no *more* reason to distinguish between inherited and earned income. (ibid., 104; italics in original)

The basic motivation that might be harmed is the desire to create a family position "that tendency to accumulate in order *not* to consume" (ibid., 105;

italics in original). This might be different in another hundred years, but it is still important.

Of course, if there were no alternatives to cover the budget deficit an increase in the inheritance tax would have to be considered. But as long as this is not the case, hardly anything can be said for the inheritance tax proper.

Schumpeter was always a proponent of a sales tax to solve the fiscal aspects of the problem of capital formation. In "Who Pays the Sales Tax" ["Wen trifft die Umsatzsteurer?"], he starts with the German situation, deploring that the German turnover tax had been successively reduced from 2.5 percent in 1923 to 0.75 percent in 1926 with a simultaneous abolition of luxury taxes (ibid., 107–12). Neither the reduction nor an increase to the former level would be noticed by anyone. Arguments against it were political, not economic. This is still true today. Much of the opposition against a value-added tax (VAT) comes from an unholy alliance of the right and the left, the former opposing the tax precisely because it is so easy to collect and yields so much revenue (which might tempt government to increase spending too freely); the latter because of its supposed regressivity.[13]

A major purpose of this article was to teach the readers something about tax shifting and the economic processes through which tax shifting proceeded. In his opinion, an increase in the tax from 0.75 percent to 1.5 percent left the turnover tax proportional, and in any case its universality did not really make it an indirect tax.

He did not deny certain difficulties, for example, that the tax did not affect own consumption (which at the time was more widespread than now)[14] and that it raised problems in international trade. The VAT successfully meets the last difficulty.

Schumpeter does not consider the VAT or the problem of cascading in this article, but he does so in his lectures[15] where he considers briefly the Austrian

[13] Schumpeter's arguments were, of course, not in terms of a value-added tax, but in terms of a turnover tax. He thought perhaps also of the Austrian approximation to a VAT known as *Phasenumsatzsteuer* which he discussed in his lectures but not specifically in his *Deutsche Volkswirt* articles. On the other hand, Gustav Stolper specifically proposed the *Phasenumsatzsteuer* as part of his tax reform package, which Schumpeter supported.

[14] This point illustrates Schumpeter's insistence that a (moderate) income tax was *the* ideal tax for a healthy intact capitalism, illustrated by the Gladstonian era and policy. When such a stage of economic development has not yet been reached, such an income tax is technically virtually impossible—see the case of many LDCs where the income tax can be collected only from civil servants and a few foreigners. But an indirect tax in LDCs also meets with very narrow limits precisely because a reversal to subsistence production is quite feasible. Of course, the productive use of any tax collected plays a major role in defining the economically justifiable limits of taxation in LDCs. The problem exists also in developed countries where it appears on other levels.

Imputed rents of owner-occupied houses are part of the income tax base in some European countries. If the income tax is *the* tax of a bourgeois society, the sales tax evidently is *the* tax for an economy whose major problem is capital formation.

[15] I have the typewritten lecture notes on Schumpeter's course on Public Finance, Finanzwissenschaft, given in Bonn in the winter semester of 1928–1929. The notes were made by the renowned Cläre Tisch, which guarantees their accuracy.

approximation to the VAT, the Phasenumsatzsteuer, or phased turnover tax, in which commodities were grouped according to the number of phases they ran through from raw material to finished product, with tax rates applying to a phase or group, and the cascaded rate never amounting to more than 5–5.5 percent.[16]

A general sales tax shared with the income tax that in principle, if not always in fact, all sources were taxed equally. All taxes could be partly shifted, none were shifted entirely. Exceptions are mentioned but not important or realistic.

Generality of a tax reduces its shiftability but does not eliminate it. There will be changes in the structure of production. Complete shifting would involve a general price rise which a "sound" monetary policy would make impossible. So there will be a tendency—Schumpeter mentions Alfred Marshall in this context—to shift production toward industries working under conditions of increasing and away from industries working under conditions of decreasing returns. But it remains true of this tax that "*to a large extent it is not shifted and in this respect it differs much more from consumption taxes proper* [i.e., specific excises] *than from the income tax*" (ibid., 111; italics in original).

However, there is even an advantage in a tax which is collected at every stage because it enforces adaptation in small and frequent steps. "Only taxation by inflation has this property *even* more. It is precisely the absence of any merely thought-of (ausgedacht) rational distribution which makes this tax so much a *skin* which always fits better than the best *clothing*" (ibid., 111–12; italics in original). Schumpeter never deviated from his opinion about the virtues of a general sales tax, defended it in letters, suggested it as the proper wartime tax.

Schumpeter wrote a letter early in 1941 to Seymour Harris arguing for a sales tax. I have not found this letter but I have found Harris's answer of June 20, 1941, which quotes from Schumpeter's letter and voices opposition to two points, one of which may have validity: the proposed sales tax would have to be a multiple of the 1.5 percent on the basis of which Schumpeter wrote his earlier article. The other deals with the more general point of shiftability and regressivity/proportionality.

> Dear Joe:
>
> I have postponed answering your interesting letter about the sales tax because I heard that you were to be in town this week. Of course, you are free to say anything you please in behalf of the sales tax. I need not add that I am heartily in disagreement with you about the advisability of such a tax. You say, and I quote, "I believe that about 4 billion could be raised by a sales tax without anyone being perceptibly worse off." You add, however, that "One or two billions would have to be applied to indemnify the states and local authorities who levy sales taxes

---

[16] A VAT was at the time not yet generally thought of, though Austria had developed an approximation to it. R. A. Musgrave discovered, however, that it was proposed already in 1919 by v. Siemens.

now." May I point out, and I take the figures from an estimate submitted to the Ways and Means Committee Hearings on *Revenue Revisions of 1941* pages 332–335, that 4 billion dollars of revenue can be obtained in the following alternative ways: (1) a sales tax including taxes on food of 8.9 per cent, (2) a general sales tax without taxes on food of 14.4 per cent. Do you really believe that such a tax is politically possible?

I should also like to quote to you two items in the memorandum which you signed. "While we believe that the defense program must include other taxes—in particular adequate excess profits taxes and certain regulatory taxes—we are convinced of the need for taxes along the lines of our proposal if the government is to raise enough revenue to stop inflation without needlessly discouraging production either for defense or for civil needs and without distributing the burden unfairly." "No workable system of 'indirect' taxes, whether sales or excise taxes, can do the like. Indirect taxes, furthermore, are direct deterrents to production." Our position has been that we would like to have a flexible tax program because we ought to get ready for the time when more tax revenues are required and at the same time not introduce excessive tax measures. Furthermore, the idea was to broaden the base of taxation considerably. We did not, however, go so far as to suggest a sales tax, which is most inequitable in its incidence, particularly since our present tax system does not become progressive until we reach the $3000–5000 limit. Our view was also that if we prepared tax measures now we would ward off pressure for a sales tax later on, for a sales tax can be imposed with much less preparation than many more equitable taxes.

With best wishes. I am

Sincerely yours
sgnd Seymour
Seymour E. Harris

In Western European countries we now have VATs with rates from about 14 percent to 34 percent, which differentiate between different groups of commodities. We also have the solution of the crossing of frontiers. And Schumpeter mentioned that the French had in 1928 a substantial sales tax and politically used the lowness of sales taxes in Germany.[17]

---

[17] "It is of the essence of any tax that it is a foreign element in the capitalistic economic process and that it must damage it. Nevertheless the turnover tax is the right tax for Germany of today—and since France has such a tax, and a high one at that, there are also other than purely economic arguments for such a tax, a point which we always overlook to be then surprised about the consequences of this overlooking and to assign it to all kinds of other causes."

To illustrate the orders of magnitude that are involved in Schumpeter's proposals: The American GNP for 1991 is estimated at $5,670.80 million in current prices. Total consumption of goods and services is estimated at $3,841.80. A VAT of 10% on all consumption expenditures would wipe out the federal deficit and more. Food consumption is estimated at $644.60 million. If it were excluded from the VAT, the remaining $3,247.40, taxed at 10%, still would suffice to wipe out the federal deficit. Whatever adjustments one might wish to make in detail—for example, substantially increased taxation of alcoholic beverages and tobacco, perhaps of gasoline to European levels and lower taxation of other items or exemption of some services like medical expenses—the orders of magnitudes for the VAT involved would be less or comparable to the lowest taxes accepted as a matter of course in Europe.

"What Can a Fiscal Reform Achieve?"

By 1929, the economic situation of Germany had further deteriorated and signs of a world depression were appearing. Gustav Stolper's *Finanzplan* had appeared and Schumpeter's next articles supported it and in part referred to its proposals. The first of this group of articles was "What Can a Fiscal Reform Achieve?" ("Was Vermag eine Finanzreform"; Schumpeter 1985, 112–23). It is a plea for a thoroughgoing fiscal reform. At the same time, Schumpeter continued to teach economic thinking at its best. As almost always Schumpeter starts with historic comments on English developments in the nineteenth century. The point is made that there are moments in the history of a country when fiscal policy is so central that compared to it everything else is a side issue—a statement of the problem that clearly referred specifically to Weimar Germany, but which applies also, I believe, to the United States of today.

The incipient depression which in Germany was in 1929 already almost two years old and really came after only a single year of "normal" prosperity, was evidently not the "normal" cyclical phenomenon as shown by the fact that long-term interest rates did not fall. The question to be answered was to what extent "fiscal policy can help solve the problem on whose solution depends the economic fate of all interests, among them the maintenance and even more (vollends) the expansion of our social achievements . . . the answer is *capital formation*" (ibid., 114; italics in original).

Schumpeter proceeds systematically. Starting with Marshall's representative firm we have first to arrive at [gross] value added.[18] One should then deduct depreciation, here strictly defined as what is necessary and sufficient to maintain the existing plant and equipment. But in addition there ought to be the *reserve* "which from our standpoint is what the recipients of wages or dividends save individually" (ibid., 115; italics in original).

One of Schumpeter's most important points is first broached in a footnote: "Notice that class interests attach only to the distribution of consumption expenditures but not to the reserve. In other words, no one can be indifferent whether he or someone else *consumes*, but everyone can be indifferent about who reserves, as long as reserves there are" (ibid., 115, note 2; italics in original).

The point is central to Schumpeter's view of the economic process and its fate, that the real conflict was between the present and the future. The point has been stressed in the discussion of the coming of socialism, with laborism becoming the villain in the piece, or, more broadly, a class that sees only its own present welfare important and neglects the future; more generally, a

---

[18] Schumpeter actually refers to Marshall in a footnote. The English "added value" is used. The German "Wertschöpfung" was then evidently not yet in common use. It also must be remembered that this discussion appeared before Kuznets's pathbreaking work on national income or Walther Hoffmann's work on German data, and the common understanding of the various concepts of national accounting. So this discussion was at that time more than mere popularization.

situation in which income distribution becomes more important than income creation.

The reserve is necessary to renew the capital structure at higher levels rather than simply maintain existing plant and equipment. It does involve a sacrifice of present consumption, but is, first:

> [A] sacrifice of all in favor of the future of all. *Second*, the process is wrongly formulated by stating that the reserved amounts are withheld from consumption. They are withheld from the consumption of *those* who otherwise would have consumed them. But the reserved sums are spent and become income. . . . *Third*, the fruits of the sacrifice . . . do not ripen in the distant future but as a rule in a few years, just as the consequences [of not reserving] appear not in the distant future but extraordinarily quickly—in such phenomena as those under which the German economy suffers at present. (ibid. Italics in original; my translation)

It is easy to show the parallels between the German situation in the 1920s and early 1930s, and the American situation in the 1980s and 1990s: lack of increase in productivity, stubborn levels of unemployment, refusal of long-term interest rates to decline, increasing budget deficits, dependence on capital imports to take the place of lacking domestic savings.[19]

How, then, can fiscal policy help? Schumpeter first gives German and English estimates of "reserves," that is, gross savings, which are found to be much below prewar levels. Government expenditures can not be compressed very much, though their growth must be at least temporarily reduced.

All taxation affects savings rates, but consumption taxes have greater effects than personal taxes.

> *And here small sums in absolute terms may have a disproportionate effect.* . . . From which it follows that even without a reduction of the total [tax] burden and by relatively minor changes in its distribution very much can be achieved, in some cases (unter Umständen) the economy can be helped over a dead point and a period of expansion can be started in which increased money wages *become possible* and increases in real wages *must necessarily occur* regardless of whether anyone wants them or not. (ibid., 117–18; italics in original)

As in the theoretical analysis, the rate of interest gets a central role. As in the theoretical analysis, it is symptom more than cause. One of the more frightening aspects of the never-ending calls for reductions in interest rates by monetary policy alone is that no distinction is made between whether interest falls because the supply of savings has increased or whether it falls because the demand for funds has slackened. Schumpeter's discussion of this point is, of course, adapted to the actual conditions of the time: the favorable situation created by the Young Plan's reduction in reparations pay-

---

[19] There are, of course, also enormous differences, chief of which is that the United States won a major war and had large foreign assets which could be drawn down. Even so, the lack of capital formation shows in the fact that the United States has within an incredibly short period of time changed from the largest international creditor to largest debtor nation.

ments, but on the other side of the ledger the large foreign indebtedness which limited the freedom of action of the Reichsbank as it has in the 1980s and 1990s of the Federal Reserve. In the German case, prices also were inflexible "because the most important cost are politically fixed" (ibid., 119).[20]

One does not understand Schumpeter's point if one thinks this analysis merely of historical interest. For his point—inadequate savings—simply appears in other circumstances in other spots of the economy. Real estate prices are not fixed in the United States, but when they fall as the result of the end of a speculative boom liberally financed by S&Ls or commercial banks, these prices are—less rather than more successfully—maintained by bailouts and the Resolution Trust which is given the literally impossible task to liquidate the excesses without losses.

The issue in these cases is not to prevent large bankruptcies. This is applying equilibrium analysis. The issue is to change the *structure* of the tax system so as to allow the economy to *grow out of the problem*.

"Growing out" has, of course, become a code word of the so-called supply-side economics, but the actual policy pursued does not in fact allow it to do so. It is the slogan which is valid, not the reality. Of course, there should be tax cuts during a recession, and it is a sign of the failed past policies that the budget situation does not allow the right policy to be made. This was also the case in Germany, and Schumpeter explicitly made this point.

Indeed—and again in a footnote—Schumpeter points out that the anti-capitalistic (i.e., anti-savings) policy in fact favored capitalists by keeping interest rates high. "Economic history knows more such paradoxes" (ibid., note 6). In other contexts Schumpeter spoke of history making jokes in questionable taste.

The specific taxes Schumpeter proposed followed Gustav Stolper's *Finanzplan* which Schumpeter completely supported. The details are not of interest here. But the plan had two starting points: It did *not* require a significant reduction in public expenditures and it proposed a tobacco monopoly as a major source of consumption taxation.[21]

[20] It was at the time estimated that already under Brüning there were more than 80,000 fixed prices. And, of course, wages were very sticky. Under Hitler, in 1936, there was a complete price stop which was, however, broken through time and again so that by 1945 no one knew any more what was what. Exchange depreciation or fluctuating exchanges were at the time in Germany simply not in the cards, which even Hitler recognized. But the experiences in the 1970s, 1980s, and 1990s suggest that while fluctuating exchange rates can for a while mitigate the effects of lacking savings, they become in the longer run useless. The present freedom of action of the Federal Reserve is still limited by lack of savings and the real effects which that lack causes.

[21] The Stolper proposals were expressions of Schumpeterian views, so that agreement was hardly surprising. The proposed tobacco monopoly was modeled on the Austrian monopoly, the oldest in Europe and known for its excellent cigarettes using "Turkish," i.e., Balkan and Levant tobaccos. This proposal was one of the difficulties facing the enactment of the proposals, because the Socialists resented that Stolper as a known defender of markets and capitalism was considered unfair and "illogical" in proposing it. The monopoly was not opposed by Reemtsma, one of the biggest tobacco firms whose owners were liberal democrats. I know this from my own experience.

The plan proposed a shift to consumption taxation and a reduction—elimination would have been preferable but politically not feasible—of corporate income taxation; no reduction of capital gains taxes but basically the conversion of the existing income tax into an expenditure tax so as to free from taxes the nonconsumed parts of income (ibid., 121; italics in text), which Schumpeter considered technically quite feasible.[22]

Schumpeter's comments on suggestions to continue in the old ways and perhaps increase regulation and criminal penalties for violators, to refuse to ease the tax burden on "unpopular shoulders," is biting: "Whoever considers this path to have a chance of success deserves admiration but no further discussion . . . neither the reduction of the burden on higher incomes nor higher consumption taxation are *avoidable*, and all attempted changes in detail come always *back* to this point" (ibid., 122; italics in original).

I may perhaps characterize the principles of Schumpeter's tax policy in the following manner: Given the particular problem of insuficient capital formation and the desire for long-term growth, as well as for an adequate social policy, if the choice is between working or not working, the tax system should encourage working. If the choice is between consuming or saving, the tax system should bias the choice toward savings. In general you should be encouraged to make as much money as you can, and you can even keep it provided you do not consume but save and invest it.[23]

It is logical that Schumpeter turned next to an analysis of the "Economics and Sociology of the Income Tax" ("Oekonomie und Soziologie der Einkommensteuer"; ibid., 123–32). Schumpeter's position is stated at the very beginning: "The income tax is our most beautiful and best instrument of fiscal policy, the backbone of our—and every civilized—tax system, but we have put too great a burden on it and we must for the near future lighten its burden somewhat" (ibid., 124).

Schumpeter repeats his proposal for an expenditure tax. "Only the consumption-income tax is a true income tax. Its technical difficulties . . . are great, but not anywhere near as great as generally asserted" (ibid., 125).

Much of this article is devoted to answering the question whether the income tax is indeed the most beautiful and best tax for all times. The answer has been expounded before: The tax is a child of the bourgeois world, and part of a world consisting of a competitive economy with many small and medium-sized firms; of private property; of free trade; of an automatic gold standard, of small government expenditures whose payment requires only a small portion of income; of a peaceful nonimperialist and noncolonialist policy and of limited military expenditures. When tax rates are moderate they

---

[22] *The Economist* called the proposed American reduction of capital gains taxes "pure snake oil," and Felix Rohatyn in the *New York Review of Books* referred to it as just churning around the same old stuff. Making distinctions by the source of income violates all sound principles of taxation. An expenditure tax distinguishes uses of income, not sources. All this is explicit in Schumpeter.

[23] One may thus view Schumpeter's proposals as an expression of the Protestant ethic.

are accepted as fair and just, and there is no incentive to shift it. A good income tax also requires that *all* income sources are treated equally. When income tax payments amount to "a fifth or a fourth or even more of incomes they change the whole economic man and everything he does" (ibid., 130).

Many of the preconditions which, given low rates and nondiscrimination by income source, make this tax "the fiscal policy of an abstinence of economic policy (wirtschaftspolitische Enthaltsamkeit), of *anti-interventionism*, are at *present* not given (ibid.; italics in original). The conclusions are, however, evolutionary.

> Of course, the income tax will not disappear for a long time. Too strong forces including a set expert opinion support it. As every social institution, every tax survives the epoch of its economic and psychological appropriateness (Zweckmässigkeit). But as with all other social institutions no tax system survives its non-appropriateness for ever. Slowly the stream of development washes away at its roots. Thus the income tax, too, will disappear with the economic form and mentality whose tax-political child it was. (ibid., 132)[24]

FISCAL POLICY AS DESTINY

By 1930, it was clear that a depression had hit Germany badly. Nevertheless some people tried to deny this, insisting that all economic problems including unemployment and capital formation were due to "rationalization" and "misdirection" of capital respectively. Schumpeter dealt with these analyses in a prophetic article on "If the Fiscal Reform Fails . . . ?" ("Wenn die Finanzreform misslingt . . ."; ibid., 133–43).

The first part of this article dealt with the analysis of the cyclical situation, Schumpeter's point being that one dealt not with a "normal" depression, that is, a reaction to a preceding expansion which indeed would require a process of adaptation and which was a recurrent phenomenon. With lacking savings and capital formation and an expansion based essentially on consumption which in Germany (as in the United States in the 1980s) could be traced back to fiscal policy, there "had to follow a depression characterized not by adaptation but by financial anemia, a phenomenon unknown by a normal cyclical movement" (ibid., 139).

Of course, there would then be calls for easier money and increased consumption expenditures and, of course, such expenditures would ease the situation temporarily, the limit being when all resources were exhausted. When they are, real incomes must fall. *Or* there must be domestic inflation— and/or the foreign value of the Reichsmark must become untenable.[25]

---

[24] In Soviet style economics, income taxes are insignificant.

[25] This is a paraphrase of the arguments on pp. 136–141. Schumpeter suggests that public tolerance of inflation or exchange depreciation would suddenly snap. This was indeed the case. Even Hitler did not dare to devalue because of that psychological barrier. (On this point, see H.

The article ends with a political prognosis, something Schumpeter rarely did. If fiscal policy did not change before it was too late there ought to be a sharp swing of the political pendulum to the left, followed by as sharp a swing to the right. In too many cases the answer to a bad fiscal policy would be that it was not bad enough—a phenomenon with which anyone working in LDCs is all too familiar. And there Schumpeter reverted to the impossibility of socialism at the time.

> The pleasure of both extremes would be short-lived. Both would get a lesson in the economic interpretation of history and would have to learn that the economic system (Wirtschaftsverfassung) of a period is not something accidental, that it can be ruined but not arbitrarily molded (gemodelt). To the one side it would show the sober truth that social democracy can, for the next hundred years, be a power only within the capitalist system or none at all, and that it must observe the necessities of capitalist life as much as any other party—it may sound paradox: *more* than any other because only a capital-saturated capitalism can lead to successful socialism—to the other the no less sober truth that the most beautiful dictatorship cannot change anything essential in the fundamental facts of today which one must deal with successfully or die. Finally for *all parties* (Beteiligte)— who will ask themselves, if neither favorable accidents nor fate (Bestimmung) prevent the development of the described causal nexus and when we should find ourselves after a while impoverished though educated about where we are now, will perhaps ask: couldn't we have had all that more cheaply?—that the historic fact that in the causal chain which leads through the French revolution and the Napoleonic wars, a failed fiscal reform or also political incompetence to undertake a fiscal reform stands in a crucial place. (ibid., 142–43; Italics in original; my translation)

In the Christmas issue of the *Deutsche Volkswirt* of 1931, Schumpeter had explained his theoretical views of the cyclical situation ("Daueɪ Krise?"; ibid., 202–10), which I discussed before. Schumpeter referred back to this analysis which had stressed that no interpretation of the existing situation could do without a cyclical analysis, but that no analysis was complete without a stress on the specific noncyclical aspects. Early in 1932, he discussed the relation between the world crisis and fiscal policy ("Welt Krise und Finanzpolitik"; ibid., 143–56). Specifically Schumpeter wanted to explain what German fiscal policy since 1924 had to add to the explanation of the existing state of affairs, neglecting all other specific elements such as reparations payments which were still poisoning the air, Russian, Chinese, and Indian events, and even the "immeasurably overestimated gold problem."

Schumpeter starts with the Brüning policy of simultaneous reduction of

James 1986.) Expansion without devaluation required exchange controls which started before Hitler but were built into an all-encompassing system by him. With exchanges freely fluctuating, the expression of the same troubles has shifted to the phenomenon of stagflation and shifts of the so-called Philipps curve. This is just said to point out that, with the proper adjustments for changed circumstances, the Schumpeterian analysis retains its significance. Then as now solutions are always tackled at the most superficial level.

prices and incomes (ibid., 144). Evidently, if everything were reduced equally, the policy would be senseless and useless. No recourse to theory is necessary to show "that a policy of reducing prices and incomes by political fiat (Eingriff), would by itself suffice immediately to create a depression even in the midst of a boom" (ibid., 145).

The only "good" effect of such a policy would be to make imports more difficult and exports easier. But this would have only a temporary effect. A brief section on "Price Reduction and Politics" dealt explicitly with another Brüning policy to deflate drastically so as to make reparations payments possible, or perhaps better, to show the impossibility of such payments by carrying the deflation to its ultimate conclusion. "And the beautiful thing is that . . . this policy is quite honest and faithful to international obligations (Vertragstreue) and undertakes only to be effective through the logic of things" (ibid., 146).

The trouble was that the *only* (italicized in the original) sense of such a policy was "foreign-exchange-political" and "reparations-political," that in any case it could have only temporary effects and that it had enormous cost. It is worth quoting in extenso, for here Schumpeter turned out to be a very good prophet.

> [T]he economic ravages which it causes will after a while and with a necessity beyond anyone's will bring this policy to an end. Just as an increase in the Bank Rate tends temporarily to reduce prices but in the long run produces disruptions of production which work in the opposite direction, so the effect of this policy must eventually lead through a field of economic corpses to its reversal and, quite aside from the social consequences must result in a complete paralysis of the economy. It is the great weakness of this policy . . . that the opponent knows this just as well. The policy may be temporarily sensible and successful if used at a well-chosen moment. Only, one has to understand when to stop it immediately and to throw around the economic rudder in the moment in which success has been achieved or turns out to be impossible. (ibid., 147)[26]

The final and longest section of this article is entitled "Fiscal Policy as Destiny," and it deals in detail with what would have happened if a pro-saving fiscal policy had been made. The economic expansion would have lasted longer, the depression would have been milder and, importantly, the Reich would have had the fiscal means to combat or at least to mitigate it. Interest rates would have fallen because of increased liquidity. Capital imports would have been smaller. Unemployment would never have risen to the actual levels and then only after 1929. "The Federal Government, the States and communities in the United States may economically do anything they like, France may waste the achievements of Poincaré's government, England may undermine its financial position—but for Germany the finances are *destiny*, a rational economy a matter of life or death" (ibid., 149; italics in original).

The whole analysis has a frightening and direct relevance to the American

---

[26] For details of the Brüning policy see James (1986).

policies of the 1980s and 1990s, not only on the purely economic level, but on the political level as well. There is an inability to pursue one's political aims actively and to support them economically. There is the increasing and very serious danger of, on the one hand, putting the whole blame for what is happening on the misbehavior of other countries—Japan bashing, for example—instead of looking first at oneself.

There is (or at least was until the collapse of the Soviet Empire), on the other hand, a dangerous and almost exclusive reliance on military might. To be sure, there is now a multilateral foreign policy, while at the same time stressing that the United States cannot be the world's policeman. Yet the example of the late Soviet Union suggests that it is dangerous only to be feared without being loved, to be respected mainly for military might rather than right. Ultimately the war is won on the economic field, which means what a government can do for its people domestically as well as protecting it from foreign enemies.

Fiscal policy is not everything. But in Schumpeter's analysis it is a, if not even *the*, central policy which makes the achievement of all other aims possible. And here is the point at which the view of the capitalistic process as a whole becomes truly central. Schumpeter's essential point is that every economic and political measure derives its meaning only from the total context *which includes* the whole of society: its state of affairs, its tendencies. One needs to remember Schumpeter's praise of Gladstonian policies as an ideal expression of an intact bourgeois society, and of his analysis of the tendency toward socialism which, let it be remembered, means something very specific if also complicated and which it has taken me three chapters to analyze. You cannot make a sound fiscal policy by just stressing one historical element. The weakness of the American policy since the end of the Second World War was its antisaving aspect. Considering that it took the Soviet Empire seventy years (and a devastating war on its own soil) to collapse by its own stupidity, it is no wonder that the much richer United States will take much longer to feel the ultimate consequences of its antisaving policies and, more importantly, preserve for some time the ability to reverse course.

There is a comprehensive view in Schumpeter's conservativism (as he understood the term) which is much closer to liberalism in the European sense: The gold standard with its fixed exchange rates, a small government, an anti-inflationary (and certainly also anti-deflationary) monetary policy which meant essentially reserving credit creation for innovative investments, free trade, peace in the world, a small army, and no imperialistic-colonial adventures.

But it is no more possible to reverse developments in society which have occurred without asking for a catastrophe than it is to force socialism on a society not yet ready for it. Marx was right: there is logic in development. He was wrong in his analysis of what this development implied economically.

Mises was right. The market, and only the market, will deal with many problems. He was wrong to make the market the defining element of capitalism. He was quite fatally wrong, not only to define what the market said as anything business wanted to do, but that the economic system which is inherently "turbulent"—and I believe that Mises saw this—can be preserved in all eternity if only government's role is abolished or at least restricted essentially to law and order.

Hayek is right in fearing and disliking the end of a beautiful era. But Schumpeter, who shared this like and the dislike of what he saw coming, is right: Hayek basically wants to preserve this state of affairs, particularly the individual freedom it seems to guarantee. He fails to see how this state of affairs has arisen and what its inherent tendencies foreshadow. But *no* state of affairs can be preserved forever, not even for a long time. Even the very learned and (to me) attractive *Constitution of Liberty* has a very time-less ahistoric aura.

Only Schumpeter's evolutionary vision seems right without any major qualifications that can be seen now, though no one can foresee what the future holds in this respect as in any other. Obviously, there are many details on which Schumpeter can be challenged, details of history, not of logic. No doubt the time will come when this vision, too, will be superseded. It is not yet on the horizon. But, as The Preacher says: This, too, will change.

Epilogue

BIOGRAPHERS HAVE SPENT much space on Schumpeter's flamboyant private life, including many scandalous stories. I do not doubt that Schumpeter was in his youth a most virile man and that many of the stories are true. Perhaps he felt himself above conventional behavior and delighted in shocking bourgeois society. I doubt, however, that he would commit unaesthetic sins. Even where true, their importance can be judged only in a much wider frame of reference which is perhaps better left to first-class poets and novelists.[1]

In any case, how much time can even the most virile of men, which Schumpeter evidently was, spend on affaires du coeur and produce at the same time so much outstanding work? Perhaps the real clue to his behavior is expressed in a few pages about a proposed novel first reproduced by Smithies[2] in his *Memorial of Schumpeter*.

The last two paragraphs of the *Outline* seem relevant here. They certainly fitted the friend so many knew:

> More important than country means class—but he did not with subconscious allegiance belong either to society or the business class or the professions or the trade union world, all which provided such comfortable homes for everyone he knew. Yes—his mother's corner of society had been his as long as she lived.
>
> Doing efficient work without aim, without hope. . . .
>
> No Family. No real friends. No woman in whose womanhood to anchor.

In other words, Schumpeter was a romantic, and Goethe would have understood better than to interpret his behavior merely as the desire to shock. So would have saints. For, as he wrote in one of his "Aphorisms," if you understand everything there is nothing to forgive.

Schumpeter also had an excellent classical education, and he read, for example, Euripides in the original to the last. In his knowledge of architecture

[1] This is not far-fetched. Wolfgang Köhler, one of the founders of Gestalt psychology, told me what a wonderful time he had reading poetry in preparing a set of lectures on motivation, since the poets had much greater insight into that subject than most psychologists. In my private lingo I think of Schumpeter as having spent his youth in the Venusberg, only to repent and redeem himself in later years. Before judging on facts alone, it ought be relevant that both Kierkegaard and George Bernard Shaw paint Don Juan as a tragic rather than as an immoral figure, pursued by fate; and even Mozart's Don Giovanni (the subject of Kierkegaard's essay) is not without tragic pride. It was his pride which prevented him from repenting, which in the end condemned him, not his many sins.

[2] Smithies (1950). The outline of the novel is reproduced also in Swedberg 1991b, and in Allen (1990), vol. 2, 10–11.

or theology, he was an amateur in the eighteenth-century sense of the word, before it became synonymous with dilletantism.

While exuberance and romanticism of a fin-de-siècle kind might explain a good part of his early personality, there was also tragedy in his life, and it is tragedy which dominated his later years.

As Smithies pointed out, though of middle-class origin, "he was neither aristocrat nor bourgeois, but he had no resentments as did Marx. And he had great intellect" (Smithies 1950, 635). His really beloved Austro-Hungarian Monarchy collapsed irrevocably, and with this he became an eternal wanderer, deraciné, though after the Second World War he found some sort of peace in the United States.

Having to adjust first to the First World War, which he felt was a major tragedy, then to the disappearance of his beloved Double Monarchy, then to his failures as minister and investment banker which left him with heavy debts and an unjustly tarnished reputation, seeing the tragedy of Weimar, must have put a heavy strain on his energies and on his psychological equilibrium, as it did on those of so many others.

He might have mastered even these blows of history if personal tragedy had not destroyed the last moorings of his inner self. His mother died in 1926, and with it he lost that "corner" of reality. That same year his wife, his great love, died together with their newborn son. Only work remained, and I believe that he transferred some of his need to and for love to his students. There really remained only the never-ending search for truth.

Since I am neither a saint nor a novelist nor a poet and since it seemed to me that virtually none of the more lurid stories give any clue to the development of Schumpeter's thought and actions, discretion seemed to be the better part of wisdom.

On the other hand, I felt it necessary to go more deeply into the fact that Schumpeter was a man not only virile and certainly enormously gifted, but also like everyone born at a particular time into a specific environment and history which no one can choose and everyone has to come to terms with, whether by passively accepting it or by actively trying to influence it. He may escape class and nationality, but there is no way to escape history. I therefore thought it necessary to go more deeply into the historic background into which Schumpeter was born and to which he reacted. I still believe that his writings and actions reveal essential features of the man, but only if seen in a historic and social context.

This historic context may be political or economic and, in the case of an academic which Schumpeter was most of his life, the state of his chosen field, specifically economic theory. The importance of the historic context is the real content of Schumpeter's apparently cynical statement that "the fastest way to complete nonsense is to be ruthlessly logical"; it is literally true. No theory can possibly hedge against every historic fact, against future changes. Every application needs adaptation.

But in addition there is a shying away from ultimate conclusions if asserted with absolute certainty, because no scholar is God, because one may be wrong somewhere in the chain of events (not just of logic) and indeed one is bound to be wrong if the conclusions are far in the future. How far? Even this no man can know for certain. In "normal" circumstances perhaps fifty to one hundred years, but it is impossible to know whether circumstances are that "normal." No one I know, certainly not I myself, expected the collapse of the Soviet Empire to come exactly when it did, and to lead so swiftly to the dissolution of a super power. Abram Bergson or Andrei Amalrik, to mention only the foremost American scholar of Soviet economics and one of the more prominent Soviet dissidents, had pointed to the "sickness unto death" of the USSR, but the exact moments of death, even the beginning of the final agony of death, were hidden even from them. It is a lesson of history which would have struck awe into the heart of a man like Schumpeter.

To put the cause of that breakdown on the absence of a "free" market seems frighteningly simplistic, particularly as that "free" market is one with international textile agreements, "voluntary" car export quotas, export restrictions, and huge defense expenditures. The semantic confusion in this phrase is similar to that produced in the former Soviet Union where free meant not free and democratic meant dictatorial. What happened to the Soviet Empire can happen to anyone who neglects the lessons of history. And it may well be not only that he who neglects the lessons of history is fated to repeat it, but that this will also be fate of him who does know the lessons. (I forgot who said that first. I believe it was Santayana.)

The proper reaction to the victories which Schumpeter would have had is awe, not pride. It is the fear of God, not the pride in one's own achievement— and Schumpeter turned out to be a closet Christian. The Old Testament is a better guide to understanding what is happening than Mises, or Hayek, or Marx.

It is, I believe, in this context that Schumpeter's theory and actions derive their meaning. Schumpeter's is a theory, a theoretical model. It is open in the sense that it establishes a new paradigm which is capable of, even cries for, further work and development. Like history itself, it is not final. It does not produce immediate answers applicable at all times and places without adaptation, but it does give a framework to work out what the answers in particular times and places might be. Schumpeter's policy and political views provide illustrations, and I believe even clues, how the underlying view of reality may be transformed in ever changing actual situations.

Of course, the "facts" of a situation may be insufficient, inexact, even false. The answer is better facts: more historical research if the quest is directed towards the past; greater, better, and quicker availability of statistics if the quest is directed toward the (immediate) future.

Of course, the advice given—but not the analysis of a situation—necessarily depends on the direction in which you want to go. To want the impossible is merely quixotic. It becomes important to try and understand how a situation has come about, where it is likely to go, and what are the degrees of freedom on any action which history allows at any moment on time.

One way is, of course, to preach restraint in one's actions. One reviewer of my *Planning Without Facts* accused me—correctly—of being a risk averter. When head of the Economic Planning Unit of the Nigerian Federal Ministry of Economic Development in Lagos, I felt very strongly that Nigeria had troubles enough without my adding to them by advice based on ignorance of facts, which is something very different from unavailability of statistics. So I advised caution, primary attention to the recurrent budget and the balance of payments, and often not acting in preference to doing something which might or more likely would not work. This is partly a matter of temperament.

But it is also one of scholarly conscience, and in any case it was based, as it should be, both on a theoretical approach which was definitely Schumpeterian in its evolutionary stance and its emphasis on fiscal policy as the major planning tool, and on the best assessment of the facts in the existing situation that could be made. When asked, as was frequently the case, how I knew that my decisions were optimal, the answer was simple: I didn't. I just did the best I could with the facts and the time available. As Alchian put it, the choice is never among all possible courses of action. To consider Schumpeter's contribution to theory to be simply "the dynamic entrepreneur" is a caricature of his work.

This is the basic reason why I believe that the account of Schumpeter's political activities and policy advice tells more about the man as well as his theories than all the juicy stories, even when they are true. Unlike sketching a complicated personality which Schumpeter undoubtedly was and which I did not feel comfortable in drawing, I feel strongly that Schumpeter's writings, which are as complicated as his personality, can be safely interpreted in the light of history on the one hand and on the basis of later theoretical developments in and outside of economics on the other.

And here I hope to have convincingly shown that Schumpeter's is a truer vision than most, even all, others (though I have been at pains to give credit where credit is due, a rule of behavior which is Schumpeterian to the core, but which is perhaps simple decency). The evolutionary view is, I believe, more of a radical break with the past than appears at present when many of the originally revolutionary ideas have been accepted to such a degree that their origin is forgotten. It was felt to be such a break in 1911 and even as late as 1932. It is as radical as Marx, but not being a Marxist, I prefer Schumpeter's vision.

There is a fundamental difference between creative and adaptive acts with fundamentally different consequences, even when paradoxically adaptive acts involve creativity. It remains true that adaptation is also "creative" but the meaning of the word is subtly changed. It now means finding a personal solution to adapting to ideas and facts which someone else has first developed. Since knowledge is "personal," there is no simple way of imitating. But the idea to which the adaptation is required still comes from someone else who has successfully shown that something is feasible. "Creative" may or may not involve a complete break with the past in more than some details. But it certainly involves the whole man and it involves the whole activity. Johann Sebastian Bach did not, as far as I know, invent any particular new form of music; he was in this respect "traditional." His sons considered him something of an old fogey. But in his hands a fugue, counterpoint, was transformed to the height of perfection which human beings are allowed to achieve.

This difference to other thinkers is of the essence. Schumpeter himself wrote to Gottfried Haberler that he felt like Moses who was allowed to see but not to enter the Promised Land.[3] The analogy is instructive: Jews and Christians consider Moses the founder of Judaism, not Abraham or any other of the Patriarchs, nor the later prophets. It was Moses who was allowed to do the creative act, based on predecessors to be sure; and prophets were developers of the original idea.

The second central achievement of Schumpeter is the integration of history and theoretical analysis in a manner which remained only programmatic in the German historical school and different with the American institutionalists. Schumpeter did not refer to Commons in either *Business Cycles* or the *History of Economic Analysis*, but in his assessment of Schmoller's approach he compared it with that of Mitchell, whom he esteemed very highly personally and professionally.

Because of his insistence on historic uniqueness, the policy writings as well as his personal behavior must be interpreted in the light of their contemporary situation which in turn is not understandable unless it is described how that situation has come about. It is certainly wrong to interpret actions and views of the past in terms of present knowledge and attitudes. We know how things have turned out, but this knowledge was not available in the past, and in any case it was not the only outcome possible. History, it has been said, is written by the victors. It is all too often also written by great-grandchildren in terms of attitudes and the knowledge of the writing historian, who all too often mixes up his better knowledge of facts and logical relationships with moral superiority and higher intelligence. Schumpeter was singularly free of this particular sin of seeing the past in terms of the present, and it is this, together with his theoretical insights, which distinguishes him from many of his contemporaries.

Thus, Schumpeter is different, but difference implies neither that there are not intellectual forebears nor contemporaries with related ideas. To say that Schumpeter did not succeed in formalizing his views is true but it is less of an indictment than appears at first blush. The means to do so simply did not exist at his time. Only linear dynamics was available at his time, which is com-

---

[3] Letter to Gottfried Haberler, dated March 20, 1933, in the Harvard University Archives, reproduced in Swedberg 1991b, 214. Ragnar Frisch, in his contribution to the second Festschrift for Schumpeter, thought that Schumpeter was too modest, that he did enter the Promised Land. Of course, Schumpeter's letter antedates *Business Cycles*, Frisch's assessment postdates it. And both wrote before the appearance of the computer and nonlinear mathematics of higher order.

pletely deterministic. Should he therefore have adapted his "vision," his insights to the technical means available to express them formally? This would have meant to cut out its very life in order to fit it into too short a Procrustean bed. There probably is even at present an inherent limit to formalizing his approach because the changes in the basic parameters of the model which must not be assumed away change for reasons which are as yet only imperfectly understood and for this reason resist modeling. The model of the economic style may be at present the best we have. And the contributions of "chaos" and "complexity" mathematicians seem to this nonmathematician to point to an exciting and fruitful future.

Of course, Schumpeter's mathematical knowledge was inadequate. There is, however, in the Harvard Archives a handwritten comment on Marschak's review of *Business Cycles* which, as far as I know, has not been published.[4]

Marschak had sent Schumpeter a draft of his proposed review for comment. The comments from which I quote are seven handwritten pages. I have not found a typescript of these comments, and thus I do not know whether Marschak actually saw them. There is, however, the evidence that the published review differs from the draft, for example, in only describing but not actually reproducing the equations which in Marschak's view might have formalized Schumpeter's thoughts.

In the system of exact models, Prof. M. has actually most to teach me. My own relation to them has always seemed to me most unsatisfactory. I simply have no such model to offer and in the hope that Prof. M. might be able to do so I will only state the reasons why.

But first I want to explain in what sense my system does, and in what sense it does not, seem to me to be a "closed" one. I think it is closed if "closed" means the same as endogenous. Though I am prepared, in interpreting any given case, to take account of all the outside factors I can see, my theory does not rely on outside factors, that is, on factors outside the logic of business cycles. Enterprise is inside the economic system, an internal, if you so please, source of energy. It is not of the nature of erratic shocks, it is part of the system that could not live without it and the main categories of which are keyed to its occurrence. But my system is not closed, if that means "causal" in the sense of Birkhoff and Lewis. For that source of energy is (it is formal so far) refractory to quantification so that the system subject to this impulse is ex ante indeterminate and in this sense "open." If you will allow me to deviate so far from your strict principles, there is something of évolution créatrice about it (as there is I think—another confessio fidei—about every true evolution, a biological "sport" for instance or de Vries' "mutation").

Now this is perhaps the most fundamental reason why I have never attempted to get my system into equations—except for individual bits of mechanics: if you have a system of interdependent quantities you will always be able to describe surface mechanical relations (everything has always also such mechanical effects, e.g. the effect of spending upon prices) as disturbed by my process by partial sets

[4] Marschak's review appeared in the *Journal of Political Economy*, 1940, vol. 40, no. 6.

of conditions which in the "partial" system may even be quite determinate. Therefore I do not feel any contrast between those schemata (Frisch–Tinbergen–Roos–Amoroso–Kalecki–Keynes–and many others) and my way of thinking: they simply move on planes different from mine and I feel perfectly free to use any of them for those peripheric problems for which they are intended.

But there are other reasons:

First, there are objections to what I call aggregative analysis which seems to me precisely to exclude the very source of my process, in particular the highly characteristic inter-firm disequilibria which are compatible with ideal equilibrium in an industry as a whole, still more in an economic domain when defined aggregatively. Couldn't you do something about that—i.e., express that kind of disequilibrium as between innovating and petrified firms as an element of the total economy?[5]

Second, however, there are no simple relations between aggregates that would suit my purposes. Take the attempt which you have made yourself. I would contest the relations which you try to fit to my thought. I would neither accept No. 2 because it lacks the element of the rate of spending (also a lag would have to be inserted). No. 3 is quite off my rail (?). No. 4 I would accept only as a first approximation and No. 5 is one of those propositions I am most hostile to— thinking as I do little of the role of price movements as primary factors. That is not to say that that schema is uninteresting or "wrong." I should much like to see it worked out. But causally interpreted those relations are far removed from my way of thinking.

Third, there are, as you point out correctly, difficulties about statistical constants. There are not enough invariant relations to make them theoretically significant. For instance, there is no unique relation between the movement of credit creation for some innovations and its importance, e.g., the amount of disturbance which it will (the innovation) cause in the industrial organism. The same investment might cause quite different effects according, for instance, the degree to which the additional product which it brings forth is more or less competitive to existing products (or methods). It might throw out of operation the whole industry and start a downward spiral. Or its effects might be so distributed as to be difficult to trace and easy to absorb.

Again the period of gestation has something to do with the duration of prosperity. But there is no unique relation. No period of gestation of a single firm could be of much importance; neither would some weighted average of those individual periods. For how long that time of preponderance of spending over repaying lasts (you mention one factor only) depends on so very many other circumstances—how rapidly the "last" follows the "leaders," how great the advantages of the new things over the old are, how much rebuilding is involved in adaptation and so on.

---

[5] This is, of course, the basic approach followed by Nelson and Winter, who could not have known this letter. Or of Dahmén. See chapter 6 above.

Undoubtedly, the future will show that Schumpeter was often wrong in his assessment of facts and possibilities. This is the fate of most people. This biography has not hidden that aspect, for example his belief held for the briefest of moments that the Austrian situation could be saved in 1919, or that the kind of treaty which the Treaty of St. Germain represented was so far from the long-term interest of the victors that it would not come about. But no one can doubt that Schumpeter was very sensitive to the facts of an actual situation.

Thus, I come to the conclusion that Schumpeter deserves to be considered one of the greatest economists "dead or alive" (to quote Schumpeter's assessment of Tinbergen), not so much for purely technical achievements (which at present are equated—perhaps too much—with mathematical formulations) but for giving economics a push in new and quite different directions from the past. And his importance is by now attested by the fact that many of his "visions" have become so commonplace that the present generation can hardly imagine how radical they once were. It is the research which he has inspired and which he continues to inspire which is his greatest legacy and his finest monument.

• R E F E R E N C E S •

WORKS BY JOSEPH ALOIS SCHUMPETER

Article Collections

Schumpeter (1951) *Essays of J. A. Schumpeter*, edited by Richard V. Clemence. Cambridge, Mass.: Addison-Wesley Press. Reprinted with a new introduction by R. Swedberg, New Brunswick, N.J.: Transaction Publishers, 1989.

———. (1952) *Aufsätze zur ökonomischen Theorie*, edited by Erich Schneider and Arthur Spiethoff. Tübingen: J.C.B. Mohr (Paul Siebeck).

———. (1953) *Aufsätze zur Soziologie*, edited by E. Schneider and A. Spiethoff. Tübingen: J.C.B. Mohr (Paul Siebeck).

———. (1954) *Dogmenhistorische und Biographische Aufsätze*, edited by E. Schneider and A. Spiethoff. Tübingen: J.C.B. Mohr (Paul Siebeck).

———. (1985) *Aufsätze zur Wirtschaftspolitik*, edited by W. F. Stolper and Christian Seidl. Tübingen: J.C.B. Mohr (Paul Siebeck).

———. (1987) *Beiträge zur Sozialökonomik, Herausgegeben, übersetzt und eingeleitet von Stephan Böhm. Mit einem Vorwort von Gottfried Haberler.* Köln and Graz: Böhlau Verlag Wien.

———. (1991a) *The Economics and Sociology of Capitalism*, edited by Richard Swedberg. Princeton, N.J.: Princeton University Press.

———. (1992) *Politische Reden*, edited by Christian Seidl and W. F. Stolper. Tübingen: J.C.B. Mohr (Paul Siebeck).

———. (1993) *Aufsätze zur Tagespolitik*, edited by Christian Seidl and W. F. Stolper. Tübingen: J.C.B. Mohr (Paul Siebeck).

Books

———. (1908) *Das Wesen und der Hauptinhalt der theoretischen Nationalökonomie.* Munich and Leipzig: Duncker and Humblot.

———. ([1911] 1926) *Theorie der wirtschaftlichen Entwicklung.* 2d rev. ed. Berlin: Duncker & Humblot.

———. (1918) *Die Krise des Steuerstaats.* Reprinted in Schumpeter (1953). English translation by R. A. Musgrave and W. F. Stolper in *International Economic Papers*, vol. 4, edited by A. Peacock et al. London: Macmillan, 1954. Reprinted in *The Economics and Sociology of Capitalism*, edited by Richard Swedberg. Princeton, N.J.: Princeton University Press, 1991.

———. (1934) *The Theory of Economic Development.* Cambridge, Mass: Harvard University Press. Translated by Redvers Opie with Joseph A. Schumpeter from the second German edition; revised by Joseph A. Schumpeter.

———. (1939) *Business Cycles.* 2 vols. New York: McGraw-Hill.

———. (1942) *Capitalism, Socialism and Democracy.* New York: Harper and Brothers.

———. (1950) *Capitalism, Socialism and Democracy.* 3d enlarged ed. With Schumpeter's posthumous "March into Socialism." Reprinted with a new introduction by Tom Bottomore. New York: Harper Torchbooks, 1970.

———. (1951) *Imperialism and Social Classes*, edited and introduced by Paul M. Sweezy; translated by Heinz Norden. New York: Augustus Kelley Inc.

——. (1954) *History of Economic Analysis*. New York: Oxford University Press.

——. (1970) *Das Wesen des Geldes*. Göttingen: Vandenhoeck und Ruprecht. Edited and introduced by Fritz K. Mann. (Posthumous publication of unfinished manuscript.)

Reviews

——. "Review of Keynes, *General Theory*." Reprinted in Schumpeter 1951.

——. (1946) "Review of F. A. Hayek, *Road to Serfdom*." *Journal of Political Economy*, June.

Letters (see sender's name for letters to Schumpeter)

Letter to President Conant, December 7, 1936. In the Harvard University Archives.

Letter to Ragnar Frisch, November 3, 1932. In the Harvard University Archives.

Letter to J. K. Galbraith, October 28, 1948. In the Harvard University Archives.

Letter to Gottfried Haberler, March 20, 1933. In the Harvard University Archives.

Letter to Irving Fisher, February 10, 1933. In the Harvard University Archives.

Letter to Irving Fisher, December 6, 1940. In the Harvard University Archives.

Letter to Irving Fisher, March 17, 1942. In the Harvard University Archives.

Letter to Charles A. Gulick, August 7, 1944. In the Harvard University Archives.

Letter to Alvin Johnson, August 22, 1940. In the Harvard University Archives.

Letter to Hugh J. Kelly, McGraw-Hill, June 24, 1937. In the Harvard University Archives.

Letter to Taljin Koopmans, August 22, 1940. In the Harvard University Archives.

Letter to J. Marschak. Handwritten draft. In the Harvard University Archives.

Letter to Wesley C. Mitchell, May 7, 1937. In the Harvard University Archives.

Letter to Redvers Opie, from Cambridge, Mass., Saturday. Probably 1933.

Letter to Redvers Opie, May 12, 1937. Made available by Loring Allen.

Letter to David C. Pottinger, Harvard University Press, June 4, 1934. In the Harvard University Archives.

Letter to Albert Pratt, May 12, 1937. Reprinted in Swedberg, (1991).

Letter to D. H. Robertson, Cambridge, Mass., December 24, 1932. In the Harvard University Archives.

Letter to Karl Renner, n.d. (1919). Reprinted in Schumpeter 1985.

Letter to Walt W. Rostow, March 12, 1940. In the Harvard University Archives.

Letter to Carl Snyder, October 22, 1932. In the Harvard University Archives.

Letter to Walter F. Spahr, February 1, 1941. In the Harvard University Archives.

Letter to George Stocking, September 19, 1949. In the Harvard University Archives.

Letter to Gustav Stolper, May 28, 1926. In Stolper Nachlass, Bundesarchiv, Koblentz.

Letter to Gustav Stolper, March 15, 1927. In the Stolper papers, Bundesarchiv, Koblentz.

Letter to Gustav Stolper, May 8, 1931, Bonn, with an account of Schumpeter's letter to Ministialdirektor Richter, of the Prussian Ministry of Education. In the Stolper papers, Bundesarchiv, Koblentz.

Letter to Gilbert Walker, May 19, 1937. In the Harvard University Archives.

Letter to E. B. Wilson, May 13, 1937. In the Harvard University Archives.

Unpublished Works

——. (1928) "Der neueste Stand des Konjunkturproblems." *Vortrag* von Professor Dr. J. Schumpeter, Bonn, Münster, Saturday, Nov. 24. Uncorrected typewritten transcript. In the Harvard University Archives.

———. (1928–1929) *Finanzwissenschaft*. Notes on Schumpeter's lectures on public finance, by Cläre Tisch, winter semester, University of Bonn. Typewritten.

———. (1932a) "Soziale und wirtschaftliche Entwicklung." Vortrag in der sozialphilosophischen Arbeitsgemeinschaft am 28.IV. Typewritten. My lecture notes.

———. (1932b) "Tendenz zum Sozialismus." *Vortrag* vor der PAV. Bonn: July 18. Typewritten. My lecture notes.

Unpublished Documents concerning Schumpeter

Schumpeter's negotiations with the Handelshochschule, Berlin. File, partly typewritten, partly handwritten. In the Archive of the Humboldt University, (East) Berlin.

File of faculty discussions concerning a possible appointment of Schumpeter to the University of Leipzig, 1916.

File of the Banking Comission concerning the Biedermann Bank in the Archiv der Republik.

Protocols of the faculty discussion concerning a possible appointment of Schumpeter to Berlin. Typewritten. Archives of the Humboldt University, (East) Berlin.

Verbatim Report of the Interrogation of Schumpeter by the District Attorney of Vienna (Staatsanwaltschaft Wien I) concerning the Braun-Stammfels case. March 10, 1928. Typewritten. In the Archive of the City and Land Wien, Vienna. City Hall, Vienna. File No. S XVI 5689/224/27.

Verbatim Report of Judgment against Schumpeter in the case of the Kaufmannsbank. *Neue Freie Presse*, July 11, 1925.

Report to parliament by Hofrat Stern of the Banking Commission, concerning the Biedermann Bank, together with an interrogation of various officials. Typewritten. In the Archive of Parliament (1925). Kept secret at the time.

Sozialiesierungskommission, österreichische. Typewritten documents, all the in Archiv der Republik.

Miscellaneous

The Secret Memoranda are reprinted in Schumpeter (1985).

All articles that originally appeared in the *Deutsche Volkswirt* are reprinted in Schumpeter (1985).

All budget speeches are reprinted in Schumpeter (1985), except one, which is reprinted in Schumpeter (1993).

The letters to Count Harrach are reprinted in Schumpeter 1992.

Works by Other Authors

Allen, R. Loring (1990) *Opening Doors: The Life and Work of Joseph Schumpeter.* New Brunswick: N.J.: Transaction Publishers, 2 vols.

Amalrik, Andrei. (1970) *Will the Soviet Union Survive until 1984?* New York: Harper and Row.

Arthur, W. Brian. (1990) "Positive Feedbacks in the Economy." *Scientific American* 262, no. 2: 92–99.

Ashmead-Bartlett, E. (1923) *The Tragedy of Central Europe*, London: Thornton-Butterworth Ltd.

Augello, Massimo M. (1990) *Joseph Alois Schumpeter. A Reference Guide.* Berlin, New York, Tokyo: Springer Verlag.

Bak, Per, and Chen, Kan (1991) "Self-Organizing Criticality." *Scientific American* (January).

Baumol, W. J., and Benhabib, J. (1989) "Chaos: Significance, Mechanism and Application." *Journal of Economic Perspectives* 3, no. 1: 77–105.

Bauer, Otto. (1921) *Der Weg zum Sozialismus, 1918* 12th ed.

———. (1929) *Die österreichische Revolution*. Vienna, n.p.

Benhabib, J. See Baumol, W. J.

Biedermann Bank. *See under* Schumpeter, Documents concerning Schumpeter.

Brock, W. A. (1992) *Pathways to Randomness: Emergent Nonlinarity and Chaos in Economics and Finance*. Santa Fe, Santa Fe Institute. Draft 93–02–006, dated December 28.

Brussati, Alois. (1967) "Die wirtschaftlichen Folgen des Ausgleichs von 1867." In *Der Oesterreichisch-Ungarische Ausgleich von 1867. Vorgeschichte und Wirkungen*, edited by Peter Berger. Wien, München: Verlag Herold.

Butterfield, Herbert. (1942) "Capitalism and the Rise of Protestantism." (Review of Archbishop Temple's *Christianity and Social Order*.) *The Cambridge Review*, May 23.

———. (1979) *Writings on Christianity and History*. Edited by C. T. McIntire. New York: Oxford University Press.

———. (1955) *The Whig Interpretation of History*. New York: W. W. Norton & Co.

Carlson, Bo, and Rolf G. H. Henriksson, ed. (1991) *Development Blocks and Industrial Transformation. The Dahménian Approach to Economic Development*. Stockholm: The Industrial Institute for Economic and Social Research.

Carver, Earlene. (1986) "The Emigration of Austrian Economists." *History of Political Economy* (HOPE), 18, no. 1.

Chen, Kan. *See* Bak, Per.

Churchill, Lord Randolph. (1910) "Tory Democracy." In " *Encyclopaedia Britannica*, 11th ed.

Clemence, Richard V., ed. (1951) *Essays of J. A. Schumpeter*. Cambridge, Mass.: Addison-Wesley Press.

Coal Socialization. (1919) *Vorläufiger Bericht der Sozialisierungskommission über die Frage der Sozialisierung des Kohlenbergbaus. Abgeschlossen am 15. Februar 1919*. E. Schenck, Berlin: R.v. Decker Verlag.

———. (1920) *Bericht der Sozialisierungskommission über die Frage der Sozialisierung des Kohlenbergbaus vom 31. Juli 1920*. Berlin: Verlag Hans Robert Engelmann.

Dahmén, Erik. (1986) "Schumpeterian Dynamics." In *The Dynamics of Market Economics*, edited by R. H. Day and G. Eliasson. Reprinted in Carlson and Henriksson (1991).

———. (1989) "'Development Blocks' in Industrial Economics." In *Industrial Dynamics, Technological Organizational, and Structural Changes in Industries and Firms*, edited by Bo Carlson. Reprinted in Carlson and Henriksson (1991).

Djilas, Milan. (1969) *The Unperfect Society. Beyond the New Class*. New York: Harcourt, Brace and World.

Dönhof, Marion Gräfin. (1988) "Selbstbeschränkung ist keine Unfreiheit" (Interview with Adolf Löwe). *Die Zeit* no. 21 (May 20).

Ekeland, Ivar. (1988) *Mathematics and the Unexpected*. Chicago: Chicago University Press.

Feynman, Richard P. (1986) *You Can't Be Serious, Mr. Feynman*. New York: Bantam Books.

———. (1989) "The Value of Science." In *What Do You Care What Other People Think? Further Adventures of a Curious Character*. New York: Bantam Books.

Fischer, Fritz. (1961) *Griff nach der Weltmacht, Die Kriegszielpolitik des kaiserlichen Deutschland, 1914–1918*. Düsseldorf: Droste Verlag.

Friedman, Milton. (1990) "Bimetallism Revisited." *The Journal of Economic Literature* 4, no. 4 (Fall).

Frisch, Helmut, ed. (1982) *Schumpeterian Economics*. Eastburne, Sussex, London: Praeger Special Studies.

Frisch, Ragnar. (1931) Letter to J. A. Schumpeter, dated July 5. In the Harvard University Archives.

———. ([1933] 1967) "Propagation Problems and Impulse Problems in Dynamic Economics." In *Essays in Honour of Gustav Cassell, October 20th 1933*. London: Frank Cass & Co., in cooperation with Allen and Unwin. Reprint. New York: Augustus Kelly.

———. (1934) *Forslesninger holdt 1933 II og 1934 over Makrodynamik av Professor Ragnar Frisch*. Oslo. Mimeo.

Gerlich, Rudolf. (1980) *Die gescheiterte Alternative. Sozialisierung in Oesterreich nach dem 1. Weltkrieg*. Wien: W. Braumüller.

Gerschenkron, Alexander. (1957) *A Schumpeterian Analysis of economic Development*. (Review article of Dahmén). *The Review of Economics and Statistics*, vol. 19. Reprinted in Gerschenkron, Alexander, *Continuity in History and Other Essays*. Cambridge, Mass.: Belknap Press of Harvard University Press, 1968. Reprinted in Carlson and Hendriksson (1991).

Goodwin, Richard M. (1947) "Dynamic Coupling with Special Reference to Markets Having Production Lags." *Econometrica* 15, no. 2 (July).

———. (1990) "Walras and Schumpeter. The Vision Confirmed." In *Evolving Technology and Market Structure. Studies in Schumpeterian Economics*, edited by A. Heertje and M. Perlman. Ann Arbor: University of Michigan Press.

———. (1991) "Schumpeter, Keynes and the Theory of Economic Evolution." *Journal of Evolutionary Economics*, 1: 28–47.

Gulick, Charles A. (1948) *Austria from Habsburg to Hitler*. 2 vols. University of California Press.

Haberler, Gottfried. (1927) *Der Sinn der Indexzahlen*. Tübingen: J.C.B. Mohr (Paul Siebeck).

———. (1951) "Schumpeter's Theory of Interest." In Harris (1951).

———. (1986) "Hayek's Theory of the Business Cycle Revisited." Washington, D.C.: The Cato Institute. Mimeo. Revised January 24.

———. *See also* Koo, Anthony Y. C.

Harris, Seymour E. (1941) Letter to J. A. Schumpeter, dated June 20. In the Harvard University Archives.

———, ed. (1951) *Schumpeter. Social Scientist*. Cambridge, Mass.: Harvard University Press.

Hayek, F. A. v. (1944) *The Road to Serfdom*. Chicago: Chicago University Press.

———. (1960) *The Constitution of Liberty*. Chicago: Chicago University Press.

Heertje, Arnold, ed. (1981) *Capitalism, Socialism and Democracy 40 Years After*. Eastbourne, Sussex, London: Praeger, Special Studies.

Heertje, Arnold, and Mark Perlman, ed. (1990) *Evolving Technology and Market*

Structure. Studies in Schumpeterian Economics. Ann Arbor: University of Michigan Press.

Heilbronner, R. (1986) *The Worldly Philosophers.* 6th ed. New York: Simon and Schuster.

Henriksson, Rolf G. H. (1989) "The Institutional Base of the Stockholm School. The Political Economy Club (1917–1951)." *H.E.S. Bulletin,* 11, no. 1 (Spring).

———. *See also* Carlson, Bo, and Rolf G. H. Henriksson, ed.

Hill, Polly. (1970) *Studies in Rural Capitalism in West Africa.* Cambridge: Cambridge University Press.

Hoensch, Jörg K. (1984) *Geschichte Ungarns 1867–1913.* Stuttgart, Berlin, Köln, Mainz: W. Kohlhammer.

James, H. (1986) *The German Slump. Politics and Economics 1924–1936.* Oxford: Clarendon Press.

Jellinek, Georg. (1919) *Die Erklärung der Menschen- und Bürgerrechte.* 3rd ed. Munich and Leipzig: Duncker and Humblot.

Kauffman, Stuart. (1991) "Antichaos and Adaptation." *Scientific American* 265 (August): 78–84.

Keynes, J. M. (1924) *A Tract on Monetary Reform.* London: Macmillan.

———. (1930) *A Treatise on Money.* London: Macmillan. 2 vols.

———. (1935) *The General Theory of Employment, Interest and Money.* London: Macmillan. American Edition New York: Harcourt Brace, 1936.

Koo, Anthony Y. C., ed. (1985) *Selected Essays of Gottfried Haberler.* Cambridge, Mass.: MIT Press.

Kuhn, Thomas. (1970) *The Structure of Scientific Revolutions.* Chicago: University of Chicago Press.

Kunwald, G. (1932) Letter to G. Stolper, dated January 27. In the Stolper papers in the Bundesarchiv, Koblentz. Reprinted in Schumpeter (1985).

Lane, Frederic C., and Jelle C. Riemersma. (1953) "Introduction to Arthur Spiethoff." In *Enterprise and Secular Change. Readings in Economic History,* edited by Frederic C. Lane and Jelle C. Riemersma. Homewood, Ill.: Richard D. Irwin, Inc.

Lederer, Emil. (1919) Letter to Otto Bauer, handwritten, dated May 21. Published in full in translation in W. F. Stolper (1985).

Le Duan. (1970) *La Revolution Vietnamesienne. Problèmes Fondamentaux. Taches Essentielles.* Hanoi: n.p.

Leontief, W. W. (1971) "The Trouble with Cuban Socialism." *The New York Review of Books,* January 7, 1971.

Lewis, C. S. (1926) *Dymer. A Poem.* London: Macmillan.

Löwith, Karl. (1989) *Mein Leben in Deutschland vor und nach 1933. Ein Bericht. Fischer Taschenbuch.* Frankfurt: Fischer Taschenbuch Verlag.

Marschak, J. (1940) "Review of J. A. Schumpeter, *Business Cycles.*" *Journal of Political Economy,* vol. 40, no. 6.

Marshall, Alfred. (1956) "Social Possibilities of Economic Chivalry." In *Memorials of Alfred Marshall,* edited by A. C. Pigou. Reprint, New York: Kelly and Millman.

März, E. (1983, 1991) *Joseph Alois Schumpeter—Forscher, Lehrer und Politiker.* Verlag für Geschichte und Politik, Vienna, 1983. English translation as *Joseph Schumpeter. Scholar, Teacher and Politician.* Preface by James Tobin. New Haven, Conn.: Yale University Press.

McCraw, Thomas K. (1991) "Schumpeter Ascending." *The American Scholar* (Summer): 371–92.

McNeil, William. (1982) *The Pursuit of Power, Technology, Armed Force and Society since AD 1000.* Chicago: Chicago University Press.

Mises, L. (1920) "Die Wirtschaftsrechnung im sozialistischen Gemeinwesen." *Archiv für Sozialwissenschaft und Sozialpolitik* 47.

———. (1926) "Interventionismus." *Archiv für Sozialwissenschaft und Sozialpolitik* 56, no. 3.

———. (1951) *Socialism. An Economic and Sociological Analysis.* New Haven, Conn.: Yale University Press.

———. (1962) *The Ultimate Foundation of Economic Science. An Essay on Method.* Princeton, N.J., Toronto, New York, and London: D. Van Nostrand.

Morgan, Theodore. (1983) Letter to *The Economist* dated London, July 24.

Müller, Klaus O. W. (1990) *Joseph A. Schumpeter, Oekonom der Neunziger Jahre.* Berlin: Erich Schmidt Verlag.

Nelson, Richard R., and Sidney P. Winter. (1982) *An Evolutionary Theory of Economic Change.* Cambridge, Mass., and London: Belknap Press of Harvard University Press.

Niehans, Jürg. (1981) "Economics, History, Doctrine, Science and Art." *Kyklos* 35: 165–77.

———. (1990) *A History of Economic Theory. Classic Contributions 1720–1980.* Baltimore and London: The Johns Hopkins University Press.

North, Douglass C. (1978) "Structure and Performance: The Task of Economic History." *Journal of Economic Literature* 16 (September): 963–78.

———. (1981) *Structure and Change in Economic History.* New York: W. W. Norton.

Olson, Mancur. (1982) *The Rise and Decline of Nations. Economic Growth, Stagflation and Social Rigidities.* New Haven and London: Yale University Press.

Omodeo, Adolfo. (1951) *Die Erneuerung Italiens und die Geschichte Europas 1700–1920.* Zürich: Artemis Verlag.

Perlman, Mark. *See* Heertje, Arnold, and Mark Perlman, ed.

Polanyi, Michael. (1958) *Personal Knowledge. Towards a Post-Critical Philosophy.* Chicago: University of Chicago Press.

Renner, Karl. (1919) Letter from Paris in response to Schumpeter speech. Reprinted in Schumpeter (1993).

Riemersma, Jelle C. *See* Lane, Frederic C., and Jelle C. Riemersma.

Richter, Rudolf. (1989) *Money. Lectures on the Basis of Equilibrium Theory.* Berlin: Springer Verlag. Translated from idem, *Geldtheorie.*

Robertson, Hector Monteith. ([1933] 1959) *Aspects of the Rise of Economic Individualism. A Critique of Max Weber and his School.* New York: Kelly and Millman, Inc.

Rogers J. H. (1925) Letter to Professor L. S. Marshall, dated September 29. In the Manuscript Collection of Yale University.

Roll, Eric, Lord. (1988) *Crowded Hours.* London: Faber and Faber.

Röpke, Wilhelm. (1948) "Muss der Sozialismus kommen? Zu Josef Schumpeters Buch *Kapitalismus, Sozialismus und Demokratie.*" *Ordo Jahrbuch*, vol. I. Helmut Küpper, vormals Georg Bondi.

Rostow, Walt W. (1990) Foreword to Allen (1990).

Rothbard, Murray. (1987) "Catallactics." In *The New Palgrave.* London: Macmillan, and New York: Stockton Press.

Samuelson, Paul A. (1947) *The Foundations of Economics.* Cambridge, Mass.: Harvard University Press.

———. (1982) "Schumpeter as an Economic Theorist." In *Schumpeterian Economics*, edited by Helmut Frisch. Eastbourne, Sussex, and London: Praeger Special Studies.

———. (1986) *Collected Scientific Papers*, vol. 5, Cambridge, Mass.: MIT Press.

Scherer, F. M. (1992) *International High-Technology Competition* Cambridge, Mass.: Harvard University Press.

Schmiedtchen, Dieter. (1990) "Preise und spontane Ordnung—Prinzipien einer Theorie ökonomischer Evolution." In *Studien zur evolutorischen Oekonomik. Schriften des Vereins für Sozialpolitik. Gesellschaft für Wirtschafts-und Sozialwissenschaften, Neue Folge 195/1*, edited by Ulrich Witt, 75–113.

Schüller, Richard. *Diary*. Typewritten, in English. In the Haus-, Hof- und Staatsarchiv, Wien. Entries for 1919.

Scitovski, Tibor de. (1941) "Theory of Protection." *Review of Economic Studies* (November).

Shionoya, Yuichi. (1990a) "Instrumentalism in Schumpeter's Methodology." *History of Political Economy* 22, no. 2.

———. (1990b) "The Origins of the Schumpeterian Research Program: A Chapter Omitted from Schumpeter's *Theory of Economic Development*." *Journal of Institutional and Theoretical Economics* 146, no. 2 (June): 314–29.

Simon, Oskar, ed. (1919) *Materialien zur Sozialisierung*. Erstes Heft. Berlin: Carl Heyman's Verlag. Abgeschlossen 30.

Slutsky, E. (1933) "The Summation of Random Causes as the Source of Cyclical Processes." Conjuncture Institute of Moscow, vol. 3, no. 1. In Russian with English summary as quoted by Ragnar Frisch.

Smithies, Arthur. (1950) "Memorial. Joseph Alois Schumpeter 1883–1950." *American Economic Review* 40, no. 4: 628–44.

Socialization Commission. (1919). *Vorläufiges Gutachten über die Sozialisierung der Hochseefischerei, erstattet von der Sozialisierungskommission* (10 März). Berlin: R.v. Decker's Verlag. G. Schenck.

Somary, Felix. (n.d.) *Erinnerungen aus meinem Leben*. Zürich: Manesse Verlag.

Spiethoff, Arthur. (1925) Letter to Gustav Stolper concerning Schumpeter, dated August 14. In the Stolper papers in the Bundesarchiv, Koblentz. Partially reproduced in Schumpeter (1985).

———. (1933) "Die Allgemeine Volkswirtschaftslehre als Geschichtliche Theorie. Die Wirtschaftsstile." In *Festgabe für Werner Sombart*, edited by Arthur Spiethoff. Munich and Leipzig: Duncker und Humblot.

———. (1948) "Anschauliche und reine Volkswirtschaftstheorie und ihr Verhältnis zueinander." In *Synopsis. Festgabe für Alfred Weber, 30. IV. 1865–30. VII. 1948*, 569–664. Heidelberg: Verlag Lambert Schneider.

———. (1953) "Pure Theory and Economic Gestalt Theory. Ideal Types and Real Types." Translation of selections from Spiethoff's various methodological writings, particularly from *Synopsis* (1948). In Lane and Riemersma (1953).

———. *See also under* Schumpeter (1952, 1953, 1954), edited by Erich Schneider and Arthur Spiethoff.

Stolper, Gustav. (1918) *Das Mitteleuropäische Wirtschaftsproblem*. Leipzig and Vienna: Franz Deuticke Verlag.

———. (1919) Letter to Dr. Kurt Singer, dated Wien, 5 Dezember. Schriftleitung des Wirtschaftsdienstes, Hamburg. Reproduced in Schumpeter (1985).

———. (1929) *Ein Finanzplan. Vorschläge zur Deutschen Finanzreform*. Originally a series of articles in the *Deutsche Volkswirt*, June 21–August 30. Berlin: Verlag des Deutschen Volkswirts.

———. (1932a) Letter to Ministerialdirektor Richter, dated January 29. In Stolper papers in the Bundesarchiv, Koblentz.

———. (1932b) Letter to G. Kunwald, dated January 21. In the Stolper papers, in the Bundesarchiv, Koblentz.

———. (1932c) "Sombart als Prophet. Oder: Die Zukunft des Kapitalismus." *Der Deusche Volkswirt* 6, no. 22.

Stolper, Wolfgang F. (1963) "The Economic Development of Nigeria." *The Journal of Economic History* 23, no. 4 (December).

———. (1970) "Economic Growth and Political Stability in Nigeria: On Growing Together Again." In *Growth and Development of the Nigerian Economy*, edited by Carl K. Eicher and Carl Liedholm. East Lansing: Michigan State University Press.

———. (1979) "J. A. Schumpeter. A Personal Memoir." *Challenge* 21, no. 6.

———. (1984) *The Relevance of Schumpeter's Ideas for Economic Policy*. Kieler Vorträge, Tübingen: J.C.B. Mohr (Paul Siebeck).

———. (1985) "Schumpeter and the German and Austrian Socialization Attempts of 1918–1919." In *Research in the History of Economic Thought and Methodology*, edited by Warren J. Samuels. vol. 3. Greenwich, Conn.: Jai Press.

———. (1988) "Development Theory and Empirical Evidence." In *Evolutionary Economics*, edited by H. Hanusch. New York: Cambridge University Press.

———. (1991) "The Theoretical Bases of Economic Policy: The Schumpeterian Perspective." *Journal of Evolutionary Economics* 3: 189–205.

Streissler, Erich. (1982) "Schumpeter's Vienna and the Role of Credit in Innovation." In *Schumpeterian Economics*, edited by Helmut Frisch. Praeger Special Studies.

Swedberg, Richard. (1989) Introduction to *Essays*, by Joseph A. Schumpeter. New Brunswick, N.J.: Transaction Publishers. Reprint of Schumpeter (1951).

———. (1991a) *Joseph A. Schumpeter. The Economics and Sociology of Capitalism*. Princeton, N.J.: Princeton University Press.

———. (1991b) *Schumpeter. A Biography*. Princeton, N.J.: Princeton University Press.

Sweezy, Paul M. (1935) "Economics and the Crisis of Capitalism." *Economic Forum*, New York.

———. (1942) *The Theory of Capitalist Development*. Oxford, 1942. Reprint *The Monthly Review Press* 1961 and later.

Twain, Mark. (1904) "Stirring Times in Austria." In idem, *How to tell a Story and other Essays*. New York and London: Harper and Brothers Publishers.

Verosta, St. (1978) "Joseph Schumpeter gegen das Zollbündnis der Donaumonarchie mit Deutschland und gegen die Anschlusspolitik Otto Bauers (1916–1919)." In *Festschrift für Christian Broda*, edited by M. Neider. Vienna: Europa Verlag, 374–404.

Viner, Jacob. (1991) "Schumpeter's History of Economic Analysis." In *Essays on the Intellectual History of Economics*, edited by Douglas A. Irwin. Princeton, N.J.: Princeton University Press.

Vogelstein, Theodor. (1950) *Joseph A. Schumpeter and the Sozialisierungskommission. An Annotation to Gottfried Haberler's Memoir of Schumpeter*. Typewritten, with an accompanying letter to G. Haberler. December 4, Paris.

Walré de Bordes, L. van (1924) *The Austrian Crown*. London: P. S. King & Co.

Weber, Max. (1918) *Der Sozialismus*. Vienna: Phöbus Kommissionsverlag Dr. Viktor Rimmer.

———. ([1904] 1922) "Die Objektivität sozialwissenschaftlicher und sozialpolitischer Erkenntnis." Reprinted in *Gesammelte Aufsätze zur Wissenschaftslehre von Max Weber*. Tübingen: J.C.B. Mohr (Paul Siebeck).

———. N.d. Letter to the Vienna faculty concerning Schumpeter. Made available by Richard Swedberg.

Wieser, F.v. (1919) *Tagebuch* (Diary) Typewritten, in German. In the Haus- Hof- und Staatsarchiv Vienna. Excerpt reprinted in Schumpeter 1992.

Wilson, E. B. (1943) Letter to J. A. Schumpeter, November 4. In the Harvard University Archives.

Winter, Sidney P. (1984) "Schumpeterian Competition in Alternative Technological Regimes." *Journal of Economic Behavior and Organization* 5, no. 3–4 (September, December): 287–320.

———. *See also* Nelson, Richard R. and Sidney P. Winter.

Winterberger, G. (1983) "Ueber Schumpeter's Geschichtsdeterminismus." Walter Eucken Institute. *Vorträge und Aufsätze*. No. 95. Tübingen: J.C.B. Mohr (Paul Siebeck).

Wiebel, Martin. (n.d.) *Der Systemgedanke in der Geldtheorie von Ricardo bis Schumpeter*. Breslau: Verlag Dr. Hermann Eschenberger.

Zitelmann, Rainer. (1987) *Hitler. Selbstverständnis eines Revolutionärs*. Hamburg and New York: Berg Publishers, Ltd.